Problems in Applied Ethics

SEE ALSO FROM BLOOMSBURY:

Debating Christian Religious Epistemology edited by John M. DePoe and Tyler Dalton McNabb
Introduction to Applied Ethics by Robert L. Holmes
Problems in Epistemology and Metaphysics edited by Steven B. Cowan
Problems in Value Theory edited by Steven B. Cowan

Problems in Applied Ethics

An Introduction to Contemporary Debates

EDITED BY

STEVEN B. COWAN

BLOOMSBURY ACADEMIC
LONDON • NEW YORK • OXFORD • NEW DELHI • SYDNEY

BLOOMSBURY ACADEMIC

Bloomsbury Publishing Plc, 50 Bedford Square, London, WC1B 3DP, UK
Bloomsbury Publishing Inc, 1359 Broadway, 12th Floor, New York, NY 10018, USA
Bloomsbury Publishing Ireland, 29 Earlsfort Terrace, Dublin 2, D02 AY28, Ireland

BLOOMSBURY, BLOOMSBURY ACADEMIC and the Diana logo are trademarks of Bloomsbury Publishing Plc

First published in Great Britain 2026

Copyright © Steven B. Cowan and Contributors, 2026

Steven B. Cowan and Contributors have asserted their rights under the Copyright, Designs and Patents Act, 1988, to be identified as Authors of this work.

For legal purposes the Acknowledgments on pp. xvi constitute an extension of this copyright page.

Cover Image: Photograph © Busà Photography / Getty Images

All rights reserved. No part of this publication may be: i) reproduced or transmitted in any form, electronic or mechanical, including photocopying, recording or by means of any information storage or retrieval system without prior permission in writing from the publishers; or ii) used or reproduced in any way for the training, development or operation of artificial intelligence (AI) technologies, including generative AI technologies. The rights holders expressly reserve this publication from the text and data mining exception as per Article 4(3) of the Digital Single Market Directive (EU) 2019/790.

Bloomsbury Publishing Plc does not have any control over, or responsibility for, any third-party websites referred to or in this book. All internet addresses given in this book were correct at the time of going to press. The author and publisher regret any inconvenience caused if addresses have changed or sites have ceased to exist, but can accept no responsibility for any such changes.

A catalogue record for this book is available from the British Library.

A catalog record for this book is available from the Library of Congress.

ISBN: HB: 978-1-3504-5216-9
PB: 978-1-3504-5217-6
ePDF: 978-1-3504-5218-3
eBook: 978-1-3504-5219-0

Typeset by Deanta Global Publishing Services, Chennai, India
Printed and bound in Great Britain

For product safety related questions contact productsafety@bloomsbury.com

To find out more about our authors and books visit www.bloomsbury.com and sign up for our newsletters.

Contents

List of Contributors ix
Acknowledgments xvi

Introduction *Steven B. Cowan* 1
   Normative Ethical Theories 3
   About the Essays 5
   For Students and Instructors 16

1 Abortion 19
   A Case for the Moral Permissibility of Abortion *Amy Berg* 19
   Unborn Human Beings Have Fundamental Rights *Patrick Lee* 31

   Responses 42
   Response to Berg on Abortion *Patrick Lee* 42
   Response to Lee on Abortion *Amy Berg* 45

2 Physician-Assisted Suicide/Euthanasia 51
   The Case for Mercy Killing and Physician-Assisted Suicide *Arthur Schafer* 51
   Against Physician-Assisted Suicide and Euthanasia *Scott B. Rae* 62

   Responses 74
   Response to Schafer on Physician-Assisted Suicide and Euthanasia *Scott B. Rae* 74
   Response to Rae on Physician-Assisted Suicide and Euthanasia *Arthur Schafer* 77

3 Capital Punishment 83
   The Case for Capital Punishment *Joseph M. Bessette and Edward Feser* 83
   The Death Penalty: Against *Lloyd Steffen* 95

   Responses 110
   Response to Bessette and Feser on Capital Punishment *Lloyd Steffen* 110
   Response to Steffen on Capital Punishment *Joseph M. Bessette and Edward Feser* 114

4 Human Genome Editing 120

The Case in Favor of Intentional Genetic Modification *Colin Farrelly* 120
Human Genetic Enhancement: A Bridge Too Far *C. Ben Mitchell* 133

Responses 146
Response to Farrelly on Human Genome Editing *C. Ben Mitchell* 146
A Response to Mitchell on Human Genome Editing *Colin Farrelly* 149

5 The Right to Health Care 154

Stability, Liberty, and the Right to Health Care *Robert C. Hughes* 154
There Is No Right to Health Care *Trevor Burrus* 164

Responses 176
Response to Hughes on the Right to Health care *Trevor Burrus* 176
Response to Burrus on the Right to Health Care *Robert C. Hughes* 180

6 Vaccine Mandates 184

For Vaccine Mandates *Shlomo Cohen* 184
Against Vaccine Mandates *Gabriël A. Moens* 197

Responses 211
Response to Cohen on Vaccine Mandates *By Gabriël A. Moens* 211
Reply to Moens on Vaccine Mandates *Shlomo Cohen* 215

7 Animal Rights 221

A Non-Consequentialist Defense of Animal Rights *Molly Gardner* 221
Animal Ethics and the Substance View *Bruce P. Blackshaw* 231

Responses 244
A Response to Gardner on Animal Rights *Bruce P. Blackshaw* 244
A Response to Blackshaw on Animal Rights *Molly Gardner* 247

8 Immigration/Open Borders 252

A Case for Immigration *Michael Huemer* 252
On the Incoherence of Libertarian Open Borders Theory *Daniel Demetriou* 264

Responses 279
Response to Huemer on Open Borders *Daniel Demetriou* 279
Response to Demetriou on Open Borders *Michael Huemer* 284

9 Gun Control 290

There Is No Right to Own a Gun for Self-Defense *Nicholas Dixon* 290
The Right to Bear Arms *Benjamin L. Mabry* 303

Responses 315
Response to Dixon on Gun Control *Benjamin L. Mabry* 315
Respone to Mabry on Gun Control *Nicholas Dixon* 320

10 War and Peace 325

War Can Be Morally Justified *Steven B. Cowan* 325
Pacifism and Peacemaking *Timothy Paul Erdel* 336

Responses 349
Response to Cowan on War and Peace *Timothy Paul Erdel* 349
Response to Erdel on War and Peace *Steven B. Cowan* 352

11 Reparations 358

For Reparations for Past Injustices *Federico Lenzerini* 358
The Case Against Slavery Reparations *Andrew Bernstein* 370

Responses 382
Response to Lenzerini on Reparations *Andrew Bernstein* 382
Response to Bernstein on Reparations *Federico Lenzerini* 386

12 Free Speech 390

Free Speech Absolutism *Onkar Ghate* 390
There Should Be Legal Limits to Free Speech *Andrei Bespalov* 402

Responses 415
Response to Ghate on Free Speech *Andrei Bespalov* 415
Response to Bespalov on Free Speech *Onkar Ghate* 419

13 Same-Sex Marriage 424

Against Same-Sex Marriage *James S. Spiegel* 424
A Case for Same-Sex Marriage *Christopher Arroyo* 434

Responses 446
Response to Spiegel on Same-Sex Marriage *Christopher Arroyo* 446
Response to Arroyo on Same-Sex Marriage *James S. Spiegel* 450

14 Transgender Rights 455

The Case for Trans Rights *Jasper Heaton* 455
Against Transgender Rights *David S. Crawford* 466

Responses 479
Response to Heaton on Transgender Rights *David S. Crawford* 479
Response to Crawford on Transgender Rights *Jasper Heaton* 483

15 Drug Legalization 489

For Drug Legalization *Chris Meyers* 489
Eat, Drink, and Be Sober: The Case for Drug Prohibition *Timothy Hsiao* 500

Responses 517
Response to Meyers on Drug Legalization *Timothy Hsiao* 517
Reply to Hsiao on Drug Legalization *Chris Meyers* 522

Index 527

Contributors

Christopher Arroyo (PhD, Fordham University) is Professor of Philosophy at Providence College in Providence, Rhode Island, and Associate Editor of *New Blackfriars*. His scholarship focuses on two areas, namely, a philosophical critique of Catholic sexual ethics and Philippa Foot's account of natural goodness. He has published one book: *Kant's Ethics and The Same-Sex Marriage Debate: An Introduction* (2017). His work has appeared in academic journals such as *Philosophy* and the *European Journal of Philosophy*. He has a chapter, "Teaching Ethics at a Catholic College," in *A Companion to Doing Ethics* (2025).

Amy Berg (PhD, University of California-San Diego) is Assistant Professor of Philosophy at Rice University. She specializes in ethics and political philosophy. Her work has appeared in *Philosophical Studies*, the *Journal of Political Philosophy*, and the *Journal of Moral Philosophy*, among others. Her book on the well-rounded life is under contract with Princeton University Press.

Andrew Bernstein (PhD, City University of New York) taught for many years at SUNY Purchase and at Marist College. He is the author of *The Capitalist Manifesto: The Historic, Economic, and Philosophic Case for Laissez-Faire*; *Heroes, Legends, Champions: Why Heroism Matters*; *Why Johnny Still Can't Read or Write or Understand Math—And What We Can Do About It*; and numerous other books and essays. He has lectured across the United States and around the world on numerous philosophical topics.

Andrei Bespalov (PhD, Pompeu Fabra University) is a postdoctoral fellow at Pompeu Fabra University and Barcelona Institute of Analytic Philosophy supported by a María de Maeztu Unit of Excellence grant. He specializes in political philosophy with a focus on theories of public reason and their implications for the justification of religious exemptions, civil disobedience, and policies regulating the spread of conspiracy theories and fake news. His work is published and forthcoming in the journals *Law and Philosophy*, *Res Publica*, *Oxford Journal of Law and Religion*, *Jurisprudence*, and *Social Theory and Practice*.

Joseph M. Bessette (PhD, University of Chicago) is Alice Tweed Tuohy Professor Emeritus of Government and Ethics, Claremont McKenna College, where he taught for three decades. He specializes in democratic theory, American government and politics, the American founding, the American presidency, crime and punishment, and the death penalty. He has coauthored two textbooks on American government and politics and is the author of *The Mild Voice of Reason: Deliberative Democracy and American National Government* (1994) and, with Edward Feser, *By Man Shall His Blood be Shed: A Catholic Defense of Capital Punishment* (2017). He has also co-edited and contributed to three books on the Presidency and the Constitution. He is currently completing a book on capital punishment in the United States and, with Gary Schmitt, a major new study of the creation of the American presidency, 1775–1817.

Bruce P. Blackshaw (PhD, University of Birmingham) was recently awarded his PhD in the ethics of abortion and is an adjunct researcher at the University of Notre Dame, Sydney. He specializes in bioethics and also has interests in the philosophy of religion and the philosophy of science. He has published widely in bioethics and is a co-editor of *Agency, Pregnancy and Persons: Essays in Defense of Human Life* (2022). He is also a co-founder of a successful software company.

Trevor Burrus (JD, University of Denver, Sturm College of Law) is a constitutional lawyer and the former editor-in-chief of the *Cato Supreme Court Review*. His research interests include legal philosophy, legal history, political philosophy, economics, and the intersection of science and public policy. He has filed hundreds of briefs in the US Supreme Court and his scholarly work has appeared in law journals such as the *Harvard Journal of Law and Public Policy* and the *NYU Journal of Law and Liberty*. His popular writing has appeared in numerous outlets, including the *Washington Post*, *Forbes*, and the *New York Times*. He is also the editor of two books: *Deep Commitments: The Past, Present, and Future of Religious Liberty* (2017) and *A Conspiracy Against Obamacare: The Volokh Conspiracy and the Health Care Case* (2013).

Shlomo Cohen (PhD, Hebrew University) is Chair of the Department of Philosophy and Associate Professor of Philosophy at Ben-Gurion University of the Negev, Israel. He specializes in normative and applied ethics, areas in which he has published numerous academic articles. He is the author of *The Concept and Ethics of Manipulation* (2025).

Steven B. Cowan (PhD, University of Arkansas) is Assistant Dean of the School of Arts, Humanities, and Social Sciences. and Professor of Philosophy and Religion at Lincoln Memorial University. He specializes in the philosophy of religion and the metaphysics of free will, areas in which he has published numerous articles in academic journals, including *Faith and Philosophy*, *Religious Studies*, and *Philosophia Christi*. He has edited or authored several books, including *Problems in Epistemology and Metaphysics* (2020), *Problems in Value Theory* (2020), and (with James Spiegel) *Idealism and Christian Philosophy* (2016) and *The Love of Wisdom: A Christian Introduction to Philosophy*, 2nd ed. (forthcoming).

David S. Crawford (JD, University of Michigan; STD, Lateran University) is Academic Dean and Associate Professor of Moral Theology and Family Law at the John Paul II Institute for Studies on Marriage and Family at the Catholic University of America. He specializes in human action, natural law, sexual ethics, and the anthropological foundations of modern civil law, areas in which he has published numerous academic articles. He is the author of *Marriage and the Sequela Christi*. Dr. Crawford has served as a theological advisor on the United States Conference of Catholic Bishops' Subcommittee for the Promotion and Defense of Marriage and for Vatican Delegation Meetings at the Pontifical Council for the Promotion of Christian Unity. His writings have been translated into several languages, and he has lectured on several continents.

Daniel Demetriou (PhD, University of Colorado-Boulder) is Professor of Philosophy at the University of Minnesota-Morris. An ethicist and social-political philosopher, he has specialties in honor ethics, monument ethics, sex ethics, and non-liberal moral psychology. He is the co-editor of *Honor in the Modern World* (2016).

Nicholas Dixon (PhD, Michigan State University) is Professor Emeritus of Philosophy at Alma College in Michigan. He specializes in applied ethics and has published articles in such journals as *Social Theory and Practice*, *Journal of Social Philosophy*, *Philosophical Forum*, *The Monist*, *Public Affairs Quarterly*, *Hastings Center Report*, and *Journal of the Philosophy of Sport*. He served as editor of *Journal of the Philosophy of Sport* and president of the International Association for the Philosophy of Sport.

Timothy P. Erdel (PhD, University of Illinois at Urbana-Champaign) is Archivist for the Missionary Church Archives & Historical Collections at Bethel University, Indiana, where he was Professor of Religion & Philosophy & in the Committee on Humanities, as well as Alumni Association Distinguished Professor. He coauthored *Religions of the World*, 2nd ed. (1988), compiled *Guide to the Preparation of Theses*, 4th ed. (2013), and wrote *Grace upon Grace* (2020), and has published dozens of scholarly articles and chapters in books.

Colin Farrelly (PhD, University of Bristol) is Sir Edward Peacock Professor of Political Theory in the Department of Political Studies (cross-appointed with Philosophy) at Queen's University in Canada. He has published many journal articles on the ethics of longevity science and the genetic revolution in journals in science, medicine, and bioethics. His books include *Biologically Modified Justice* (2016), *Genetic Ethics: An Introduction* (2018), and *Aging and the Ethics of Longevity Science* (forthcoming).

Edward Feser (PhD University of California at Santa Barbara) is Professor of Philosophy at Pasadena City College. He is coauthor, with Joseph M. Bessette, of *By Man Shall His Blood be Shed: A Catholic Defense of Capital Punishment* (2017). He has also authored or edited thirteen other books on topics in political philosophy, philosophy of religion, philosophy of mind, metaphysics, and history of philosophy.

Molly Gardner (PhD, University of Wisconsin) is Assistant Professor of Philosophy at the University of Florida. She has published academic articles and book chapters on a number of ethical issues, especially pertaining to the non-identity problem, animal ethics, and future generations. She has also co-edited the book *The Ethics of Policing and Imprisonment* with Michael Weber (2018).

Onkar Ghate (PhD, University of Calgary) is Chief Philosophy Officer and Senior Fellow at the Ayn Rand Institute (ARI). He specializes in Ayn Rand's philosophy of Objectivism and serves as ARI's lead instructor and editor. He is a contributing author to many books on Rand's fiction and philosophy, including *Foundations of a Free Society: Reflections on Ayn Rand's Political Philosophy* (2019), *A Companion to Ayn Rand* (2016), *Concepts and Their Role in Knowledge: Reflections on Objectivist Epistemology* (2012), and *Essays on Ayn Rand's "We the Living"* (2012).

Jasper Heaton is Instructor in the Philosophy Department at Langara College in Vancouver BC, and a PhD candidate in the Philosophy Department at the University of British Columbia. They specialize in epistemology and transfeminist philosophy, with a particular focus on epistemic violence and epistemic resistance. They have published on the APA Blog for Women in Philosophy, exploring the commonalities between cis and trans people's relationship to gender-affirming care, and their work has been cited as part of an Amicus Brief to the US Supreme Court. Jasper is interested in bringing philosophy to the public and frequently gives talks in the Vancouver area. They are also a leading member of the Philosophy Exception, a research group that aims to make philosophy a more inclusive discipline for students and faculty.

Timothy Hsiao (M.A., Florida State University) is Fellow at the Firearms Research Center at the University of Wyoming College of Law. He specializes in applied ethics and political philosophy, with more than thirty scholarly publications and forty popular articles to his name. He also serves as Adjunct Associate Professor of Philosophy at Johnson County Community College and is a sworn law enforcement officer.

Michael Huemer (PhD, Rutgers University) is Professor of Philosophy at the University of Colorado at Boulder. He is the author of more than eighty academic articles in ethics, epistemology, political philosophy, and metaphysics, as well as about twelve brilliant and amazing books that you should immediately buy, including *Knowledge, Reality, and Value* (2021), *Progressive Myths* (2024), and *Dialogues on Ethical Vegetarianism* (2025).

Robert C. Hughes (PhD, University of California, Los Angeles) is Associate Professor of Professional Practice in the Department of Management and Global Business at Rutgers Business School. His research concerns the ethics and just regulation of business and other economic activities, such as the financing of health care. His publications include articles in *The Journal of Ethics*, *Law and Philosophy*, *Bioethics*, *Journal of Medical Ethics*, *Journal of Business Ethics*, and *Business Ethics Quarterly*.

Patrick Lee (PhD, Marquette University) is the John N. and Jamie D. McAleer Professor of Bioethics and Philosophy, and the Director of the Center for Bioethics at Franciscan University of Steubenville. He specializes in bioethics and foundations of ethics. He has published numerous articles in academic journals, including *Faith and Philosophy*, *Philosophy*, *Bioethics*, and *American Catholic Philosophical Quarterly*. He authored or coauthored three books: with Robert P. George, *Body-Self Dualism in Contemporary Ethics and Politics* (2008); *Abortion and Unborn Human Life* (2010); with Robert P. George, *Conjugal Union, What Marriage Is and Why It Matters* (2014).

Federico Lenzerini (PhD, International Law) is Full Professor of International Law and International Human Rights Law at the Department of Political and International Sciences of the University of Siena (Italy). He is also Professor at the LLM Program in Intercultural Human Rights at the St. Thomas University School of Law, Miami (FL), United States, and Professor at the Tulane-Siena Summer School on International Law, Cultural Heritage and the Arts. He has been Consultant to UNESCO (Paris) (2001–14) and has been Counsel to the Italian Ministry of Foreign Affairs for international negotiations related to cultural heritage (2001–4). He is the Chair of the Garifuna Reparations Working Group (GRWG), St. Vincent and the Grenadines. He is the author of *The Culturalization of Human Rights Law* (2014) and the editor of *Reparations for Indigenous Peoples, International and Comparative Perspectives* (2008; also published in paperback in 2009). He has published over 140 academic works and held more than 100 academic lectures in over twenty countries.

Benjamin L. Mabry (PhD, Louisiana State University) is Program Director and Assistant Professor of Political Science at Lincoln Memorial University. His primary areas of research include the intersection of politics, philosophy, and religion, especially the study of ideologies, ideals, and belief systems. His work can be found in publications including the *Observer and Review Journal*, *First Things*, and the *American Mind*.

Chris Meyers (PhD, Loyola University-Chicago) worked for twelve years at the University of Southern Mississippi, where he was eventually promoted to full professor but quit so that he could live full time with his family in Washington, DC. He then worked as a visiting professor at George Washington University until funding for the position was cut. He specializes in moral theory, moral psychology, and applied ethics. His books include *Drug Legalization—A Philosophical Analysis* (2023) and *A Moral Defense of Homosexuality: Why Every Argument against Gay Rights Fails* (2015). He has recently published several articles on philosophy and drugs, including two articles in the *Palgrave Handbook of Philosophy and Psychoactive Drug Use* (2024).

C. Ben Mitchell (PhD, University of Tennessee-Knoxville) is a moral philosopher with an academic concentration in medical ethics. He has done additional study in genetics for non-scientists at the Cold Spring Harbor Laboratories, Cold Spring Harbor, New York, and has twice been a visiting scholar at Green-Templeton College, the medical college of Oxford University. Mitchell held the Graves Chair in Moral Philosophy for over a decade at Union University, where he also served for three years as Provost and Vice President for Academic Affairs. In 2020, he served on the NIH Human Fetal Tissue Research Ethics Advisory Committee. He has been a consultant with the Center for Genetics & Public Policy at Johns Hopkins University, Co-Director and Fellow for the Council for Biotechnology Policy in Washington, D.C., and a fellow of the Institute for Biotechnology and a Human Future at Illinois Institute of Technology, Chicago-Kent School of Law. For over twenty years, he was editor of *Ethics & Medicine: An International Journal of Bioethics*. Among other publications, he is the author of *Ethics and Moral Reasoning: A Student's Guide* (2013) and *Bioethics and Medicine: A Short Companion* (2025).

Gabriël A. Moens AM (PhD, University of Sydney) is Emeritus Professor of Law, the University of Queensland. He served as Pro Vice Chancellor, Dean and Professor of Law, Murdoch University. He also served as Head, Graduate School of Law, The University of Notre Dame Australia; Garrick Professor of Law, The University of Queensland; and Professor of Law, Curtin University. In 1999, Professor Moens received the Australian Award for University Teaching in Law and Legal Studies. In June 2019, he was appointed a Member of the Order of Australia (AM) for services to the law and higher education. He has coauthored several books, including *Foundations of the Australian Legal System: History, Theory and Practice*, (2023); *Emergency Powers, Covid-19 Restrictions and Mandatory Vaccination: A "Rule-of-Law" Perspective* (2022); *Law of International Business in Australasia* (2nd ed), (2019); *The Constitution of the Commonwealth of Australia Annotated* (9th ed), (2016). He writes opinion pieces and commentary for various magazines and newspapers.

Scott B. Rae (PhD, University of Southern California) is Senior Advisor to the President, Biola University, Dean of Faculty and Professor of Christian Ethics, Talbot School of Theology, Biola University. His primary interests are medical ethics and business ethics, dealing with the application of Christian ethics to medicine and the marketplace. He is author/editor of eighteen books (including *Moral Choices; An Introduction to Ethics*, 5th edition forthcoming, *Body and Soul: Human Nature and the Crisis in Ethics*, with JP Moreland, and *Business for the Common Good*, with Kenman L. Wong) and numerous articles and chapters in edited works.

Arthur Schafer (B.Litt., Oxford) is Founding Director of the Centre for Professional and Applied Ethics at the University of Manitoba. He specializes in professional and applied ethics, with a special focus on biomedical conflicts of interest. He has published numerous articles in bioethics journals, including *The Journal of Medical*

Ethics and Bioethics, as well as many book chapters on topics ranging from privacy and medically assisted death to prisoners' right to vote. His 1962 article "The Ethics of the Randomized Clinical Trial" (*New England Journal of Medicine*) generated widespread and continuing discussion within the medical research community. He has edited or authored several books, including *The Buck Stops Here: Reflections on Moral Responsibility, Democratic Accountability and Military Values*; *Fragile Freedoms: The Global Struggle for Human Rights*; and *Ethics and Animal Experimentation*.

James S. Spiegel (PhD, Michigan State University) is Executive Director of the Geneva College Center for Faith and Life. He has taught at Taylor University, Hillsdale College, and Indianapolis Theological Seminary and has published eleven books and over 100 articles and book chapters. His publications, which primarily explore issues in ethics, philosophy of religion, and virtue epistemology, have appeared in such scholarly journals such as *Philosophia*, *Metaphilosophy*, *Faith and Philosophy*, *Sophia*, *Science and Engineering Ethics*, and the *International Journal for Philosophy of Religion* as well as popular periodicals such as *Christianity Today*, *First Things*, *The Federalist*, and *Touchstone*. Spiegel's books include *The Benefits of Providence* (Crossway), *Faith, Film, and Philosophy* (Intervarsity), *Hell and Divine Goodness* (Cascade), and the two-volume *Idealism and Christianity* series (Bloomsbury).

Lloyd Steffen (PhD, Brown University) is Professor of Religion, Culture, and Society, University Chaplain, and Director of both the Center for Spirituality and Dialogue and the Lehigh Prison Project at Lehigh University in Bethlehem, PA. A former Fulbright specialist in Brazil, he has written or edited a dozen books in ethics and the philosophy of religion, including *Ethics and Experience: Ethical Theory from Just War to Abortion* (2012), *Executing Justice: The Moral Meaning of the Death Penalty* (2006), and *Christianity and Violence* (2021). He served seven years as the NGO representative to the United Nations for the Religious Coalition for Reproductive Choice.

Acknowledgments

I wish to express my appreciation to the staff at Bloomsbury Publishing for allowing me the opportunity to produce this book. I especially want to thank Colleen Coalter, Suzie Nash, and Aimee Brown for their expert advice and support in seeing this project through to completion, and to my son, Oliver Cowan, who helped to compile the "For Further Reading" lists and the index. I owe much thanks as well to all of the contributors who gave much of their professional time and energy (and patience!) to make this book happen. I dedicate the book to all of my students over the years, especially those in my ethics classes whose insightful questions and challenging arguments have deepened and sharpened my own understanding of the complex issues discussed herein.

Introduction

Steven B. Cowan

Human beings make decisions every day. We usually begin our day deciding whether or not to hit the "snooze" button on the alarm clock one more time. Then follows a myriad of other decisions concerning, for example, what to have for breakfast, what route to take to avoid traffic on the way to work, how to respond to an email query from a co-worker, what TikTok videos to watch during lunch, whether to watch a TV show after supper, or read that sci-fi novel you've been wanting to get to for weeks.

Those decisions are rather mundane and trivial. But often we have to make decisions that are *moral* in nature. For example, you may have to choose whether or not to lie to your boss about why you're late for work. Or maybe you're tempted to shoplift that diamond necklace at the jewelry store. Or suppose you just found out that you're pregnant and you need to decide whether or not to get an abortion. Perhaps you are a member of your state legislature and you have to decide whether or not to vote for a bill to legalize recreational drugs. When it comes to questions like these, you are in the realm of ethics and, more specifically, *applied ethics*.

Ethics is a major branch of philosophy that deals broadly with the nature of morality and questions of moral right and wrong. As an academic discipline, ethics may be subdivided into three main areas:

1. *Metaethics*. This area addresses fundamental questions about the nature and justification of morality per se. As philosopher Jonathan Wolff puts it, metaethics concerns "the nature of value, where the rules of ethics come from, and how we can learn about them."[1] So, metaethical questions include: Is anything really right or wrong at all? Do moral terms like "rightness" and "wrongness" refer to anything objectively real? What do we *mean* when we say that something is right or wrong? Are moral properties natural (e.g., pleasure, self-interest) or are they nonnatural (e.g., abstract entities like Plato's forms)? Does morality depend in some way on God? As you may surmise, by its very nature, metaethics has significant overlap with other major branches of philosophy such as metaphysics (the study of being or reality) and epistemology (the study of knowledge), as well as the philosophy of language and the philosophy of religion.

2. *Normative ethics.* As the name suggests, normative ethics seeks to delineate the correct moral norms or standards. To quote Wolff again, "Normative ethics . . . is the branch of ethics that asks: What moral rules, principles, or doctrines should we accept?"[2] The rules and principles that Wolff has in mind are those that enable us to make morally right decisions. They are, that is, *action-guiding principles*. Approached from a different angle, we can say that normative ethics sets forth "principles, concepts, and ideals that can be cited in support of ethical judgments about cases."[3] In other words, supposing you think, "I ought to do X," normative ethics helps you answer the question, "*Why* ought you to do X?" As we will discuss later, there are numerous normative ethical theories, each of which lays out different (often conflicting) moral principles.

3. *Applied ethics.* At the risk of oversimplification, applied ethics has to do with *the application of normative ethical theories to real-world moral issues*. As noted at the beginning of this introduction, you might be interested in answering questions like:

- Is abortion ever morally permissible?
- Should the state employ capital punishment for murder?
- Do citizens have a right to government-sponsored healthcare?
- Should we allow same-sex marriage?
- Should universities engage in affirmative action in their admissions practices?

These are the kinds of questions that fall within the domain of applied ethics. Sometimes a number of questions cluster around a particular discipline or area of society, thus creating a sub-field of applied ethics such as bioethics, medical ethics, business ethics, environmental ethics, and the like. In any case, the attempt to provide a thoughtful, principled answer to such questions is to do applied ethics. This usually involves answering the question at issue in terms of what one takes to be the best normative ethical theory.[4] So, for example, suppose you think that utilitarianism is the correct moral theory (see below). Then you would answer each of these questions yes or no depending upon which answer would bring about the most happiness for the most people. However, if one held a deontological theory (again, see below), then one might answer each question in terms of what rights are upheld and/or violated by the proposed action.

This book, of course, is a work in applied ethics. It includes chapters dealing with several specific moral problems. Each of the authors of these chapters approaches their assigned problem from a particular theoretical perspective. It will prove helpful to the reader, then, before delving into these chapters, to have a basic understanding of the major normative ethical theories.

Normative Ethical Theories

In the history of moral philosophy, there have been three broad approaches to normative ethics. Each of these approaches admits of several variations, some of which I will mention, but the discussion that follows will of necessity be somewhat general in nature.[5]

Consequentialism

For consequentialist theories, the focus of moral assessment is on the *consequences of action*. That is, the rightness or wrongness of an action is determined by whether the results of the action are good or bad. So, for the consequentialist, the "end justifies the means." Put more formally, *consequentialism* is the view that

(C) An action is morally right if and only if it produces the best overall consequences.

The question arises, of course, as to what counts as "the best overall consequences"? Different consequentialist theories are distinguished by their answers to this question. According to *Ethical Egoism*, what counts as a good consequence is "whatever serves my self-interest." For *Act Utilitarianism* (by far the most popular consequentialist theory), the right action is the one that "maximizes utility"—where "utility" has to do with bringing about the most overall happiness for those affected by the action. And according to *Rule Utilitarianism*, the right action is one performed in accordance with a rule that, when followed, usually maximizes utility.

Deontology

A different approach to normative ethics focuses not on consequences but on rights and duties. This approach is called *deontology* (from the Greek *deon*, meaning "duty"). For the deontologist, the end never justifies the means. Rather, actions (or action-types) are *intrinsically* right or wrong. That is, actions are right or wrong in themselves independent of their consequences. For this reason, deontological theories are duty-based and rule-centered. What matters morally is performing the right duty or following the right rule. With all of this in mind, we may state the approach of deontology as follows:

(D) An action is right if and only if it is done in accordance with a *bona fide* moral rule.

Obviously, various deontological theories will be distinguished by what they take to be bona fide moral rules and/or how they are known. The most well-known deontological theory is that of Immanuel Kant. According to *Kantianism*, the only *bona fide* moral rule is the so-called *categorical imperative*, which he formulated in multiple ways. One version is the *principle of universalizability*, according to which a right action is one that follows a universalizable maxim (i.e., can be followed by everyone without contradiction). Another version is the *principle of humanity*, which states that a right action is one that treats people as "ends in themselves" rather than as "mere means."

According to the *Divine Command Theory*, an action is right insofar as it comports with the commands of God—commands that are revealed either in Scripture or nature. Similarly, the *Natural Law Theory* holds that right actions are those done in accordance with moral principles implanted in human nature by God and discovered by rational intuition. And W. D. Ross famously proposed that there are a number of prima facie duties, known intuitively, that may be overridden when one duty comes into conflict with another. Lastly, according to the *Social Contract Theory* of morality, actions are morally right if and only if "they are permitted by rules that free, equal, and rational people would agree to live by, on the condition that others obey these rules as well."[6]

Virtue Ethics

A third broad approach to ethical theory takes the focus off of actions and places it instead on the *character* of the moral agent. According to *virtue ethics*, what matters most in ethics is not the question, "What should I *do*?" but "*What kind of person should I be?*" And the answer to that question is simply: a virtuous person—a person who inhabits the moral *virtues* (e.g., patience, honesty, courage, and humility). A virtuous person, of course, is a person who is strongly disposed, by virtue of his character, to *act* virtuously. For example, a person who has the virtue of courage, when faced with danger, will typically act courageously on that occasion. So, while the virtue ethicist places actions secondary to matters of character and character-building, they do after all have an action theory. As Shafer-Landau puts it,

(VE) An act is morally right just because it is one that a virtuous person, acting in character, would do in that situation.[7]

Obviously, virtue ethics puts forward the virtuous person as a moral exemplar or role model. As such, assuming they can be identified, moral guidance can be obtained on controversial issues by looking to what the virtuous person does or would do.[8]

About the Essays

This book is the third volume in a series, the other two being *Problems in Epistemology and Metaphysics* and *Problems in Value Theory* (both published by Bloomsbury, 2020). The essays in the previous volumes were designed to introduce students to some of the most important and interesting philosophical problems and the ways in which philosophers have attempted to solve them. This volume has a similar intent, though the essays contained here are concerned exclusively with problems in applied ethics. Also like the previous volumes, each chapter in this book contains a "point-counterpoint" debate, two major essays by contemporary philosophers arguing for contrary answers to the moral issue addressed in the chapter. After each set of point-counterpoint essays, the authors also offer critical responses to their opponent's essay.

The fifteen problems/topics included in the book cover both old, perennial moral issues as well as problems of more contemporary concern. No doubt some readers will wish I had chosen some other topics that have not been included. There are several that I myself would have included but for limitations of space (affirmative action and the ethics of climate change, for example). But, alas, decisions had to be made. The book is not intended to be comprehensive; it is an introduction to *some* contemporary debates in applied ethics. Moreover, it is not intended to present essays defending every possible perspective on these topics or every argument that may be offered for and against the various views. Each contributor presents what he/she takes to be the best arguments for his/her position and against his/her opponent's position. No doubt, some readers (and this editor, too!) will have preferred that a particular contributor had used a different approach and/or different arguments for some favored viewpoint. But I hope that in such cases all readers will appreciate the diversity with which these difficult topics may be addressed.

In what follows, I provide a brief overview of the fifteen problems and the thirty point-counterpoint essays.

Abortion

The question of the moral permissibility of *abortion* has been at the top of the list in applied ethics for more than fifty years. Despite (or because of) the recent Supreme Court ruling overturning *Roe v. Wade*, the debate has only become more intense. *Abortion*, of course, is the intentional termination of a (human) pregnancy—which always involves the killing of the unborn zygote, embryo, or fetus, either by chemical or surgical means. The question, of course, is whether or not aborting an unborn human organism is morally permissible and, if so, under what conditions?

In Chapter 1, Amy Berg takes up the case for the "pro-choice" position, namely that abortion is morally permissible in most cases. She argues that, because fetuses are importantly different from most other human beings (e.g., with regard to cognitive capacities), they lack a right to life. Moreover, even if human fetuses have the right to life, abortion is still morally permissible because the right to life does not include the right to be kept alive by someone else's body.

Patrick Lee, on the contrary, defends the "pro-life" view that unborn humans do have a right to life that cannot be trumped by the mother's right to bodily autonomy. He contends that human beings, from the moment of conception, are subjects of rights in virtue of the fundamental kind of thing we are. Unlike the pro-choice view, our value is grounded in our fundamental nature, rather than some attributes that we acquire at some time after we come into being. Hence, abortion is not morally permissible except when the mother's life is endangered.

Physician-Assisted Suicide/Euthanasia

When a person has a terminal illness and suffers intensely as his/her disease progresses, what can be done to end or ease his/her suffering? Many such patients desire to end their lives rather than endure further suffering "to the bitter end." *Euthanasia*, or "mercy killing," has to do with ending the life of a suffering person. *Passive euthanasia* is relatively uncontroversial since it only involves the removal of extraordinary life-sustaining measures and allowing the patient to die from the underlying effects of his/her disease. What *is* controversial is *active euthanasia*—taking active steps to intentionally kill the patient (e.g., by administering a lethal dose of medication). When a medical professional is enlisted to aid in active euthanasia, that is called *physician-assisted suicide* (PAS). Do suffering terminally ill patients have the moral right to engage in active euthanasia? Should they be able, legally, to request PAS?

Arthur Schafer answers yes to these questions in Chapter 2. Allowing voluntary active euthanasia and PAS (hereafter PAS/E), he argues, promotes the values of self-determination and patient well-being. He relies primarily on the *argument from autonomy* (sometimes called the "right-to-die argument"): People have a fundamental right to personal autonomy in making important life decisions. This right should only be infringed when its exercise can be shown to cause harm to third parties or society. Schafer does not think that allowing PAS/E causes any such harm, and therefore they should be legally permitted with certain reasonable safeguards.

Opposing PAS/E and euthanasia, Scott B. Rae argues that it is always wrong to take an innocent human life. Furthermore, the right to personal autonomy, if taken as an absolute, would justify PAS/E not just for terminally ill patients but *for any reason*. Rae also highlights the concern that voluntary PAS/E would slide into *involuntary* PAS/E and the right to die would transform into a *duty* to die for the sick and elderly. So, rather than PAS/E, we have an obligation to pursue and improve the hospice and palliative care of terminally ill patients.

Capital Punishment

Chapter 3 addresses the issue of *capital punishment*, the state-sanctioned killing of people convicted of very serious crimes such as murder and treason. As of this writing, fifty-five nations retain the death penalty, including the United States. But what is the purpose of capital punishment? Does it satisfy justice or deter other would-be criminals better than other forms of punishment? Is it "cruel and unusual"? These and other questions prompt the central question of this chapter: Is capital punishment morally permissible?

Joseph M. Bessette and Edward Feser argue that capital punishment is morally appropriate for the most heinous murderers. Justice demands that punishment must be proportionate to the crime, and for the worst aggravated murders, nothing short of the death penalty will do. Additionally, capital punishment reinforces in society the belief in an objective moral order and a revulsion to murder. And there are good reasons to believe that capital punishment is an effective deterrent to at least some would-be murderers. According to Feser and Bessette, a society that abolishes capital punishment is in danger of losing these valuable benefits.

Lloyd Steffen, however, argues that capital punishment is a terrible injustice. Beginning with the presumption that the government should not, as a general rule, kill its own citizens, he holds that advocates of capital punishment must provide a very strong justification to claim an exception to the rule. To show that this burden cannot be met, Steffen cites statistical evidence that the death penalty is unusual and inequitably administered. More egregiously, innocent people may (and have been) executed. For these and other reasons, life imprisonment is preferred to capital punishment.

Human Genome Editing

Advances in biotechnology have turned science fiction into science fact. With the mapping of the human genome and the invention of the CRISPR tool has come the ability to do genetic editing—the modification of an organism's DNA. One use of this new technology is *gene therapy* which has to do with correcting or replacing defective genes so as to treat or cure diseases such as sickle cell anemia and Parkinson's. Such therapy is relatively uncontroversial morally. However, *gene enhancement* is the subject of considerable debate. The idea is to modify a person's genetic profile as a way (putatively) to enhance or "improve" his/her quality of life usually as defined by current societal standards. Genetic enhancement, therefore, might be used to modify hair and eye color, height, body type, intelligence, memory, and even personality. Human genome editing in general and gene enhancement in particular are challenged on moral grounds. The specter of "designer babies" (which implies the commodification and exploitation of children) is the most well-known worry. But other concerns include safety issues and the long-term effects of genetic engineering on society in general.

In Chapter 4, Colin Farrelly argues that the benefits of genome editing greatly outweigh any such moral concerns. These benefits include not only curing but preventing disease, as well as curtailing the aging process and minimizing disparities caused by the genetic effects of lifestyle and environment. Farrelly also thinks that most objections to "enhancements" are rooted in an unwarranted and inconsistent preference for the biological "given."

C. Ben Mitchell contends that, despite the potential benefits, genetic enhancement is "a bridge too far." One reason is that our ability to diagnose genetic anomalies will lead to discrimination against those who are so diagnosed. Another reason is that proposed germline therapies (modification of sperm and egg cells), besides having potential unintended side effects, are morally problematic because the future generations affected by the therapies cannot give informed consent. Mitchell also warns of the dangerous potential for eugenics posed by genome editing, as well as other possible dystopian futures.

Right to Health Care

Suppose you become deathly ill with some serious disease that can only be treated with a very expensive drug or surgery. But suppose also that you do not have the money to pay for this treatment or to afford any insurance that would cover it. Do you have a *right* to receive this treatment anyway regardless of your ability to pay? No one seriously denies that you have a right to *acquire* this treatment if you can afford it—the doctors, for example, cannot turn you away because of your race or gender or religious beliefs. But do you have a right to the treatment *itself*, money or no money? The question is: *Do we have a right to health care?* This question is closely related to another: Should the government subsidize a system of universal health care for all its citizens? Many nations—Canada and the UK, for instance—have implemented such systems. The United States so far has not.

Chapter 5 addresses the topic of whether there is a right to health care. Robert C. Hughes argues in the affirmative. He bases his case not on concerns about social justice but on the values of social stability and liberty. As he sees it, a government's failure to provide equal access to health care poses a threat to both social order and individual freedom. It threatens the latter because people who are dependent on others for their basic needs are not free. It threatens the former because such needy people may be forced to get what they need through unethical means.

Trevor Burrus argues the negative. A "right" to health care, if it exists, would be a *positive* right as opposed to a negative right. Whereas negative rights require merely an omission from a duty-holder, a positive right requires an *action* from a duty-holder. Burrus argues that the very notion of a positive right is fraught with philosophical and moral problems. Thus, the idea of a "right" to health care is likewise morally problematic, entailing logical absurdities and requiring duties of individuals and governments that cannot reasonably be required of them.

Vaccine Mandates

The moral issue of *vaccine mandates* took center stage during the recent Covid-19 pandemic. A vaccine mandate is a state-enforced requirement for citizens to receive a vaccination against some infectious disease. Of course, the primary impetus behind vaccine mandates has to do with concerns for public safety. Those who oppose these mandates are also concerned about safety, specifically the safety of the vaccines themselves, as well as matters related to individual liberties.

Shlomo Cohen, in Chapter 6, argues that vaccine mandates are morally justified. While granting that the value of liberty creates a presumption against vaccine mandates, he contends that this presumption is trumped by concerns for public safety—after all, a refusal to be vaccinated has implications for other people and *their* personal autonomy. Specifically, Cohen appeals to the Harm Principle, the promotion of the common good, and the principle of fairness to justify vaccine mandates.

Gabriël A. Moens, using the example of the mandates implemented in Australia, argues that vaccine mandates do not, in fact, override individual liberties and are not morally justified. He claims that the mandates enforced in Australia and elsewhere represent a tyranny that undermines the rule of law, violates the individual's right to voluntary consent to medical treatment, and leads to a two-tier society that discriminates against the unvaccinated. These problems are exacerbated when the required vaccines are insufficiently tested and arguably unsafe.

Animal Rights

Many nonhuman animals are clearly sentient—that is, they can sense, feel pain, experience emotions, have desires, and so on. But is being sentient enough for them to have moral rights as human beings do? No one thinks that animals are moral *agents*; they have no moral obligations, are not subject to moral praise and blame. When a wolf attacks a sheep, or even a human, we do not think that it has acted immorally even if we decide to "put it down" for safety reasons. But while they are not moral agents, perhaps they are moral *patients*—objects, that is, of our moral obligations. Perhaps we have duties to at least some animals to not mistreat them, experiment on them, or even eat them.

The question of *animal rights* is the subject of Chapter 7. Molly Gardner defends animal rights on the basis of two premises: (1) Except in special circumstances, it is wrong to harm some individuals for the sake of others, and (2) Most instances of factory farming, testing on animals, and hunting or trapping for sport or fashion are cases of harming some individuals for the sake of others. The implication is that most factory farming, animal experimentation, sport hunting, and the like are morally impermissible.

According to Bruce P. Blackshaw, an adequate account of the moral status of animals must satisfactorily address three issues: (1) It must explain the wrongness of inflicting gratuitous pain on animals, (2) It must resolve the problem of wild animal suffering, and (3) It must account for our intuition that the wrongness of killing human beings—even "marginal" human beings—is weightier than the wrongness of killing nonhuman animals. He argues that a modified substance view of persons can meet these requirements. On this view, all human beings have a high moral status and animals have a real, but lower, moral status. So, while animals do not have rights, it is wrong to cause (but not necessarily wrong to not prevent) their suffering without a good reason.

Immigration/Open Borders

During President Joe Biden's term as US president, an estimated eleven million illegal immigrants entered the United States.[9] In response to this statistic, you might ask: "So what?" What is wrong with people crossing the borders of a nation without permission? Why should that be illegal? Why do we even have borders at all? Why shouldn't people be allowed to freely come and go to any country as they please without interference from the government? The *problem of illegal immigration* and the question of *open vs. closed borders* have been at the forefront of political debate for some time, but especially in recent years, not only in the United States but around the world.

In Chapter 8, Michael Huemer contends for open immigration and open borders. His argument is straightforward. Immigration restrictions, he claims, are harmful and coercive, and anything that is harmful and coercive is prima facie wrong. Immigration restrictions enforced by government agents are clearly coercive, and keeping immigrants from crossing a border harms them because it prevents them from meeting economic and other needs. Huemer responds to reasons given for border restrictions to show that they are either false or insufficient to justify the harm done to migrants.

Daniel Demetriou argues against open borders on two grounds. First, he argues that advocates of open borders either don't understand or refuse to be clear about what they are defending—are they defending "open access" or "open residence"? This ambiguity leads to confusing and sometimes misleading arguments for "open immigration." Second, defenders of open border policies either depend on radical libertarian views of political (non)authority, or, to fix problems implied by that, they inconsistently resort to authoritarian measures.

Gun Control

Gun violence is a serious social problem, especially in the United States.[10] Some countries (e.g., the UK and Australia) either ban or severely restrict private gun ownership. Gun violence in these countries is, as we would expect, quite rare comparatively.[11] Accordingly, *gun control* advocates surmise that the gun violence and gun-related deaths in the United States would be greatly minimized by stringent restrictions on gun ownership, and that the government is obligated to implement such restrictions. Of course, strong gun control measures are hotly contested by those who believe that private gun ownership is a bulwark against government tyranny and vital to upholding the individual's right to self-defense—a perspective they believe is enshrined in the Second Amendment to the *US Constitution*.[12]

Nicholas Dixon, in Chapter 9, argues that there is no right to gun ownership for self-defense. He first makes the utilitarian argument that the prevalence of guns in society is a determinant of gun violence, and thus gun control is justified in order to reduce the number of gun deaths. In response to the rights-based argument for gun ownership based on the right to self-defense, Dixon argues that gun control does not violate the right to self-defense because in a society without guns, the need to use guns in self-defense will be greatly diminished. Moreover, like other rights, the right to self-defense has limits. Specifically, due to the social harm caused by the prevalence of guns, the right to self-defense does not entail the right to own a gun.

Against gun control and in defense of gun rights, Benjamin L. Mabry maintains that the "right to bear arms" is partly constitutive of what it means to be a free and equal citizen. By definition, he argues, a free citizen essentially resists acts that would nullify one's freedom, and philosophers and lawyers (who make the laws) are incompetent to judge the legitimate means to such resistance. Moreover, arguments about costs and benefits of civil rights, and concerns about public safety, are irrelevant to ethics. What matters is justice, and justice is not a matter of utility.

War and Peace

"War is hell," as the saying goes. It is the source, that is, of untold death and misery. All good people rightly prefer peace. Indeed, we believe that we are obligated to strive for peace, to prevent war and put an end to war. But can war ever be morally justified? At the two ends of the moral spectrum on this question are Just War Theory and pacifism. The latter, *pacifism*, claims that war is never morally justified. The violence and destruction involved in war make it morally unthinkable. *Just War Theory*, on the other hand, holds that war may, under certain conditions, be morally justified. Indeed, sometimes justice demands that war be waged.

In Chapter 10, Steven B. Cowan (yours truly) defends the Just War Theory. I argue that human beings have a natural right to life that includes the right to use deadly force in self-defense. Further, government exists to secure the natural rights of citizens, including their right to life. That entails that government has an obligation to wage war to defend its citizens (and perhaps the citizens of other nations) against unjust foreign aggression. I also explain and defend the criteria demanded by justice before, during, and after a war is fought.

Timothy Paul Erdel argues for pacifism. He maintains that many pacifists have four virtues that make war unjustifiable: daring imaginations, strong moral convictions, the willingness to face facts, and the courage to fail. Those who see war as justifiable, he says, fail to imagine better alternatives. They also fail to adequately appreciate the inherent wrongness of killing, that killing only makes matters worse, not better, and that killing adversely affects the character of the killer. Moreover, the pacifist alone is willing to face the brutal facts of war, which have to do with the horrendous suffering inflicted on innocent civilians. And, lastly, the pacifist is not afraid to fail. Even when the pacifist response to violence fails to stop violence, he knows at least that he was unwilling to kill to achieve his goals.

Reparations

Chapter 11 takes up the topic of *reparations* for past injustices. Take, for example, the treatment of Black Africans in the not-too-distant past. Millions of them were enslaved by Europeans (and others), forcibly removed from their homelands and forced into hard and degrading servitude. Fortunately, the slave trade and slavery itself were eventually abolished—for example, in Britain, by an act of Parliament; in the United States, by a bloody civil war. Now, it is a universally held principle of justice that reparations should be made to those who suffer an unjust loss. In other words, the injustice is to be "repaired" by giving the victim some form of compensation (i.e., money, land, etc.). So, it is uncontroversial that the freed slaves should have received reparations for their enslavement. But what about their *descendants* several generations removed? The contemporary debate focuses on this question. Should people alive today whose ancestors were enslaved receive reparations?

Federico Lenzerini argues that past injustices do in fact call for contemporary reparations. The purpose of reparations is not, in his view, simply to correct past acts of injustice but, more importantly, to heal present societal wounds and fractures. This point works to undermine the common objection that no one alive today was a slave who deserves reparations and no one alive today owes any reparations. Also, while no individual citizen of a country that once permitted slavery may be guilty of an injustice, the government as an institution with a past *is* guilty of having once allowed slavery and benefited from its existence. Moreover, while no one alive today directly caused or suffered the injustice of slavery, there are many who are *indirectly* affected by the past enslavement of their predecessors.

Andrew Bernstein insists that moral responsibility is individual and volitional, not collective. This implies that actual slave owners owe reparations to actual slaves. But, with regard to past US slavery, neither slaves nor slave owners presently exist. So, there are no African Americans today who deserve reparations for past slavery, and no white Americans owe anyone reparations for past slavery. Bernstein also points out apparent absurd consequences of the notion of collective responsibility. For example, if I am responsible for the past crimes of my ancestors, then am I not responsible also for their past achievements? Don't non-whites, then, owe me (a white man) restitution for the benefits they receive from my ancestors' accomplishments? There is the further difficulty of discerning who among the current white population are descended from slave owners and, more importantly, which African Americans are descended from slaves.

Free Speech

The right to *free speech* is considered fundamental to the existence of a free society. Thus, the US Constitution, in its First Amendment, famously stipulates, "Congress shall make no law abridging the freedom of speech, or of the press." But are there no limits to free speech? What if the speech harms, or threatens to harm, some person or group of people? Everyone knows that you cannot rightly shout "Fire!" in a crowded theater unless there really is a fire. Out of concern especially for people who have been the targets of unjust discrimination, many countries (including some that have traditionally championed free speech) have enacted "hate speech" laws in order to curtail what is perceived to be harmful speech. Are such laws morally justified? Are they violations of an inviolable right to free speech? Do they cause more harm than good?

In Chapter 12, Onkar Ghate contends for *free speech absolutism*. Free speech is an absolute right that no state should have the power to regulate. In a free society, the government exists solely to secure the rights of individuals—rights they have prior to and independent of the state. Hate speech laws, which limit free speech in the public interest, are the expression of a power that government does not legitimately possess. To cede this power to the government is to allow government officials to decide for me what is true and good and thereby relinquish control of my life and happiness. The only appropriate response to hateful speech is to walk away from the speaker or engage in counterspeech.

On behalf of the thesis that there are limits to free speech, Andrei Bespalov points out that even advocates of free speech grant that clearly dangerous speech—threats of harm, incitements to violence, libel, and so on—are rightly prohibited by law. He argues that hate speech is no less seriously harmful and, in fact, jeopardizes the very values that are protected by the right to free speech. Therefore, hate speech laws are justified because any benefits of not restricting hate speech are outweighed by the benefits of eliminating hate speech.

Same-Sex Marriage

Until very recently, most people in the West believed in what is now called the "traditional view of marriage," namely that marriage involves the union of one man and one woman. But many people and many nations have now come to recognize the legitimacy of *same-sex marriage*. For example, in 2015, the US Supreme Court's decision in *Obergefell v. Hodges* made same-sex marriage legal in all fifty US states, overriding several states' laws forbidding it. Despite its current legality, however, debate still rages. Legality does not equal morality and those who continue to hold the traditional view of marriage continue to argue that same-sex marriage is wrong and ought to be illegal.

James S. Spiegel, in Chapter 13, defends the traditional view of marriage, arguing first that the principal argument for same-sex marriage makes a false assumption, namely that banning same-sex marriage constitutes the unequal treatment of homosexuals, denying them a right that others enjoy. On the contrary, traditional marriage laws treat everyone equally because they grant to everyone the equal right to marry a person of the opposite sex. Second, Spiegel maintains that same-sex marriage is inherently unjust because it undermines the special social value of heterosexual unions. Traditional, heterosexual marriage has special social value because of its procreative function. But the legal recognition of same-sex marriage is tantamount to a rejection of this special value, which is unjust.

The case for same-sex marriage is made by Christopher Arroyo. He begins by providing historical evidence against the view of most traditional marriage advocates that marriage has an unchanging essence that has persisted throughout history. There have been, he claims, many forms of marriage at different times and places. He goes on to argue that marriage is a human convention in which two people make promises to each other, something that is essential to human flourishing because it enables people to live and thrive together. As such, promises are a human good. And, Arroyo contends, since there are no differences between a different-sex marriage and a same-sex marriage relevant to the goodness of marriage, same-sex marriage must be a human good if different-sex marriages are.

Transgender Rights

As I write, the Trump administration is attempting to enforce a ban on transgender biological males from competing in women's sports or utilizing women's bathrooms. All transgender individuals are being purged from the US armed forces. Also, the Supreme Court of the UK recently ruled that the legal definition of "woman" is to be based on biological sex. Prior to these developments, over the last decade or so, DEI initiatives in many universities, corporations, and governments required the use of people's "preferred pronouns." Hospitals, except where prohibited by law, offer "gender-affirming care" to transgender individuals who wish to transition physically to their self-identified gender. It is difficult to imagine a more controversial ethical and political issue.

According to its advocates, a *transgender* (or trans) person is someone who has a gender identity different from the gender associated with their biological sex. The opposite of transgender is *cisgender*, which describes persons whose gender identity matches their biological sex. This, of course, is precisely where the controversy lies. Is a "transwoman" really a woman trapped in a man's body? Or does that person suffer from a mental disorder known as "gender dysphoria?"[13] Are there really only two genders, or is gender a fluid, multifaceted phenomenon? More germane to this book's purposes, the question is: *What rights do trans people have?* Do they have the moral right to use the restroom of their choice? Should trans women be allowed to participate in women's sports? Are cisgender people obligated to recognize their trans identities?

In Chapter 14, Jasper Heaton argues that trans people have a right to have their gender identities respected. This does not mean that people are required always to *believe* what trans people believe about themselves, but it does mean that trans people should be regarded as *epistemic interdependants*—which involves accepting their first-person authority regarding their experiences of their bodies and claims about their gender identities. Once this requirement is understood, Heaton thinks it will be evident that cis people often do not meet the conditions for ethically dissenting to trans people's gender identities.

David Crawford points out that transgenderism is rooted in a fragmented view of human persons according to which the relation of the sexually dimorphic body to a person's internal subjective state is seen as arbitrary and thus implying that persons lack integral wholeness. He argues that such a view of humanity leads inevitably to the eradication of sex itself (i.e., maleness and femaleness). For example, if a woman can have male sex organs, then we can no longer speak of "male" and "female" sex organs. This view also assumes that human beings and their bodies do not possess an organic unity but are just amalgamations of disparate parts. Therefore, the call for "transgender rights" is a call to universalize this false and fragmented understanding of human persons which will bring harm to people and society, including those it purports to help.

Drug Legalization

Chapter 15 takes up the ethical problem of *drug legalization*. Many people consume so-called "recreational" drugs—psychoactive drugs that are consumed for nonmedical purposes (e.g., for pleasure, to relieve anxiety or depression, etc.). These include alcoholic beverages and nicotine products (cigarettes, cigars), which are generally legal for adults. But there are many recreational drugs that are (or have been) illegal: marijuana, cocaine, methamphetamine, heroin, LSD, and more. Many of these drugs are addictive and can impair one's judgment. Do such dangers justify keeping these drugs illegal? Or does prohibiting them amount to an unwarranted intrusion into people's private lives?

Chris Meyers makes the case for legalizing all recreational drugs. He begins by arguing that the burden of proof is on anyone who desires to punish people for recreational drug use. He then offers evidence that drug use is not as harmful as prohibitionists think, and yet, even if it was harmful, punishing users amounts to an unjustified paternalism. In response to the charge that recreational drug use harms *others*, Meyers agrees that those who actually harm others by drug use should be punished, but the drug use itself should not be criminalized any more than other activities that might lead one to harm others (e.g., playing video games). Meyers also argues for the legalization of selling (and thus enabling the regulation of) recreational drugs on the grounds of public safety.

Timothy Hsiao argues for the strict regulation of some recreational drug use and the outright prohibition of others. His argument is grounded in the fundamental value of human freedom. The exercise of freedom requires rational agency—sober cognitive function and self-control. But the use of intoxicating drugs impairs and sometimes destroys a person's rational agency and thus undermines his freedom. So, the government has the duty to protect freedom by carefully regulating drugs that have the potential (when used in excess) for immediate cognitive impairment (e.g., alcohol). And a substance (e.g., marijuana, cocaine) that is consistently and deliberately used to induce a "high" that undermines rational agency demands prohibition.

For Students and Instructors

To aid both students and instructors, I have also included in the book some pedagogical features. First, at the beginning of each essay, I have provided a list of "**Study Questions**." These questions are designed primarily to facilitate reading comprehension, to help the reader follow the author's train of thought and understand the major points and arguments presented. They can also be used by instructors to enable students' classroom preparation.

Second, at the end of every chapter are "**Questions for Reflection**." These questions require students to critically evaluate what they have read in the chapter and to explore additional related issues. These questions can be utilized to facilitate classroom discussions or provide small group exercises. They could also be used for writing assignments.

Third, also at the end of each chapter, I have provided a list "**For Further Reading**." Each list is composed of books and articles that will allow the student to expand his knowledge of the specific applied ethics problem addressed in that chapter.

Bloomsbury Publishers provides some additional **online resources** for students and instructors to accompany this book. First, there is an article called **"The Philosopher's**

Toolkit" which outlines the three principal methods or "tools" that philosophers (including ethicists) use in discussing and solving philosophical problems: arguments, definitions, and thought experiments. Second, you will find an essay entitled **"How to Write a Philosophy Paper."** Instructors who assign students to write essays or term papers should direct their students to read this essay for helpful guidance for completing their assignment. You can find both of these online resources at the following link:

https://www.bloomsbury.com/us/problems-in-applied-ethics-9781350452176/

Notes

1. Jonathan Wolff, *An Introduction to Moral Philosophy*, 2nd ed. (London: W. W. Norton & Company, 2018), 7.
2. Ibid., 8.
3. Stephen L. Darwall, "Theories of Ethics," in *Contemporary Debates in Applied Ethics*, 2nd ed., ed. Andrew I. Cohen and Christopher H. Wellman (Malden: Wiley-Blackwell, 2014), 14.
4. The relationship between normative and applied ethics is actually more complex than this. For example, as Darwall points out (see Ibid., 14–15), a philosopher may start with some considered judgment on a particular moral problem (e.g., torturing children is morally wrong) and then use that judgment in evaluating the acceptability of some normative ethical theory.
5. For more detailed treatments of normative ethical theories, see Darwall, "Theories of Ethics"; Wolff, *An Introduction to Moral Philosophy*; Louis P. Pojman and James Fieser, *Ethics: Discovering Right and Wrong*, 8th ed. (Boston: Cengage, 2017); and Russ Shafer-Landau, *The Fundamentals of Ethics*, 6th ed. (Oxford: Oxford University Press, 2023).
6. Shafer-Landau, *The Fundamentals of Ethics*, 189.
7. Ibid., 279.
8. As with consequentialism and deontology, there are different versions of virtue ethics. The differences, however, are far more finely grained, so I do not mention them here. For a discussion of various virtue ethics theories, see Rosalind Hursthouse and Glen Pettigrove, "Virtue Ethics," in *The Stanford Encyclopedia of Philosophy* (https://plato.stanford.edu/entries/ethics-virtue/).
9. See official stats at https://www.cbp.gov/newsroom/stats/southwest-land-border-encounters.
10. According to the John Hopkins Center for Gun Violence (https://publichealth.jhu.edu/center-for-gun-violence-solutions/research-reports/gun-violence-in-the-united-states), in 2022, there were 48,204 firearms deaths in the United States (over half of these were suicides). That translates into one violent gun death every eleven minutes.
11. For example, in 2023/24, there were only twenty-two firearms-related homicides in England and Wales (See the statistics at https://www.statista.com/statistics/288166/homicide-method-of-killing-in-england-and-wales-uk/).

12 The Second Amendment states, "A well regulated Militia, being necessary to the security of a free State, the right of the people to keep and bear Arms, shall not be infringed."

13 See "What Is Gender Dysphoria?" American Psychiatric Association (https://www.psychiatry.org/patients-families/gender-dysphoria/what-is-gender-dysphoria).

1

Abortion

A Case for the Moral Permissibility of Abortion[1]

Amy Berg

Study Questions

1. What is Berg's "cognitive capacities view" of the right to life? What are its three advantages?
2. What is Marquis's "future-of-value view"? Why does Berg reject it?
3. What is the "Violinist Case"? What does Berg think it shows?
4. Describe the "Case of the People seeds." What does Berg think it shows?
5. Why does Berg believe that abortion should be legal even for cases in which it is immoral?

Here's a common argument that abortion is morally impermissible and that, therefore, it should be illegal:

(1) The fetus has the right to life.

(2) If the fetus has the right to life, then abortion is morally impermissible.

(3) Therefore, abortion is morally impermissible. (from 1 and 2)

(4) If abortion is morally impermissible, then it should be illegal.

(5) Therefore, abortion should be illegal. (from 3 and 4)

This argument is simple and plausible. Fetuses are human beings, just as you and I are, and we have the right to life. That right is what makes killing us so wrong, one of the worst crimes a person can commit. Just as the law protects us against being murdered, so it should protect fetuses against abortion.

In fact, however, each key premise—1, 2, and 4—is weaker than it looks. We'll tackle each in order. First, we'll look at premise 1, the claim that the fetus has a right to life. Once we see why we—you and I—have this right, we'll see that because fetuses are different in key ways, most of them lack the right to life. From there, we'll move on to premise 2. Even if some or all fetuses have the right to life, we'll see that abortion is still morally permissible, because the right to life does not include the right to be kept alive by someone else's body.

That gives us two reasons for thinking that abortion is morally permissible—that is, in most cases. There may be some times when fetuses do have the right to life *and* when the right to life includes the right to use someone else's body to stay alive. That's where premise 4 comes in. It might seem like we should outlaw morally impermissible abortions—after all, these may have the same moral status as murder. At the same time, the complex, fast-moving circumstances of pregnancy mean that we should err on the side of keeping abortion legal even when it's morally impermissible.

Premise 1

One of the most common reasons for thinking that abortion is wrong is that fetuses, like most or all other human beings, have the right to life. That's what makes it wrong to kill us, and it's also what makes abortion morally impermissible. At first glance, this makes sense. Yet nonhuman animals are alive too, and most people are perfectly okay with eating a chicken sandwich—and trees, slime molds, and insects seem even less likely to have the right to life. To know whether premise 1 is true, we need to know what living beings actually have the right to life.

So, what makes us different from insects, trees, and maybe animals? An easy answer is that we are human beings, and only human beings (including fetuses) have the right to life—but this easy answer is too simple. Imagine that we make contact with aliens who are very similar to us—they're capable of reasoning and making moral decisions, they feel pain, they form relationships, they have senses of humor, and they're roughly as intelligent as we are. They don't pose any threat to us. The only real difference is that they aren't human. Most people would say it would be wrong for us to kill these humanlike, but not human, aliens—they have the right to life, just as we do.

The Cognitive-Capacities View

If those aliens-like-us have the right to life, *why*? The major thing we have in common with them is the set of cognitive capacities that let us reason, form relationships, make jokes, and so on (capacities not shared with insects, trees, and slime molds). These capacities may include consciousness, reasoning, self-motivated activity (i.e., activity involving our own choices and agency), communication, self-awareness,[2] emotions,[3] and organized cortical brain activity.[4] We'll call this the *cognitive-capacities view* of the right to life.

The capacities on this list do a good job explaining why we have the right to life. Common explanations for why it's wrong to kill us include: (1) killing is painful, (2) killing would leave your friends and family to grieve your death, (3) killing means you won't get to have any future experiences, and (4) killing creates an atmosphere of fear. Nearly all of these rely on at least one of the cognitive capacities listed in the previous paragraph. True, even beings without our sophisticated cognitive capacities can experience pain—but we tend to think killing is wrong even when it's painless, and many people don't think it's wrong to kill animals even when this causes them pain. But grief requires us to be able to reason and feel emotions; having future experiences requires consciousness; fearing death requires emotions, self-awareness, and reasoning; all of the above require organized cortical brain activity.[5] Beings who lack these cognitive capacities include trees, insects, slime molds . . . and most fetuses. If the cognitive-capacities view is correct, then abortion appears to be morally permissible.

You might object to the cognitive-capacities view by pointing out that there are many beings who lack some or all of our cognitive capacities, yet whom we believe it's wrong to kill. These may include infants, elderly people with late-stage dementia, and people who are in comas. If we think that abortion is permissible, but we also think it's wrong to kill elderly people with dementia, aren't we being inconsistent?

First, the cognitive capacities we listed a minute ago are best understood as what philosophers call a "cluster concept": no single item on the list is necessary or sufficient for the right to life, but some number of them are jointly sufficient.[6] Elderly people with late-stage dementia may have diminished capacities for reasoning and self-motivated activity, but they still have organized cortical brain activity and feel emotions. You don't need all of these capacities to have the right to life; you just need enough of them.

This helps, but it doesn't fully solve the problem. People in reversible comas lack nearly all of these capacities, yet we almost all think it would be wrong to kill these people.[7] It seems to most of us that it would be wrong to kill very young infants, and yet the cognitive capacities of very young infants are surely not very different from the cognitive capacities of fetuses who are just days from being born.[8] Can the cognitive-capacities view of the right to life explain this difference?

Proponents of this view have a few options. One is to claim that very small infants and people with very severe dementia really do not have the right to life. Some philosophers have argued for this, but most people find it unacceptable.[9]

A second option is to claim that very small infants, and so on, do not have the right to life but hold that we should treat them as if they do, because doing otherwise will create a culture in which we feel free to harm people who do have the right to life. Yet evidence for this claim is lacking. Plenty of people don't think animals have the right to life, but this doesn't make them very likely to murder their fellow human beings. We would need some evidence to support the idea that killing beings who don't have the right to life makes us more likely to harm or kill beings who do.

The most promising response is to accept the cognitive-capacities view of moral status and to recognize that some fetuses do have the cognitive capacities that give them the right to life. In at least some cases, then, abortion is morally impermissible. Insofar as organized cortical activity is one of the criteria determining moral status, fetuses who have acquired this capacity (somewhere between the twenty-fifth and thirty-second week of gestation) have the right to life;[10] fetuses who lack this capacity (and the other cognitive capacities that depend on it) do not have the right to life. This view has at least three advantages: (1) it shows why nearly all abortions are morally permissible (since the vast majority of abortions take place well before twenty-five weeks of gestation);[11] (2) it shows why it is wrong to kill all the people we think it's wrong to kill, since people with very severe dementia, infants, and even some coma patients have organized cortical brain activity; (3) we keep a plausible view of what it is that gives us the right to life in the first place.

The Future-of-Value View

If you disagree with this, you'll need a better answer to this last part: What do adults and fetuses—but not trees, slime molds, insects, and maybe animals—share that makes it wrong to kill them? An alternative answer is that what matters is not our actual, but rather our potential, cognitive capacities. This is at the heart of Don Marquis's very influential argument against abortion. According to Marquis, what makes it wrong to kill us is not any fact about us as we are right now, but rather facts about our futures: killing is wrong because it means we will lose out on all of the projects, relationships, and activities we would have experienced in the future.[12] While fetuses do not currently have the capacity to value their futures, they do have futures they will have reason to value once they've developed these cognitive capacities. Therefore, it is wrong to kill them, for just the same reason that it's wrong to kill us.[13] Call this the *future-of-value view* of the right to life.

The future-of-value view is compelling—but, ultimately, the cognitive-capacities view of moral status is more persuasive. Start with what we already believe: few of us think that the death of a fetus is morally equivalent to the death of a person who's already been born. It's likely that around half of all human beings die as a result of pregnancy loss, most extremely early in pregnancy. If the death of a fetus is the moral equivalent of the death of a human being, miscarriage is the greatest public health crisis of our time—and yet practically no one treats it that way.[14]

Likewise, imagine a situation in which a fire breaks out at a fertility clinic: you can save either one fertility doctor or five embryos, but you don't have time to save everyone.[15] If you would choose to save the fertility doctor, even if you recognize that the loss of the embryos is a tragedy, this indicates that you think the death of someone who's been born is a greater loss than the death of someone who hasn't yet been born.

Of course, this isn't necessarily strong evidence against the future-like-ours view. All of us have some inconsistent and poorly reasoned beliefs; our beliefs about death and miscarriage may fall into this category. Yet there's good reason for us not to view these two kinds of deaths as equivalent. While fetuses do have futures of value, they don't seem to have the same kind of relationship to those futures that you and I do. There are specific projects, relationships, and commitments each of us has reason to value; fetuses have much fuzzier futures, and so it's less clear what, specifically, they lose if they never experience those futures. Maybe, then, killing is wrong when it cuts us off from futures we are currently capable of valuing.

Marquis acknowledges this objection, but he argues that my current valuing of my future can't be what makes killing wrong. It would be wrong to kill me when I'm sleeping, even though when I'm asleep, I'm not valuing anything at all.[16] It would be wrong to kill someone who is deeply depressed and so doesn't currently value their future.

But this response isn't satisfactory. Each of us, whether awake or asleep, has all sorts of desires we're not aware of. You may desire that you pass this class, for example. You can't hold all your desires in your head at once, but that doesn't mean they're alien to you—if someone asked you, "Do you want to pass this class?", you wouldn't have to puzzle long and hard about how to answer that question.[17] It's the capacity to have those desires that matters—we are the kind of beings who can have desires about our future whether we are awake or asleep, whether or not we currently desire to stay alive. Marquis is right that the wrongness of killing has to do with our futures—but the best explanation has to do with the cognitive capacities we have now that make us the kind of beings who can value those futures.

That may not satisfy you—you may still think it's the fact that you have a future, not the attitude you have toward it, that explains why killing is wrong. But beings who have this future of value, and yet are incapable of valuing it, lack the right to life. Suppose you are the owner of a future-of-value machine. Anything that enters the machine will, within nine months, develop into a being with projects, relationships, and on and on—all the things that give us reason to value our futures. Now, choose something you believe doesn't have the right to life—a slime mold, say. Imagine that it's right outside the machine and moving toward it; if you do nothing, the slime mold will slither into the machine.[18] Without your intervention, that is, the slime mold has a future of value. Would it be wrong for you, right now, to move the slime mold away from the machine, thereby denying it a future of value?

The answer seems to be no: it wouldn't be wrong. You don't owe the slime mold anything in particular because it isn't wrong to deny a being its future of value when it lacks the right kind of capacities at the present moment. The best explanation of why killing is wrong, when it's wrong, is still the cognitive-capacities view: it's wrong to kill beings who *currently* have the cognitive capacities they need in order to be able to form desires, relationships, and commitments that will stretch into the future.

So, to summarize: it initially seemed plausible that fetuses have the right to life, because they're human beings just like us, and it's usually wrong to kill us. We saw, though, that it isn't our status as human beings that makes it wrong to kill us; instead, it's the cognitive capacities that distinguish us from other living beings. These are cognitive capacities nearly all fetuses lack, making abortion morally permissible in nearly all circumstances. Setting the bar at a low level of cognitive capacities gets all the cases right, allowing us to say that elderly sufferers of severe dementia, some coma patients, and fetuses who are very close to birth have the right to life, while most fetuses, and adults with persistent very low levels of brain activity (people in very deep and irreversible comas, for example), do not.[19]

Premise 2

At this point, you may be unconvinced that premise 1 is false. Maybe you think Marquis's future-of-value view is more plausible than I've argued, or maybe you disagree with that view but find the cognitive-capacities view problematic too. Let's move on, then, to premise 2: "If the fetus has the right to life, then abortion is morally impermissible." This premise, as we'll see, is false: even if fetuses have the right to life, abortion is still (usually) morally permissible.

The Violinist Case

To see why this is, let's examine a situation that's very similar to abortion, but where the person involved unquestionably has the right to life—and then we can see whether it's permissible to allow that person to die. The most famous attempt to do this (one of the most famous thought experiments in all of ethics) is Judith Jarvis Thomson's *violinist case*:

> You wake up in the morning and find yourself back to back in bed with an unconscious violinist. A famous unconscious violinist. He has been found to have a fatal kidney ailment, and the Society of Music Lovers has canvassed all the available medical records and found that you alone have the right blood type to help. They have therefore kidnapped you, and last night the violinist's circulatory system was plugged into yours, so that your kidneys can be used to extract poisons from his blood as well as your own. The director of the hospital now tells you, "Look, we're sorry the Society of Music Lovers did this to you—we would never have permitted it if we had known. But still, they did it, and the violinist now is plugged into you. To unplug you would be to kill him. But never mind, it's only for nine months. By then he will have recovered from his ailment, and can safely be unplugged from you."[20]

If anyone has a right to life, the violinist surely does. Yet Thomson thinks that you are, of course, permitted to unplug yourself from the violinist. That's not because the violinist loses his right to life when the Society of Music Lovers kidnaps him, nor because your right to life outweighs his—it's because the right to life does not include the right to use someone else's body to stay alive.[21] If the only way to stop him from using your body to stay alive is to take an action that will let him die, you are permitted to do this.

Compare this to abortion. A person who's pregnant is not permitted to ensure that a fetus dies—if it is viable outside the womb, she should have the fetus removed in a way that preserves its life. But if the only way to stop a fetus from using your body without consent is to remove it in a way that will result in its death, abortion is morally permissible. This is true, the violinist analogy shows us, even if fetuses do have the right to life—because just the same thing would be true in the case of the violinist.

You've probably noticed that the violinist case is different from many pregnancies in some key ways. Some of these differences strengthen the case for the permissibility of abortion. For one thing, although you have to stay in the hospital in the violinist case, we are never told that you're in any physical danger from the process. Pregnancy isn't like this: its complications range from annoying to potentially fatal.[22] If you're permitted to unplug yourself from the violinist even when his use of your body poses no risk to you, you surely are permitted to have an abortion when a fetus's use of your body poses a serious risk to you. For another, if you support the violinist for nine months, you and he go your separate ways for the rest of your lives. While adoption is an option, most people who carry pregnancies to term choose to keep their children.[23] That means that their responsibilities for those children last at least eighteen years in most cases. That's a significant additional cost.

But you've probably also noticed that there are some differences between the violinist case and many pregnancies that seem to push us in the opposite direction. Most people who are pregnant aren't confined to a hospital bed, so the person in the violinist case bears an extra cost. Perhaps most significantly, in the violinist case, you are kidnapped—you had absolutely no say in the circumstances that put you in the hospital, hooked up to the violinist. In contrast, most pregnancies—some 95 percent— are the result of consensual intercourse.[24] The violinist case may only tell us that abortion is permissible when a pregnancy results from nonconsensual intercourse.

This would still permit more abortions than the future-of-value view does. That view told us that it's wrong to kill anything with a future of value; the vast majority of fetuses have futures of value, regardless of how they were conceived. Moreover, many of the states that have passed restrictive abortion measures since the US Supreme Court's *Dobbs* decision in 2022 do not include exceptions for rape.[25] If we're allowed to unhook ourselves from the violinist, then abortion in cases of rape is very likely to also be morally permissible.

The Case of the People-Seeds

Yet many people believe that abortion is permissible even when pregnancy is the result of consensual intercourse. To support this claim, Thomson offers analogies that are meant to be more like the average pregnancy. Consider the *case of the people-seeds*:

> . . . people-seeds drift about in the air like pollen, and if you open your windows, one may drift in and take root in your carpets or upholstery. You don't want children, so

you fix up your windows with fine mesh screens, the very best you can buy. As can happen, however, and on very, very rare occasions does happen, one of the screens is defective; and a seed drifts in and takes root. Does the person-plant who now develops have a right to the use of your house?[26]

Thomson says that the answer to this question is no—the people-seed does not have a right to use your house. Sure, there are things you could have done to make it impossible for a people-seed to drift in: "you *could* have lived out your life with bare floors and furniture, or with sealed windows and doors."[27] But it is unreasonable to expect that a person who doesn't want a baby live her life in such a constrained way. Likewise, although you *could* prevent abortion by having a hysterectomy, this is an unreasonable constraint on your exercise of your right to bodily autonomy.[28]

If this analogy works, then any time a person takes precautions (condoms, the pill, an IUD) to prevent herself from getting pregnant—and most women do use contraceptives[29]—abortion is morally permissible. By taking steps to prevent a fetus from using her body, the person has shown that she does not intend to give up her right to control her own body—and so, as in the case of the violinist, she's not required to let the fetus use her body without her consent. The violinist case shows us that a being's having a right to life does not automatically mean it has the right to use someone else to stay alive; the people-seeds case shows us that even when someone is partly responsible for a being's coming into existence, that being still cannot use her body to stay alive without her consent.

Again, we can ask how well this analogy truly extends to abortion. Are there relevant differences between living in a world where people-seeds float around in the air and engaging in consensual, protected sex? Thomson seems to be relying on the idea that sex is a normal, permissible way for a person to exercise her bodily autonomy; if you disagree, then this analogy may not work. Or is having consensual, protected sex more akin to inviting a fetus in (doing something to induce it to enter) than it is like having a window open and letting a people-seed drift in? Thomson doesn't think so—by using protection, you are affirming that you do not intend to use your body to shelter a fetus. If she's wrong about that, then the people-seeds analogy is weaker.

Finally, we've seen that the people-seeds case is more closely analogous to most pregnancies than the violinist case is. But what if a person buys screens for her house, but she doesn't take the time to put them up properly? If she's not permitted to uproot the people-seed here, then someone who's pregnant may not be permitted to have an abortion in a case where she sometimes forgot to take the pill. What about someone who takes no precautions at all? If you think people in the people-seeds world must accept the consequences if they leave their doors wide open, then people who have completely unprotected sex may not be permitted to have abortions. Thomson acknowledges that some abortions are unjust—maybe she's thinking of cases like these.[30] Still, in any case where a person does not want to be pregnant and takes effective steps to avoid becoming pregnant, the people-seeds case gives us reason to think that she has not given up the right to control her body. Even if fetuses have the right to life, this does not include the right to use someone else's body to stay alive without that person's consent.

Premise 4

We've seen that many abortions are morally permissible—but not all. When we examined the cognitive-capacities view, we saw that most fetuses lack the right to life—but some have the cognitive capacities that give them that right. When we examined the violinist and people-seeds cases, we saw that even fetuses with the right to life do not normally have the right to use someone else's body to stay alive— but if a woman has waived her right to bodily autonomy, it may be impermissible for her to have an abortion. The vast majority of abortions aren't like this. Nearly all take place in the first trimester, and most women who don't want to become pregnant use contraceptives. If abortion is ever morally permissible, then the vast majority of abortions are probably morally permissible.

What about when they aren't? Should morally impermissible abortions be illegal? Even though the law is often based on morality, what's moral and what's legal come apart. Telling your friend a malicious lie is immoral, but most of us don't think this should be illegal. Driving on the left side of the road is illegal in the United States, but this isn't immoral in and of itself (British people are not committing immoral acts every time they drive). Yet morally impermissible abortion may be tantamount to murder. Surely, if anything is illegal, murder should be.

Yet pregnancy is distinctive because it involves significant, fast-moving health risks. Nearly everyone accepts that abortion is morally permissible if the pregnant woman, the fetus, or both will die unless an abortion is performed[31]—but laws restricting abortion are unable to make these fine moral and medical distinctions. Consider the case of the Irish dentist Savita Halappanavar. Halappanavar went to the hospital when she was miscarrying, but, at the time, Ireland did not allow abortion if the fetus still had a heartbeat. Halappanavar died of septicemia caused by the miscarriage.[32]

Could Halappanavar, or someone like her, have had morally impermissible reasons for wanting to have an abortion? Sure. But her pregnancy moved faster than the Irish legal system could, and this cost her her life. Abortion is a case where the boundaries of the legal must be wider than the boundaries of the moral. Trained medical professionals struggle with when an abortion is medically indicated and when it's not; the situations of pregnancies, especially risky ones, change very quickly.[33]

If all abortions are legal, some morally impermissible abortions will take place. But this is a cost worth bearing because the alternative is even costlier. Banning most or all abortions means that even women at serious risk of severe injury or death will not get the care they need; even restricting abortion to cases in which a woman's life is at risk means that doctors have to substitute the law's judgment for their own medical knowledge.[34] When violations of the law carry the threat of severe penalties—as many recent US state restrictions on abortion do—providers err on the side of not giving care, even when that care might be legally permissible.[35] To protect the lives and health of people seeking morally permissible abortions, we have to accept that some morally impermissible abortions may be performed.

You might wonder whether this strategy applies to similar cases. If the law should allow abortions even when they're morally impermissible, what does this tell us about infants or people in comas? There's a critical difference between pregnancy and these other cases. The reason to allow legal abortion even where it might be impermissible is that in cases such as Halappanavar's, the fetus can directly threaten the pregnant woman's life, and even medical professionals can't know for certain in advance where such a threat will develop. Very small infants and people in comas rarely pose such direct threats to their caretakers.

Conclusion

We started with this plausible argument that abortion is morally impermissible and should be illegal:

(1) The fetus has the right to life.

(2) If the fetus has the right to life, then abortion is morally impermissible.

(3) Therefore, abortion is morally impermissible. (from 1 and 2)

(4) If abortion is morally impermissible, then it should be illegal.

(5) Therefore, abortion should be illegal. (from 3 and 4)

Yet we have seen that this argument is weaker than we might have thought. Most fetuses do not have the right to life because most fetuses lack the cognitive capacities that give people the right to life. Even when fetuses do have the right to life, this doesn't mean that they can use others' bodies without consent. In the narrow band of cases where fetuses have the right to life *and* the right to use someone else's body to stay alive, abortion is indeed morally impermissible—but the fast-moving facts of pregnancy mean that it should nevertheless remain legal.

Notes

1 I'm grateful for helpful feedback from Rosa Terlazzo and Eric Wiland.
2 The first five capacities are from Mary Anne Warren, "On the Moral and Legal Status of Abortion," *Monist* 57, no. 1 (1973): 43–61.
3 Kate Greasley, *Arguments about Abortion: Personhood, Morality, and Law* (Oxford: Oxford University Press, 2017), 165.

4 Organized cortical brain activity is "electrical activity in the cerebral cortex of the sort that produces recognizable EEG readings" (David Boonin, *A Defense of Abortion* [Cambridge: Cambridge University Press, 2005], 115). Until organized cortical brain activity develops, consciousness is impossible (Ibid., 126–7). For what it's worth, Boonin doesn't accept the cluster-concept view; he thinks that organized cortical brain activity is the only criterion required for the right to life.

5 There's some evidence that animals have at least some of these cognitive capacities; for example, there's some evidence that elephants mourn their dead (see Elizabeth Preston, "Elephants in Mourning Spotted on YouTube by Scientists," *The New York Times* [May 17, 2022]). If so, then it may be wrong to kill elephants too. Remember, these theories don't make the wrongness of killing depend on whether something is or isn't human.

6 Compare having a right to life with another cluster concept, being a game. Games tend to be fun, have rules, use game pieces, end when some goal is achieved, and so on. None of these criteria on their own make something a game. Tag doesn't have an endpoint; pro basketball players aren't playing just for fun; hide-and-seek doesn't have game pieces. Most games have rules, but lots of nongames, such as driving, have rules too. If something has *enough* of these properties, though, it's a game.

7 The situation is different when a person is in an irreversible coma and lacks all but the most minimal brain activity; in these cases, it's less clear that they have the right to life. Consider the tragic case of Jahi McMath, whose parents disagreed with her hospital about whether she was legally dead and should be taken off life support (Rachel Aviv, "The Death Debate," *The New Yorker* [February 5, 2018]).

8 Greasley does argue that birth makes some difference to infants' capacities (see Greasley, *Arguments about Abortion*, 191).

9 For example, see Alberto Giubilini and Francesca Minerva, "After-Birth Abortion: Why Should the Baby Live?," *Journal of Medical Ethics* 39, no. 5 (2013): 261–3.

10 Boonin, *A Defense of Abortion*, 115.

11 Around 90 percent of abortions take place in the first trimester, that is, the first thirteen weeks of pregnancy (see Katherine Kortsmit, Antoinette Nguyen, Michele Mandel, Elizabeth Clark, Lisa Hollier, Jessica Rodenhizer, and Maura Whiteman, "Abortion Surveillance—United States, 2020," Centers for Disease Control and Prevention [November 23, 2022]).

12 Don Marquis, "Why Abortion Is Immoral," *The Journal of Philosophy* 86, no. 4 (1989): 189–90.

13 Ibid., 192.

14 Amy Berg, "Abortion and Miscarriage," *Philosophical Studies* 174, no. 5 (2017): 1217–26; Toby Ord, "The Scourge: Moral Implications of Natural Embryo Loss," *The American Journal of Bioethics* 8, no. 7 (2008): 12–19.

15 S. Matthew Liao, "The Embryo Rescue Case," *Theoretical Medicine and Bioethics* 27, no. 2 (2006): 141–7.

16 Marquis, "Why Abortion Is Immoral," 195.

17 Boonin, *A Defense of Abortion*, 65.

18 This case is a variant of one I found on Chad Vance's website: "Marquis against Abortion" (https://rintintin.colorado.edu/~vancecd/phil3160/abort.pdf, accessed

February 29, 2024). That case is itself modeled on a case from Michael Tooley, "Abortion and Infanticide," *Philosophy & Public Affairs* 2, no. 1 (1972): 60–1.
19. Boonin, *A Defense of Abortion*, 114–17.
20. Judith Jarvis Thomson, "A Defense of Abortion," *Philosophy and Public Affairs* 1, no. 1 (1971): 49–50.
21. Ibid., 56.
22. "Pregnancy Complications," Centers for Disease Control and Prevention (February 8, 2023) (https://www.cdc.gov/reproductivehealth/maternalinfanthealth/pregnancy-complications.html, accessed April 22, 2024).
23. Gretchen Sisson, Lauren Ralph, Heather Gould, and Diana Greene Foster, "Adoption Decision-Making among Women Seeking Abortion," *Women's Health Issues* 27, no. 2 (2017): 136–44.
24. Melisa M. Holmes, Heidi S. Resnick, Dean G. Kilpatrick, and Connie L. Best, "Rape-Related Pregnancy: Estimates and Descriptive Characteristics from a National Sample of Women," *American Journal of Obstetrics and Gynecology* 175, no. 2 (1996): 320–5.
25. According to KFF, a nonprofit that researches healthcare policy, fourteen states currently (as of May 2023) have abortion bans in effect (a further six have bans that are currently not in effect). Of these twenty-two total states, all have exceptions to preserve the life of the mother; sixteen have exceptions for the health of the mother (although, as we'll see in the next section, these are complicated); seven have exceptions if the fetus is diagnosed with a fatal anomaly; and eight have exceptions in the case of rape or incest. Some of these eight have additional restrictions; for example, in Idaho, a woman needs to report the alleged sexual assault to law enforcement before she can have an abortion. (See Mabel Felix, Laurie Sobel, and Alina Salganicoff, "A Review of Exceptions in State Abortion Bans: Implications for the Provision of Abortion Services," KFF [May 18, 2023]).
26. Thomson, "A Defense of Abortion," 59.
27. Ibid.
28. Ibid.
29. "Contraceptive Use in the United States," Guttmacher Institute (May 2021) (https://www.guttmacher.org/fact-sheet/contraceptive-use-united-states, accessed April 22, 2024).
30. Thomson, "A Defense of Abortion," 59.
31. Marquis, "Why Abortion Is Immoral," 194.
32. Partly as a result of the outcry over Halappanavar's death, Ireland loosened abortion restrictions in 2018 (see Megan Specia, "How Death of Woman Who Was Denied an Abortion 'Woke Up' Ireland," *The New York Times* [May 28, 2018]). Kate Cox, a Texan, experienced a similar situation when her fetus was diagnosed with severe anomalies in 2023; she was able to travel out of state for an abortion (see Greer Donley, "What Happened to Kate Cox Is Tragic, and Totally Expected," *The New York Times* [December 20, 2023]).
33. Donley, "What Happened to Kate Cox Is Tragic"; and Kavitha Surana, "Inside the Internal Debates of a Hospital Abortion Committee," *ProPublica* (February 26, 2024).
34. Donley, "What Happened to Kate Cox Is Tragic."
35. Surana, "Inside the Internal Debates."

Unborn Human Beings Have Fundamental Rights

Patrick Lee

Study Questions

1. What three points does Lee make about the human embryo at the point of conception?
2. Why does Lee think that you and I are physical organisms? What implications does this have for personhood?
3. What is the "acquired attributes view" of when human beings have a right to life? What problems does this view have according to Lee?
4. When does Lee think human beings acquire rights? Why?
5. Why does Lee think we can have interests and be harmed before we have conscious desires? What implications does this have for abortion?

The abortion issue raises both legal and moral questions. I will address here the following moral question: Do human embryos and fetuses have fundamental rights, including a right to life? Not all beings have fundamental rights. It is morally permissible intentionally to kill some things (certainly weeds and mosquitoes, for example) but not others, and it is morally permissible to use some things without serious regard for their survival and well-being, but other beings are such that we ought at least to take account of their well-being when we interact with them, and indeed treat them as we would have others treat us. The first question regarding the morality of abortion is, which kind of being is the human embryo or fetus? I will argue that human embryos and fetuses do have basic rights, and so we owe them the same type of respect that we owe to born human beings.

I. Overall Argument

The basic case can be set out briefly. You and I are subjects of rights in virtue of the fundamental kind of thing we are. That is, we are valuable because of our fundamental nature, as opposed to being subjects of rights only in virtue of some attributes that inhere in us, and that we acquire at some time after we come to be.

There is a difference between the thing that you are (or substance, to use an Aristotelian term), and the attributes or characteristics you have in addition to the thing that you are. What you *are* is a human being, a rational animal. You and I also have additional attributes such as size, shape, and degree of development. With respect to these additional attributes, you and I are constantly changing, but throughout all of these changes you and I each continue to be, that is, each of us continues as human beings.

This first point to be made is that what makes you and me intrinsically valuable as subjects of rights is not these additional attributes. Rather, what makes you intrinsically valuable is the thing that you are, the fundamental kind of being that you are.

Second, you and I are physical organisms. We are rational beings, yes. But we are not purely spiritual beings, or conscious subjects that possess physical organisms; rather, we are physical organisms, albeit physical organisms of the rational kind. From this point, it follows that we came to be when these physical organisms came to be. If we were conscious subjects that possessed or inhered in physical organisms, then the physical organism might come to be at one point, and we come to be at some later time. But since what we are is a particular type of physical organism, we came to be when these physical organisms that we are came to be.

Third, the time that a human physical organism comes to be is at fertilization. In other words, human embryos and human fetuses are human organisms.

If these points are true, then what is intrinsically valuable as a subject of rights comes to be at fertilization. What is intrinsically valuable as a subject of rights comes to be when the human embryo comes to be. Human embryos and fetuses are valuable as subjects of rights. In sum:

(1) You and I are intrinsically valuable as subjects of rights in virtue of what we are.

(2) What we are are human physical organisms.

(3) Human physical organisms come to be at fertilization.

(4) So, an entity that is intrinsically valuable as a subject of rights comes to be at fertilization.

The rest of this article clarifies and provides support for these points (treating them in reverse order).

II. A Distinct Human Organism Comes to Be at Conception

Step #3 is a question within biology or embryology. It is worth noting that some people have the mistaken impression that the position that human embryos and fetuses are human beings is only a religious belief. However, in fact, the standard texts in embryology all state that in normal cases fertilization (the union of the sperm and the ovum) marks the beginning of a distinct human organism.[1]

The evidence for this is extensive, so I will sketch only some of it here. In the case of ordinary sexual reproduction, the life of an individual human being begins with fertilization. In normal conception, a sex cell of the father, a sperm, unites with a sex cell of the mother, an ovum. Within the chromosomes of these sex cells are the DNA molecules that constitute the information that guides the development of the new individual brought into being when the sperm and ovum unite. When fertilization occurs, the twenty-three chromosomes of the sperm unite with the twenty-three chromosomes of the ovum.

When the sperm and the ovum unite, they cease to be, and their constituents enter into the makeup of a new entity. This organism, the human embryo, then begins to grow by the normal process of cell division—it divides into two cells, then four, eight, sixteen, and so on (the divisions are not all synchronous, so there is a three-cell stage, etc.). This embryo gradually develops all of the organs and organ systems necessary for the full functioning of a mature human being. His or her development (sex is determined from the beginning) is very rapid in the first few weeks. For example, as early as eight or ten weeks of gestation, the fetus has a fully formed, beating heart, a complete brain (though not all of its synaptic connections are complete—nor will they be until sometime *after* the child is born), and a recognizably human form.

Three key points should be noted about this human embryo. First, the embryo is a distinct being. The embryo is not a part of the mother or a part of the father. This is clear because it is growing in its own distinct direction. Its growth is internally directed to its own survival and maturation, a distinct end from the survival and flourishing of the mother in whose body this distinct organism resides.

Second, the embryo is human: it is a product of human parents, and it has the genetic structure characteristic of human beings.

Third, this new human embryo is a *whole* human organism, though obviously at an immature stage of development. This is a crucial point: because there is human tissue or human cells, for example, body cells or sex cells, which are human (i.e., genetically human) but are not whole human organisms. But a human embryo is quite unlike human tissue or human cells. Human tissue or a human cell is only functionally a part of a larger organism. Neither human tissue nor a human cell has the active disposition to develop itself to the mature stage of a human being. And so, each of these is only a *part* of a human being, not a whole human organism.

By contrast, the human embryo, from fertilization onward, is fully programmed actively to develop itself (himself or herself) to the adult stage of a human being. After conception, that is, from the zygote stage on, the major development of this organism is controlled and directed from within, that is, by the multicellular organism itself. And unless deprived of a suitable environment or prevented by violence, accident, or disease, this embryo will actively develop itself in its own distinct direction, to the adult stage of a human organism.

The identity of a biological entity—whether it is a cell or an organism, what type of cell or organism it is—is determined by its structure and trajectory of growth and maintenance. The structure and trajectory of the human embryo shows that it is a complete (though immature) human organism. It is not a part of the mother or of the father, unlike the sperm cells and the ova. Nor is it a disordered growth such as a teratoma. These do not have the internal resources to actively develop themselves to the mature stage of a human. Nor is it an intermediate form, something that regularly emerges into a whole (though immature) human organism but is not one yet. None of the changes that occur to the embryonic human being after fertilization during normal gestation generates a new direction of growth. Rather, all of the changes (e.g., those involving nutrition and environment) either facilitate or retard the internally directed growth of this individual. These facts are sufficient to show that the human embryo is a whole, though immature, human being, an individual member of the human species. This new organism is identical with the organism that will later be a fetus, and then an infant, a toddler, an adolescent, and so on.

III. You and I Are Physical Organisms

Now a supporter of abortion might admit that human embryos or fetuses are human beings but deny that they are *persons*. (In other words, he might deny #2 in the overall argument I set out earlier.) He might grant that the human organism comes to be when a human zygote comes to be, but still deny that you and I ever were human embryos. He might claim instead that we are persons but not human organisms. The argument would be that only persons have basic rights, but human embryos or fetuses are not persons.

However, this argument is based on a false premise. It implicitly identifies the human person with a consciousness that inhabits (or is somehow associated with) a body; the truth, however, is that we human persons are a particular kind of physical organism.

A brief argument for this point is as follows: I perform acts of sensation. Sensation is a bodily act. Just as walking is a bodily act—because one walks with one's legs as the organs with which one acts—in the same way, the act of sensing is an act one performs with external sense organs and portions of one's brain. Hence, the agent that performs the act of sensing is a bodily thing (specifically, an animal). Now, everyone—including those who deny that the person is a bodily being—refers to the entity that performs the act of understanding, and is self-conscious, as "I" or the ego. But it is clear that it must be the same agent, the same I, that performs the act of sensing, on the one hand, and that performs the act of understanding, and is self-conscious, on the other hand. When I say, "That is a horse," I directly understand what a horse is (the predicate of this assertion) by my intellect or power to understand—the same as my power of self-consciousness—and I directly apprehend what the word "that" refers to by sensation and perception. But it must be the same agent—the same I—that apprehends the subject and the predicate in a single assertion. So, the one that understands is identical with the one that senses. But since the agent that senses is a bodily being, it follows that I—the one who understands and is self-conscious—am a bodily being. Although I have a spiritual as well as a material aspect (or so I would argue), these are not two entities but are aspects of one thing, one concrete nature: what I am is a physical organism, though also a physical organism with a rational (spiritual) power.

Moreover, whether one holds that the mind (or intellect) is identical with the brain or holds that it is a distinct, nonmaterial power, the development of the brain is, from its beginning, organized toward becoming a highly complex structure that can produce sense images that are apt for providing content for conceptual or abstract thought. So, the dynamic human body and the human mind (however one conceives of the mind) are internally oriented to each other and function as a single whole. As in any animal-body the bodily parts are related to each other as parts of a single whole capable of performing the actions of a specific kind; just so with the *human* animal—its various parts, developing as it matures, cooperate in a manner to make possible a rational mode of life. Hence, the human body is related to the person, not as mere external components being used by a mind (the person), but as part of the whole body-mind composite, body and mind together being parts of a single whole. Hence, the human being is a particular type of animal, a rational animal. And so, the human person comes to be when this animal—this rational animal organism—comes to be.

III. Human Beings Are Persons and Bearers of Right in Virtue of What They Are

This is step #1 in the argument summarized above. Someone might reject this premise by saying that although you and I once were embryos and fetuses, we were not persons or bearers of rights at that time. Rather, they argue that only some human beings possess basic rights, and they possess basic rights in virtue of some accidental attribute, such as self-consciousness, or a capacity for self-consciousness, which they acquire some time after the human organism comes to be. Call this the "acquired attribute view."

The accidental attribute that qualifies one as a person involves, on this view, a mental function such as self-consciousness or rationality, since they seem to mark out humans from other entities. Also, the required characteristic will have to be a *capacity* of some sort,[2] since there is no actual behavior performed at all times by subjects of rights. People who are asleep or in reversible comas are subjects of rights but are not engaging in activities of the kind that might be a ground for moral status.

However, there are two types of capacities: proximate or radical. A *proximate capacity* is one that can be exercised right now, or at least in the immediate future. A *radical capacity* might take one some time to be in a position to exercise, or one might need to pass through several intermediate steps before one can at that point actualize it. For example, I lack the proximate capacity to speak Chinese but have the radical capacity to do so. That is, I cannot now speak Chinese but have the capacity to do so through intermediate steps. It is true that human embryos and fetuses do not have certain proximate capacities such as the capacity, right now, to reason or speak. However, human embryos and fetuses do have a radical capacity for such mental functions. Although they cannot now perform such actions, they are actively developing themselves to the stage at which they will do so. They have the structure or nature such that, provided the right environment, nutrition, and absence of violence, they will develop themselves to the stage where they will perform such actions—something not true, for example, of an unborn dog or cat.

So, why should the capacity that grounds being a subject of rights be a proximate or immediately exercisable capacity? Why wouldn't a radical capacity—which is equivalent to, or follows upon, the nature of a thing—be enough? There are, I think, compelling reasons in favor of the second alternative.

First, we treat beings with basic rights in a radically different way than we treat beings we think do not have rights. Most people believe it is permissible to use, experiment on, dismember, and even kill, for our own purposes, beings that do not have rights, even though we think we should not cause unnecessary pain to them when doing so. By contrast, we believe that, at least in general, we should not intentionally kill beings with rights, and even that we should treat them as we would have others treat us.

But it would seem that such a radical difference in the way *we treat* different classes of beings should be based on some radical difference *in reality* between those classes of beings. Now, there *is* a radical difference between individuals with a rational nature, on the one hand, and other types of entities—for example, cells or human tissue—on the other. In particular, considering the beginning of human life, we see that there is a radical difference in kind between a sperm and an ovum on the one hand, and an embryo, from the zygote stage onward, on the other. The former are mere parts of larger organisms; the latter is a human being at his or her earliest stage of development, and is the same substantial entity that will later be born, crawl, walk, talk, and eventually reason and shape his or her own life. And there is a radical difference between human organisms—at any stage of their development—and other animals. And that point applies to these different beings from the moment they come to be.

In fact, the proximate capacity for mental functions, and the radical capacity for it, are not two distinct powers: the proximate power is the same as the underlying radical power at a certain degree of development. The agent develops a radical capacity along a certain pathway, and at a certain stage of development, it can then be referred to as a proximate or immediately exercisable capacity. So, on the acquired attribute view, there is a disproportion between the ontological difference proposed as the basis for a moral difference and that moral difference itself.[3]

A second problem with the acquired attribute view is that, if it were true, then it is hard to see why it would be wrong to kill a human being who is in a temporary coma. A human being may be in a temporary coma for several weeks, and during that time, he is very much like an embryo or fetus. He lacks the proximate capacity for any mental functions. But he remains a human being. Now, the clearest reason why it is wrong to kill him is that he is the same kind of being as you or me; he is an individual possessing a nature that orients him to having self-consciousness and shaping his life by deliberate choices. But this same point is true of the unborn human being.

Someone might object that the comatose individual is different from an unborn human being, in that he *did* have consciousness and self-conscious desires in the past. And so he is a person, and a bearer of rights, and so because of that past, killing him is wrong.

But suppose I was in a coma, and we knew with certainty that, although I would regain consciousness in the future, I would not regain any of the same consciousness—not any of the same memories or mental skills that I had in the past. I would only gradually regain full consciousness, and I would have to learn everything again—how to walk, how to talk, and so on. Would it be right to kill me then?

Of course not—but that would not be because of my past consciousness or self-awareness, since all of that would be gone forever. It would be wrong to kill me because by killing me one would be depriving me of my whole future as a rational being, a being that, although not now conscious or self-aware, has a nature orienting him toward the stage where he will perform all of those distinctive human actions.[4]

What makes it wrong to kill me in such a situation is not that one would be killing something that is presently conscious or even presently able to be conscious—it is enough to have a right to life if I am identical to the thing that eventually will have rational consciousness. So, to be a bearer of basic rights, it is enough if an entity is constituted in such a way that she has an active disposition to develop herself toward acquiring rational consciousness and free choice. But the hypothetical scenario I have just referred to is in relevant respects similar to the position of human embryos and fetuses. Again, unborn human beings are the same kind of beings as you and me—and that point is the best explanation for why it is wrong to kill comatose individuals.

Thus, just as it would be wrong to kill me if I were in a coma, while I was still unconscious but slowly developing to the point where I would be conscious, so it is wrong to kill human embryos or fetuses because they are individuals actively developing themselves to the stage where they will shape their own lives by rationality and free choice—they are individuals with a rational nature.

IV. Benefits and Harm: More on Step #1

A third problem for the acquired attribute view concerns the relationship between benefits and harms to the subject helped or harmed.

Some philosophers have argued that a proximate capacity for conscious desires is required in order to have basic rights because rights are based on interests, and interests are based on desires.[5] However, even in cases where this might seem plausible, on further inspection we see that it's not the desires themselves that ground the interests and rights. Rather, a desire is reasonable and merits some type of deference only if it is for a genuine good, and a frustrated desire is bad only if the frustrated desire was for a genuine good. If John suffers from Pica—an eating disorder involving having desires to eat dirt, clay, and other non-nutritional items—his desire to eat dust grounds no duty to satisfy it, and he will likely visit a physician to try to get such desires removed.[6] Interests are not fundamentally grounded on desires, but on genuine goods. And so there is no reason to hold that one must have a desire (or a proximate capacity for one) prior to having interests. Moreover, you and I were subjects that could be benefited or harmed before we had desires or were conscious: our interests could be respected or thwarted from the time we came to be.

We understand, at least implicitly, as a prerequisite to any practical reasoning, what the basis of having a right is. When we deliberate about what to do, we begin by apprehending that some types of objects are worth pursuing for their own sake and not merely as means toward other conditions. I apprehend, for example, that life and health, knowledge, aesthetic experience, friendship, and other basic goods are worth pursuing for myself and for anyone else in a similar situation.

At the same time, I realize that I have a responsibility specified by these goods as opportunities—a responsibility to do something with my life, something worthwhile. And part of this whole awareness is a knowledge that I am a subject persisting through time, and that I myself am worthwhile. I apprehend that both the goods for the subject and the subjects themselves are worthwhile. The value of the fulfillments of a subject and of the subject herself are two sides of a single coin.

I also apprehend that the persons next to me—for example, the persons sitting with me at the dinner table, or the kids playing games with me outdoors—are similarly situated with respect to these same basic goods (life, knowledge, etc.). And so, I understand that the possibilities I view are also possibilities they view, that the basic responsibility I realize they also realize. And so, I understand that the goods worthy of pursuit include not just those that fulfill my own self, but also include the possible fulfillments of those who are presented (or can be presented) with the same type of view, and who see (or can see) the same type of responsibility. I apprehend that these other persons are worthwhile, and that they persist through time.[7]

Thus, the responsibility specified by goods understood as worth pursuing extends to the goods—that is, the being and fulfillment—of all those who either do or can (now or in the future) understand these goods as worth pursuing. Desires do not ground or justify the choice-worthiness of their objects; being a fulfillment that one's practical reason can apprehend as a good worth pursuing does. It grounds and enables one to understand the intrinsic value of the fulfillment of other agents and of those agents themselves.[8]

The beings that a person should care for—herself and all others similarly situated toward these intelligible goods—are agents, beings who persist through time—in philosophical language, *substances*. And an agent ought to care about what happens to her and to beings like her, not only when they are actually conscious but also during those periods of their lives when they are unable to respond to commands, to painful stimuli, and the like. And so, these substantial entities are valuable during those periods when, because of injury, illness, or immaturity, their capacities for rationality are not immediately exercisable.

This point becomes especially clear when we consider *harm*. Significant harm does not ultimately consist in the frustration of desires, even of all-things-considered desires. Rather, harm can only reasonably be viewed as depriving *someone of a genuine good*. And such deprivation can occur without its frustrating some previous psychological desire. The deprivation of a good is a harm independently of whether it is ever recognized as such, and independently of whether anyone previously desired what he is deprived of. And so, what fundamentally matters to an individual is *apprehended* or *recognized*, not decided upon. And what is recognized is real or possible prior to its being apprehended and does not depend on that recognition. Hence, you and I can be *harmed* before we possess conscious desires, and quite apart from our possessing them.

So, once an individual with a rational nature comes to be, then from that moment on what one does to this individual will either help or harm the very same individual who at a later time almost everyone will recognize as having basic rights. So, it is true for you and me that just as we can be helped or harmed *now*, we ourselves could have been helped or harmed at any earlier times that we existed.

Hence, the basis for distinguishing between those beings that a person should treat always as ends and never as mere means, and those that it is permissible for her to use as mere means, is the possession of a rational nature. Every rational being is a person. And since every human being is a rational being—a rational animal—that is, an animal with radical capacity for rational actions—it follows that every human being is a subject of rights.

Thus, just as it is wrong to kill a human being today, it would also have been wrong to kill that human being ten years ago, or twenty years ago, or at any point in her existence. It would have been wrong to kill her when she was an infant but also when she was a fetus, because at each point she is the same human being.

Conclusion

What is at stake in this debate about how to treat human embryos and fetuses is whether we will or will not recognize the fundamental equal dignity possessed by every human being, simply in virtue of being a human being. The pro-abortion position is in fact a denial of one of the most basic principles central to our civilization, namely, that all human beings, regardless of their inessential differences, possess an equal fundamental dignity, and no class of human beings can with justice enslave, use, experiment on, or deliberately kill, other innocent human beings for their own purposes.

It is intrinsically unjust to relegate unborn human beings to the status of non-persons, to reduce them to the status of mere inconvenient burdens. All human beings, no matter their size or degree of development, are worthwhile in themselves and bearers of inherent and equal fundamental rights.

Notes

1. See for example: Keith L. Moore, *The Developing Human: Clinically Oriented Embryology*, 7th ed. (New York: Saunders, 2003); Ronan O'Rahilly and Fabiola Mueller, *Human Embryology and Teratolgy,* 3rd ed. (New York: Wiley-Liss, 2001); Bruce Carlson, *Human Embryology and Developmental Biology,* 4th ed. (Philadelphia: Mosby, 2009); Scott F. Gilbert, *Developmental Biology* 7th ed. (Sunderland: Sinaur, 2003).
2. See Peter Singer, *Practical Ethics*, 3rd ed. (New York: Cambridge University Press, 2011), Chs. 4–6; David Boonin, *A Defense of Abortion* (Cambridge University Press, 2002), Chs. 2–3.
3. Kate Greasley claims that this argument commits the sorites fallacy. (Kate Greasley, *Arguments about Abortion: Personhood, Morality, and Law* (Oxford: Oxford University Press, 2017), 114–16; Kate Greasley and Christopher Kaczor, *Abortion Rights: For and Against* (Cambridge: Cambridge University Press, 2018), 67–73. That fallacy consists in thinking that since any addition of a small amount of X cannot make a radical difference, therefore repeated additions of small amounts of X also cannot constitute a radical difference. It gets its name from the Greek word for a heap (*soros).* For one might fallaciously reason that since the addition of one grain of sand to another cannot produce a heap, so repeated additions of grains of sand—no matter how many—will always fail to provide a heap. The fallacy ignores the fact that many additions of a small amount can produce a radical difference. But the argument here does not commit that fallacy. The argument is *not* that a human being possesses basic dignity at all stages of her existence on the grounds that there is no morally significant difference between any two *adjacent* stages in her life cycle. Rather, the argument is that the adult has the same basic dignity and rights as she does at any other stage because none of the differences between *any* two stages in her life cycle has an intelligible link to her having or not having basic dignity and rights. The point is not that the differences between any two *adjacent* stages along the developmental spectrum of the life of an individual human are too small to ground a radical moral difference, but that none of the differences between *any* two stages along a development that consists only in a greater or lesser possession of the same feature can ground a radical moral difference.
4. A point emphasized by Don Marquis, "Why Abortion is Immoral," *Journal of Philosophy* 86, no. 4 (1989): 183–202.
5. See, for example, Judith Thomson, "Abortion," *Boston Review* XX, no. 3 (1995) (https://www.bostonreview.net/forum/judith-jarvis-thomson-abortion/, accessedJune 7, 2024); or Bonnie Steinbock, *Life Before Birth*, 2nd ed. (Oxford: Oxford University Press, 2011).
6. Mark Murphy, *Natural Law and Practical Rationality* (Cambridge: Cambridge University Press, 2001), Ch. 2. Of course, at some point, even after deliberation, he might choose to eat some of the dust. But if he does, it will be for the sake of attaining some peace or internal harmony—attained by quelling the desire—an intelligible good (though only a fragment of its quelling will likely be self-defeating). The desire itself makes no normative claim on him, and the desire itself is not in any way generated by his practical grasp of, say, eating paint chips as intelligibly good—as something providing a *reason* for action, rather than a sub-rational motive.
7. The position set out here on our knowledge of basic rights is similar to that of David Oderberg's (See his *Applied Ethics, A Non-Consequentialist Approach* [Malden: Blackwell, 2000], 121–36). It is also similar to Alan Gewirth's position on the rights of

others: Alan Gewirth, "The Justification of Morality," *Philosophical Studies* 53 (1988): 245.
8 We apprehend these same points when we actively cooperate with others to pursue goods in common. When intelligently cooperating with others, I understand that some other beings are related to me as co-subjects, or as potential co-subjects. If I cooperate with others in pursuing the good of health or understanding, for example, I directly apprehend both myself and these others as subjects, as intrinsically worthwhile, and as persons for whom such goods as health, understanding, and so on, are worth pursuing.

Responses

Response to Berg on Abortion

Patrick Lee

> **Study Questions**
> 1. Why does Lee think that Berg's appeal to cortical brain activity implies that infants and the comatose lack basic rights?
> 2. Why might basing the right to life on degreed properties pose a problem for Bert's view?
> 3. How does Lee respond to the "embryo rescue" and "future-of-value machine" scenarios?
> 4. What is Lee's criterion for when causing death as a side effect is morally right? What does this imply for Berg's case for abortion?

Unborn human beings have a basic right to life because they are fundamentally the same kind of being as you or me, only at an immature stage of development. Each one is identical with the individual who—if not killed and does not die—will later crawl, walk, talk, reason, and so on. Although being a human individual is not *necessary* for having basic rights—perhaps there are other individuals with a rational nature—it is *sufficient*.

Actual Cognitive Capacities and Cortical Brain Activity

Professor Berg argues on the contrary that human fetuses up to twenty-five weeks gestation lack a right to life because they do not have "actual cognitive capacities." But why require "actual" capacities rather than "potential capacities" (those requiring intermediate steps toward actualization)? Berg's answer is that early fetuses are related differently to their futures than the way you and I are to ours, since, unlike early fetuses we have the "actual capacity" to value our futures. She then says such cognitive capacities are acquired between twenty-five and thirty-two weeks in gestation, with the appearance of organized cortical brain activity—and proposes that point as the beginning of basic rights.

However, organized cortical activity could be relevant here only if it grounded some capacity. But it is only an intermediate step in the human's self-development toward the "actual capacity" for mental acts specific to humans, a stage not reached until several weeks after birth (requiring many extensive synaptic connections). So, organized cortical activity cannot be used as a criterion to include infants and comatose patients but exclude early fetuses from having basic rights. And so, the actual cognitive capacity's view does imply—implausibly—that infants and comatose patients lack basic rights.

Degreed Properties and Basic Rights

Moreover, this cognitive-capacities view proposes a degreed property as the criterion for having basic rights. That is, on this view, a person is valuable as a subject of rights, not in virtue of what he or she is, but in virtue of possessing a property to a certain degree. However, it's not clear why an acquired property is required, nor why it should be *this* degree rather than another. By contrast, there are intelligible reasons why possessing basic rights—having any rights vs. having none at all—should be based on the fundamental kind of being that one is. And, as a consequence, one has basic rights at all stages of one's life. So, the radical difference between having vs. not having basic rights is based on a radical difference in the types of beings treated in radically different ways. True, in some other cases, the law must be drawn somewhat arbitrarily—for example, placing the legal driving age at sixteen years. However, these do not involve having vs. not having rights at all, and no radical difference nearby is ignored.

Further, if what confers intrinsic value and basic rights did vary in degrees, then intrinsic value and basic rights themselves would vary in degree—some people would be "more equal" than others. So, the proponents of a criterion that comes in degrees (such as "actual cognitive capacities") will have to choose either that option or select some threshold above which its possessors will have equal basic rights and below which they will lack them. But both options will be arbitrary, and arbitrariness in the selection of who counts as having rights violates basic justice.

By contrast, although human beings differ immensely with respect to talents, accomplishments, intelligence, and so on, they all are equal in having the same *nature*—all are individuals with a rational nature, naturally oriented toward shaping their own lives by deliberate choice. No arbitrary selection of a certain degree of a property is necessary. And the human being possesses its basic nature from the moment it comes to be.

Miscarriages, Hypothetical Scenarios, and Intuitions

Berg also cites the high percentage of miscarriages in pregnancy to suggest that most people do not actually believe that unborn humans are persons. However, it is worth noting that the standard embryology texts explain that many of these unsuccessful pregnancies (often undetected) are failures or defects in the process of fertilization and thus not deaths of human embryos. Also, some people—especially, but not only, mothers—often do deeply grieve in the event of a miscarriage. And the extent of people's grief, and its expression, may vary as a function of factors independent of what they believe about the nature of human embryos and fetuses.

This point—that factors extrinsic to the inherent worth of unborn humans can influence judgments or "intuitions"—also bears on Berg's claim about the "embryo rescue" scenario. Faced with a choice to save five embryos or one born human being, people's intuitions will be affected by various factors external to the intrinsic value of human embryos vs. unborn humans—survival chances, which ones have dependent relatives, and so on. And so, favoring saving one group over another may not reflect a belief about the intrinsic value of those individuals. Different responses to the "embryo rescue case" do not, then, cast doubt on the pro-life position.

Berg also asks us to imagine a "future-of-value machine." Whatever enters it will, within nine months, develop into a being with a future like ours. Suppose a slime mold slithers up next to the machine. You would not in that case be obliged to allow it to enter the machine. But that is supposed to show that merely having a future like ours does not confer personhood or a right to life.

However, the scenario is crucially disanalogous to abortion or the killing of a human fetus. A slime mold simply never has, and never did have, a rational life as its future. If a slime mold could be "transformed" somehow into a human being, *it* would not survive, even if some of the matter that was once in it might enter into the new individual. By contrast, a human embryo does not merely have parts that enter the makeup of a new and different being; rather, it actively develops itself, remaining the same individual throughout, to the mature stage of a human being.

Abortion and "Indirect Killing"

In a further, more extended argument, Professor Berg contends that even if what is killed in abortion does have a right to life, the mother has a right to expel the child from her womb—and even though the baby dies as a result. In effect, the argument is that many abortions are morally justified (and should be legal) because they are indirect killing—as distinct from intentional or direct killing.

However, it seems that in most abortions the baby's death *is* intended. For most abortions are chosen to avoid being responsible for a child, and abortion achieves that end only by killing the child.

True, some actions that cause death as a side effect are morally permissible. For example, self-defense can be justified as using force to stop an attack, even if one knows the force used will result in the assailant's death. But it is also clear that some indirect killings are *not* morally right. For example, if a man knew his smoking seriously worsened his wife's emphysema, it would be wrong for him to continue smoking, even though the harm to her health might be only a side effect. How does one determine when causing a bad side effect is right and when it is not? I would argue that causing death as a side effect is morally right only if the harm being avoided is comparable to the harm being caused—if not, then the act causing the harm is morally wrong and unjust. In a problem pregnancy, causing an unborn child's death as a side effect is *not* morally justified—unless the mother's life (a comparable good) is in danger, and the removal of the baby from the womb saves the mother's life.

However, by the same principle, if the mother's life *is* in danger, and removing the baby will save her, then that is morally permissible—even if doing so will result in the baby's death. In that case, the baby's death is a side effect and causing this side effect is not unjust. Such cases where continuing the pregnancy endangers the mother's life are rare, but of course they do occur. Examples are some ectopic pregnancies and chorioamnionitis. The removal of the baby in such cases is usually not referred to as an "abortion"—since it is neither a direct killing, nor an unjust causing of the baby's death (the baby cannot be saved no matter what is done).

What's legal and what's moral are of course not always the same, but, as a matter of strict justice, we as a political community should provide equal protection of the law to all persons, regardless of the color of their skin, sex, age, or degree of maturation. So, the political community should prohibit all intentional killing of human beings. And it should prohibit all causing of death as a side effect—unless life itself, or an interest comparable to it, is in imminent danger.

Response to Lee on Abortion

Amy Berg

Study Questions

1. Why does Berg think the idea of "radical capacities" is murky?
2. What three other problems does Berg raise for Lee's Radical Capacities View?
3. What advantage does Berg believe the cognitive-capacities view has for solving the temporary coma problem?
4. Why does Berg think Lee's argument against abortion is incomplete?

In this response to Lee's argument against abortion, I'll argue that, in addition to the difficulty of defining the idea of a radical capacity, there are serious problems with using radical capacities as the basis for rights. Next, I'll show that an alternative—the actual-capacities view—can handle problem cases at least as well as the radical-capacities view can. I'll conclude by pointing out that even if the radical-capacities view works, it still doesn't show that abortion is morally impermissible.

Defining Radical Capacities

Lee claims that all of us, including fetuses, have basic rights because of our radical capacities. This idea is murky. If what it means for radical capacities to be "equivalent to, or [follow] upon, the nature of a thing" (p. 36) is that they are capacities all humans have, then either there are no radical capacities, or we must falsely ascribe radical capacities to humans who lack them. Anencephaly is a rare and fatal condition in which the brain develops minimally or not at all. Anencephalic fetuses are human, but, tragically, they will never be rational or even conscious. Rationality, then, is not a radical capacity all humans share. It would be false to claim that anencephalic fetuses have the radical capacity for rationality just because they have human DNA.[1]

A better definition is that a radical capacity is one a human can develop over time because of her individual nature, not because of the nature of humans in general. (Note that this definition does not imply that all fetuses share the same basic rights, since some lack the radical capacity for rationality.) Yet it's hard to tell what radical capacities any individual person has. I'm very inflexible; maybe if I'd done enough yoga, I could develop the actual capacity (and so have always had the radical capacity) to touch my toes—or maybe I'd find I never had that radical capacity. Likewise, we may be unable to detect which fetuses have the radical capacity for rationality.

Even if we can come up with a satisfactory account of radical capacities, these capacities aren't the normal basis for rights. Instead, the basis is the capacities individuals currently have (call these "actual capacities"). Three-year-olds are denied the right to vote on the basis that they currently lack the judgment and knowledge necessary for voting; we do not grant or deny the right to vote on the basis of a radical capacity to eventually develop judgment and knowledge.[2]

It may be that we do bear some rights because of our radical capacities. Perhaps the right to life is a "basic right," and perhaps basic rights are importantly different from voting rights. But now we're owed an explanation as to why there are these distinct kinds of rights and why the right to life, unusually, depends on radical capacity.

Problems with the Radical-Capacity View

Perhaps we can resolve some of these difficulties if we look to one of the reasons given for the radical-capacity view. This is the claim that a radical difference in treatment should be based on a radical difference in reality—between zygotes and reproductive cells, or between humans and nonhuman animals. This difference is supposed to exist "from the moment [these beings] come to be" (p. 36). This would explain why zygotes have rights that sperm cells and dogs do not. I'll focus on three problems with this claim.

Identifying the "Singular Moment"

First, there's supposed to be a singular moment when zygotes become radically different from reproductive cells. Yet human reproduction is far more complex than this. There are at least ten distinct events that might count as the "moment" of conception: from when the sperm approaches the egg, to when the proteins in the egg cause the sperm to release its contents, to when the combined egg and sperm first divide to form a zygote.[3] The more we learn about the science of reproduction, the less able we are to pinpoint a non-arbitrary time at which a new human came into existence, that is, at which a radical difference occurred.

But it's even more complicated than that. Until around two weeks after conception, an embryo can divide into two or more parts ("monozygotic twins").[4] Much more rarely, two embryos which started out as fraternal twins can merge into a single entity (a "chimera") with two sets of DNA.[5] These unusual cases show that it can be unclear for weeks what radical differences, if any, have occurred.

The Same Substantial Entity?

The second problem is that the *only* radical difference relevant for basic rights is supposed to be between cells pre- and post-fertilization; the zygote is "the same substantial entity that will later be born . . . and eventually reason" (p. 36). But while each of us can trace our histories back to the zygote[6] we came from, this does not mean that we are the same substantial entities as those zygotes. An acorn is a different kind of thing from an oak tree, even though we can trace the histories of oak trees back to the acorns they developed from.[7] We can't assume that zygotes are the same substantial entities as infants or adults just because we develop from zygotes; we need to know why we should believe this.[8]

The Problem of Speciesism

The third problem is with the claim that there are radical differences between humans (at any stage of development) and other animals. Our rights cannot depend merely on the possession of human genes. A chimpanzee that develops a genetic mutation that gives it human intelligence would not share our DNA, but it would be a rights-bearer nonetheless.[9] To say otherwise would be arbitrary (some philosophers call it "speciesist").[10]

Perhaps a better way to put it is to say that any being with the radical capacity for rationality is the bearer of basic rights. This would avoid speciesism, but at the cost of once again making it hard to pin down what having a radical capacity consists in. In my main essay, I discussed the case of the slime mold about to enter the future-of-value machine. This being has the radical capacity for rationality—with just one intermediate step (slithering into the machine), it will begin to develop rationality, even though this is not typically a capacity associated with slime molds. (If you think that the slime mold lacks this radical capacity because its capacity to become rational isn't contained within its own being, consider that without a uterus to develop in, a fetus will never become rational either.)

To sum up: once we really dig into the idea of radical capacity, it's no longer clear (1) whether our radical capacities are shared by all humans or specific to us as individuals, (2) that radical capacities are a good basis for rights, (3) that we can identify a non-arbitrary radical difference between human reproductive cells and zygotes, or (4) that there is a radical difference between zygotes and nonhuman animals.

The Temporary Coma Problem

Yet, if the radical-capacity view does a better job than its competitors at justifying common intuitions about killing, then it might be better to try to repair it rather than abandon it. Lee discusses the case of a person in a temporary coma, who currently lacks most mental functions but whom it would be wrong to kill.

Fortunately, we don't need to rely on the murky notion of radical capacity to explain why this killing is wrong. When I'm awake, I have the actual cognitive capacity to speak. When I'm asleep, it's strange to say that I have the radical capacity for speech—it's not something I'm in the process of developing. I have the actual capacity for speech all the time, even when I don't happen to be exercising it. An adult in a temporary coma is more akin to a sleeping adult than to a zygote; both adults have the actual capacity for rationality.[11]

In other words, the radical-capacity and the cognitive-capacities view from before (for clarity, call it the "actual-cognitive-capacities view") give us the same result here. But the actual-cognitive-capacities view has advantages. First, it doesn't rely on the murky idea of a radical capacity. It holds that how we ought to be treated now does not depend on capacities we may (or may not) develop in the future—just as voting rights are based on our actual capacities, so is the right to life.[12] (Keep in mind that these actual capacities need not be full-fledged rationality; they could be something as basic as the actual capacity for organized cortical brain activity.[13]) Second, it allows for the possibility of substantial change from zygote to adult, just as there is substantial change from acorn to oak tree. Finally, it avoids the highly unintuitive implications of the radical-capacity view—that an early miscarriage is the equivalent of the death of a child, that we should save five embryos rather than one adult, that when an in vitro fertilization procedure results in the destruction of one or more embryos, this is equivalent to the killing of beings with full rights.

Conclusion: Back to Bodily Rights

Finally, even if everything I've said here is wrong—even if fetuses' radical capacities give them full human rights from the moment of fertilization—that doesn't show that they have the specific right *to use someone else's body to stay alive*. Even adult humans, such as violinists, may lack this right.[14] You know by now that arguments for this claim (such as Thomson's) have their critics, but this points us to a difficult task that isn't taken up here: the task of showing *which* rights adults, infants, and fetuses have. Without taking up this task, the case against abortion cannot be complete.

Notes

1. Some philosophers call this "speciesism"; we'll discuss this more later.
2. For a similar kind of case, see Stanley Benn, "Abortion, Infanticide, and Respect for Persons," in *The Problem of Abortion,* 2nd ed., ed. Joel Feinberg (Belmont: Wadsworth, 1984), 102. On children and the right to vote, see Nicholas John Munn, "Capacity Testing the Youth: A Proposal for Broader Enfranchisement," *Journal of Youth Studies* 15, no. 8 (2012): 1048–62; for a proposal that voting age should be abolished entirely, see Eric Wiland, "Should Children Have the Right to Vote?" in *Palgrave Handbook of Philosophy and Public Policy*, ed. David Boonin (London: Palgrave Macmillan, 2018), 215–24.
3. Kate Greasley, *Arguments about Abortion: Personhood, Morality, and Law* (Oxford: Oxford University Press, 2017), 115.
4. David DeGrazia, *Creation Ethics: Reproduction, Genetics, and Quality of Life* (Oxford: Oxford University Press, 2014), 20–1. Monozygotic twins are more commonly known as identical twins.
5. Human chimeras are fascinating and extremely rare (the first wasn't reported until 1953) (See Kamlesh Madan, "Natural Human Chimeras: A Review," *European Journal of Medical Genetics* 63, no. 9 [2020], 103971). They have occasionally caused legal controversy, as when Lydia Fairchild was accused of committing welfare fraud. DNA tests appeared to show that she was not the biological mother of her two children; a court officer even watched her give birth to her third child, and that child's DNA also didn't match Fairchild's. Eventually, her attorney stumbled on information about chimerism. Fairchild did indeed possess two distinct sets of DNA, and the children were found to be both legally and biologically hers. See ABC News, "She's Her Own Twin," (August 15, 2006) (https://web.archive.org/web/20140610123634/http://abcnews.go.com/Primetime/shes-twin/story?id=2315693&singlePage=true, accessed September 12, 2024).
6. Or zygotes, in the case of chimeras—although again note that chimeras are extremely rare.
7. Judith Jarvis Thomson, "A Defense of Abortion," *Philosophy and Public Affairs* 1, no. 1 (1971): 47.

8   Greasley, *Arguments about Abortion*, 131–2; Warren Quinn, "Abortion: Identity and Loss," *Philosophy and Public Affairs* 13, no. 1 (1984): 24–54.
9   I discussed a similar case in my main essay, when I argued that peaceful, intelligent aliens would have the same moral status we do.
10 On versions of the speciesism issue, see Greasley, *Arguments about Abortion*, 153; Michael Tooley, "Abortion and Infanticide," *Philosophy & Public Affairs* 2, no. 1 (1972): 60–1; and Jeff McMahan, "Our Fellow Creatures," *Journal of Ethics* 9 (2005): 353–80.
11 As you may recognize, this is very closely related to the response to Marquis's future-like-ours view that I discussed in my main essay. For more, see David Boonin, *A Defense of Abortion* (Cambridge: Cambridge University Press, 2005), 56–85.
12 See Boonin, *A Defense of Abortion*, 66–7.
13 See Ibid., 115–29.
14 Thomson, "A Defense of Abortion."

Questions for Reflection

1. Can you think of any other view of human personhood besides those defended by Berg and Lee? Is this view preferable? Why?
2. Suppose Berg's view does imply that infants lack basic rights. Would this be a devastating problem for her position? Why?
3. How might Lee respond to Berg's charge that his argument is incomplete when it comes to the question of bodily rights?

For Further Reading

Beckwith, Francis J. *Defending Life: A Moral and Legal Case against Abortion Choice*. Cambridge University Press, 2007.
Boonin, David. *Beyond Roe: Why Abortion Should Be Legal—Even if the Fetus is a Person*. Oxford University Press, 2019.
Boonin, David. *A Defense of Abortion*. Cambridge University Press, 2005.
Colgrove, Nicholas, Bruce P. Blackshaw, and Daniel Rodger, eds. *Agency, Pregnancy and Persons: Essays in Defense of Human Life*. Routledge, 2024.
Greasley, Kate. *Arguments about Abortion: Personhood, Morality, and Law*. Oxford University Press, 2017.
Greasley, Kate, and Christopher Kaczor. *Abortion Rights: For and Against*. Cambridge University Press, 2017.
Kaczor, Christopher. *The Ethics of Abortion: Women's Rights, Human Life, and the Question of Justice*, 3rd ed. Routledge, 2022.
Lee, Patrick. *Abortion and Unborn Human Life*, 2nd ed. Catholic University of America Press, 2010.

2

Physician-Assisted Suicide/Euthanasia

The Case for Mercy Killing and Physician-Assisted Suicide

Arthur Schafer

Study Questions

1. How does Schafer show that PAS and VAE are not morally different?
2. According to Schafer, what was unreasonable about the original MAiD Bill?
3. What is the Autonomy Argument for mercy killing?
4. What are the two versions of the "Slippery Slope" objection to PAS/E? How does Schafer respond to them?
5. Why does Schafer think we shouldn't be alarmed by the number of MAiD deaths?
6. Why are disability rights organizations opposed to the expansion of MAiD? How does Schafer reply to this concern?

The moral case for medically assisted dying is straightforward. When a competent adult patient who is suffering intolerably from a grievous illness makes an informed decision to die, providing them with assistance both respects their personal autonomy and ends their suffering. In the health care context, voluntary euthanasia and physician-assisted suicide promote two fundamental moral values: patient self-determination and patient well-being. There are competing approaches to ethical decision-making but, regardless of which approach one adopts, it will be axiomatic that society in general and the medical profession in particular should both respect patient autonomy and strive to minimize patient suffering.

Two major claims will be defended in this chapter: first, that there are circumstances in which mercy killing and physician-assisted suicide are morally justifiable and, second, that both ought to be legally permitted, subject to careful safeguards. In other words, assisted dying ought to be regulated rather than prohibited.

Historical Background: Assisted Suicide, Mercy Killing, and the Law

Physician-assisted suicide [PAS] was legalized in Oregon, via the Death with Dignity Act, in 1997. At present, it is also legally permitted in nine additional American jurisdictions: Washington, D.C., Washington State, California, Colorado, Vermont, New Mexico, Maine, Hawaii, and New Jersey. To be eligible, patients must be eighteen years of age or older, capable of making and communicating health care decisions for themselves and must have been diagnosed with a terminal illness that will lead to death within six months. Eligible patients must self-administer a lethal dose of medication prescribed by a physician for that purpose. By contrast, euthanasia/mercy killing, in which it is a physician who administers the lethal dose of medication to the patient, is illegal in all fifty states of the United States.

Outside the United States, almost every country that has legalized physician-assisted suicide has also legalized voluntary active euthanasia [VAE].[1] Eligibility requirements are the same for both. The phrase "assisted dying" refers to both assisted suicide and mercy killing.

Before assessing the moral case for voluntary active euthanasia,[2] it will be helpful to consider whether there is any morally significant difference between PAS and VAE that would justify legalizing the former while criminalizing the latter. Consider the following two scenarios.

> **Scenario 1:** A competent adult patient, who meets all legal requirements for PAS, requests and is granted permission to receive assisted dying. At her request, the physician prescribes a lethal dose of barbiturate. The patient arranges to have a pharmacist fill the prescription, combines the drug with orange juice, drinks the resulting cocktail, and dies. This would be a case of physician-assisted suicide.

> **Scenario 2:** A competent adult patient, who meets all legal requirements for PAS, requests and receives a prescription for barbiturate, but when she attempts to raise a glass containing the lethal cocktail to her lips, her arthritic hands are not up to the task. She requests further help, whereupon the doctor steadies her hands and moves the glass to her lips. Holding her hands and the glass, the physician pours the medication into her mouth. She swallows the mixture and dies.

Scenarios 1 and 2 are identical in every morally relevant respect. In both, the physician participates in bringing about the patient's death. In both, the decision to die is made voluntarily by a competent adult patient. In both, the patient has control over the decision to die and could change her mind until the very last moment simply by saying "no." The sole difference between PAS and VAE consists in who acts last. With PAS, it is the patient who acts last. With VAE, it is the physician.

From this, it follows that, if PAS is legally permissible (because morally justified) in Scenario 1, as it would be in Oregon and nine other American jurisdictions, then VAE, in Scenario 2, would also be morally justified and so should also be legally permissible (as it would be in the Netherlands, Belgium, and Canada). This point has practical significance because not all patients seeking an assisted death are able to swallow or otherwise self-administer lethal medication. In the ten American jurisdictions which have legalized PAS but not VAE, a physician who injected her patient with a lethal medication, in circumstances where the patient was unable to perform the task on their own, could face serious criminal sanctions. The prohibition of VAE seems a clear-cut case of wrongful discrimination against those whose disability prevents them from using their hands or swallowing.

In what follows, arguments are presented in defense of the view that PAS and VAE should be legally permitted, subject to careful safeguards. The discussion will draw on recent Canadian experience, as well as on data from Oregon and from European countries such as the Netherlands and Belgium.

A Fateful Decision by the Supreme Court of Canada

A 2015 decision by the Supreme Court of Canada, in *Carter*, ruled that a general prohibition of mercy killing is unconstitutional—because it conflicts with Section 7 of the Canadian Charter of Rights and Freedoms. "Everyone has the right to life, liberty and security of the person and the right not to be deprived thereof except in accordance with the principles of fundamental justice." The *Carter* decision compelled the Government to introduce a new law, Bill C-14. As of 2016, medical assistance in dying, which in Canada is labeled MAiD, became a legal option for competent adult patients who clearly consent to their death, so long as they meet legislated requirements.

To be eligible for MAiD, patients must have a "grievous and irremediable medical condition (including an illness, disease or disability) that causes enduring suffering that is intolerable to the individual in the circumstances of his or her condition." Parliament also added a further requirement: that natural death must be "reasonably foreseeable."[3]

Since mercy killing provides an escape route for patients who would otherwise be condemned to a life of intolerable suffering, it is easy to see how outright prohibition would conflict with an individual's right to liberty and her right to "security of the person." It seems paradoxical, however, to claim that banning assisted dying violates one's "right to life."

The paradox is more apparent than real. When medically assisted dying is prohibited, some grievously ill patients will be forced to take their own lives prematurely. If they wait until they are truly ready to die, then they may no longer be able to take their own life without assistance. By permitting medical assistance in dying, society allows patients to live as long as they still wish to do so, secure in the knowledge that assistance will be available if/when, at some later point, they need it.

The Burden of Proof

The right to make important life decisions for oneself, including the decision as to when and how one dies, is a fundamentally important human right; but it is not an absolute right. Even basic rights may legitimately be restricted or overridden if it can be demonstrated that their exercise will cause serious harm to innocent third parties or to society. That said, the burden of proof rests upon those who seek to restrict basic freedoms. They must demonstrate, with good evidence rather than mere speculation, that if society permits individuals to choose assisted dying, the result will be, overall, more harmful than beneficial.

The Canadian government defended its general ban on mercy killing by highlighting the government's obligation to protect vulnerable patients, especially racialized minorities, the poor and uneducated, and those living with disabilities. Without a blanket prohibition against assisted dying, the government claimed, it could not adequately protect vulnerable patients from the harm of wrongful death.

In response, the plaintiffs argued that a general prohibition of assisted dying was overbroad—unnecessary because less liberty-restricting protective measures are available. They adduced empirical evidence from jurisdictions that have chosen to regulate mercy killing rather than to ban it. Based on the totality of Expert Witness testimony, the SCC concluded that, so long as mercy killing is carefully regulated, vulnerable individuals can be effectively protected against abuse and exploitation.[4]

Having lost its case, the government responded with an Act of Parliament, Bill C-14 (2016), legalizing Medical Assistance in Dying [MAiD] for adult Canadians who clearly consent to their death and whose intolerable and enduring suffering results from a "grievous and incurable medical condition." Bill C-14 also imposed a further and more contentious requirement: that the patient's natural death be "reasonably foreseeable."

By excluding from eligibility patients who are not at the end of their natural life, Bill C-14 presumably intended to limit the amount of harm that could be done in the event of mistake or abuse. So, for example, when death is imminent, "miracle cures" become unlikely. When death is imminent, it is also unlikely that the patient will change his/her mind. On the other hand, the imposition of a timeframe provision denies the benefits of MAiD to patients who, though not at the end of life, are experiencing unrelievable suffering. Patients with spinal stenosis, for example, or Amyotrophic Lateral Sclerosis (ALS), can sometimes continue living long past the point when the quality of their life is acceptable to them. If they are excluded from MAiD eligibility because their natural death is not imminent, then they may be condemned to years of intolerable suffering.

It seems wrong headed to permit assisted dying for patients whose suffering will be of short duration (because their natural death is imminent) but to forbid it for those who will otherwise be forced to suffer intolerably for a much longer period. Oregon and the other American jurisdictions which have legalized PAS should consider extending eligibility to patients who have more than six months to live but who seek assisted dying because they are suffering intolerably.

Implications for People Living with Severe Disabilities

Not unexpectedly, when the "reasonably foreseeable natural death" requirement was challenged in court (*Truchon*, 2019, Superior Court of Quebec), it was found to be unconstitutional. The plaintiffs in this case were two severely disabled Quebec patients, Nicole Gladu and Jean Truchon—the former with post-polio syndrome, for which pain medication could no longer provide relief, the latter with cerebral palsy so severe that it left him in great pain, utterly dependent on caregivers and unable to engage in any of the activities that (in his judgment) made life worthwhile. Ms. Gladu and Mr. Truchon argued that, for people in their circumstances, the timeframe requirement was unfairly discriminatory. As people living with severe disabilities but not at the end of life, they were denied MAiD, while other patients, whose intolerable suffering would be of shorter duration because their natural death was imminent, were eligible for medically assisted dying. The Government responded that patients who are suffering intolerably but who are not at the end of life have other options, such as voluntarily stopping eating and drinking or unassisted suicide. However, the Court ruled that the timeframe restriction of Bill C-14 was unfairly discriminatory and therefore unconstitutional.

Having lost this court challenge, the Government passed new legislation. Bill C-7 (2021) allowed patients who, though not at the end of life, meet all other requirements, to receive MAiD; but, for patients whose natural death is not reasonably foreseeable, the new legislation imposes additional safeguards, such as a ninety-day waiting period, during which the patient's capacity can be rigorously assessed and alternatives to MAiD can be identified.

The most recently available data (2022) show that the proportion of MAiD recipients whose natural death was not reasonably foreseeable constitutes a very small proportion (3.5 percent) of total MAiD provisions, which constitute 4.1 percent of all 2022 deaths in Canada.

The Autonomy Argument in Favor of Mercy Killing

One of the *Carter* plaintiffs, Gloria Taylor, was suffering from ALS, a fatal neurodegenerative disease. Her testimony emphasizes the central justificatory role played by personal autonomy.

> What I want is to be able to die in a manner that is consistent with the way that I lived my life. I want to be able to exercise control and die with dignity and with my sense of self and personal integrity intact. I want to be able to experience my death as part of my life and part of my expression of that life. I do not want the manner of my death to undermine the values that I lived my life in accordance with . . . (Written submission of the Plaintiff, *Carter*, 2010, p 1)

Respect for the principle of autonomy is a cornerstone of liberal democracy. Indeed, it would be difficult to find any modern liberal democratic society that does not take seriously the state's duty to protect each citizen's right to make important life-and-death decisions, based on his/her own beliefs about what makes life go well.

The most famous philosophical defense of this principle is associated with nineteenth-century British philosopher John Stuart Mill. For Mill, when a person's important life choices affect only (or primarily) himself/herself, then others (including the state) ought not to interfere coercively. Actions that do not cause harm to others fall within the sphere of liberty: "The only freedom which deserves the names is that of pursuing our own good in our own way, so long as we do not attempt to deprive others of theirs or impede their efforts to obtain it."[5]

The essence of Mill's "Harm Principle" is that individuals are sovereign with respect to acts that are primarily self-regarding. Mill qualifies his doctrine, however, by explaining that it is meant to apply only to competent adults who are rational, fully informed, and acting voluntarily.

This Millian principle has been adopted by almost all jurisdictions which have legalized mercy killing, as seen by the fact that all restrict eligibility to the voluntary choices of competent adults (or "mature minors").[6] Nevertheless, proponents of mercy killing readily accept that individual liberty cannot be unfettered. The right to personal liberty, though fundamentally important, cannot be taken as absolute. When the exercise of personal liberty would result in serious harm to others or to society, then coercive restrictions may be legitimate.

Mill's key point is that the autonomous choices of a mature and competent adult should not be infringed except for proportionately exigent reasons. A discretionary weighing and balancing of benefits and harms is required. When we apply Mill's argument to patients in Gloria Taylor's situation, it follows that the choice of medically assisted dying should be respected, so long as there are safeguards in place adequate to protect vulnerable individuals from such harms as wrongful death.

How Slippery Is the Slippery Slope?

Opponents of mercy killing commonly appeal to "the slippery slope argument." Their opposition to MAiD is based on the claim that if it were legalized, its use would expand in a dangerous manner. Initially, mercy killing will be restricted to competent adult patients who experience their lives as more burdensome than beneficial, but it will quickly expand to include patients whose lives are a burden to others (or to society). At this juncture, the horrors of the Nazi so-called "euthanasia" program are typically invoked.

Traditional physician ethics has always prohibited killing one's patients. If mercy killing were to become an accepted medical procedure, so the objection goes, both doctors and society would become desensitized, brutalized even. Such an outcome would not only erode the vital bond of trust between doctor and patient but would also serve to weaken society's commitment to the sanctity of life. The process of desensitization is progressive and will, ultimately, result in wrongful death for stigmatized minorities.

Critics urge us to oppose legalization based on the fear that, despite safeguards, the practice of mercy killing will inevitably result in a precipitous slide down a very slippery slope. At the bottom of the slope: a snake pit of abuse and harm for vulnerable members of society. Legalization of mercy killing will also, it is claimed, weaken society's commitment to the sanctity of life and seriously erode the important bond of trust between doctor and patient. Equally to be feared: both doctors and society will become progressively desensitized to the value of human life. This desensitization will result, ultimately, in victimization for the most vulnerable. The harm resulting from legalization will far outweigh any possible benefits.

In response, advocates of MAiD deny that the slide from mercy to abuse is inexorable. Or, rather, they argue that, with careful safeguards in place, it will be possible to respect the individual's right to choose assisted dying while also protecting vulnerable patients from the harm of wrongful death.

To evaluate the cogency of the slippery slope argument against MAiD, one must consider two different versions of the argument. The *psychological* version, mentioned above, alleges that legalization of mercy killing will have a brutalizing effect on society in general and on the medical profession in particular.

Alternatively, or as well, it is argued that even if access to MAiD is carefully regulated, the safeguards meant to prevent abuse and exploitation will gradually become weakened or diluted. The *conceptual version* of the slippery slope argument points out that safeguards against abuse depend upon concepts that are inescapably vague. Erosion will occur because it is impossible to draw a non-arbitrary line between ethically permissible and ethically impermissible cases of MAiD.

Consider, for example, the safeguard that restricts MAiD to cognitively competent patients. "Cognitive competence" is not like an "on-off switch." Rather, it is located on a continuum. MAiD assessors will have a comparatively easy time with patients who clearly have capacity or who clearly lack capacity. But they will struggle with patients in "the grey zone." The slippery slope argument claims that once we legalize mercy killing for patients who clearly possess decisional capacity, we will then, over time, slide inexorably toward providing assisted dying for those who lack capacity and who are, in consequence, vulnerable to wrongful death. A similar problem arises when we try to distinguish patients whose suffering is intolerable from those whose suffering is tolerable, or patients whose disease is incurable from those whose disease might be cured.

In sum: Attempts to regulate mercy killing must rely upon such key concepts as patient "competence," disease "incurability," and "intolerable" suffering. Each of these concepts is vague. There will be clear-cut cases when patients fall at one or the other end of the continuum, but many cases will fall between the extremes. For grey zone cases, drawing a line between patients who qualify for euthanasia and those who should be excluded will require discretionary judgment. Because there is no non-arbitrary place to draw a line, social pressure will result in a slide toward ever-diminishing protection for the vulnerable. Slippage from voluntary to non-voluntary euthanasia is particularly to be feared because, in the latter sort of case, someone other than the patient is deciding that he/she would be better off dead.

By appealing to both the psychological and the conceptual versions of the slippery slope argument, critics of physician-assisted dying argue that even with legislated safeguards, mercy killing is morally unjustified and should be legally prohibited. Assisted dying should be opposed because it puts the most vulnerable members of society—the frail elderly, racialized minorities, the poor and marginalized—at high risk of wrongful death.

Proponents of mercy killing can respond to these slopist arguments by appealing to evidence from jurisdictions in which assisted dying has been legal for an extensive period. In none of these are socioeconomically or racially vulnerable patients disproportionately represented among MAiD recipients. Instead, what the data consistently show is that assisted dying recipients are drawn disproportionately from the most privileged sectors of the population. A substantial majority of MAiD recipients are white, rather than belonging to a racialized minority; recipients are on average wealthier and better educated than people who die without receiving MAiD. They are mostly living independently (rather than being institutionalized) and almost all have received palliative care or have had access to it but declined.

Data from every jurisdiction disconfirms the hypothesis that when MAiD is legalized, it will be provided, disproportionately, to marginalized people—those who are too poor, powerless, or ignorant to gain access to palliative care or to the other vital support services that make continued life tolerable. Although there is a strong case to be made for improved social support services, including palliative care, requests for MAiD are clearly not being driven by either socioeconomic deprivation or poor availability of social services.

Also worth noting: Most MAiD applicants (and recipients) have cancer (or some other terminal illness, such as ALS) as their underlying medical condition and almost all of them have received extensive palliative care services before requesting MAiD. This fact has special significance because it disconfirms another objection commonly raised against assisted dying: that budget-conscious governments will use the availability of MAiD as a rationale for cutting back on expensive social services. The empirical evidence simply does not support this claim.

Thus, despite dire warnings issued by MAiD opponents, empirical evidence from every jurisdiction that has legalized assisted dying shows that it is accessed with disproportionate frequency by the most privileged members of society rather than by the vulnerable and marginalized.

Should We Be Alarmed by the Number of MAiD Deaths?

We learn from the "Fourth Annual Report on Medical Assistance in Dying in Canada 2022" that

> In 2022 there were 13,241 MAiD provisions reported in Canada, accounting for 4.1% of all deaths in Canada. This figure represents a 32.1% increase in growth compared to the previous year.

Some critics argue that both the number of MAiD provisions in Canada and the year-on-year percentage increase are evidence that we are already sliding down a slippery slope toward a morally problematic destination. However, to evaluate the claim that these figures are morally troubling, we must first consider what would be a morally appropriate number of annual MAiD deaths.

International comparisons may help. In the Netherlands, for that same year, euthanasia provisions represented about 5 percent of overall deaths. In Oregon, by contrast, only an estimated 0.6 percent of overall deaths were from physician-assisted suicide. So, the percentage of MAiD deaths in Canada (2022) is somewhat lower than in the Netherlands but significantly higher than the number of physician-assisted suicides in Oregon. Should one be alarmed by these figures?

Statistics cannot, without interpretation, tell us whether the number (or rate of increase) of medically assisted deaths in a particular jurisdiction is too high, too low, or just right. If it is established that medical assistance in dying is provided exclusively to patients who satisfy appropriate eligibility criteria, and if it is provided in a manner that both respects patient autonomy and eliminates patient suffering, then, regardless of the numbers or the rate of increase, we should not find legalization ethically troubling.

In addition to statistical arguments, critics are also wont to highlight individual cases in which it is alleged, sometimes by family members of a MAiD recipient,[7] that a patient was provided MAiD despite lacking capacity to make an informed and voluntary decision or despite not suffering from a grievous and incurable medical illness. If such cases were to occur frequently, then that would be a genuine cause for concern. However, in jurisdictions which have legalized MAiD, there is generally rigorous oversight. Cases of suspected or reported abuse are reviewed by a professional body and, ultimately, they can be investigated by the police. No system involving human discretion and judgment can ever be perfect. But the infrequency of such allegations and the rarity of established wrongdoing should be reassuring.

Reasons Patients Seek MAiD

In Canada, the Netherlands, Oregon, and elsewhere, the reasons most frequently given by patients for seeking assisted dying are very similar. Loss of ability to engage in meaningful activities (89 percent) generally comes top of the list, followed by inability to perform the tasks of daily living. Inadequate control of pain (and other symptoms) is cited less frequently—perhaps because over 80 percent of MAiD applicants receive palliative care (and, almost all the remaining 20 percent had access to such care but declined). Across jurisdictions, loss of autonomy and dignity are high on the list of reasons patients give for seeking assisted dying. There are only minor differences from one country to another and from one year to the next. (The percentages cited in brackets, above, are for Canada, 2022.)

When one is considering the overall benefits of regulation over prohibition, it should be noted that the number of patients who benefit from the legalization of MAiD is actually much larger than the number who request and receive it.[8] Many patients with a serious medical condition or disability will never request assisted dying but, nevertheless, they derive a comforting sense of control from the knowledge that if their medical condition deteriorates to the point that they are experiencing intolerable suffering, a dignified and painless alternative will be available. Moreover, some seriously ill patients who might be irrationally tempted to take their lives prematurely may be less likely to act impulsively or irrationally because they know that, sometime down the road, assisted dying will be an option.

Ongoing Controversy

Public opinion surveys show that approval of MAiD in Canada is extremely high among all sectors of the population, including people with disabilities. However, since 2021, when MAiD legislation was changed to permit assisted dying for patients *who were not at the end of life*, disability rights organizations have been increasingly vocal in their opposition. People with severe and incurable disabilities whose death is not reasonably foreseeable now qualify for MAiD (so long as they are suffering intolerably and meet the other eligibility requirements). Many disability rights advocates claim that this expansion of the eligibility criteria discriminates against people with disabilities and devalues their lives. Two arguments are offered to support the charge of wrongful discrimination.

The first argument contends that by offering MAiD to disabled patients who are not dying, society is in effect devaluing their lives. But this claim ignores the fact that the choice of assisted dying must always be made by the patient herself/himself. It is individuals living with severe and incurable disabilities who get to decide when their suffering is so great that continued life is no longer worthwhile. If some people with grievous disabilities decide *for themselves* that their life has become more burdensome than beneficial, and if they possess decision-making capacity, then they should be permitted to choose assisted dying if that is their preferred option. Those who choose assisted dying are not thereby judging the lives of others who, in similar circumstances, choose to go on living.

The second argument claims that some people living with severe disabilities will opt for MAiD because society has failed to provide income support, affordable housing, and other social services that would make their lives tolerable. Instead of offering adequate social supports, society selfishly offers the less expensive option of assisted dying.

In response, let us agree that, on grounds of both distributive justice and harm reduction, social support for people with disabilities should be greatly increased. It is undeniable that socioeconomic deprivation contributes to the suffering of many disabled people, thereby making it more likely that they will choose MAiD. In a better world, every patient would have access to the housing they require and to a full range of potentially beneficial social services. Nevertheless, the fact that social services are less than ideal does not justify denying patients their right to choose MAiD. The cure for inadequate social supports is to improve such supports rather than to deny individuals who are suffering intolerably the right to make the choice that seems best to them.

Notes

1 Switzerland was the first country in the world to permit any kind of assisted death. It legalized assisted suicide in 1941. As in some American states, physicians are permitted to prescribe lethal drugs to eligible patients, who then take the medication themselves; but physicians are not allowed actively to administer such drugs, for example, by injection.

  PAS and VAE were legalized simultaneously in the Netherlands and Belgium in 2002, and in Luxembourg (2009). More recently, on June 17, 2016, the Parliament of Canada passed Bill C-14, legalizing Medical Assistance in Dying [MAiD], which encompasses both PAS and VAE.

2   Here's a working definition of the phrase "voluntary active euthanasia": VAE occurs when a physician (or other person) deliberately brings about the death of a competent patient, from the motive of mercy, at the patient's voluntary request.

3   Every American state that has legalized physician-assisted suicide requires that the patient must have a prognosis of six months or fewer to live.

4   Under the Canadian Charter of Rights and Freedoms, if government legislation violates or restricts basic individual liberties, such as the right to life, liberty and security of the person, then the *onus probandi* rests with the government. It must demonstrate that the liberty-limiting legislation in question is (a) necessary to achieve a pressing objective and that (b) there is no less restrictive means to achieve the objective. So, if regulatory safeguards will work as well as total prohibition, then the former should be preferred to the latter. The government must also demonstrate that its restrictive legislation is reasonably likely to achieve the objective being sought and that it will produce, overall, more good than harm. In Canadian jurisprudence, this is called "the Oakes test." It corresponds closely to JS Mill's discussion, in *On Liberty*, of the "Harm Principle." A good end (such as protecting the vulnerable) can potentially justify bad means (such as limiting the individual's right to choose how and when to die) but only if the means are shown to be necessary to achieve the end, are the least coercive means available, are likely to achieve their goal, and will produce more good than harm overall.

5   J. S. Mill, *On Liberty* (1859), ed. Alburey Castell, Crofts Classics (Harvard, 1947), 12, Ch. 1, (Hoboken, NJ: Wiley, 1947).

6   In Canada, no one under eighteen is currently eligible for MAiD. In the Netherlands, euthanasia is legal for children between twelve and sixteen years old, with consent required from both the child and its parents. Children between the ages of sixteen and eighteen do not require parental consent, but parental involvement in the decision-making process is expected.

7   In several well-publicized Canadian cases, patients receiving MAiD exercised their right to exclude family members from participating in their treatment decisions. Excluded family members thus have no access to the patient's medical records. Nor are they able to override the medical decisions made by an adult patient with capacity.

8   Some patients who apply for and receive a certificate entitling them to MAiD nevertheless die naturally. In some cases that is because their death occurs naturally, without the need for assistance. In other cases, patients change their minds.

Against Physician-Assisted Suicide and Euthanasia

Scott B. Rae

Study Questions

1. What is Rae's principled argument against PAS/E?
2. What are the two objections to his argument that Rae addresses? How does he respond to them?

3. What obligation does Rae claim we have to the vulnerable? Why?
4. What criticisms does Rae make of the Argument from Autonomy?
5. Why does Rae think that hospice and palliative care are more compassionate than PAS/E?

In February of 2024, former Dutch prime minister Dries van Agt and his wife of seventy years, Eugenie, died together by physician-performed euthanasia. He served as the Dutch prime minister from 1977 to 1982, founded a pro-Palestinian rights group (Rights Forum) in the Netherlands, and later served as EU ambassador to the United States and to Japan. Both were ninety-three at the time of their deaths. Both were in frail health, and what seems to be the primary motivation was their desire to avoid future suffering, especially should one partner precede the other in natural death. Their decision appeared to be fully consensual. This phenomenon of couples being administered euthanasia together is still rare in the Netherlands (twenty-six in 2020, thirty-two in 2021, and fifty-eight in 2023). Their joint euthanasia was publicized around the world in most major media outlets, giving an impetus to the euthanasia movement globally. It's already accepted widely in the Netherlands and has been for some time. According to the Dutch pro-euthanasia group, DVVE, many people express a wish for euthanasia, but it only accounts for roughly 5 percent of the total death rate in the Netherlands.[1]

A similar widely publicized case of euthanasia in the United States occurred in November 2014 in the tragic case of Brittany Maynard. She was twenty-nine when she was diagnosed with a terminal brain tumor that left her roughly six months to live. Two surgeries were unsuccessful in removing the tumor, and it is common, when attempts fail to remove tumors, that they return more aggressively. She refused all further treatments to shrink the tumor, insisting that they would compromise the quality of life she had left. She also refused hospice and palliative care, both of which are designed to keep terminally ill patients comfortable. Instead, she chose to move to Oregon in time to establish residency there so she could take advantage of Oregon's Death with Dignity Act (physician-assisted suicide was not yet legal in her home state of California, though it would become legal sometime after her death). While admitting she did not want to die, she insisted on dying on her own terms and preventing her own suffering as well as the suffering of her loved ones.[2]

Many people look at these accounts and wonder, "What's the problem with euthanasia and physician-assisted suicide (PAS)?" They see suffering people wanting to die as they see fit and are puzzled as to what could be morally or legally problematic about it. However, as heart-wrenching as these stories are, they do not substitute for reasoned argument about the merits and demerits of PAS/euthanasia.

In this chapter, we will look at the case *against* PAS/euthanasia (PAS/E). Despite the intuitive appeal that comes from narrative accounts of terminally ill patients enduring unrelieved suffering, there are good reasons that make PAS/E a bad idea, both morally and legally. We will look briefly at the history of euthanasia, both in the United States and in Europe, and point out that its history was mostly a dark one, as its modern roots were deeply embedded in the eugenics movements of the late nineteenth and early twentieth centuries. We will then examine the various arguments opposing PAS/E, and finally, propose a compassionate alternative that focuses on hospice and palliative care medicine.

A Brief History of the Euthanasia Movement[3]

In ancient times, the moral discussion was more about suicide and infanticide than euthanasia. The impact of the Hippocratic Oath during antiquity was the subject of considerable debate. It was neither widely known nor consistently adhered to by physicians in the Greco-Roman world. Some Greek philosophers condemned suicide outright—Plato and Aristotle, for example. The more predominant practice among both Greeks and Romans was infanticide, namely by exposure, that is, leaving the infant exposed to the elements to die. This was done for economic reasons at times (e.g., if the family could not support additional children). It was also done commonly when the baby was born with some sort of deformity.

Views on suicide changed in the Roman Empire under the influence of the Stoic and Epicurean philosophers.[4] They condoned both suicide and infanticide and considered them, in many cases, a reasonable, if not laudable, thing to do. However, with the coming of Christianity, that view was strongly opposed, both in theory and in practice. The Old Testament admonition, "Thou shalt not kill," was widely taken to apply to suicide as well as murder and infanticide. The early church became well-known for their practice of rescuing and adopting infants who had been left to die from exposure because they fundamentally viewed those infants, like adults, to be made in the image of God, and therefore of inestimable and intrinsic value. Though there were some examples of suicide in the Old Testament, they were committed by less than ideal moral characters (Saul, Samson, for example) and their acts were not condoned in any way.[5] In addition, there is no example in the Bible of anyone who committed or attempted suicide, or enlisted help in suicide, as a result of the suffering experienced by an advanced illness.[6] Moreover, perhaps the two most influential Christian philosophers/theologians of the early and medieval periods of Christian history, Augustine and Thomas Aquinas, both clearly and strongly condemned suicide.[7]

The general prohibition of suicide continued through the medieval period that was dominated by a Judeo-Christian framework for viewing the world. With the challenges to that worldview that arose during the Renaissance and Enlightenment eras, there were some isolated objections to the immorality of suicide, though not enough to change the moral consensus against it. For example, Thomas More not only allowed for but also encouraged suicide in the face of a terminal illness with unrelievable pain and suffering, similar to the conditions necessary for PAS/E in countries where those have been legalized.[8]

The modern PAS/E movement began in the late nineteenth and early twentieth centuries and was driven by an interest in eugenics, the movement to rid the world of genetic disease and thereby improve the overall gene pool of the human race. It did so primarily by encouraging abortion, involuntary sterilization, and euthanasia/infanticide, all seen as reasonable practices to eliminate "undesirables" from the population due to the burden of caring for them and their lack of ability to be productive contributors to society. The Nazi experience with euthanasia put this eugenic emphasis into "overdrive," with its stated ambition to further what they considered the Aryan master race. They viewed candidates for euthanasia (involuntary) as people who did not have a life worth living for reasons of disability or disease. As a result of the Nazi excesses that came to light in the aftermath of the Second World War, the euthanasia movement suffered a serious setback, only to be resuscitated in the 1970s with the advent of life-sustaining technologies that enabled medicine to keep people alive in increasingly poor quality of life circumstances. People who, in the past, simply died from chronic illnesses now could be kept alive, sometimes indefinitely. The inability of medicine to say "enough" when it came to treating terminal illnesses led to the desire to end life peacefully as opposed to a long and sometimes painful and lingering dying process. The law changed to reflect this, allowing for patients (or their families) to refuse treatments they did not want and allowing for PAS in several states in the United States and PAS/E in some countries in Europe.[9] This was the first time that PAS/E took the interests of the patient into account and the first time PAS/E had been voluntary by the patient. Up to now in the history of PAS/E, the patient's interests were rarely, if at all, considered, and most cases of PAS/E were non-voluntary. PAS/E/infanticide was done for the benefit of society or for the benefit of the families that did not want the patient because of the burden they caused to the family. This was particularly true of the developing world and its cultural preference for boys that led to millions of baby girls dying of various forms of abortion and infanticide. In that sense, PAS/E did not go down a slippery slope from beneficent purposes to non-beneficent ones. It started out with eugenic purposes and was taken to extremes by the Nazis. Only in the more recent past was the practice driven by the interests of the patient.

Arguments Against PAS/E

The arguments against PAS/E presented in this section are principled, or deontological arguments. The primary principled part revolves around the notion that it is always unethical to intend to kill an innocent person. This initial section takes into account two objections to the principled argument—that killing and allowing to die are both morally and legally distinct, and that the seriously ill, elderly, and demented are still full human persons. This is, in part, the reason why there is no recognized constitutionally protected right to die. In addition, there is a principled argument that upholds the obligation to protect the vulnerable at the end of life, not kill them. Further, this section responds to the principled argument in favor of PAS/E, the argument from personal autonomy. This section concludes with a consideration of allowing PAS/E in the context of the massive demographic shifts around the world that could result in vulnerable people being harmed by being administered PAS/E without their consent.

PAS/E Involves Killing an Innocent Human Person

At the most basic level, both proponents and opponents of PAS/E must acknowledge that the practice involves the killing of an innocent human person. Whether it is done by the hand of the patient or that of a physician is morally irrelevant, though in the eyes of the law that difference is still maintained in some countries. For example, in the US states that have legalized PAS, it is only PAS that has been legalized, explicitly not euthanasia, different from the situation in some countries in Europe, where both are legal. The reason it is morally irrelevant is that an innocent life is being taken, violating the long-standing moral principle that prohibits the intentional taking of innocent life.[10]

Killing and Allowing to Die Are Not the Same Thing

The mandate against taking innocent life distinguishes between killing and allowing to die. Even though the result is the same, the result is not all that matters in the moral assessment of an action. *Intent* is also a critical component of a moral act. In some cases, it is the only thing that distinguishes between two otherwise identical actions, such as the difference between a gift and a bribe. When refusing a treatment, for example, most patients who desire to stop such treatments do not want to die; they simply want to live out their remaining days without dependence on medical technology that will not change the downward course of their disease and may be more burdensome than beneficial. For example, my father-in-law told me clearly when I was wheeling him out of the hospital, "Don't ever bring me here again." He didn't want to die, but simply wanted to live out the rest of his life unencumbered by tubes, tests, and technologies that he didn't want. Although it is true that in many cases the patient will die soon after termination of life support, it is not usually nor necessarily the intent. By contrast, the intent in physician-assisted suicide/euthanasia is clearly to cause the patient to die.

In addition, the *cause* of death is different when refusing treatments and requesting PAS/E. In cases in which treatments, especially life-sustaining ones, are refused, the cause of the patient's death is the underlying disease that is allowed to take its natural course. At best, such treatment was only delaying an inevitable death. The disease is allowed to finish its course, unchecked by any additional treatments. Of course, when the patient chooses this course, the physician is morally obligated to provide for adequate comfort and care for the patient. But when a physician assists in suicide or administers euthanasia, his or her action is the immediate and direct cause of death.

There Is No Distinction Between a Human Being and a Human Person

The mandate not to take innocent life presumes that seriously ill patients are still full human persons, regardless of their ability to function. Some would make a distinction between human beings and persons, or between *biological* and *biographical* life,[11] which ends up being a distinction without a moral difference. Those who make this distinction often invoke a set of what they consider non-negotiable functions a human being must be able to perform before he or she can be designated a full person. This includes such functions as self-consciousness, rationality, ability to make relational connections, self-awareness, and sentience (the ability to feel sensations, such as pain but also joy). However, there are several counterexamples that render these functions irrelevant to the moral status of a full person. For example, take someone under general anesthesia, which if performed correctly (and hopefully so!!) will render the person temporarily unable to perform any of those functions deemed essential to be a person. Or take someone in a reversible coma, perhaps temporarily unable to perform those functions for a longer time period. Is it reasonable to assert that the person forfeits their moral status, and attendant rights, during the time they cannot perform those functions? The advocate for this distinction between a human being and a person will reply that since these are only temporary losses of those functions, that makes them different. But that reply presumes that *there is something else besides those functions* that grounds the full personhood of those under anesthesia or in reversible comas while they cannot perform those functions. I would suggest that there is no distinction between a human being and a human person and that one's status and right to life do not depend on the ability or inability to perform certain functions deemed critical to being persons. They are still full persons but, due to illness or other causes, no longer have the ability to actualize certain capacities.

If "having a life," as characterized by those key functions, is what gives life its value, and persons their moral standing, and if, when it is gone, essentially only a body can be said to exist, then what is to prevent us from stripping the "person" of all rights? Could we then bury the "person" and treat him like a corpse? Can we take organs with only the consent of next of kin? Can we experiment on him, again with appropriate proxy consent? One could even argue that if rights have been lost once those functions are gone, not even consent would be necessary for PAS/E. If the essentials of one's life and one's rights are tied up with biographical life, and that is lost, there does not seem to be any consistent way of preventing any of the above scenarios as long as they are done with appropriate respect for the dead.

Obligations to Care for, Not Kill the Vulnerable

This mandate not to take innocent life is heightened when the person whose life is taken is vulnerable, such as an elderly, terminally ill adult, whose competence to make his or her own decisions may be seriously compromised. Ironically, in many cultures, suicide prevention is taken very seriously—unless the person is elderly and infirm, and deemed a burden to society and their loved ones. We assume that when the average person contemplates suicide, there are serious mental health issues that must be addressed. However, with the elderly, we tend not to take these mental health issues nearly as seriously, if at all. Of course, when someone gets a terminal diagnosis or suffers losses that accompany aging and the end of one's life, not surprisingly, depression and other mental health issues arise. But in the elderly, those are rarely treated with the same seriousness as they would be with a younger adult or adolescent. The general moral obligation to protect the vulnerable, widely held throughout the Western world at least, should ensure that the elderly are not being administered euthanasia, nor given assistance in suicide.

Critique of the Argument from Autonomy

But you might ask, "Doesn't someone have the *right* to die?" What if they willingly choose PAS/E?

There Is No Constitutionally Protected Right to Die

Legally speaking, there is no Constitutional precedent for anything like a right to die. The US Supreme Court ruled on this in their landmark ruling in 1997, *Washington v. Glucksburg*,[12] that there is no right to die recognized by the US Constitution. Therefore, states are not acting in an unconstitutional manner if they prohibit PAS/E. However, the Court also ruled that states may allow PAS/E if that reflects the will of the people in that state. The key to the Court's ruling is that there is no legal basis for asserting a fundamental "right to die." They ruled that there has been a long tradition of discouraging and preventing suicide and prohibiting someone from aiding and abetting someone in suicide (the latter of which is what physicians are doing when they assist someone in PAS). They also distinguished between killing and allowing to die, insisting that morally and legally those are two distinct acts, with a different intent and a different ultimate cause of death.

Evaluating the Argument from Personal Autonomy

At the heart of the *argument from the right to die* is an assumption of personal autonomy, an extension of the pro-choice argument of "my body, my choice."

Proponents of PAS/E insist that the timing and manner of one's death is one of life's most personal issues and should be one of life's most private decisions, unencumbered by regulations from the state. This has become the main argument in favor of PAS/E, eclipsing the argument from mercy and compassion, since palliative care medicine and hospice now provide a high level of pain control for seriously ill patients.

However, the right of autonomy is not absolute. There are many things you cannot do with your own body, such as put certain drugs into it, use it for prostitution, or sell your organs to the highest bidder. In addition, if the right to die is a fundamental one, *then it must be available to any adult, regardless of the reason for requesting it*. But there are significant restrictions on the "right to die," such as competence to make the decision, being an adult, and suffering from a condition of unrelievable pain (and in some states, the person must have a diagnosable terminal illness with a prescribed time period left to live, usually six months or less). Physicians would not normally assist a young adult or college student in suicide with treatable mental health conditions, regardless of their presumed "right to die." These widely accepted restrictions on who can receive PAS/E strongly suggest that the right to die is not a fundamental right, for if it were, the reasons for requesting it wouldn't matter, nor would we even require reasons to be stated. For fundamental rights do not need reasons to justify exercising them.

In general, when there has been a conflict between autonomy and the rights of others, the rights of others normally take precedence. This is particularly the case when the exercise of autonomy results in harm coming to others. Opponents of PAS/E argue that by opening the door to PAS/E, others at the end of life are being harmed. The data from the Dutch experience with euthanasia strongly suggest that terminally ill people are being administered euthanasia without their consent. Most who advocate for PAS/euthanasia insist that the practice must be administered only with the consent of the terminally ill patient, that *non-voluntary* euthanasia is clearly immoral. However, some influential advocates for PAS maintain that consent is not always necessary and that nonconsensual euthanasia could be morally acceptable for those for whom we would presume consent, or if they cannot enjoy a threshold quality of life, such as the severely cognitively impaired or demented.[13] Others maintain that once PAS is legalized, there will be irresistible pressure to extend it to incompetent patients, including children.[14] But if by legalizing PAS/E, other terminally ill people are put at risk for non-voluntary aid in dying, this argues that the exercise of autonomy for some is bringing harm to others. In such cases, the reality of harm should override the right to privacy and personal liberty.

PAS/E in the Context of Seismic Demographic Shifts

This concern is magnified by the demographic shifts that have taken place in the Western world in the past decade. It is widely known that the baby boomer generation has reached retirement age, and for the next twenty or so years, societies in the United States and Europe will have unprecedented numbers of men and women over the age of sixty-five in their populations, with a shrinking working population to help support them. In addition, the average elderly person will spend roughly half of their lifetime medical expenses in the final year of their lives, when it arguably will do them the least amount of good. The pressure on these societies to curb health care costs will be intense and has already begun to occur. For example, British philosopher Kevin Yuill points out the explicit connection being made between support for PAS and the numbers of elderly that will populate the Western countries in the next several decades. Yuill describes himself as a typical European liberal on abortion, but he opposes legalizing PAS due to its open eugenics agenda. British social commentator Brendan O'Neill, in the foreword to Yuill's book, points out that

> Time and again, thinkers and activists who claim only to support the exercise of individual autonomy at the end of life talk openly about the fact that letting people die will save society money and resources. Indeed, this has become one of the key implicit arguments for assisted suicide, since in the words of British journalist and disability activist Melanie Reid, "it is ridiculous that a society in crisis, a society filled with more old, demented people than have ever existed before, has failed to legalize the ending of sick people's lives [by PAS/euthanasia]."[15]

In addition, British Baroness Mary Warnock, a very influential person in bioethics in Europe and a well-known advocate for PAS, has insisted that the elderly should exercise their duty to die if they have become a burden to others or to the state. She states, "If you are demented, you are wasting the resources of the National Health Service."[16] In the United States, the strain on the health care system has been echoed by *New York Times* columnist David Brooks (who was not recommending legalizing PAS/E), who was drawing attention to economic conditions following the financial crisis in 2008–10, when he said, "The fiscal crisis is about many things, but one of them is our inability to face death—our willingness to spend our nation into bankruptcy to extend life for a few more sickly months."[17] O'Neill concludes that, "Indeed today, to insist on the right to continue living despite the economic or environmental cost of one's life, despite the 'uselessness' of one's life in comparison with the lives of other, more able-bodied individuals—is surely regarded as immoral—after all, it sins against the new moralities of environmental awareness and generational responsibility."[18] His fear is that the right to die might become a duty to die as the resources necessary to take care of the growing number of elderly reach the breaking point.

Some of the potential abuses about which opponents are concerned could come out of the application of some of the values that PAS/E proponents strongly hold. For example, the *argument from compassion*, if taken too far, could lead to non-voluntary euthanasia. If it's a matter of mercy, then whether or not someone has the ability to consent to it is less relevant. In addition, the argument from autonomy, if taken to its logical conclusion, could lead to euthanasia for virtually any reason, especially since it would be considered a fundamental right to die.

PAS/E and Harm to Oneself

PAS/E being available legally can also cause harm to the patient himself or herself. Should the "right to die" mutate into a "duty to die," this would undoubtedly impact the poor and vulnerable segments of the population much more than the financially well-off, potentially putting good, or even adequate, end-of-life care into the category of a luxury item, available only to those with the means to afford it. In addition, often there are mental health issues that affect the elderly and seriously ill that often go untreated in those populations. For example, in a paper published in early 2016, Dr. Paul Applebaum of Columbia University Department of Psychiatry studied the increasing incidence in the Netherlands of euthanasia being requested by those with psychiatric disorders. Since 2010, the number of deaths by euthanasia has increased by roughly 75 percent. From published material on euthanasia by Dutch authorities from 2011–14, Dr. Applebaum concluded that roughly one in five patients who had requested euthanasia and had a psychiatric disorder had not been hospitalized for that disorder. This "raises concerns about eliminating people from the population as an alternative to providing them with the medical care and social support they need." Dutch supporters of euthanasia insist that these cases are consistent with the law that allows for aid in dying for "unbearable suffering with no prospect of improvement."[19]

Frequently, other social conditions, such as where one lives, access to family and other important relationships, and having a sense of purpose for one's remaining days, significantly influence the elderly person's sense of well-being and, sometimes, the desire to continue to live. Given the demographic pressures on societies, it is not hard to imagine scenarios in which individuals are coerced by their conditions to choose PAS/E even though they would desire to continue to live. For example, a Canadian elderly man, who required institutionalized long-term care because of his disabilities, was refused by the government health care program to live in a facility near his family. He did not want to die but regarded the prospect of living far away from his loved ones to be worse than continuing to live.[20] A second example, also from Canada, involves an elderly man of limited means, whose rental residence was being sold and he could not find another affordable place to live. He chose PAS/E not because he wanted to die, but because he feared being homeless worse than death.[21] It is not hard to imagine in these cases that family members could consider caring for their loved ones a significant burden and work together to "persuade" their loved one to accept PAS/E, even though their loved one may want to continue living. Even putting the elderly in the position of having to justify their continued existence would be inconsistent with their fundamental right to life.

Conclusion—A Compassionate Alternative of Hospice and Palliative Care

The case against PAS/E is based on the fact that it is killing an innocent person; recognizes a moral and legal difference between killing and allowing to die; denies the distinction between a human being and a human person; sees the obligation to protect the most vulnerable among us, namely the elderly; denies a fundamental or constitutional "right to die"; and is concerned about the movement from voluntary to non-voluntary PAS/E, especially given the unprecedented percentages of populations over sixty-five in many societies. The alternative of palliative care/hospice is a good and compassionate one, which has essentially moved the argument from mercy to the background of the debate. Take this example of Dr. Ian Haines, a medical oncologist and a professor in the Department of Medical Oncology at Cabrini Monash University in Australia, who has gone public about how his thinking has changed about euthanasia. He states, "As an oncologist with 35 years' full-time experience, I have seen palliative care reach the point where the terminally ill can die with equal or more dignity than euthanasia will provide. It is now very effective and increasingly available . . ." Haines goes on to describe the importance of advanced care planning and the right to refuse life-sustaining treatments. He opposes legalizing PAS/E on the grounds that the right to die will become a duty to die and become less of a problem for society. He states that "it [legalizing euthanasia] will be the wrong choice. It is not necessary and it will inevitably increase the pressure for some chronically ill patients to move on and stop being a burden."[22]

Notes

1 Kelly Kasulis Cho, "Duo Euthanasia: Famous Couple . . .," *Washington Post* (February 13, 2024) (https://www.washingtonpost.com/world/2024/02/13/netherlands-duo-euthanasia-dutch-prime-minister/).

2 For further reading on Maynard's story, see Brittany Maynard, "My Right to Death with Dignity at 29," *CNN* (November 2, 2014) (http://www.cnn.com/2014/10/07/opinion/maynard-assisted-suicide-cancer-dignity/); Olga Khazan, "Brittany Maynard and the Challenge of Dying with Dignity," *The Atlantic* (November 3, 2014) (http://www.theatlantic.com/health/archive/2014/11/brittany-maynard-and-the-challenge-of-dying-with-dignity/382282/).

3 In this historical section, I am indebted to the work of Richard Weikart, *Unnatural Death: Medicine's Descent from Healing to Killing* (Seattle: Discovery Institute, 2024).

4 Ibid., 21–3.

5 Ibid., 177, n. 25.

6 Ibid., 24–5.

7 Ibid., 29–30.

8   Ibid., 34–5.

9   See the landmark cases of Karen Ann Quinlan (the first person legally allowed to refuse life-sustaining treatment (355 A.2d 647 (1976)), and Nancy Cruzan (the first person legally allowed to refuse medically provided food and water (497 US 261; 110 S. Ct. 2841 (1990)). The US Supreme Court ruled on PAS, leaving it essentially a matter for the individual states to decide based on the will of their voters and thereby denying that there is a constitutionally protected "right to die" (Washington v. Glucksberg, 521 US 702 (1997).

10 There are some widely recognized exceptions to the mandate not to take life—combatants in a just war, acting in self-defense, and for some, the death penalty. In these cases, the person whose life is taken is not considered innocent, and there can be justification for taking life in these circumstances. This is why it's important to recognize that the modifier "innocent" must be included in the mandate not to take life—it's not to take *innocent* life.

11 See for example, James Rachels, *The End of Life* (New York: Oxford University Press, 1984).

12 521 US 702 (1997).

13 See for example, Margaret Battin, *The Least Worst Death: Essays in Bioethics at the End of Life* (New York: Oxford University Press, 1994), 120.

14 See for example, Norman Cantor, "On Kamisar, Killing and the Future of Physician Assisted Death," *Michigan Law Review* 102 (2004): 1825. Recently, Dutch law has extended the minimum age for euthanasia candidacy to 12.

15 Ibid.

16 Kevin Yuill, *Assisted Suicide: The Liberal, Humanist Case Against Legalization* (London: Palgrave Macmillan, 2013), xi.

17 David Brooks, "Death and Budgets," *New York Times* (July 14, 2011), A23 (http://www.nytimes.com/2011/07/15/opinion/15brooks.html), cited in Yuill, *Assisted Suicide*, xi. See also Daniel Callahan and Sherwin B. Nuland, "The Quagmire," *The New Republic* (May 18, 2011) (https://newrepublic.com/article/88631/american-medicine-health-care-costs).

18 Yuill, *Assisted Suicide*, xv.

19 "The Number of Mentally Ill Seeking Help to Die Is Rising. Are the Rules Being Twisted?" *The Economist* (June 15, 2016) (http://www.economist.com/news/international/21700506-between-life-and-death-number-mentally-ill-seeking-help-die-rising-are).

20 "Ontario Man Asks for MAiD Based on Long Term Care Access" (https://alexschadenberg.blogspot.com/2022/12/ontario-man-asks-for-maid-based-on-long.html, accessed December 14, 2022), cited in Weikart, *Unnatural Death*.

21 Cynthia Mulligan and Meredith Bond, "Ontario Man Applying for Medically-Assisted Death as Alternative to Being Homeless," *Toronto City News* (https://toronto.citynews.ca/2022/10/13/medical-assistance-death-maid-canada/, accessed December 14, 2022), cited in Weikart, *Unnatural Death*.

22 Ian Haines, "I Believed that Euthanasia Was the Only Humane Solution. I No Longer Believe That," *The Sydney Morning Herald* (November 20, 2016) (http://www.smh.com.au/comment/i-believed-that-euthanasia-was-the-only-humane-solution-i-no-longer-believe-that-20161118-gss921.html).

Responses

Response to Schafer on Physician-Assisted Suicide and Euthanasia

Scott B. Rae

> **Study Questions**
>
> 1. What are the areas of agreement shared by Rae and Schafer?
> 2. Why does Rae object to the term "mercy killing"?
> 3. How does Rae respond to Schafer's appeal to the principle of autonomy to justify PAS/E?
> 4. Why does Rae think that prohibiting PAS/E is not inconsistent with respect for autonomy?

I am grateful for the opportunity to respond to the thoughtful defense of euthanasia and physician-assisted suicide in this chapter by Arthur Schafer. I have a practice of avoiding critique of a position with which I disagree until I can represent the opposing position clearly and to the satisfaction of the proponent. Since I don't have the chance for actual conversation with Schafer, I will presume that I am representing his position accurately. Schafer is making two principal points in his advocacy for his position. First, that under certain circumstances, both euthanasia (which he terms "mercy killing") and physician-assisted suicide are morally justifiable. Second, both mercy killing and physician-assisted suicide should be legalized, but are subject to guardrails, to prevent the practice from being abused. In short, he argues for regulation, not prohibition, of mercy killing and physician-assisted suicide. He makes the case based on the moral and legal principle of personal autonomy, the right of individuals to make life's most important and personal decisions apart from government intrusion. He further argues that the concern about a legal slippery slope is overstated and that both practices can be adequately regulated with a set of procedural safeguards. I trust I have represented his position fairly.

Points of Agreement

Before critique of his argument, I want to point out several insightful places in his essay with which I agree. First, he rightly recognizes that the United States is an outlier among countries where euthanasia (referred to from now on as VAE—voluntary active euthanasia) and physician-assisted suicide (PAS) are treated differently. Most countries that have legalized one have also legalized the other. I agree with Schafer that there is no morally relevant difference between the two practices, and to be consistent, both should either be prohibited or allowed legally.

A second area of agreement is the recognition that personal autonomy, though the basis for his position, is not absolute. There can be valid restrictions on personal autonomy, such as harm to others. We could also point out that most would agree that autonomy can be restricted in order to provide a benefit to others (paying taxes for police and fire departments) and a benefit to oneself (mandatory education). The debate here is over the application of a principle, personal autonomy, on which we both agree, to the choice for VAE/PAS. A final agreement regards the designation of physician-assisted *suicide*. Most advocates of PAS avoid the term "suicide" to refer to the practice, when in reality, that is precisely what is occurring when PAS is chosen. I appreciate that Schafer has not shied away from using the term "suicide" instead of the other euphemisms that are commonly used. Similarly, using the term "mercy killing" to describe VAE also accurately describes what it is—the actual killing of a human being.

Points of Criticism

The first point of critique of Schafer's argument actually comes from the title of his essay and the use of the term "mercy killing" to describe VAE. The term suggests that the patient is in unbearable pain and suffering and that allowing VAE/PAS is the only alternative a compassionate person could think possible. Framing it this way can make the opponent of VAE/PAS seem callous to the pain and suffering of patients at the end of life. However, as Schafer admits, the argument from mercy is rarely mentioned today by VAE/PAS advocates because of the effectiveness and availability of palliative care medicine, which can control virtually all pain a patient experiences at the end of life. He cites figures that 80 percent of VAE/PAS recipients had received palliative care and the remaining 20 percent were offered it and declined. This is not to say that there are not some pain management cases that are particularly challenging, but in today's environment, those are rare exceptions to the general rule. He also points out that even in disadvantaged communities without access to social services, including palliative care, that is not determinative when it comes to the choice for VAE/PAS. What this suggests is that mercy has little to do with the argument for VAE/PAS—it's personal autonomy that is driving it.

This raises the second point of critique which has to do with the underlying moral principle of autonomy that supports VAE/PAS. This puts the choice for VAE/PAS in the category of a fundamental right. According to John Stuart Mill, such rights can only be overridden in cases where the exercise of that autonomy causes harm to others. However, surely there are some beliefs about what makes life go well that we would not want to recognize as valid. Some life choices we clearly don't want to affirm, for reasons beyond the fact that they cause harm to others.[1] But the more important point is that if VAE/PAS is a fundamental right, based on autonomy, then why should there be any criteria for eligibility? To be fair, Schafer does not spell out any specific criteria that he supports, but makes reference to some common ones, such as competence of the patient, disease, incurability, and intolerable suffering, pointing out that all of these criteria are vague and not particularly helpful. But he offers no other criteria for eligibility that would prevent the practices from being abused. I would argue that having any criteria for eligibility is inconsistent with the principle of personal autonomy. For if exercising VAE/PAS is a fundamental right, the reason why one wants to exercise it is, and should be, irrelevant. After all, we don't generally require reasons why someone wants to exercise other fundamental rights, nor do we have criteria for eligibility for who can exercise them. Why should VAE/PAS be restricted to persons with serious illness? Or a certain level of pain and suffering? Or someone with six months or less to live? If the choice for VAE/PAS is a fundamental right, to be consistent, it should be available to any adult (minors can be legitimately excluded) for any reason. But in my view, as a society, we don't actually believe that. That's why the societies where this is being considered also have a strong and admirable tradition, with many supporting features, of suicide prevention. But why, for example, should the person who has been "left at the altar" and lost the love of his or her life, or the person who failed to accomplish one of their major life goals that made their life worth living, be any less of a candidate for VAE/PAS than someone with a terminal illness, if it's based on personal autonomy? In my view, one can generally hold to the importance of autonomy and prohibit VAE/PAS at the same time.

Here's the reason that's not inconsistent. As I pointed out in my essay, there is harm that results from legalizing VAE/PAS, and there is empirical evidence to support it, particularly from some of the earlier adopters in Europe, such as in Belgium and the Netherlands. The slope from voluntary to non-voluntary VAE/PAS is real and suggests that the requirement that every proponent maintains—that the request for VAE/PAS be entirely voluntary—is impossible to enforce. This argument was made some time ago by Hastings Center founder, Daniel Callahan, when he stated, "I see no way, even in principle, to write or enforce a meaningful law that can guarantee effective procedural safeguards. . . . The euthanasia transaction will take place within the boundaries of the private and confidential doctor-patient relationship. No one can possibly know what takes place in that context unless the doctor chooses to reveal it."[2] Similarly, imagine family members continually attempting to talk their loved one into accepting VAE/PAS, wearing him or her down until eventually the loved ones agree to it, effectively having been coerced into a non-voluntary decision for VAE/PAS. Here's the major question—who will ever know that these coercive conversations have taken place? How will the most basic requirement, that virtually everyone agrees on, be enforced? I maintain that it cannot.

A final critique is recognizing a major omission in the argument. Schafer maintains that legalization of VAE/PAS can only be justified with a set of "careful safeguards" that prevent the prospect of abuse. But nowhere in the essay does he spell out what those safeguards are and how they might be enforced. Neither does he suggest any criteria for eligibility for VAE/PAS. Without these being made clear, in my view, the slide down the slope becomes quite slippery.

Notes

1 For example, imagine a person whose goal in life is to be the most effective provider of sadomasochistic sex for willing clients. Or take the person who wants to be the world's leading producer of pornography.
2 Daniel Callahan, "When Self-Determination Runs Amok," *Hastings Center Report* 22, no. 2 (March–April 1992): 52–5, at 54.

Response to Rae on Physician-Assisted Suicide and Euthanasia

Arthur Schafer

Study Questions

1. Why does Schafer object to Rae's comparing PAS/E to Nazi eugenics?
2. How does Schafer respond to Rae's absolute prohibition against killing innocent people?
3. What response does Schafer make to Rae's slippery slope arguments?
4. What does Schafer think of Rae's palliative/hospice alternative?

Scott B. Rae has argued against the morality of Physician-Assisted Suicide and Euthanasia (PAS/E). In this response, I offer a critique of the main arguments on which he relies.

Nazism and the Eugenics Movement

Several hundred thousand physically and mentally impaired infants, children, and adults were systematically murdered by the Nazi regime under the pretense that these were acts of "euthanasia." It is highly misleading, however, for Rae to conflate the Nazi so-called euthanasia program with PAS/E. From the moral point of view, killing people *involuntarily*, because others regard their lives as burdensome, could not be more different from PAS/E, which respects the *voluntary* wish of competent adults for assistance in dying.

Rae's Case Against PAS/E

Rae claims that PAS/E is inherently wrong because it violates an absolute rule that "it is always unethical to intend to kill an innocent person." His deontological approach to ethics assigns transcendent value to human life—even when it is irreversibly vegetative or blighted by unrelievable suffering. By contrast, many people regard irreversibly comatose life as having no intrinsic value, and intolerable suffering as a fate worse than death.

If we ask why the deliberate killing of an innocent human being is morally wrong, the most obvious answer is that killing innocent people directly causes grave harm to the person killed and causes indirect harm to all who are dependent upon or closely connected to the victim. However, if a patient has been suffering intolerably from a grievous and incurable medical condition and has made a voluntary and informed request for assistance in dying, then helping them to die should be counted as a morally justifiable "act of mercy."

Those committed to the "sanctity of life" view will respond that the inherent value attaching to every human life, regardless of its quality, overrides both patient autonomy and the relief of intolerable suffering. But are they entitled coercively to impose their (quasi-religious) views on those who do not share them? In liberal secular societies, the answer to that question is "no." No one should be killed because others regard their life as not worth living. Equally, no one should be denied assistance to die when they meet morally appropriate safeguards.

In the section titled "Obligations to Care for, Not Kill the Vulnerable," Rae correctly notes that patients who are elderly and/or terminally ill are vulnerable to abuse. Their decisional competence may be compromised by age or infirmity. They may also suffer from mental health problems. Rae then offers us a version of the slippery slope argument, claiming that if we legalize PAS/E for mentally competent patients, we will inevitably end up killing patients who lack competence. He concludes that only a total ban on assisted dying can protect vulnerable patients.

Against this argument, it should be noted that all the jurisdictions which permit PAS/E as an end-of-life option successfully protect vulnerable patients by means of stringent eligibility criteria. In Canada, for example, the mental competence of MAiD patients must be ascertained both when they are granted a MAiD certificate and at the time when MAiD provision occurs. Patients who lack capacity are refused MAiD. The blanket prohibition of PAS/E advocated by Rae, though intended to be protective of vulnerable patients, turns out, in practice, to be discriminatory against and stigmatizing of everyone who happens to be frail and elderly.

The Moral Limits of Personal Autonomy

Proponents of PAS/E regard the timing and manner of one's death as highly personal issues. It does *not* follow, however, that they reject state regulation. Even though personal autonomy is accepted in all liberal societies as a fundamental value, it may be legitimately restricted or overridden when it conflicts with other, equally basic, values. This means that when the state proposes seriously to restrict personal autonomy, it must demonstrate that the restrictions are both necessary and sufficient to achieve other equally or more important social goals. The *onus probandi* lies upon those who propose to restrict basic liberties.

So, for example, if legalizing the right of competent patients to choose assisted death could result in the wrongful death of incompetent patients, then governments will have to consider how best to respect the autonomy of competent patients while not endangering the lives of patients who lack decisional capacity. That said, any government which proposes seriously to restrict the liberty of patients, by imposing a total ban on assisted dying, must demonstrate, with good evidence, that vulnerable patients cannot otherwise be adequately protected. If the lives of vulnerable patients can be protected by means of regulatory safeguards, then a total ban would not be warranted. The experience of Oregon, Canada, and other jurisdictions which have legalized PAS/E demonstrates that carefully drafted eligibility criteria can simultaneously respect the self-determination of competent patients and protect vulnerable patients against wrongful death.

Against this, critics of PAS/E cite data from the Netherlands which show that Dutch doctors sometimes administer PAS/E to patients who have not made an explicit request. The Dutch label such cases "LAWER": Life Ending Actions Without Explicit Request. The existence of LAWER deaths is alleged to show that a total ban is necessary because safeguards do not work.

Some context is necessary here. Although *non-voluntary* mercy killing is illegal everywhere, LAWER cases occur *both* in countries that ban and those that permit PAS/E with safeguards. Significantly, however, the number of LAWER cases appears to be *lower* in countries that permit PAS/E than in countries that prohibit it.[1] Available evidence, though not conclusive, suggests that legalization of PAS/E, with safeguards, decreases the incidence of LAWER. A reverse slippery slope.

Those who worry that legalizing voluntary active euthanasia will inevitably, over time, lead to legalizing non-voluntary (or even involuntary) euthanasia should take comfort from the fact that neither Oregon, which legalized PAS in 1997, nor Canada, which legalized PAS/E in 2016, has moved to legalize non-voluntary euthanasia. Rae's unfounded speculation about what *might* happen in the future leads him to the false claim that "the exercise of autonomy for some *is* bringing harm to others" (p. 69, emphasis mine).

It is possible, of course, that the legalization of PAS/E might, in the future, cause harm to vulnerable patients. If that were to happen, then society would have to assess whether the best balance of benefits and harms is likely to be achieved by the reintroduction of a total ban or by the improvement of existing safeguards. At present, we can say with some confidence that the preponderance of empirical evidence supports the conclusion that careful safeguards are more effective than total prohibition at both protecting basic human rights and minimizing human suffering. That was the unanimous conclusion of the Supreme Court of Canada when it decided the *Carter* case in 2015, and data from subsequent years have been strongly confirmatory.

Another Slippery Slope?

Rae speculates that in rapidly aging societies, such as North America and Europe, the pressure to curb health care costs will become ever more intense. Cost-cutting pressure will, he fears, cause a precipitous slide down the slippery slope in those jurisdictions which have legalized PAS/E. At the bottom of the slope: not the more compassionate and respectful society we had sought to achieve but a society in which frail elderly patients will be seen as disposable waste products. Voluntary euthanasia will transmogrify into non-voluntary euthanasia.

It is impossible to prove that the benefit/harm ratio will always favor allowing competent patients to make their own end-of-life decisions. The nightmare scenario sketched by Rae could become a reality at some time in the future. That said, the jurisdictions which have legalized PAS/E tend to be those with the best-developed and most humane social services and palliative/hospice care. Based upon their dystopian fears and imaginings, critics of PAS/E wish to deny competent patients the option of choosing when and how they will die. So far, the evidence seems to contradict those fears.

One final point. Poor social conditions—such as inadequate housing, food insecurity, poverty, and loneliness—can and do contribute to the suffering experienced by some patients. We can agree that it is a moral imperative and should become a political imperative for wealthy societies to improve social conditions, especially for the most disadvantaged members of society. But the data from every country that has legalized PAS/E show that those who receive assisted dying are disproportionately the most privileged and best educated members of society. If we delay the introduction of

PAS/E until we have solved all our serious social problems, we will merely increase unnecessary suffering.

Rae's Preferred Solution

Rae believes that palliative/hospice care has improved to such a degree that intolerable suffering is now a thing of the past. The need for PAS/E has been eliminated. Unfortunately, however, Canadian experience, like that in Oregon and elsewhere, shows that this belief is naïve. Even the highest quality palliative/hospice care cannot always eliminate intolerable suffering. Indeed, the majority of applications for PAS/E come from patients who are suffering intolerably despite having received palliative/hospice care.

Note

1. See J. Bilsen, J. Cohen, K. Chambaere, et al., "Medical End-of-Life Practices under the Euthanasia Law in Belgium," *New England Journal of Medicine* 361, no. 11 (2009): 1119–21; and A. van der Heider, L. Deliens, K. Faisst, et al., "End-of-Life Decision-Making in Six European Countries: Descriptive Study," *Lancet* 362 (2003): 345–50.

Questions for Reflection

1. Compare and contrast Schafer's and Rae's discussion of the Slippery Slope Argument. Who makes the better case? Why?

2. Is Rae correct that having any criterion for eligibility for PAS/E is inconsistent with personal autonomy? Why?

3. A principle known as the *doctrine of double-effect* states that, if you know an action will have two effects, one good and one bad, you may perform the action so long as your intent is to bring about the good one. How might this principle apply to a case in which a patient suffers intolerable pain?

For Further Reading

Jones, David A., Chris Gastmans, and Calum MacKellar, eds. *Euthanasia and Assisted Suicide: Lessons from Belgium*. Cambridge University Press, 2018.

Paterson, Craig. *Assisted Suicide and Euthanasia: A Natural Law Ethics Approach*. Routledge, 2008.

Sumner, L. W. *Physician-Assisted Death: What Everyone Needs to Know.* Oxford University Press, 2017.

Weikart, Richard. *Unnatural Death: Medicine's Descent from Healing to Killing.* Discovery Institute, 2024.

Young, Robert. *Medically Assisted Death.* Cambridge University Press, 2007.

Yuill, Kevin. *Assisted Suicide: The Liberal, Humanist Case Against Legalization.* Palgrave Macmillan, 2013.

3

Capital Punishment

The Case for Capital Punishment[1]

Joseph M. Bessette and Edward Feser

Study Questions

1. What is the three-stage process for deciding who merits the death penalty in the United States? What "emerges" from this process?
2. What three points are demonstrated by Bessette's and Feser's historical survey?
3. What are the "key facts" about the forty-three executed killers cited by Bessette and Feser? How are these relevant to capital punishment?
4. Why do Bessette and Feser believe that capital punishment for the "worst of the worst" is simply what justice demands?
5. In what ways is capital punishment a moral teacher?
6. What do Bessette and Feser think would be the consequence of abolishing capital punishment?

In the 1970s, David Alan Gore and his cousin Fred Waterfield began abducting and raping women in and around Vero Beach, on the Atlantic coast in central Florida.[2] Waterfield paid Gore $1,000 to find pretty victims. In the early 1980s, their crimes escalated to murder. In February 1981, Gore flashed a badge he had from his job as an auxiliary sheriff's deputy and tricked a seventeen-year-old girl into getting into his car. He then drove the girl to her home, abducted her mother, and took the two of them to a citrus orchard where he and his cousin raped and murdered them, killing the mother by tying her up in such a way that she slowly choked herself to death while struggling to break free. Five months later, he kidnapped a thirty-five-year-old woman by playing the role of a Good Samaritan after he had disabled her vehicle. He met his cousin at the orchard where they raped and killed the woman and "fed her to the alligators" by throwing her into a swamp. Pleased with Gore's choice, Waterfield paid him $1,500. Within a few weeks of this crime, police arrested Gore for armed trespass when they found him crouched in the back seat of a woman's car with a pistol, handcuffs, and a police scanner. He served two years in prison for this crime. Two months after his release, Gore and Waterfield picked up two fourteen-year-old female hitchhikers and raped and murdered them. They dismembered one body, burying it in a shallow grave, and dumped the other in a nearby canal.

Two months after their fifth murder, the two men picked up two teenage girls, fourteen and seventeen, who were hitchhiking to the beach. They took the girls to Gore's parents' house, where Gore bound the girls and placed them in separate bedrooms. Gore sexually assaulted each girl several times. At one point the older girl escaped and ran from the house naked, with her hands still tied behind her back. A teenage boy on a bicycle saw Gore chase down the girl, drag her back toward the house, and shoot her twice in the head. The boy's mother called the police, who were able to rescue the fourteen-year-old and arrest Gore (his cousin had fled).

The state of Florida executed Gore by lethal injection on April 12, 2012, one of forty-three murderers executed in the United States that year. The case for capital punishment turns on the answer to a simple question: Do vicious killers like David Alan Gore deserve to die for their crimes?

With about 20,000 homicides each year in the United States and thousands of murder convictions, how is it decided which murderers merit the punishment of death? In the decades since the Supreme Court addressed the constitutionality of the death penalty in the 1970s, a three-stage process has developed. First, state legislatures decide whether to authorize the death penalty for certain kinds of murders, like rape murders or murders of multiple victims. Currently, twenty-seven American states and the federal government provide for capital punishment. Second, in those cases where a defendant is charged with a death-eligible murder, a prosecutor (usually locally elected), relying on the details of the crime and/or the violent background of the offender, must specifically request the death penalty. Third, in nearly every state, a 12-person jury, familiar with all the relevant facts, including the aggravating and mitigating circumstances, must decide unanimously that the offender merits death for his crime. (A very few states allow nonunanimous jury recommendations.) From this three-stage filtering process there emerge what are sometimes called "the worst of the worst" offenders.[3]

Sorting Out Who Deserves to Die in the Foundational Laws of Western Society

This chapter addresses the appropriateness of the death penalty only for aggravated murders and only under the legal procedures currently in place in the United States. As far back as the records of Western legal systems go (nearly four millennia), lawmakers have distinguished more heinous killings from the less heinous and, with few exceptions, have reserved the penalty of death for the more aggravated homicides. Although modern American lawmakers (in the states that retain capital punishment) limit the death penalty to a narrower class of murderers than was common earlier in Western history, they embrace the same principle that guided much of penal law in the West for thousands of years: some murders are so heinous that death is the fitting punishment. Here we briefly summarize some of the ways in which the oldest legal systems in the West sorted out the kinds of murders that merited the death penalty from those that did not.

The Code of Hammurabi

The most extensive set of laws to have survived from the ancient world is the Code of Hammurabi, named after the king of Babylon who ruled from approximately 1792 to 1750 BC.[4]

The Code identifies several types of homicide for which the offender must die, and others for which he is spared. Capital murders included, for example, a man and woman arranging to have their spouses murdered and a builder constructing an unsafe home that collapsed and killed its owner. Less serious homicides meriting less serious punishments included, among others, striking a man during a quarrel so that he died and failing to properly secure an ox known to be dangerous, which escaped and killed a free man. In these mitigated cases, the offender was required to pay a specified amount of monetary compensation.[5] Scholars hold that the underlying common law of Babylon almost certainly imposed the death penalty for intentional murders.

For assaults and personal injuries, Hammurabi's Code stipulated that the punishment must be equal to the offense: "If a man put out the eye of another man, his eye shall be put out";[6] "If he break another man's bone, his bone shall be broken;"[7] and "If a man knock out the teeth of his equal, his teeth shall be knocked out."[8] This is the *lex talionis*—or "law of retaliation"—which requires that as much as possible the punishment should mirror the offense. We might think, then, that every unlawful killing would result in the execution of the offender. Yet, as we have seen, in ancient Babylon some homicides were sufficiently mitigated as not to justify a death sentence.

The Mosaic Law of the Ancient Israelites

In Jewish tradition, God gave the law to Moses, who presented it to his people after their escape from Egypt. It is found in the first five books (the Torah, or Pentateuch) of the Old Testament (or Hebrew Bible). The Mosaic Law rested its criminal provisions explicitly and repeatedly on the *lex talionis*. Here is the provision from Deuteronomy:

> [Y]ou shall do to [a false witness] as he had meant to do to his brother; so you shall purge the evil from the midst of you. And the rest shall hear, and fear, and shall

never again commit any such evil among you. Your eye shall not pity; it shall be life for life, eye for eye, tooth for tooth, hand for hand, foot for foot. (Deut. 19:19-21)[9]

Nearly identical provisions appear in Exodus (21:23-25) and Leviticus (24:17-20). Elsewhere, as well, the law seems to require that all killers must die for their act. In Exodus: "Whoever strikes a man so that he dies shall be put to death" (21:12); and twice more in Leviticus: "He who kills a man shall be put to death" (24:17, 24:21).

Though this is the general rule, the Mosaic Law did not, in fact, impose the death penalty on all those who unlawfully killed a fellow human being. In general, capital killings were those that resulted from enmity or hatred. Here is a characteristic provision:

And if he stabbed him from hatred, or hurled at him, lying in wait, so that he died, or in enmity struck him down with his hand, so that he died, then he who struck the blow shall be put to death; he is a murderer; the avenger of blood shall put the murderer to death, when he meets him. (Num. 35:20-21)

The phrase "lying in wait"—which shows premeditation—still appears in the capital punishment statutes of several American states. The use of a deadly weapon—such as "an instrument of iron," a "stone," or a "weapon of wood"—also elevated a killing to a capital offense (Num. 35:16-18).

In general, accidental killings in which there was no enmity toward the victim did not warrant death. Examples include swinging an axe in a forest to cut wood when the head flew off and killed someone (Deut. 19:5) and throwing a stone that unintentionally struck someone, not seen by the hurler, killing him or her (Num. 35:22-23).

One provision of Israel's law seems to contemplate killings that result from fights that got out of hand: "But if he stabbed him suddenly without enmity," the death penalty would not apply (Num. 35:22). This sounds like the classic "heat of passion" killing that in American law would generally be classified as "voluntary manslaughter." Because a knife is a deadly weapon, this seems to be an exception to the general rule that killings with deadly weapons call for the execution of the offender. It follows, then, that the Mosaic Law exempted a wide range of homicides from a death sentence: purely accidental killings, most negligent homicides, and, apparently, "heat of passion" killings. It would not be surprising if most homicides in ancient Israel fit into one of these non-capital categories.

Classical Athens and Ancient Rome

In the laws of classical Athens (of the fifth and fourth centuries BC) and ancient Rome (from the founding of the Republic, traditionally dated to 509 BC, up through the reforms of the Emperor Justinian in the early sixth century AD), homicides were generally placed into one of three categories: (1) intentional, (2) unintentional but involving some culpability on the part of the offender, and (3) purely accidental or justified. The death penalty was reserved for intentional killings. In Athens, convictions for homicides in the middle category required exile, but no forfeiture of property, and the offender could return if pardoned by the victim's family. In Rome, such homicides required only the symbolic sacrifice of a ram.[10]

This brief summary of early homicide law in the West demonstrates three related points.

> First, the principle of proportionate punishment was deeply embedded in the Western legal tradition. Simple justice demanded that offenders suffer a harm equivalent in severity to the harm they inflicted.
>
> Second, this principle of just punishment created, at a minimum, a strong presumption, if not an absolute demand, that those who willfully and maliciously killed others should die for their crimes.
>
> Third, all four ancient societies recognized that homicides vary in degree, and, therefore, that some killers merited death while others did not. The early codes varied in how fully they identified and defined these mitigated homicides and did not always agree on exactly where to draw the line between capital homicides and lesser homicides.

This sorting out of who deserves to die from among all those who unlawfully kill a fellow human being—so central to the foundational legal systems in the West—continues in twenty-first century United States in the legal systems of just over half the states and the federal government.

Who Actually Dies for Murder in Twenty-first-century United States?

As noted above, David Alan Gore was one of forty-three murderers executed in the United States in 2012. For an earlier project we examined in great detail thousands of pages of legal proceedings that constituted the extensive and time-consuming appellate record for the forty-three offenders. (The time from sentence to execution averaged seventeen years.) From this mass of material, we can form an accurate portrait of the crimes committed, the prior records, and the malicious character of the offenders. There is no reason to believe that the forty-three killers executed in 2012 were at all atypical of the 1009 executed in the United States between 2000 and 2024—their crimes more or less heinous, their criminal histories more or less violent and extensive.

If murderers are the worst criminals our justice system confronts, then the forty-three executed in 2012 were surely among the worst of the worst. Yet, even among this group of vicious killers, some stand out for exhibiting a degree of cruelty and depravity that is almost unimaginable: *Gore*, certainly, but also:

- *Edwin Hart Turner*, who with an accomplice entered a convenience store at 2:00 a.m. and then shot the clerk in the chest and, when the clerk was on the floor pleading for his life, placed the barrel of his rifle to his face and shot and killed him. A few miles away at a gas station, Turner ordered a man pumping gas to the ground, took cash from his wallet, and shot him in the head as he was pleading for his life, killing him;

- *Robert Brian Waterhouse*, who raped and beat a 29-year-old woman with a hard object before dragging her into the water where she drowned;

- *Timothy Shaun Stemple*, who murdered his wife to collect her life insurance by beating her in the head with a baseball bat, driving a truck over her head, beating her again, driving the truck over her chest, and then killing her by driving over her at 60 miles per hour (while awaiting trial, Stemple tried to get other inmates to arrange the death of several witnesses in his case);

- *Henry Curtis Jackson*, who, in an attempt to steal money from his mother's home, murdered a two-year-old girl, a two-year-old boy, a three-year-old boy, and a five-year-old girl (Jackson also stabbed a one-year-old girl, leaving her unable to walk);

- *Daniel Wayne Cook*, who, with an accomplice, killed a 26-year-old man after beating, torturing, and sodomizing him over 6–7 hours, and then a few hours later sodomized and strangled to death a sixteen-year-old boy;

- *Robert Wayne Harris*, who in retaliation for being fired from a car wash for exposing himself to a customer, murdered the manager and four other employees by shooting them in the back of the head at close range while they were kneeling on the floor (Harris left another victim with permanent disabilities and he later led police to the remains of a woman he previously abducted and murdered); and

- *Richard Dale Stokley*, who, with an accomplice, abducted two 13-year-old girls from a campsite, drove them to a remote area, raped them, stabbed them in the eye, killed them by stomping on their necks, and then threw the naked bodies down an abandoned mineshaft.

We provide more detailed descriptions of these crimes and of others committed by those executed in 2012 elsewhere.[11] It is grim reading, but it is the details of the crimes that justify elevating a first-degree murder to a capital offense. Statistical descriptions of the crimes and of the histories of the offenders can be useful, but they can never capture the full reality of the heinous acts that justify the death penalty to prosecutors and juries.

Nonetheless, statistics can demonstrate how the capital punishment system in the United States selects the worst offenders for the ultimate punishment. Here are some key facts about the forty-three killers executed in 2012 (with comparisons to data for all murders, if available).

- Twelve of the forty-three offenders (28 percent) killed more than one person, and five (12 percent) killed more than two: one killed three, two killed four, one killed five, and one killed nine. By contrast, fewer than 5 percent of all homicide incidents in the United States involve multiple murder victims, and fewer than 1 percent involve three or more murder victims.[12]

- Eight (19 percent) had killed at least one person prior to the capital crime that resulted in their execution, totaling thirteen prior homicide victims.

- Ten (23 percent) had committed a sexual assault in the past; ten (23 percent), robbery; eighteen (42 percent), a felony assault (also called aggravated assault); and two (5 percent), a kidnapping. Altogether, twenty-nine (fully two-thirds) had in the past committed a homicide, sexual assault, robbery, felony assault, or kidnapping. (And these are only the known offenses.)

- At least 35 percent of the murders that resulted in executions in 2012 involved the rape of the murder victim or of another person by the executed offender or his accomplice. Yet, among all homicides in the United States in recent decades, only about 1 percent involved a sexual assault.[13]

- Of the seventy murder victims for which the forty-three offenders were executed in 2012, sixteen (23 percent) were under 18 years old and nine (13 percent) were under 9 years old. The first figure is about two and one-half times higher than among all murder victims in the United States, and the second figure is three times higher. Four of the offenders raped and murdered a total of eight young girls and minors (ages nine, twelve, thirteen, thirteen, fourteen, fourteen, seventeen, and seventeen).

That Justice Be Done

If the principle that justice requires proportionate punishment means anything at all, it means that murderers of the sort executed in the United States in 2012 must die for their crimes. The loved ones of a murder victim feel the loss most acutely and most painfully. To many, it is an affront to justice that the one who took the life of their mother, father, brother, sister, son, or daughter, often in a particularly calculated or brutal way, should continue to live, even in the confines of a maximum security prison. For these family members, the disorder created by the offense and the demands of justice to balance the crime with a proportionate punishment are not abstract philosophical principles but palpable realities.[14]

Of course, not every loved one of every murder victim demands the death penalty for the offender. Yet the comments by the family members in the proceedings that surrounded the sentencing and punishment of those executed in 2012 are eloquent testimony to the strength of the principle of just deserts.[15] "In the end I hope and pray justice will be served"; "I just hope justice can be done as soon as possible"; "I'm glad this is finally over and justice is served for my late husband"; "My father deserves justice"; "We are sorry for watching Mr. Cleve Foster die, but the justice is done"; "Finally, justice for Becky after 22 years and five months and 23 days"; and "For over 25 years we have waited for justice to be served and for this sentence to be carried out." Finally, "I would beg this court and this jury to see that justice is done. And justice to us is no less than the death penalty."

Several family members noted that the justice of the offender's death would bring closure, at least of a certain kind, and foster healing. The sister of the woman killed by her husband with a baseball bat and a truck so that he could collect on her life insurance said, after the execution, that the day was "about justice, finality and closure for my gorgeous sister, Trisha, and my family." Others expressed a similar view: "Today, we got that justice. . . . We're glad that it's finally over. Be at peace. The race is finally over." Others also pointed out that, even though the execution of the offender would not bring back their loved one, justice demanded it: "It's not going to change what happened[,] . . . [b]ut justice will be served." Thus, achieving justice could promote healing. The father of a rape murder victim said, "In this particular case, when justice is carried out, it will be a vindication of my daughter's life." By "vindication" he seemed to mean that, by imposing the ultimate punishment on the murderer, public authority was making a statement about the worth of his daughter's life. To allow the offender to live out his days in prison would be to undervalue the life he took in such a brutal way.[16]

In our book-length defense of capital punishment, we present the words of dozens of family members and loved ones who commented on many of the nearly seven hundred executions that occurred between 2000 and 2011 (often after witnessing the execution).[17] These illustrate just how very deep and pervasive is the sense among ordinary people that capital punishment is, for the most heinous crimes, simply what justice demands. This desire to see offenders get their just deserts is not only natural to human beings but is, in itself, a positive good. Men and women rightly get angry when family members, other loved ones, or members of their community are harmed, and they naturally wish to see malefactors receive the punishment they deserve for their evil deeds.

Strikingly, three of the offenders who were executed in 2012 acknowledged the justice of their punishment. A week before his execution, Donald Palmer said that "I believe in justice and I believe that the victims, their hatred, their anger, they need to have justice."[18] Eric Robert, who waived all appeals and met his fate just a year after sentencing, wrote that "I do not want or desire to die, instead I deserve to die; this I have always stated. . . . [The families] needed swift justice."[19] And Donald Moeller, who had abducted, raped, and killed a nine-year-old girl, announced in a court hearing that

"I killed the little girl. It's just that the punishment be concluded. I believe it's a good thing, that the death penalty does inhibit further criminal acts." He added, "I killed. I deserve to be killed."[20]

Altogether, eighteen of the forty-three offenders expressed sorrow or contrition for what they had done (often in the days or moments just before execution): eleven mentioned God; six specifically invoked Jesus Christ; and at least three received Catholic sacraments at some point before execution. Of course, this does not mean that they agreed that their sentence was just, but it does demonstrate that they came to believe that what they had done was grievously wrong.

We cannot overstate just how dramatic some of these transformations were. Men guilty of the most despicable acts that one human being can commit against another, who exhibited at times a depravity of soul that seems almost beyond comprehension, became profoundly remorseful and sorry for what they had done and, in several cases, positively affirmed the justice of their punishment. What can account for such a radical transformation if not the murderer's consciousness that he had done great wrong? And what societal act more effectively teaches the wrongness of murder than the imposition of the ultimate penalty on those most deserving of it?

Capital Punishment as Moral Teacher

Capital punishment is uniquely able to reinforce within society both a horror of murder and confidence in the reality of an objective moral order. The lawyer, judge, and legal historian James Fitzjames Stephen famously made this point in the middle of the nineteenth century. "Some men," he wrote, "probably, abstain from murder because they fear that, if they committed murder, they would be hung." But "[h]undreds of thousands" of others "abstain from it because they regard it with horror. One great reason they regard it with horror is, that murderers are hung."[21] Here Stephen argues for both (a) the deterrent effect that comes from calculating whether a criminal act is worth the potential cost, which does restrain some men, and (b) the deeper, and more widespread, restraining effect that results from the moral revulsion of murder that is taught and reinforced by executing murderers.

Similarly, both sociologist Steven Goldberg and philosopher Ernest van den Haag argue that the death penalty may have greater crime reduction effects by reinforcing deep-seated moral values than by influencing the rational calculations of would-be killers. For Goldberg, "[If] the death penalty deters, it is likely that it does so through society's saying that certain acts are so unacceptable that society will kill one who commits them; the individual internalizes the association of the act and the penalty throughout his life, constantly increasing his resistance to committing the act."[22] And for van den Haag, "[D]eterrence does not depend on rational calculation . . . . [It] depends on the likelihood and on the regularity—not on the rationality—of human responses to danger; and further on the possibility of reinforcing internal controls by vicarious external experiences."[23]

While we generally agree with Goldberg and Van den Haag, we also hold that criminals often behave much more rationally than many concede. One clear case was recounted in the journal *Criminology* in 2009. Two robbers had broken into the home of a professor's mother in Westchester County, New York, to steal her collectibles. They had bound the woman to a chair, and as they were about to leave one asked the other, "She has seen us and can identify us, should we kill her?" "No," he answered, "we don't want to risk the death penalty."[24] (New York was then, but is not now, a death penalty state.)

More generally, many killers will plead guilty to murder in exchange for a life sentence rather than go to trial and risk conviction and a death sentence. Also, only a tiny fraction of those sentenced to death (perhaps 4–5 percent) "volunteer" for the death penalty by prematurely ending the appeals process.[25] Given the choice, condemned murderers would rather live out their lives behind bars than face execution. Like the rest of us, hardened criminals want to live, and they will often adjust their behavior accordingly. Abolish the death penalty entirely and what incentive does a "lifer" have not to kill while in prison or, if he escapes, while on the run? We should not be reluctant to draw on our own commonsense when thinking about the deterrent effect of capital punishment. After all, this is how men and women have been reaching such judgments for thousands of years.[26]

For David Gelernter, the Yale computer scientist who was maimed by a bomb sent by "Unabomber" Ted Kaczynski, when "we execute murderers . . . [we] make a communal proclamation: that murder is intolerable. . . . Among possible responses, the death penalty is uniquely powerful because it is permanent and can never be retracted or overturned. An execution forces the community to assume forever the burden of moral certainty. . . . Deliberate murder, the community announces, is absolutely evil and absolutely intolerable, period."[27] The finality and, therefore, the irrevocability of the death penalty (often singled out by opponents) is part of what makes it such a powerful teacher of the utter immorality of murder. Here justice and deterrence of this deeper sort meet. The most brutal murderers deserve to pay for their crimes with their lives. When we execute them, we reaffirm in a public and definitive way the absolute evil of their deeds. In so doing, we inculcate and reinforce the moral norms that make it less likely that those growing up in such a society would ever even consider murdering a fellow human being in the first place.

The political scientist Walter Berns saw in Shakespeare's *Macbeth* eloquent testimony to the poet's understanding that the moral law demands death for heinous murders. Driven by his "vaulting ambition," Macbeth, either by his own hands or by ordering others, killed Duncan (his kinsman and king), the king's guards, his friend Banquo (a general in the king's army), and the nobleman Macduff's wife and children (and others at Macduff's castle). By the end of the play, Macbeth must die for his crimes. Could the play have ended any other way? It is a "dramatic necessity," writes Berns: "Because of justice, Macbeth has to die."[28] A moral universe demands no less:

In *Macbeth* the majesty of the moral law is demonstrated to us; . . . it teaches us the awesomeness of the commandment, thou shalt not kill. In a similar fashion, the punishments imposed by the legal order remind us of the reign of the moral order; not only do they remind us of it, but by enforcing its prescriptions, they enhance the dignity of the legal order in the eyes of moral men. . . . Reenforcing the moral order is especially important in a self-governing community, a community that gives laws to itself.[29]

Conclusion

If in the end, capital punishment is absolutely rejected even for the most heinous offenses, the fundamental principle that an offender deserves a punishment proportional to his crime will be fatally undermined. Society will lose sight, first of the idea of proportionality, then of the idea of desert, and finally of the idea of punishment itself. And when the idea of punishment goes, the very idea of justice will go with it, replaced by a therapeutic or technocratic model that treats human beings as cases to be managed and socially engineered rather than as morally responsible persons. Nothing less is at stake in the death-penalty debate.[30]

Notes

1. A longer version of this article appeared in *The Elgar Companion to Capital Punishment and Society*, ed. Benjamin Fleury-Steiner and Austin D. Sarat (Edward Elgar Publishing, 2024). Edited and reprinted with permission, Cheltenham, UK.
2. For a fuller discussion of Gore, see Edward Feser and Joseph M. Bessette, *By Man Shall His Blood Be Shed: A Catholic Defense of Capital Punishment* (San Francisco: Ignatius Press, 2017), 215–17, 237–8, 306.
3. As of July 1, 2024, there were 2,213 murderers in the United States under sentence of death. Of these, forty-six were held under federal jurisdiction. See Death Penalty Information Center, "Factsheet" (https://deathpenaltyinfo.org/factsheet.pdf, accessed September 17, 2024).
4. This account draws from G. R. Driver and John C. Miles, *The Babylonian Laws*, 2 vols. (Oxford: Oxford University Press, 1952), especially their highly detailed 450-page "Legal Commentary" in Volume I, and from the standard English translation by L. W. King, *The Code of Hammurabi* (1915) (http://www.general-intelligence.com/library/hr.pdf, accessed September 17, 2024).
5. See King, *Code of Hammurabi*, laws #153, 206, 207, 229, and 251.
6. Ibid., law #196.
7. Ibid., law #197.
8. Ibid., law #200.
9. All biblical quotations are from the Revised Standard Version. Though not directly relevant to our point here, it is important to recognize that the *lex talionis*, which

can seem draconian to the modern ear, also had a restraining function: for while it required that the punishment be as severe as the harm, it also held that it be *no more severe* than the harm.

10 At times, both classical Athens and ancient Rome provided permanent exile (a kind of civic death) as an option to the death penalty for capital murders. But in neither case did this reflect an ideological opposition to the death penalty as too severe a punishment for intentional killings.

11 See Feser and Bessette, *By Man Shall His Blood Be Shed*, 215–232.

12 See Erica L. Smith and Alexia Cooper, *Homicide in the U.S. Known to Law Enforcement, 2011*, 14, Table 5 and Figure 22, Bureau of Justice Statistics, December 2013, NCJ-243035 (https://www.google.com/url?client=internal-element-cse&cx=015849196504226064512:8qeg8tt4g1g&q=https://bjs.ojp.gov/content/pub/pdf/hus11.pdf&sa=U&ved=2ahUKEwikn4nDhMuIAxW7I0QIHVedNjkQFnoECAEQAQ&usg=AOvVaw0p2HPvXldrBbuDEwGfb1VE, accessed September 17, 2024); and Alexia Cooper and Erica L. Smith, *Homicide Trends in the United States, 1980–2008*, 24–5, Bureau of Justice Statistics, November 2011, NCJ-236018 (https://www.google.com/url?client=internal-element-cse&cx=015849196504226064512:8qeg8tt4g1g&q=https://bjs.ojp.gov/content/pub/pdf/htus8008.pdf&sa=U&ved=2ahUKEwiqtrPPhsuIAxW9EkQIHfpal98QFnoECAIQAg&usg=AOvVaw0_H9jSUH_klu4G9AwAsOpM, accessed September 17, 2024).

13 The figures on rape murders, robbery murders, and age of murder victims for all homicides in the United States are based on calculations from data published in the annual FBI publication, *Crime in the United States*, covering the years 1978–2011. Publications from 1995–2019 are online at http://www.fbi.gov/about-us/cjis/ucr/ucr-publications#Crime. Printed copies of these and earlier volumes are published by the US Government Printing Office.

14 Of course, it is important that the death penalty can be defended on rigorous philosophical grounds. See, for example, Edward Feser, "The Justice of Capital Punishment," in *The Palgrave Handbook on the Philosophy of Punishment,* ed. Matthew C. Altman (London: Palgrave Macmillan, 2023), 725–46; and Feser and Bessette, *By Man Shall His Blood Be Shed*, 17–95.

15 The following quotations are from Feser and Bessette, *By Man Shall His Blood Be Shed*, 236–53.

16 Several family members asserted that they were seeking justice, not vengeance. For a detailed discussion of the relationship of vengeance to justice in punishing murderers, see Feser and Bessette, *By Man Shall His Blood Be Shed*, 40–3, 66–70, 213–14, and 303–12.

17 Ibid., 241–52.

18 Ibid., 252.

19 Ibid., 253.

20 Ibid.

21 James Fitzjames Stephen, *A General View of the Criminal Law of England* (London and Cambridge: Macmillan, 1863, reprinted in 2014 by Cambridge University Press), 99.

22 Steven Goldberg, *When Wish Replaces Thought* (Buffalo: Prometheus Books, 1991), 26–7.

23 Ernest van den Haag, "On Deterrence and the Death Penalty," in *Punishment and the Death Penalty: The Current Debate*, ed. Robert M. Baird and Stuart E. Rosenbaum (Amherst: Prometheus Books, 1995), 127.

24 Kenneth C. Land, Raymond H. C. Teske, Jr., and Hui Zheng, "The Short-Term Effects of Executions on Homicides: Deterrence, Displacement or Both?" *Criminology* 47, no. 4 (2009): 1016–17.

25 Charles Keckler, "Life v. Death: Who Should Capital Punishment Marginally Deter?" *Journal of Law, Economics and Policy* 2, no. 1 (2006): 82.

26 For more extensive defenses of how the death penalty saves lives through deterrence, see Feser and Bessette, *By Man Shall His Blood Be Shed*, 312–35; Louis P. Pojman, "Why the Death Penalty Is Morally Permissible," in *Debating the Death Penalty: Should America Have Capital Punishment?*, ed. Hugo Bedau and Paul Cassell (New York: Oxford University Press, 2004), 58–67; and Paul Cassell, "In Defense of the Death Penalty," in *Debating the Death Penalty*, ed. Bedau and Cassell, 189–97.

27 David Gelernter, "What Do Murderers Deserve?" *Commentary* (April 1998) (https://www.commentary.org/articles/david-gelernter/what-do-murderers-deserve/, accessed September 2024).

28 Walter Berns, *For Capital Punishment: Crime and the Morality of the Death Penalty* (New York: Basic Books, 1979), 167.

29 Ibid., 169.

30 We acknowledge, of course, that a punishment that is just and beneficial might be rejected because it is not possible, for whatever reasons, to administer it fairly and accurately—charges that modern critics often make against the use of the death penalty in the United States. We answer these and other criticisms in some detail in Feser and Bessette, *By Man Shall His Blood Be Shed*, 61–78, and 338–74.

The Death Penalty: Against

Lloyd Steffen

Study Questions

1. What do reasonable people agree on regarding the state? What implications does Steffen say this has?
2. Why does Steffen think that capital punishment is not really about an "eye-for-an-eye" as many of its supporters claim?
3. Why does Steffen claim that the death penalty is a "misdirected" punishment?
4. What reasons does Steffen give for why life imprisonment is a better alternative to capital punishment?
5. How does Steffen appeal to contractualism to argue against capital punishment?
6. What are the ways that government may abuse the execution power?
7. What are the "justice concerns" that Steffen raises?

The death penalty is a moral issue for a simple reason: it involves the intentional and willful killing of a human person, a fully endowed member of the moral community. By "fully endowed," I mean that the person put to death is a conscious[1] agent not afflicted with cognitive impairments that would interfere with rationally understanding why he or she was being killed.[2] Supporters of the death penalty, and there are many, do not usually trouble themselves with the moral issues involved in the death penalty, for their support is built upon the assumptions that those being executed are receiving justice and that the killing that takes place is justified. But a moral inquiry must examine those assumptions. Is justice being served? Is the killing justified? This chapter argues that it is a terrible thing for the moral community to authorize the destruction of one of its members through an act of willful violence. Examining the death penalty from a moral point of view will show it to be an unjust instrument—and an instrument of injustice—best kept away from those who wield what I shall discuss below as "the execution power."

Where Agreement Is to Be Found

Although not often acknowledged in death penalty debates, a meaningful discussion about the ethics of the death penalty must begin by recognizing that an execution is a presumably wrongful act. Reasonable people of good will can agree that the state ought not to kill its own citizens, a claim not controversial even for those who hold views favoring the death penalty.[3] Executions, however, do take place, so when they do, they should be understood as exceptions to this common moral understanding. From a moral point of view, executions will necessarily require strong and convincing justification to overcome the presumption against such killing.

Governments and their criminal justice system claim authority to punish those who commit violent and antisocial offenses, the most serious being the killing of one person by another. But a moral community will not ordinarily act intentionally and with premeditation to kill even the offender who kills. Evidence for this claim can be supported by a commonsense interpretation of some statistics; and statistics, it should be noted, come to play an important part in evaluating the moral meaning of the death penalty. Consider, for instance, that in 2022, the FBI reported 21,156 homicides, murders, and unintentional killings[4] in the United States, a number 10 percent higher than 2023.[5] Every one of those homicides was one person in the moral community killing another. In that same year, 2022, twenty-one death sentences were handed down and eighteen men (they were all male) were actually executed (with seven of those executions having been described as "problematic").[6] One oft-heard justification for the death penalty is that an "eye for an eye" notion of retributive justice demands that persons who take a life must forfeit their own life in recompense for the life taken, but these numbers refute such a claim. In the face of over 21,000 homicides, eighteen executions and 20 new death sentences hardly meet a "life-for-a-life" ethical requirement.[7] There are many questions to ask in light of these statistics, but the first one might be this: "How unlucky do you have to be to receive a death sentence?" That question can be put another way: "What kinds of factors affect the execution outcome, when one person receives the death penalty yet others guilty of the same offense do not?"

With those questions we open up the death penalty to a justice interrogation. How can it be claimed that the death penalty serves justice when it would appear on the basis of statistics alone that it is an "unusual" penalty freakishly applied?—the word "freakish" appeared in the *Furman v. Georgia* Supreme Court decision that in 1972 put a stop to executions in the United States, temporarily as it turned out.[8] To describe a legal remedy as serious as execution as "freakishly" applied seems on the face of it to be problematic and lacking in the evenhandedness justice requires. So, when legal review of the death penalty draws such a conclusion, justice questions take center stage. In moral arguments about the death penalty, justice issues are clearly at the heart of the debate.

The justice issues involved in the death penalty usually focus on such matters as race and gender discrimination, cruelty, wrongful executions, concern for victims, irrevocability, and even the brutalizing effects of executions. Not all who take a stand on the death penalty, however, do so on the basis of justice issues. Some people hold to positions on the basis of religious beliefs or a philosophical commitment to an overarching principle that would oppose any killing for any reason, some version of a "reverence for life" ethic. Those who endorse this kind of death penalty "pacifism" are not to be denied or diminished, but for present purposes, those perspectives, valuable as they may be, are not engaged with the justice questions that arise in ethical debate.

Attention must be given to the justice issues involved in the death penalty, and that is the task at hand. In the context of raising those questions, a few broader philosophical issues should be mentioned as reasons for opposing the death penalty.

A Misdirected Punishment

Persons who commit a serious, violent, or antisocial crime misuse their freedom. If criminal behavior is a misuse of freedom, a just deserts idea of punishment would logically require that freedom be taken away. Incarceration does exactly that. Depriving an offender of freedom imposes a serious punishment while also provoking a possible deterrence effect since the prospect of prison life is an unpleasantness much to be avoided. In enlightened prison systems, incarceration may actually focus beyond retribution to correction, providing opportunities for rehabilitation and opening an avenue for the offender's return to society as a responsible citizen.[9]

But an execution kills. Execution destroys the physical supports for conscience, intentionality, and the will, which are clearly the sources of violence and antisocial behavior. Execution destroys the body. Defenders of the death penalty would hold to an idea of personhood where body and mind are so intricately connected that they cannot be separated for purposes of this punishment, and of course the body is involved in taking direction and performing actual acts of wrongdoing. But maybe some separation between body and will is called for. A body is itself neither bad nor evil. A quadriplegic could lack the ability to commit an offense by means of bodily action yet still, with a perverse will, conspire with able-bodied persons to commit a crime such as murder. The quadriplegic involved in such a scenario would be morally responsible for an unjust act, liable to legal prosecution and subject to punishment, perhaps even execution. What this admittedly bizarre example illustrates is that wrongdoing springs not from the body but from the will, the mind, the person's intentionality and that aspect of agency whereby persons make decisions to engage in wrongful conduct. So, if wrongdoing is a misuse of freedom and the logical response ought to be to remove freedom from its misuser, why destroy the body?

The body is an accomplice in acts of wrongdoing, but the moral supports of agency are not matters of the body. The body is not the moral source of an intention to harm others; it is a servant of the will. The body is not the locus of wrongdoing; it is not the culprit. Yet when an execution occurs, it is the body that bears the brunt of the punishment, the assumption being that the body misused freedom and was apparently free to misuse it. The body, however, is in many ways not free or even capable of free action. It is constrained by nature, by society, by direction from a person's will, desire, intentionality, and by countless factors in an individual's life story. Yet the death penalty holds the body in a sense ultimately responsible for a person's wrongdoing, for it holds the body responsible for the misuse of freedom. To obliterate the body is to direct responsibility for wrongdoing to the wrong place. The argument can be made in opposition to the death penalty that destroying the body is not a just means of punishing a person whose crime is an act of will and a misuse of freedom, for the body cannot itself be responsible for a person's wrongdoing to the degree that justice demands its destruction.

Another "mislocation" issue regards punishment and the death that results from execution. Execution destroys the possibility for remorse, rehabilitation, restitution, and even retribution if one aim of retribution is for the offender to experience a harm equivalent to the one visited on the victim, the "eye-for-an-eye" effect. If death is the intended effect, the criminal facing execution experiences all that leads up to the death, which may be horrible, even torturous, but does not experience the ostensible end of capital punishment, death, for the offender is, when punished, beyond experience. An ordinary, commonsense notion of capital punishment is that the actual punishment is the loss of life, the death, not the process leading up to it. The loss of life is a great loss to the person executed, but the executed person does not experience that loss except prospectively and imaginatively. The killing process may be terribly painful and cause enormous suffering, but it can be argued that the death result so often pointed to as the punishment sought actually provides relief from the killing process,[10] for it is in that killing process where the infliction of pain and suffering associated with punishment takes place and is actually experienced. The death penalty fails, then, to deliver an experienced punishment except by inflicting pain, loss, and suffering through a killing process, which may be lengthy and torturous. The punishment in capital punishment, then, is in all that leads up to death, not in achieving the end of a punishment, death, which the offender cannot experience as punishment.

Alternatives to Execution

Many death row inmates have done terrible, even despicable things, and many would pose a continuing threat if released back into society. The death penalty is sometimes defended as a way to ensure societal safety. Fifty years ago, many incarcerated for killing could expect to be released due to parole policies, which, in some jurisdictions, came under heavy criticism for being too lenient. Crime entered political campaigns as a major issue, and concern about crime often expressed the fear that releasing serious offenders from prison posed a threat to the safety and well-being of society. Following the 1973 Supreme Court moratorium on the death penalty, the concern for safety increased and led to the expansion of a "life-without-possibility-of-parole" sentence. Today 50,000 people are serving this sentence in America's prisons.[11] Although there are strong reasons for opposing the policy, including cruelty and undermining the safety of prison employees, removing the possibility of release back into society does meet the demand for protecting society. It does so without resorting to intentional killing, which is always morally problematic and more difficult to justify than incarceration—taking away freedom from those who abuse their freedom.

Despite the many problems with America's prisons and policies of mass incarceration, it can be said without undue controversy that incarceration does present a reasonable and morally preferable alternative to the deliberate killing of the death penalty. Three issues are worth noting:

- First, for those who want an offender to experience maximum pain and suffering for their misdeeds, the loss of freedom and condemnation to prison should be recognized as meeting that goal. Incarceration is a terrible fate. John Stuart Mill, a nineteenth-century English defender of capital punishment, believed the harshest possible punishment was depriving an offender of freedom. Mill, however, defended the death penalty, even an "acceptable loss" view of wrongful executions, but he did so on the grounds that the death penalty actually reflected "effeminacy" on the part of those who demanded it. "For what else than effeminacy is it to be so much more shocked by taking a man's life than by depriving him of all that makes life desirable or valuable."[12] What makes a life valuable, Mill thought, is freedom. For those seeking the death penalty on the justice demand that terrible crime should meet with a terrible sentence, Mill thought imprisonment worse than death.

- Second, those who think a maximum-security prison where capital offenders are held is akin to a country club experience have never visited such a facility or seen the cruel and debilitating effects of death row and solitary confinement. It is a severe setting and a coercive way of life no reasonable person would ever choose. In the Commonwealth of Pennsylvania, three executions have occurred since the Supreme Court moratorium on executions was lifted in 1976. All three were "volunteers." All three inmates, unable to endure prison, dropped their appeals and volunteered for execution. Prison has been described as torturous confinement for maximum security offenders on death row, and for some the worse punishment was continuing to live in prison confinement—death was preferable.

- Third, suicides are not uncommon on death row,[13] another indication of the severity of incarceration; and for those who want an offender dead as retribution for their crime, the "life-without-parole" penalty actually does deliver that, for life-without-parole is a death sentence—it is simply a longer ride to the end of life than what executions bring, but it ends in the death of the offender.

Alternatives to capital punishment that satisfy the desire of death penalty supporters for harsh retribution and the death of an offender exist. The death penalty as a killing process is a punishment that delivers pain and suffering through a harsh sentence, even the harshest if one follows Mill's thought that freedom is necessary for life to have meaning. Those wanting to maximize an offender's suffering by imposing a death sentence should remember that execution shortens the punishment while incarceration extends the suffering of the killing process. The "life-without-parole" sentence meets the societal concern for citizen safety, and the incarceration alternative, problematic though it may be, does deliver a harsh punishment without involving all of society in the willful and premeditated killing of selected offenders unable to defend themselves as the state, in the name of the people, assumes the right to kill and then proceeds to do so. Societal safety is a legitimate concern that can be accomplished by incarceration. Recognizing this fact is the reason Pope John Paul II finally declared that the Roman Catholic Church would generally oppose the death penalty, and Pope Francis pushed even further to deny that the death penalty could ever serve the cause of justice.[14]

A Human Rights Abuse? Execution of the Innocent

The moral community is comprised of rational and autonomous agents capable of moral deliberation, and membership in this community includes even those facing execution. One moral theory, contractualism, holds that members of the moral community are bound together in a "social contract" as "free and equal citizens."[15] This social contract theory holds that if an act is to be deemed permissible, it must be "justifiable to everyone affected by it."[16]

Contractualist theorists take seriously that there are instances where innocent persons are convicted of capital crimes. One interpretation of the contractualist theory holds that the death penalty as a punishment cannot be justified to those wrongfully sentenced to death. That the criminal justice system allows extensive appeals in death penalty cases is recognition that mistakes can happen; and the American criminal justice system recognizes this possibility and seeks through mandatory appeals to review capital cases to prevent the moral horror of an innocent person being executed.

Still, it can happen. Since 1973, more than 197 capital convictions have been overturned because of evidence of innocence, almost four "mistakes" per year.[17] So substantial evidence exists that capital trials are error-prone and imperfect, a general claim supported by the number of errors recognized on appeal and the many exonerations and releases from death row for reasons of actual innocence. The contractualist view of ethics holds that if a punishment is not justifiable to everyone affected by it, it is not morally permissible. Clearly, wrongfully condemned persons are affected by the death penalty punishment, and clearly, they cannot consider their own executions justifiable. Moreover, the injustice of a wrongful execution affects the entire moral community. The death penalty on this view can be justified neither to the condemned nor to the entirety of the moral community.

A utilitarian, however, could argue against this view. Holding that the right thing to do depends on calculating the greatest good for the greatest number, the utilitarian could argue that the occasional error is inevitable but a price worth paying due to overriding societal benefits, like the death penalty's deterrence value. Leaving aside the debate over deterrence—there is no proof that the death penalty deters crime—[18] a wrongful execution, on this view, is of course regrettable, but the benefits outweigh any negative results from eliminating the death penalty altogether. The problem with this view is that utilitarianism, because it affirms that all persons are of equal value, must then be committed to the logic that *any* innocent person is then eligible for that "permissible error" spot, including the defender of the "permissible error" view, or the defender's son or daughter, parent or grandparent, spouse, friend, or loved one. Such a defense of the death penalty is irrational.

Philosopher Corey Brettschneider has drawn on contractualism to address the death penalty as it affects the person as citizen. He argues that the state may employ a power of coercion over criminals to curtail certain rights, like disallowing free speech in prison to prevent planning for a prison riot. The state, however, cannot justifiably impose death as a punishment and thereby cancel the criminal's status as citizen, which is not relinquished even by the commission of a terrible deed, such as murder. By holding offenders' lives disposable, the death penalty discounts criminals' dignity as persons and subverts their very humanity by subjecting them to willful killing, leading Brettschneider to conclude that an offender's status as citizen—a live citizen— establishes the grounds for a "right not to be executed."[19] To execute a citizen on this view constitutes an illegitimate exercise of political power.

The question of the death penalty's legitimacy, and the claim of a right not to be executed, opens up the question of human rights. Although the United States views capital punishment through a legal lens, many international treaties view it as a human rights issue. *The International Covenant on Civil and Political Rights* adopted by the United Nations in 1966 asserts that "no one shall be arbitrarily deprived of life," and abolition of the death penalty worldwide is an announced goal in a later protocol signed on by ninety nations.[20] That the death penalty violates an inherent right to life possessed by persons due to their status as human beings has gained wide international currency, and it may be among the reasons that in the United States executions have declined 80 percent over the last quarter century.[21] The human rights prohibition on "arbitrary" executions raises issues about the meaning of the execution power, since the case could be made that "legitimate" governments act in accordance with the rule of law and thus do not impose the death penalty "arbitrarily." The arbitrary deprivation of life identifies for some the death penalty's central human rights violation.

The Execution Power

Debate over the ethics of the death penalty usually assumes a context of political legitimacy. Also assumed is that the person facing execution is a criminal who has received a death sentence in accordance with recognizable standards of justice, legal due process, and a society's legally enshrined standards of decency. But this framing of execution within legal sanctions and recognized societal legitimacy overlooks that the execution power extends far beyond the boundaries of legal and societal authority. Those who face execution may also be dissidents, political subversives, heretics, or opponents otherwise believed to threaten social stability, political power, or even religious order. When the execution power is exercised to remove threatening persons, groups, and even viewpoints and thereby protect a power structure, it provokes questions about human rights; and even legitimate governments and legal structures can fall into this category.

The fact is that the execution power has often been used in an arbitrary fashion, that is, outside the framework of moral justification even if covered by governmental legitimacy. Executions are defended as a protection of life and cherished values, but many of humanity's horrors can be traced to arbitrary uses of the execution power even if cloaked with the mantle of legitimacy. Genocide could not proceed without it. The execution power was employed in the slaughter of Jews in Nazi Germany and of Armenians in the Ottoman Empire, and in the mass killings in Darfur, Rwanda, Bosnia, and Cambodia. White supremacist communities in the United States, mainly in the South but elsewhere as well, terrorized and oppressed Black citizens by means of lynching, immoral killings outside the law that often proceeded with local law enforcement officials looking on, sometimes in front of courthouses. Local communities justified lynching as protecting themselves from undesirable persons threatening the community, and "legitimate" government did not stop it. Lynchings were only criminalized under federal law in the Emmet Till Anti-Lynching Bill of 2022.

Executions go on today under the guise of "legitimate violence," but execution killings often constitute human rights abuses. Saudi Arabia executed eighty-one people in a single day, March 12, 2022,[22] the Saudi Specialized Criminal Court sentencing one man to death for tweets that criticized Saudi authorities.[23] The Chinese government executes political dissidents and Falun Gong followers for religious beliefs and does so for the purpose of harvesting organs to sell for transplantation.[24] Organizations like Amnesty International and Human Rights Watch address execution as a fundamental abuse of human rights and appeal to the *Universal Declaration of Human Rights* adopted by the UN in 1948 to condemn the death penalty—and the execution power—for violating the right of persons to life and the right to live free from torture and cruel, inhuman and degrading treatment or punishment.[25] Despite political and legal legitimacy, sentences of death and actual executions carried out through the American criminal justice system are often subject to scrutiny and criticism by human rights organizations on the grounds of human rights violations. A candidate for inclusion might be the US Supreme Court decision in *Herrera v. Collins* (506 US 390 [1993]), which denied a claim of actual innocence. The decision prevented a retrial where exculpatory evidence could have been introduced because the Court ruled no procedural errors were made in the original trial. The petitioner, Leonel Torres Herrera, was executed by lethal injection a few months after the decision. The case could be made that, when a "legitimate" government prevents a person condemned to death from every opportunity to escape a possibly wrongful execution, it thereby engages in a human rights violation.

The Major Justice Concerns

The execution power is subject to abuse. Throughout history it has been used to eliminate enemies and perceived threats to political and social power, and such uses continue to this day. As a topic for ethical debate, we noted at the outset that the state ought not kill its citizens, a noncontroversial justice claim for which we assumed common moral agreement. Executions are therefore presumed to be impermissible from a moral point of view, and the low number of executions relative to the number of homicides confirms a deep reluctance to resort to the death penalty. That reluctance, however, does not equal an absolute prohibition, which means that, theoretically, the execution practice could be justified if it satisfies the demands of justice. The death penalty requires serious moral justification to lift the presumption against its use, and various justice considerations should be examined to see if this can be accomplished. Below are justice-related concerns that would deny any effort to establish a workable theory of "just execution." Without adequate moral justification to overrule the presumption against executions, the death penalty is a wrongful act and should be abolished.

The Wrongful Execution

The possibility of persons innocent of the crime that has brought them to death row is the most powerful reason for opposing the death penalty. There has been one exoneration and release from death row for every 8.2 executions.[26] Although wrongful prosecutions will never be as frequent as those that show up in entertainment programs like *Matlock* or *Perry Mason* (in which every defendant is wrongfully accused), the fact is that there are persons wrongfully accused, wrongfully convicted, and wrongfully put to death. Couple these legalized "legitimate" execution possibilities with the "illegitimate" extermination policies of the Nazis[27] or Pol Pot or the terrorist lynching of Blacks in the United States, and the effect of the execution power as unjust is unmistakable and inescapable. If a justice system is so imperfect as to subject innocent persons to wrongful death and one lends that system support, then one must be prepared to include oneself as a potential victim along with any other innocent person. This reason alone—simple self-interest—should be a primary reason for opposing the death penalty. If it can happen to an innocent person, it can happen to any innocent person, including me.

Discrimination and Fair Imposition

A convincing case can be made that the death penalty is not fairly applied, that it is imposed arbitrarily and with discrimination due to class, gender, and race.

Death rows are overwhelmingly populated with poor people[28] and males. On the gender issue, it can be argued that women commit fewer capital crimes, with even fewer of the aggravating circumstances required for a death sentence. Yet an issue of "chivalric attitudes" could be at play for the 2 percent female death row population: "Because women are stereotyped as weak, passive, and in need of male protection, prosecutors and juries seem reluctant to impose the death penalty upon them."[29]

Race presents a long-standing discrimination issue that has not really changed since the Supreme Court initiated efforts to eliminate arbitrariness with an "objective" aggravating and mitigating circumstances calculus in sentencing. This is what allowed the death penalty to be reinstated in 1976. The US population is 12 percent Black, but since 1976, Blacks have made up 34 percent of those actually executed. Whites have made up 81 percent of victims. Although twenty-one white defendants were executed for killing a Black person, 299 Black defendants were executed for killing a white person.[30] The Supreme Court in *McCleskey v. Kemp* (481 US 279) reviewed an exhaustive study by David Baldus that showed that Black defendants were twenty-two times more likely to receive a death sentence for killing a white person than Black defendants for killing a Black person; and a white victim increased the likelihood of a death sentence seven times over instances where the victim was Black. All of this is to say that racial bias in the application of the death penalty appears most strongly in relation to the race of victim. The Court struggled with this evidence but understood that accepting it as an indictment of the capital punishment system would necessarily implicate the entire criminal justice system in racial bias, and this the Court would not do. While not denying the research findings of the Baldus study, the Court resolved the issue by requiring defendants to prove discrimination in their individual cases, thus allowing the system to continue. Racial bias continues to affect the entire criminal justice system, from policing, to prosecution, to sentencing, and to questions about who winds up on death row. The US Accounting Office in 1990 reported that "In 82% of the studies [reviewed], race of the victim was found to influence the likelihood of being charged with capital murder or receiving the death penalty, i.e., those who murdered whites were found more likely to be sentenced to death than those who murdered blacks."[31] The death penalty is applied arbitrarily and discriminatorily.

The claim that in the capital justice system all juries can ignore race and achieve objectivity in imposing a death sentence based on aggravating versus mitigating circumstances is simply illusory. Opposing bias and unfairness is a legal issue for a justice system dedicated to fairness, nondiscrimination, equal protection, and due process, but it is also a profound moral issue. It is morally wrong to demand a death as a just punishment when the system of justice delivery itself presents evidence of racial arbitrariness and class and gender bias in arresting, charging, trying, sentencing, and then selecting individuals for execution. The legacy of racial discrimination in the United States goes so deep that creating a color-blind criminal justice system, a dream perhaps of death penalty supporters, is simply beyond reach. A punishment system that is error-prone and that by an irretrievable action—killing—eliminates the possibility of correcting inevitable injustices simply increases the possibility of injustice, even if in particular cases there are no errors in matters of fact and procedure. Human beings, however, cannot be certain of perfection in their actions or in the fallible systems of justice they create, but is perfection not demanded when a life is at stake?

Other justice issues involved in the death penalty could extend this discussion. Worth mentioning are botched executions—those seven "problematic" executions in 2022 mentioned earlier. It turns out that it is sometimes difficult to kill a person via execution. Electric chair victims have actually caught on fire, lethal injections have missed usable injection sites due to technician inexperience (physicians and nurses are prohibited by their professional ethics codes from participating in executions), and problems can attend all the methods—poisoning, suffocation (nitrogen), shooting, electrocution, gassing, hanging. The Death Penalty Information Center has listed sixty botched executions since 1976,[32] and this identifies cruelty in the killing itself. The punishment in execution is not designed to torture but to dispatch—it is the death not the killing that is supposed to be the punishment—and to the extent that the modes of dispatch deliver unnecessary and often unexpected pain and suffering, the execution itself comes under moral scrutiny as a torturous act worthy of condemnation by persons of good will.

Conclusion

The death penalty should be abolished. There is no societal benefit from it. It does not deliver justice but enacts vengeance, reinforcing the illusion that family members of a murder victim will receive some sense of closure when the offender is dead. Perhaps that happens sometimes, but sometimes, the execution process can postpone grief and confrontation with loss. Once the offender is dead, the family so set on revenge is left alone to grieve a loss that no punishment could ever recompense or repay.

The death penalty fails to recognize the humanity of every person. No one is ever nothing more than the worst thing they have done. Those who take a life should be punished, but the imbalance created by an offender's unjust killing cannot be put right by a killing pursued through an eye-for-an-eye mentality. When an Iranian woman was disfigured for life by a spurned acid-throwing pursuer, her call for eye-for-eye retribution—throwing acid on her attacker—was condemned worldwide.[33] It was considered by the civilized world—the moral community—as an act of barbarism. The death penalty sends the message that societal problems can be solved with violence. As one of the only actual "eye-for-eye" punishments still in existence, the death penalty is defended as a powerful response to injustice, but it is the state subjecting human beings to a lengthy, arbitrary, and torturous killing process that itself merits description as a barbaric agent of injustice and violence. Continued use of the death penalty is unworthy of the people of good will who aspire to build communities of justice and peace.

Notes

1. Witnesses to the execution of John Spenkelink in Florida have reported that he was either already dead when strapped into Florida's "Old Sparky" or that he was alive but unconscious. See UPI Archives, "A Priest Who Witnessed the 1979 Execution of John. . ." (March 5, 1981) (https://www.upi.com/Archives/1981/03/05/A-priest-who-witnessed-the-1979-execution-of-John/8591352616400/).

2. Ricky Ray Rector had killed a police officer in Arkansas, then turned the gun on himself, leaving him "lobotomized" and unable to understand his execution. He set aside his dessert before being taken to his lethal injection, believing he would be returning, and said he would vote for Governor Bill Clinton's gubernatorial reelection. Clinton refused to grant clemency due to his fear that he would appear "soft on crime" during his presidential bid, a charge that helped sink his party's previous candidate Michael Dukakis. See Nathan J. Robinson, "The Death of Ricky Ray Rector," *Jacobin* (November 5, 2016) (https://jacobin.com/2016/11/bill-clinton-rickey-rector-death-penalty-execution-crime-racism/).

    The US Supreme Court considered a possible right not to be executed for those suffering severe mental illness. The Court's opinion did not attempt to define the mental illnesses that make a person ineligible for the death penalty. Justice Lewis

Powell's concurring opinion would have held the prohibition applicable only for those who are unaware of the punishment they are about to suffer and why they are to suffer it. (*Ford v. Wainwright*, 477 US 399 [1986] at 420 ff.) See also: https://constitution.congress.gov/browse/essay/amdt8-4-9-7/ALDE_00000972/.

3 A 2021 Pew survey revealed that 60 percent of Americans support capital punishment but 78 percent believe there is a risk of executing innocent people. Pew Research Center, "Most Americans Favor the Death Penalty Despite Concerns about Its Administration" (June 2, 2021) (https://www.pewresearch.org/politics/2021/06/02/most-americans-favor-the-death-penalty-despite-concerns-about-its-administration/). A Gallup Poll in 2019 indicated 55 percent public support for the death penalty, with 60 percent saying they would choose a penalty other than execution. Death Penalty Information Center, "Fact Sheet" (updated February 2024) (https://dpic-cdn.org/production/documents/pdf/FactSheet.pdf).

4 An unintentional killing is a crime in which a person is killed by the action of another, but the killing was unintended, which means without malice. Involuntary manslaughter is such a crime. Killing resulting from texting while driving, driving under the influence of drugs or alcohol, and firing a weapon accidentally in an argument are actions that meet with legal penalties, including imprisonment and fines.

5 "Number of Reported Murder and Nonnegligent Manslaughter Cases in the United States from 1990 to 2022," *Statistica* (https://www.statista.com/statistics/191134/reported-murder-and-nonnegligent-manslaughter-cases-in-the-us-since-1990/#:~:text=How%20many%20criminal%20homicides%20werereported%20in%20the%20previous%20year).

6 Khaleda Rahman, "Every Death Row Prisoner Executed in 2022," *Newsweek.com* (https://www.newsweek.com/every-death-row-prisoner-executed-2022-1769611). Another word for "problematic" is "botched"—executions that did not go according to plan and were "visibly problematic."

7 Over 9,800 death sentences have been imposed since 1972, and of those 4,732 were reversed, 1,542 were executed, and 734 died in prison. The Death Penalty Information Center, "The DPIC Death Penalty Census" (https://deathpenaltyinfo.org/facts-and-research/death-penalty-census).

8 A 5-4 Supreme Court majority found in *Furman v. Georgia* (408 US 238, Potter Stewart opinion) that the application of capital punishment was "harsh, freakish, and arbitrary." On that finding, the Court ruled that the death penalty as practiced in the United States was in violation of the Eighth Amendment's prohibition on cruel and unusual punishment.

9 Many people who kill another person actually regret having done so, and remorse can effect change. The time spent in prison awaiting execution has affected lives to the point that occasionally even death penalty supporters call for clemency due to the dramatic change in a person's life, as happened in the celebrated case of Carla Faye Tucker, for whom prison was the most stable environment she had ever known. Gustav Niebuhr, "Execution in Texas: Religious Debate; Tucker Case May Split Evangelical Christians," *New York Times* (February 4, 1998), Section A, 20 (https://www.nytimes.com/1998/02/04/us/execution-in-texas-religious-debate-tucker-case-may-split-evangelical-christians.html).

10. After thirty-six years on the Tennessee death row, the last words of David Earl Miller were that the impending electrocution "beats being on death row." Associated Press, "Tennessee Inmate Executed 37 Years after Crime Said It 'Beats Being on Death Row,'" WTHR, Associated Press (https://www.wthr.com/article/news/nation-world/tennessee-inmate-executed-37-years-after-crime-said-it-beats-being-death-row/531-b0ddf3a2-845b-4c9c-ab43-63ebbf5aca92).

11. Ashley Nellis, "Life Goes On: The Historic Rise in Life Sentences in America, The Sentencing Project" (September 18, 2013) (https://www.sentencingproject.org/reports/life-goes-on-the-historic-rise-in-life-sentences-in-america/).

12. Quoted in Lloyd Steffen, *Executing Justice: The Moral Meaning of the Death Penalty* (Eugene: Wipf & Stock Publishers, 1999), 60–1.

13. Suicides on death row are about ten times that of the general population in the United States, and six times more than the prison population. See David Lester and Christine Tartaro, "Suicide on Death Row," *Journal of Forensic Sciences* 47, no. 5 (2002): 1108–11.

14. John Paul II wrote (*Evangelicum Vitae* [1995]) that the death penalty is defensible only "in cases of absolute necessity, in other words, when it would not be possible to defend society." Pope Francis said in a speech to ambassadors to the Vatican (January 22, 2022), "The death penalty cannot be employed for a purported state justice, since it does not constitute a deterrent nor render justice to victims, but only fuels the thirst for vengeance." See "Pope Francis Condemns Iran for Using Death Penalty Against Demonstrators," *Reuters* (January 9, 2022) (https://www.reuters.com/world/europe/pope-francis-condemns-iran-using-death-penalty-against-demonstrators-2023-01-09/).

15. There is also a related moral theory, contractualism, associated with T. M. Scanlon, author of *What We Owe To Each Other* (Cambridge, MA: Harvard University Press, 2000). It has its roots in Rousseau and it bases morality on reason, rational agency, and the equality of persons. Another theory, contractarianism, grounded in Hobbes, emphasizes mutual self-interest in the social contract. Hobbes held that a person loses the protections of citizenship and the social contract with a crime like murder and could justifiably face a death sentence.

16. Elizabeth Ashford and Tim Mulgan, "Contractualism," in *The Stanford Encyclopedia of Philosophy* (Summer 2018 Edition), ed. Edward N. Zalta (https://plato.stanford.edu/archives/sum2018/entries/contractualism/).

17. Death Penalty Information Center, "Fact Sheet."

18. National Institute of Justice, U.S. Department of Justice, "Five Things about Deterrence." This is according to National Academy of Sciences, "Research on the deterrent effect of capital punishment is uninformative about whether capital punishment increases, decreases, or has no effect on homicide rates" (https://www.ojp.gov/pdffiles1/nij/247350.pdf).

19. Corey Brettschneider, "The Rights of the Guilty: Punishment and Political Legitimacy," *Political Theory* 35, no. 2 (2007): 175–99.

20. Death Penalty Information Center, "Sentencing Data" (https://deathpenaltyinfo.org/policy-issues/human-rights).

21. Death Penalty Information Center (https://deathpenaltyinfo.org/facts-and-research/sentencing-data).

22 Human Rights Watch, "Saudi Arabia: Mass Execution of 81 Men: Rampant Abuses in Criminal Justice System Make Fair Trials Highly Implausible" (March 15, 2022) (https://www.hrw.org/news/2022/03/15/saudi-arabia-mass-execution-81-men).

23 Amnesty International, "Saudi Arabia: 100 People Executed as Authorities Continue Relentless 'Killing Spree'" (September 8, 2023) (https://www.amnesty.org/en/latest/news/2023/09/saudi-arabia-100-people-executed-as-authorities-continue-relentless-killing-spree/).

24 See Ethan Gutmann, *The Slaughter: Mass Killings, Organ Harvesting, and China's Secret Solution to Its Dissident Problem* (Guilford: Prometheus Books, 2014), 253ff.

25 Amnesty International, "Death Penalty" (https://www.amnesty.org/en/what-we-do/death-penalty/).

26 Death Penalty Information Center, "Key Findings" (https://deathpenaltyinfo.org/facts-and-research/death-penalty-census/key-findings).

27 Martin Luther King, Jr., "Letter from Birmingham Jail" (August 1963): "We can never forget that everything Hitler did in Germany was 'legal' and everything the Hungarian freedom fighters did in Hungary was 'illegal.' It was 'illegal' to aid and comfort a Jew in Hitler's Germany" (https://www.csuchico.edu/iege/_assets/documents/susi-letter-from-birmingham-jail.pdf), 3.

28 Office of the High Commissioner of Human Rights, United Nations, "Death Penalty Disproportionately Affects the Poor, UN Rights Experts Warn" (October 6, 2017) (https://www.ohchr.org/en/press-releases/2017/10/death-penalty-disproportionately-affects-poor-un-rights-experts-warn).

29 Jeremy Carnes, "Why Are So Few Women Sentenced to Death?" *Alive* (May 1, 2019) (https://www.11alive.com/article/news/why-are-so-few-women-sentenced-to-death/85-9b773762-1f21-4cdb-83ef-47ba3c0954e9).

30 Death Penalty Information Center, "Executions by Race and Race of Victim" (https://deathpenaltyinfo.org/executions/executions-overview/executions-by-race-and-race-of-victim).

31 Ibid.

32 Death Penalty Information Center, "Botched Executions" (https://deathpenaltyinfo.org/executions/botched-executions).

33 Reza Sayah, "Woman Blinded by Acid Wants Same Fate for Attacker," CNN, n.d. (https://www.cnn.com/2009/WORLD/meast/02/19/acid.attack.victim/).

Responses

Response to Bessette and Feser on Capital Punishment

Lloyd Steffen

> **Study Questions**
>
> 1. Why does Steffen think that Bessette's and Feser's appeal to history begs the question?
> 2. What response does Steffen make to Bessette's and Feser's "consequentialist arguments"?
> 3. Why does Steffen believe that retribution does not justify capital punishment?

Joseph M. Bessette and Edward Feser have presented a defense of capital punishment, and I am grateful to them for their substantive contribution to this volume. The issues they raise for consideration are significant and worthy of response.

Three Pro-Capital Punishment Arguments

The authors present three essential arguments that they believe provide adequate justification for supporting the continued use of the death penalty in our American criminal justice system. Those arguments are as follows:

1. The authors reference legal systems in the West that have historically sanctioned capital punishment, thus rendering capital punishment a morally defensible tool of criminal justice.

2. The authors discuss execution as a way to bring closure to a victim's family and loved ones. They argue that the death penalty is a proportionate punishment that reduces crime through a deterrent effect and teaches the horror of murder. They fear that without this punishment, society will lose sight of the idea of punishment itself.

3. The authors defend a just-desert position. Capital punishment, they argue, is restricted to only the vilest offenders, the "worst of the worst," who deserve death due to their depraved acts of murder. The authors' retributive justice perspective appeals to a principle of proportionality.

These are all valid issues, but each has difficulties deserving of a response.

A Question-Begging Historical Appeal

The historical fact that the death penalty has been an accepted part of legal codes in the West is simply question-begging with respect to moral meaning. Slavery, too, was defended in ancient legal codes, in Roman and Greek law, in sacred scriptures (condoned in the New Testament Epistle to Philemon), and in the original American Constitution. American law recognizes that what is morally acceptable in society can change in accordance with "evolving standards of decency" (*Weems v. United States*, 217 US 349 (1910)). As evidence of its place in our moral and legal thinking, this standard has steered the efforts to kill capital offenders more humanely, which was the original justification for moving to lethal injection.[1]

The history of capital punishment does not establish moral meaning, but it can allow insight into how and why it was used in a particular society. For instance, the Code of Hammurabi, mentioned by the authors, did enunciate the *lex talionis* retribution notion of "eye for an eye, tooth for a tooth, death for a death," but it was in a society where a personal injury demanded a tribal response. The *lex talionis* was a reform move designed to restrict the violence of revenge so that resolving a conflict did not create broad social chaos, clan against clan. A Babylonian justification from 3,700 years ago is not relevant today when society can be protected and retribution effected without resorting to state-sponsored execution. Although "eye for eye" thinking is often assumed to be a just response to injury and injustice, modern punishments are retributive without resorting to like-for-like punishment responses. To illustrate this, I raised the example of the Iranian woman who was disfigured for life by a disgruntled suitor who attacked her with acid then demanded of a Sharia court that the attacker himself be sprayed with acid the same way. The prospect of such a punishment was greeted worldwide as a cruel and barbaric response.[2] Retribution has a place in law and in punishment ethics, but the *lex talionis* is contemptible as a moral standard.[3]

Execution has historically been used to dispose of those deemed undesirable in societies, and although it has been used outside of the law, as in the lynching of Blacks or in the elimination of political enemies, as a legal punishment it has a history of being imposed arbitrarily, with race, gender, and economic status playing a discernible role.[4] Moral meaning must attend to the ways the death penalty has actually been used. The authors do not seem to acknowledge the relevance of these concerns.

Furthermore, it is hard to restrict the death penalty to just one crime when so much cultural subjectivity—"arbitrariness" in legal language—is involved in determining which offenses merit death. The Mosaic Law imposes the death penalty for intentional killing, yes, but it also included three dozen other capital crimes, such as cursing one's parents, homosexuality, and working on the Sabbath. In one case, the offense involved gathering wood on the Sabbath (Num. 15: 32-36). The 1994 Federal Death Penalty Act established sixty new death penalty offenses, so how many "worst of the worsts" can there be?

So, what constitutes "worst of the worst" and who decides? A nurse at one of the local hospitals in Bethlehem, Pennsylvania where I live, Charles Cullen by name, was arrested in 2003 for having dispatched forty people in medical centers in Pennsylvania and New Jersey. It is suspected that he killed many more, possibly as many as 400 patients, by injecting lethal drugs in the IV bags of elderly and dying patients. The authors bolster their defense of capital punishment by mentioning individual cases that are beyond any question stupefyingly horrendous. But is Cullen not one of the worst? Do a possible 400 victims not qualify for such a designation? What happened in Cullen's case is that he negotiated with prosecutors to avoid the death penalty, agreeing to admit to other killings, and that, in my view, blunts adherence to a "worst of the worst" justice standard.

Faulty Consequentialist Arguments

In response to the authors' various consequentialist arguments, let me offer these points. On deterrence: That the death penalty deters crime, specifically murder, is a case often made, but "The consensus in the scientific community, including the National Academy of Science, National Research Council's 2012 report, is that there is no reliable evidence of a deterrent effect of the death penalty on homicide rates."[5]

On a second point: States that have the death penalty have higher murder rates than those that do not, and murders typically increase in states following a well-publicized execution. These facts count against capital punishment being a tool that teaches the horror of murder.

Third: Families of murder victims caught up in the years-long efforts to see the murderer of their loved one executed will seek closure, of course. The reality, however, is that after an execution, when the attention of the media and prosecutors suddenly vanishes, victim survivors are left to confront a grief that has in many ways been postponed. Although not always the case, a "life for a life" execution will not ordinarily put things back in balance for those who have lost a loved one.

The Injustice of Retributive Capital Punishment

The authors' most serious moral issue is the proportionality and just deserts argument, namely, that persons who murder justly forfeit their own life by their act. Retribution does not need to operate on a *lex talionis*, eye-for-eye calculus, however, and our justice system in the main does not do so. The loss of freedom is a harsh form of retribution.[6] It does not endorse the view that violence is the appropriate way to respond to violence, which is a lesson capital punishment does teach. And incarceration has the benefit of holding open the possibility that an injustice in an offender's conviction might yet be corrected. "Since 1973, 200 former death-row prisoners have been exonerated of all charges related to the wrongful convictions that had put them on death row."[7]

The authors concentrated on victims and the horrible crimes that have led a select few to death row. I understand this emphasis, but I also believe justice systems make mistakes, and we ought not to act as if they were infallible. As the moral point of view necessarily imposes a test of universalizability, my strongest reason for opposing the death penalty is this: if one grants that mistakes happen and a wrongful execution can occur, and then also grants that an occasional mistake is an acceptable loss because the societal benefits of capital punishment far outweigh the moral deficit created by killing an innocent person, it logically follows that that innocent person could be *any* innocent person—you, me, the authors of the response to my article, my reader's mother or father, sister, or brother, or loved one—or any innocent person. Correcting mistakes and not killing the innocent is a demand of justice. Correcting a justice mistake is only possible if the condemned is alive to receive the correction. Justice demands that the possibility of correction be kept open for that one mistake, even if there is no doubt about the guilt of all the others presently on death row.

Conclusion

I have not responded to every point the authors have made, nor have they to mine. But in the end, from a moral point of view, the prospect of executing wrongfully one innocent person, a prospect that is inevitable and unavoidable, suffices in my view to collapse the whole execution system and rob it of moral justification.

Notes

1 See "Lethal Injection," *Britannica* (https://www.britannica.com/topic/electrocution): "Lethal injection—now the most widely used method of execution in the United States—was first adopted by the U.S. state of Oklahoma, because it was considered cheaper and more humane than either electrocution or lethal gas."

2 "Iran Acid Attack: Ameneh Bahrami's Quest for Justice," *BBC News* (June 2, 2011) (https://www.bbc.com/news/world-middle-east-13578731).

3 For those who cannot accept anything short of death for a murderer, a sentence of life in prison without chance of parole is a death sentence—it is an extended death sentence, to be sure, but the sentence is designed to inflict punishment up to and including the death of the condemned.

4 Readers should consult The Death Penalty Information Center for more information and resources: https://deathpenaltyinfo.org/.
5 Jeffrey Fagan, "Capital Punishment & Deterrence," ACLU (February 2, 2022), 2 (https://www.aclu.org/sites/default/files/field_document/2022_4_feb_fagan_deterrence_report.pdf).
6 Incarceration is a severe punishment, so much so that suicides are the most frequent cause of death in US prisons. See Katherine LeMasters, Jennifer Lao, Meghan Peterson, Michael F. Behne, and Lauren Brinkley-Rubinstein, "Suicides in State Prisons in the United States: Highlighting Gaps in Data," *PLOS One* (May 21, 2023) (https://journals.plos.org/plosone/article?id=10.1371/journal.pone.0285729). I mentioned in my article the Pennsylvania death row inmates who dropped appeals and "volunteered" for execution, seeing it as preferable to continued incarceration.
7 "DPIC Database: Innocence Database," Death Penalty Information Center (https://deathpenaltyinfo.org/policy-issues/innocence, accessed October 7, 2024).

Response to Steffen on Capital Punishment

Joseph M. Bessette and Edward Feser

Study Questions

1. How do Bessette and Feser respond to Steffen's claim that there is a presumption against the death penalty?
2. How do Bessette and Feser answer the charge that capital punishment is "freakish and arbitrary"?
3. Why do Bessette and Feser disagree with Steffen's argument that life imprisonment is preferable to capital punishment?
4. According to Bessette and Feser, why do the abuses of tyrants not undermine capital punishment?
5. How do Bessette and Feser respond to the "justice issues" Steffen raises?

In his call for abolishing the death penalty for murder in the United States, Lloyd Steffen makes a variety of related arguments. Here we address what seem to be the most important. Some of these are more theoretical and others more practical, and Steffen weaves these kinds of arguments together throughout his essay.

Is the Death Penalty Presumably Wrongful?

Steffen holds that the death penalty cannot be just because it is immoral. Why immoral? He starts by maintaining that "execution is a presumably wrongful act." "Reasonable people of good will," he writes, "can agree that the state ought not to kill its own citizens" (p.96). But of course. No state should kill its citizens unless there is a good reason for doing so. Who would disagree with that? Yet, for thousands of years—and until about a century ago—Western societies presumed that those who intentionally kill their fellow human beings should themselves be put to death. And they should be put to death because they deserve to be punished in a way commensurate with the evil act they committed. This is the presumption that characterized Western law as far back as records go. While most democratic nations have now rejected capital punishment, the US federal government has not, nor have more than half the American states and such major democracies as India, Japan, and South Korea.

Is the Death Penalty Freakish and Arbitrary?

Steffen rightly notes that, currently, in the United States, there are relatively few death sentences and executions, compared to the number of homicides. He concludes that this demonstrates that the death penalty is applied "freakishly" and "arbitrarily" (pp. 97, 105). But it simply does not follow logically that if a punishment is applied rarely, it is applied arbitrarily. Consider the process in the American states by which some murderers are selected for capital punishment—something that Steffen never mentions. First, the state legislature must decide whether to have the death penalty at all. Second, states with the death penalty must define which kinds of murder, such as multiple murders or rape murders, make an accused killer eligible for the death penalty. Third, the prosecutor, usually an elected district attorney, must judge whether a qualifying murder is so heinous or the accused's prior record so violent that the offender merits the death penalty. Finally, if a jury unanimously convicts the accused of the murder, it must determine, after a special sentencing hearing, whether the aggravating circumstances of the crime outweigh any mitigating circumstances, and, therefore, whether to recommend death.

But this is not the end of the process. Every defendant sentenced to death has the right to appeal his conviction or sentence, first to the state courts and, if unsuccessful there, to the federal courts. It is hard to imagine a less "arbitrary" or "freakish" process.[1] In our main essay, we showed through a close examination of the forty-three murderers executed in 2012 that the death penalty system does in fact select the "the worst of the worst" for the ultimate punishment, especially rape murderers, those who kill multiple victims, those who have killed in the past or have a long history of violent crime, and those who kill the very young or very old.

Is Life without Parole Preferable?

Steffen, like many opponents of capital punishment, endorses "life without parole" in prison as a "morally preferable alternative" to the death penalty. It "deliver[s] a harsh punishment," he writes, "without involving all of society in the willful and premeditated killing of selected offenders" (p. 100). Not only harsh, but, in his view, *even harsher* than execution; for "execution shortens the punishment while incarceration extends the suffering of the killing process" (Ibid).

What is odd here is that Steffen is seemingly calling to replace the death penalty, which he claims is immoral because it is excessively harsh, with another penalty—life without parole— which he claims, is *even harsher*. If he is right about the harshness of life in prison, then he should be denouncing its immorality along with that of the death penalty itself. And, make no mistake, if the nation were to abolish the death penalty, the next target of the opponents would be life without parole. Note that while Steffen cites Pope Francis's opposition to the death penalty, he does not mention the Pope's adamant opposition to life sentences, which Francis calls "hidden death sentences."[2] Indeed, Steffen himself calls life without parole "problematic." Why problematic?[3]

Do Abuses by Tyrants Undermine the Death Penalty?

To demonstrate the dangers of the death penalty—what Steffen calls "the execution power"—he cites such abuses as Nazi Germany's genocide of the Jews, the Ottoman Empire's oppression of Armenians, and the Chinese government's execution of dissidents. Tyrants will, of course, use whatever means they can to achieve their ends. But what has any of this to do with a constitutional democracy imposing death for the most heinous murders and the most vicious murderers following carefully elaborated rules and procedures and under the watchful eye of state and federal courts? No responsible person, for example, would reject incarceration as a punishment for crime because tyrants jail their political opponents.

What about the Possibility of Executing the Innocent?

Steffen holds that "the most powerful reason for opposing the death penalty" (p. 104) is the possibility of an innocent person being sentenced to death. He makes two main arguments. First, he seemingly embraces a moral theory that holds that "if a punishment is not justifiable to everyone affected by it, it is not morally permissible" (p. 101). Because wrongly condemned persons do not consider their punishment justified, it is immoral and must be rejected. Under this logic, however, no punishment for criminal offenses would ever be "morally permissible" if there was any possibility—as there always will be—that a single innocent person might be convicted and punished. Later, Steffen makes a similar point in the language of self-interest. If a wrongful death "can happen to an innocent person, it can happen to any innocent person, including me" (p. 104). "Simple self-interest," he concludes, should be enough to oppose capital punishment. Yet, according to Gallup, clear majorities of Americans have favored the death penalty for murder all forty-six times Gallup has asked the question since 1967.[4] Also, other surveys show that at least 70 percent of Americans support the death penalty for the most aggravated types of murder, such as raping and killing a child (80 percent), killing someone after torturing him or her (73 percent), and killing at least one person by setting off a bomb in a public place (70 percent).[5] Clearly, most Americans have a very different understanding of their self-interest, and of what justice requires, than does Steffen.[6]

Steffen asks, "but is perfection not demanded when a life is at stake?" (p. 105). No reasonable defender of the death penalty denies the possibility of errors in the criminal justice system run by fallible human beings. Would Steffen deny guns to half a million police officers in the United States because a few may negligently, or even intentionally, take an innocent life? Perfection is not to be seen in human beings and human institutions. We arm fallible police officers because it serves a larger social good, a good that cannot be achieved without the risk of an innocent person being harmed or killed. Similarly, the death penalty serves a larger social good that cannot be achieved without the risk, however small, of an innocent person being executed. Fortunately, among the 1,600 executions that have taken place since the Supreme Court reinstated the death penalty in 1976, there is no compelling evidence that a single innocent person has been wrongly executed.

Is the Death Penalty Racist?

As for the charge that the death penalty is applied in a racially biased way, consider these data from the US Bureau of Justice Statistics. From 1990 to 2013, whites were 46 percent of those arrested for murder, but 56 percent of those sentenced to death, and 64 percent of those executed. In other words, Blacks arrested for murder were *less likely* than whites to be sentenced to death or executed. This is hardly the mark of a racist criminal justice system.[7]

Are There No Social Benefits to the Death Penalty?

Steffen concludes that the death penalty should be abolished because "[t]here is no societal benefit from it" (p. 106). He could not be more wrong. Here are some of the benefits that opponents refuse to recognize. First, it helps to protect prison guards and other inmates from being killed by those serving life terms for previous murders. Second, it protects members of the community by giving lifers who escape from custody powerful reasons not to kill while on the run. Third, it almost certainly has a deterrent effect on at least some potential murderers by threatening to take from them that which they value most: their lives. Fourth, it powerfully reinforces society's condemnation of murder, making it less likely that those growing up in a community with capital punishment would even consider killing someone in the first place. Fifth, it anchors the entire schedule of punishments for serious crimes to the principle of "just deserts," helping to ensure that retributive punishment remains a key element in punishing crimes. Sixth, it reassures the families of murder victims that they live in a just society that shows respect for the lives of their loved ones. Finally, it promotes belief in and respect for the majesty of the moral order and for the system of human law that both derives from and supports that moral order.[8]

Notes

1. Though Steffen notes that in 1972 the US Supreme Court, in a 5-4 vote, temporarily overturned the death penalty throughout the nation because of the perceived arbitrariness of its application, just four years later, in a 7-2 vote, the Court upheld new laws from several states that channeled discretion in the application of the death penalty so as to minimize the risk of arbitrary or capricious action. In other words, the problem of arbitrariness it had identified in 1972 (over the dissent of four justices) had been rectified by new laws upheld by the Court a mere four years later. In the decades since, the Court has struck down the death penalty for rapists who do not murder, for those under eighteen, and for those suffering from mental retardation; but it has not held that in the twenty-seven states that retain capital punishment, death sentences are handed down to adult killers of sound mind in an arbitrary, capricious, or "freakish" way.

2. Quoted in Edward Feser and Joseph M. Bessette, *By Man Shall His Blood Be Shed: A Catholic Defense of Capital Punishment* (San Francisco: Ignatius Press, 2017), 188.

3. Moreover, Steffen is simply wrong if he means to imply that most of the 2,200 now on death row in the United States would prefer death to living out their lives in prison. We know this because nearly all of them appeal their sentences until all hope is lost. Perhaps 4–5 percent "volunteer" for death by suspending their appeals. Also, each year dozens of those charged with a capital murder plead guilty in exchange for a life sentence, revealing their preference for life, even in prison, over death. Convicted murderers, like common citizens, recognize that execution is a harsher punishment than life in prison. Not only is it closer in severity to the crime of murder it punishes, but it is also likely to be a more effective deterrent than a prison sentence, even one for life. (See our discussion of deterrence in our original essay.)

4. See https://news.gallup.com/poll/1606/death-penalty.aspx

5. Joseph M. Bessette and J. Andrew Sinclair, "How Many Americans Support the Death Penalty? Results of National Surveys in 2019 and 2020," Rose Institute of State and Local Government, Claremont McKenna College, at https://roseinstitute.org/crime-justice/.

6. Of the more than 8,500 people sentenced to death in the United States since the past half century, the number who were later shown to be factually innocent of the murder is closer to three dozen, or so, than to the nearly 200 Steffen cites. In all these cases, appellate courts discovered the error, so none of these individuals was executed. See Feser and Bessette, *By Man Shall His Blood Be Shed*, 339–55.

7   For a fuller discussion of this issue, see Feser and Bessette, *By Man Shall His Blood Be Shed*, 355–67.
8   Feser and Bessette, *By Man Shall His Blood Be Shed*, 381–2.

Questions for Reflection

1. Some have argued that retribution is synonymous with revenge. Do you agree? Why?

2. How would you respond to the charge that capital punishment is just "legalized murder," that is, it violates the murderers' right to life?

3. Could the death penalty be rightly extended to punish other crimes besides murder? Why?

For Further Reading

Bedau, Hugo, and Paul Cassell, eds. *Debating the Death Penalty: Should America Have Capital Punishment?* Oxford University Press, 2004.

Feser, Edward, and Joseph M. Bessette. *By Man Shall His Blood Be Shed: A Catholic Defense of Capital Punishment.* Ignatius Press, 2017.

Fleury-Steiner, Benjamin, and Austin D. Sarat, eds. *The Elgar Companion to Capital Punishment and Society.* Edward Elgar Publishing, 2024.

Hood, Roger, and Carolyn Hoyle. *The Death Penalty: A Worldwide Perspective,* 5th ed. Oxford University Press, 2015.

Kramer, Matthew H. *The Ethics of Capital Punishment: A Philosophical Investigation of Evil and its Consequences.* Oxford University Press, 2014.

Steffen, Lloyd. *Executing Justice: The Moral Meaning of the Death Penalty.* Wipf & Stock Publishers, 1999.

4

Human Genome Editing

The Case in Favor of Intentional Genetic Modification

Colin Farrelly

> ### Study Questions
>
> 1. What is the "genetic lottery"? What are examples of the disadvantages influenced by genetic inheritance?
> 2. What is "epigenetics"? What promise does it have of offering ethical gene modification?
> 3. What is the primary ethical concern with germline modification? How does Farrelly address this concern?
> 4. What is "epigenetic inheritance"? What ethical implications does it have?
> 5. How does Farrelly summarize the moral reasons for pursuing IGM?

In 2020, Emmanuelle Charpentier and Jennifer Doudna won the Nobel Prize in Chemistry for their discovery of CRISPR/Cas9,[1] a gene editing tool that has accelerated innovation in the biomedical sciences. The first FDA-approved treatment to utilize a novel genome editing technology (called Casgevy) was authorized in 2023, as a treatment for sickle cell disease, an inherited blood disorder that is more common in African Americans.[2] Genome editing involves adding, editing, or removing DNA in the genome, and it offers the promise of a more precise form of genetic manipulation than gene therapy. The first gene therapy experiment in humans, which was performed on children who suffered from a rare genetic disease called adenosine deaminase (ADA) deficiency, took place in 1990.[3] And since that time the number of gene therapy clinical trials has grown to over 2,500 trials worldwide.[4]

Scientific advances in human genetics have made the prospect of what Russell Powell and Allen Buchanan call "Intentional Genetic Modification"[5] (hereafter referred to simply as IGM) a reality in the twenty-first century. IGM involves, among other things, directly intervening in our DNA through applying gene therapy or genome editing in persons, and, potentially, to embryos and fetuses in utero.[6] However, new insights into what is known as "epigenetics"—which studies how behaviors (e.g., exercise) and environment (e.g., diet and stress) also affect the *expression* of genes (i.e., turning genes "on" or "off")—compel us to expand our understanding of what constitutes *direct* and *indirect*, as well as "unintentional" and "intentional," genetic modification. In doing so, the way we conceptualize the moral landscape, in terms of the potential strategies available to prevent harm and redress health disparities, will also need to be revised.

A competent ethical analysis of IGM cannot be constructed in the abstract, by simply appealing to our moral intuitions about the potential pros and cons of scientific innovations, especially when the latter still involves a lot of *uncertainty* concerning the safety and effectiveness of different types of genetic intervention, like genome editing. And the moral issues at stake in IGM can vary significantly depending on the type of intervention under consideration. Measures that propose "environmental enrichment," like improved living conditions that can alter (whether intentionally or unintentionally) gene expression, may be very different in terms of cost, safety, and efficacy than measures that involve genome editing. Likewise, the moral interests at stake in the regulation of an experimental gene therapy designed to treat an early onset, fatal disease may be quite distinct from the moral interests and potential harms that may arise when deploying experimental genome editing to reduce the risks of late-life morbidity (risks that may be reduced by other, less risky, types of interventions). This essay provides a summary of the *provisional* ethical reasons in favor of pursuing (safe and effective) scientific innovation that could make new forms of IGM a reality, with an emphasis on the most pressing harms and health disparities such innovations may help redress.

The "Genetic Lottery": Single-Gene Disorders and Biological Aging

Each person begins life with their own unique *genetic inheritance*, receiving two copies of most genes—one from the biological mother and one from the biological father. Genes are the fundamental physical and functional units of heredity; they "specify the proteins that form the units of which homoeostatic devices are composed."[7] It is estimated that over 400 million people worldwide have been diagnosed with one of about 7,000 Mendelian diseases, disorders generally thought to be caused by mutations in a single gene.[8] Many of those single-gene disorders cause significant harm, including early-life mortality, for the children born with these conditions. Highlighting the devastating impact the genetic lottery of life can have on those born with the genes that negatively impact health and well-being helps frame the moral imperative to pursue the scientific innovation for intentional genetic modification (IGM). The cause of these genetic disadvantages, and their accompanying health and lifespan disparities, is the genetic lottery of life, a lottery determined by evolution by natural selection. Thus, following Powell and Buchanan,[9] we can call this evolutionary process of natural selection *unintentional genetic modification*.

A child born with Fragile X syndrome, for example, has a change in a gene that can cause developmental delays, learning difficulties, and behavioral problems. While the disease can affect both males and females, the intellectual disability it causes in males is usually more severe (ranging from mild to severe).[10] Cystic fibrosis (CF) is a recessive genetic disease, which means a child born with the disease inherits both copies of the CF gene. If a child only inherits one copy of the gene, they are a CF carrier but do not develop CF. CF causes thick mucus to form in the lungs and is a life-threatening condition. Medical treatments for CF have improved survival significantly over the past few decades. The median survival age for a child born in the United States with CF was age 4–5 years in the 1950s, but it is now 48.4 years.[11] However, a diagnosis of CF still means a reduction of several decades below the average life expectancy at birth, which makes it a significant health and lifespan disparity that ought to be redressed if possible.

Alzheimer's disease (AD) is another disease in which genetics can play a significant factor in the development of the disease. A type of progressive dementia, AD impacts cognition (e.g., memory and thinking) and behavior. For most forms of AD, there are multiple risk factors, especially advanced age. But there are three rare, single-gene variants known to cause AD.[12] There is a 50 percent probability that parents with one of these gene variants will pass them along to their offspring, which would put the offspring at a high risk for developing AD before age sixty-five.

Genetic inheritance can also impact hearing and vision. Over 130 genes are associated with deafness and "gene therapy represents a promising prospect for ameliorating, preventing or even curing hereditary hearing loss that affects millions of people worldwide."[13] Inherited retinal diseases are caused by mutations in over 300 genes.[14] Because of the role genes play in the degradation of vision, which is often irreversible by other forms of intervention, gene therapy is also being explored as a potential treatment for some forms of inherited eye diseases.[15]

Genetic inheritance can influence not only an individual's level of health and disease over their lifespan but also their vision, cognition, muscle development, and mobility. While single-gene disorders constitute clear instances where genetic inheritance can *strongly influence* morbidity and mortality risks, they are rare conditions. This might lead one to conclude that, at best, IGM is only morally permissible to pursue when limited to the narrow range of the most severe, early-onset single-gene disorders. But the influence of the genetic lottery is much more expansive than simply the inheritance of single-gene disorders. For the most prevalent diseases, like cancer and heart disease, the risk factors typically cover a broad spectrum of issues, such as age and the interaction of genes, behavior, and environment. With *multifactorial* diseases, one's genetic inheritance does not, by itself, cause the development of pathology. However, genetic inheritance can influence the risks of these complex diseases which, in combination with particular behaviors and environmental risk factors over many decades, can lead to pathology.

Biological aging, defined as "the progressive loss of function accompanied by decreasing fertility and increasing mortality with advancing age,"[16] can be profoundly influenced by genetics (as well as environment and lifestyle, which is the focus of the next section on "epigenetics"). A comparison between the extreme cases of the accelerated aging of children born with progeria and the decelerated rate of aging among centenarians and supercentenarians (age ≥ 100 and age ≥ 110, respectively) makes this most apparent. About one in four million children are born with the rare and fatal disorder of progeria (called Hutchinson-Gilford syndrome), which is caused by a genetic mutation in the LMNA gene. Children with this extreme form of premature aging have an average life expectancy of only thirteen to fourteen years.

In contrast to the accelerated aging of progeria, some (rare) individuals can survive over a century of disease-free life, and there is good reason to believe some protective genetic mutations likely play a more significant role in exceptional healthy aging. Estimates suggest about 25 percent of the variation in the human lifespan is due to genetics; however, for the oldest of the old, genetics plays a higher role (but is not deterministic, nor due to a specific genetic mutation).[17] Having a centenarian sibling, for example, increases one's chances of survival to very old age.[18]

The prevalence of multi-morbidity in late life is due, at least in part, to the fact that the force of evolution by natural selection declines in later life (which is *Unintentional Genetic Modification* or UGM). The evolutionary biologist Michael Rose describes this evolutionary process as follows, which explains why progeria is so rare but late-onset diseases like cancer are so prevalent:

> Natural selection discards bad genes, genes like those that cause fatal childhood progeria. Bad genes cause these effects by producing inborn errors of metabolism: letting toxins accumulate, impairing brain function, and so on. Many of the diseases that kill infants are the products of such bad genes . . . Natural selection keeps genes with such devastating early effects rare, because the afflicted individuals die before reproducing. Bad genes destroy themselves when they kill the young . . . But at later ages, the force of natural selection becomes weak. It leaves genes with late bad effects alone, because natural selection has stopped working. Its force has fallen toward zero. Bad genes that only have late effects will not be removed by natural selection. They can accumulate. There is no more automatic Darwinian screening.[19]

A potential benefit of shifting from UGM to IGM, argue Powell and Buchanan, is that the latter "can avoid or ameliorate the harms that humans suffer as a result of UGM's insensitivity to their post-reproductive quality of life".[20] But the case in favor of IGM extends beyond promoting the scientific innovation needed to make safe, effective, and affordable gene therapy and genome editing a reality. Findings from what is called *epigenetics* reveal the importance of reconceptualizing many traditional preventive health measures (e.g., exercise) and some of the social determinants of health (e.g., healthy childhood development, etc.), as well as potential applied gerontological interventions designed to slow biological aging, as forms of *indirect* IGM.

Epigenetics and Indirect Intentional "Genetic Modification"

Rather than limiting the ethical focus of IGM to only direct forms of genetic modification—like genome editing—it is important to recognize that newly emerging scientific insights into "epigenetics" (and "epigenetic inheritance," covered in the following section), as well as the prospect of RNA-editing, require us to broaden our understanding of "genetic modification" to encompass both "direct" and "indirect" forms of genetic modification. Gene therapy and genome editing constitute forms of *direct* intentional genetic modification because they alter DNA by making precise edits to genes or the genome itself. And these modifications are made with the intention of altering the RNA molecules (a nucleic acid that is structurally similar to DNA) and proteins expressed by genes. Some RNAs are involved in gene expression.[21] RNA-editing is now a potential (though very recent) intervention. Reardon notes that in 2019 researchers published more than 400 papers on the topic.[22] Rather than making permanent alterations to the DNA to alter RNA molecules in cells, RNA-editing could "allow clinicians to make temporary fixes that eliminate mutations in proteins, halt their production or change the way that they work in specific organs and tissues."[23] If RNA-editing proves to be a more safe and effective intervention than genome editing, then the case for "indirect" genetic modification via RNA-editing would trump the ethical case for direct IGM through (irreversible) gene therapy and genome editing.

Gene expression can also be influenced by environmental, behavioral, and pharmacological interventions that do not directly alter genes (but alter gene expression). The "epi" in "epigenetics" is Greek for "above" or "beyond," and it refers to "any process that alters gene activity without changing the DNA sequence, and leads to modifications that can be transmitted to daughter cells (although experiments show that some epigenetic changes can be reversed)."[24]

"Epigenetic mechanisms contribute to the regulation of physiology and disease by changing gene expression, and epigenetic changes occur as a result of the interplay between DNA and environmental factors."[25] Unlike the permanence of direct IGM like gene therapy and genome editing, epigenetics "represents a reversible mechanism in regulating the function of the genome without altering the underlying DNA sequence of the genome."[26] Consider, for example, the impact nutrition, exercise, and stress can have on human health. The food we consume,[27] our physical activity or inactivity,[28] and the stressors of our environments,[29] actually alter the expression of genes which impact both physical and mental health. In the past, before we had a better understanding of the interaction between environment and genes, the prescriptions of diet, exercise, and safe environments were *unintentional* genetically modifying health prescriptions. Such interventions alter the expression of genes to bring about more positive health outcomes, but medical researchers were not aware of the epigenetic mechanisms at play. As our understanding of epigenetics increases and expands, these interventions ought to be construed as forms of (indirect) IGM.

Studies in animal models involving dietary sodium intake suggest epigenetic changes such as DNA methylation might be involved.[30] Sodium intake affects blood pressure, increasing the risks of heart disease, stroke, kidney disease, and so on. While not a form of genetic modification via genome editing, modifying one's diet can alter metabolism and gene expression. If done with the intention of bringing about more favorable health outcomes, I suggest it can be considered a form of (indirect) IGM. So, one form of a morally laudable IGM would be the consumption of a diet that is not excessively high in sodium. In most contexts and for most people, this is likely a safe and inexpensive intervention that could reduce the risks of hypertension. However, this aspiration may be challenging to implement in practice, especially in the long term, given the prevalence of highly processed foods high in sodium. Hence the reason why hypertensive medications are often prescribed, though the compliance rate for such medications is low.[31]

With respect to physical exercise, "numerous studies have reported the influence of exercise on the genome-wide DNA methylation in different tissues including skeletal muscle, adipose tissue and blood."[32] And in experiments on laboratory animals[33] "environmental enrichment" interventions—such as larger than standard cages, mazes, and toys, and so on.—have been shown to improve metabolism, learning and cognition, anxiety and depression, and immunocompetence. While diet, exercise, and environmental enrichment may not, historically, have been pursued with the purposeful intention of modulating the expression of genes, as our knowledge of epigenetics improves, such interventions move from the category of "unintentional" to "intentional" forms of genetic modification.

"Based on the molecular mechanisms underlying cellular senescence and aging, a series of therapeutic strategies, many of which are closely related to epigenetic regulations, have been proposed,"[34] and these should also be construed as other (indirect) forms of IGM. Arguably one of the more promising strategies is the development of what are known as gerotherapeutics, "drugs that target pathways involved in aging with the aim of reducing the burden of aging-related diseases and increasing lifespan and healthspan."[35] Two candidate drugs currently being explored to target aging in humans are metformin and rapamycin. Both of these drugs have been used for decades in the treatment of other conditions. Metformin has been used as a pharmacological intervention to control type 2 diabetes, but it has also been shown to improve both healthspan and lifespan in different animal models.[36] Rapamycin was first developed as a drug to help prevent the rejection of transplanted organs for patients undergoing organ transplant, but it was later discovered that rapamycin could affect aging and age-related diseases in mice.[37] For example, in experiments with rapamycin on mice, researchers found there were "gene expression changes that were similar to potent longevity interventions and were opposite to age-related changes, with males better preserving these effects across the life span."[38] Targeting aging with repurposed drugs, versus experimental genome editing, has two important benefits. The first is that such drugs have been extensively studied in humans for many decades, which means the potential risks of harm are lower. Second, drugs that are off-patent are substantially cheaper to produce, and thus the prospect that such a gerotherapeutic could be a *widely diffused* intervention for the world's aging populations (especially in developing countries) is much higher than the (currently) prohibitive costs of genome editing.

While gerotherapeutics are not a form of direct genetic modification, it is important to recognize that there are other, indirect and reversible, ways of modifying the expression of genes which may be more feasible and ethical to pursue than the direct and irreversible form of (at least still experimental) genome editing.

Germline Modifications and Epigenetic Inheritance

The moral analysis developed so far, with respect to the reasons in favor of pursuing safe and effective forms of both direct and indirect IGM, has been limited to interventions that only impact the biological development of *existing* persons. These types of genetic interventions are called *somatic* interventions; they only change the cells of the person undergoing the procedure (but not *germline* genes, which are passed on to offspring). However, IGM can also influence the biological development of future generations through both germline genetic intervention as well as epigenetic inheritance. Those who do not yet exist obviously cannot consent to having their inherited genetic endowments modified, and so the case of germline genetic modification raises some unique ethical concerns.

In 2018, the first genetically edited babies (twins) were born from a Chinese germline genome editing experiment of embryos. In this experiment the gene CCR5 was disabled; this gene is "a key player in HIV infection due to its major involvement in the infection process."[39] Some rare people are naturally born with this gene disabled, which provides protection against HIV/AIDS. The researcher of the Chinese study, He Jiankui, made international news when he announced the birth of the twins from the experiment—Lulu and Nana (pseudonyms to protect their identity). One child was born with both copies of the gene disabled, meaning they may be highly resistant to HIV. The couples recruited for the experiment were those where the potential father was HIV positive, but the mothers were not. Thus, they were prospective parents who were aware of the stigma of living with HIV. Though, as I explain below, their potential children were not at serious risk of contracting HIV as there are other ways to reduce the risk of transmission that do not involve the risks of experimental germline genome editing of embryos.

The international scientific community condemned the He experiment, with swift calls for a global moratorium on germline genome editing.[40] And He was sentenced to three years in prison for "illegal medical conduct."[41] Most of the moral condemnation of He's experiment took issue with its failure to adequately meet the requirement that there be a reasonable balance between the potential risks and benefits given the number of "unknowns" (e.g., potential "off-target" effects) with heritable genome editing. Furthermore, He experimented on healthy embryos to protect potential children from (what is now) a manageable chronic condition. Some of He's critics worried that the disabled gene could be important for protection against viruses that people would be more likely to encounter in Asia, and thus the experimental intervention might increase some other health risk for the children born from the experiment.[42] Greely argued:

> The healthy adults known to have no functional CCR5 gene are from Northern Europe. They have a different environment, diet, set of microbial exposures, and (to some extent) other human genetic variations than people in China. Is that important? We do not know. And neither does He Jiankui.[43]

Other critics pointed to some empirical findings which suggested that the deletion of the CCR5 gene might shorten lifespan, though the study contending that was subsequently retracted.[44] Nonetheless, the plurality of "unknowns" led many scientists to condemn the experiment for not taking the potential risks seriously enough. Much more research is needed before genome editing of embryos should be considered, especially for embryos where the risk of serious harm to the potential children is low.

Furthermore, while the potential fathers recruited for He's experiment were HIV positive, the risk of father-to-child HIV transmission in IVF is significantly minimized with "sperm washing."[45] In other words, the prospective parents in the experiment would have already reduced the risk of HIV transmission to their offspring with sperm washing alone given they were undergoing IVF. Adding germline genome editing of the embryo simply added risks with minimal expected therapeutic benefits (as the unedited embryos were healthy). Prospective fathers can also reduce their viral load to "undetectable" levels by taking antiretroviral therapy drugs, thus reducing the risks of transmission to their partner and potential offspring.

Finally, while a serious health condition, advances in medical treatment have altered the prognosis of HIV from a fatal infectious disease in the 1980s to a manageable chronic condition today. According to the World Health Organization, "Antiretroviral therapy continues to transform the lives of people living with HIV. People living with HIV who are diagnosed and treated early, and take their medication as prescribed, can expect to have the same health and life expectancy as their HIV-negative counterparts."[46]

Unfortunately, the media headlines and news coverage of He's 2018 germline genome experiment can detract from the compelling moral reasons to (safely and cautiously) explore embryonic genome editing in cases where the risks and benefits may be favorable. Several organizations, like the US National Academies of Sciences, Engineering, and Medicine (NASEM), the American Society of Human Genetics, and UK Nuffield Council on Bioethics have considered the case of germline genetic intervention in embryos and "recommendations from all of these bodies support future clinical trials of human germline genome editing, but only for compelling medical needs, with credible preclinical and clinical evidence on risks and potential health benefits and subject to comprehensive oversight protecting the research subjects and their descendants."[47]

The main reason for considering the pursuit of embryonic germline genetic interventions is that it may overcome a limitation of postnatal somatic gene therapy, namely that the latter intervention often occurs *after* the onset of disease, the harmful effects of which may be irreversible. In utero somatic gene editing may prove to be effective without editing the genetic inheritance of the offspring.[48] However, in cases of inheritable diseases, the additional benefit of a germline intervention is that this could prevent the transmission of a disease gene onto future generations (thus reducing the need for future in utero and postnatal somatic gene editing).

One last consideration to note with respect to direct germline interventions, which may compel us to reevaluate some of the ethical resistance to tolerating any potential risks with direct germline genetic interventions, concerns recent findings from another newly emerging field of study: *epigenetic inheritance*.[49] While still in the early stages of research as a discipline of study, this area of study may compel us to reconsider what constitutes intentional and unintentional forms of germline genetic modification since the line between the two may be blurred as more discoveries of epigenetic inheritance are made.[50]

Traditionally, heritability was thought to be a feature of only the genetic material of an organism (i.e., the passing on of DNA). "However, it is now clear that inheritance not based on DNA sequence exists in multiple organisms, with examples found in microbes, plants, and invertebrate and vertebrate animals."[51] There is mounting evidence that life experience and environment can influence biological alterations in offspring over several successive generations. This means that the health prospects of future generations are influenced not only by the genetic endowments passed on to them but also by the environmental exposures their ancestors experienced, exposures which can alter the expression of the genes of future generations. Evidence for this conjecture comes from studies in both humans and nonhumans.

For example, a study in male mice found that paternal exposure to cocaine prior to coitus resulted in offspring that displayed deficits in sustained attention and spatial working memory (when they bred with females that were drug-free).[52] The study concluded that a potential explanation for why the cognitive functioning of the offspring would be impacted by paternal drug exposure before coitus is that chronic exposure to cocaine may cause brain-changing effects by interfering with the gene-imprinting patterns in male gametes. In other words, specific types of environmental exposure prior to coitus may alter the gene expression of future generations.

In human studies, there is evidence that a paternal grandfather's food access in pre-puberty predicts his male (but not female) grandchildren's all-cause mortality, and Vågerö et al. found that cancer mortality contributes strongly to this pattern.[53] Vågerö et al. contend that their results lend support for the existence of a male-line transgenerational pathway, which means that events during the paternal grandfather's slow growth period trigger mechanisms (the details of which are still not well understood) that influence the cancer risks of their future descendants. And a number of studies have explored how exposure to traumas like the Holocaust may result in the intergenerational transmission of trauma effects, stemming from epigenetic mechanisms.[54, 55]

What studies on epigenetic inheritance reveal is that "germline inheritance" should not simply be equated with "genetic inheritance," and this has significant ethical implications for how we think about the duty to prevent harm and redress health disparities. As Lewens points out, noting that concerns about the ethics of genome editing that can impact future generations apply to many other types of interventions:

> the ethical problems it raises for this technology apply not only to genome editing, but to nutritional advice designed to provoke epigenetic modifications to the germline, and even to urban planning, or to changes in the organization of schooling and specified educational curricula, that are meant to better the lot of future individuals. Here, too, we find interventions whose effects are uncertain, whose effects may also persist over several generations, and to which those affected by the changes—because they may not exist until after these structures have been put in place—cannot consent.[56]

Recent findings from epigenetic inheritance should not alter the importance of ensuring that any potential germline genetic intervention is safe and effective for future generations, but it does require us to acknowledge that life experience and environment also alter the gene expression of future generations, in both potentially beneficial and harmful ways. The latter constitute a form of (unregulated) indirect germline genetic modification, and that should inform our baseline about what constitutes a reasonable level of safety for regulating direct forms of germline modification. As our understanding of the mechanisms affecting epigenetic inheritance expands, so too may our understanding of what constitutes IGM and the potential strategies that are most effective in ameliorating the harms and inequalities of both genetic and non-genetic inheritance.

Conclusion

This chapter has made the provisional case for pursuing the biomedical innovation necessary to make safe and effective IGM more of a reality than it currently is. The moral reasons for aspiring to do so are twofold: (1) genetic inheritance and aging can cause *harm*—for example, disease and other health vulnerabilities; and (2) genetic inheritance also influences *disparities* in health and well-being. The argumentation deployed in this essay also drew attention to the fact that insights from epigenetics compel us to expand our understanding of the moral landscape and what constitutes "genetic modification." Behavior and environment can constitute *indirect* genetic modification by altering the expression of different genes, through exercise, diet, exposure to different types of stress, and so on. So IGM encompasses not only biomedical interventions that edit the human genome but also lifestyle and environmental interventions, as well as pharmacological interventions which alter gene expression (e.g., to target aging itself). As our scientific understanding of the different ways we can influence human health and well-being progresses, so too must our understanding of the moral landscape and the theories of morality and justice advanced by philosophers.[57]

Notes

1. NobelPrize.org. Nobel Prize Outreach AB 2024 (Friday, January 5, 2024) (https://www.nobelprize.org/prizes/chemistry/2020/press-release/).
2. FDA News Release (December 8, 2023) (https://www.fda.gov/news-events/press-announcements/fda-approves-first-gene-therapies-treat-patients-sickle-cell-disease).
3. L. Walters and J. Palmer, *The Ethics of Human Gene Therapy* (New York: Oxford University Press, 1997).
4. S. L. Ginn, A. K. Amaya, I. E. Alexander, M. Edelstein, and M. R. Abedi, "Gene Therapy Clinical Trials Worldwide to 2017: An Update," *Journal of Gene Medicine* 20, no. 5 (2018): e3015.
5. R. Powell and A. Buchanan, "Breaking Evolution's Chains: The Prospect of Deliberate Genetic Modification in Humans," *Journal of Medicine and Philosophy* 36, no. 1 (2011): 6–27.
6. C. N. Z. Mattar, J. K. Y. Chan, and M. Choolani, "Gene Modification Therapies for Hereditary Diseases in the Fetus," *Prenatal Diagnosis* 43, no. 5 (2023): 674–86.
7. B. Childs, *Genetic Medicine: A Logic of Disease* (Baltimore: The Johns Hopkins University Press, 1999), 5.
8. National Human Genome Research Institute, "NIH Funds New Effort to Discover Genetic Causes of Single-gene Disorders" (July 15, 2021) (https://www.genome.gov/news/news-release/NIH-funds-new-effort-to-discover-genetic-causes-of-single-gene-disorders).
9. Powell and Buchanan, "Breaking Evolution's Chains."

10 Centers for Disease Control and Prevention, "What is Fragile X Syndrome?" (https://www.cdc.gov/ncbddd/fxs/facts.html).
11 K. A. McBennett, P. B. Davis, and M. W. Konstan, "Increasing Life Expectancy in Cystic Fibrosis: Advances and Challenges," *Pediatric Pulmonology* 57, Suppl 1 (2022): S5–S12.
12 National Institute on Aging, *Alzheimer's Disease Genetics Fact Sheet* (https://www.nia.nih.gov/health/genetics-and-family-history/alzheimers-disease-genetics-fact-sheet).
13 A. E. Amariutei, J.-Y. Jeng, S. Safieddine, and W. Marcotti, "Recent Advances and Future Challenges in Gene Therapy for Hearing Loss," *Royal Society Open Science* 10 (2023): 230644, at 3.
14 M. L. Hu, T. L. Edwards, F. O'Hare, D. G. Hickey, J. H. Wang, Z. Liu, and L. N. Ayton, "Gene Therapy for Inherited Retinal Diseases: Progress and Possibilities," *Clinical Experimental Optometry* 104, no. 4 (2021): 444–54.
15 W. Chiu, T. Y. Lin, Y. C. Chang, Lai H. Isahwan-Ahmad Mulyadi, S. C. Lin, C. Ma, A. A. Yarmishyn, S. C. Lin, K. J. Chang, Y. B. Chou, C. C. Hsu, T. C. Lin, S. J. Chen, Y. Chien, Y. P. Yang, and D. K. Hwang, "An Update on Gene Therapy for Inherited Retinal Dystrophy: Experience in Leber Congenital Amaurosis Clinical Trials," *International Journal of Molecular Sciences* 22, no. 9 (2021): 4534.
16 T. Kirkwood and S. Austad, "Why Do We Age?" *Nature* 408, no. 9 (2000): 233–8, at 233.
17 Z. D. Zhang, S. Milman, J. R. Lin, S. Wierbowski, H. Yu, N. Barzilai, V. Gorbunova, W. C. Ladiges, L. J. Niedernhofer, Y. Suh, P. D. Robbins, and J. Vijg, "Genetics of Extreme Human Longevity to Guide Drug Discovery for Healthy Aging," *Nature Metabolism* 2, no. 8 (2020): 663–72.
18 T. Perls, C. G. Wager, J. Vijg, and L. Kruglyak, "Siblings of Centenarians Live Longer," *The Lancet* 351, no. 9115 (1998): 1560.
19 M. Rose, *The Long Tomorrow* (New York: Oxford University Press, 2005), 42.
20 Powell and Buchanan, "Breaking Evolution's Chains," 11.
21 National Human Genome Research Institute, "Ribonucleic-Acid (RNA)" (July 15, 2021) (https://www.genome.gov/genetics-glossary/RNA-Ribonucleic-Acid).
22 S. Reardon, "A New Twist on Gene Editing," *Nature* 578 (2020): 24–7.
23 Ibid., 25.
24 B. Weinhold, "Epigenetics and the Science of Change," *Environmental Health Perspectives* 114, no. 3 (2006): A160–A167, at A163.
25 M. Liang, "Epigenetic Mechanisms and Hypertension," *Hypertension* 72, no. 6 (2018): 1244–54, at 1244.
26 K. Wang, H. Liu, Q. Hu, et al., "Epigenetic Regulation of Aging: Implications for Interventions of Aging and Diseases," *Signal Transduction and Targeted Therapy* 7, no. 374 (2022): 1.
27 H. Landecker, "Food as Exposure: Nutritional Epigenetics and the New Metabolism," *Biosocieties* 6, no. 2 (2011): 167–94.
28 G. Wu, X. Zhang, and F. Gao, "The Epigenetic Landscape of Exercise in Cardiac Health and Disease," *Journal of Sport and Health Science* 10, no. 6 (2021): 648–59.

29 K. Gudsnuk and F. A. Champagne, "Epigenetic Influence of Stress and the Social Environment," *ILAR Journal* 53, no. 3–4 (2012): 279–88.

30 S. Kidambi, X. Pan, C. Yang, et al., "Dietary Sodium Restriction Results in Tissue-Specific Changes in DNA Methylation in Humans," *Hypertension* 78, no. 2 (2021): 434–46.

31 S. M. Hamrahian, O. H. Maarouf, and T. Fülöp, "A Critical Review of Medication Adherence in Hypertension: Barriers and Facilitators Clinicians Should Consider," *Patient Prefer Adherence* 16 (2022): 2749–57.

32 Wu, Zhang, and Gao, "The Epigenetic Landscape of Exercise in Cardiac Health and Disease."

33 N. J. Queen, Q. N. Hassan, and L. Cao, "Improvements to Healthspan Through Environmental Enrichment and Lifestyle Interventions: Where Are We Now?" *Frontiers in Neuroscience* 14 (2020): 605.

34 Wang, Liu, Hu, et al., "Epigenetic Regulation of Aging," 10.

35 D. G. Le Couteur and N. Barzilai, "New Horizons in Life Extension, Healthspan Extension and Exceptional Longevity," *Age and Ageing* 51, no. 8 (2022): afac156, at 1.

36 M. G. Novelle, A. Ali, C. Diéguez, M. Bernier, and R. de Cabo, "Metformin: A Hopeful Promise in Aging Research," *Cold Spring Harbor Perspectives in Medicine* 6, no. 3 (2016): a025932.

37 R. Selvarani, S. Mohammed, and A. Richardson, "Effect of Rapamycin on Aging and Age-Related Diseases-Past and Future," *GeroScience* 43, no. 3 (2021): 1135–58.

38 A. V. Shindyapina, Y. Cho, A. Kaya, A. Tyshkovskiy, J. P. Castro, A. Deik, J. Gordevicius, J. R. Poganik, C. B. Clish, S. Horvath, L. Peshkin, and V. N. Gladyshev, "Rapamycin Treatment During Development Extends Life Span and Health Span of Male Mice and *Daphnia magna*," *Science Advances* 16, no. 8(37) (2022): eabo5482, at 6.

39 L. Lopalco, "CCR5: From Natural Resistance to a New Anti-HIV Strategy," *Viruses* 2, no. 2 (2010): 574–600, at 574.

40 E. S. Lander, et al., "Adopt a Moratorium on Heritable Genome Editing," *Nature* 567 (2019): 165–8.

41 D. Cyranoski, "What CRISPR-baby Prison Sentences Mean for Research," *Nature* 577 (7789): 154–5.

42 H. Ledford, "CRISPR Babies: When Will the World be Ready?" *Nature* 570, no. 7761 (2019): 293–6, at 295.

43 H. T. Greely, "CRISPR'd Babies: Human Germline Genome Editing in the 'He Jiankui Affair'," *Journal of Law and the Biosciences* 6, no. 1 (2019): 111–83, at 155.

44 X. Wei and R. Nielsen, "CCR5-Δ32 is Deleterious in the Homozygous State in Humans," *Nature Medicine* 25, no. 6 (2019): 909–10.

45 M. Zafer, H. Horvath, O. Mmeje, S. van der Poel, A. E. Semprini, G. Rutherford, and J. Brown, "Effectiveness of Semen Washing to Prevent Human Immunodeficiency Virus (HIV) Transmission and Assist Pregnancy in HIV-discordant Couples: A Systematic Review and Meta-analysis," *Fertility and Sterility* 105, no 3 (2016): 645–55.e2.

46 World Health Organization, "New WHO Guidance on HIV Viral Suppression and Scientific Updates Released at IAS 2023" (https://www.who.int/news/item/23-07

-2023-new-who-guidance-on-hiv-viral-suppression-and-scientific-updates-released-at-ias-2023).

47 D. P. Wolf, P. A. Mitalipov, and S. M. Mitalipov, "Principles of and Strategies for Germline Gene Therapy," *Nature Medicine* 25 (2019): 890–7, at 895.
48 W. H. Peranteau and A. W. Flake, "The Future of In Utero Gene Therapy," *Molecular Diagnosis & Therapy* 24, no. 2 (2020): 135–42.
49 E. A. Miska and A. C. Ferguson-Smith, "Transgenerational Inheritance: Models and Mechanisms of non-DNA Sequence-Based Inheritance," *Science* 354, no. 6308 (2016): 59–63.
50 T. Lewens, "Blurring the Germline: Genome Editing and Transgenerational Epigenetic Inheritance," *Bioethics* 34, no. 1 (2020): 7–15.
51 Miska and Ferguson-Smith, "Transgenerational Inheritance," 59.
52 F. He, I. A. Lidow, and M. S. Lidow, "Consequences of Paternal Cocaine Exposure in Mice," *Neurotoxicol Teratology* 28, no. 2 (2006): 198–209.
53 D. Vågerö, P. R. Pinger, V. Aronsson, and G. J. van den Berg, "Paternal Grandfather's Access to Food Predicts All-cause and Cancer Mortality in Grandsons," *Nat Communication* 9, no. 1 (2018): 5124. Erratum in: *Nature Communication* 12, no. 1 (1954).
54 R. Yehuda and A. Lehrner, "Intergenerational Transmission of Trauma Effects: Putative Role of Epigenetic Mechanisms," *World Psychiatry* 17, no. 3 (2018): 243–57.
55 N. P. Daskalakis, C. Xu, H. N. Bader, et al., "Intergenerational Trauma is Associated with Expression Alterations in Glucocorticoid- and Immune-Related Genes," *Neuropsychopharmacology* 46, no. 4 (2021): 763–73.
56 Lewens, "Blurring the Germline," 12.
57 C. Farrelly, "How Should We *Theorize* About Justice in the Genomic Era?" *Politics and the Life Sciences* 40, no. 1 (2021): 106–25.

Human Genetic Enhancement: A Bridge Too Far

C. Ben Mitchell

Study Questions

1. What is "genetic diagnosis"? What ethical concerns does it raise?
2. What moral problems does Mitchell think germline modifications have?
3. What is "eugenics"? Why might genetic technologies raise the specter of a new eugenics movement?
4. How does gene enhancement differ from gene therapy? What are the controversial ways that enhancement technology may be used?
5. What moral concern does Mitchell highlight regarding genetic enhancements?
6. Why does Mitchell think proponents of genetic enhancements conflate happiness with flourishing?

Never before in human history has there been more power and promise of altering the human genome than today. New developments in genetic technology have opened doors for the modification of the human genetic blueprint that could not have been imagined when the Augustinian priest, Gregor Mendel (1822–44), began his experiments with pea plants in the nineteenth century.

Remarkably, in 2012, Jennifer Doudna and colleagues published a study in the journal *Science* that effectively revolutionized gene editing.[1] She and one of her colleagues, Emmanuelle Charpentier, subsequently jointly won the Nobel Prize in Chemistry "for the development of a method for genome editing"[2] known by the acronym CRISPR (Clustered Regularly Interspaced Short Palindromic Repeats). According to Michael La Page of *New Scientist* magazine, the method is relatively simple: ". . . it's a way of finding a specific bit of DNA inside a cell. After that, the next step in CRISPR gene editing is usually to alter that piece of DNA. However, CRISPR has also been adapted to do other things too, such as turning genes on or off without altering their sequence."[3] Prior to CRISPR there were other ways of manipulating genes, but CRISPR made the process more efficient, precise, and, therefore, less expensive, and potentially less risky.

CRISPR has already been used to identify pathological genes as well as to develop therapies for a variety of genetically based diseases. Future applications could include editing the genes of human gametes and human embryos to eliminate certain diseases or even to enhance human beings genetically. Like nearly all new technologies, speculations about the future of CRISPR run from the fantastic to the dystopian. This chapter will explore some of the ethical, legal, and social issues that attend human genetic modification.

The Human Genome

Every individual human being is genetically unique. Of course, *Homo sapiens* as a species share many common traits such that we can speak meaningfully about the human genome as the human genetic blueprint. Yet each member of the species is genetically distinct. We are all carbon-based, upright, bipedal psychophysiological life forms, but we each have our own particular genetic information that can be read out on the 20,000–25,000 genes in the thirty trillion or so cells that make up our bodies. Like snowflakes, each one of us is one of a kind. Our genetic legacy has become a cottage industry in American culture. 23andMe, MyHeritageDNA, and LivingDNA are only a few direct-to-consumer genetic test kits that are capitalizing on the popular interest in knowing more about one's genetic background and potential health risks.

The genes inside our body's trillions of cells contain codes for proteins that are responsible for certain phenotypic traits. Today we know, for example, that there are single genes that control the formation of ear lobes, the ability to curl one's tongue, or whether one has a widow's peak at the hairline of the forehead. Most of our genetically linked traits and diseases, however, are multifactorial or polygenic. That is, they are the result of the combination of two or more genes working together to produce either malign traits or sometimes lethal diseases. For instance, two genes (BRCA1 and BRCA2) have been identified as associated with early-onset breast cancer. Women who have mutations in these genes are significantly more likely to develop breast cancer. And it turns out that mutations in these genes in men may increase their risk of developing breast cancer, prostate cancer, and pancreatic cancer.

To much fanfare on April 14, 2003, the International Human Genome Sequencing Consortium announced the successful completion of the Human Genome Project, the mapping of the human genetic blueprint. Since then, physicians and patients increasingly rely on genetic diagnoses to identify the causes of the symptoms patients are experiencing or even to identify pre-symptomatic conditions such as cystic fibrosis, Duchenne's muscular dystrophy, Huntington's chorea, thalassemia, Down syndrome, heart disease, and a growing menu of others.

By some reckonings, there are more than 6,000 known genetic disorders in human beings. But this is a moving target (1) because we are learning more daily about how genes and proteins work (proteomics) in human cells, and (2) because "disorder" is a value-laden term. More about that below.

Genetic Diagnosis

Our ability to diagnose genetic anomalies continues to improve. There are currently four basic methods for detecting genetic conditions:

Carrier testing: A blood test showing whether you or your reproductive partner carry a mutation linked to a genetic disorder. This is increasingly being recommended for everyone considering pregnancy, even if there is no family history of a genetic disease.

Preimplantation genetic diagnosis (PGD): A lab procedure used in conjunction with *in vitro* fertilization (IVF) to detect genetic conditions in an embryo that may code for certain proteins associated with certain traits, positive or negative.

Prenatal screening: A blood test from a pregnant woman that reveals how likely it is that her fetus could have a common chromosomal condition.

Prenatal diagnostic testing: Sampling fluid from the uterus through amniocentesis, doctors can discover whether the developing fetus faces a higher risk for certain genetic disorders such as Down syndrome and spina bifida.

Newborn screening: Sampling a newborn baby's blood from a heel prick within forty-eight hours of birth to detect genetic disorders. Newborn screening is mandatory in the United States for a defined set of genetic diseases, although the exact tests differ from state to state. Newborn screening programs may screen for up to fifty diseases, including phenylketonuria (PKU), sickle cell disease, and hypothyroidism.

Although the information gained through screening can be valuable in helping families anticipate their own needs and the needs of their children, most genetic disorders do not have a cure yet. In some cases, there may be treatments that slow disease progression or lessen their impact on a person's life, but the lack of a remedy leads to what is sometimes referred to as the "diagnosis/therapy gap," the gap in time between being able to diagnose a genetic anomaly and our ability to do anything to alter that anomaly or to provide a treatment to protect against its deleterious effects.

For the foreseeable future, we will have far greater abilities to diagnose genetic conditions than we will have therapies or cures for those conditions. For example, we now know that the mutation associated with Huntington's Disease (HD) is on gene HTT, also known as IT-15. HD can be detected with a simple blood test administered to an adult, child, or even a fetus in the uterus. HD is an ultimately fatal disease that affects the central nervous system. Symptoms include movement disorders, including clumsiness, loss of coordination, and loss of balance. Cognitive problems are typical, including difficulty remembering, keeping track of things, and making decisions. Irritability, depression, and lethargy are common psychological problems. Eventually, the disease results in severe dementia and progressive motor dysfunction, and finally, death.

HD is a late-onset disease, meaning that its symptoms do not usually manifest until a person is in his or her forties or fifties. The diagnostic/therapy gap means that a person could live with the knowledge of his or her diagnosis from even before they were born without any meaningful treatment or hope for a cure on offer. Some people report that they would not want to know their HD status early in their lives for fear that the diagnosis would change the way they live and think about their future. Others say they would want to know.

Genetic Discrimination

Genetic diagnosis raises profound ethical, legal, and social questions. One concern associated with genetic diagnosis is the potential for discrimination. Since an increasing number of genetic conditions will become diagnosable, that information could have profound implications. People worry that the information will affect their life insurance, for example.[4] After all, insurance companies use sophisticated actuarial data to assess risk, including risks of developing debilitating illnesses and death. Data from genetic tests would prove very valuable to life insurers. Even coverage for health care could be impacted, despite a person not being symptomatic. These concerns led the US federal government in 2008 to pass the Genetic Information Nondiscrimination Act (GINA) that makes it illegal to discriminate against someone because of their genetic profile, including in healthcare and employment.[5] Genetic discrimination still exists,[6] however, and that fact increases the urgency to find ways to modify deleterious genetic conditions.

Discrimination extends to human embryos as well. Preimplantation genetic screening and diagnosis provide information that leads to some embryos generated through IVF to not be selected for transfer and ultimately discarded. Typically, in IVF, a dozen or so ova are fertilized in hopes of developing a number of viable embryos for potential transfer. After the embryos develop to the six-to-eight cell stage, they can be biopsied to discover if they have either the desired genes or the undesired genes.

The loss or destruction of human embryos is an important ethical concern. Living human embryos are members of our species *Homo sapiens*. That is precisely why they are so acutely desired by potential parents. Sorting out the ethical obligations we have to other members of our species is a crucial part of protocol and policy in the use of PGD and IVF.[7]

CRISPR may eventually reduce discrimination by making it possible to provide therapeutic gene editing in embryos. In 2017, Shoukhrat Mitalipov, a reproductive and developmental biologist at Oregon Health & Science University in Portland, along with colleagues in California, Korea, and China, developed a CRISPR-based method to remove a genetic mutation in embryos linked to heart failure later in life.[8] Clinical trials are underway using CRISPR to modify genes to eliminate some forms of cancer, blood disorders, eye disease, and several other conditions.

Germline Genetic Alteration

These scenarios point to another significant problem, namely, the problem of altering the human germ cells. Germ cells are the reproductive cells: sperm and egg. Some genetic anomalies are present in either one or both of the reproductive cells. The hope would be that modifying the germ cells would end a heritable disease in a family line by altering the anomaly in some way to prevent it from being passed on to the next generation. This technique has created controversy since it was first hypothesized. Long before the possibility of genetic modification, the late bioethicists Paul Ramsey and Joseph Fletcher engaged in a book-length debate on genetic enhancement in the 1970s in the form of Ramsey's, *Fabricated Man: The Ethics of Genetic Control*, and Fletcher's, *The Ethics of Genetic Control: Ending Reproductive Roulette*. The titles reveal the perspectives taken by each of them.

Although it might prevent future generations of a family from having a particular genetic disorder (e.g., sickle cell anemia or hemophilia), the manipulation of the germ cells might also work in unanticipated ways to create other unforeseeable problems. It is well-known, for instance, that the gene for sickle cell anemia also provides some protection from malaria. Modifying the gene might make future generations more susceptible to contracting malaria. No one really knows at this point, and once the germline has been modified, there is no known way of reversing the procedure. So, what if, instead of making things better, the modification of the germline resulted in acute or even fatal anomalies? What would the recourse look like? Either the genetic modification would have to be reversed before it was passed to the next generation or, somehow, the individuals would have to be prevented from procreating so as not to pass it on.

One of the canons of contemporary medical research is informed consent. Patients are deemed to have a right to make decisions about their own health care, including participation in research protocols. In the United States, parents may offer proxy consent for their children. In research, proxy consent for children is only justifiable when it is given for a living child's well-being and only for his or her benefit. Because the outcomes of the research cannot be predicted accurately and because future children cannot consent to having their genome altered, germline modifications are not funded by federal dollars in the United States. Although there is no regulation that bans germline gene editing conducted through private funding in the United States, any therapies that might result would still have to be approved by the FDA through clinical studies of safety and efficacy before being brought to market.

Germline genetic modification is banned by several other countries, including Australia, Belgium, Denmark, Sweden, France, and others. Art. 5(b) of the United Nations "Universal Declaration on the Human Genome and Human Rights" states that "In all cases, the prior, free and informed consent of the person concerned shall be obtained. If the latter is not in a position to consent, consent or authorization shall be obtained in the manner prescribed by law, guided by the person's best interest." With respect to germline modifications per se, the declaration states that germline interventions "could be contrary to human dignity" (Art. 24).[9] Likewise, the "European Convention for the protection of Human Rights and Dignity of the Human Being with regard to the Application of Biology and Medicine: Convention on Human Rights and Biomedicine" provides that "an intervention seeking to modify the human genome may only be undertaken for preventive, diagnostic or therapeutic purposes and only if its aim is not to introduce any modification in the genome of any descendants" (Art. 13).[10]

Despite these restrictions, in 2018, He Jiankui stunned the world when he announced at a scientific conference that, without appropriate ethical review, he had modified a gene in human embryos that would purportedly confer resistance to HIV. At least three babies were born with this modification, and He and some of his colleagues were convicted for conducting "illegal medical practices" and sentenced to three years in prison.

Although there is no universal support for a complete ban, in 2019, in the wake of the He Jiankui controversy, National Institutes of Health director Francis Collins stated that human germline modification experiments were irresponsible and unethical and called for a five-year moratorium on its use. A significant number of leaders in science, medicine, and ethics, including CRISPR inventor Emmanuelle Charpentier and specialists from seven countries, published a comment in the international journal, *Nature*, calling for a global moratorium on germline editing.[11]

A New Eugenics

Eugenics, the study of the role of genetics in improving the human species through reproductive choice, has had a less-than-stellar history. In early twentieth-century England and America, eugenics was thought to be good science and policy. Under the leadership of social engineers Francis Galton in the UK and Charles Davenport in the US, the eugenics movement was a powerful cultural force. Because it was impossible to modify human genes in the lab, the eugenics movement encouraged better humans through better breeding. In the United States, so-called "Fitter Family" contests were held across the country. A "fit family" was one with few instances of physical or mental disability, at least average IQ, and with marriages within the appropriate ethnic group. Mary T. Watts, founder of the first Fitter Family contest at the Kansas Free Fair in Topeka in 1920, said proudly, "While the stock judges are testing the Holsteins, Jerseys, and whitefaces in the stock pavilion, we are judging the Joneses, Smiths, and Johns."[12]

Even more tragically, so-called "undesirables" were not only discouraged from reproducing, but in many cases mandatorily sterilized without their consent. From 1907 to 1935, eugenically supported sterilizations increased from about 3,000 to over 22,000. By the 1930s, most states had laws supporting mandatory sterilization. In one now famous case in Lynchburg, VA, a young cognitively impaired girl, Carrie Buck (1906–83), was given a "choice" either to be sterilized or return to her asylum. Because both her grandmother and mother had suffered from the same cognitive disability, in the court case, *Buck v. Bell*, the famous jurist Oliver Wendell Holmes declared, "Three generations of imbeciles is enough," ordering that she be sterilized.[13] In 2002, a historical marker was placed to memorialize Carrie Buck and the sad legacy of eugenics.

The power of the new genetic technologies raise the specter of eugenics again. Disability rights activists have long been some of the most vocal opponents of germline genetic modification because of the notion that there are "good genes" and "bad genes" and the question of who decides which is which. For instance, members of the Deaf community argue that deafness is not a disability but a different way of inhabiting the world. As David Ludden explains,

> From the perspective of the hearing majority, deafness is a disability that isolates its sufferers from mainstream society. And yet, that's not the way deaf people view themselves. They certainly understand that they're outsiders in the hearing world, and no matter how good their skills at speaking and lip-reading, they may never completely fit in. But within their Deaf communities, they lead rich and happy lives full of meaningful relationships with others who share the same experiences

and worldview. If the deaf don't see deafness as a disability, why then should the hearing community treat it as one?[14]

Therapy versus Enhancement

Although it is notoriously challenging to locate a bright line between therapy and enhancement, it is possible to distinguish them. Sometimes the argument is made that everyone obviously favors human enhancements. The evidence offered is eyeglasses and hearing assist devices. Of course, a moment's reflection will identify these not as enhancements but therapies that bring one's diminished capacities of sight and hearing up to (hopefully) species-typical norms. Likewise, the use of caffeine or modafinil to help one stay awake and alert is offered as an example. Although these do improve alertness, they do not do so beyond species-typical norms and they have associated side effects that make their overuse harmful. So, they are not enhancements in the way proponents of genetic enhancements generally mean.

Genetic enhancement refers to the aim of augmenting the human genome in such a way as either to enhance one person's species-typical capacities and abilities or, more often, to enhance the entire species *Homo sapiens*. There would be essentially three venues for manipulating human genetics for enhancement. First, scientists might manipulate the human genetic material in germ cells—sperm and egg. We know, for example, that a cleft chin is a single-gene dominant trait passed from one generation to another through normal procreation. That gene could potentially be "turned off" in the germ cell so that trait would stop being expressed at some point in a family line. Likewise, any gene for a desirable trait could be "turned on" in the germ cells so it would more reliably occur in the next generation.

In his volume, *Choosing Children: Genes, Disability, and Design*, Kings College London philosopher-ethicist Jonathan Glover argues that we have a moral obligation to use genetic technology for therapeutic purposes and cannot rule out the possibility of enhancement.[15] Similarly, in *Better Than Human*, Allen Buchanan has written, "Once we appreciate that some enhancements will bring broad social benefits, including increased productivity, we must abandon the comforting assumption that the risk of state-driven eugenics is a thing of the past."[16]

As Nicholas Agar has argued, however, the new eugenics should not be mandated by law as it was in Nazi Germany. It would be, according to the title of one of his books, *Liberal Eugenics*. Liberal eugenics would be a kinder, gentler eugenics encouraged by public opinion, shaming, and through government incentives. Although in a subsequent volume, *Truly Human Enhancement: A Philosophical Defense of Limits*, he recognizes possible abuses, he nevertheless calls for genetic modification to be used to enhance human capacities.

Julian Savulescu and colleagues have not only argued that it is permissible to attempt to enhance human beings but it is also morally obligatory. Cognitive, mood, physical, lifespan, and even moral enhancements should be developed to make better humans, or even make people better than human.[17] Says Savulescu, "Once technology affords us with the power to enhance our children's lives . . . I want to argue that far from being merely permissible, we have a moral obligation or moral reason to enhance ourselves and our children. Indeed, we have the same kind of obligation as we have to treat and prevent disease. Not only can we enhance, we should enhance."[18] Glover, Buchanan, Savulescu, and others do not want only to enhance individual children. That would be, among other things, too labor-intensive. Rather, they want to enhance families of human beings and ultimately the entire species. This would have to be done by manipulating the germline.

Human germline modification is highly controversial and does not receive support through government funding in the United States and other countries. But some jurisdictions, including the UK,[19] are warming to the idea, at least with respect to the therapeutic uses of germline manipulation. In 2015, for instance, UNESCO's International Bioethics Committee called for a moratorium on germline genetic modification stating that "Interventions on the human genome should be admitted only for preventive, diagnostic or therapeutic reasons and without enacting modifications for descendants" because germline modifications "jeopardize the inherent and therefore equal dignity of all human beings and renew eugenics."[20]

Second, the genetic material of a human embryo might be selected or manipulated using CRISPR or some other technology *in vitro*. Oxford philosopher and director of the Future of Humanity Institute, Nick Bostrom, explores this kind of project in his volume, *Superintelligence: Paths, Dangers, Strategies*.[21] For instance, Bostrom writes: "Embryo selection does not require a deep understanding of the causal pathways by which genes, in complicated interplay with environments, produce phenotypes: it requires only (lots of) data on the genetic correlates of the traits of interest."[22] In other words, because some traits are multifactorial—a combination of genetics and environmental factors—it might be difficult to identify the exact origins of something like IQ. But precision is not necessary if what he calls the "genetic correlates" of higher IQ among embryos could be identified through data analysis. So Bostrom maintains that with, say, 1,000 selection cycles, it might be possible to gain 24.3 IQ points among the embryos selected. More sophisticated technologies, Bostrom believes, might result in even better results. Embryonic stem cell selection or synthetic biology might increase the potency and reliability of improving human cognition. One might avoid the manipulation of genetics altogether and move toward brain-computer interfaces, Bostrom speculates, but that would take this chapter in a different direction.

Conclusion

There are good reasons for supporting somatic cell gene research and modification, as long as the canons of informed consent and safety are carefully followed. Those modifications would only affect a single patient, not the genome of an entire family or clan. The potential for biological harm would be mitigated in the same way it is limited in other forms of human subjects research.

Genetic modification for enhancement, however, remains problematic both as a means and end. The means to achieve significant physical, cognitive, and other enhancements would inevitably require germline modification. The ethical problems associated with those applications of genetic engineering have been well documented, including in the excellent work of the US president's Council on Bioethics report, *Beyond Therapy: Biotechnology and the Pursuit of Happiness*.[23] Chaired by Leon R. Kass, MD, the report of the council of medical, legal, scientific, theological, and social experts pointed to manifold potential risks associated with genetic enhancement.

In the report's final section, "'Beyond Therapy': General Reflections," the Council affirms that a wide variety of technologies are being, and increasingly will be, developed for therapeutic purposes. Only later will they be applied for human enhancement. Therefore, it will likely be impossible to consider the subsequent enhancements "piecemeal and independently of one another."[24] Instead, the Council recommends that "we should, as a matter of public understanding, try to see what they might all add up to, taken together."[25] Biotechnology, they opine, deserves to be considered as a whole, not in fragments.

Some of the familiar concerns the Council identifies of emerging biotechnological enhancement, including human genetic enhancement, include (1) issues of health and safety, (2) unfair advantage, (3) equality of access, and (4) freedom from coercion, both overt and subtle. In addition, the Council suggests that there are other essential sources of concern: (1) hubris or humility and respect for "the given," (2) the use of "unnatural" means and the dignity of human activity, (3) identity and individuality, and (4) partial ends and full flourishing. They formulate those concerns in the following way:

- In wanting to become more than we are, and in sometimes acting as if we were already superhuman or divine, we risk despising what we are and neglecting what we have.

- In wanting to improve our bodies and our minds using new tools to enhance their performance, we risk making our bodies and minds little different from our tools, in the process also compromising the distinctly human character of our agency and activity.

- In seeking by these means to be better than we are or to like ourselves better than we do, we risk "turning into someone else," confounding the identity we have acquired through natural gifts cultivated by genuinely lived experiences, alone and with others.

- In seeking brighter outlooks, reliable contentment, and dependable feelings of self-esteem in ways that bypass their usual natural sources, we risk flattening our souls, lowering our aspirations, and weakening our loves and attachments.

- By lowering our sights and accepting the sorts of satisfactions that biotechnology may readily produce for us, we risk turning a blind eye to the objects of our natural loves and longings, the pursuit of which might be the truer road to a more genuine happiness.[26]

These reflections highlight the fact that many of the proponents of genetic enhancement conflate human enhancement with human flourishing. Just because certain human capacities are magnified in no way guarantees human happiness. In fact, many people with a variety of physical, emotional, cognitive, and other challenges often seem to be happier than those without those challenges. That is not meant in any way to diminish the challenges, but to recognize and celebrate the resilience of the human spirit.

Moreover, for many, enhancement is not really the end game. Bostrom, Sanders, Savulescu, Kurzweil, and others have been prophets of *transhumanism*, a movement that aims to use multiple technologies to "liberate" humans from their mortal coil by freeing them from their humanity to become *posthuman*.[27] There is something both philosophically and existentially suspicious about the notion that the best path for human flourishing is to escape our very humanity. For these and other reasons outlined in this chapter, human genetic enhancement is a bridge too far.

Notes

1. Martin Jenik, Krzysztof Chylinski, Ines Fonfara, et al., "A Programmable Dual-RNA–Guided DNA Endonuclease in Adaptive Bacterial Immunity," *Science* 337, no. 6096 (2012): 816–21 (https://www.science.org/doi/10.1126/science.1225829).
2. See https://cen.acs.org/biological-chemistry/gene-editing/CRISPR-genome-editing-2020-Nobel/98/i39. For Doudna's own account of the development of the technique see, Jennifer A. Doudna and Samuel H. Sternberg, *A Crack in Creation: Gene Editing and the Unthinkable Power to Control Evolution* (Mariner Books, 2017: Boston, MA).
3. Michael La Page, "What is CRISPR?" *New Scientist* online (https://www.newscientist.com/definition/what-is-crispr/).
4. Jenny Kleeman, "Why Our Genetic Code Should Remain Off-Limits to Life Insurers," *New Scientist* (March 20, 2024) (https://www.newscientist.com/article/2422777-why-our-genetic-code-should-remain-off-limits-to-life-insurers/).
5. Fact Sheet: Genetic Information Nondiscrimination Act, Issued September 9, 2014 (https://www.eeoc.gov/laws/guidance/fact-sheet-genetic-information-nondiscrimination-act).
6. Yann Joly and Gratien Dalpe, "Genetic Discrimination Still Casts a Large Shadow in 2022," *European Journal of Human Genetics* 30, no. 12 (December 22, 2022): 1320–2.
7. See *Davis v Davis* (1992) in which the Tennessee Supreme Court overruled a district court about the disposition of "spare embryos." The district court decided the case based on custody law, deeming human embryos to be persons. The Tennessee Supreme Court deemed human embryos to be property and made a determination

about the disposition of the embryos using property law (https://law.justia.com/cases/tennessee/supreme-court/1992/842-s-w-2d-588-2.html). In 2024, the Alabama Supreme Court ruled that frozen embryos are children for whom someone should be held accountable for their destruction (https://law.justia.com/cases/alabama/supreme-court/2024/sc-2022-0579.html).

8 Heidi Ledford, "CRISPR Fixes Disease Gene in Viable Human Embryos," *Nature* 548 (2017): 13–14.

9 See https://www.ohchr.org/en/instruments-mechanisms/instruments/universal-declaration-human-genome-and-human-rights.

10 See https://www.coe.int/en/web/conventions/full-list?module=treaty-detail&treatynum=164.

11 Eric Lander, Françoise Baylis, Feng Zhang, Emmanuelle Charpentier, Paul Berg, et al., "Adopt a Moratorium on Heritable Genome Editing," *Nature* 567 (March 13, 2019): 165–8.

12 Steven Selden, "Transforming Better Babies into Fitter Families: Archival Resources and the History of American Eugenics Movement, 1908–1930," *Proceedings of the American Philosophical* Society 149, no. 2 (2005): 199–225.

13 Cf. Paul A. Lombardo, *Three Generations, No Imbeciles: Eugenics, the Supreme Court, and Buck v. Bell* (Johns Hopkins University Press, 2022: Baltimore, MD); Elof Axel Carlson, *The Unfit: A History of a Bad Idea* (Cold Spring Harbor Laboratory Press, 2001: Woodbury, NY); Wendy Kline, *Building a Better Race: Gender, Sexuality, and Eugenics from the Turn of the Century to the Baby Boom* (University of California Press, 2001: Oakland, CA).

14 David Ludden, "Is Deafness Really a Disability? A View from the Deaf Perspective," *Psychology Today* (February 1, 2018) (https://www.psychologytoday.com/gb/blog/talking-apes/201802/is-deafness-really-disability).

15 Jonathan Glover, *Choosing Children: Genes, Disability, and Design* (Oxford University Press, 2008 & amp).

16 Allen Buchanan, *Better Than Human: The Promise and Perils of Enhancing Ourselves* (Oxford: Oxford University Press, 2011).

17 Julian Savulescu, Ruud ter Meulen, and Guy Kahane, eds., *Enhancing Human Capacities* (Wiley-Blackwell, 2011). A helpful commentary on the penchant for enhancement in American culture and medicine is Carl Elliot's, *Better Than Well: American Medicine Meets the American Dream* (W. W. Norton & Company, 2004: Malden, MA, New York).

18 Julian Savulescu, "New Breeds of Humans: The Moral Obligation to Enhance," *Reproductive BioMedicine* 10, Supp I (December 9, 2004): 36–9.

19 Cf., *Genome Editing and Human Reproduction: Social and Ethical Issues* (London, 2018) Nuffield Council on Bioethics.

20 See https://www.unesco.org/en/articles/unesco-panel-experts-calls-ban-editing-human-dna-avoid-unethical-tampering-hereditary-traits.

21 Nick Bostrom, *Superintelligence: Paths, Dangers, Strategies* (Oxford: Oxford University Press, 2014).

22 Ibid., 37.

23 President's Council on Bioethics, *Beyond Therapy* (Washington, DC, 2003). https://bioethicsarchive.georgetown.edu/pcbe/reports/beyondtherapy/fulldoc.html. Although not restricted to genetic technologies, cf. C. Ben Mithcell, Edmund Pellegrino, Jean Bethke Elshtain, John F. Kilner, and Scott B. Rae, *Biotechnology and the Human Good* (Washington, DC: Georgetown University Press, 2007).

24 Biotechnology and the Human Good, 276.

25 Ibid.

26 Ibid., 300.

27 Cf. Calum MacKellar and Trevor Stammers, eds., *The Ethics of Generating Posthumans: Philosophical and Theological Reflections on Bringing New Persons into Existence* (London: Bloomsbury Academic, 2022) and Ray Kurzweil, *The Singularity Is Nearer: When We Merge with AI* (Viking, 2024).

Responses

Response to Farrelly on Human Genome Editing

C. Ben Mitchell

> **Study Questions**
>
> 1. Why does Mitchell think that the issue of informed consent is a serious problem for germline modification?
> 2. Why does Mitchell think that "liberal eugenics" is no less worrisome than the older Statist eugenics?

Colin Farrelly offers an elegant defense of intentional genetic modification (IGM) in his essay. He is surely correct that developments in epigenetics will continue to help scientists refine genetic modification. From my perspective, the troublesome aspects of IGM arise primarily in the arena of germline genetic modification.

Germline Modification and Consent

Farrelly accurately distinguishes between somatic cell genetic modification and germline genetic modification. Our somatic cells are those cells in the body that are exclusive of germ cells or stem cells. Somatic cells reproduce other somatic cells: skin is replaced by skin cells, neurons are replaced by neurons, and old bone cells are replaced by new bone cells, for instance.

Germ cells, however, are totipotent cells that give rise to reproductive cells (sperm and egg) that are passed from one generation to another. Modification performed in somatic cells only impacts the individual in whom those cells are altered. Modification performed in germ cells carries those modifications to offspring indefinitely. As Farrelly points out, one of the ethical concerns raised by germline modification is consent. With somatic cell modification, consent may be given by the patient or, in the case of minors, the parents, to have his or her own cells modified. Though still rare, there are several examples of successful somatic cell genetic therapy.[1] The modification only affects that individual patient. Given appropriate informed consent protocols with evidence of safety and efficacy, this seems to be a promising way forward.

Germline genetic modification presents a more challenging scenario vis-à-vis consent. Lindsay Wiley and colleagues at Wake Forest University Center of Bioethics identify informed consent as one of several major issues in the ethics of human embryo editing via CRISPR-Cas9 technology.[2] Since the modifications will be performed in one generation and passed to the next generation, how can anyone offer meaningfully informed consent for future generations?

Why would informed consent be a cause for concern for future generations? Problems already identified in my original essay should be obvious—such as eugenics, enhancement, and justice concerns. Perhaps most problematic is the potential for harm to future generations from off-target mutations.

Let's assume for the sake of a thought experiment that germline genetic modification is performed on an embryo who is brought to term and delivered as a baby. And let's further assume the modification was performed to provide a therapy for an inheritable condition that would result in health problems later in that person's life (e.g., Huntington's chorea, a neurodegenerative disease that manifests symptoms typically when individuals are in their thirties or forties). What happens, however, if in the effort to provide a therapy, an unintentional, off-target mutation results that is at least as debilitating as the genetic condition being targeted? And what if, worse, it is even more debilitating or potentially lethal? Because this mutation occurs in the germ cell, it will be passed to the next generation through normal human procreation. An entire family and, eventually, possibly an entire clan may suffer from the deleterious effects that are the result of an intentional genetic modification. Agency and culpability loom large here. Who is responsible for subjecting the family or clan to suffering what, as far as anyone could know, would not have occurred if the germline had not been altered? The parents? The research scientists? Moreover, who is responsible for providing compensation for the additional financial and other burdens resulting from intentional germ cell genetic modification?

Additionally, what alternatives would there be to prevent this individual from transmitting this deleterious new genetic condition to his or her offspring and from them to their offspring, ad infinitum? To complicate matters further, the health, emotional, and social burden of the anomaly would not only be borne by the individual, but the individual's family, the community, and the healthcare system.

There is no guarantee that the new anomaly would be reversible. Even if it were, a different anomaly might occur in the next person whose germline is modified. There seems to be no way of ensuring that multigenerational harm could be limited. After all, preventing this deleterious condition from being passed to another generation would require either that the person voluntarily agree not to procreate or that legal authorities resort to the unimaginable options of mandatory sterilization or sequestering the person in some way.

Eugenics Concerns

Even though it seems impossible to imagine a second era of forced sterilization in Western society (so-called Statist eugenics), Nicholas Agar has defended what he describes as liberal eugenics.[3] Agar claims that his eugenics is better understood by what it permits than by what it bans, allowing parents to select the traits of their offspring, and not allowing the state to interfere. Yet, we all know there are third-party and cultural means of restraining the conception of offspring with markers for genetic disabilities. Tax benefits for "healthy" children, insurance penalties for "unhealthy" children, and social stigmatization, while not administered by the government per se, are nevertheless powerful forces. Liberal eugenics may seem kinder and gentler, but it is no less worrisome.

Osagie K. Obasogie is the Haas Distinguished Chair and professor of law at the UC Berkeley School of Law and holds a joint appointment in the Joint Medical Program and School of Public Health. In 2018, he and his colleagues blew the whistle on a $2.4 million project at UC Berkeley to "support research and education on policies, practices and technologies that could 'affect the distribution of traits in the human race,' including those related to family planning, infertility, assisted reproduction technologies, prenatal screening, abortion, gene editing and gene modification."[4] This revelation and Obasogie's "Legacies of Eugenics" project are powerful reminders of the persistence of a eugenic mindset in American culture.[5] Whether it is Statist or liberal, the history of the American eugenics movement must not be allowed to repeat itself.

Germline genetic modification seems to be a classic case in which the ends do not justify the means.

Notes

1. Saeideh Razi Soofiyani, et al., "Gene Therapy, Early Promises, Subsequent Problems, and Recent Breakthroughs," *Advanced Pharmaceutical Bulletin* 20, no. 2 (2013): 249–55 (https://pmc.ncbi.nlm.nih.gov/articles/PMC3848228/).
2. Lindsay Wiley, et al., "The Ethics of Human Embryo Editing via CRISPR-Cas9 Technology: A Systematic Review of Ethical Arguments, Reasons, and Concerns," *HEC Forum* (September 20, 2024) (https://doi.org/10.1007/s10730-024-09538-1).
3. Nicholas Agar, *Liberal Eugenics: In Defence of Human Enhancement* (Malden: Blackwell, 2004).
4. Teresa Watanabe, "UC Berkeley s Disavowing Its Eugenic Research Fund after Bioethicist and Other Faculty Call It Out," *Los Angeles Times* (October 26, 2020) (https://www.latimes.com/california/story/2020-10-26/uc-berkeley-disavows-eugenics-research-fund).
5. Osagie K. Obasogie, "Legacies of Eugenics: An Introduction," *Los Angeles Review of Books* (April 17, 2024) (https://lareviewofbooks.org/article/legacies-of-eugenics-an-introduction/).

A Response to Mitchell on Human Genome Editing

Colin Farrelly

Study Questions

1. How does Farrelly characterize Mitchell's methodological approach? What alternative does Farrelly favor?
2. Why does Farrelly reject "bioconservatism"?
3. What does Farrelly think will be the most significant biomedical innovation in the near future? Why is this topic the biggest point of disagreement with Mitchell?

Peter Medawar, who won the Nobel Prize in Medicine in 1960, argued that scientific reasoning consists of a dialogue between two voices.[1] One voice he called *the imaginative*, the other the voice of *the actual*. The first voice represents "the possible," and as such it endorses the spirit of proposal and conjecture concerning what might be true. By contrast, the conservative voice endorses what currently is "in fact the case." Within bioethics, many of the debates between proponents and critics of biomedical "enhancement" mirror this same type of debate between "the imaginative" and "the conservative."

Taken to an extreme, I think appeals to imagination and conservatism are both problematic. To ascertain what constitutes the judicious "middle ground" between "the imagined" and "the actual" is, I believe, the authentic orientation of *epistemic* and moral *virtue* and is not something that can be determined in the abstract. Instead, it necessitates undertaking the careful and painstaking work of determining the specific benefits and risks associated with any particular type of biomedical innovation, including new potential enhancements. An inquisitive and "attentive to the relevant facts and details" approach to bioethical debates often results, at best, in *provisional normative conclusions* as one may need to revise judgments and recommendations as new empirical discoveries and moral insights are made.

I suspect there are many issues Mitchell and I agree on when it comes to the ethics and regulation of new biomedical technologies, such as the importance of safety and accessibility. But I will focus my comments here on what I perceive as potential points of disagreement concerning biomedical enhancements.

A Methodological Disagreement

Unlike Mitchell, who applauds the approach taken by the US president's Council on Bioethics report *Beyond Therapy: Biotechnology and the Pursuit of Happiness* for its attempt to assess biotechnology "as a whole" (rather than assessing it in fragmented parts), I find such a methodology inherently problematic. The risks and potential benefits of any type of enhancement should be considered on the merits and demerits of each specific case, rather than lumped into the general category of "enhancements" that is then assessed in the abstract.

Respect for the "Given"?

Michell also applauds the Report's recommendation that we should have respect for "the given" and be concerned about "means that are unnatural." Such sentiments, which are expressive of the viewpoint commonly referred to as "bioconservatism," have, in my estimation, impoverished rather than enhanced the quality of public deliberations and debates about biomedical enhancement. As a political ideology or moral temperament, conservatism encourages appreciation for "what is available rather than wish for or look to something else: to delight in what is present rather than what was or may be."[2] Michael Oakeshott contends that this temperament prefers "the familiar to the unknown," "the tried to the untried," "fact to mystery," "the actual to the possible," "the near to the distant," "the sufficient to the abundant." Is such a stance a helpful or desirable one to take with respect to biomedical innovation? Since conservatives emphasize the wisdom we can learn from history, I suggest we consider some historical examples.

Perhaps the most significant "biomedical enhancements" developed to date are vaccinations. Immunization against smallpox, diphtheria, tetanus, pertussis, polio, measles, mumps, rubella, and Covid-19 all constitute "enhancements" to the human immune system rather than "treatments for disease." Immunizations help improve population health by reducing the risks of infection and/or reducing the severity and mortality risks from infection. It is part of "normal species functioning" for humans to be vulnerable to the over 1,400 infectious organisms[3] that cause disease. This is "the given" of evolution by natural selection in a world full of extrinsic mortality hazards. Luckily for humanity, infectious disease researchers imagined that it would be possible to enhance the human immune system, and in doing so helped reduce our susceptibility to infectious disease fatality (especially in early life).

Many people hold anti-vaccination attitudes and the reasons for doing so are varied, but some echo the worries expressed by bioconservatives in opposition to biomedical enhancements. In their study of vaccination attitudes, for example, Martin and Petrie[4] found four distinct attitudes expressed among those who opposed vaccination:

(1) mistrust of vaccine benefit,

(2) worries about unforeseen future effects,

(3) concerns about commercial profiteering, and

(4) preference for natural immunity.

Eschewing scientific innovations one takes to be "unnatural" is a way to prime the intuitions behind worry (2), while appeals to appreciating "the given" can amplify anti-vaccination attitudes which invoke attitude (4). Indeed, appeals to the gift of "the given" were commonly invoked to rationalize the historically high rates of infant and child mortality from infectious disease. In his 1903 article entitled "The War Against Disease," C.-E. A. Winslow (1877–1957)—the first chairperson of Yale University's School of Public Health—noted that many of his contemporaries believed that plagues and pestilences were "a merciful provision on the part of Providence to lessen the burden of the poor man's family."[5] Improving sanitation and boosting the human immune system through vaccinations may strike some as "unnatural" and an expression of disregard for "the gift of keeping a poor man's family small," but we now view such sentiments as archaic and an obstacle to critically important health innovations. If new, safe biomedical enhancements are developed, either through deploying gene editing or drugs that mimic the effects of gene mutations, I suspect future generations will view the conclusions of the *Beyond Therapy Report* in a similar light.

I believe that the most feasible and significant biomedical innovation likely to be developed in the foreseeable future is *gerotherapeutics*: "drugs that target pathways involved in aging with the aim of reducing the burden of aging-related diseases and increasing lifespan and healthspan."[6] Some may perceive intervening in aging to be "unnatural" and something that threatens our appreciation for "the given." For example, the theory that aging is a programmed trait that is beneficial to the species has intuitive appeal to many. In 1891, August Weismann espoused such a view, contending that aging was a programmed trait that was beneficial to the species:

> To put it briefly, I consider that duration of life is really dependant upon adaptation to external conditions, that its length, whether longer or shorter, is governed by the needs of the species, and that it is determined by precisely the same mechanical process of regulation as that by which the structure and functions of an organism are adapted to its environment.[7]

The programmed theory of aging has been refuted by insights in biogerontology,[8] but the view persists as "folkbiology." This means it forms part of the "everyday understanding of the biological world that contains "rudimentary" or "inchoate" elements of more sophisticated scientific concepts."[9] If aging truly served as a general mechanism for population control, we would expect to observe more senescent animals in the wild, and there would be ample opportunity to see this mechanism in action, as senescence should be an obvious and widespread killer.[10] But this is not the case.

In *The Case Against Perfection: Ethics in the Age of Genetic Engineering*, Michael Sandel, a key member of the *Beyond Therapy Report*, argues that a quest to perfect our biology "threatens to banish our appreciation of life as a gift, and to leave us with nothing to affirm or behold outside of our own will."[11] There is some common ground between my stance and that of Sandel (and I suspect Mitchell's) in that I do believe certain aspirations or "communicative frames" championed by some "pro-longevity science" proponents can be unhelpful and even harmful. Frames that pathologize chronological aging (e.g., suggestions that aging be classified as a disease), or that catastrophize population aging and perpetuate ageism, or marginalize the benefits often associated with more time and experience in life (such as wisdom, gratitude, resilience, etc.) are ones I consider problematic. Population aging is a major *success story*, only made possible because of dramatic decreases in the historically high rates of early and mid-life mortality. One can be "pro" biomedical enhancement AND have appreciation for "the given." But when it comes to "biological aging," the reality of "the given" is that evolution by natural selection has left people at high risk of multi-morbidity, frailty, and disability in late life. And if medical science can help us redress these vulnerabilities, I believe there are compelling reasons for doing so.

Methodology Again

My focus on an aging drug reveals perhaps the biggest point of disagreement between my stance and Mitchell's—the contention that "enhancements" can, and ought to be, assessed as a whole. For me, the devil is really in the details. The societal benefits of reducing disease, frailty, and disability in late life through interventions that extend healthy lifespan are quite different from those that may be achieved via cognitive enhancement or interventions that modulate mood or "human nature." I think each specific type of enhancement must be assessed on its own merits/demerits. To simply group so varied a range of interventions into one grand meta-normative analysis risks activating intuitions or knee-jerk emotive responses rather than attentive judgments reached via consideration of the relevant benefits and harms at stake in each distinct case of biomedical enhancement.

Notes

1. P. Medawar, "Science and Literature," *Perspectives in Biology and Medicine* 12 (1969): 529–46.
2. M. Oakeshott, *Rationalism in Politics and Other Essays* (Indianapolis: Liberty Fund, 1991), 408.
3. L. Taylor, et al., "Risk Factors for Human Disease Emergence," *Philosophical Transactions of the Royal Society of London B* 356 (2001): 983–9.
4. L. R. Martin and K. J. Petrie, "Understanding the Dimensions of Anti-Vaccination Attitudes: The Vaccination Attitudes Examination (VAX) Scale," *Annals of Behavioral Medicine* 51, no. 5 (2017): 652–60 (https://doi.org/10.1007/s12160-017-9888-y).
5. C. E. A. Winslow, "The War Against Disease," *Atlantic Monthly* 91 (1903): 43–52, at 42.

6   D. G. Le Couteur and N. Barzilai, "New Horizons in Life Extension, Healthspan Extension and Exceptional Longevity," *Age and Ageing* 51, no. 8 (2022): afac156, at 1.
7   A. Weismann, E. B. Poulton, S. Schoenland, and A. E. Shipley, *Essays upon Heredity and Kindred Biological Problems* (Oxford: Clarendon Press, 1891), 9.
8   A. Kowald and T. B. L. Kirkwood, "Can Aging Be Programmed? A Critical Literature Review," *Aging Cell* 15, no. 6 (2016): 986–98 (https://doi.org/10.1111/acel.12510).
9   D. Medin and S. Atran, *Folkbiology* (Cambridge, MA: MIT Press, 1999).
10 T. B. Kirkwood and S. Melov, "On the Programmed/Non-programmed Nature of Ageing Within the Life History," *Current Biology* 21, no. 18 (2011): R701–R707 (https://doi.org/10.1016/j.cub.2011.07.020).
11 M. Sandel, *The Case Against Perfection: Ethics in the Age of Genetic Engineering* (Cambridge, MA: Harvard University Press, 2007), 99–100.

Questions for Reflection

1. One concern with genome editing is the prospect of "designer babies" (parents selecting for personally or socially desirable enhancements for their children). What, if anything, is morally problematic about this?

2. How might Farrelly respond to the potential problem of "off-target" mutations that Mitchell emphasizes?

3. Would allowing gene enhancement lead to a two-tiered society in which the unenhanced are discriminated against? Would such a society be morally problematic? Why?

For Further Reading

Baer, Neal. *The Promise and Peril of CRISPR*. John Hopkins University Press, 2024.
Baylis, Francoise. *Altered Inheritance: CRISPR and the Ethics of Human Genome Editing*. Harvard University Press, 2019.
Davies, Kevin. *Editing Humanity: The Crispr Revolution and the New Era of Genome Editing*. Pegasus Books, 2020.
Glover, Jonathan. *Choosing Children: Genes, Disability, and Design*. Oxford University Press, 2008.
National Academies of Sciences, Engineering, and Medicine. *Human Genome Editing: Science, Ethics, and Governance*. The National Academies Press, 2017.
Sandel, Michael J. *The Case Against Perfection: Ethics in the Age of Genetic Engineering*. Harvard University Press, 2007.
Walters, LeRoy, and Julie Gage Palmer. *The Ethics of Human Gene Therapy*. Oxford University Press, 1997.

5

The Right to Health Care

Stability, Liberty, and the Right to Health Care

Robert C. Hughes

> **Study Questions**
>
> 1. Why does Hughes think that social stability depends on citizens having the right to universal health care?
> 2. Why does Hughes think that unequal access to health care presents a threat to liberty?
> 3. According to Hughes, if the government provided universal health care, why would people's dependence on the decisions of doctors and government officials *not* be a serious threat to liberty?
> 4. How does the importance of social stability lead to a *right* to health care?
> 5. How does the importance of liberty lead to a *right* to health care?

Many countries' governments guarantee all citizens access to health care, either by providing public health care, by providing a public health insurance plan, or by subsidizing private health insurance for low-income citizens. In some of these countries, the quality of universally provided health care is high. In others, health care provided or paid for by the government is basic, and people generally prefer to get privately provided health care or private health insurance if they can afford it. Still other countries, notably including the United States, do not guarantee universal access to health care, even at a basic level. Is this variety of policies a morally permissible reflection of different countries' cultures, resource limitations, and priorities? Or is failure to provide health care equally to all citizens a violation of a moral right?

This essay will argue that everyone who lives in a society that has law and government has a moral right to health care. The moral right to health care is a right against one's government. The government has a moral duty to provide health care to its citizens and its long-term residents. Moreover, the government has a duty to provide medically necessary treatment on an equal basis. It must ensure that citizens' and long-term residents' ability to get the medical treatment they need does not depend on their ability to pay. Others have defended a right to universal health care on grounds of justice.[1] People disagree intensely, and perhaps intractably, about what justice requires. Instead of relying on the deeply contested concept of justice, this essay will defend a right to health care based on two other values: the value of social stability and the value of liberty.[2] A government's failure to provide equal access to health care creates a constant threat to social order and to citizens' freedom.

Health Care and Social Stability

If a country's government does not provide universal, equal access to medical treatment, there will be many people who cannot get the medical treatment they need. People who need medical treatment cannot always get it through work. Many jobs do not provide health insurance that covers everything workers and their families need, nor do they pay enough for workers to be able to cover health care costs out of pocket. Many people who need medical treatment are unable to work. (Sickness tends to get in the way of work.) Sometimes people who need medical treatment and cannot afford it are able to get the treatment they need through charitable aid, either from a loved one or from an organization. Many cultures have social norms requiring people to help close relatives in need, and many cultures encourage generosity toward strangers, either by giving directly to the needy or through charitable organizations. Nevertheless, charity is unreliable. People who need expensive medical treatment and do not have wealthy relatives cannot count on getting the financial help they need from strangers. When people cannot get the treatment they or their families need through work or through charity, they will face a difficult decision about whether to get health care through ethically problematic means.

The psychologist Lawrence Kohlberg told a story about someone who chose to get medical treatment for a loved one through theft. Kohlberg wrote this story as part of an interview designed to study how children and teenagers reason about difficult moral questions. The story was first published in 1963, when $2,000 was a much more valuable sum than it is today.

> In Europe, a woman was near death from a special kind of cancer. There was one drug that the doctors thought might save her. It was a form of radium that a druggist in the same town had recently discovered. The drug was expensive to make, but the druggist was charging ten times what the drug cost him to make. He paid $200 for the radium and charged $2000 for a small dose of the drug. The sick woman's husband, Heinz, went to everyone he knew to borrow the money, but he could only get together about $1000 which is half of what it cost. He told the druggist that his

wife was dying and asked him to sell it cheaper or let him pay later. But the druggist said: "No, I discovered the drug and I'm going to make money from it." So Heinz got desperate and broke into the man's store to steal the drug for his wife. Should the husband have done that?[3]

Kohlberg used this story to study moral reasoning because it raises a difficult moral question. People disagree about whether Heinz was justified in stealing the drug to save his wife. It is reasonable to think that Heinz's theft was justified. Heinz faces a conflict between two moral duties: the duty to save his wife and the duty to respect property law.

In a society that makes medical care available on the basis of ability to pay, many people will face similarly conflicting duties. Some religious traditions and some influential moral theories (such as Kantian ethics) hold that there is a moral duty of self-preservation. On this view, it is morally important to try to maintain one's own health. To neglect a serious, treatable illness rather than seeking treatment for it would show a culpable lack of self-respect. Some people doubt that there are any self-regarding duties. Even if all moral duties are duties to other people (not to oneself), people clearly have moral duties to protect their loved ones. Parents have moral duties to protect their children, for instance. Married people and other people in committed relationships have a duty to protect their spouses or partners. If one's child, spouse, or partner needs medical treatment, one should help them get the treatment they need. Sometimes the only way to help a loved one get the treatment they need may be to steal medicine or the money to pay for it. Perhaps more commonly, it may sometimes be possible to help a relative get needed treatment only by taking out a loan one knows one will not be able to repay. It is normally wrong to make a promise knowing one cannot keep it.[4] Unequal access to health care forces some people to choose between neglecting the health of their loved ones and engaging in other ethically problematic conduct, such as stealing or making insincere promises.

Unequal provision of health care presents a threat to social stability. One component of social stability is the reasonable expectation that legally defined rights to resources will be widely respected. Thefts occur in every human society, as do breaches of promises to repay debts. In a stable society, people can reasonably expect theft and breach of contract to be rare. This expectation is reasonable in two senses. First, theft and breach of contract, such as nonpayment of debt, will rarely occur. Second, theft and breach of contract will rarely be justified.

In a society with unequal provision of health care, it will be typically unreasonable in both senses to expect property rights and contractual rights to be widely respected. First, it is likely that many people will pay for their own medical care or their loved ones' medical care by taking out loans they do not expect to be able to repay, and it is not unlikely that some needy people will resort to theft or to other forms of lawbreaking. Wealthy people and organizations are likely to turn to harsh methods of debt collection and draconian forms of law enforcement to protect their resources from the needy.

Second, in a society with unequal provision of health care, people morally ought to find it tempting to make insincere promises or even to steal. Helping loved ones to obtain medical care they need is a moral duty, and if theft or insincere promising is the only way to provide this help, there is a moral reason to engage in this problematic conduct. Whether or not theft or insincere promising is justified, all things considered, it ought to be at least a temptation. A society in which people morally ought to be tempted to break important laws and social norms is a society with a serious problem.

Universal provision of health care within a society reduces or eliminates this threat to social stability. To the extent that health care is provided to everyone, regardless of ability to pay, people will have no reason to steal or to make insincere promises to obtain health care for themselves or their loved ones. There is thus a clear reason of social stability for government to provide at least basic medical care to everyone who needs it.

Unfortunately, it is often impossible to provide all medically necessary treatment to everyone who needs it. When a medical resource is inherently limited (such as organs for transplant), it will enhance social stability to ensure that people's finances do not affect their access to this resource. When there are economic obstacles to providing all the medical treatment people need, government faces a difficult choice: Should it allow people to purchase access to expensive medical treatment, or should it take some expensive treatments off the market even though some people need them? No doubt the answer should depend partly on how private availability of expensive treatment will affect people's health. Allowing a private market for expensive treatment will enable some people to get what they need, but it may reduce the availability of necessary treatment for others (e.g., because doctors choose to do less work for the public system and more work for private patients). There is another reason to limit the availability of expensive treatment on the private market: the possibility of paying for expensive but necessary medical treatment creates a temptation to pay for treatment through insincere promises to pay, through theft, or through other forms of lawbreaking or breach of contract.[5]

Social stability thus gives everyone an interest in the equal provision of medical treatment within their society. It is not only the sick and the financially less well-off who have this interest. Rich, healthy people also have an interest in the equal provision of health care. Their property rights and their contractual rights are more secure if everyone can meet their needs and their loved ones' needs without breaking laws or breaching contracts. When it is impossible to give everyone the health care they need when they need it, it benefits everyone (including the rich) to ensure that the ability to pay does not affect people's access to the care they need.

Health Care and Liberty

Inequality in access to health care also presents a threat to liberty. If access to medical care depends on financial resources, some people's ability to get things they genuinely need without violating social norms (e.g., by breaking the law or by making insincere promises) will depend on whether other people feel like being generous. Needy people who are either unwilling or unable to meet needs by violating social norms will be dependent on others' generosity. People who are dependent on generosity for the satisfaction of basic needs are unfree.

Consider a person who has fallen on hard times and cannot put a roof over his head. Whether because of a bad job market, a disability, or some other form of bad luck, he has been unable to find work that pays enough to cover rent. He lacks sufficient coverage from unemployment insurance or disability insurance, and public aid is unavailable to him. The only way to avoid being homeless is to live with a relative. Since he is a guest, not a tenant, the relative is legally free to kick him out of the house at any time and for any reason. The relative will be able to make demands on the guest and to impose rules. The host's demands may be eminently reasonable, they may be misguided attempts at paternalism, or they may be arbitrary. In any case, the guest will have to comply with these demands on pain of homelessness. Because the guest is subject to the relative's rules and dependent on the relative's good opinion, the indigent guest is not truly free.

Likewise, if someone is sick and can get necessary health care only if a wealthier relative pays for it, the dependent patient is unfree. A relative who pays for health care is perhaps less likely to attach rules or conditions to this aid than a relative who takes in an indigent guest. (The burden of having a guest is more than financial, and trying to force an indigent guest to find work that pays well is perhaps more likely to seem worthwhile than trying to force a medical patient to find a new job with good insurance.) Nevertheless, a patient whose access to health care depends on one individual's generosity is vulnerable because the benefactor has the power to take away what the patient needs. This vulnerability undermines the patient's freedom even if the benefactor is highly likely to provide financial help without attaching conditions.

Perhaps some readers will doubt that the patient receiving financial help from a relative is unfree. The patient appears to be free in two important senses. First, no one (including the generous relative) is actively preventing the patient from getting the treatment they need, nor is anyone threatening to prevent the patient from getting the treatment they need. The absence of coercive interference is one kind of freedom (sometimes called "negative freedom"). Second, the patient is in fact able to get what they need. The ability to do what one needs or wants to do is an important kind of freedom (sometimes called "positive freedom"). But there is a third kind of freedom the patient lacks. The patient is unfree *because they are subject to someone else's goodwill.*

The civic republican and Kantian traditions in political philosophy both explain why non-domination, or freedom from subjection to others' will, is a distinct and important form of freedom. A standard example these traditions use to distinguish non-domination from other forms of freedom is the example of the privileged slave.[6] Imagine that a wealthy landowner in ancient Rome decides to give one of his slaves permission to do whatever the slave likes. The slave is now able to do many things, including some things people who are legally free but less well-off cannot do. The slave's choices are not currently constrained by force or by threats of penalties. Yet the slave has not been freed, since the landowner can withdraw the grant of permission at any time and for any reason. As another example, offered by Elizabeth Anderson, consider the king's favorite courtiers in an absolute monarchy.[7] Being the king's favorites, they can do many things other people cannot do. Their choices are not currently constrained by force or threats. (Even the threats embodied in criminal law may not constrain them if it is understood that the king likes these courtiers so much that he would pardon them for any crime.) Yet the king could throw the courtiers in the dungeon on a whim. The courtiers enjoy some important forms of freedom, but because everything they do is subject to the king's goodwill, they are in an important sense unfree. They are subject to the king's domination.

A patient whose access to life-saving medical care depends on another individual's generosity is not thereby a slave or a subject. Still, they are vulnerable to their benefactor's continued goodwill in much the same way as the relatively privileged slave or the favored courtier. What about the patient whose access to medical care depends on the generosity of a group, rather than an individual benefactor? If the patient raises money for health care through crowdfunding, the small donors who contribute will not be able to attach conditions to their gifts in the way that a sole benefactor can attach conditions to a gift. Nevertheless, the patient's access to needed health care will still depend on the whims of donors. The patient will be vulnerable to strangers' emotional reactions to their illness, to their need, and to the way they publicly present themselves and their plight. Dependence on the whims of strangers for the satisfaction of a basic need makes one unfree.

Universal provision of health care addresses this threat to freedom. Suppose the government ensures that citizens' and residents' access to health care does not depend on their ability to pay. Then patients' ability to get health care they need will not depend on the whims of any private donor or any group of private donors. Their ability to get health care will still depend on other people's choices, in three ways. First, they will not be able to get most forms of medical treatment and most other medical interventions (e.g., vaccines) unless a medical professional judges the treatment or other intervention is suitable for them. Second, public officials (potentially including both legislators and executive branch officials) will make decisions about what the public health care system or the public insurance system will cover. If the government ensures equal access to medical treatment by subsidizing the purchase of private insurance, public officials will make decisions about what subsidized private insurance plans are required to cover. Finally, the overall level of funding for the system depends on choices of the legislature, as does the continued existence of the system.

These forms of dependence on others' choices do not threaten freedom in the same way as dependence on the goodwill of donors. Donors are legally free to decide whether to give or to withhold aid however they like. There may be a strong social expectation that wealthy people will help family members in need, but in most societies, aid to strangers (and acquaintances) is both socially and legally discretionary. A potential donor need not give a reason for choosing to withhold aid from a particular person or organization; the decision whether to donate can be made on a whim. By contrast, a doctor's decisions about providing treatment may be judgment calls, but they are not discretionary. Strong legal and social norms prohibit doctors from making treatment decisions on a whim, and doctors can be held to account for making decisions that depart from professional standards. Likewise, an executive branch agency's decisions about what insurance will cover are subject to legislative oversight and perhaps also to review by the courts. A legislature's decisions about funding levels and coverage requirements for public insurance may be discretionary in the sense that there is no constitutional requirement to maintain funding. Still, in a moderately well-functioning democracy, even one that departs significantly from the ideal, there will be public pressure for legislators to explain major policy changes. Social norms will not allow radical policy changes to be made on a whim.

Dependence on the judgment calls of doctors, executive branch officials, and legislators can undeniably be problematic. Because all three forms of dependence have an associated accountability mechanism, they do not present the same power asymmetry or the same deep threat to freedom as dependence on private donors' whims. If one's access to medical care or other necessities depends on private donors' goodwill, one is dominated by one's potential benefactors. One is therefore unfree. Thus, government can protect people's freedom by providing a guarantee that everyone will have access to a broad range of medical services, regardless of ability to pay.

Again, resource constraints sometimes make it impossible for everyone to get the medical treatment they need when they need it. For government to prevent citizens' finances from affecting their access to needed health care, public funding of health care for the less well-off will not be enough. It will also be necessary to limit private markets for health care and health insurance. There is a trade-off here among the three kinds of freedom discussed earlier. Limiting health care markets limits what financially better-off people can do with their money (a component of their positive freedom). If the limits on markets are coercively enforced, these limits also reduce negative freedom. By preventing people from becoming dependent on private charity for their health care needs, limits on health care markets protect people from domination. There is a difficult balance to strike here. If Kantians and civic republicans are right to identify non-domination as the most important form of freedom, then limits on health care markets are freedom-enhancing.

There is no such difficult balance to strike where the government's decision to provide universal health care is concerned. Providing health care to all citizens and long-term residents protects people from domination. It increases the positive freedom of the financially less well-off by enabling them to get health care they otherwise could not have gotten. It may reduce the positive freedom of wealthier people who face higher taxes. But wealth has diminishing marginal utility: "a gain of one thousand ducats is more significant to a pauper than to a rich man though both gain the same amount."[8] Thus, taxes that fund a public health care system enhance positive freedom overall unless they are so burdensome that they substantially reduce society's aggregate wealth. If tax law and property law are both coercively enforced, changes in tax law (or property law) that affect the distribution of wealth do not affect the amount of coercion in society and thus do not reduce negative liberty.[9] So universal health care, funded via taxation, enhances people's liberty overall.

From Stability and Liberty Interests to a Right

The argument so far shows that a government's failure to secure equal access to health care is bad in two ways. It undermines social stability by creating an incentive for people to seek health care through theft or through insincere promises to repay debts. It also makes sick and financially less well-off citizens and residents unfree by making their ability legally to obtain health care dependent on the goodwill of potential donors. This section will explain why people's interests in social stability and liberty ground a governmental duty to provide health care and a corresponding right that it be provided. The stability-based argument will be presented first and in more detail.

The Stability-Based Argument

The first step is to recognize governments' role in making needy people vulnerable to private resource owners' discretionary decisions. Governments do this in several ways. Most obviously, governments decide whether to provide a social safety net and how strong that safety net will be. For example, governments decide whether to provide universal health insurance and, if not, whether to provide free or subsidized health insurance coverage to people who are financially struggling. Governments also influence needy people's vulnerability by making policy choices that influence the overall distribution of wealth. For example, tax law influences both society's overall level of wealth and how much wealth inequality there is. These features of the economy in turn affect the likelihood that patients in need of expensive care they cannot afford will be able to get care through charity, and whether they will be dependent on a small pool of potential donors.

Perhaps less obviously, the moral duty not simply to take what one needs is largely a product of law and government. There may be a universal moral duty not to steal, but law determines what counts as stealing. Most of the forms of property that account for differences in wealth owe either their existence or their legitimacy to the law. Money and financial instruments, such as stocks and bonds, are creations of the legal system. It is only possible to buy or lease real estate because governments record land ownership and determine the conditions under which land may be acquired and transferred. Law also determines when, if ever, people may use other people's resources without getting permission. Many legal systems allow for a right of necessity under limited circumstances. For instance, in the United States, a ship may dock during a dangerous storm without the dock owner's permission, though the ship owner will owe the dock owner compensation for any damage to the dock.[10] Governments could choose to grant a wider right of necessity and to excuse people like Heinz who resort to theft to obtain medical care for a family member. The decision not to expand the right of necessity may be a good decision, but it is a decision nonetheless.

The next step of the argument concerns the moral duties of individuals. If government makes some people's ability to fulfill true needs (such as medical needs) dependent on private charity, then government foreseeably creates conflicts between legal duties and law-independent moral duties. Because charity is inherently unreliable, in a society that gives some people no way other than charity to meet their needs, some of these people will face dilemmas like the dilemma Heinz faced. They will be able to obtain medical treatment they need, or the treatment a relative needs, only by stealing either the treatment itself or the money to pay for it. There is arguably a moral duty to preserve one's own health. There is undeniably a moral duty to help loved ones, including one's spouse and one's children, to get the medical care they need. So, in a country with an inegalitarian health care system, for some people the legal duty not to steal will conflict with a law-independent moral duty. For other people, who can obtain health care for themselves or for loved ones only by taking out loans they expect not to repay fully, the moral duty to preserve one's own health or the moral duty to help loved ones will conflict with fulfillment of one's contractual obligations. There is some complexity here about whether contractual obligations are legal duties. Arguably, governments *should* treat breach of contract as breach of a legal duty in most cases.[11] If a government does this, and if it allows citizens' financial resources to determine whether they can get medical care they need, it will make it impossible for some people to fulfill their moral duties without breaching legal duties to fulfill contracts.

The last step of the argument concerns the moral duties of government. Governments should prevent foreseeable conflicts between the legal duties it imposes and the moral duties people have independent of law. Governments should not demand that people do things that are morally wrong, and governments should not prohibit people from doing things that are morally required. It is normally wrong for anyone to tell someone else to do something wrong. So, it is normally wrong for lawmakers and enforcers of law to tell people to do things that are wrong. It is especially objectionable to tell someone to do something wrong and to back up this demand with coercive force or threats. Many legal requirements are backed with a threat of legal sanctions or other forms of coercive enforcement. It is seriously wrong to use or to threaten coercion to get someone to do something wrong. So, it is important to make the coercively enforced requirements of law compatible with morality. When legal requirements are imperfectly enforced, they are less likely to influence people's conduct if they make immoral demands.

So, considerations of social stability ground a governmental duty to prevent people's ability to get necessary health care from depending on their ability to pay. If government does not do this, it will foreseeably create conflicts between people's legal duties (such as the duty to respect property rights) and their moral duties. Since government has a duty not to create foreseeable conflict between legal duties and moral duties, government has a duty to prevent citizens' financial resources from affecting their ability to get necessary health care.

The Freedom-Based Argument

Government also has a duty grounded in freedom to provide health care on an egalitarian basis. The first step of the argument for this duty is the same as the first step of the stability-based argument: a government that chooses not to provide health care on an egalitarian basis thereby makes some citizens' (and residents') ability to fulfill basic needs depend on other citizens' discretionary decisions to give or to withhold charity. The second step, defended in the previous section, is that dependence on private charity for the fulfillment of basic needs makes people unfree. That is true whether or not charity is likely to be forthcoming. The third step is simply that government has a duty not to make people unfree.

Conclusion: The Right to Health Care

Both the value of social stability and the value of freedom support a governmental duty to provide health care on an egalitarian basis. Government has a duty to ensure that medical care people need to live or to be reasonably healthy is equally available to citizens and long-term residents, regardless of their ability to pay. Because this duty is owed to citizens and residents, citizens and residents have a corresponding right. This right is not a right to receive any specific medical treatment. It is a right to a *system* that enables everyone to receive medical treatment on an egalitarian basis. Since the right is grounded partly on the value of social stability, and since everyone benefits from social stability, everyone has this right, and everyone benefits when government honors it. Rich people as well as poor people benefit when government provides health care on an egalitarian basis. Rich people as well as poor people have a right to a health care system that gives equal access to the rich and to the poor.

Notes

1. For a summary of some of these arguments, see Norman Daniels, "Justice and Access to Health Care," in *The Stanford Encyclopedia of Philosophy* (Winter 2017 Edition), ed. Edward N. Zalta (https://plato.stanford.edu/archives/win2017/entries/justice-healthcareaccess/).
2. I have presented a similar liberty-based argument before. See Robert C. Hughes, "Egalitarian Provision of Necessary Medical Treatment," *The Journal of Ethics* 24 (2020): 55–78.

3 Lawrence Kohlberg, "The Development of Children's Orientations Toward a Moral Order: I. Sequence in the Development of Moral Thought," *Human Development* 51 (2008): 8–20, at 12. Reprint of *Vita Humana* 6 (1963): 11–33.

4 In the Kantian ethical tradition, making an insincere promise to get a loan is one of the central examples of immoral behavior. Immanuel Kant, *Groundwork of the Metaphysics of Morals*, in *Practical Philosophy*, ed. and trans. Mary J. Gregor (Cambridge: Cambridge University Press, 1996), 74, Ak. 4:422.

5 In the United States, breach of contract has legal consequences, but the law typically does not treat it as a violation of a legal obligation. See Seana Valentine Shiffrin, "The Divergence of Contract and Promise," *Harvard Law Review* 120 (2007): 708–53.

6 Frank Lovett, *The Well-Ordered Republic* (Oxford: Oxford University Press, 2022), 14–15; Arthur Ripstein, *Force and Freedom* (Cambridge, MA: Harvard University Press, 2009), 15.

7 Elizabeth Anderson, *Private Government: How Employers Rule Our Lives (and Why We Don't Talk about It)* (Princeton: Princeton University Press, 2017), 46.

8 Daniel Bernoulli, "Exposition of a New Theory on the Measurement of Risk," trans. Louise Sommer, *Economeetrica* 22 ([1738] 1954): 23–36, at 24.

9 For a similar argument that redistributive taxation enhances the overall level of positive liberty and has no effect on negative liberty, see D. W. Haslett, "Is Inheritance Justified?" *Philosophy & Public Affairs* 15 (1986): 122–55.

10 *Vincent v. Lake Erie Transp. Co.*, 109 Minn. 456, 124 N.W. 221 (1910).

11 Shiffrin, "The Divergence of Contract and Promise."

There Is No Right to Health Care

Trevor Burrus

Study Questions

1. What practical and moral concerns does Burrus raise regarding universal health care systems in his introduction?
2. What is a "right"? What is the distinction between positive rights and negative rights?
3. Why does the fact that positive rights are neither absolute nor scalable cause problems for the idea that there is a right to health care?
4. Why does belief in a positive right to health care create a problem for those who believe in political borders?
5. Why does the fact that positive rights are neither composible nor universal cause problems for the idea that there is a right to health care?
6. What does Burrus see as the positive benefit of not having a "right" to health care?
7. Why does Burrus think that the "right" to health care is immoral?

In 2017, Britain's National Health Service (NHS)—sometimes considered a gold standard for so-called "universal" health care systems or a "right" to health care—decided that smokers and the obese would have less of a "right" to health care. In the words of a CNN article:

> For an indefinite amount of time, it plans to ban access to routine, or non-urgent, surgery under the National Health Service until patients "improve their health," the policy states, claiming that "exceptional clinical circumstances [will] be taken into account on a case-by-case basis."[1]

Why did they do this? Because the resources of the NHS are constrained, and decisions must be made about who has access to those resources. Those decisions are made by political systems, but such questions are unavoidable in "universal" health care systems. Who can get a knee replacement? Who can get cosmetic surgery? How much health care is owed to people?

Whatever you think about smokers, the obese, or the wisdom of the policy, it's worth asking whether the British NHS is functionally conveying a "right" to health care. Rights are generally considered to be universal and inalienable, not to be played with by the whims of politicians. What are your unhealthy habits? What happens if they become politically unattractive? Forty years ago, when far more of the upper class of British society smoked, that policy would not have been passed. What happened to smokers' "right" to health care? The answer: it was never a right.

There is no "right" to health care. That claim, of course, depends on the definition of a "right." That definition is mostly what this essay will explore. I argue that the claim, "I have a right to health care," is usually synonymous with the claim "I am owed some amount of health care from some people in a politically contingent context," and I will then argue why that claim does not properly describe a "right."

Importantly, this essay is not about whether health care is essential to human flourishing. Obviously, it is. There are many things that are essential to human flourishing, such as love of family, love of friends, and intellectual stimulation. But I argue that things that are essential to human flourishing are not the same as "rights."

I argue that the word "right" describes a relationship between those who are owed and those who owe. Or a "right" describes a moral relationship between someone who is owed a duty and someone who is obliged to perform that duty. If someone says they have a "right," they are also claiming that others have a duty.

Understanding the relationship between a right and a duty helps delineate the difference between what philosophers often call positive and negative rights. A *negative right* requires an omission from the duty-holder. A *positive right* requires an action from the duty-holder. A negative right to life requires the duty-holder to not kill the right-holder—an omission. A positive right to life requires the duty-holder to help the right-holder—a duty of action. These are very different concepts.

One can argue that we all have a "right" to life. I would agree. If you're a duty-holder, you can't kill other right-holders. You have a duty to omit killing. But when a tiger kills a man in the jungle, it hasn't violated his rights because the tiger is not a duty-holder. Similarly, when a tornado kills people in a terrible storm, it hasn't violated anyone's rights because the tornado is not a duty-holder. It is still a tragedy, but it doesn't implicate rights.

Do mice have a right to life, and do you violate that when you kill them with a mousetrap? Perhaps. If mice do have that right, do cats violate that when they kill them? What entities are the duty-holders and what entities are the right-holders? And what is required of duty-holders? Also, importantly, does the fundamental moral calculus change if government is involved? Democratic governments are a purported way of amalgamating preferences (i.e., "what the people want"), but does that change the underlying moral question?

I put quotation marks around "right" because the meaning of that concept is the question that is being discussed. The claim of a "right" is often used to mean something similar to "important." In that claim, the sentence "everyone has a right to clean water" would essentially be the same as "clean water is important to everyone." I will not dispute the second claim on its face—clean water is important to everyone—but I do dispute that importance creates a right. I will also discuss who is included in the term "everyone," such as people in other countries. That claim would also, of course, depend on the definition of "clean water," which varies, and the definition of "important," because we all view things as having different levels of importance.

Ultimately, I hope to show that positive rights are a different concept than negative rights. If someone wants to use the word "right" to describe a positive right, then they must deal with the inevitable moral quandaries that will result. Namely, that positive rights are not and can't be absolute; they are not scalable with different sizes of human societies; they draw distinctions based on arbitrary lines (such as borders and citizenship); they can't co-exist together easily with other positive rights (or, in other words, they are not "compossible"); and the duties they impose are not universally shared. Fundamentally, the concept of a positive right to health care still needs to answer basic questions of moral philosophy: what we owe other people, how much we owe, who we owe, who owes, and what we are obliged to do to fulfill that obligation.

A negative right to life answers all those questions. A positive right to health care answers none of them, and it raises more questions than it answers.

What Is a Right?

As mentioned in the introduction, a right is a different type of moral claim than other types of moral claims. For example, we can argue that things are "unfair," such as an income distribution, but it is unclear who would have the duty to fix that unfairness. We often also claim that something is "unfair" because we didn't deserve it, such as being struck by lightning or being afflicted with a sudden medical condition like a stroke. But we wouldn't say that anyone's rights have been violated in those unfortunate situations.

To have a right violated requires a violator who is also a duty-holder. When Robinson Crusoe was alone on the desert island, there were no other duty-holders around him. He was subject to the elements and the predations of animals, but none of those are duty-holders. One could argue that Robinson Crusoe had no rights on the island because there was no one who could hold a duty, but that is a somewhat abstract, metaphysical point that is a little far from this discussion.

When Friday arrives on the island, however, there is now a two-place relationship between Crusoe and Friday. They are both duty-holders and right-holders simultaneously. It is generally not disputed that both had a right to life and a correlating duty not to kill the other person. That is a negative right, with a correlating duty of omission (not to kill). It becomes a much different question, however, if we postulate a duty of help—in other words, a positive right. If they are struggling to find water, does Friday have a duty to give Crusoe his last drop of water? If Friday is caught in quicksand, does Crusoe have a duty to help him even if it imperils his own life? These are significantly more difficult questions, and they are not solved by simply saying the word "right." (I will discuss later whether the amount of resources available changes those obligations).

And I'm only discussing a two-person situation. The difficulties that occur when a society and a government are involved become infinitely more complex. And just like Friday and Crusoe, the moral problems are not solved—or even mitigated—by invoking the word "right." Next, I will discuss how these problems play out in the real world and why it matters to distinguish between positive and negative rights.

Negative Rights Are Absolute; Positive Rights Are Not, and Cannot Be

We think of rights as a kind of absolute claim of moral authority: "I have a right!" But, as noted above, a claim to a negative right, such as the right to life, is very different than a claim to a positive right, a right to care and/or help. Right now, if no one is killing you, assaulting you, or otherwise violating your body and possessions, you are fully enjoying your negative rights to life, property, and bodily autonomy. Everyone who is not killing you is completely fulfilling their duties as a duty-holder. Simultaneously, by not killing anyone, you are doing the same. You are absolutely enjoying your rights and fulfilling your duties.

But let's return to the Robinson Crusoe situation, or any desert island situation you want to imagine. Let's expand the population of the island to 100 people. My interlocutor might think this unfair because I'm creating an artificial thought experiment, but I believe political philosophy should begin with moral philosophy and, as Tim Scanlon famously asked, "what we owe each other."[2] So, now that there are 100 people on the island, we can posit that no one is killing each other, so their absolute negative rights to life are being respected by all relevant duty-holders. Now, suppose someone gets sick, say, an infection from stepping on sharp coral. They need help from the others. The others should certainly help if they are able—that's a different type of moral claim—but could the sick person claim an "absolute" right to life such that the others are obliged to help them?

On one level, that claim seems not only absurd but actually impossible. Whereas every duty-holder can absolutely avoid killing everyone else—as most of us do every day—how much you must help someone can never be "absolute." In the reductio ad absurdum sense, it would require all other people on the island to stop doing anything else to keep the sick person alive for even one more day. They would need to stop caring for themselves and their families to provide health care for the sick person. But I'm not making a *reductio* argument here. Rather, I'm pointing out a literal impossibility, which illuminates a crucial distinction between negative and positive rights. How the correlating duty can be fulfilled is unclear when it comes to positive rights; it is clear with negative rights.

Negative Rights Are Scalable; Positive Rights Are Not

With negative rights, the duty-holders' obligations are entirely and infinitely *scalable*—that is, they can be accommodated by groups of different sizes or scales. With, for example, the negative right to life, the rule is simple: if you are a duty-holder, you have the duty not to kill everyone (or thing) that is a right-holder. Everyone has a right to life, and everyone doesn't kill anyone, basically all the time (self-defense would be the exception, which is a different conversation). That's true if there are two people, ten people, eight billion people, or eighty trillion people. If no one is killing you, then it shows how the right is scalable.

But with a positive right to health care, it becomes very difficult to see how the right can be scaled. Some people will be cared for to some extent, and others will have the obligation to care for them. But the obligations are not universal on either side. The rights are not held equally; the duties are not held equally. A person can hold an infinite number of negative duties (how many things are you not doing right now?). But a person can only hold a finite number of positive duties (how many things can you do right now?). A duty to care for someone will run up against resource constraints and competing obligations. In terms of our desert island example, someone could spend time and resources to take care of the sick person or spend time and resources gathering food for himself and others. Which obligations control? Does the invocation of the term "right" answer the question?

None of these questions becomes easier when we scale up the desert island example to 10 or 100 people. They become more difficult. But with negative rights, the question never becomes more difficult because they are scalable.

A Positive Right to Health Care Tends to Endorse Political Boundaries That Are Morally Irrelevant to the Underlying Claim

This argument is somewhat related to the scalability claim but looks more specifically at the nature of borders, political systems, and citizenship. This might muddy the waters a bit in this discussion, but it is a relevant point.

With a *negative* right to life—as a duty-holder—I can't kill *anyone* in the world, regardless of borders or citizenship. But believers in a *positive* right to health care tend to strangely draw lines that correlate with borders and citizenship. People who are born on one side of a line (a border) deserve some health care provided by some other people (but not everyone) that are also born on that side of the line, but those born on the other side of the line apparently don't have that right. If you believe in a positive "right" to health care, it would be strange, for example, to argue that the borders drawn by the Treaty of Guadalupe Hidalgo—which ended the Mexican-American War and created the modern southern borders of the United States—has a moral significance that overcomes a claim of a right.

Now, I don't mean to impute a claim to my interlocutor—who may be as against borders as I am—I only mean to point out that drawing such lines undercuts a claim to universality and supports my argument for scalability. For the negative rights argument, the right to life is truly universal. I can't cross the border and kill a Mexican, but our political system delineates who has the "right" to health care through Medicare or Medicaid and who has the duty to provide that health care (i.e., people over a certain income level). If we truly cared about the underprivileged and believed in a universal "right" to health care, we'd be advocating for sending all our Medicare and Medicaid money to South Sudan, currently ranked as the poorest country in the world.[3] Yet most people who are enamored with "universal" health care systems are also supportive of borders that distinguish who has the "right." Where you are born—and treaties made 176 years ago—should not determine your rights.

Of course, the best counterargument here is feasibility: it would be simply impossible to have a country that invests as much in other countries as it invests in its own. But that argument only underscores my basic point: a positive "right" to health care simply means: "some people (depending on borders and citizenship [and citizenship is a pliable concept]) are owed some amount of health care provided by some people (usually "rich" people [another pliable concept]) in a politically contingent context (such as whether you are obese or a smoker)." Negative human rights are truly universal; positive rights are not. Whether and how a country allows certain immigrants to receive health care coverage from a centralized health care service is a political question. How much a country supports the health care of other countries like South Sudan is a political question. None of this resembles the typical, classical liberal definition of a human right.

Negative Rights Can Exist Together; Positive Rights Cannot

Someone—a duty-holder—can maintain an infinite number of negative duties (omissions) but only a finite number of positive duties (actions). If you have the duty to provide for your kids, take care of your own health, work your job, and then also provide for someone else's health, those duties will inevitably come into conflict. In philosophical terms, they are non-compossible duties, based on the finite nature of time and resources. They can't fully exist together.

This might seem like a ticky-tacky argument, but it is a crucial point. Many Western European countries declare things like a right to a vacation. They also declare a right to health care. But what happens when the doctor's right to a vacation conflicts with the patient's right to health care? And what happens when a society can no longer pay for a "right"?

Sometimes, it seems as if supporters of a positive right to health care primarily support the idea because modern societies enjoy abundance, especially compared to the impoverished societies that we all lived in before about 1800. This is an interesting argument but again shows the odd reasoning of those who argue for a positive right to health care. The claim is apparently that the positive right comes into existence when a certain per capita income is acquired, or maybe when some people have extremely high wealth. And, as will be discussed below, the duty to provide health care is not equally shared in most conceptions of positive rights. Usually, the richer people are the ones who supply the resources for the health care of the poorer.

But relative abundance shouldn't be the basis of the definition of a right. Do you somehow acquire a right to health care when a certain level of per capita income is achieved? Even in societies that enjoy abundance, there are constant fights over how that abundance should be used. When tax revenue goes down, should we diminish health care for the poor or the elderly? (Depends on the voters.) Or maybe we should take the revenue from education (something that is also often claimed to be a right)? Or maybe we should take the revenue from housing subsidies (another oft-claimed right)? In the end, politicians courting voters will decide. What a weird conception of a right.

In a society where there is a proclaimed right to health care, education, housing, and other things, these difficulties are unavoidable. This demonstrates that positive rights do not exist comfortably together. If all those things are "rights," then they are competing with each other. On the other hand, negative rights never have to compete against each other because they don't require a claim on inexorably limited resources. The duties required by duty-holders are only omissions, and we can all take on an infinite amount of those.

Negative Duties Are Universally Shared; Positive Duties Are Not

In a system of negative rights, everyone who is a duty-holder has the exact same duties. Neither a rich person nor a relatively poor person can violate others' bodily autonomy or property. Negative rights recognize no differentiation between those who hold duties. Who has a duty to respect my rights to life, bodily autonomy, and property? The answer is simple: everyone, everywhere, all the time. Negative rights do not recognize borders, differences in income, or other politically contingent distinctions (such as who counts as "rich").

Countries that have declared a right to health care often have progressive taxation. The level of health care that is provided by the government is unequally funded by wealthier citizens. That means that the duty is not universal but depends on the whims of the body politic. Whatever that is, it's not a right.

The obvious counterargument depends on the diminishing marginal utility of income, that is, that $10 is worth a lot more to someone who is starving than to a billionaire. That argument might be true, but it doesn't entail that it creates a right. At most, it entails that, when there are disparities in wealth, governments might have a duty to redistribute those disparities. But who they take those resources from, who they give them to, and how much they give, are questions not answered by the invocation of the word "right." They are answered by politics. Again, whatever that is, it's not a "right."

Positive Right to Health Care Is a Politically Contingent Claim and Cannot Properly Be Called a Right

To reiterate my basic point that I hope this essay conveys: positive and negative rights are so fundamentally different that we shouldn't use the same word for the concepts. The word "right" is often seen as a trump card in political philosophy, but before we use that word indiscriminately, we should discuss what it means.

It is possible that the wealthier have obligations to the less wealthy. Most of the world's biggest religions have been making that point for millennia. But they don't use the word "right." If we don't properly define "right," everyone is apparently owed some amount of health care or owes some amount of health care depending on where they sit in the current political zeitgeist: smoker, obese, rich, poor, an immigrant, an "undesirable" race. That's not a right.

Real human rights—and duties—are what we have because of our status as human beings, not as the playthings of political currents.

What Happens When There Is No "Right" to Health Care?

It might seem like I'm being coarse or heartless when I describe why I think there is no right to health care. If someone is dying on the street or suffering from a severe malady, shouldn't we do something? Yes, we should. We should give to the homeless. We should help those who can't help themselves. None of those statements entail that there is a "right" involved. Be a good person, please. You don't need the concept of "rights" to figure out that problem.

Yet there is another important factor: innovation and cost reduction. For most of human history, people lived on the edge of starvation.[4] They worked hard constantly, mostly farming, to eke out a living and keep their families alive.[5] If anyone argued there was a universal "right" to food, they probably would have responded, "then you farm my field and feed my family!" The only thing that changed the situation was innovation. From the plow to the threshing machine to fertilizers to modern scientific farming, we made food cheap, for the most part. As has been often observed, those advances created the first societies where the problem was that poor people were fat, not starving.

We can criticize fast food and other easy-access, unhealthy foods another time. My point here is that innovation creates access. Once, only rich people ate meat regularly. Most people's diet consisted of cheap, starchy foods like potatoes and rice. Spices were a luxury. Innovation changed that; it made meat and spices broadly accessible.

The same is possible in health care if we let innovation and markets work. So much of the discussion around a right to health care focuses on distribution and accessibility: whether some class has more than another class. It should focus on what mechanisms we need to make treating cancer a $20 pill, and then many distribution problems solve themselves.

For centuries, one of the primary medical treatments was bloodletting, draining the blood out of people. The problem then was not whether bloodletting was used more by the rich and not available to the poor, or whether there was a "right" to bloodletting; it was the fact that they were practicing bloodletting. We needed innovation, not more equitable bloodletting. And, as I argue below, if countries create a "right" to health care—and that makes it more expensive, less equitable, and less innovative—then it could be immoral.

Is a "Right" to Health Care Immoral?

In the preceding sections, I hope to have made a somewhat compelling argument for why there is not a right to health care. Health care is vital—tautologically so—but that, as I've argued, is not a good definition of a right as a concept in political philosophy. I will now elaborate on some of the implications of my argument.

One is that restrictions on the right to access private health care are immoral. A few countries fully restrict access to private health care—meaning access to health care outside of the single-payer system is prohibited. This is rare, but often an implication of single-payer health care systems.

The second implication is that things that even impair access to fundamentally important things, like health care or food, are also immoral. On one level, this is obviously true: Stalin killed millions of people by essentially forcing starvation upon them by restricting their ability to cultivate food for their families. If producing food is a human right, which I would argue it is, then blocking or even impairing that right is immoral.

In the following syllogism, "X" could be whatever you think is vital to human well-being, for example, water, clean air, and so on. Here's the syllogism:

(1) X is vital to human well-being.

(2) Y makes it more difficult or impossible to access X.

(3) Therefore, Y is immoral.

Some might wonder about my definition of "immoral." I think that is immaterial to my argument here, and a longer discussion of the metaphysics of ethics would be beyond the scope of this article. My argument relies only upon whatever your theory of ethics is—deontology, utilitarianism, virtue, and so on.

My argument here is also, admittedly very empirical, and I do not have the space to elaborate on the policy arguments about the effects of a "right" to health care. Whether a certain policy makes health care more or less efficient is to be debated in economic journals and research papers. But, if it is true that countries that "guarantee" a "right" to health care make health care more difficult to access, make it more expensive overall, and diminish innovation in medicine, then the syllogism would be valid. This is all very abstract, so I want to tell a couple stories to help elucidate the ideas.

First: In 2005, the Canadian Supreme Court decided the case of *Chaoulli v. Quebec*.[6] The question was whether Quebec's prohibition on providing private health insurance violated the fundamental rights of Quebecois. The case was brought by a doctor who wanted to take private health insurance to provide medical services, particularly to those who were on long waitlists for public health care. The province prohibited this practice. In a split decision, the Court decided that the prohibition on access to private insurance violated fundamental rights. It made Quebecois wait in pain for needed medical procedures. The decision was limited to Quebec's ban on private insurance tied with the long wait times created by the single-payer system. This decision helps illustrate the concept that a malfunctioning right to health care—coupled with a prohibition on obtaining private insurance—can violate human rights.

Second: In 2007, the US Court of Appeals for the D.C. Circuit decided the case of *Abigail Alliance for Better Access to Developmental Drugs v. von Eschenbach*.[7] Abigail Burroughs was a college student diagnosed with head and neck cancer. She wanted to take a drug that the FDA had not yet approved for use to treat her type of cancer. She argued that the Constitution protected the right of terminally ill patients to try drugs that could help them. She ultimately lost her case (and her life).

Neither of these examples create an open-and-shut argument against the right to health care. I use them as real-world stories about how it is possible for a controlled health care system to violate human rights. There are of course many difficult questions about how to regulate a private health care system or how to approve prescription drugs. Yet those questions should be addressed with a focus on protecting human rights (real human, negative rights, as I've argued in this essay).

These questions are not necessarily limited to the so-called single-payer health care system. I say "so-called" because there are many ways that countries can control and direct a health care system. Some are almost entirely centralized, like the NHS in the UK. Some are industries that come to depend on Medicaid and Medicare, which may or may not be good programs, but have fundamentally restructured the health care system in the United States.

Moreover, there are many restrictions on who can provide health care and what health care can be provided. The Food and Drug Administration (FDA) decides what drugs and medical procedures you're allowed to take. State licensing boards get to decide who can give you treatment.

Most people who believe in a positive right to health care believe that the right can be effectively mediated by the political system. I've already discussed how politically created borders cannot morally create a class of "those who are owed health care" and "those who owe health care," and that whatever that is, it's not a "right." Borders and restrictions on providing health care are difficult moral concepts, but it would also be weird if a purported right to health care depended on how a country defines "doctor" or "nurse." Those definitions are based on current licensing systems that are often corrupted or controlled by existing licensees who have vested interests in controlling the access to their profession. Same with FDA approval of drugs and who can access them. The pharmaceutical industry has immense influence over the FDA, and certain organic drugs—like smoked whole leaf marijuana—will never be approved as medicine, partially because it can't be patented. To the FDA, approving whole leaf marijuana as medicine would be like approving chicken soup as medicine.

A proper appreciation of universal human rights would take these questions into consideration. It wouldn't turn the definition of "human right" into a question about how bureaucracy should function. A real human right exists without bureaucracy. But opening up the health care system to diminish or eliminate harmful government programs, reduce licensing restrictions, and allow access to potentially life-saving drugs is rarely discussed.

It's time for a new perspective on health care and time to stop talking about how it is a "right."

Notes

1 Meera Senthillingam, "No Surgery for Smokers or the Obese: Policy in UK Stirs Debate," *CNN.com* (October 31, 2017) (https://www.cnn.com/2017/10/31/health/smokers-obese-no-surgery-nhs-uk/index.html).

2 T. M. Scanlon, *What We Owe Each Other* (Cambridge: Belknap Press, 2000).

3 Cherry Gupta, "Top 10 Poorest Countries in the World in 2024: African Countries have the Lowest GDP Per Capita," *The Indian Express* (September 9, 2024) (https://indianexpress.com/article/trending/top-10-listing/top-10-poorest-countries-in-the-world-in-2024-by-gdp-per-capita-9557753/).

4 Deirdre McCloskey, "The Great Enrichment," *Discourse Magazine* (July 13, 2020) (https://www.discoursemagazine.com/p/the-great-enrichment).

5 Ibid.

6 (AG) [2005] 1 S.C.R. 791, 2005 SCC 35.

7 495 F.3d 695 (D.C. Cir. 2007).

Responses

Response to Hughes on the Right to Health care

Trevor Burrus

> **Study Questions**
>
> 1. Why does Burrus think that Hughes's arguments, even if cogent, do not establish a *right* to health care?
> 2. What is the difference between Burrus's "minimalist" conception of rights and Hughes's "maximalist" conception? What problem does Hughes's view have according to Burrus?
> 3. What difficulties might Hughes's view have when it comes to defining health care needs?
> 4. What are the "further basic disputes" that Burrus has with Hughes and how does he address them?

I appreciate Professor Hughes's erudite essay on whether there is a right to health care. His approach is novel and doesn't depend on arguing that something is a "right" because it is "important" or that its denial is declared to be somehow "unfair." His argument is cogent, although I disagree with it.

Good Policy Doesn't Establish a Right

Most of Hughes's argument is what I would describe as a "policy" argument rather than a "rights" argument—that is, it is a good idea for the government to guarantee some amount of health care to the citizens, and it should do this by making some citizens pay for it. He argues it creates a type of stability and a type of freedom, which is also a cogent argument. In some situations, that would be true: meaning it could create *some* amount of stability for *some* people and *some* people would feel more free if *some* other people were obliged to pay for that health care. That would depend on the nature of the implementation. Would *some* people feel more stable if "the government" (really, other taxpayers) provided their "needed" health care? Of course.

Would *some* people feel more free if they didn't have to worry about their access to "needed" health care? Of course. It would be absurd for me to dispute those claims.

But does that make it a "right"? Or is it just a politically contingent claim to *some* amount of health care for *some* people as provided by *some* other people?

His argument is heavily empirical. Whereas my essay mostly focuses on the definition of a "right," his argument focuses on good policy, but not on the definition of a right. His argument is empirical because, if many of the claims he makes are not true—if, for example, a government is incapable of providing a "right" to "needed" health care, or impedes access to effective and affordable health care—then his argument would not hold weight. I'm doubtful that people in North Korea feel like they have a meaningful "right" to health care, although their system of law and government purportedly "guarantees" them one. Thus, his argument depends, to some extent, on government efficacy. That's a weird definition of a right.

In a broad sense, his argument is similar to the claim that it is a good idea for governments to have a military and a police force. I don't dispute those claims in the abstract (but it would somewhat depend on the use—or misuse—of military and police), but I do dispute whether a "good idea" for a policy establishes a "right."

There might be many good ideas for government policy. It might be a good idea for the government to mow your lawn, supply government-funded entertainment and art, or support agricultural industries. Those policies might create a more stable and free society, but do they establish a "right"?

Minimalist Vs. Maximalist Conceptions of Rights

Our fundamental disagreement has to do with a minimalist vs. maximalist conception of "rights." As I argued in my original essay, rights are fairly minimalist concepts that should begin with the relations between individual people—who is owed, who owes, what is owed—thus my Robinson Crusoe example. Hughes's arguments are rooted in a concept of an existing and functioning government, whereas my arguments begin at an individual level.

After starting at an individual level, we can move to questions about what duties governments may owe, but we start with individual relations and moral philosophy. This is similar to the classic Lockean concept of government: the government has no powers or duties that are not transferred to it by the people as they would exist in a state of nature.

Yet Hughes argues that "everyone who lives in a society that has law and government has a moral right to health care" (p. 154). It is difficult to unpack this sentence. What level of "law and government" is needed to create a purported right to health care? Does it exist in a fairly lawless society like South Sudan? Does it matter how much relative wealth the society has? Does the government have an obligation to prioritize a right to health care over a right to food? Or education over health care? Resources are limited, and it is unclear who is owed, who owes, and what is owed. Does the word "right," as used by Hughes, answer any of these questions?

Hughes may respond that bringing up examples of dysfunctional governments doesn't properly respond to his argument, any more than his bringing up examples of dysfunctional markets in health care would respond to my argument. This is a good point. But if governments are prone to systematically distort and corrupt health care markets, then his argument fails. To his credit, Hughes elaborates more on this argument, but his baseline argument is still subject to every criticism I make in my original essay.

What Medical Care Is Needed?

Hughes claims that "the government has a duty to provide medically necessary treatment on an equal basis" (p. 155). It might seem easy to define the health care someone "needs." Removing an inflamed appendix is quite necessary to preserve life. Same with cutting off a gangrenous limb. But providing beta blockers—a drug for reducing high blood pressure and other heart conditions—is a more difficult question. Vitamins? Painkillers? Antidepressants? Knee surgery? Cosmetic surgery? Mammography? Colonoscopy? Vision correction? That's just a short list. Invite twenty doctors into a room and see if they can agree on what is "necessary treatment." Much of the debate over health care depends on a concept of "need," but that concept is rarely well-defined.

For example: vision correction, massively important for health and quality of life. Lasik laser eye surgery was once very expensive and is now available to even poor Americans. It hasn't been heavily subsidized nor covered by most insurance. The goal of health care policy should be to create the best system to make health care cheap and innovative.

Most advocates for national health care systems are content to let bureaucrats define health care "needs," and those "needs" somehow become "rights." Those bureaucrats might be doctors, true, but when in government they become bureaucrats who have control over your purported "rights." And they will disagree. I don't put any aspersions on the character of these people; I'm just describing the reality of the situation. Whatever that is, it's not a "right."

Some Further Basic Disputes

In this section, I will quote from Hughes's essay and make some short responses:

> *"Health care provided or paid for by the government is basic."*

"The government" is a collection of people and it funds services through taxation. "The government" isn't paying for anything; some people are. Who pays and who gets it depends on political currents.

> "Still other countries, notably including the United States, do not guarantee universal access to health care, even at a basic level."

Through Medicaid and Medicare, the US "government" does provide a "basic level" of health care, but of course that means just some taxpayers supply that "right" to health care. And that "basic" level of health care varies depending on who controls the government. The debate over the provision of abortion and IVF is one example of many. The purported "right" is a leaf on the political wind.

> "The government has a moral duty to provide health care to its citizens and its long-term residents."

In my original essay, I argue that defining a "right" to health care based on citizenship or "long-term residents" is extremely difficult to justify morally. Borders shouldn't have moral significance for a "right," nor should the shifting laws that determine the definition of "long-term residents." Rights transcend borders.

> "Many legal requirements are backed with a threat of legal sanctions or other forms of coercive enforcement. It is seriously wrong to use or to threaten coercion to get someone to do something wrong."

To this I ask only whether threatening someone with legal force to provide someone else's health care is wrong? Would Hughes do it himself? Would he threaten violence against another person to make him supply health care to someone else? That's the reality of government enforcement. Whatever that is, it's not a right.

Conclusion

I agree with Professor Hughes that there are some important things that governments should do to promote social stability and freedom. Top of that list is the classic group of "life, liberty, and property." But "life" here means protecting you from predation, not giving you a "right" to health care.

As I describe in my original essay, the instantiation of positive rights (rights where other people owe you a positive duty of action) inevitably creates conflict. Education? Food? Health care? Choose. This is not a coherent theory of rights. A coherent theory of rights begins with the relations between individuals and doesn't use the government as a proxy for deciding how *some* people have to give to *some* other people *some* things depending on politics. That's how it works in the real world. When the next election comes, your "right" may be gone. But rights exist before government, not after. Government is not magic; it's about the relations between people.

Response to Burrus on the Right to Health Care

Robert C. Hughes

Study Questions

1. How does Hughes clarify what he means by the "right to health care"? How does this help him reply to some of Burrus's objections?
2. What does Hughes say in response to the concern that government-funded health care is subject to the whims of politicians?
3. Why does Hughes think that Burrus's argument that limits on private health insurance are immoral is unsound?

Trevor Burrus's arguments against a right to health care raise three important questions. First, what does it mean to say that people have a right to health care? Second, if health care is provided by government, is the provision of health care necessarily subject to the whims of voters? Third, is it ethical or just for a government to limit people's ability to purchase medical treatment or health insurance on the private market? My answers to all three questions are different from Burrus's.

What Is the Right to Health Care?

Burrus's argument against a right to health care presupposes a particular view about what a right to health care would be, if there is such a right. He argues that for there to be a right to anything, there must be someone who has a corresponding duty. For negative rights, the corresponding duty is a duty not to do something. The duty corresponding to the right to life, for instance, is the duty not to kill, a duty everyone has. For positive rights, the corresponding duty is a duty to do something, or to provide something. What would be the duty corresponding to the right to health care? Burrus suggests it would be a duty to provide the specific forms of health care that each patient needs. Implicitly, Burrus assumes that a right to health care would be a right to whatever specific treatments and preventive measures one needs.

If the right to health care is a right to have all one's health care needs fulfilled, Burrus is correct to argue that there can be no right to health care. As he points out, resources are limited. Sometimes it is simply impossible to fulfill everyone's health care needs. For instance, during an outbreak of a dangerous infectious disease, there may not be enough vaccine doses to protect everyone who is in danger. Sometimes it is possible to fulfill a need, but it is unreasonable to try, because devoting enough resources to fulfill this need would involve directing resources away from other things people need or deeply want.

There is another way of understanding the right to health care, however. It is a right to a *system* of health care that makes health care reasonably accessible. What services should this system provide? The answer depends on the resources available to the people who have a duty to support the system. Since the right to a system of health care is sensitive to resource limitations, it does not face Burrus's main objection to a right to health care.

Who has a duty to support the system of health care? I argue that this duty falls on every institution and every individual who helps to establish and maintain the social norms that govern the allocation of resources. It is wrong to make people dependent when they do not have to be dependent. It is wrong to create rules of resource allocation that make people dependent on others' generosity for the satisfaction of basic needs. In modern societies, governments create the rules that determine who may use what resources in what ways. These rules include the law of property and tax law. Governments have a moral duty to ensure that the laws they establish and enforce do not make people dependent on others' generosity. To do this, they must ensure that people's ability to get genuinely necessary medical care does not depend on their ability to pay. If there is no publicly supported health care system, some people's ability to get health care they need will depend on whether resource owners feel like helping them. People will often fall into that form of dependence through no fault of their own.

What about the Whims of the Body Politic?

Though Burrus's argument about resource limitations does not challenge this conception of a right to health care, he raises another question that presents a serious worry. Isn't government-funded health care subject to "the whims of politicians" or "the whims of the body politic"? If yes, then a public health care system does not protect people from dependence. People's ability to get health care they need through the public system will depend on the whims of bureaucrats, legislators, and voters. How is that better than being dependent on the whims of private resource owners who could choose to donate or not to donate to the provision of health care for others?

My answer is that in a democracy that is functioning well, major policy decisions are not made on a whim. The lawmaking system is set up so that establishing a public health care system or making major changes to it requires more than a bare majority vote. It requires the cooperation of different lawmaking bodies that represent the country in different ways, such as the House of Representatives and the Senate in the United States. It may require a supermajority in one of these lawmaking bodies. Establishing a health care system should require discussion and deliberation. (No doubt there will be some horse-trading as well.) Once the system is established, it must operate as the law requires, even if the current leader of the executive branch would prefer to shut it down.

Since legislatures cannot work out all the details of a health care system when they establish it, there will also be a need for administrative rulemaking in the executive branch of government. There should be procedures for administrative rulemaking that protect patients (and taxpayers) from the whims of the current head of government. Deliberation and discussion should be required to change the rules. With these procedural protections in place, people's access to health care will be less vulnerable to others' whims than it would be if access to health care were determined by ability to pay.

May Government Limit Private Insurance?

To ensure that people's access to health care does not depend on their ability to pay, it is not enough to provide a publicly funded health care system. It is also necessary to place limits on private funding of health care, as Canada still does, the decision in *Chaoulli* notwithstanding.[1] Burrus argues that such limits are immoral, using the following argument:

(1) X is vital to human well-being.

(2) Y makes it more difficult or impossible to access X.

(3) Therefore, Y is immoral.

Burrus argues that restrictions on private insurance (Y) can sometimes make it difficult or impossible to access medical treatments people need (X). For example, if there is a long waiting list for hip replacements in the publicly funded system, prohibiting private insurance makes it difficult or impossible for people to get hip replacements quickly.

Burrus's three-step argument is unsound. To see why, suppose that a country has a publicly funded health care system with limits on private insurance. Suppose all or almost all the surgeons trained to provide hip replacements are operating at or near capacity. Offering surgeons a higher price for their services will not substantially increase the number of hip replacements that are done. If the country decides to allow private payment for hip replacements, some patients will jump the queue for hip replacements by paying surgeons for early access. This will force financially less well-off patients to wait longer for hip replacements. Thus, allowing private insurance or private payment for health care (X) makes it more difficult for some people to access medical treatment they need (Y). Burrus's argument implies that government acts wrongly whether it allows or prohibits privately funded health care. That implication shows that the argument does not work.

Burrus is right to point to the importance of resource limitations. When we collectively have limited resources to devote to health care, we face a choice. Will we allow wealth to determine who lives and who dies, who is healthy and who is sick? Do we want rich people to be able to make life-and-death choices for others, by choosing to give or to withhold aid? Or do we want access to scarce necessities to be determined democratically, with public discussion and debate about the rules of access?

Note

1. The government of Quebec responded to the court decision in *Chaoulli* by enacting a law that permits private insurance plans that cover only the specific services the plaintiffs were seeking in *Chaoulli*. (See Ifran Dhalla, "Private Health Insurance: An International Overview and Considerations for Canada," *Healthcare Quarterly* 10 [2007]: 89–96.) In Quebec and several other provinces, physicians who wish to accept private payment must opt out of the public system and cannot legally receive payment from Medicare. The number of doctors who have opted out in Quebec remains low. (See Damien Contandriopoulos and Michael R. Law, "Policy Changes and Physicians Opting Out from Medicare in Quebec: An Interrupted Time-Series Analysis," *CMAJ* 193, no. 7 [2021]: E237–E241.)

Questions for Reflection

1. Has Hughes adequately addressed the concern that government-funded health care is subject to the whims of politicians (consider Burrus's examples of smokers and the obese)? Why?

2. What would (or could) Burrus say to a person who cannot afford the health care (or insurance) he needs? Would this be the right answer? Why?

3. What would you say to a person who claims that it is immoral for the government to tax her to fund a government health care system? Why?

For Further Reading

Colton, David. *The Case for Universal Healthcare*. Clarity Press, 2019.
Jasinski, Lukasz. *Markets vs Public Health Systems: Perspectives from the Austrian School of Economics*. Routledge, 2023.
Kelley, David. "Is There a Right to Healthcare?" The Atlas Society, 2010. https://www.atlassociety.org/post/is-there-a-right-to-health-care.
Pipes, Sally C. *The False Promise of Single-Payer Health Care*. Encounter Books, 2018.
Rhodes, Rosamond, Margaret P. Battin, and Anita Silvers, eds. *Medicine and Social Justice: Essays on the Distribution of Health Care*, 2nd ed. Oxford University Press, 2012.
Wolff, Jonathan. *The Human Right to Health*. W. W. Norton & Company, 2012.

6

Vaccine Mandates

For Vaccine Mandates

Shlomo Cohen

Study Questions

1. What value or principle puts the burden of proof on the proponent of vaccine mandates?
2. What is the "Harm Principle"? How, and under what conditions, does it justify vaccine mandates?
3. How does Cohen answer the charge that vaccine mandates based on the Harm Principle are paternalistic?
4. How does concern for the common good support vaccine mandates?
5. What is the principle of fairness? How, and under what conditions, does it justify vaccine mandates?
6. How does the reality of infectious diseases provide a basis for collective responsibility and a more robust justification of vaccine mandates?

Immunization is a cornerstone of public health policy. Alongside smallpox, which was eradicated following the introduction of vaccination, many other diseases that were previously responsible for the majority of childhood deaths have become very rare in countries with high vaccination coverage.[1] It is estimated that roughly four million deaths worldwide are prevented by childhood vaccination every year,[2] and much disability and misery are averted. In a deep sense, vaccines have substantially transformed the frightening human experience of living surrounded by pathogens. Given how beneficial vaccines are, their high safety profile,[3] and the fact that (in communicable diseases) the benefits are conferred not only on the vaccinated but on the wider community, it may be surprising that people would not vaccinate or that there should be any substantial ethical controversy raised by vaccination. And yet there is controversy, and many refuse vaccination or delay and miss vaccinations due to "vaccine hesitancy."[4] The aim of this chapter is to present central ethical considerations in favor of mandating vaccination (of oneself as well as one's children).

Vaccine Mandates and Liberty

Liberal culture hallows personal liberty (hence its name). The value of liberty requires noninterference with personal affairs—an expression of respect for personal autonomy. Vaccine refusal can surely be an exercise of personal autonomy. This constitutes a presumption against vaccine mandates, which is yet reinforced by the importance of respecting people's sovereignty over their bodies. All that being granted, no society protects individual freedom to an absolute degree. Accordingly, any argument for vaccine mandates must show that it is sometimes reasonable to override respect for autonomous refusals for the sake of counterbalancing moral considerations. Generally speaking, the more weight we put on the duty to safeguard others, and the less weight we put on the autonomy consideration, the easier it is to find mandated vaccines justified. We will examine the moral arguments for this position and chart its boundaries.

Imagine a limit case. A terrible epidemic has begun. The infectious agent is highly contagious, and contracting it results in certain death. Fortunately, it turns out that a vaccine has been developed. It is 100 percent safe, offers 100 percent immunity for the individual, and blocks transmission completely. Now imagine that despite this wonderful news, a non-negligible portion of the population refuses to be vaccinated. Should they be mandated to get the vaccine?

Historically, liberal democratic countries (our relevant reference point) have indeed been employing vaccine mandates. The UK Vaccination Act of 1853 was the first, and nowadays most European countries have mandates.[5] In the United States, where the protection of civil liberties was enshrined in the Fourteenth Amendment, the constitutionality of vaccine mandates was nonetheless affirmed in *Jacobson v. Massachusetts* (1905),[6] in which the Supreme Court ruled that states may require vaccination via mandates accompanied by a criminal fine. This ruling set a precedent that remains in effect today. Clearly, laws and legal rulings are subject to moral review and criticism. Our task in this chapter is to examine how vaccine mandates can be ethically justified. I will present three justifications below, based on non-harming, on promoting the common good, and on fairness. First, however, let us dwell for a moment on the main moral hurdle for vaccine mandates.

Respect for Individual Autonomy

The first moral consideration in assessing vaccine mandates is the (*pro tanto*) duty to respect the autonomous decisions of individuals. This consideration must be weighed on the moral scales against countervailing (*pro tanto*) duties.[7] Since we are dealing here not merely with individual moral judgment, but with ethics of public policy, it is useful to remind ourselves of a general truth: government by its very nature exercises coercive authority. The law as such is binding and enforceable regardless of whether particular citizens agree with or consent to it. Excluding the small minority of anarchists, people by and large endorse such coercion in principle. This means that we accept violations of citizens' autonomy in the interest of promoting competing values—the question is only which values and under what circumstances. We should likewise remember that mandatory vaccination is but one of a set of coercive measures for fighting epidemics available to a government. These include: required screening, unconsented-to surveillance and contact tracking, isolation, quarantine, directly observed therapy, closure of facilities, travel restrictions, and more. Though we will not discuss these, parallel questions of justification can be raised with regard to each of them.

Vaccine refusals have various grounds. These include fears of iatrogenic diseases, preferences for natural lifestyles, religious opposition to vaccines, attributing greater salience to the small risks of vaccines compared to the risks of exposing one's children to infectious diseases, and more.[8] We will here treat the duty to respect the autonomy of vaccination refusals not only as a given but as of constant magnitude or weight. This is not because all decisions to refuse are in fact autonomous (some could, for instance, result from sustained brainwashing), nor is it because they all exhibit the same level of autonomy (some will be less informed, more manipulated, more related to phobias, etc., than others, and so less autonomous; in turn, the duty to respect them may be weaker). Rather, the reasons to treat refusal decisions as equally fully autonomous are two: (1) public health deals with the general population; ascertaining the (level of) autonomy of each citizen's decision is therefore impractical. This being the case, our (defeasible) default ought to be to treat each decision by an otherwise competent adult as autonomous. (2) Analyzing the various considerations that can affect the autonomous nature of personal decisions is a complex topic that is not connected to the issue of vaccination specifically. Discussing it would therefore take too long and divert us from our main topic.

Let us then review the main moral reasons that may counterbalance the duty to respect autonomous refusals. Each of these reasons may be most compelling under somewhat different circumstances, and so they may together offer justification for vaccine mandates under a wide range of circumstances. Alternatively, since these reasons need not be mutually exclusive, then to the extent that they hold, the justification of vaccine mandates can be overdetermined.

The Harm Principle

The most influential principle for balancing personal liberty with social welfare in the liberal tradition is John Stuart Mill's "Harm Principle." The principle states: "The only purpose for which power can be rightfully exercised over any member of a civilized community, against his will, is to prevent harm to others."[9] In a civilized society, liberty does not mean license; liberty must come hand in hand with a duty not to expose others to (non-negligible and easily preventable) harm. The safety of others sets the limit to one's freedoms. The harm referred to in the Harm Principle is ordinarily understood to include exposing others to increased *risk* of harm. This is not only a matter of moral duty for the individual but also—and most relevantly for us—a fundamental principle of the liberal morality governing public policy and legislation. This principle can justify vaccine mandates.

Now the precise prescriptions of the Harm Principle are anything but obvious. This is both due to philosophical disagreements as to the meaning of "harm" and (more relevantly here) due to ethical disagreements as to the principle's adequate application and precise scope. While these grand questions obviously cannot be settled here, I would like briefly (1) to establish that the application of the Harm Principle to vaccine mandates has initial plausibility, and (2) to discuss conditions for its appropriate application.

The logic of the Harm Principle allows implementing coercive measures to secure public safety. By this logic, we accept the prohibition against "shouting 'Fire!' in a crowded theater" as legitimate,[10] or, closer to our interest in public health, the legitimacy of prohibiting smoking in public places. Vaccine mandates may similarly be appropriate, given that the more people are vaccinated, the less morbidity and mortality there will be in the population. We all accept enforceable regulations for dealing with hazardous materials. A lab worker who goes out to the street carrying a jar full of dangerous viruses is thereby wronging passersby (and is liable to punishment by law). It is prima facie plausible to argue that society has a compelling interest in enforcing vaccinations to prevent people from (perhaps unknowingly) roaming the streets with parallel "*internal* jars" full of dangerous viruses.[11]

There are three different epidemiological conditions, and in all of them vaccines can reduce risks of harm to others. (a) During epidemics, vaccines reduce the number of contagious people. The pertinence of the Harm Principle here is further supported by the fact that one carrier can infect many people. (b) Vaccinations help prevent epidemics through the creation of herd immunity. (Herd immunity is the situation where enough people in a community are immune from a certain infectious disease that those not vaccinated are indirectly protected, because the high immunization rate stops person-to-person transmission.) (c) In a state of already existing herd immunity, continued vaccination helps prevent the constant risk of falling below the Herd Immunity Threshold (with certain pathogens, e.g. measles, it is *easy* to fall below the threshold, since it can approach 94 percent of the population; and remember that a portion of the population cannot be vaccinated for medical reasons).

Under which conditions does the general duty not to harm actually materialize as a vaccine mandate? We need parameters that would help us strike a reasonable balance between respecting autonomy and preventing harm to others. Four main parameters are the following.[12]

(1) *The severity of the threat.* This refers to the severity of the disease, its level of contagiousness (in a given locale), and the effectiveness of available treatments, if any.

(2) *The effectiveness of the available vaccine.*

(3) *The level of safety of the vaccine.* Vaccines must have a very favorable safety profile for it to be ethical to mandate them; the ethicality of mandates is proportional to their level of safety.

(4) *The mandate must be the least coercive effective alternative.*

Although there is much to articulate about the details of these four parameters, the first three are basically self-explanatory, while the fourth, a little less so; hence, I will dwell on the fourth. That a mandate must be "the least coercive effective alternative" means that a mandate is justified only if it is the last resort, that is that milder forms of influence are not similarly effective in resulting in vaccination. This follows from the understanding that coercion is *pro tanto* wrong, and so must be rejected in favor of non/less coercive yet equally effective alternatives. The notable milder measures are: education, nudging, and providing incentives. (Influence is a continuum, and the four options I am mentioning—i.e., including coercion—are not discrete; they overlap. Thus: much education involves subtle nudging; at least some incentives may be classified as nudges; payment for vaccination is likely viewed as an incentive, while withholding benefits—e.g., tax breaks—may be viewed as coercive, but others would claim that these ought to belong in the same category; etc. Nevertheless, it is instructive to view them as separate options.)

Education, if effective, is ethically optimal. However, public education campaigns often have too little effect, are sometimes ineffective, and at other times backfire.[13] It is very unlikely that public education will be effective against those who have strong beliefs against vaccines or who feel no incentive to actively seek them. In addition, education takes time, so this venue may be impractical during an epidemic. Questions of effectiveness are mostly empirical, and we obviously cannot here provide definitive answers to them; our business here is to illustrate conditions under which mandates are probably justified. "Nudging" refers to using insights from behavioral sciences to influence people to react and choose in predictable ways, without eliminating or burdening available options.[14] Thus, if changing the default of school vaccination from "opt in" to "opt out" would raise vaccination rates satisfactorily, then mandates are not necessary, and so are forbidden.[15] Other kinds of nudging include: changing the way outcomes are framed, changing the salience of available information, invoking social norms to create peer pressure, and more.[16] Reports about the efficacy of nudging are mixed, but even when nudging seems to help, its effects seem rather small. For instance, a large study of nudging by text-messaging prior to primary care visits found an average of 5 percent increase in vaccination rates.[17] In addition, it is claimed that the effects of nudges tend to be less long-lived.[18] An alternative method for increasing vaccination rates is by monetary incentives. The sums cannot be large both because it is impractical vis-à-vis entire populations and because the larger the sum, the more potentially coercive is the offer. Modest payments, however, seem to have rather small effects (e.g., 4 percent increase).[19] To the extent that mandating is much more effective than nudging or incentivizing, mandating vaccines may well be morally justified to prevent harm. Finally, not all coercions are equal. A higher fine may be more coercive than a smaller one, and forcefully vaccinating people (the limit case) is more coercive than limiting access to schools or services. As the last example suggests, level of coercion is determined not only by the intensity of pressure but also by the *scope* of rights violated: a mandate's overriding the freedom to choose need not violate freedom relating to bodily integrity.

I spoke above of coercion as "last resort," but this is inaccurate. "Effectiveness" is not a binary parameter: there is greater and lesser effectiveness. Accordingly, there can be lesser coercion with lesser efficacy or greater coercion with greater efficacy, and—once we reject the absolute priority of minimization of coercion—we will have to judge which is the morally better trade-off. For instance, if mandates to wear a face mask in public or stand six feet away from others are less coercive but also less effective than vaccine mandates, then we'll have to weigh the differences in coercion versus efficacy to choose the morally optimal policy.

Having explained the basic considerations relevant for deliberation on the justification of vaccine mandates by the Harm Principle, where do we draw the threshold of legitimacy? The precise threshold, I believe, is not set a priori or indeed philosophically; it is determined by a society's moral perspective and way of life. Importantly, this does not mark an end to rational deliberation; to the contrary—it requires much deliberation. Vaccine mandates ought to be justified or rejected in view of our considered judgments regarding analogous cases of coercion so as to fit within a coherent overall view. I can here merely illustrate how justification might work. For instance, it may be argued that in prohibiting smoking in public places, we curtail freedom by disallowing the exhalation of hazardous substances. If we accept this restriction, it may seem reasonable to disallow exhalation of dangerous microorganisms too (which is *more* dangerous, since victims need to inhale cigarette smoke for *years* for it to harm them), and this may only be achievable by vaccination. Another example: If we allow restricting liberty by prohibiting driving under the influence of alcohol or other sedatives (as well as impose speed limits, seat belts, etc.), then it makes sense to restrict freedom by vaccine mandates given that the lifetime odds of dying from a motor vehicle accident are *much* lower than the lifetime odds of dying from an infectious disease in a pre-vaccination society.[20] These examples are not final pronouncements—they merely show how deliberation could proceed rationally.

A reasonable challenge to the harm-based justification of vaccine mandates asks who exactly is put at risk by vaccine refusals. The answer, it is argued, is that risk befalls the one refusing as well as the other refusers she comes in contact with, for they are the ones who aren't protected. But if that is the case, then vaccine refusers harm *themselves* only, not others. Vaccine mandates therefore turn out to be paternalistic, and so do not meet the burden of justification required to offset respect for refusers' autonomy. This indeed reduces the weight of the argument from harm, but it does not cancel it. This is because there are many who *cannot* get immunized, and so remain involuntarily unprotected (those under vaccination age, the immunosuppressed, those allergic to the vaccine, and those whose immune systems react inefficiently to vaccines).[21] In addition, remaining unvaccinated poses not only the risk of direct contagion but also indirect risks of harm to others. An epidemic breaking out can have terrible consequences for the economy (e.g., the US GDP contracted in 2020 by hundreds of billions of dollars due to Covid-19),[22] and this translates to significant economic harm, especially to the socioeconomically vulnerable; fears and social isolation cause increased incidence of mental health problems; travel restrictions disrupt chains of supply, causing shortages of products and goods; lockdowns disrupt effective education; and so on. These are substantial harms.

The Common Good

Beyond an obligation not to harm, many acknowledge moral obligations to do what is positively good (duties of beneficence). Vaccine mandates can be justified on this basis. Pope Francis called vaccination an "act of love,"[23] and while moral agents are not obligated to perform those generally, duties to do positive good *are* widely recognized—most notably in rescuing those in imminent danger, when costs to oneself are relatively insignificant.[24] This is affirmed by commonsense morality and also follows directly from utilitarianism, which demands doing the greatest expected good overall. Utilitarianism demands that we aggregate all considerations relevant for promoting the overall good and seek to do the (kind of) act that maximizes it. Importantly, the value of noninterference with personal decisions does not stand out as a protected autonomy right that can be defeated, if at all, only by the enormity of bad consequences. Rather, utilitarianism requires that we view the moral landscape holistically. The consideration against interfering with personal liberty, though surely important, is but one among others—it lacks the theoretically privileged status of being the hinge around which justifications for intervention are given.

Utilitarianism is a prominent moral theory, and even those who deny its claim to the status of universal moral theory often accept it as guiding moral judgment when collective considerations are paramount, as in the case of public health policy. This is further accentuated during epidemics, where failure to prioritize the consideration of consequences could lead to massive preventable loss of life.[25] In *Jacobson v.*

Massachusetts, the Court accordingly stressed the central importance of promoting the common good in upholding a vaccine mandate. The majority opinion read: "the liberty secured by the Constitution of the United States to every person within its jurisdiction does not import an absolute right in each person to be, at all times and in all circumstances, wholly freed from restraint. There are manifold restraints to which every person is necessarily subject *for the common good*. On any other basis, organized society could not exist with safety to its members."[26]

Once we adopt the general welfare-maximizing consequentialist scheme of utilitarianism, moral reasoning relies heavily on empirical cost-benefit analysis, and this favors vaccination quite overwhelmingly. Utilitarianism therefore seems to support vaccine mandates, so long as alternative measurements to augment vaccination levels do not approach similar cost-benefit ratios. Vaccinations are among the most cost-effective health investments there are,[27] and *all* childhood immunization programs are cost-saving.[28] For example, a cost-saving analysis of the vaccination program with diphtheria, tetanus, and acellular pertussis (DTaP) found a US$27 return for each dollar invested.[29] In poorer countries too, a large study of immunization against ten pathogens found a 26.1 ratio of return on investment.[30] These impressive figures are most probably underestimations, since the usually narrow views on the disease-preventing effects of vaccination do not take into account broader effects of health on welfare and economic growth, such as that healthier children perform better at school, that healthy adults are more productive at work, that disease-free countries attract more tourism, and so on.[31] Moreover, over and above the return-on-the-dollar consideration, vaccines save lives and prevent disability and agony. These effects obviously have a tremendous impact on the common good.

A major criticism of utilitarianism (and consequentialist views more generally) is that it may require far-reaching sacrifice of individual interests for the sake of the collective good. The case of vaccine mandates is a rather appealing instance of utilitarian thinking in that it does not make such a demand. The case is in fact typically the *opposite* of personal sacrifice: For the great majority, getting vaccinated for the common good coincides with a favorable personal cost-benefit function in terms of health. Immunization against dangerous diseases is gained for the price of the nuisance of a jab, and sometimes mild discomfort and malaise for a day or two. More serious side effects are very rare. Those with known risks of suffering more substantial side effects can and of course should be exempt from vaccination. This is not a concession that utilitarianism makes out of respect for individual interest but is consistent with promoting the maximization of the good, since the exemption of the few with a negative personal cost-benefit ratio should not interfere with achieving or maintaining herd immunity. Hence, vaccine mandates can ideally maximize the common good while simultaneously maximizing individuals' personal good.

Now certain individuals oppose being vaccinated despite an objectively favorable cost-benefit ratio in terms of personal health, and in those cases, utilitarianism indeed prescribes overriding personal preference for the sake of maximizing the collective good. Utilitarianism therefore legitimizes the coercion involved in vaccine mandates. Having said that, to the extent that utilitarianism aims at maximizing preference satisfaction, the level of ideological resistance to vaccination in a given society is a relevant consideration. Hence, theoretically, in a society where a significant part of the population prefers not to be vaccinated despite objective personal health benefits, this may well tilt the utilitarian calculus against vaccine mandates. If, on the other hand, the idea of welfare with which utilitarianism works is (not preference satisfaction, but) an "objective list" view that includes the promotion of health as an objective good,[32] then utilitarianism may advocate vaccine mandates even when many in the population oppose them ideologically.

Fairness

Justice and fairness are among the most basic moral values. A strong argument has been made that they ground the ethicality of vaccine mandates. The idea stems from the following intuitions. Everyone, in any given population, has an interest in removing the risks imposed by dangerous infectious diseases. The removal of such risks can indeed be achieved by herd immunity, yet herd immunity cannot be accomplished by individual action or the action of the few—it necessitates the collective efforts of a substantial portion of society. Now *the principle of fairness* holds that if many in a population make a cooperative effort to produce benefits that in fact benefit everyone, including non-cooperators, then it is unfair if the latter do not rise up to participate in the effort.[33] As John Rawls put it succinctly, "We are not to gain from the cooperative labors of others without doing our fair share."[34] According to this logic, individuals have a moral duty of fairness to make their own contribution to the public good of herd immunity that was, or is being, achieved by the cooperative efforts of many in their society.

This argument from fairness has attracted criticism. Robert Nozick argued: "One cannot, whatever one's purposes, just act so as to give people benefits and then demand or seize payment. Nor can a group of persons do this."[35] You cannot, for instance, thrust a book—not even one in which I have much interest—into my hand and then demand payment in return. Moreover, and more importantly for us, even if under certain conditions I *would* have a duty to reciprocate a benefit that is conferred on me without my asking or consenting to it, the claim is that complying with such a moral duty is not *enforceable*; and that is all that is needed to counter the fairness argument for vaccine mandates.

Proponents of the argument from fairness do not deny that there is no *general* duty to reciprocate benefits that are imposed on one, but they argue that under certain conditions, such a duty of fairness does in fact exist and is enforceable too. Here are three central conditions,[36] and their application to vaccine mandates.

(1) *Non-excludability.* Suppose that produce prices have skyrocketed, and so the village residents decide to form a cooperative that can buy seeds, fertilizers, and so on collectively and grow vegetables much more cheaply. If a certain family prefers not to pay coop dues and to forgo its benefits, it is just to allow them to exclude themselves. There are public goods, however, from which it is *impossible* to be excluded. When the state, through its legal system and police force, provides law and order, this in a sense necessarily applies to all citizens. Similarly, no individual dissenter can be excluded from the state of affairs in which unpolluted air or border security prevails. Herd immunity too is a non-excludable public good: it is impossible to exclude a vaccine refuser from benefiting from herd immunity. Hence there are only two options: free ride on the efforts of others or contribute your fair share. The principle of fairness demands that you do the latter.

(2) *Indispensability for a satisfactory life.* The benefit in point cannot be any random benefit; it has to be a benefit that is indispensable for a satisfactory life for virtually any reasonable person. Hence, a book—even one in which I have much interest—does not qualify as far as this parameter is concerned, whereas, for example, having access to clean water does. Similarly, breathing air that does not contain potentially lethal microorganisms is indispensable for a satisfactory life. We can accordingly assume bona fide that everyone actually does benefit from herd immunity.

(3) *Justice.* The benefits and burdens ought to be fairly distributed in the population. Hence, the logic of "No taxation without representation." This is relevant to vaccination in that people with higher health risks from being inoculated with the vaccine should not be expected to contribute their share, for that would not be a *fair* share.

When all these conditions hold, contributing to the cooperative effort of herd immunity is not only a moral duty but is enforceable too: a government is then *just* in expecting everyone to do their fair share of contributing to herd immunity. This spells out vaccine mandates.[37]

Interconnectedness and Solidarity

The duty of fairness emphasized the basic decency in shouldering the efforts of the collective in which you are a member and which bestows benefits on you. This basic decency is expressed in assuming collective responsibility. How do we calibrate this burden of responsibility? How does it measure on the balance against the right to act autonomously to realize personal preferences? There are good reasons to believe that questions about precise thresholds and balances have no a priori moral answers but refer ultimately to ideas about the human condition, in which ethics is rooted. Our relevant conceptions will determine the baselines against which ideas of "harming" are assessed or the stringency of one's duty to act for the common good is evaluated. While these topics obviously exceed our scope, there is an element of the human condition that involves infectious diseases specifically and that relates to collective responsibility and can consequently shed light on the legitimacy of vaccine mandates.

The stringency of the duty to maximize the common good and even its sheer validity are a function of our interpretation of and attitude toward social solidarity (these would also help determine the optimal balance between rights of self-expression and obligations to not harm others). An extreme solidaristic interpretation of utilitarianism was offered in John Harris's "Survival Lottery."[38] It suggested that whenever there are two or more patients at risk of dying who can be saved by organ transplantation, yet no organs are available, a healthy individual should be chosen by lottery and sacrificed to save the greater number of innocent lives. This would maximize the common good. The survival lottery idea is almost universally rejected—we humans do not see ourselves as a collective web of organs. In contrast, in the domain of infectious diseases, it may well be reasonable to view ourselves as cooperators in a collective web of infectivity. This idea was developed comprehensively by Margaret Battin and colleagues, and it can ground a theory of deep collective responsibility.[39]

Battin and colleagues remind us that the basic reality of infectious diseases essentially involves the *interconnectedness* of all individuals as far as the transmissibility of infections is concerned. Our collective fate rests on the fact that everyone is simultaneously both a potential victim of infection and a potential vector of transmission to others, and that the spread of infectious diseases is constant, beyond our control, and potentially highly consequential. The reality of interconnectedness is also expressed in the development of antibiotic resistance, where one person's irresponsible use of antibiotics can result in a resistant strain killing other persons, and it is surely expressed in the effect of one's vaccination on others: the development of herd immunity. It is our inescapable existential condition that, as physically located bodies, we are always embedded in potential circumstances of exchange. In this shared predicament, "the consequences to others of possible contagious disease are part of the patient's *own* interests."[40] (In a similar vein, it was shown that advanced economies would gain financially from financing vaccines for developing economies.)[41] Unlike the artificiality of Harris's idea of organ swapping, in the domain of infectious disease ethics specifically, the basis for collective responsibility and solidarity is rather naturally anchored in our existential condition. It is reasonable that with the right education, this can be leveraged to a society's self-imposition of vaccine mandates, and it offers mandates a more robust justification.

Conclusion

To conclude, I presented three different justifications for vaccine mandates, based on: (1) the prohibition against harming, (2) the duties of beneficence and advancing the common good, and (3) the duty of fairness. I then offered a description of the human condition vis-à-vis infectivity that offers extra force to these arguments. These justifications can act in concert or complement one another under different circumstances (for instance, the argument from harm can be seen as more forceful when there is no herd immunity, whereas the argument from fairness is precisely the opposite, and vice versa). A discussion of these further intricacies will have to wait for another day.

Notes

1. WHO, Global Vaccine Action Plan 2011–2020 (2013) (https://www.who.int/teams/immunization-vaccines-and-biologicals/strategies/global-vaccine-action-plan).
2. CDC (2023) (https://www.cdc.gov/globalhealth/immunization/data/fast-facts.html).
3. CDC (2023) (https://www.cdc.gov/vaccinesafety/vaccines/index.html).
4. Ève Dubé, et al., "Vaccine Hesitancy, Acceptance, and Anti-vaccination: Trends and Future Prospects for Public Health," *Annual Review of Public Health* 42, no. 1 (2021): 175–91.
5. Manon Haverkate, et al., "Mandatory and Recommended Vaccination in the EU, Iceland and Norway: Results of the VENICE 2010 Survey on the Ways of Implementing National Vaccination Programmes," *Eurosurveillance* 17, no. 22 (2012): 1–6.
6. 197 US 11 (1905).
7. Robert I. Field and Arthur L. Caplan, "A Proposed Ethical Framework for Vaccine Mandates: Competing Values and the Case of HPV," *Kennedy Institute of Ethics Journal* 18, no. 2 (2008): 111–24.
8. Alberto Giubilini, "Vaccination Ethics," *British Medical Bulletin* 137, no. 1 (2021): 4–12.
9. John Stuart Mill, *On Liberty* in *On Liberty and The Subjugation of Women* (New York: Henry Holt & Co., 1879), 23.
10. *Schenck v. United States*, 249 US 47 (1919).
11. B. Bambery, M. Selgelid, H. Maslen, et al., "The Case for Mandatory Flu Vaccination," *American Journal of Bioethics* 13 (2013): 38–40.
12. For somewhat different lists see, e.g., Carmel Shachar and Dorit Rubinstein Reiss, "When are Vaccine Mandates Appropriate?" *AMA Journal of Ethics* 22, no. 1 (2020): 36–42; Julian Savulescu, "Good Reasons to Vaccinate: Mandatory or Payment for Risk?" *Journal of Medical Ethics* 47, no. 2 (2021): 78–85.
13. Anthony Pratkanis and Elliot Aronson, *Age of Propaganda* (New York: Henry Holt, 2001), chaps. 2–4.

14 Richard Thaler and Cass Sunstein, *Nudge: Improving Decisions about Health, Wealth, and Happiness* (New Haven: Yale University Press, 2008).

15 A. Giubilini, et al., "Nudging Immunity. The Case for Vaccinating Children in School and Day Care by Default," *HEC Forum* 31 (2019): 325–44.

16 Mark Donald C. Reñosa, et al., "Nudging toward Vaccination: A Systematic Review," *BMJ Global Health* 6, no. 9 (2021): e006237.

17 Katherine L. Milkman, et al., "A Megastudy of Text-Based Nudges Encouraging Patients to Get Vaccinated at an Upcoming Doctor's Appointment," *Proceedings of the National Academy of Sciences* 118, no. 20 (2021): e2101165118.

18 N. T. Brewer, G. B. Chapman, A. J. Rothman, et al., "Increasing Vaccination: Putting Psychological Science into Action," *Psychological Science in the Public Interest* 18, no. 3 (2017): 149–207.

19 Pol Campos-Mercade, et al., "Monetary Incentives Increase COVID-19 Vaccinations," *Science* 374, no. 6569 (2021): 879–82.

20 Data on the lifetime odds of dying from a motor vehicle crash is from the National Safety Council at: https://injuryfacts.nsc.org/all-injuries/preventable-death-overview/odds-of-dying/. The odds of dying from infectious diseases before widespread vaccination is based on the fact that in the year 1900, 797 out of every 100,000 died per year in the United States from infectious diseases (Gregory L. Armstrong, Laura A. Conn, and Robert W. Pinner, "Trends in Infectious Disease Mortality in the United States during the 20th Century," *Jama* 281, no. 1 [1999]: 61–6). The lifetime probability to die is then given by the expression $1-(992/1000)^n$ (where n stands for mean longevity). I thank Dr. Noam Cohen for help with calculating the probability.

21 Thomas May and Ross Silverman, "Free-Riding, Fairness and the Rights of Minority Groups in Exemption from Mandatory Childhood Vaccination," *Human Vaccines* 1, no. 1 (2005): 12–15.

22 See https://www.macrotrends.net/countries/USA/united-states/gdp-gross-domestic-product.

23 https://www.vaticannews.va/en/pope/news/2021-08/pope-francis-appeal-COVID-19-vaccines-act-of-love.html.

24 Peter Singer, "Famine, Affluence, and Morality," *Philosophy and Public Affairs* 1, no. 3 (1972): 229–43.

25 Julian Savulescu, Ingmar Persson, and Dominic Wilkinson, "Utilitarianism and the Pandemic," *Bioethics* 34, no. 6 (2020): 620–32.

26 *Jacobson v. Massachusetts* 197 US 11, 26 (1905) (my emphasis).

27 Jenifer Ehreth, "The Value of Vaccination: A Global Perspective," *Vaccine* 21 (2003): 4105–17.

28 Tammy O. Tengs, et al., "Five-Hundred Life-Saving Interventions and their Cost-Effectiveness," *Risk Analysis* 15, no. 3 (1995): 369–90.

29 Donatus U. Ekwueme, et al., "Economic Evaluation of Use of Diphtheria, Tetanus, and Acellular Pertussis Vaccine or Diphtheria, Tetanus, and Whole-Cell Pertussis Vaccine in the United States, 1997," *Archives of Pediatrics & Adolescent Medicine* 154, no. 8 (2000): 797–803.

30 So Yoon Sim, et al, "Return On Investment from Immunization Against 10 Pathogens in 94 Low-And Middle-Income Countries, 2011–30," *Health Affairs* 39, no. 8 (2020): 1343–53.

31 David E. Bloom, David Canning, and Mark Weston, "The Value of Vaccination," in *Fighting the Diseases of Poverty*, ed. Philip Stevens (New York: Routledge, 2017), 214–38.

32 Guy Fletcher, "Objective List Theory," in *The Routledge Handbook of Philosophy of Well-being*, ed. Guy Fletcher (New York: Routledge, 2015), 148–60.

33 H. L. A. Hart, "Are There Any Natural Rights?" *Philosophical Review* 64 (1955): 175–91, at 185.

34 John Rawls, *A Theory of Justice* (Cambridge, MA: Harvard University Press, 1971), 112.

35 Robert Nozick, *Anarchy, State, and Utopia* (New York: Basic Books, 1974), 95.

36 This is adapted from George Klosko, *Political Obligations* (New York: Oxford University Press, 2005).

37 For an example of basing vaccine mandates on fairness see, e.g., A. Giubilini, "An Argument for Compulsory Vaccination: The Taxation Analogy," *Journal of Applied Philosophy* 37 (2002): 446–66.

38 John Harris, "The Survival Lottery," *Philosophy* 50 (1975): 81–7.

39 Margaret Battin, et al., *The Patient as Victim and Vector: Ethics and Infectious Disease* (Oxford: Oxford University Press, 2008).

40 Ibid., 465.

41 Cem Çakmaklı, et al., *The Economic Case for Global Vaccinations: An Epidemiological Model with International Production Networks*, No. w28395 (Cambridge: National Bureau of Economic Research, 2021).

Against Vaccine Mandates

Gabriël A. Moens

Study Questions

1. Why does Moens believe that the Covid-19 vaccine mandate "sits uncomfortably" with the Australian High Court's jurisprudence?
2. What does Moens say about vaccine mandates when approached from the perspective of the dignity and privacy of individuals?
3. What standards should vaccines meet? How does the Covid-19 vaccine fail to meet these standards?
4. Why does Moens think that the Covid-19 vaccine mandates were draconian and tyrannical?
5. What are the adverse consequences of the vaccine mandates that Moens cites?

During the Covid-19 pandemic, governments throughout the world imposed vaccine mandates as the way out of lockdowns. The mandates were often enforced rigidly by compliant police forces. The unvaccinated were routinely warned that they would enjoy less freedom to travel and to associate with other people, or even to go to restaurants or attend football matches. Now that the pandemic has receded, and most vaccine mandates have been lifted, it is appropriate to consider whether these mandates were legal, efficacious, and ethical. As I am located in Australia, I will argue in this essay that vaccine mandates violated Australian law, especially the Australian Constitution, and were incompatible with international law, and based on poor policy which failed to defeat the pandemic and facilitate a return to normal life.

The first part of this essay discusses the imposition of vaccine mandates, and the second part offers an assessment of the legality, efficacy, and ethics of these mandates, concentrating on the Australian Constitution and international law. Finally, before offering closing comments, part three deals with the consequences of the imposition of vaccine mandates.

The Imposition of Vaccine Mandates

Although the policy of the Australian federal government was that Covid-19 vaccinations were "voluntary," most state and local governments, and private organizations adopted vaccine mandates. Any assessment of the legality of vaccine mandates, understandably, should start with a review of the relevant section of the Australian Constitution. Section 51(xxiiiA) of the Constitution stipulates that "The Parliament shall . . . have power to make laws for the peace, order and good government of the Commonwealth with respect to . . . pharmaceutical, sickness and hospital benefits, medical and dental services (but not so as to authorize any form of civil conscription)."

The High Court first considered the concept of "civil conscription" in 1949 in *British Medical Association v Commonwealth*.[1] The Court ruled that requiring doctors to comply with professional standards to receive Medicare payments did not amount to civil conscription. But the Court also decided that legislation requiring that medical practitioners use a particular Commonwealth prescription form was invalid as a form of civil conscription. Justice Dudley Williams, in his judgment, stated that "the expression invalidates all legislation which compels medical practitioners or dentists to provide any form of medical service."[2]

In 2009, in *Wong v Commonwealth; Selim v Professional Services Review Committee*,[3] Chief Justice Robert French and Justice William Gummow held that "civil conscription" is a "compulsion or coercion, in a legal or practical sense, to carry out work or provide services."[4] The "no conscription requirement" to be found in that constitutional provision thus amounts to an explicit limitation on mandating the provision of medical services, for example, compulsory vaccination, which remains governed by the contractual relationship between patients and doctors.

Hence, a government directive, addressed to the medical profession to mandatorily vaccinate people, would constitute an unconstitutional civil conscription. Such a directive would interfere with the relationship between the doctor and the patient—a relationship that is based on contract and trust.

However, according to constitutional law commentators, any claim that section 51(xxiiiA) prohibits mandatory vaccinations is "pseudo-legal nonsense" because the section does "not grant people individual 'rights'"; it merely "prevents the federal government from forcing people to do work as doctors and dentists." For example, Luke Beck argued that "There's nothing in the constitution that would prevent a law making COVID vaccination mandatory."

Similarly, Professor George Williams argued that section 51(xxiiiA) "would not prevent the Commonwealth from requiring citizens to be vaccinated." For him, the section could be relied upon to prevent the Commonwealth, but not the states, from compelling medical practitioners to take part in mass vaccination programs.[5]

Justice Robert Beech-Jones of the New South Wales Supreme Court provided judicial support for these academic views in *Kassam v Hazzard; Henry v Hazzard*.[6] In *Kassam*, the plaintiffs challenged the New South Wales public health orders requiring vaccination in certain circumstances on the ground that the legislation infringed section 51(xxiiiA) of the Constitution. Justice Beech-Jones opined that the term "civil conscription" in that section was "directed to compulsory service in the *provision* of medical services as opposed to the acquisition of services such as vaccinations by a patient." The Court, dismissing the plaintiffs' challenges, also noted that section 51(xxiiiA) "is directed to the legislative power of the Commonwealth not the states."[7]

Nevertheless, the implementation of mandatory Covid-19 vaccination sits uncomfortably with the High Court's jurisprudence. There are two constitutional challenges to overcome when attempting to interpret section 51(xxiiiA) as allowing vaccine mandates: (i) the construction of the section as granting a constitutional right to patients to refuse vaccinations, and (ii) the applicability of the section to the states.

The first challenge relates to the construction of section 51(xxiiiA) as conferring constitutional right on individuals to refuse vaccination. If that section were to be interpreted as allowing mandatory vaccination, then the contractual relationship between doctor and patient would be effectively abolished because the ability of patients to enter a contract for the receipt of vaccination services would be fatally compromised. Yet, Justice Michael Kirby opined in 2009, in *Wong v Commonwealth; Selim v Professional Services Review Committee*,[8] that the purpose of prohibiting the civil conscription in section 51(xxiiiA) was to ensure that the relationship between medical practitioner and patient was governed by contract. For him, the test whether civil conscription has been imposed is "whether the impugned regulation, by its details and burdens, intrudes impermissibly into the private consensual arrangements between the providers of medical and dental services and the individual recipients of such services."[9]

Justice Kirby's point reveals that compulsory vaccination destroys the contractual relationship between doctors and patients and, therefore, it imposes an impermissible obligation on people to accept a medical procedure which they can refuse on constitutional grounds. Section 51(xxiiiA) could thus be regarded as an implied constitutional right of patients to refuse vaccinations. Hence, a medical treatment which is imposed upon a person without his or her informed consent is a trespass upon that person. In *Bowater v Rowley Regis Corp*,[10] Lord Justice Scott explained that consent to treatment, including vaccination, is needed to proceed with the treatment:

> a man cannot be said to be truly 'willing' unless he is in a position to choose freely, and freedom of choice predicates, not only full knowledge of the circumstances on which the exercise of choice is conditioned, so that he may be able to choose wisely, but in the absence from his mind of any feeling of restraint so that nothing shall interfere with the freedom of his will.

The second challenge relates to the applicability of section 51(xxiiiA) to the Australian states. Although a state government can institute its own public health orders, any component of such an order cannot impermissibly intrude into any matter which may be regarded as coming within the sole legislative authority of the Commonwealth Parliament. When this occurs, of course, the state must make application to the Commonwealth to enact that specific component of the health order. Accordingly, the issue of vaccine mandates is not whether an Australian state can issue a public health order, but rather whether such state is constitutionally authorized to issue a public health order which unreasonably intrudes into a matter that comes within the sole purview of the Commonwealth.

Furthermore, if unvaccinated Australians were to face serious restrictions of rights and freedoms, these restrictions would violate the democratic principle of equality before the law. Accordingly, in *Leeth v Commonwealth*,[11] Justice William Deane and Justice John Toohey referred to the Preamble to the Constitution to support their view that the principle of equality is embedded impliedly in the Constitution. They argued that "the essential or underlying theoretical equality of all persons under the law and before the courts is and has been a fundamental and generally beneficial doctrine of the common law and a basic prescript of the administration of justice under our system of government."[12]

It is also worth approaching the matter from the perspective of the dignity and privacy of individuals. Governments should avoid relying on the *parens patriae* doctrine according to which government will decide what is good for people: it would be a textbook example of the operation of the Nanny State that removes any sense of individual responsibility and human dignity. There is a danger of excessive state paternalism when citizens are not allowed to make personal decisions about their own medical treatment, including the decision of whether to take a Covid-19 vaccine. This was highlighted in *Airdale National Health Service Trust v Bland*,[13] where Lord Justice Mustill expounded on this danger:

> If the patient is capable of making a decision on whether to permit treatment and decides not to permit it his choice must be obeyed, even if on any objective view it is contrary to his best interests. A doctor has no right to proceed in the face of objection, even if it is plain to all, including the patient, that adverse consequences and even death will or may ensue.

Furthermore, the right of an individual to refuse vaccination is also supported by the *Nuremberg* Code—an ethics code—relied upon during the Nazi doctors' trials in Nuremberg. This Code has as its first principle the willingness and informed consent by the individual to receive medical treatment or to participate in an experiment. However, it has been argued that an attempt "to apply the code to COVID-19 vaccines is incorrect and misleading." The argument notes that the Nuremberg Code only addresses human medical experimentation and does not apply to "approved vaccines."[14] The analysis thus turns on the fact that Covid-19 vaccines do not involve human experimentation, but instead have been approved—in Australia by the Therapeutic Goods Administration—for emergency use. But it is precisely the experimental nature of the Covid-19 vaccines and the widespread disagreement about the capacity of vaccines to provide protection against the virus that is responsible for the lack of confidence in their effectiveness. Indeed, in a climate of uncertainty, characterized by a demonstrable lack of confidence, a program of mandatory vaccination cannot be regarded as consensual. The unvaccinated, in relying on health implications for the purpose of refusing the vaccine, may thus ironically invoke the same argument used by proponents of vaccinations who, to promote the vaccine, also rely on health grounds. Hence, people's refusal to be vaccinated may be based on the ground that the Covid-19 vaccines are still experimental and their long-term effects and safety on its recipients are still largely unknown, but nevertheless real.

Moreover, there is evidence of a correlation between excess mortality and Covid vaccination. In a thoughtful article entitled "COVID Vaccine-Associated Mortality in the Southern Hemisphere," Professor Wendy Hoy and Professor Augusto Zimmermann point to a comprehensive comparative research study that found that "COVID vaccines are directly associated with the disturbing rise in the mortality rate among countries of the Southern Hemisphere."[15] The researchers found that in the seventeen countries studied, covering 9.2 percent of the world's population, the research "invariably exhibited an unprecedented and relatively sharp peak or surge in all-ages deaths during or after January-February 2022, which was synchronous with or immediately preceded by a rapid rollout of a COVID vaccine booster dose 3 or 4, depending on the country." The researchers stated that "If vaccines prevented transmission, infection or serious illness, then there should have been decreases in mortality following vaccine rollouts, not increases which were observed in every elderly group subject to rapid booster rollouts." The research study concluded that "The scientific tests for causality are amply satisfied, as extensively demonstrated" in the following sections of the study.[16]

   Covid-19 vaccines can cause death

   Absence of excess mortality until the Covid-19 vaccines are rolled out

   The Covid-19 vaccines did not save lives and appear to be lethal toxic agents

   Strong evidence for a causal association and vaccine lethal toxicity

   Causality in excess mortality is amply demonstrated

   Assessing other interpretations of the cause of the excess mortality

   Implications regarding age-dependence of fatal toxicity of Covid-19 vaccines

The "rule of law" would be undermined if mandatory vaccination were mandated in circumstances where constant government changes undermine the confidence of people in the efficient administration of the vaccine rollout and the effectiveness of the vaccines. In fact, research confirms that these vaccines are not able even to stop the spread of Covid-19. In other words, those who are vaccinated can still catch and transmit Covid-19. As evidence of the inefficacy of these vaccines, in a recent study supported by Centers for Disease Control and Prevention contracts, members of the Upper Midwest Regional Accelerator for Genomic Surveillance founded by the Rockefeller Foundation, concluded that vaccinated people can still catch and transmit Covid-19 and, once infected, the vaccinated are as likely to infect others as the unvaccinated.[17]

An Assessment of Vaccine Mandates

The lack of confidence in the efficacy of vaccines, and consequently vaccine mandates, is exacerbated when one considers the standards that vaccines should exhibit. There are at least five medical requirements that need to be met: (i) the vaccine must result in a measurable reduction in the number of sick people afflicted with the Covid-19 virus, (ii) the vaccine must be capable of protecting recipients for a significant time, thereby possibly avoiding booster shots, (iii) the vaccine should have few negative side effects, (iv) the vaccine must be effective against newer variants of the virus, and (v) the vaccine must substantially reduce transmission rates. There are four logistical requirements: (i) a low cost to produce the vaccine, (ii) the vaccine can be produced quickly on the required scale, (iii) the vaccine can be efficiently distributed, and (iv) it is easy to administer.

Arguably, the most important requirement is that the public, medical professionals, and politicians confidently trust the vaccine. Obviously, the Covid-19 vaccines on offer do not meet this important requirement of trust. It is now patently clear that the vaccines have prevented neither infection nor transmission. The assumed "protection" provided by these vaccines has been shown to be of extremely limited duration, and now "boosters" are being promoted, potentially for life.

Nevertheless, Dr. John Ioannidis, professor of medicine and epidemiology at Stanford University, believes that the average rate of death for Covid-19, when adjusted for a wide age range and unreported cases, could be as low as 0.05 percent, similar to that of influenza.[18] He also explains that more than a majority of those who contract the virus have no symptoms or these symptoms are actually very mild. Even the World Health Organization (WHO) acknowledges that "Most people infected with the virus will experience mild to moderate respiratory illness and recover without requiring especial treatment."[19]

With such low risks for most people, why were populations coerced to be vaccinated with defective Covid-19 vaccines? So, given the already known potential harms of the novel vaccines, of which myocarditis is just one, and the entirely unknown potential long-term adverse effects which may become known only in the future, the decision to vaccinate everyone, including small children, regardless of age or health conditions, is highly problematic and not scientific. Neither is it moral nor ethical, because there are profoundly serious risks attached to any new drug. As an article from the *British Medical Journal* explains:

> From a public health standpoint, it makes poor sense to impose vaccine side-effects on people at minimal risk of severe COVID-19. The argument that it protects others is weak or contrary to evidence. This conclusion suggests a policy of targeting vaccination to those at highest risk, allowing broader post-infection immunity to provide community protection.[20]

The fact is that the response to the spread of the virus certainly struck a very heavy blow at democracy by undermining the "rule of law" and confidence that people have in the ruling classes, particularly in members of the legal, medical, and political professions. It has also fatally compromised the rights and freedoms of people and jeopardized the economies of the free world. As Ian Hanke pointed out:

> These extraordinary powers are arbitrary and extreme. They are a draconian attack on civil liberties the like of which Australia has never seen before. Further because all laws are overridden there would appear to be little recourse to any excesses by an authorised officer or their civilians co-opted by them. These laws are so broad and ill-defined that you could be detained for almost anything.[21]

The view that the imposition of Covid-19 vaccine mandates (and also lockdowns) was draconian and often tyrannical is strengthening throughout the world. For example, Human Rights Watch has accused the UK government of setting aside "human rights for the sake of political expediency" and criticizes it for its "worrying disdain for the rule of law."[22] In Italy, authors Piero Stanig and Gianmarco Daniele have argued that the worst possible thing a government could do during the pandemic "when dealing with a highly infectious disease that spreads almost exclusively indoors and targets the elderly is to lock old people up inside their homes . . . and ban citizens from spending time in arguably the safest place of all: outdoors."[23] In Australia, the authors of *Fault Lines: An Independent Review into Australia's Response to COVID-19*, published on October 20, 2022, argued that the response failed the nation because "too many of Australia's lockdowns and border closures were the result of policy failures in quarantine, contact tracing, testing, disease surveillance and communicating effectively the need for preventative measures like mask wearing and social distancing."[24] Similarly, pondering the fact that Australian governments have failed to make a cost-benefit analysis of lockdowns, Professor Gigi Foster estimates that the cost of lockdowns has been "at least 68 times greater than the benefits they delivered."[25] How could this happen in Australia, which always prided itself on protecting the rights of people?

One plausible explanation is that, because of the peculiarities of Australia's Westminster system, it became possible for the executive to assume quasi-dictatorial powers, which a politicized police force brutally enforced. Professor Augusto Zimmermann has argued that the concentration of unrestrained political power in the Executive is the result of the imperfect implementation of the separation of powers doctrine, according to which power should be divided among the legislative, executive, and judicial branches of government. But in Australia, the doctrine only provides for the separation of the judiciary from the executive and legislative branches of government. The executive is able to wield almost unrestricted powers because it is backed by a majority of members of the parliament. This means that the government can do as it pleases because it is backed by a parliament that fails to provide effective parliamentary oversight of executive decisions. Zimmermann fittingly calls this an "elective dictatorship."[26]

In addition, the parliament often delegated its legislative power to unelected health administrators who made decisions that dramatically affected the freedoms of people during the pandemic. Although this delegation diminishes the legislative function of the parliament, the High Court has never restricted the elaboration of what is known as the "delegated powers doctrine." In fact, this doctrine is a logical concomitant of the imperfect implementation of the separation of powers doctrine under a Westminster system because it facilitates the exercise of administrative power by the Executive without adequate parliamentary oversight.

In any case, the idea that rights emanate from the parliament or the executive is problematic because it overlooks the view that rights, embedded in the natural law tradition, are "inalienable," a view that some members of the Australian High Court also seem to have accepted. For example, in *Re Bolton; Ex Parte Beane*,[27] Justice Gerard Brennan admitted that "Many of our fundamental freedoms are guaranteed by ancient principles of the common law or by ancient statutes which are so much part of the accepted constitutional framework that their terms, if not their very existence, may be overlooked until a case arises which evokes their contemporary and undiminished force." Justice William Deane agreed with this sentiment when he stated that these principles "are the very fabric of the freedom under the law which is the prima facie right of every citizen and alien in this land. They represent a bulwark against tyranny."

This imposition of vaccine mandates is a gross violation of the "rule of law," the ultimate goal of which is to provide "an umbrella concept for a number of legal and institutional instruments to protect citizens against the power of the State."[28] First coined by Plato and later refined by Aristotle, the concept of the "rule of law" was further elaborated by St Thomas Aquinas, who stated: "Once the government is established, the government of the kingdom must be so arranged that opportunity to tyrannize be removed. At the same time, his power should be so tempered that he cannot easily fall into tyranny."[29] According to the American legal philosopher, Charles Rice, who taught at the University of Notre Dame, "Aquinas' analysis is a prescription for limited government, providing a rational basis on which to affirm that there are limits to what the state can rightly do. His insistence that the power of the human law be limited implies a right of the person not to be subjected to an unjust law."[30]

In this context, the *United Nations Universal Declaration of Human Rights* recognizes, in its preamble, the critical role of the rule of law in preserving the inalienable rights of the individual: "Whereas it is essential, if man is not to be compelled to have recourse, as a last resort, to rebellion against tyranny and oppression, that human rights should be protected by the rule of law."

Public international law recognizes that, during extraordinary circumstances, governments may enact emergency powers that suspend ordinary rule-of-law protections, with the exception of "non-derogable rights." The importance of preserving these rights of the individual is recognized in an extensive range of international human rights treaties. For example, support for the inalienability of "non-derogable rights" is provided by the *Siracusa Principles on the Limitation and Derogation Provisions in the International Covenant on Civil and Political Rights* ("Siracusa Principles"). A document produced by the American Association for the International Commission of Jurists, the Siracusa Principles explicitly state that,

> No state party shall, even in time of emergency threatening the life of the nation, derogate from the Covenant's guarantees of the right to life; freedom from torture, cruel, inhuman or degrading treatment or punishment, and from medical or scientific experimentation without free consent; freedom from slavery or involuntary servitude . . . the right to recognition as a person before the law; and freedom of thought, conscience and religion. These rights are not derogable under any conditions even for the asserted purpose of preserving the life of the nation.[31]

Consistent with the Siracusa Principles, in a climate of uncertainty, characterized by a demonstrable lack of confidence, a program of mandatory vaccination cannot be regarded as consensual. From the perspective of international law, the right to informed consent is the bedrock principle of ethical standards in medicine. According to Article 6:1 of UNESCO's *Universal Declaration on Bioethics and Human Rights* (2005):

> Any preventive, diagnostic and therapeutic medical intervention is only to be carried out with the prior, free and informed consent of the person concerned, based on adequate information. The consent should, where appropriate, be express and may be withdrawn by the person concerned at any time and for any reason without disadvantage or prejudice.

In this context, Dr. Rocco Loiacono comments:

> For any government either by itself or via corporate proxy to attempt to mandate vaccines in circumstances were there has not been adequate testing and analysis of risks as well as benefits would constitute not only a violation of the principle of informed consent . . . but a violation of Australia's obligations under international law with respect to medical experimentation.[32]

As noted earlier, international human rights legislation explicitly prohibits the removal of non-derogable rights even in situations of an alleged "emergency." This prohibition encompasses any form of compulsion subjecting individuals to mandatory medical or pharmaceutical services, including vaccination. Hence, any law that requires vaccine mandates either directly or indirectly is not only constitutionally invalid but also constitutes a violation of Australia's obligations under public international law and codes of medical ethics.

Consequences of the Imposition of Vaccine Mandates

Writing about Australia's management of the Covid-19 pandemic, Garrick Professor of Law, James Allan, commented "that in a decade or less we will look back on this as the worst public policy failure in this country's history . . . it will take a few years for the ruinous outcomes . . . to become clear." In this context, Allan also opined that the damage to the economy is not caused by the Covid-19 virus itself "but by the political response to it" that "shows the economic effects of ignoring freedom-concerns."[33] Now that Australia, and most other countries (perhaps reluctantly) have returned to its pre-Covid routine, it is appropriate and timely to assess Allan's confident assertion that the management of the Covid-19 pandemic, especially the imposition of vaccine mandates, is the worst policy failure of the decade.

The decline in civility and the toxicity generated by the response to the Covid-19 pandemic provide ample evidence of the failure of Australian authorities to protect the basic rights of people. The government's responses have fueled the media's doomsday predictions that point to the development of a two-tier Australian society. When the vaccine mandates were imposed, the former Premier of New South Wales warned, "Unvaccinated people in New South Wales could be barred from locations and denied movement freedoms even after the state achieves 80% double dose vaccination" and that, "vaccine-hesitant residents . . . will not be able to let everybody else do the hard work and then turn up for equal freedoms."[34] In the same vein, the then Deputy Premier of New South Wales boldly declared that businesses that accept unvaccinated people will be subject to exceptionally heavy fines.

Private employers were encouraged to require their workforce to be vaccinated. For example, Qantas required the vaccination of all people who wanted to fly internationally, including its workforce. These were draconian edicts, which facilitated the creation of a two-tier Australia where some people were more privileged than others, involving the distribution of burdens and benefits simply on the ground of people's vaccine status.

The policy failures of the federal, state, and territory governments demonstrate the validity of President Ronald Reagan's comment that, "government is not the solution to our problem; government *is* the problem."[35] Indeed, a review of the management of the Covid-19 pandemic reveals that Australia has become a nation of slave-like people with elected politicians acting more as masters, without providing the servant leadership that a free people expect of their leaders. That this bold comment does not belong to the world of fiction is evidenced by the adoption by state governments, following the expiry of the state of emergency, of temporary emergency legislation (which may well become permanent). For example, the Western Australian parliament adopted the Emergency Amendment (Temporary COVID-19 Provisions) Act 2022, which confers power on the police commissioner, acting on the advice of the Chief Health Officer, to declare a state of emergency, removing the need for parliamentary oversight. On October 12, 2022, the Queensland Labor government—with support from the Liberal-National Party opposition—passed similar legislation that allows the Chief Health Officer to make public health directions. Queensland also adopted the Health Practitioner Regulation National Law and Other Legislation Amendment Act 2022 that potentially threatens medical practitioners with deregistration if they do not accept, or adhere to, the government's health directives. The inability of the government to address the demonstrable evisceration of the rights of people is unforgettable and unforgivable.

As the long-term adverse consequences of the Covid-19 fiasco are enduring, Professor Allan's opinion that the management of the pandemic is the worst policy failure of the decade is credible for at least three reasons. First, there is the enviable—probably impossible—task to restore the trust that people place in government. It can be expected that the level of trust, as it existed in pre-pandemic times, will never be restored to the same level.

Second, the government's management of the pandemic has created a two-tier state where some people are more privileged than others, involving the distribution of burdens and benefits simply on the ground of people's vaccine status. The emergence of a two-tier society proves that Australia (and comparable nations around the world) has irretrievably changed because fundamental rights are ever more dependent on the government's generosity and could quickly be taken away at the slightest provocation, ostensibly to protect the health of Australians. The legacy of Covid-19, especially the imposition of vaccine mandates, is defacing Australia, while potentially, if not actually, transforming it into an illiberal state.

Third, the vaccine mandates and other Covid-19 measures have now created a toxic society where persons, as soon as they have a cold, are urged (sometimes coerced by those around them) to test for the virus, thereby making it difficult to live normally as in pre-Covid days. Hence, there is an assumption that any physical discomfort requires the application of various measures, for example, masking.

Conclusion

One of the most contentious practices of the Covid-19 pandemic in Australia, and throughout the world, was the imposition of vaccine mandates. In Australia, the imposition of these mandates, which had a devastating impact on the livelihood of people and caused dislocation and trauma, is likely to be unconstitutional. It is also a practice that, in international law, offends against the right of people to consent to medical treatment, including vaccinations. The deliberate exclusion of unvaccinated Australians from participation in certain activities discriminates against them on the grounds of vaccine status. This raises problems of unequal treatment and contributes to society's slide to authoritarianism.

Notes

1. *British Medical Association v Commonwealth* (1949) 79 CLR 201.
2. Ibid., 287 (Williams J).
3. *Wong v Commonwealth; Selim v Professional Services Review Committee* (2009) 236 CLR 573.
4. Ibid., 62.
5. The views of Luke Beck and George Williams are discussed in: *AAP FactCheck*, "Does a constitutional clause ban vaccine mandates in Australia?" (July 26, 2021) (https://www.aap.com.au/factcheck/constitutional-clause-doesn't-ban-vaccine-mandates-in-australia/).
6. *Kassam v Hazzard; Henry v Hazzard* (2021) NWSC 1320.
7. Ibid., 275.
8. *Wong v Commonwealth; Selim v Professional Services Review Committee* (2009) 236 CLR 573.
9. Ibid., 151.
10. *Bowater v Rowley Regis Corp* (1944) KB 476:479 (Scott LJ).

11 *Leeth v Commonwealth* (1992) 174 CLR 455.
12 Ibid., 8.
13 *Airdale National Health Service Trust v Bland* (1993) AC 789: 889. (Mustill LJ). Similarly, in that same case, Lord Judge Goff remarked at 866: "[I]t is established that the principle of self-determination requires that respect must be given to the wishes of the patient, so that, if an adult patient of sound mind refuses, however unreasonably, to consent to treatment or care by which his life would or might be prolonged, the doctors responsible for his care must give effect to his wishes, even though they do not consider it to be in his best interests to do so: To this extent, the principle of sanctity of human life must yield to the principle of self-determination."
14 *AAP FactCheck*, "The Nuremberg Code Doesn't Apply to COVID-19 Vaccinations" (June 9, 202) (https://www.aap.com.au/factcheck/the-nuremberg-code-doesnt-apply-to-COVID-19-vaccinations/).
15 Wendy Hoy and Augusto Zimmermann, "Excess Mortality and COVID Vaccination: Is There a Correlation?," *The Spectator Australia* (November 23, 2023) (https://www.spectator.com.au/2023/11/excess-mortality-and-COVID-vaccination-is-there-a-correlation/).
16 Denis G. Rancourt, Marine Baudin, Joseph Hickey, and Jérémie Mercier, "COVID-19 Vaccine – Associated Mortality in the Southern Hemisphere" (September 17, 2023) (https://correlationcanada.org/research/ https://denisrancourt.ca/ https://www.researchgate.net/profile/Jeremie-Mercier2 https://ocla.ca/COVID/ https://www.jeremie-mercier.com/ https://denisrancourt.substack.com/).
17 Kasen K. Riemersma et al., "Vaccinated and Unvaccinated Individuals Have a Similar Viral Loads in Communities with a High Prevalence of the SARS-CoV-2 Delta Variant," *MedRxiv* (July 31, 2021) (https://www.medrxiv.org/content/10.1101/2021.07.31.21261387v1?).
18 John P. A. Ioannidis, "A Fiasco in the Making? As the Coronavirus Pandemic Takes Hold, We Are Making Decisions Without Reliable Data," *Statnews* (March 17, 2020) (https://www.statnews.com/2020/03/17/a-fiasco-in-the-making-as-the-coronavirus-pandemic-takes-hold-we-are-making-decisions-without-reliable-data/).
19 World Health Organization, "Coronavirus Disease (COVID-19)" (https://www.who.int/health-topics/coronavirus#tab=tab_1).
20 David Bell and Roland Salmon, "Public Health Logic of COVID-19 Vaccinations," *The British Medical Journal* (September 6, 2021) (https://www.bmj.com/content/374/bmj.n2180/rr-4). See also: "COVID-19: JCVI Opts Not to Recommend Universal Vaccination of 12–15 Year Olds," *The British Medical Journal* (September 3, 2021) (https://www.bmj.com/content/374/bmj.n2180). A recent study has revealed that people who suffer from myocarditis after receiving their Covid-19 vaccination continue to suffer from the symptoms six months after the diagnosis of the disease: see *Long term follow up and outcomes of Covid-19 vaccine associated myocarditis in Victoria, Australia: A clinical surveillance study*; Naveen Athrapully, "Over Half of Post-COVID Vaccine Myocarditis Patients Still Had Symptoms After 6 Months: Study," *The Epoch Times* (December 29, 2023) (https://www.theepochtimes.com/health/over-half-of-post-COVID-vaccine-myocarditis-patients-still-had-symptoms-after-6-months-study-5555188).

21 Ian Hanke, "Daniel Andrews' Plan for Indefinite Detention—and More," *The Spectator Australia* (September 18, 2020) (https://www.spectator.com.au/2020/09/daniel-andrews-plan-for-indefinite-detention-and-more/). See Augusto Zimmermann and Gabriël Moens AM, *Emergency Powers, COVID-19 Restrictions & Mandatory Vaccination: A "Rule of Law' Perspective"* (Connor Court Publishing, 2022: Cleveland, Queensland, AU).

22 Gabriël A. Moens, "Why Was Australia Allowed to Impose Such Draconian COVID-19 Restrictions?" *The Epoch Times* (March 31, 2023) (https://www.theepochtimes.com/opinion/why-was-australia-allowed-to-impose-such-draconian-COVID-19-restrictions-5162320).

23 Ibid.

24 Peter Shergold AC, Jillian Broadbent AC, Isobel Marshall, and Peter Varghese AO, *Fault Lines: An Independent Review into Australia's Response to COVID-19*, 2.

25 Gigi Foster, "Australia's COVID Response Cost 68 Times More than the Benefits Delivered," UNSW, *Businessthink* (January 3, 2023) (https://www.businessthink.unsw.edu.au/articles/COVID-lockdowns-government-policy-analysis).

26 Augusto Zimmermann, "Constitutional Monarchy or Elective Dictatorship?" *Quadrant* (March 15, 2023) (https://quadrant.org.au/opinion/liberty/2023/03/constitutional-monarchy-or-elective-dictatorship).

27 *Re Bolton; Ex Parte Beane* (1987) 162 CLR 514.

28 Adriaan Bedner and Jacqueline A. C. Vel, "An Analytical Framework for Empirical Research on Access to Justice," *The Journal of Law, Social Justice and Global Development* 1 (2010): 21.

29 St Thomas Aquinas, *De Regimine Principum*, trans. Gerald B. Phelan (New York: Sheed & Ward, 1938), Bk I, Ch. 2, 55.

30 C. E. Rice, *50 Questions on the Natural Law* (San Francisco: Ignatius Press, 1999), 85.

31 United Nations Economic and Social Council, United Nations Sub-Commission on Prevention of Discrimination and Protection of Minorities, Siracusa Principles on the Limitation and Derogation of Provisions in the International Covenant on Civil and Political Rights, Annex, UN Doc E/CN.4/ (1984) [58].

32 Rocco Loiacono, "Most COVID Patients at Israeli Hospital Fully Vaccinated? What Does This Mean for Australia?" (August 12, 2021) (https://www.spectator.com.au/2021/08/most-COVID-patients-at-israeli-hospital-fully-vaccinated-what-does-this-mean-for-australia/).

33 Rocco Loiacono and Augusto Zimmermann, *Deconstructing Scomo: Critical Reflections on Australia's 30th Prime Minister* (Underwood, Queensland: Locke Press, 2022), viii.

34 Elias Visontay, "NSW Unvaccinated Could be Denied Freedoms at 80% Target, Premier Says, as 1,257 COVID Cases Recorded," *The Guardian* (September 13, 2021) (https://www.theguardian.com/australia-news/2021/sep/13/nsw-unvaccinated-could-be-denied-freedoms-at-80-target-premier-says-as-1257-COVID-cases-recorded).

35 Ronald Reagan, Inaugural Address (January 20, 1981) (https://speakola.com/political/ronald-reagan-first-inaugural-speech-1981).

Responses

Response to Cohen on Vaccine Mandates

By Gabriël A. Moens

Study Questions

1. According to Moens, what is the problem with Mill's view of the Harm Principle? How does this apply to the issue of vaccine mandates?
2. Why does Moens think that Cohen fails to achieve the desired balance between respecting individual rights and preventing harm to others?
3. What does Moens think is problematic with Cohen's appeal to utilitarianism?
4. How does Moens respond to Cohen's fairness and solidarity arguments?

Shlomo Cohen presented three justifications for vaccine mandates. The first concerns the prohibition against harming. The second relates to the duty of advancing the common good, and the third deals with the duty to fairly contribute to the public good. Interestingly, the paper's arguments offer a "generalized" defense of vaccine mandates and do not specifically deal with Covid-19 vaccine mandates. I make this point because Covid-19 vaccine mandates certainly spawned a contentious and widespread discussion on the ethical and legal propriety of imposing these mandates.

It can be argued that the three arguments, listed above, in favor of the imposition of vaccine mandates, collapse into one argument. This is because the promotion of the common good and the duty to act fairly are embedded in the prohibition against harming. Indeed, the implementation of the Harm Principle is inevitably motivated by the desire to contribute fairly to the "common good." Hence, this response paper will concentrate on the "harm" principle.

The Illusory Nature of "Harm"

John Stuart Mill succinctly states the "harm" principle in his essay *On Liberty*: "The only purpose for which power can be rightfully exercised over any member of a civilized community against his will is to prevent harm to others."[1] The problem with Mill's argument is that "harm" is an illusory concept, the meaning of which depends on people's subjective perception of what constitutes "harm." If so, in relying on the Harm Principle to contribute to the perceived "common good," the principle unavoidably involves harm-shopping to justify the imposition of a vaccine mandate. As such, a subjective evaluation of competing claims of harm is inevitably involved in the harm-shopping process which, in turn, has the capacity to eviscerate a person's right to "individual autonomy." Moreover, vaccines, mandated by the ruling health authorities, themselves could cause harm, which would complicate any attempts at justifying their imposition on people.

As Cohen indicates, those in favor of mandates usually argue that a *risk* of suffering harm is sufficient to activate the power of the state to impose vaccine mandates "to secure public safety." Proponents of this argument advocate that the Harm Principle thus allows coercive mandates even if the risk has not yet materialized or manifested itself in society. If it is justifiable to implement the Harm Principle whenever a risk of harm surfaces, then all vaccine mandates become acceptable because life is inherently risky, and any attempt at maintaining individual autonomy would effectively be extinguished.

The association of vaccine mandates with the avoidance of "harm" and the promotion of the "common good" thus involves the use of vague, indeterminate notions, the meaning and content of which are fundamentally unclear. This is ironic because people who seek exemptions from vaccine mandates are usually required to provide convincing and demonstrable proof that vaccination would harm their health. Hence, if vaccines are to be mandatory, it is necessary to demonstrate the actual, as opposed to the perceived, existence of harm, and their potential to secure the "common good."

Cohen's Four Parameters and the Problem of Consent

Nevertheless, the power of the state to order mandatory vaccination appears to rest on solid legal foundations. For example, in *Jacobson v Massachusetts*, the Supreme Court of the United States ruled in 1905 that states may mandatorily vaccinate people and that a refusal could result in the imposition of punishments.[2] This judgment relies on the earlier case of *Crowley v Christensen*,[3] where the Court indicated that "The possession and enjoyment of all rights are subject to such reasonable conditions as may be deemed by the governing authority of the country essential to the safety, health, peace, good order, and morals of the community" and that "Even liberty itself, the greatest of all rights, is not unrestricted license to act according to one's own will. It is only freedom from restraint under conditions essential to the equal enjoyment of the same right by others. It is, then, liberty regulated by law."

Even if the constitutional validity of vaccine mandates is incontestable in the United States, the issue of where to draw the line between freedom to consent to medical treatment, on the one hand, and the need to protect the community, on the other, remains a concern.

In this context, Cohen seeks to strike a reasonable balance between respecting individual autonomy and preventing harm to others by establishing four parameters: the severity of the threat, effectiveness of the vaccine, level of the vaccine's safety, and the choice of the least coercive effective alternative. Of course, the issue as to who will evaluate these parameters is highly problematic because of the subjectiveness involved in the process. This is exemplified by Cohen's claim that "the more people are vaccinated, the less morbidity and mortality there will be in the population" (p. 187). Such a claim is optimistic at best, and egregiously wrong at worst. The further claim that "During epidemics, vaccines reduce the number of contagious people" (Ibid) is equally contentious.

These parameters must be subject to the consent of the individual to receive the vaccination. It is certain that, from an international law point of view, consent is an unconditional requirement. For example, the S*iracusa Principles on the Limitation and Derogation Provisions in the International Covenant on Civil and Political Rights* ("Siracusa Principles") explicitly state that "No state party shall, even in time of emergency threatening the life of the nation" compromise the rights of people to freely consent to medical or scientific experimentation, "even for the asserted purpose of preserving the life of the nation." Consistent with the Siracusa Principles, in a climate of uncertainty, characterized by a demonstrable lack of confidence, a program of mandatory vaccination cannot be regarded as consensual. From the perspective of international law, the right to informed consent is the bedrock principle of ethical standards in medicine. According to Article 6:1 of UNESCO's Universal *Declaration on Bioethics and Human Rights* (2005):

> Any preventive, diagnostic and therapeutic medical intervention is only to be carried out with the prior, free and informed consent of the person concerned, based on adequate information. The consent should, where appropriate, be express and may be withdrawn by the person concerned at any time and for any reason without disadvantage or prejudice.

The *Nuremberg* Code—an ethics code—relied upon during the Nazi doctors' trials in Nuremberg also supports the right to refuse vaccination. This Code has as its first principle the willingness and informed consent by the individual to receive medical treatment or to participate in an experiment. This Code, in requiring consent to receive medical treatment, discloses that lack of confidence in the vaccines' effectiveness is a sufficient reason to reject vaccination. Indeed, in a climate of uncertainty, as amply demonstrated by the vaccine hesitancy in many countries, a vaccine mandate violates the rights of people as it simply cannot be regarded as consensual and based on a contractual relationship between doctors and patients.

Which Utilitarianism?

As stated before, the duty of beneficence to contribute to the common good is a restatement of the Harm Principle because, if vaccine mandates are necessary to avoid harm, they will inevitably support the common good. Mr. Justice Harlan offers this justification in *Jacobson v Massachusetts*, where the court said that "There are manifold restraints to which every person is necessarily subject for the common good."[4] Cohen attempts to justify the duty of beneficence by relying on the principle of utilitarianism which "demands that we aggregate all considerations relevant for promoting the overall good and seek to do the (kind of) act that maximizes it" (p. 190). Hence, a cost-benefit analysis of the implementation of this principle of utilitarianism may yet result in a rejection of vaccine mandates.

However, this understanding of the principle of "utilitarianism" disregards the likelihood that repeated reliance on it prejudices a competing version of utilitarianism, according to which extensive violations of people's individual autonomy may result in a breach of the "rule of law"—a rule that protects the rights of people even in a climate that demands submission to, and conformity with, the health edicts of the relevant authorities.

Fairness and Solidarity?

The argument based on fairness holds that it is not fair for people to reject vaccination by failing to make their own contribution to the public good—a moral duty. As such, this argument also constitutes a variant of the Harm Principle. Cohen notes that "There are public goods . . . from which it is *impossible* to be excluded," and that the state's "legal system and police force" monitor people's contribution to those goods (p. 193). Surely, such an approach may facilitate a slide to a totalitarian situation where the rights of individuals would be subservient to the interests of the state. Moreover, the claim that such an approach is acceptable to secure a satisfactory life is putting the bar too high because it is most unlikely that vaccine mandates could ever meet this requirement.

Cohen suggests that an expectation of basic decency and the interconnectedness of all people support the duty of fairness. He also opines that, in our complex world, acceptance of vaccine mandates is an expression of solidarity with other people. He confidently states that "the basis for collective responsibility and solidarity is rather naturally anchored in our existential condition" (p. 194). These opinions, while undoubtedly well-intended, are more appropriately used in a utopian environment where vaccine mandates are heralded as the savior of the common good at the expense of individual integrity.

Notes

1 John Stuart Mill, *On Liberty* in *On Liberty and the Subjugation of Women* (New York: Henry Holt & Co., 1879), 23.
2 *Jacobson v Massachusetts*, 197 US 11 (1905).
3 *Crowley v Christensen*, 137 US 86, 89 (1890).
4 *Jacobson v Massachusetts*, 197 US 11, 26 (1905).

Reply to Moens on Vaccine Mandates

Shlomo Cohen

Study Questions

1. What preliminary points does Cohen make in response to Moens?
2. In what four ways does Cohen think that Moens is guilty of hyperbole in his claim that vaccine mandates are gross violations of the rule of law?
3. How does Cohen reply to Moens's view that vaccine mandates would interfere with the doctor-patient relationship?
4. How does Cohen respond to Moen's vaccine safety concerns?

That protecting civil liberties is extremely important is indisputable. The dispute that does exist refers to the circumstances under which basic civil liberties may, or indeed should, be overridden out of concern for basic public interests—specifically, in our case, those circumstances under which emergency measures for safeguarding public health can override individual liberties.

Preliminary Issues

I should start with two preliminary remarks to demarcate the debate. First, Moens's chapter discusses vaccine mandates in the case of the Covid pandemic. To the extent that his arguments are restricted to that specific case, nothing he says needs to contradict my arguments: he could theoretically be right that vaccine mandates *in the specific case of the pandemic* were unethical, without this affecting my general arguments for vaccine mandates when the appropriate conditions *are* met. My response will therefore focus on the general ethical ideas expressed in his chapter, to the extent that they transcend the historical peculiarities of the Covid pandemic.

Second, Moens sets out to examine "whether these mandates were legal, efficacious, and ethical" (p. 198). I will set aside arguments regarding the law (I have nothing to say about the legality of vaccine mandates in Australia) and regarding the relevant scientific facts (the efficacy of Covid vaccines, etc.) as such; I will concentrate only on what is pertinent to the ethical debate.

A Gross Violation of the "Rule of Law"?

Moens's main idea revolves around the argument that the "imposition of vaccine mandates is a gross violation of the 'rule of law'." This sounds hyperbolic, and I think it really is. Moens explicates his view through his discussion of a cluster of important ethical concepts: inalienable rights, equality, informed consent, and dignity. These concepts and the issues they raise are interrelated; I will comment briefly on each.

Inalienable Rights

The idea of "the inalienable rights of the individual" is often rejected by consequentialist moral thinking. When the consequences of upholding individual rights become catastrophic, many deontologists too reveal that they are not truly absolutists about "inalienable rights"; they rather support the idea of a threshold level of badness of consequences beyond which those individual rights are overridden. The question is where to draw the threshold. This dilemma is known, for example, from the literature on the permissibility of torture in "ticking bomb scenarios," where torture is the only way to get a terrorist to reveal the location of a bomb he planted in a populated area. Non-absolutists may hold, in analogy, that there is a threshold of public health risk that justifies coercive measures against vaccine objectors. (And since getting vaccinated or suffering relatively minor sanctions for not doing so is orders of magnitude less severe than being tortured, the threshold of bad consequences is correlatively lower.) This expresses a general recognition that balancing opposing moral considerations can be inescapable, even with respect to so-called "inalienable rights." I think this is correct; Moens seems to disagree (see his discussion of the Siracusa Principles).

Equality

Moens argues that "if unvaccinated Australians were to face serious restrictions of rights and freedoms, these restrictions would violate the democratic principle of equality before the law" (p. 200). However, it is hard to see why vaccine mandates should be *essentially* inegalitarian. Justice surely demands that we treat similar cases similarly; but which are the relevant parameters of "similarity"? Why must society view the vaccinated, who help protect public health as relevantly equal to vaccine objectors who impose health risks on others?

Moens writes of "draconian edicts, which facilitated the creation of a two-tier Australia where some people were more privileged than others, involving the distribution of burdens and benefits simply on the ground of peoples' vaccine status" (p. 207). This language is reasonable with respect to *arbitrary* discrimination, such as on the basis of skin color or ethnicity; it is misplaced when referring to vaccination ultimatums given to employees who provide face-to-face services to the public, as in one of Moens's examples. Compensating pro-social behavior while punishing antisocial behavior is sensibly meritocratic; it is not arbitrary discrimination. It need not therefore be unjust.

Informed Consent

Moens also argues that "the right to informed consent is the bedrock principle of ethical standards in medicine" (pp. 205–06). I would qualify that it is *a* bedrock principle, alongside others that can qualify its stringency. This qualified view follows notably from the principle pluralism theory of Tom Beauchamp and James Childress—the most influential system of medical ethics during the past four decades.[1] It is likewise expressed in many works in bioethics that support medical paternalism under certain conditions. The same logic applies to the advocacy of coercive public health measures under certain conditions—such as during pandemics. This ethical view finds expression in vaccine mandate laws in most liberal democracies.

The question of *when* infringement of personal liberty can be justified is of course crucial, and specifically, whether and when it applies to the decision not to get vaccinated. Imagine a person who—due to a brain tumor, say—gets fits of pathological rage, where he becomes dangerous to his environment. That person may be legally speaking considered a competent decision-maker during these fits, and he may refuse treatment. Despite his legal competence, we may be morally justified in restraining him forcibly during those rage attacks to protect his surroundings. We may think of the danger of infectivity as analogous, if the level of risk is sufficiently high, and thus view vaccine mandates as reasonable.

Dignity

Moens further argues that "when citizens are not allowed to make personal decisions about their own medical treatment," as in the case of vaccination, that is "a textbook example of the operation of the Nanny State that removes any sense of individual responsibility and human dignity" (p. 200). Indeed, state paternalism can fail to respect human dignity, but paternalism is not the issue here. Referring to decisions regarding vaccination as merely "personal decisions" is a strange denial of reality: with regard to infectious pathogens, we are all—whether we admit it or not—potential vectors of infectivity and therefore of harm to others. That the state intervenes in behaviors that pose potential harm to others does not make it a Nanny State—that is the state's *raison d'être* and fundamental responsibility.

Some Additional Points

All the above referred to the basic constitutional issue of individual liberties. I now turn to a couple of extra points.

The Doctor-Patient Relationship

According to Moens, mandating vaccination by law "would interfere with the relationship between the doctor and the patient—a relationship-which is based on contract and trust" (p. 199). Now the question of how trust is affected is ultimately an empirical matter, not a matter of philosophical speculation. I am leaving aside the technical issue that the implementation of vaccination (especially during pandemics) can be managed by the government without needing to pass through one's primary care physician, and that at any rate, the patient may well realize that the physician is fettered by the law.

Rather, the more essential points are different. First, (to the extent that one's doctor *is* instrumental in the vaccination program) we would surely expect an injury to trust if the doctor's actions flout the patient's inalienable rights, including that of informed consent, treat the patient as ineligible to egalitarian justice, and disrespect the patient's human dignity. We have seen, however, that none of those terrible things need apply. Second, even if the patient did feel subject to a certain paternalism, trust is a function of various parameters, such as trust in the doctor's wisdom or her caring attitude toward the patient.[2] The different parameters of trust may point in opposing directions, and the potential decline in trust due to one parameter may be more than offset by enhanced trust due to another parameter. Preserving trust by respecting patient autonomy is surely very important; it just isn't the alpha and the omega of trust, and may not be the decisive factor determining its level.

Safety Concerns

Finally, Moens argues that "people's refusal to be vaccinated may be based on the ground that the COVID-19 vaccines are still experimental and their long-term effects and safety on its recipients are still largely unknown, but nevertheless real" (p. 201). I agree that the question of the relative safety of vaccines is a valid consideration when contemplating vaccine mandates. Moens claims that Covid vaccines "have prevented neither infection nor transmission" (p. 203). I saw other facts,[3] but this is not the forum to debate the science. Rather, I want to make two points. (1) The optimal balance between levels of safety and of prevention of widespread disease is to be negotiated between all stakeholders. (2) Whether a decision to vaccinate was ethical or not should be determined according to the scientific data existing *at the time* of decision-making—in retrospect, it is unfairly easy to be all the wiser. In real time, public health authorities are always between a hammer and a hard place: they could be justly condemned if they recommend too much intervention but also if they recommend too little.

Conclusion

Individual liberty is of foundational importance, and Moens's perspective does well to remind us of this. But for all that, I believe it is wrong to cling too strongly to any single value. Such total devotion to one supreme value paves the way to fundamentalism; and fundamentalism is the mother of all political trouble. We should rather acknowledge the plurality of basic values and find the optimal balance between them.

Notes

1. T. L. Beauchamp and J. F. Childress, *Principles of Biomedical Ethics*, 8th ed. (Oxford: Oxford University Press, 2019).
2. Shlomo Cohen, "Potential Challenges to Doctor-Patient Trust Posed by Personalized Medicine," in *Can Precision Medicine Be Personal; Can Personalized Medicine Be Precise?*, ed. Yechiel Michael Barilan, Margherita Brusa, and Aaron Ciechanover (Oxford: Oxford University Press, 2022), 161–72.
3. For instance: Iván Martínez-Baz, et al., "Effect of COVID-19 Vaccination on the SARS-CoV-2 Transmission among Social and Household Close Contacts: A Cohort Study," *Journal of Infection and Public Health* 16, no. 3 (2023): 410–17.

Questions for Reflection

1. Where do you think the line should be drawn in balancing individual autonomy and the public good? Why?
2. Is the issue of informed consent as serious as Moens claims when it comes to vaccine mandates? Why?
3. What ethical principles (e.g., personal autonomy, beneficence, justice, harm prevention, etc.) do you think are most relevant when evaluating the morality of vaccine mandates?

For Further Reading

Battin, Margaret P., et al. *The Patient as Victim and Vector: Ethics and Infectious Disease,* 2nd ed. Oxford University Press, 2021.

Dershowitz, Alan. *The Case for Vaccine Mandates.* Hot Books, 2021.

Giubilini, Alberto. "An Argument for Compulsory Vaccination: The Taxation Analogy." *Journal of Applied Philosophy* 37 (2002): 446–66.

Heckenlively, Kent. *The Case against Vaccine Mandates.* Hot Books, 2021.

Steinhoff, Uwe. "The Case against Compulsory Vaccination: The Failed Arguments from Risk Imposition, Tax Evasion, 'Social Liberty,' and the Priority of Life." *Journal of Medical Ethics* (October 2024): 1–7.

Zimmerman, Augusto, and Gabriël A. Moens. *Emergency Powers, COVID-19 Restrictions & Mandatory Vaccination: A "Rule-Of-Law" Perspective.* Connor Court Publishing, 2022.

7

Animal Rights

A Non-Consequentialist Defense of Animal Rights

Molly Gardner

> **Study Questions**
>
> 1. What is Gardner's non-consequentialist argument for animal rights?
> 2. What is the No Harming Principle? What is Gardner's argument in defense of it?
> 3. What are the "special circumstances" in which harming may be morally permissible?
> 4. What evidence does Gardner give in support of the second premise of her argument?
> 5. What two objections to her argument does Gardner address? How does she respond to them?
> 6. How does Gardner explain the connection between the No Harming Principle and animal rights?

Many people who defend what we might loosely refer to as "animal rights" do not, strictly speaking, believe in animal rights at all. They are *utilitarians*: they believe that for humans and for animals, morality is about promoting well-being and reducing suffering, not respecting rights. Nevertheless, they are easily mistaken for animal rights proponents because they tend to arrive at the same practical conclusions we associate with the animal rights movement. For example, utilitarians usually conclude that factory farming is wrong; that most animal testing is wrong; and that hunting and trapping animals for sport or fashion is wrong.

If you have sympathy for the animal rights movement, you might be tempted to align yourself with utilitarianism. Once you accept the utilitarian starting point, it is easy to defend the relevant prescriptions. It is plainly true that if we all ate vegan hamburgers instead of regular hamburgers, conducted sound experiments without using animals, and wore fake fur instead of real fur, there would be much less suffering in the world. Nevertheless, there is something unsettling about aligning yourself with a view whose practical consequences you agree with, but whose starting premises you might not really accept.[1]

Can we derive the same conclusions about factory farms, animal testing, and hunting or trapping from a *non-consequentialist* starting point? This might seem like more of a challenge. Many people associate non-consequentialism with the philosopher Immanuel Kant, who was famously opposed to giving animals any direct moral consideration at all. The non-consequentialist philosopher Tom Regan vehemently defended animal rights, but he has been criticized for going too far. On his view, for example, it would be wrong to test on animals no matter how many lives we could save.[2] However, I believe that we can build upon the insights of philosophers like Kant and Regan to construct a more plausible non-consequentialist defense of treating animals better than we currently do. More precisely, we can argue for the same practical conclusions I mentioned above—that factory farms are wrong; that most animal testing is wrong; and that hunting or trapping animals for sport or fashion is wrong—without appealing to premises that are hard to accept, either because they assume the truth of utilitarianism or because they assume an implausible absolutism.

In what follows I will develop that argument. It has two main premises. The first premise is that, except in special circumstances, it is wrong to harm some individuals for the sake of others. I will defend the first premise by showing how it has more plausible implications than utilitarianism and fits better with our understanding of the moral significance of the distinction between doing and allowing harm. The second premise is that in the present circumstances, most instances of factory farming, testing on animals, and hunting or trapping for sport or fashion qualify as cases in which we are harming some individuals for the sake of others. I will defend the second premise against the objection that special circumstances nevertheless make it permissible to harm animals in these cases. I will then consider two further objections to my argument: that harms to animals do not matter as much as harms to human beings, and that without practices like factory farming and animal testing, many animals with lives that are at least worth living would never come into existence at all. Finally, I will discuss the concept of "rights" and explain why my view can be understood as a non-consequentialist, non-absolutist defense of animal rights.

The No Harming Principle

Recall that the first premise of my argument is that, *except in special circumstances, it is wrong to harm some individuals for the sake of others*. I will refer to this principle as the *No Harming Principle*. When I say it is wrong to harm some individuals, I mean that it is wrong to cause harm to them or to do harm to them; I hold that harming, doing harm, and causing harm are all the same thing. However, harming is not the same as allowing harm. Even if there is something I fail to do that would have prevented someone from suffering a harm, this does not mean that I caused the harm. Suppose you ate some potato salad and suffered a stomachache, and I could have prevented all of this by throwing your plate of potato salad into the trash. You suffered harm, but by failing to throw your plate into the trash, I did not harm you; I merely allowed you to suffer harm.

When I talk about harming some "for the sake of others," I intend to refer to cases where harming some would benefit others, either by increasing their well-being from an already happy baseline, or by saving them from harm. Since the No Harming Principle implies that (absent special circumstances) it is wrong to harm some individuals as a way of saving others from harm, it is not a principle about minimizing the total amount of harm in the world. Indeed, the No Harming Principle sometimes implies that we are morally required to act in such a way that there is ultimately more harm in the world, rather than less. For example, we are not permitted to kill one person in order to procure his healthy organs for transplantation, even if transplanting his organs into other people's bodies is the only way we can save five others from the harm of death. In such a case, our failure to save those who need organ transplants is like my failure to throw your plate of potato salad into the trash. Just as, by not acting, I allow you to suffer stomach pain but do not cause that pain, so it is that by not killing the one, we allow the five to suffer the harm of death but do not kill them. The No Harming Principle implies that we are morally required to let these five people die, for we are not permitted to kill the one.

The best argument for accepting the No Harming Principle is that it explains a wide array of moral judgments that many people feel strongly about. It is part of commonsense morality that we may not kill a healthy person in order to procure his organs for transplantation. It is also part of commonsense morality that we may not force unwilling individuals to fight to the death for our entertainment, no matter how much enjoyment spectators might get from watching the fight. It is wrong to give sleeping pills to a baby so that we can leave him at home without a babysitter, no matter how much fun we would have on our night out. It is wrong for us to conduct secret medical experiments on people, even if doing so would advance scientific knowledge. It is wrong to steal money from our neighbors, even if we want to give that money to a charity that feeds starving children. In all of these cases, the fact that our actions would benefit ourselves or others does not justify doing the harm. The No Harming Principle explains why.

A utilitarian might object that the No Harming Principle is not the best explanation of our judgments about these cases. Instead, a better explanation is that when we do harm in these cases, we are not doing the best that we can do to promote overall well-being. The aggregated benefits of each action are smaller than the harm we cause; therefore, the total amount of well-being in the world would be higher in each case if we prioritized not harming over procuring the benefits. But this way of explaining our judgments seems wrong. First, in many of these cases, it is not at all clear that the aggregate benefits are smaller than the harms. Second, at least in the cases I described above, we do not need to aggregate the benefits of each action and weigh them against the magnitude of each harm to know that the benefits do not justify causing the harm. In these cases, it is the simple fact that we would be doing harm (and not merely allowing harm) that makes each action wrong, not the relative magnitude of that harm in comparison with the resultant benefits.

That said, there are some cases in which the relative magnitude of the harm we cause matters. Although I may not kill you to save five others, it would be morally permissible for me to pinch you on the arm to save five others. Although I may not drug my child so that I can have a fun night out, it would be morally permissible for me to apply duct tape to my baby's mouth to prevent his loud crying from revealing to the Nazis where an entire family is hiding. Even killing one person might be permissible if this were the only possible way to save an extremely large number of other people from dying. What explains why the ratio of harm to benefit matters in some cases but not in others? Perhaps it is the same principle that explains why, although I am not required to devote every moment of my life to helping other people, I am required to help a stranger in need in a case where the cost to me is minimal and the benefit to the stranger is large. It appears to be a basic feature of morality—albeit a strange one—that what we are morally permitted or required to do can change when the ratio of cost to benefit reaches a certain threshold. I mean to allow for this possibility with my use of the term "special circumstances." A case where you could save the lives of five people by pinching one victim on the arm is one of those special circumstances in which it is not wrong to harm one for the sake of others.

There are a few other situations that also fall into the category of special circumstances. First, if a competent, informed adult consents to being harmed for the sake of others, then it seems morally permissible for us to do the harm. Second, there might be cases where a wrongdoer deserves to be punished, and in those cases, we might be morally justified in punishing—and thereby harming—the wrongdoer for the sake of others. Third, there might be cases where the victim will suffer harm no matter what we do, but at least if we harm the victim ourselves, we can benefit others. Because these are all special circumstances, harming in these cases is not prohibited by the No Harming Principle. But in all other cases, doing harm, even to only one individual, is morally worse than allowing harm to many individuals. Our commonsense moral judgments support the principle that, except in special circumstances, it is wrong to harm some individuals for the sake of others.

How Our Practices Harm Animals

I have so far defended the No Harming Principle, which was the first premise of my non-consequentialist argument in support of treating animals better than we currently do. Recall that the second premise of my argument is the following: *In the present circumstances, most instances of factory farming, testing on animals, and hunting or trapping for sport or fashion qualify as cases in which we are harming some individuals for the sake of others, and in which the relevant special circumstances do not obtain.*

To see why the second premise is true, first consider what we do to animals on factory farms. Typically, factory farming involves confining animals in small, uncomfortable spaces; frustrating their natural instincts; performing painful procedures on them such as debeaking, castration, tail docking, and branding; failing to treat them for chronic health conditions and other debilitating injuries; and finally slaughtering them, sometimes in painful or terrifying ways, while they are still relatively young. Although many people think that opponents of factory farms object only, or mainly, to the practice of killing animals for food, factory farming harms animals in many other ways besides killing them. Indeed, for some factory-farmed animals, their death might be the least of the harms they suffer. Perhaps we can characterize the most objectionable harm of factory farming as *the harm of living a restricted life*. When we engage in factory farming, we are causing that harm: we are subjecting each animal to the immense harm of a restricted life.

Next consider animal testing. We conduct tests on animals for a variety of reasons, including to further our understanding of basic physiological processes; to train students; to find new ways to prevent or treat diseases or injuries; and to determine the toxicity of fragrances, pesticides, or other commercial products. These tests often require that we injure animals or that we sicken them with pathogens or toxic substances. Many of the experiments are painful, and the animals are killed afterward while they are still relatively young. But even in cases where the tests themselves are not painful or the deaths are not especially harmful, the animal test subjects have often been confined for their entire lives in cages, living restricted lives akin to the lives of animals on factory farms. Animal testing is usually very harmful to animals.

Finally, consider hunting or trapping animals for sport or fashion. Unlike factory farming and animal testing, hunting and trapping do not typically involve captive animals, although there are some hunting ranches where animals are imported and confined. Still, the primary harm suffered by animals who are hunted or trapped is death itself—and the pain and suffering associated with the manner in which that death comes about—rather than the harm of living a restricted life.

In any case, when we engage in factory farming, animal testing, hunting, or trapping, there is at least one clear harm we cause animals, whether it is the harm of a restricted life, the harm of pain and suffering, or the harm of death. Moreover, when we engage in these activities, we are harming animals for the sake of others. In the case of factory farming, the benefits to others are the abundant supply of inexpensive meat for meat-eaters and the profits people make from the sale of meat. In the case of animal testing, others benefit by gaining new knowledge—usually about physiology, medicine, or the toxicity of certain chemicals. And in the case of hunting or trapping, the benefits to others are food, entertainment, trophies, or fashionable clothing. None of these benefits are to the animals. Therefore, all of these activities are prohibited by the No Harming Principle.

Here one might object that we have not yet considered whether there are special circumstances that would invalidate the prohibition on harming. Are there special circumstances that make it permissible to harm animals in these ways? Recall the special circumstances I described in the previous section. I suggested there that they seem to fall into four categories. First, there are cases in which the ratio of harm to benefit reaches a certain threshold, such that the harm to the victim is a mere fraction of the benefit to others. Second, there are cases in which competent adults consent to being harmed for others' sake. Third, there are cases in which the harm is deserved. And fourth, there are cases in which the victim would suffer the harm regardless of what we did.

When it comes to how we treat animals, it seems clear that the second, third, and fourth categories do not apply. None of the animals we harm when we engage in factory farming, animal testing, hunting, or trapping consent to being harmed, nor are they capable of consenting. Nor do any of the animals deserve to be harmed. If we refrained from subjecting farm and laboratory animals to restricted lives, they would not live restricted lives at all. If we refrained from hunting and trapping animals, they would still die at some point, but they would not die the specific deaths that we caused them.

This leaves us only with the first category of special circumstances. Thus, to determine whether special circumstances apply when it comes to factory farming, testing, and hunting, we must consider whether the harm we do to animals when we engage in these activities is relatively minute in comparison with the benefits of these activities. Remember that this is not the same as the question of whether the benefits of the activities are greater than the harms. Arguably, the benefits of killing someone for his organs are five times as great as the harm to him, assuming that his organs could save five lives. Yet in that case, the ratio of harm to benefit is not sufficiently vast to render killing permissible. Therefore, factory farming would not be permissible even if it were like killing the one to save the five in the organ transplantation case. Factory farming would be permissible only if it were more like pinching someone on the arm to save five lives.

But factory farming is not like pinching someone on the arm to save five lives. If we are to stick with the pinching and killing analogies, factory farming is much more like killing one person to prevent another person from being pinched. As I mentioned above, the benefits of factory farming are the abundant supply of meat and the profits people get from meat sales. To procure those benefits, we cause each animal the immense harm of a restricted life. Each person who benefits from factory farming obtains a benefit whose magnitude is only a fraction of what each animal suffers. Perhaps if we consider not only the benefit to each person, but also the numbers of people who benefit from factory farming, we might think that the benefits of factory farming are greater. But in that case, we should also consider not only the harm to each animal but also the numbers of animals we are harming. If we take the numbers of people and animals into account, the ratio of harm to benefit does not significantly change. Instead of killing one person to prevent another person from being pinched, the case is now like killing millions of people to prevent millions of other people from being pinched. The ratio of harm to benefit is still the direct opposite of what the No Harming Principle's "special circumstances" clause refers to.

Similar reasoning applies to animal testing, hunting, and trapping. The knowledge we gain from testing on animals is a significant benefit, but in most cases, it is not so significant as to completely swamp the harm of pain, suffering, or living a restricted life. The value we get from hunting or wearing fur is also significant, but its magnitude does not come close to the magnitude of harm that an animal suffers when it dies a painful, early death. It seems, then, that just as the "special circumstances" clause does not apply to factory farming, it does not apply to hunting, trapping, or most cases of animal testing.

Objections and Replies

The No Harming Principle says that, except in special circumstances, it is wrong to harm some individuals for the sake of others. I have argued that we should accept this principle because it is the best explanation for a wide variety of our moral judgments about doing and allowing harm. I have also argued that this principle implies that factory farming, hunting, trapping, and most cases of animal testing are wrong, and I have replied to the objection that these practices involve special circumstances. In this section, I will consider and respond to two further objections.

Harming Animals Is Not as Bad as Harming Humans

The first objection is that harms to animals do not matter as much as harms to human beings. There are two ways to interpret this objection. First, it might be thought of as a challenge to the No Harming Principle. The objection might be that a better explanation of our moral judgments is a principle with a more restricted scope, such as the following: except in special circumstances, it is wrong to harm some human beings for the sake of others. Call this the *No Harming Humans Principle*.

However, the No Harming Humans Principle is not a better explanation of our moral judgments, for it cannot explain as many of our moral judgments as the No Harming Principle can. Many of us believe it is wrong, not only to force unwilling humans to fight to the death for our entertainment, but also to force roosters and dogs to do so. It would also be wrong to kill our pets or chain them up in the basement so that we could leave home without a pet sitter, no matter how much fun we would have on our vacation. If you thought your food had been contaminated with deadly bacteria, it would be wrong for you to test it on your dog before eating it. The No Harming Humans

Principle does not explain why these actions would be wrong, but the No Harming Principle does.

Perhaps the objection is not to the No Harming Principle itself, but to my argument for the claim that it is not the case that animals are harmed less by factory farming, testing, and hunting than people are benefited. The objection might be that animal harms are always small. Because animals lack full self-awareness, rationality, moral agency, or some other feature that adult humans have, the harm they suffer is insignificant. The death of a healthy adult human being might be a massive harm for her, but the death of a healthy adult cow is barely a harm for that cow at all. Likewise, living a restricted life would be an immense harm to a human being, but living a restricted life would not be much of a harm to a chicken. Thus, contrary to what I said earlier, factory farming is not like killing one person to save another from being pinched. Instead, it is like pinching one person to save five people from death.

Understood in this way, however, the objection is still implausible. Human babies and children are more similar to animals than adults are, so if animal harms are always small, we should expect harms to human babies and children to be relatively small as well. But they are not. Think back to a time when you were a child and you suffered from pain, injury, or sickness. Because you were a child, you lacked the self-awareness and rationality that you now have as an adult. Perhaps you were so young that you did not understand morality. But the harm you suffered then was not small. It was not like a pinch on the arm. It seems clear, then, that when we engage in factory farming, animal testing, hunting, or trapping, the harms we cause animals are not small either. They are large enough in magnitude to make these actions morally wrong.

Living a Restricted Life Is Better than Never Living at All

Here is another objection to my overall argument. The No Harming Principle tells us that except in special circumstances, it is wrong to harm some individuals for the sake of others. However, it does not tell us that it is wrong to harm some individuals for *their own sake*. Imagine, then, that we continue to engage in factory farming and animal testing, but we change our intentions. Instead of engaging in these practices for human benefit, we do it for the animals. We reason that for an animal, living a restricted life is still better than never living at all: the animals on factory farms and in laboratories still have lives worth living. We also reason that if we did not engage in factory farming and animal testing, it would not be economically feasible to bring such large numbers of animals into existence. Factory farming and animal testing benefit animals by giving them lives worth living, and while they also harm the animals, it is entirely possible for us to inflict those harms for the sake of the benefits to the animals themselves; all we have to do is intend those benefits. Therefore, even if the No Harming Principle is true, it does not necessarily follow that factory farming and animal testing are wrong.

In response, I will grant that causing someone to exist who will have a worthwhile life is a way of benefiting them. I also agree with the objection that it is often permissible to harm an individual for his or her own sake. It is permissible for a surgeon to harm me by cutting me open if his goal is to treat an even more harmful condition, and it is permissible for a parent to gently punish a child in order to teach that child a valuable lesson. Nevertheless, to qualify as harming someone for their own sake, you must do more than merely intend to benefit them. In cases where we can truly say that we are harming an individual for his or her own sake, the action that causes the harm must also be the action that causes the benefit. In the cases of factory farming and animal testing, the various individual actions that cause harm to the animals are not at all identical to the actions that bring these animals into existence.

Consider, for example, the action of castrating a pig. This particular action happens to the pig after he has already been born. It would take a wild leap of the imagination—and a belief in backward causation—to maintain that this action was the cause of the pig's existence. The same can be said for other actions like confining pigs in gestation crates, debeaking chickens, branding cattle, confining chickens in crowded sheds, and so on. The more general action I described earlier—causing the animals to live restricted lives—is also performed after the animals are born and is therefore not the cause of their existence. One might object that although castrating a particular pig (or causing him to live a restricted life) does not cause him to exist, it indirectly causes other pigs to exist by keeping costs down on the farm. However, harming a pig for the sake of other pigs is not the same thing as harming a pig for his own sake. Pigs are no more interchangeable than humans are. The No Harming Principle prohibits harming some for the sake of others whether those others are humans, pigs, or any other animal.

From No Harming to Animal Rights

Earlier I described my view as a non-consequentialist, non-absolutist defense of animal rights. I have so far appealed to a principle about harming to argue that most cases of factory farming, animal testing, hunting, and trapping are wrong. At this point, you may be wondering why this argument is a view about rights. What does harming have to do with rights?

Here is what I take the connection to be. One common conception of rights holds that rights considerations take priority over utility considerations. This means that it is more important to respect people's rights than it is to promote their well-being. Even if we could bring about more happiness in the world by infringing upon people's rights than we could by respecting their rights, true rights proponents say it would be wrong to infringe upon people's rights. But what if respecting people's rights would lead to the complete destruction of civilization? At this point, proponents of rights can be divided into two further camps. The absolutists contend that basic rights must never be infringed upon, even if respecting these rights will lead to the destruction of civilization. I find absolutism to be implausible, so I side with those who say that once we reach a certain threshold of impending harm, it becomes permissible to infringe upon people's rights for the sake of preventing that harm.

Notice that this discussion of rights has the same structure as my discussion of the No Harming Principle. In my discussion of that principle, I argued that even if we could bring about less harm in the world by harming someone, in the absence of special circumstances it would be wrong to harm that individual. My view is therefore equivalent to the view that individuals have a basic right to not be harmed. But my view is also a non-absolutist view because I allow for special circumstances in which we can permissibly harm those who have a right against being harmed.

Not only is my view about rights, generally, but it is also about animal rights, in particular. My argument that animals belong within the scope of the No Harming Principle is equivalent to an argument for the claim that animals have rights. More precisely, I believe that animals have a basic right against being harmed, just as people do. My argument has also shown that animals have derivative rights. That is, they have derivative rights against being raised on factory farms, against being used as test subjects in laboratories, and against being hunted and trapped for sport or fashion.

Conclusion

I have argued that, in virtue of violating the No Harming Principle, many of our practices violate animal rights. Such practices include factory farming, testing on animals, and hunting or trapping for sport or fashion. But what about the practice of eating meat? Certainly, eating meat is not the same thing as farming, and not all animals are raised on factory farms. I take it that my argument here can be extended to a practice like eating meat (factory-farmed or otherwise) if it can be shown that the practice in question also causes harm and thereby violates the No Harming Principle. I suspect that in many cases the relevant causal relationship will hold.[3] However, if it does not, the wrongness of eating meat will depend on whether there are other plausible moral principles that condemn such a practice.

Notes

1 The starting premises I have in mind have to do with utilitarianism's contention that aggregate welfare is the only thing that really matters from a moral perspective. Opponents of utilitarianism have objected that other considerations matter in themselves, apart from whether our feelings about them contribute to aggregate welfare; they point to considerations like justice, rights, and integrity. For some influential critiques of utilitarianism, see Tom Regan, *The Case for Animal Rights* (Berkeley: University of California Press, 2004); Bernard Williams, "A Critique of

Utilitarianism," in *Utilitarianism: For and Against*, by J. J. C. Smart and Bernard Williams (Cambridge: Cambridge University Press, 1973), 77–150; and John Rawls, *A Theory of Justice* (Cambridge, MA: Harvard University Press, 1971).

2 Tom Regan, "The Dog in the Lifeboat: An Exchange," *New York Review of Books* (April 25, 1985): 56–7.

3 For more on my view about whether the relevant causal relationship holds in other cases of collective harm, see Molly Gardner, "A Deontological Approach to Future Generations," in *The Oxford Handbook of Intergenerational Ethics*, ed. Stephen M. Gardiner (Oxford: Oxford University Press, 2022) (https://doi.org/10.1093/oxfordhb/9780190881931.013.3).

Animal Ethics and the Substance View

Bruce P. Blackshaw

Study Questions

1. What strong intuitions does Blackshaw say we have regarding nonhuman animals? What might this imply?
2. What important issues are raised by the possibility that we have moral obligations to animals?
3. What are the three accounts of moral status that Blackshaw discusses? What moral significance does each give to animals?
4. Why does Blackshaw think that each of the accounts of moral status is problematic?
5. What are "time-relative interests"? How does this concept resolve the embryo rescue and other problems?
6. How does Blackshaw modify the substance view to develop his Dual-Aspect Account? What implication does his view have for animal suffering?

In this essay, I highlight three important issues regarding animals that accounts of moral status must deal with. First, they must account for the wrongness of inflicting gratuitous pain on animals. Second, they must deal with the problem of wild animal suffering. Finally, they must account for our intuitions regarding the comparative wrongness of killing nonhuman animals compared to human beings. I then examine how three distinct accounts of moral status address these issues, primarily focusing on the substance view of persons. I explain that the wrongness of inflicting gratuitous pain on animals is problematic for the substance view and propose a modification of the account as a solution.

The Problem of Animal Suffering

We have a strong intuition that inflicting gratuitous pain on a nonhuman animal is morally wrong for the animal's own sake, and this implies animals enjoy some sort of moral considerability. Mary Anne Warren's widely used definition states that if moral agents have moral obligations toward an entity for its own sake, that entity has *moral standing*.[1] The stronger the obligations toward it, the higher its *moral status*, and so the claim regarding gratuitous animal pain implies that at least some nonhuman animals possess a degree of moral status, even if they do not possess the moral status of adult human beings.

However, if moral agents such as ourselves have moral obligations toward animals, this raises two important issues. First, *factory farming*. As DeGrazia observes, "factory farming routinely causes massive harm to animals,"[2] including pain and distress, and this is well documented. The number of animals being farmed far exceeds the human population. For example, in 2014, it was estimated that the global livestock population consisted of nearly 1.5 billion cattle, almost 2 billion sheep and goats, a billion pigs, and almost 20 billion chickens.[3] More recently, the Food and Agriculture Organization of the United Nations estimated that the global population of chickens was around thirty-three billion birds.[4] Accounts that award moral status to nonhuman animals will need to address factory farming.

The second important issue is *wild animal suffering*. Kyle Johannsen explains that not only do animals predate on each other but many animals produce huge numbers of offspring, "the majority of who die from disease, starvation, injury, exposure or predation soon after birth."[5] This is suffering and death on a vast scale,[6] and if we have a moral obligation to reduce animal suffering or protect their rights, then wild animal suffering is an important problem that accounts of moral status must address.

There are two caveats regarding obligations we might have to alleviate wild animal suffering. First, ecosystems are extremely complex, and any substantial intervention on behalf of one species is likely to have unexpected detrimental effects on others. Interventions may even result in an overall increase in wild animal suffering, or possibly extinctions. Nicolas Delon and Duncan Purves[7] call this uncertainty the *epistemic problem* of interventions to prevent wild animal suffering: we do not know what effect our interventions will have. This does not mean nothing can be done about wild animal suffering. Delon and Purves suggest that we begin by developing models that can "predict the effects of interventions (or any human activity) on biodiversity, ecosystem functioning, and animals' well-being."[8]

Second, if we accept there is a distinction between doing and allowing harm, such that it is harder to justify the former, then reducing the suffering involved in factory farming *may* be a higher priority than addressing wild animal suffering, *ceteris paribus*. However, the figures I have cited do indicate that there are far more wild animals than there are livestock, and this should also be taken into account.

If an account of moral status entails that animals have a similar moral status to our own, or that their suffering is as important as ours, then the vast numbers of animals involved in factory farming and in the wild animal population entail that we have a *prima facie* obligation to address the issues. Of course, such accounts typically highlight the issue of factory farming, but say much less regarding reducing wild animal suffering. If we are skeptical that wild animal suffering is an urgent problem that should take priority over human suffering, this undermines the plausibility of accounts that have this implication.

Animals Versus Human Beings

If animals do possess moral status, it raises the question of how their moral status compares to that of human beings, particularly marginal cases: human beings whose psychological capacities are well below those of many animals. This includes anencephalic babies, profoundly intellectually disabled human beings, and those whose psychological capacities have been erased by disease or physical trauma.

On accounts of moral status that are predicated in some way on psychological capacities, this implies that killing such animals is morally more serious than killing these human beings. McMahan points out that this is a challenge for such accounts, noting that it is common to believe that killing even an anencephalic infant is as serious (or almost so) as killing an adult human being.[9]

Three Accounts of Moral Status

Different accounts of moral status present diverse perspectives on the ethical significance of animals. The substance view of persons[10] does not assign animals any moral status, while accounts such as that of Peter Singer argue that the interests of animals deserve equal consideration to those of humans.[11] Tom Regan maintains that animals have rights similar to our own, and therefore should not be used as a means to human ends.[12]

Singer's Utilitarian Account

One of the most well-known accounts that entails that nonhuman animals are morally significant is Peter Singer's.[13] His utilitarian approach seeks to maximize the satisfaction of preferences or interests. Accordingly, he argues that the interests of all beings capable of suffering or experiencing well-being should be given equal consideration. As a result, he believes that harming sentient animals is immoral, regardless of their species. In addition, Singer also believes that animals with more advanced psychological capacities are more valuable than those with lesser capacities.

He is clear that this means some nonhuman animals will be more valuable than some human beings, such as infants born with severe brain damage.[14]

Regan's Rights-Based Account

Contra Singer, Tom Regan argues that animals possess rights.[15] He uses an inductive approach to identify a property that all human beings possess to determine what is the basis for possessing rights, including marginal cases such as infants. He infers that this property is their being "experiencing subjects of a life."[16] Although animals may not possess rationality, they have beliefs, desires, a sense of the future, a psychological identity over time, pleasures, and pains. Since we grant rights to all human beings, Regan concludes that being a *subject-of-a-life* is the property that grounds rights, and as many animals are also subjects-of-a-life, they too have rights. This includes a right to life, a right to liberty, and a right to be treated with respect.

Problems for Singer and Regan

Clearly, neither Singer's nor Regan's account has any difficulty in explaining why inflicting gratuitous pain on animals is immoral. In fact, both accounts entail that veganism is a moral obligation. However, wild animal suffering is a problematic issue. Singer's account entails that we are obligated to deal with wild animal suffering, and given its vast scale, the task is one of highest priority. Regan tries to avoid the issue, arguing that because animals are not moral agents, they do not have duties toward other animals, and therefore animal predation is not an issue for his account.[17] Critics have responded to point out that even though on his account animals have no duties to respect the rights of other animals, as moral agents *we* have a duty to intervene.[18] The intractability of wild animal suffering is also not an adequate defense for inaction. As Delon and Purves suggest, there is much research to be undertaken to determine effective solutions.[19] As I have noted, it seems absurd that we have such a duty, and consequently this issue undermines the plausibility of Singer's and Regan's accounts.

Singer's and Regan's accounts also have counterintuitive implications for marginal human cases. As anencephalic infants are unable to feel pain, they have no moral status on Singer's utilitarian account, implying it is permissible to kill them. Intellectually disabled human beings and those with conditions such as Alzheimer's disease can experience suffering, and so they have a higher moral status. However, on Singer's account it is not wrong to kill them painlessly. On Regan's account of rights, anencephalic infants are not subjects-of-a-life, entailing that they possess no rights and that killing them is not a serious wrong. More broadly, the moral status of human beings that possess psychological capacities much less than that of many animals is correspondingly lower than these animals on Regan's account, again a problematic conclusion contrary to what is widely believed.

The Substance View of Persons

The *substance view of persons* is a metaphysical account of the nature of human beings developed by the medieval theologian and philosopher, Thomas Aquinas. On the substance view, moral status is based on the possession of rationality, or the capacity to develop rationality. Accordingly, all human beings are regarded as moral persons from conception, irrespective of their stage of development. Proponents of the substance view have little to say regarding the moral status of animals. As nonhuman animals are not rational, the implication is that they have no moral status. David Oderberg is an exception: while he makes no explicit reference to the moral status of nonhuman animals, he argues that they have no rights and that human beings have no duties to nonhuman animals.[20] As a result, the substance view cannot easily explain why inflicting gratuitous pain on animals is morally wrong. On the other hand, wild animal suffering clearly is not an issue for the account.

In the sections that follow, I examine the substance view in more detail, including these implications for animal ethics. I conclude that, appropriately modified, it can adequately address the problem of gratuitous pain in animals.

The Substance View Explained, Modified, and Defended

The substance view of persons is based on Aristotelian metaphysics. An Aristotelian substance is an entity capable of existing in its own right, such as an animal or human being. Aquinas adopted his understanding of "person" from sixth-century Aristotelian commentator Boethius, who defined a person as "an individual substance of a rational nature."[21] To have a rational nature is to have the capacity to develop rationality; it does not require actual possession of rationality. All human beings have this capacity, no matter what stage of development they are at, from conception onwards.

The substance view is not just a metaphysical account of human beings. It also makes a claim about their moral worth. According to Aquinas, human beings are persons possessing "high dignity," which provides the basis for our high moral value.[22] Modern substance view proponents believe that this entails that all human beings are persons of high moral value. As a result, it is widely defended by philosophers who are opponents of abortion.[23]

The Substance View and Animals

Aquinas also argued that reason is required to discern between good and evil actions. As nonhuman animals lack reason and free will, they are unable to make such discernments and thus are not capable of moral action. Nonhuman animals, because they lack moral agency, do not deserve moral consideration.[24] Oderberg expands on this argument to argue that a rational nature is required for possession of rights. According to Oderberg, the basis of morality is to do good and avoid evil.[25] But, he argues, this requires knowledge of the good that should be pursued, and the ability to freely choose to do so.[26] These seem plausible conditions for being a moral agent, but Oderberg insists that they are also necessary for being a moral patient.[27] Consequently, he believes nonhuman animals cannot be rights bearers, and we have no duties toward them. Using the same reasoning, Timothy Hsiao argues that without a rational nature, there can be no moral standing or moral status.[28]

Aquinas is clear that nonhuman animals can be used for our benefit.[29] Hsiao[30] takes the argument further, claiming that on the substance view, practices such as industrial farming of animals and trophy hunting are not necessarily cruel or morally wrong.[31] Oderberg similarly believes that causing suffering to animals is not an injustice against them.[32] Since it is widely believed that inflicting gratuitous suffering on animals is morally wrong, Hsiao and Oderberg require an alternative explanation for this belief that does not rely on animals possessing moral status.

Aquinas supplies an answer, citing the Old Testament, to argue that cruelty to animals was prohibited so that the Israelites would be "less inclined to be cruel to other men, through being used to being kind to beasts."[33] Similarly, Immanuel Kant argued that animals are only indirectly morally considerable and that we should not mistreat them out of respect for human virtue, rather than for the sake of animals themselves.[34] In other words, according to both Aquinas and Kant, mistreating animals is only instrumentally immoral. Hsiao and Oderberg take this approach, claiming that animal cruelty is wrong because it corrupts our character and disposes us to be cruel to other human beings.[35] It is not wrong for the sake of the animals, but for ourselves.

An important difficulty for this position is acknowledged by Hsiao: that what is cruel for one person may not be cruel for another.[36] This means that inflicting gratuitous pain on animals may or may not be cruel, depending on the person. If it is not necessarily cruel, then it is not necessarily wrong. For example, it implies it would not be immoral to own an automated factory farm that causes terrible suffering to animals while requiring no direct human involvement. Given our strong intuitions that inflicting gratuitous pain on animals is always morally wrong,[37] this conclusion casts doubt on the credibility of this account.

In the light of these challenges, I propose that the substance view be modified. Any changes will need to maintain the central premise that moral personhood requires a rational nature; otherwise, the substance view is being replaced rather than modified. However, I propose that it should also allow that beings without a rational nature may still be awarded moral status of a lesser degree, discarding its "all or nothing" account of moral status.

Before developing this account, I will address Oderberg's (and Aquinas's) argument that nonhuman animals have no rights and we have no duties toward them. As we have seen, Oderberg argues that knowledge of purpose and free will are necessary conditions for the possession of rights. As animals possess neither knowledge of purpose nor free will, he believes they cannot be rights holders, and he implies they have no moral status. Hsiao is clearer on this latter point, stating that "in order for a being to have moral status of any kind, it must have the capacity to reason."[38]

I agree with Oderberg and Hsiao that the capacity to reason is required for moral *agency*, but they also claim that this is required to be a moral *patient*—an entity that is the recipient of moral concern. A difficulty for this claim is that newborns, infants, and severely intellectually disabled human beings lack the capacity to reason, implying that they must also lack moral status and rights. However, Oderberg and Hsiao are clear that *all* human beings have rights, including these cases.[39] This, they argue, is because they are the *kind* of entity that has the capacity for rationality—that is, they possess a rational nature. Of course, this is the primary claim of the substance view. However, this does entail that actual possession of rationality is not necessary for moral status and rights—the *potential* for rationality is sufficient. However, their original argument claimed morality was concerned with doing good and avoiding evil, something which requires actual rationality. Clearly, even if we grant that a rational nature grounds the moral status of human beings, it does not entail that all human beings are moral agents. Therefore, an entity may have moral standing without being a moral agent. Nonhuman animals, although they are not moral agents, might possess moral standing based on something other than a rational nature.

It is also worth noting that the problem of gratuitous animal suffering is not the only difficulty for the substance view. In the section below, I outline what is called the *embryo rescue argument*. Its relevance here is that several ethicists have suggested modifying the substance view in order to better cope with this argument. Drawing upon their suggestion, I proposed a formal account of moral status.[40] I present it below and explain that it also provides a plausible explanation for why causing animal suffering is immoral.

The Embryo Rescue Argument

The embryo rescue argument has been raised many times as an objection to the plausibility of the substance view. A thought experiment, it poses a scenario of a burning building that contains a ten-year-old child and some frozen embryos. A rescuer entering the building cannot save both the embryos and the child because they are in different locations. Intuitively, it seems that the child should be saved rather than the frozen embryos. The implication is that a child's moral worth is greater than that of multiple embryos. This is contrary to the substance view, which entails that all human substances are persons of equal moral worth from conception.

To account for this intuition, both Henri Friberg-Fernros[41] and S. Matthew Liao[42] have suggested incorporating the use of *time-relative interests*.

Time-Relative Interests

Jeff McMahan[43] developed the concept of time-relative interests in an attempt to explain widely held intuitions regarding the badness of death. For example, death seems to be worse for a younger person than an older person, all other things being equal, because death deprives the younger person of more future good. However, it is also common to believe that the death of a fetus is not as bad as the death of an adult, even though the fetus potentially has far more good in its future. Similarly, the death of a very early fetus does not seem as bad as the death of a late-term fetus. This puzzle led McMahan to propose his *time-relative interest account* of the badness of death. It addresses the apparent contradiction in the above examples by adjusting the value of future events in a life by a multiplier based on the concern an individual has for their own interests. Early fetuses, having no mental life, have no concern for their future interests, and so their time-relative interests are zero. Although infants have a very weak concern for their future interests, it is greater than that of fetuses, and so their time-relative interests are greater. Adults, with a very rich mental life, have even stronger time-relative interests.

More formally, time-relative interests are scaled according to the degree of *psychological unity* between the individual now and in the future. An individual's time-relative interests are a function of the expected good their future contains if they continue living, and their degree of psychological unity. This explains why the death of an early fetus does not seem as bad as that of an infant: because it has no mental life, there can be no psychological unity between the fetus now and in the future. Consequently, it has no time-relative interests. It also explains why the death of someone who is elderly with a terminal disease is not as bad as the death of someone much younger—the elderly person has limited future interests.

McMahan then proposes that killing is wrong because it frustrates the time-relative interests of the victim, calling this the time-relative interest account of the wrongness of killing. As a result, the killing of a fetus is not as wrong as the killing of an infant or an adult.

In my earlier work,[44] I suggested that our intuitions regarding who to save in an embryo rescue scenario might be based on time-relative interests rather than moral worth. As embryos have no time-relative interests and children have significant time-relative interests, our intuitions suggest saving the child. This is because embryos are not conscious and cannot experience pain, while we can easily identify with the interests of children and their parents. Therefore, even though they have equal moral worth, our intuitions mislead us into acting as if they do not.

Time-relative interests can also explain why it is commonly believed that infanticide is worse than abortion, and why killing an older child is worse than infanticide. The more developed the human being, the stronger their time-relative interests. Infants have greater psychological capacities than fetuses, and children have greater psychological capacities than infants.

Nonhuman animals also have time-relative interests, but they are weak in comparison to human adults. Nonetheless, their time-relative interests can explain why it is wrong to inflict gratuitous pain on animals, given that there is no corresponding benefit to our own interests that might justify this. This suggests combining time-relative interests with the substance view in some way.

Modifying the Substance View

McMahan's account of the wrongness of killing recognizes moral persons. After developing his time-relative interest account, McMahan notes that it is widely believed that the killing of persons is equally wrong, no matter what time-relative interests they might have. Given this belief, his time-relative interest account must be rejected for persons. Instead, he believes that the wrongness of killing persons is grounded in a failure to respect a person's intrinsic worth. Above a certain level of psychological development, called the *threshold of equal worth*, all individuals have equal worth and command respect as persons. He also refers to this as the *threshold of respect*.

McMahan combines these two accounts into what he calls the *Two-Tiered Account* of the morality of killing, describing it as involving two spheres of morality. The time-relative interest account governs the morality of killing below the threshold of respect, while the intrinsic worth account applies above the threshold. Below the threshold the morality of interests applies, while above the threshold is the morality of respect. In McMahan's view, since fetuses and infants do not reach the threshold of equal worth, they are not persons, and the morality of killing them is governed by time-relative interests. Older children and adults exceed this threshold and are persons, and killing a person is seriously wrong.

The wrongness of killing is closely related to moral status. As McMahan notes, the higher an individual's moral status, the more seriously objectionable it is thought to kill them.[45] On his account, the wrongness of killing is directly related to psychological capacities, as it is these that determine the strength of time-relative interests and whether an individual reaches the threshold of respect. Those who lie in the morality of interests sphere have lower moral status than individuals in the morality of respect sphere.

On McMahan's account, nonhuman animals such as mammals lie in the morality of interests sphere. They have moral status because they "have memories, beliefs, desires, and other psychological states that form connections that unify their lives over certain periods of time."[46] However, they do not enjoy the moral status of human persons, as their psychological capacities are not nearly as well developed, and they lie well beneath the threshold of respect. According to what McMahan describes as a gradualist view of moral status, the higher an animal's psychological capacities, the higher their moral status. Nonhuman animals that are not sentient have no moral status on McMahan's account.

The Dual-Aspect Account

McMahan's *Two-Tiered Account* of the morality of killing illustrates how an account can combine two different spheres of morality. Based on this approach, I have developed what I call the *Dual-Aspect Account* of the morality of killing.[47]

Instead of using tiers, the Dual-Aspect Account of killing employs the morality of interests and the morality of respect simultaneously. It uses the substance view of persons to ground respect, rather than reaching a threshold of psychological capacities. Consequently, the Dual-Aspect Account utilizes the morality of respect from conception onwards in the case of human beings. All human beings possess full moral status and are rights holders. However, the time-relative interest account also contributes to the wrongness of killing, implying it is more wrong to kill children than infants or fetuses. In other words, the Dual-Aspect Account calculates the wrongness of killing by combining the badness of death for an individual and their intrinsic worth as a human substance.

There are three direct implications of the Dual-Aspect Account. First, all human beings are moral persons, as per the substance view. Second, the wrongness of killing human beings, while always seriously wrong (because they are persons and possess rights), does vary depending on the victim's time-relative interests. Third, although they are not persons, nonhuman animals possess time-relative interests. This entails it is wrong to kill them without sufficient reason, implying they have a degree of moral status.

That all human beings are moral persons solves an important difficulty I noted earlier for McMahan's account, as well as Singer's and Regan's. Many animals have psychological capacities exceeding those of human beings with very severe intellectual disabilities or at early stages of development. The implication of these accounts is that killing such animals is morally more serious than killing these human beings. McMahan, however, notes that it is common to believe that killing even an anencephalic infant is as serious (or almost so) as killing an adult human being.[48] In fact, as infants are not persons, these accounts also imply that it is permissible to sacrifice an infant to save older children. McMahan states that these implications "are even more shocking to common sense than I have so far acknowledged."[49] The Dual-Aspect Account, by contrast, regards all human beings as moral persons, and so none of these challenges apply: you cannot sacrifice infants to save older children or adults, and it is worse to kill an anencephalic infant than a nonhuman animal.

Implications for Animal Suffering

Awarding nonhuman animals a degree of moral status solves the problem of gratuitous animal suffering. Their moral status means we are obliged to take their interests into consideration for their sake. Even though they do not have rights, inflicting suffering for no good reason is not permissible, and neither is killing them.

Of course, there may be circumstances that can justify killing or inflicting suffering on mammals—after all, we can justify inflicting pain on other human beings for reasons such as health. For example, ensuring a food supply that is sufficient for our dietary needs and population *might* justify factory farming on a large scale. However, there are three points to consider. First, it is well documented that factory farming causes a great deal of harm to animals. Second, as DeGrazia argues, for many, perhaps most people, this harm is unnecessary, because we have reasonable alternatives to factory-farmed animal products.[50] The implication is that current methods of factory farming of animals are incompatible with animals possessing moral standing, and so must be phased out or reformed in such a way that animals do not experience unjustifiable pain prior to and in the process of being killed. If we decide that meat can be part of our diet, it must be ethically sourced. Finally, we must consider whether we require meat or animal products in our diets at all. It might be that a vegetarian or a vegan diet is sufficient for our needs.

The issue of wild animal suffering is not as problematic on the Dual-Aspect Account as it is on Singer's and Regan's accounts. Nonhuman animals are not persons, and so they do not have the moral status of human beings. They do not have rights to defend. It is significantly more important to intervene on behalf of human death and suffering than it is for nonhuman animals.

Conclusion

The substance view of personhood, while aligning with our intuitions about the moral status of infants and humans with limited psychological abilities, faces challenges in justifying the immorality of inflicting gratuitous pain on nonhuman animals. In this chapter, I have proposed the Dual-Aspect Account of moral status, a modification of the substance view that incorporates time-relative interests. The account grants significant moral status to nonhuman animals with psychological capacities. Although they are not recognized as moral persons, the Dual-Aspect Account implies that inflicting gratuitous pain on nonhuman animals is not permissible. A corollary is that the account implies that practices such as factory farming must be reformed in such a manner that unnecessary pain and suffering for nonhuman animals is eliminated. Wild animal suffering is not a primary concern for the account.

Notes

1 M. A. Warren, *Moral Status: Obligations to Persons and Other Living Things* (Oxford: Clarendon Press, 1997), 3.

2 D. DeGrazia, "Moral Vegetarianism from a Very Broad Basis," *Journal of Moral Philosophy* 6, no. 2 (2009): 153.

3   T. P. Robinson, G. R. W. Wint, G. Conchedda, T. P. Van Boeckel, V. Ercoli, E. Palamara, et al., "Mapping the Global Distribution of Livestock," *PLoS ONE* 9, no. 5 (2014): e96084.

4   Food and Agriculture Organization of the United Nations, *Gateway to Poultry Production and Products: Chickens* (2024) (https://www.fao.org/poultry-production-products/production/poultry-species/chickens/en/).

5   K. Johannsen, *Wild Animal Ethics: The Moral and Political Problem of Wild Animal Suffering* (New York: Routledge, 2020), 1.

6   Adding mammals and other sentient species would significantly increase this number.

7   N. Delon and D. Purves, "Wild Animal Suffering is Intractable," *Journal of Agricultural and Environmental Ethics* 31 (2018): 239–60.

8   Ibid., 252.

9   J. McMahan, *The Ethics of Killing* (Oxford: Oxford University Press, 2002), 230.

10 F. Beckwith, "The Explanatory Power of the Substance View of Persons," *Christian Bioethics* 10, no. 1 (2004): 33–54; P. Lee, "The Pro-life Argument from Substantial Identity: A Defence," *Bioethics* 18, no. 3 (2004): 249–63.

11 P. Singer, *Animal Liberation, 40th Anniversary Edition* (New York: HarperCollins, 2015).

12 T. Regan, *The Case for Animal Rights* (Berkeley: University of California Press, 1983).

13 Singer, *Animal Liberation*.

14 Ibid., 50–4.

15 Regan, *The Case for Animal Rights*.

16 T. Regan, "A Case for Animal Rights," in *Advances in Animal Welfare Science*, ed. M. W. Fox and L. D. Mickley (Washington, DC: The Humane Society of the United States, 1986), 187.

17 Regan, *The Case for Animal Rights*, 357.

18 J. B. Callicott, "The Search for an Environmental Ethic," in *Matters of Life and Death: New Introductory Essays in Moral Philosophy*, ed. Tom Regan (New York: McGraw-Hill, 1993), 352–3; M. Torres, "The Case for Intervention in Nature on Behalf of Animals: A Critical Review of the Main Arguments against Intervention," *Relations. Beyond Anthropocentrism* 3, no. 1 (2015): 37–8.

19 Delon and Purves, "Wild Animal Suffering is Intractable," 239–60.

20 D. Oderberg, *Applied Ethics: A Non-Consequentialist Approach* (Malden: Wiley-Blackwell, 2000), 138–9.

21 S. Ebbesen, "Boethius as an Aristotelian Commentator," in *Aristotle Transformed: The Ancient Commentators and Their Influence*, ed. Richard Sorabji (Richmond: Duckworth, 1990), 403–422; Boethius, "A Treatise Against Eutyches and Nestorius," in *The Theological Tractates*, trans. H. F. Stewart (London: Heinemann, 1918), 93.

22 T. Aquinas, *The Summa Theologica*, trans. Fathers of the English Dominican Province, I, Q29, A3.

23 Oderberg, *Applied Ethics*; Beckwith, "The Explanatory Power of the Substance View of Persons"; Lee, "The Pro-life Argument from Substantial Identity."

24 Aquinas, *The Summa Theologica*, II.I, Q1, A1.

25 Oderberg, *Applied Ethics*, 128.

26 Ibid., 121–36.

27 Ibid., 128.
28 T. Hsiao, "Industrial Farming is Not Cruel to Animals," *Journal of Agricultural and Environmental Ethics* 30, no. 1 (2017): 44.
29 Aquinas, *The Summa Theologica*, II.II, Q24, A1.
30 Although Hsiao does not explicitly refer to the substance view, he argues that possession of a rational nature is necessary for moral status, and he cites Boethius in footnote 16.
31 Hsiao, "Industrial Farming Is Not Cruel to Animals"; and "A Moral Defense of Trophy Hunting, Sport," *Ethics and Philosophy* 14, no. 1 (2020): 26–34.
32 Oderberg, *Applied Ethics*, 140.
33 Aquinas, *The Summa Theologica*, I.II, Q102, A6.
34 I. Kant, *Lectures on Ethics*, ed. P. Heath and J. B. Schneewind (Cambridge: Cambridge University Press, 1997), 212 [Ak 27: 459].
35 Hsiao, "Industrial Farming is Not Cruel to Animals," 49.
36 Ibid.
37 Scott Hill states that "the theory that rationality is required for any sort of moral status at all violates intuition badly and goes against tradition" (S. Hill, "Animals Deserve Moral Consideration," *Journal of Agricultural and Environmental Ethics* 33 [2020]: 184).
38 Hsiao, "Industrial Farming is Not Cruel to Animals," 44.
39 Oderberg, *Applied Ethics*, 40; and Hsiao, "Industrial Farming is Not Cruel to Animals," 47.
40 B. P. Blackshaw, "The Ethics of Killing: Strengthening the Substance View with Time-Relative Interests," *The New Bioethics* 25, no. 4 (2019): 332–48.
41 H. Friberg-Fernros, "A Critique of Rob Lovering's Criticism of the Substance View," *Bioethics* 29, no. 3 (2015): 211–16.
42 S. M. Liao, "The Organism View Defended," *The Monist* 89, no. 3 (2006): 334–50.
43 McMahan, *The Ethics of Killing*.
44 Blackshaw, "The Ethics of Killing."
45 J. McMahan, "Suffering and Moral Status," in *Rethinking Moral Status*, ed. Steve Clarke, Hazem Zohny, and Julian Savulescu (Oxford: Oxford University Press, 2021).
46 Ibid., 32.
47 Blackshaw, "The Ethics of Killing."
48 McMahan, *The Ethics of Killing*, 230.
49 Ibid., 359.
50 DeGrazia, "Moral Vegetarianism from a Very Broad Basis," 153.

Responses

A Response to Gardner on Animal Rights

Bruce P. Blackshaw

Study Questions

1. What is the main problem that Blackshaw has with Gardner's No Harming Principle?
2. What difficulties might Gardner's principle have when it comes to *allowing* harm?
3. Why does Blackshaw think the No Harming Principle is vague?

Molly Gardner and I are in broad agreement that factory farms are wrong, most animal testing is wrong, and that hunting and trapping animals purely for sport or fashion is wrong. In her essay, she explains that it is easy to defend the view that these practices are wrong under utilitarianism, as Peter Singer does, as they involve suffering, and reducing suffering increases overall well-being. It is, Gardner claims, more of a challenge to derive this view from a non-consequentialist account. She notes that Kant gives no moral consideration to animals at all, while Tom Regan's "subject-of-a-life" account seems to go a step too far, as it entails that many animals have the same rights as human beings.

In my essay, I explained that the traditional substance view of persons, like Kant, also does not give moral consideration to nonhuman animals. However, on the Dual-Aspect Account that I have developed, based on the substance view, the interests of animals must also be taken into account. Human beings have a special moral status as moral persons, but nonhuman animals also have moral status. As a result, inflicting unnecessary or gratuitous suffering on animals is impermissible, and as these practices involve a degree of gratuitous suffering, they are wrong. Notably, though, because they are not persons, the Dual-Aspect Account does allow that the interests of animals can be sacrificed for the benefit of human beings. It's worth noting that the account from which the Dual-Aspect Account is also derived, McMahan's *time-relative interest account*, also has no difficulty explaining why practices such as factory farming are wrong, because of the gratuitous suffering they involve.

Gardner's No Harming Principle

Gardner takes a different approach, basing her moral theory on what she calls the *No Harming Principle: except in special circumstances, it is wrong to harm some individuals for the sake of others*. According to Gardner, this explains a wide range of moral judgments that comprise commonsense morality. For example, we don't sacrifice an individual in order to obtain their organs to save others, and we shouldn't steal money from others to save lives. In certain situations, however, harming individuals for the sake of others is not wrong. Gardner believes that when the relative magnitude of the harm caused is small compared to the harm prevented, it can be permissible to cause harm. For example, it might be permissible to kill one person if a very large number of other people are saved. Another scenario in which it is permissible to cause harm is when an individual has consented to it.

Next, Gardner explains how factory farming, animal testing, and hunting for sport or fashion violate the No Harming Principle. All of these practices inflict pain and shorten the lives of the animals involved. Factory farming and animal testing also inflict *the harm of living a restricted life*: forcing animals to live in uncomfortable, confined conditions for their entire lives. Further, these harms are for the sake of others, and Gardner explains that the ratio of harm to benefit does not justify them.

Problems with the No Harming Principle

As I have said, I have no disagreement regarding many of the harms associated with these practices that Gardner cites, based on my views regarding animal moral status. However, one important point of difference is that Gardner's No Harming Principle *does not allow us to distinguish between nonhuman animals and human beings*. She addresses this in her discussion of the first objection she considers, that harms to animals do not matter as much as harms to human beings. Contra Gardner, this is a self-evident claim: if we must choose between sacrificing a human being or a nonhuman animal, we always choose to sacrifice the animal. Also, Gardner notes that babies are more similar to animals than adults, but we don't sacrifice babies for the sake of animals. This seems to be a major issue for the No Harming Principle.

By contrast, my Dual-Aspect Account elevates the moral status of human beings far above that of nonhuman animals, ensuring that it is wrong to sacrifice human beings for animals. However, by recognizing that animals do enjoy some moral status, the account has no difficulty agreeing that inflicting gratuitous harm on animals is immoral. The wrongness of the practices Gardner identifies is because they do inflict gratuitous harm on animals. We could easily eat far less meat and avoid factory-farmed meat altogether. Painful experiments on animals in order to perfect cosmetic products seem unnecessary, as is hunting for enjoyment alone. Nevertheless, the Dual-Aspect Account does allow that animal experiments that yield medical advances that benefit human beings are permissible, something the No Harming Principle does not allow unless the relative magnitude of benefit to harm is very high. The Dual-Aspect Account also allows for the eating of meat, provided the animals supplying the meat lead good lives and are killed painlessly.

I have some other concerns with the No Harm Principle. Gardner is clear that harming is different from allowing harm, a distinction with which I am in agreement. However, in cases where we have a strong intuition that allowing harm is wrong, such as a drowning child that we can easily save, the principle has nothing to say, even though Gardner acknowledges we are required to act.

There's a further issue with allowing harm. We don't directly harm animals by consuming factory-farmed meat, or by benefiting from animal experiments—others cause the harm. Does this mean as long as we are not directly involved in these practices, we have no obligation to oppose them? Gardner states that the No Harming Principle, by including animals in its scope, implies that animals have rights, particularly the right not to be harmed. Perhaps this right implies that we do have a duty to take action to protect animals from being harmed by others, but if it does, it raises *the problem of wild animal suffering*. As I explained in my essay, wild animal suffering exists on a vast scale, and far outweighs that inflicted by factory farms, animal experiments, and hunting. If animal rights are sufficiently strong that we must demand action on factory farming, then Gardner must also deal with wild animal suffering.

My final issue with the No Harming Principle is *its vagueness*. First, it doesn't tell us which individuals it is wrong to harm. Is it only mammals like ourselves, who have similar physiology to human beings, or does it include amphibians, reptiles, and fish? Must we avoid harming insects? Plants can certainly be harmed, so are they included in its scope? Second, it does not distinguish between lesser and greater harms. This means that harm cannot be inflicted on one individual in order to benefit another individual, no matter what the benefit. Gardner's special circumstances exemption does not apply unless there is an extremely high ratio of benefit to harm. This means that confining a cow to a pasture and milking it for your own benefit violates the No Harm Principle—even though the harm to the cow is small, the benefit is not large. Third, by not distinguishing between human beings and nonhuman animals, Gardner's principle implies we cannot benefit from animals at all. For example, hunting for food is not permissible, even in situations where a person has no alternative food source and would otherwise die. In a situation where someone is trapped on a lifeboat with a cow and a lamb, the No Harm Principle appears to rule out consuming the animals, which seems absurd. Even if animals lead happy lives, Gardner believes death itself is an important harm for animals, and so they cannot be painlessly killed and consumed.

Conclusion

In conclusion, while I believe the No Harming Principle is *prima facie* plausible, it cannot account for many of our moral intuitions, principally because it fails to provide a way to recognize differences in moral status between different kinds of individuals, such as human beings and nonhuman animals. The principle is instead based on harm, and makes no allowances for the different ways individuals can be harmed. The harm suffered by a plant when it is destroyed is very different from the harm suffered by an animal, and human beings suffer most of all, as they are deprived of a future of valuable experiences. Further, the No Harming Principle is absolutist: it does not permit harm to one individual, no matter how minor, to outweigh the harm to another, except in extreme circumstances. As a result, the No Harm Principle produces some counterintuitive moral judgments, particularly when it comes to scenarios involving humans and nonhuman animals.

A Response to Blackshaw on Animal Rights

Molly Gardner

Study Questions

1. How are Gardner's and Blackshaw's views alike? In what two important ways do they diverge?
2. How is Gardner's view simpler than Blackshaw's? Why might this matter?
3. How does Gardner respond to the objection that her view doesn't explain why our obligation to alleviate human suffering is greater than our obligation to alleviate wild animal suffering?
4. Why does Gardner think that time-relative interests are irrelevant to moral status?

In this response, I note some points of agreement and disagreement between my own view and Bruce P. Blackshaw's view. One of the main points of disagreement has to do with moral status. Although Blackshaw contends that a difference in moral status explains why our obligations to animals are weaker than our obligations to other humans, I contend that we can explain the strength of our obligations to humans and animals without appealing to the concept of moral status at all.

Agreements and Differences

Blackshaw argues for what he calls the "Dual-Aspect Account of the morality of killing." His view is like mine in some important respects. Both of our views entail that there is a morally significant distinction between killing and letting die. This implies that we both reject utilitarianism and believe, instead, that at least some individuals have rights that take priority over utilitarian concerns. At the practical level, we are both opposed to factory farming practices that inflict gratuitous pain and suffering upon animals.

Nevertheless, there are at least two important ways in which our views diverge, especially at the theoretical level. First, Blackshaw focuses on killing, whereas my focus is on harming, more generally. I agree with Blackshaw that theories of when and why it is wrong to kill can sometimes cast light upon when and why harming is wrong, but I also think that an unduly narrow focus on killing will sometimes lead us astray. I will return to this point at the end of the essay.

Second, Blackshaw's view is ultimately a view about moral status. He argues that although animals have some moral status, they do not have full moral status the way that humans do. He takes this account of moral status to be what primarily explains why, when it comes to how we treat wild or domesticated animals, we have some obligations but not others.

In my view, this explanatory work can be done much better by moral principles that make no explicit mention of moral status. One of those is the principle that, other things being equal, it is worse to do harm than to allow harm. Another is that the degree of harm to everyone involved also matters to the strength of our obligations: To the extent that the harm an individual faces is greater, we have a stronger obligation to save him or her from it. Nevertheless, our overall obligation to save an individual from harm gets weaker to the extent that saving him or her involves doing or allowing harm to ourselves or others.

Blackshaw on the Wrongness of Killing

To see why I think these principles constitute a better explanation of our moral obligations than an appeal to moral status, let us now look at Blackshaw's view in more detail. Blackshaw argues that there are two fundamental considerations that contribute to the wrongness of killing an individual. The first consideration is whether the individual in question has a rational nature. Blackshaw argues that all and only human beings have a rational nature, and he holds that this rational nature is what explains why it is wrong to kill any human being, whether that human being is an embryo, a fetus, or an adult. The second consideration is the degree to which killing the individual frustrates his or her time-relative interests in staying alive. Although it is always wrong to kill a human being, it is worse to kill a human being who has strong time-relative interests than it is to kill a human being whose time-relative interests are weak. On the other hand, if a nonhuman individual has time-relative interests to at least some extent, then he or she will have at least some degree of moral status. However, Blackshaw holds that an individual who has time-relative interests but not a rational nature will never have full moral status.

To defend his Dual-Aspect Account of the morality of killing, Blackshaw highlights what he takes to be the main problems with alternative accounts that accept only one of the two aspects. For example, some accounts hold that the morality of killing is determined *only* by interests. On these accounts, it does not matter whether you are human or nonhuman; your death is bad to the extent that it frustrates your interests. Blackshaw argues that the main problem with these accounts is that they implausibly entail that our obligations to alleviate wild animal suffering are extremely strong. On the other hand, Blackshaw argues that some accounts of the morality of killing make the opposite mistake. Since these accounts hold that only humans matter, they wrongly imply that there is nothing morally objectionable about factory farming. Blackshaw concludes that his Dual-Aspect Account strikes the best balance between these two extremes: It entails that we have obligations toward animals that make factory farming wrong, but it does not entail that our obligations toward animals are so strong that we ought to prioritize wild animal suffering over human suffering.

Problems with Blackshaw's View

A Simpler Explanation

I agree with Blackshaw that we have, for example, a stronger obligation to refrain from raising chickens on factory farms than we do to save wild herbivores from carnivorous predators. However, I disagree with Blackshaw that we need to appeal to the idea that animals lack full moral status in order to explain this difference in the strength of our obligations. Instead, I take the explanation to be as simple as this: Other things being equal, it is worse to do harm than it is to allow harm. Therefore, it is worse (holding other considerations roughly equal) to harm animals by engaging in factory farming than it is to allow predation.

Blackshaw might object that this is not the only observation his view is meant to explain. Not only do we need to explain why our obligation to save wild herbivores from predation is weaker than our obligation to refrain from raising chickens on factory farms, but we also need to explain why our obligation to alleviate wild animal suffering is weaker than our obligation to alleviate human suffering. An appeal to the distinction between doing and allowing harm will not work to explain the latter, for failing to alleviate wild animal suffering and failing to alleviate human suffering *both* qualify as instances of allowing harm.

However, I contend that, even in this case, the distinction between doing and allowing is still relevant. To save humans from the harm of poverty, we can make economic interventions that are beneficial to everyone involved. When we fight poverty, no harm needs to be done to anything other than poverty itself. However, to save animals from the harm of predation (and possibly other harms), we need to intervene in the ecosystem, rather than the economy, and interventions in the ecosystem are much more likely to involve harmful tradeoffs.[1] For example, to help wild zebras, we might have to capture or kill wild lions. Or to help some deer right now, we might have to eliminate wolves, and this could paradoxically harm other deer in the future, if their population grows unsustainably large.

If the cost of saving humans from harm is minimal and the cost of saving animals from harm is high, it is easy to see why the overall obligation to help humans is stronger than the obligation to help animals. Indeed, if the cost of saving some animals involves not just allowing harm, but *doing* harm (say, to other animals), then we may well be obligated *not* to intervene at all. We can therefore explain why there is a stronger obligation to alleviate human suffering than there is to alleviate wild animal suffering without appealing to a difference in moral status between humans and animals.

The Irrelevance of Time-Relative Interests

Disagreement about the explanatory role of moral status is one of the two main differences I pointed out earlier between Blackshaw's view and my own. The other difference has to do with Blackshaw's focus on killing, rather than harming. Blackshaw endorses the view that there are various correlations between the wrongness of killing, the strength of an individual's time-relative interests, and the individual's level of moral status. He concludes that having time-relative interests is sufficient for having some degree of moral status.

However, insofar as we employ the concept of moral status at all, I think we should reject the view that moral status has something to do with time-relative interests. For one thing, I doubt that time-relative interests really do factor into the wrongness of killing.[2] But more importantly, even if time-relative interests are relevant to the wrongness of killing, this does not mean they are relevant to the wrongness of harming, more generally. Killing may well be harmful because it deprives you of something in your future, and time-relative interests are, of course, indexed to the future. However, other harms are not necessarily indexed to the future, so they may have very little to do with time-relative interests at all. And if moral status is about anything, it is about the wrongness of harming, in general, rather than the wrongness of killing, in particular.

Notes

1 I develop another argument for the claim that we should be hesitant to intervene in nature to reduce wild animal suffering in Molly Gardner, "Suffering and Meaning in the Lives of Wild Animals," *Midwest Studies in Philosophy* 46 (2022): 355–71.

2 For more on my view about whether time-relative interests can ground a difference in moral status between humans and animals, see Molly Gardner, "Persons, Animals, and Psychological Unity," *Philosophical Studies* 180, no. 4 (2023): 1197–209.

Questions for Reflection

1. What, if anything, could Gardner say in response to Blackshaw's criticism of her No Harming Principle?

2. How might Blackshaw extend his view to cover the wrongness of harming generally rather than just killing?

3. Consider what other theoretical perspectives (e.g., social contract theory or virtue ethics) might have to say about animal rights. Are these views preferable to either Gardner's or Blackshaw's? Why?

For Further Reading

Carruthers, Peter. *The Animals Issue: Moral Theory in Practice*. Cambridge University Press, 1992.

Cohen, Carl, and Tom Regan. *The Animal Rights Debate*. Rowman and Littlefield, 2001.

Johannsen, Kyle. *Wild Animal Ethics: The Moral and Political Problem of Wild Animal Suffering*. Routledge, 2020.

McMahan, Jeff. *The Ethics of Killing: Problems at the Margins of Life*. Oxford University Press, 2002.

Regan, Tom. *The Case for Animal Rights*. University of California Press, 2004.

Singer, Peter. *Animal Liberation*, 40th anniversary ed. Harper Collins, 2015.

Sunstein, Cass R., and Martha C. Nussbaum. *Animal Rights: Current Debates and New Directions*. Oxford University Press, 2005.

Warren, M. A. *Moral Status: Obligations to Persons and Other Living Things*. Clarendon Press, 1997.

8

Immigration/Open Borders

A Case for Immigration

Michael Huemer

> **Study Questions**
>
> 1. What is Huemer's core argument against immigration restrictions? How does he defend the first premise?
> 2. What is the "Starving Marvin" thought experiment? How does it support the second premise of Huemer's argument?
> 3. What objection does Huemer address? How does he respond to it?
> 4. According to Huemer, why is the desire to limit economic competition *not* a good reason to restrict immigration?
> 5. Why does Huemer think that the preservation of culture is not a good reason to restrict immigration?
> 6. What other reasons are given for immigration restrictions? How does Huemer reply to them?
> 7. What does Huemer say in defense of *illegal* immigration?

Many Americans today are gravely concerned about migration across the nation's southern border. President Biden has been (exaggeratedly) accused of instituting a policy of "complete open borders."[1] At the risk of disappointing readers, I confess that I do not favor literally complete open borders. I do, however, support *relatively* open borders for the United States,[2] meaning that the great majority of people who wish to immigrate should be allowed to do so. I would make exceptions for individuals who are at especially high risk of committing serious crimes or of carrying communicable diseases. But the overwhelming majority of migrants, I believe, fall in neither category and should be free to do as they wish. Most reasons for restricting movement are terrible reasons, and the current regime of restrictions is among our country's worst policies.

I. The Prima Facie Case

My core reasoning is as follows:

(1) Harmful coercion is prima facie wrong.

(2) Immigration restrictions are harmful and coercive.

(3) So, immigration restrictions are prima facie wrong.

A. Premise 1

To explain the first premise, I believe that in general, one should not deploy force against other people in a way that harms them, without having a good reason for doing so. For instance, you should not walk up to a stranger on the street and punch them. Coercion also includes *threatening* people with force. Thus, you also should not go up to a stranger and *threaten* to punch them. This strikes me as a fairly minimal ethical principle—if coercively harming people for no good reason isn't wrong, then I don't know what is.

There may be cases of *beneficial* (paternalistic) coercion. For instance, you forcibly take someone's crack pipe away from them. I am not saying anything, one way or the other, about such cases. There are also cases of non-coercive harms. For instance, you might harm someone by successfully outcompeting them in business. Again, I am not saying anything about such cases. I am only discussing cases in which your treatment of another person is both coercive *and* harmful.

I have said only that such behavior is "*prima facie* wrong," rather than simply "wrong." By this, I mean that there is a moral *presumption* against coercively harming others—we can start from the assumption that such behavior is wrong, in the absence of sufficiently good reasons in favor of it. One can certainly think of cases in which harmful coercion is justified. For instance, in a boxing match to which both parties have agreed, it is permissible to punch your opponent in the face. Or suppose that a criminal on the street attacks you with a knife. It is permissible to respond by pulling out your gun and shooting the criminal. This shows that consent and self-defense are (sometimes) good enough justifications for harmful coercion. There are undoubtedly other reasons that suffice to justify harmful coercion; my point is simply that a justification is needed.

So, my argument as given above only claims to show that immigration restrictions are wrong *unless* we have sufficiently good reasons for them. In Section II below, we'll consider what those reasons might be. For now, let's just focus on the prima facie case against restriction.

B. Premise 2

Turning to my second premise: Are immigration restrictions *coercive*? Of course they are. The government imposes them, not by making polite requests, but by hiring armed guards to patrol the border. When the government discovers people in the country illegally, they forcibly take those people captive and move them across the border. Compliance is compulsory. This is precisely what proponents of immigration restriction advocate for.

Are immigration restrictions *harmful*? Yes, they are. Imagine that someone kidnapped you at gunpoint, flew you to Nicaragua, then forced you to spend the rest of your life there. Would that person be harming you? If you answered "yes," consider that that is the same harm that would-be immigrants suffer from immigration restrictions. I have an example to illustrate the main point:

> *Starving Marvin:* Marvin is hungry and short on food. Fortunately, he has a way to obtain food: he plans to walk to a nearby marketplace. If he reaches the marketplace, he will be able to trade for some food. Unfortunately, he is accosted on the road by Sam, who is carrying an M16. Sam explains that he has some nephews and nieces who trade in that marketplace, and Sam doesn't want them to be able to trade with Marvin. Sam forcibly blocks Marvin's progress and sends him back home, where Marvin starves.

Did Sam harm Marvin? Did Sam act wrongly? The answer to both is clearly yes. Sam isn't responsible for the fact that Marvin was hungry to begin with, nor is he responsible for the fact that Marvin has no other options for obtaining food. Nevertheless, when Sam forcibly prevents Marvin from remedying the problem, he thereby makes himself responsible for Marvin's starvation. This illustrates the point that, to count as harming someone, it is not necessary that one be the originating cause of the harm that they suffer; it is enough that one forcibly prevent them from taking steps to avert a harm. If Sam had no good reason for interfering with Marvin, then he did something very wrong.

This is analogous to what the US government does to potential immigrants. Migrants have economic and other needs, which they could satisfy through voluntary trade if they were to reach the United States. The government does not want the migrants to do so, so it bars the way with fences and armed guards and forces the migrants to return to or remain in their countries of origin. As a result, millions of potential immigrants continue to suffer severe economic hardship and oppression. By coercively intervening to prevent them from remedying their current hardship, the government harms these potential immigrants. If it has no good reason for doing so, then the government, like Sam in the above example, is doing something very wrong.

C. An Objection

Some would object that the United States does not actively *harm* potential immigrants by refusing them entry but merely *fails to benefit* them. This matters because it is widely considered *worse* to harm someone than it is to fail to benefit them. For instance, stealing food from a poor person is much worse than merely refusing to give them food.

Let's see how the objection would go. I have claimed that acting to *prevent someone from remedying* a harm counts as harming them, even if you are not the original source of the harm they seek to avoid. But there is one exception to this: if a person is going to obtain a benefit *from you*, and you actively intervene to stop them from getting that benefit, that counts as merely *refusing to benefit* that person, not harming them. For example, suppose that Marvin is about to enter my kitchen, where he will take some of my food out of the refrigerator and eat it. I forcibly stop him from entering, thereby depriving him of food that he would otherwise have had. In this case, I am *not* actively harming Marvin; I am merely *refusing to help* him, since the good I deprive him of would have come from me.

Similarly, you might think that in denying Marvin entry to the United States, the United States merely *refuses to help* potential immigrants because the goods that they are prevented from obtaining would have come *from the United States itself*. If we stop immigrants from moving to Canada, *then* we're harming them; but if we stop them from moving to our *own* country, then we are merely refusing to benefit them.

To address this objection, it is essential to distinguish different agents within the United States. In particular, we need to distinguish *the US government* from the various *private actors* in the United States. In denying entry to potential immigrants, the government prevents those potential immigrants from obtaining various benefits from the US government, such as welfare payments or public schooling. But those are not the benefits that my argument is concerned with; as far as my argument goes, there is nothing wrong with the government's denying immigrants *those* goods. The problem is that *the government* prevents potential immigrants from obtaining goods *from private citizens* who would like to trade with those immigrants. Thus, the government is not merely refusing to benefit immigrants; it is actively harming them by stopping *other people* from helping them. This point is obscured by the tendency to confuse the government with the country by ambiguously labeling the government and/or the rest of the country "the United States."

II. Reasons for Restriction

As I've indicated, the above is only a prima facie case for open immigration: it shows why it is wrong for the government to restrict migration *unless* they have a good reason for doing so. Let's turn to the reasons for restricting migration and assess how good they are.

A. Economic Competition

Traditionally, the most popular rationale for restricting migration is to limit economic competition. It is said that immigrants "steal jobs" from native-born workers and cause wages for some kinds of labor to drop.

The overwhelming majority of economists view immigration as an overall boon to the economy, not a drag.[3] We don't have time to discuss the reasons for this in detail, but in general, free trade almost always benefits both parties. Low-cost labor results in low-cost goods and services, which benefit almost everyone.

If you find it intuitive that adding more immigrant workers to the labor force would harm the economy, you should ask yourself why adding more *native-born* workers to the labor force wouldn't harm the economy. When teenagers first become old enough to work, is that bad for the rest of us? Why not? Well, roughly speaking, work produces valuable goods and services, which is the actual point of having an economy. Trying to stop people from working is essentially trying to stop people from producing benefits. This is equally true regardless of the workers' origin; the effect of a new worker entering the labor force is the same regardless of whether that worker is native born or an immigrant.

Nevertheless, not *everyone* benefits from immigration. There is evidence for a slight decrease in wages for the least-skilled workers (especially high school dropouts) as a result of immigration, essentially because these are the only workers who are substantially in competition with immigrant workers.[4] Is this enough to justify restricting immigration?

To gauge this, let's return to the example of Starving Marvin. Imagine that, after learning of what Sam did to Marvin, you confront Sam:

> You: Hey Sam, it looks like you really harmed Marvin a lot. Why did you do that?
> Sam: Well, you see, I have some nephews and nieces who also like to trade in that marketplace. If Marvin got there, he might bid up the price of food, and then some of my nephews and nieces might have to pay slightly higher prices. Clearly, I couldn't allow that to happen.

This reason would obviously fail as a justification. The desire to grant someone economic advantages by protecting them from market competition is not a sufficient justification for harmful coercion. There are many other illustrations of this point. Just as one may not forcibly prevent someone from buying food in order to keep food prices down, one may not use force to stop other people from applying for a job that one wants, nor may one vandalize a competitor's store to stop them from competing for one's customers.

Some argue that the government has special duties to its own citizens; therefore, it must prioritize the welfare of American workers over foreign workers. Some also hold that the government should prioritize the welfare of its *poorest* citizens over that of wealthier citizens. Does this provide a reason for restricting migration to protect the economic prospects of the poorest citizens?

It does not. When one takes on special duties to a particular person or group, these duties can *restrict* one's options, but they cannot *create new options* to do things that previously would have been wrong merely because one would thereby help that person or group. For example, people have special duties to take care of their family members, which they do not owe to ordinary strangers. Thus, Sam might have special duties to his nephews and nieces, which might obligate Sam to spend some of his money to ensure that his nephews and nieces have enough to eat. But this would not make it permissible for Sam to steal money from third parties in order to give the money to his nephews and nieces. Nor, similarly, may Sam forcibly prevent third parties from trading in the marketplace, merely to procure economic advantages for his nephews and nieces.

If you're not sure that an uncle has a duty to provide for his nephews and nieces, you can imagine that Sam also signed a contract promising to ensure that all his nephews and nieces were well-fed. This still does not make it okay for him to coercively harm third parties, even if his doing so would help him feed his nephews and nieces.

Similarly, the government's obligation to attend to the interests of its citizens would not give it the right to coercively harm third parties, even if its doing so would procure advantages for its own citizens.

B. Preserving Culture

Some say that we must restrict immigration in order to protect our culture from the influence of people from foreign cultures.

To begin with, I do not believe American culture is in danger of being destroyed by exposure to other cultures. On the contrary, I think that when American culture comes into contact with other cultures, it is the *other* cultures that tend to get assimilated or destroyed. It is far more likely that American culture is going to take over the rest of the world than that it will be destroyed by foreigners. The same is true of Western culture more generally.

I also doubt that preservation of culture is a sufficient reason for harmful coercion. Again, imagine confronting Sam about his interference with Marvin:

You: Hey Sam, why did you harm Marvin like that?
Sam: Well, Marvin worships the wrong God, eats weird food, wears funny clothes, and speaks a language I'm not familiar with. I was worried that if he was able to reach the marketplace, he might influence people there to take up some of his practices. So naturally, I had to forcibly bar the road. It's too bad for Marvin, but it's a small price to pay for preserving the marketplace's culture.

Again, this justification seems completely inadequate. No one has the right to coercively interfere with other people just to stop them from influencing the culture. The culture of your society is a matter of the practices adopted by other people. Where these practices are non-rights-violating (for instance, speaking a certain language), you have no legitimate complaint about them, and no right to demand that others take up or continue the practices that you prefer. For example, since you have no right to have other people practice your preferred religion, you may not use force against other people to prevent them from spreading a religion that you disprefer.

Likewise, the state lacks a right to harmfully coerce people to prevent them from influencing the culture. Since individuals may not do this on their own behalf, they also cannot delegate to the state the authority to do this on their behalf.

C. Control of Public Property

Another rationale for immigration restrictions is to prevent foreign nationals from using public property or receiving government benefits.[5] For instance, immigrants may drive on the roads, send their children to public schools, and call for police protection against criminals. These resources belong to the public collectively, that is, to the current citizens of the country. The citizens therefore have a collective right to decide how to use these resources, including a right to decide not to share them with people from foreign countries. It happens, however, that the only practical way to stop foreign-born people from using public resources is to bar them from entering the country. Thus, the argument goes, the current citizens of a nation have the right to bar foreigners from entering, if they so choose. The way they do this (in a democratic society) is through their agent, the government.

There is a Starving Marvin illustration for this argument too.

> You: Sam, why did you harm Marvin?
> Sam: I have a charity program whereby I give free food to everyone in the marketplace. But I didn't want to give free food to Marvin. So I had to stop him from getting there.

This justification obviously fails. If Sam doesn't want to give food to Marvin, he can refuse to do so (changing his current policy). But he cannot forcibly stop Marvin from voluntarily trading for food with other people in the marketplace, solely to prevent *himself* from voluntarily giving Marvin some food.

Now, you might think this analogy fails because Sam can easily withhold food from Marvin even if Marvin enters the marketplace. This is similar to how the US government can and does withhold welfare benefits from recent immigrants. However, there are other goods that cannot be so easily withheld. For instance, anyone who lives in the territory of the United States benefits from its national defense apparatus, in the sense that they are safe from foreign military attacks. They benefit also from the general provision of law and order and from the maintenance of roads. It would be impossible or impractical for the government to stop people who are living in the country from receiving these "public goods" (as the economists call them).[6] The only practical way to refrain from giving those benefits to immigrants, therefore, is to exclude them from the country entirely.

To accommodate this point, let us imagine another program for Sam:

> You: Sam, why did you harm Marvin?
> Sam: I recently set up some speakers in the marketplace to play beautiful music for people. But I didn't want to entertain Marvin. It's *my* music system, so I don't have to provide it for anyone I don't want to provide it for! It happens that the only way to stop Marvin from enjoying the music was to completely exclude him from the marketplace, so that's what I did.

Surely this doesn't give Sam the right to block Marvin from entering the marketplace. Sam can't stop Marvin from getting food from other people in the marketplace merely because Marvin would at the same time get some other benefit caused by Sam.

D. Fiscal Burdens

Perhaps the problem is not that we wish to stop certain people from *benefiting* at our hands (which would be a peculiarly malicious motive). Perhaps the real problem is that we want to stop certain people from *adding to our costs*. As the population increases, perhaps the costs of government services increase. Imagine that somehow, Sam's entertainment system became more costly to maintain, the more people were in the marketplace. Wouldn't Sam then have some recourse?

The way governments usually handle these costs is by collecting taxes. As the population increases, the government's costs increase. But the government's *revenues* also increase proportionately, due to a larger number of taxpayers. So, in general, there is no *net* cost from population increase.

In the case of immigration, however, there may be an increase in tax burdens for native-born citizens, owing to the fact that most immigrants are low-income workers.[7] Because of the progressive tax structure of America, low-income individuals tend to be a net burden on high-income individuals. That is, poor taxpayers pay *less* into the system than the government spends on them, while wealthy taxpayers pay more. Therefore, to avoid increasing tax burdens, wealthy Americans might wish to stem the flow of immigrants.

To take account of this point, imagine another defense offered by Sam for his exclusion of Marvin:

You: Sam, why did you harm Marvin?

Sam: Well, I had previously decided that I'm going to take money mostly from wealthy people and use it to benefit people in the marketplace. Marvin is poor. Therefore, if he reached the marketplace, I would take some additional money from rich people to help (in part) Marvin. To stop myself from doing that, I had to block Marvin from getting there.

Again, I don't think this defense succeeds. If Sam is concerned about taking from the wealthy to help *Marvin*, he can change his policies regarding Marvin, so that Marvin's arrival wouldn't impose a greater burden on the wealthy. This does not provide a good reason to completely exclude Marvin from the area. One cannot, in general, justify harmfully coercing someone merely on the grounds that you have decided that if you don't harmfully coerce that person, you are going to increase your harmful coercion of someone else.

Analogously, if the government is concerned about burdening taxpayers, it could change its policies so as to either collect more taxes from immigrants or provide fewer government services to them, such that their arrival would be fiscally neutral. The availability of this option obviates any reason for excluding them from the country.

E. Freedom of Association

Individuals have a right to choose whom to associate with or, more to the present point, whom *not* to associate with. If you don't want to work for someone, or live with someone, or be friends with someone, you don't have to. You don't even need a good reason; you can simply decide that you don't feel like associating with them.

Perhaps citizens of a nation also have a right to choose not to "associate" with foreign-born people in the sense of sharing a country with them. The citizens would exercise this right collectively, through their government, by banning immigration. Imagine how this reasoning would go with Sam and Marvin:

You: Sam, why did you harm Marvin?

Sam: I have a right to decide whom to associate with! I sometimes use that same marketplace, and I did not want to associate with Marvin in the sense of sharing a marketplace with him.

This sounds like a very lame justification. The main problem is that merely using the same marketplace as someone else (where you don't have to actually trade with them or even talk to them) is such a tenuous "association" that it is implausible that one would have a significant right to control associations of that kind. Meanwhile, Sam is interfering with much more significant association rights—the rights of Marvin and his would-be trading partners to trade with each other.

Similarly, the "association" that consists merely of residing in the same country as someone else is so tenuous that it is implausible that individuals have a significant right to control whom they associate with in that sense. Much more important are the associations between immigrants and the trading partners, friends, and other people they would interact with voluntarily in their desired destination country. Many native-born citizens are happy to interact with immigrants, and those who do not wish to do so are not compelled to interact with them in any significant way merely by virtue of their residing in the country. Thus, freedom of association overall tends to support open immigration.

F. Political Influence

Conservative commentators have expressed concern that immigration threatens to upset the political balance in America because immigrants tend to lean more to the left rather than the right side of the political spectrum.[8] Indeed, some accuse Democratic politicians of attempting to import more Democrat-friendly voters to give the Democratic Party permanent control of government.[9] Such a plan could be disastrous, converting America essentially into a one-party democracy. With no significant competition, the single dominant party could easily become tyrannical.

Unlike the previous rationales for restricting immigration, this one cites a harm that really might plausibly justify harmful coercion against potential immigrants, if such coercion were needed to avert the harm.

Fortunately, it is not. The government could easily admit migrants as legal residents without granting them voting rights. This is the situation of millions of green card holders in the United States presently, and no one seems to regard this as a problem.

Granted, the children of these immigrants might, in twenty years' time, start voting more Democratic than Republican. However, there are at least two reasons why this is unlikely to lead to a permanent Democratic majority. First, the Democratic slant of the descendants of immigrants tends to diminish over the generations—second-generation immigrants are less slanted than first-generation immigrants, and third-generation immigrants are less slanted than second-generation immigrants.[10]

Second, the rough political balance between the two leading parties in the United States has been maintained for over 150 years, despite enormous changes in the demographics of the electorate, in the overall character of society, and in the political issues of the day. This is not plausibly viewed as coincidental. The best explanation is that the two parties adjust their positions so as to maintain that balance. If one party starts dominating elections, the other party alters its position and/or image to capture more of the vote. Note that this does not depend on assuming that there is only one dimension of voter preference, or even that voter preferences are solely over policy positions. This explanation works as long as the two parties can identify voter preferences; they can alter the positions and other qualities of candidates over which voters have preferences, and each party seeks to maximize its own votes. So, the political balance will probably continue to be maintained in the face of future demographic shifts.

III. In Defense of Illegal Immigration

One perhaps tangential question concerns the morality of illegal immigration. Given that most people are prohibited from immigrating to the United States, is it morally permissible to violate the law and migrate anyway?

Many political leaders appear to be outraged by such behavior.[11] However, the behavior appears to be both rational and morally blameless. To see this, we must first reflect on why individuals are thought to be obligated to obey laws in the first place.

The most popular theory of this is the *social contract theory*. It says that there is a kind of implicit agreement between citizens and the state whereby citizens obey the law and pay taxes in exchange for the government's protection and/or provision of social services.

On this theory, the obligation to obey the government is a contractual obligation, which depends upon one's receiving benefits from the government in return. One cannot be contractually obligated to do something that would inherently exclude one from obtaining any benefits from the contract. For instance, one could not have a valid employment contract that required the employee to never cash any of his paychecks. Nor could there be a valid lease that required the tenant to never use the apartment he is renting. Likewise, there could not be a valid *social* contract that required one to exclude oneself from getting any benefits from the relevant society. If potential immigrants were to obey the laws that prohibit them from migrating to their desired destination, they would be excluding themselves from obtaining any benefit from the society that made those laws. So, no valid social contract could require them to do that.

In other words, under the social contract theory, foreign-born individuals would not be bound by our laws unless and until they had already joined our society and received benefits from it. So, they are not doing anything morally wrong when they illegally cross the border.

There are other theories of the obligation to obey the law. For example, that obedience shows proper gratitude for the benefits provided by the state, that disobedience is unfair to other citizens, or that obedience shows proper respect for the equality of all citizens. However, these other theories also generally require that the person who is supposed to be bound by a given state's laws should have received a fair share of the benefits provided by that state. This rules out arguing that one is obligated to obey a law that would exclude one from obtaining any such benefits.

IV. Conclusion

Human beings have a natural suspicion of foreigners. The most likely explanation is that this is a holdover from our evolutionary past, during which there were frequent wars among neighboring primitive tribes, and people from other tribes were highly likely to kill you when given the opportunity.[12]

Fortunately, we no longer live in such conditions. Yet we still have background emotional tendencies adapted to that situation. Our evaluation of immigration policies is shaped by those emotional tendencies, leading to an instinctive sense that people from other societies are dangerous or harmful. It is important to identify this dynamic so that we can overcome the bias.

Foreign-born people have the same rights that we do. Their lives and well-being are not less important than ours, and they do not deserve to be forced to spend the rest of their lives in conditions of poverty or oppression merely because they had the bad luck to be born in the wrong geographical location.

Notes

1 See John Daniel Davidson, "Without Debate, President Biden Has Decided on Complete Open Borders," *New York Post* (March 8, 2021) (https://nypost.com/2021/03/08/without-debate-president-biden-has-decided-on-complete-open-borders/).

2 This expression is from Joseph Carens, "Aliens and Citizens: The Case for Open Borders," *Review of Politics* 49 (1987): 251–73, at 252.

3 See Julian Simon, *The Economic Consequences of Immigration* (Oxford: Blackwell, 1989), 357–61; Bryan Caplan, *The Myth of the Rational Voter* (Princeton: Princeton University Press, 2007), 58–9.

4 See National Research Council, Panel on the Demographic and Economic Impacts of Immigration, *The New Americans: Economic, Demographic, and Fiscal Effects of Immigration*, ed. James P. Smith and Barry Edmonston (Washington, DC: National Academies Press, 1997), 6–7; George Borjas, *Heaven's Door: Immigration Policy and the American Economy* (Princeton: Princeton University Press, 1999).

5 See Stephen Kershnar, "There Is No Moral Right to Immigrate to the United States," *Public Affairs Quarterly* 14 (2000): 141–58.

6 In economics, a "public good" is a good that must be provided to either all or none of the members of some preexisting group; see David Friedman, *The Machinery of Freedom*, 3rd ed. (Independently Published, 2014), 131.

7 National Research Council 1997, 10; Congressional Budget Office, "The Impact of Unauthorized Immigrants on the Budgets of State and Local Governments" (Washington, DC: Congressional Budget Office, 2007) (http://www.cbo.gov/doc.cfm?index=8711).

8 See Byron York, "Study Finds More Immigrants Equals More Democrats—and More Losses for GOP," *Washington Examiner* (April 15, 2014) (https://www

.washingtonexaminer.com/opinion/1858893/study-finds-more-immigrants-equals-more-democrats-and-more-losses-for-gop/).

9 See Tucker Carlson's Twitter post of July 19, 2022 (https://twitter.com/TuckerCarlson/status/1549576493189283846).

10 Kathleen Ronayne and Emily Swanson, "Young Voters from Newer Immigrant Families Lean More Liberal, Poll Shows," PBS News Hour (September 8, 2016) (https://www.pbs.org/newshour/politics/immigrant-young-voters-liberal).

11 See, e.g., Rep. Raul Labrador's remarks quoted by National Public Radio, "Rep. Labrador Could Shape House Plan On Immigration" (February 7, 2013) (http://www.npr.org/2013/02/07/171345273/rep-labrador-could-shape-house-plan-on-immigration).

12 See Steven Pinker, *The Better Angels of Our Nature* (New York: Penguin, 2012); Phil Thomson and John Halstead, "How Violent Was the Pre-Agricultural World?" (October 2, 2022), SSRN: https://ssrn.com/abstract=4466809.

On the Incoherence of Libertarian Open Borders Theory

Daniel Demetriou

Study Questions

1. How do open borders advocates equivocate on the term "open borders"? What implications does this confusion have according to Demetriou?
2. What is the Migrant-Citizen Symmetry Argument? Why does the equivocation on "open borders" pose a problem for this argument?
3. How does Demetriou respond to the "Starving Marvin" thought experiment?
4. What practical problems does vetting migrants present?
5. What are the "keyhole solutions" offered by open borders advocates? What problems does Demetriou have with these?
6. According to Demetriou, what must the LOBOTs do to be taken seriously?

In the main, restrictionist responses to open borders theory have been defensive insofar as they don't interrogate open borders theory itself. So although I would be happy to discuss how restrictionist pessimism has been vindicated by what we're seeing today in countries that have experimented with quasi-open borders (elevated crime rates,[1] soaring housing costs,[2] higher taxation and debt to pay for impoverished migrants,[3] unsustainable burdens on public services,[4] more social discord,[5] increased racial and religious animus,[6] reactionary extremist politics,[7] growing government censorship,[8] and so forth), I will instead take aim at open borders theory on a more theoretical level.

I focus specifically on open borders theory's ablest exponents, libertarian open borders theorists (LOBOTs), and what I take to be their two biggest problems.

I will first show that LOBOTs don't even understand what they're defending. For there are two disambiguations of "open borders," and some LOBOT (libertarian open borders theory) arguments defend one interpretation, some the other. Since the deficiencies of LOBOT become (even more) apparent once we recognize the conflation of these two meanings of "open borders," I'll begin this essay by making plain the difference between saying that *countries should have uncontrolled borders* and saying that *anyone should be allowed to migrate to the countries of their choosing*.

Second, LOBOTs tend to veer wildly between the ditches of extreme libertarianism and eyebrow-raising state authoritarianism. Regarding the former, any LOBOT must be premised on radical libertarian views about the limits of political authority, since the position denies the collective right of peoples to control their territories. So, although LOBOTs often sell their defense of open borders as commonsensical, a bit of consideration reveals that it cannot be more commonsensical than their extreme libertarianism is. Regarding their authoritarianism, LOBOTs, when faced with obvious real-world negative consequences for their vision, often retreat to fixes or "keyhole" solutions that are (by leftist lights) discriminatory and inegalitarian, and certainly authoritarian in ways that even conservatives will blanch at. Admittedly, their keyhole solutions aren't feasible either. But that's cold comfort, since that fact means an open borders policy of any significant length irreparably harms any nation foolish enough to adopt it.

I. Equivocations of the Term "Open Borders"

What are libertarian open borders advocates even advocating for? Is it, as the title to Michael Huemer's influential essay suggests, a strong prima facie "right to immigrate"?[9] Or is it, as the branding connotes, literal open borders, or a strong prima facie moral right to free movement across borders?[10] Let's peel apart the view that people have a strong moral right to freely cross international borders, or *open access*, from the view that non-citizens have a strong prima facie right to immigrate to wherever they please, which I will call *open residence*.[11]

The distinction between open access and open residence is a genuine one that, at times, even open borders advocates seem to acknowledge. Here is Huemer, early in his 2010 paper, defending open borders:

> Few would question the state's right to exclude at least some potential migrants. For example, the state may deny entry to international terrorists or fugitives from the law. The interesting question concerns the vast majority of other potential immigrants—ordinary people who are simply seeking a new home and a better life. Does the state have the right to exclude these ordinary people?[12]

This means it is consistent with this canonical text of open borders philosophy for the state to deny entry to terrorists, criminals, and fugitives. There is, however, no way to detect and "deny entry" to terrorists, criminals, or fugitives other than to stop entrants at the border or some other controlled space, such as at the international terminal of their departure airport. This means that open borders are compatible with strict border control. Thus, at least in this passage, we charitably read Huemer as arguing for open residence, not open access.[13]

Another open borders advocate, Chris Freiman, had this to say about open borders in an interview.

> It is important to keep in mind what exactly an advocate of open borders is arguing for. "Open borders" is a bit of a misnomer—it's more "light borders" or "porous borders" or something like that. So it isn't that there would be *no* checkpoints or *no* restrictions on immigration. [. . .] So I think most open borders folks would be happy saying that if you are a wanted violent criminal, that might exclude you from immigrating, [or] if you have some particularly deadly contagious disease, and so forth. But other than that, ordinary peaceful migrants should be able to come to the States.[14]

This "exact" explanation confuses more than it clarifies, since obviously we cannot keep violent criminals out unless we know which migrants are violent criminals. And if lots of migrants want to come to your country, and if your nation is prepared to let millions in, that means it needs a massive security apparatus at its borders. Freiman downplays this with his talk of there being at least *some* checkpoints but, in fact, to process and vet the many millions of migrants open borders advocates call for, desirable destination countries like the US, UK, or Sweden would need unprecedented border protections (including coastal defenses that violently turn back migrant boats), not to mention an enormous bureaucracy for vetting would-be migrants. (Migrants today typically dump their IDs, and their home countries have horribly unreliable bureaucracies, so "vetting" is moonshine in any event.) Thus, when pressed, it seems that advocates of open borders appreciate the distinction between open access and open residence, and do not take themselves to be defending open access.

However, the student of open borders is justifiably confused by *other* statements about what open borders consist in. For instance, here is Freiman in another defense of open borders:

> Before I go any further, I should clarify what I mean by "open borders." A nation with an open border is not the same thing as a nation with *no* border. Rather, it is a nation with very few restrictions on entry. To illustrate, we might say that Arizona and California share an open border. Arizonans can enter California to live and work without government-imposed restrictions. Similarly, an open border between, say,

the United States and Mexico reduces or eliminates restrictions on movement between the two nations.[15]

Here we have another confusing "clarification" by Freiman, because there are no walls, fences, or security checkpoints of any kind at the border between Arizona and California (yet). Someone afflicted with any sort of disease, carrying any sort of contraband, or transporting any number of terrorists can drive straight into California from Arizona, and no one would know, and it's no one's job to stop them at the border. If *this* is what Freiman means by "porous borders," then porous borders sound like open access. So it seems we're back to square one, unsure of whether "open borders" means not only a relatively unrestricted legal right to immigrate but also unimpeded travel into a nation's territory.

Sometimes you can tell what a strange thing *is* by figuring out what it's *for*. Since LOBOTs do such a bad job of telling us what they're calling for, maybe we should look to their arguments for open borders to determine what they want? Some, such as Bryan Caplan, seem strongly motivated by the *Productivity Argument*. Caplan and other LOBOTs believe that by moving to productive Western states, the poorest people from around the world will be tremendously more productive and we'll all get richer.[16] Granting this rosy picture for argument's sake, most or all of the alleged productivity benefits of "open borders" would be achieved by open residence, and little to none from open access. So maybe they're only calling for open residence.

But at times Caplan and certainly other LOBOTs are also moved by two additional rationales. One concerns the *Freedom of Movement Argument*, which says it's prima facie wrong to keep migrants out because migrants, like everyone else, have a right to move around wherever they please. Another related but distinct argument we can call the *Migrant-Citizen Symmetry Argument*.[17] It's tough to say precisely what libertarians think of citizenship, but in migration discussions it clearly doesn't mean much, because it seems like they operate with the principle that if you can't do something to a citizen, you shouldn't do it to a migrant. These two rationales are often blended together. For instance, in one debate with Rishi Joshi,[18] LOBOT Peter Jaworski argues for international migration on the grounds of the reasonableness of internal migration for co-nationals:

> To make this personal again, consider my situation for a minute. I live in Arlington, Virginia. Arlington is very rich, votes Democratic, is very educated, has excellent education and health care systems, and is, in general, a wonderful place to live. Our crime rates and unemployment figures are low. Our educational attainment is very high. We are mostly a white-collar crowd, and we drink our tea with a pinky in the air. Tangipahoa, Louisiana, is none of those things. It is very poor, is uneducated, votes Republican, has poor education and health systems, and is, in general, dramatically different from Arlington. The crime rates are higher, and job prospects are relatively a great deal poorer. Culturally, we are very different. And yet, there

is nothing stopping someone from Tangipahoa from getting in her car and driving straight up to Arlington. No one will check to make sure that she shares our culture, that she won't steal Arlingtonian jobs, that she shares our commitment to gender equality, that she practices a religion sufficiently similar to ours, that she believes in the First Amendment, and so on. No one will check her car for weapons, except if she is pulled over by the highway patrol, but this isn't guaranteed. There is no border in her path from her parish to my county. There are plenty of administrative borders, but no physical barrier where we can ensure the preservation of Arlingtonianness. Shouldn't there be a border separating us? [. . .] I don't have a problem with people from Tangipahoa getting in their car and moving to Arlington. But, then again, I don't have a problem with people from Tamaulipas, Mexico, getting in their car and driving straight up and east to Arlington.[19]

So Jaworski is advocating for open access on the grounds of free movement and treating foreigners as one does co-nationals.

Oh wait, no, he doesn't. Since if you *read on*, when he's forced to respond to Joshi's discussion of the astounding difference in crime rates between recent "refugees" (i.e., economic migrants, especially from East Africa, the Middle East, and Central Asia) to Western countries, Jaworski offers what LOBOTs call a "keyhole solution"—that is, a narrow fix that maximizes migration while allegedly answering the restrictionist concern in question. "If crime is a problem, don't keep them all out: instead, exclude single, young men, fourteen to thirty years old, and let everyone else in," Jaworski writes.[20] Yet where would we "exclude" these men? Presumably, at a controlled border, and (as we discussed) an awfully robust border in cases where lots of people want, and shall be allowed, to get in. That means walls, fences, barbed wire, guys with guns, dogs, drones, and so on.

Or consider this passage from Bas van der Vossen and Jason Brennan:

Jason lives in Northern Virginia, has a great job, but is getting tired of the traffic. Bas lives in North Carolina and has been telling Jason about how wonderful a place it is to live. Jason decides to move to North Carolina. This was not Bas's intention, and so he decides to prevent Jason from coming. When Jason tries to come anyway, Bas meets him on the road with his gun and threatens to shoot Jason unless he turns around. Again, the restriction is wrongful. Even though Jason had a wonderful life in Washington, DC, Bas still violates his rights when he prevents Jason from moving. Bas uses force to stop Jason from interacting with others who wish to interact with him. The point seems clear, then. The kinds of force and interference involved in limiting people's freedom of movement stands in need of justification. Unless Bas [has] some very good reason for stopping Jason, [he] need[s] to step aside and let him be on his way. By analogy, the same seems true for modern governments and immigrants.[21]

This version of the intrastate/interstate travel analogy has a subtle wrinkle Jaworski's does not, insofar as it stresses that Brennan has a good life in DC. By this, van der Vossen and Brennan are suggesting that a mere right to freedom of movement supports open borders, that open borders aren't justified only by its alleged benefit of improving the material fortunes of migrants. And importantly, this alleged right weighs in favor of open access, not just open residence. So, it seems LOBOTs support open access after all?

When advancing the migrant-citizen symmetry rationale, LOBOTs criticize restrictionists for excluding people of a certain sort—Muslims, the unemployable, the low-skilled, and so on—but not imposing similar treatment on citizens of the same sort. For instance, in this excerpt from a lecture, Brennan suggests that bans on groups with (statistically well-established) worse reputations for criminality would be unjustified because we wouldn't exile male citizens, despite their being predictably more criminal.

> [Restrictionist arguments based on criminality] *treat native-born citizens and people born elsewhere differently.* No one would make the argument that I, by being male, am statistically more likely to commit crime than the women in here, therefore by virtue of that we should kick me out.[22]

Unfortunately for LOBOTs who think we should treat migrants and citizens the same, the migrant-citizen symmetry rationale is a sword that cuts both ways. If migrant-citizen symmetry is correct, then a LOBOT who asserts that we *should* keep out known criminals or known Ebola carriers would be forced to say, presumably, that we ought to exile *citizen* criminals or *citizen* Ebola carriers. We restrictionists aren't particularly soft-hearted, but even we would not advise *exiling* citizens who steal cars or suffer from a communicable disease. But LOBOTs outright say we may bar migrants with these traits. As we will see later, some say we may bar people of certain faiths (say, Muslims) from entry, entailing that (if the migrant-citizen symmetry argument holds) we ought to exile Muslim citizens?

II. Marvin, Marketplaces, and Migration Ethics

Let us focus on Huemer's account in particular for a moment. According to him, "[O]rdinary, noncriminal migrants who wish to leave their country of origin for morally innocent reasons, whether to escape persecution or economic hardship, or simply to join a society they would prefer to live in" have a right to immigrate. And early in his famous essay for this position, he tells us that his arguments will be non-ideological, driven by intuitions about cases.

> A word about theoretical assumptions. In my view, most general theories or theoretical approaches in political philosophy—liberal egalitarianism, contractarianism,

utilitarianism, and so on—are too controversial to form a secure basis for reasoning. It is not known which, if any, of those theories are correct. I have therefore sought to minimize the reliance on such theories. This does not mean that I assume that all such broad theories are false; I merely refrain from resting my arguments on them. Thus, I do not assume utilitarianism, contractarianism, libertarian rights theory, liberal egalitarianism, nor any general account of harm or rights. Nor do I assume the negation of any of those theories. Instead, I aim to rest conclusions on widely shared ethical intuitions about relatively specific cases. The method is to describe a case in which nearly everyone will share a particular, clear intuitive evaluation of some action, and then to draw a parallel from the case described to some controversial case of interest.

Huemer then offers the case of "Starving Marvin," which has become an influential thought experiment for open borders philosophy:

Marvin is in desperate need of food. Perhaps someone has stolen his food, or perhaps a natural disaster destroyed his crops; whatever the reason, Marvin is in danger of starvation. Fortunately, he has a plan to remedy the problem: he will walk to the local marketplace, where he will buy bread. Assume that in the absence of outside interference, this plan would succeed: the marketplace is open, and there are people there who are willing to trade food to Marvin in exchange for something he has. Another individual, Sam, is aware of all this and is watching Marvin. For some reason, Sam decides to detain Marvin on his way to the marketplace, forcibly preventing him from reaching it. As a result, Marvin returns home empty-handed, where he dies of starvation. What is the proper assessment of Sam's action?

Analogizing countries as marketplaces is something a libertarian might like, but few others. I, and perhaps you, think of countries as *homelands*, not marketplaces. But let's contemplate where this marketplace analogy leads and see how amenable even it is to open borders.

Given the freedom to do so, businesses can be picky about who they let into their premises. Stores and restaurants, for example, will keep out people they feel are bad for their images, profits, or working environment. Upscale ones have dress codes. On NYC's Fifth Avenue and Beverly Hills's Rodeo Drive, stores selling haute couture can be found in which customers must be "buzzed in" by employees in an effort to keep out the riffraff. Golf clubs used to serve only WASP or Jewish clientele as a matter of policy. I don't know if any country clubs still do that, but I know of a dive bar in Ohio that, wishing to exclude Black customers, became a "private club" that handed out keycards only to whites. In many shops in depressed areas, owners post signs declaring their legal right to refuse service to anyone. Now, although the legality of such policies is questionable today, these discriminatory policies are something libertarians would have to be okay with, given their commitment to free association.

So, on a libertarian rationale that analogizes a nation to a business, or wishes national borders to be treated like the entrances to businesses, there is an embarrassment of flexibility when it comes to restricting access, and even restricting residence.[23]

Maybe we shouldn't analogize countries to stores but to marketplaces such as malls, and see individuals as analogous to the particular shops within? Even so, we should bear in mind that malls have entryways and hours of operation. Some, in high-crime areas, have metal detectors or security guards at the doors. Again, many malls have "no shirt, no shoes, no service" policies. Likewise, "Mall of America" may demand those interested in trading with its individual buyers and sellers to enter through the border in an orderly manner. In analogy to what malls do, nations may, perhaps with the aid of biometrics, bar people who have no ability to fend for themselves, make the place less livable, or carry in firearms.

Here Huemer will demur. Huemer dislikes the idea of an authority that tells the various economic agents who they can and cannot deal with. As best I can tell, Huemer wants us to understand our nations as something like informal outdoor markets located in some sort of no-man's-land oppressed by shady mafiosos (in America's case, "Sam"). In this scenario, every merchant-resident can hire and sell to whom they like. In other words, Huemer's marketplace analogy doesn't resemble any actual marketplace because (to Huemer) there is no analogous just authority regulating sellers and consumers in an actual country.[24] Which is, of course, something only someone with a radical libertarian position on state authority will say.[25] This position *may be true*, for all we'll argue here. But given that Huemer's case for open borders relies upon it, Huemer's particular LOBOT cannot be any more attractive than his radical libertarian positions about the (non-)extent of political authority.[26]

Here is another way to show that Huemer's view is only as strong as his extreme libertarianism. Note that the moral heft of Starving Marvin's right to enter the marketplace is not his freedom of movement per se, but his prima facie right to do business to survive.[27] Conceiving of the marketplace (Huemer's words and analogy) as a physical space,[28] the Marvin thought experiment does not justify Marvin's arrival merely to enjoy the benefits of the market's air conditioning, better set of people, or security. Thus, nothing in the case obliges us to accept (say) so-called "climate refugees," social migrants (e.g., retirees), or asylum-seekers. Insofar as Huemer wishes to defend the migration of such groups, the Marvin case is, without supplementation, insufficient for that task.[29] So how can we get from the Marvin case to a right to immigrate for all other reasons Huemer also recognizes?

As it happens, libertarians don't privilege economic association: whether it's business, marriage, friendship, or anything else, on libertarian grounds, it's not the state's right to interfere with our consensual relationships. Thus, on libertarian grounds, Marvin doesn't really need to be starving, or even have anything of value to trade, to justify his entrance. If Marvin was invited by a lonely Denver or Arlington resident to a backyard barbecue, then on LOBOT ethics, Sam has no right to bar his way. If a *non-citizen* in Denver or Arlington wants Marvin to come join him in a backyard barbecue,

LOBOTs have to say that Sam shouldn't be able to stop him. If a non-citizen in Denver or Arlington wants 10,000 Congolese to join him in a barbecue for no good reason at all (maybe it would make a funny social media post?), LOBOTs have to say that Sam has no right to stop them. After all, as migrant-citizen symmetrists will point out, if *you* wanted to invite 10,000 of your *countrymen* to your barbecue, you could, and it isn't *your* legal obligation to make sure they have housing! When you consider that NGOs are established to give aid to migrants, you see that all the developing world has technically been invited to a barbecue in your homeland.[30]

Or do migrants even need an invitation? The LOBOT doctrine of migrant-citizen symmetry, paired with their interpretation of our right to freedom of movement, means that we have no right to exclude millions of migrants wishing to occupy our lands even if no one invited them or wanted to deal with them. Even if millions of Marvins dislike us, or even hate us, we cannot bar their way because, as seen above, millions of hypothetical co-nationals who hate us *might* have moved next door, or millions of our co-nationals *might* have suddenly hated everything about us.[31] These, dear reader, are the non-ideological commonsense intuitions of libertarian open borders theory.

III. Authoritarian Keyhole Solutions

Now *actual* common sense says that open access, at least, would be suicidal and morally irresponsible. Insofar as they are able, governments should bar the entrance of deadly drugs, sex slaves, poached animal contraband (such as ivory or rhinoceros horn), terrorists, criminals, and predictable public charges. Thus, for any state determined to admit millions of migrants, borders must be controlled and migrants vetted. LOBOTs seem to allow as much, at least when directly challenged about these obvious concerns. I ask: Where exactly do these migrants live while they are waiting to be vetted? What sort of walls, wire fences, armed boats, and so on, are we willing to build and maintain to facilitate open residence without open access? How many desperate migrants attempting to get past these barriers are we willing to shoot? How many nurses and doctors do we hire to evaluate and treat illnesses? Since migrants often lie about their past and bring forged documents (and children, who may or may not be trafficked), how many interrogators and investigators do we hire to ensure (as if we could) that the criminals are kept out and that the kids they bring aren't trafficked? In the meantime, if we do separate adults from children, who babysits these hundreds of thousands of kids? How much biometric information do we gather and share with other governments? How many clerks and support staff will be needed to process all this paperwork? Never have I seen an open borders economist tally up those numbers, say who's going to pay for it, or address the authoritarian measures these institutions would require to function. They need to, as this list of costly and authoritarian measures is predictable given a restricted access + open residence regime. In contrast, a restrictionist (restricted access + restricted residence) regime that refused entry to anyone merely showing up at the border (be they "refugees" or not), that dealt violently with anyone attempting to cross its borders illegally, and that jailed nationals who hired illegals, would not attract hordes of migrants to its borders, thereby destabilizing its neighbors and necessitating the above unsustainable, manifestly ineffectual, coercive, and at least equally violent bureaucracies. Migrants are not foolish: they will not waste their time and money traveling to lands where their attempts are bound to fail.

That said, LOBOTs will concede that even the (alleged) right to migrate (i.e., open *residence*) may be outweighed by other harms. If these harms prove real, they'll usually say the correct response isn't to reestablish a restrictionist regime, but rather to make the smallest practicable change to open borders policy necessary to obviate the downside in question—their so-called "keyhole solutions."

For instance, restrictionists point out that migrants are likely to have values that vary dramatically from those of their receiving countries. Many migrants bring values that those in receiving countries find sexist, patriarchal, racist, fundamentalist, undemocratic, and illiberal. Open access could easily result in migrants outnumbering natives, meaning a complete change in political priorities. What should be done? One keyhole solution Huemer and others endorse in that eventuality is not letting them vote.[32] And nothing in particular obliges a LOBOT to allow even the children of migrants to vote, if their children manifest the same tendencies.

Or consider medical care. All popular receiving countries provide taxpayer-funded medical care to needy migrants. It is easy to imagine millions of people moving to a rich nation just for the medical care, even if they despise its culture and people. Given the high costs of medical care, this is unsustainable. The LOBOT keyhole solution is, of course, simply to deny migrants this public service.[33] Caplan even considers charging migrants higher taxes, requiring migrants to pay higher tuitions at state colleges, or charging them to enter the country (in his graphic book, *Open Borders: The Science and Ethics of Immigration*, one panel depicts a migrant handing a bag of money over at . . . a border crossing).[34] Caplan approvingly quotes LOBOT Alex Nowrasteh saying that we should "build a wall around the welfare state, not the country." He also suggests that forcing migrants to learn English or pass "rigorous civics tests" before becoming citizens would be better than restricting their migration.

Now LOBOTs think some of these keyhole solutions are bad, but morally superior to the alternative of keeping migrants out. But they think some are justified. For instance, Caplan seems to think that mass migration from Muslim countries could have a negative effect on liberal values. To this, he suggests not admitting Muslims or at least limiting Muslim migrants to a certain sustainable percentage by bringing in proportionately more non-Muslims. Likewise, everyone knows that a skewed sex ratio can foment social discord, so if there are too many males coming across the border, Caplan advises bringing in more females. If too many "future Democrats" are coming in, bring in more "future Republicans" to balance them out, and so on. How, then, is this to be accomplished, exactly? Shall we ask migrants whether they're Muslim or not? Muslim migrants aren't stupid; if they know there's a ban or a limit on Muslims, many will lie. If *we* aren't stupid, we'd better not take anyone at their word. Can anyone walk us through the process of determining whether someone is a Muslim? Do we find pictures of them doing Muslim things? If they say they recently abandoned the faith, do we believe them? Or how do we determine if someone is a "future Democrat" or "future Republican" (how about "future Green Party voter"?—there are a lot of parties out there!). By their demographic profile? Imagine the toxic politics behind calibrating immigration quotas on this logic. Imagine how cynical and racially loaded political parties would become under this scenario. Gone would be even an attempt at persuading our fellows to change their views: democracy would be nothing but a demographic head count in which party leaders agitate to reject or attract foreigners based on their race or their sex in order to win elections.[35] And none of this, of course, is compatible with migrant-citizen symmetry, since, as Huemer points out, we cannot limit the number of *natives* who convert to Islam[36] or wish to vote for a party we disagree with.[37]

Conclusion

I am aware that restrictionist solutions have (to many) counterintuitive consequences as well. In my view, any sustainable restrictionist solution will seem heartless, at least until the alternatives are widely appreciated. There are no easy answers in a world where hundreds of millions have the desire and means to migrate. My point is that LOBOT is not some morally elegant solution to the problem of mass migration. To deserve to be taken seriously, LOBOTs must acknowledge the need for tight border control and abandon any arguments (such as *Freedom of Movement* and *Migrant-Citizen symmetry*) that entail open access. They need to be clear about their libertarian commitments and the essential role these play in their advocacy for even mere open residence. Finally, they need to acknowledge the tensions, if not outright inconsistencies, between their libertarian values and keyhole solutions, and square both with the real-world constraints of group dynamics and human psychology.

Notes

1 Where migrants come from, and where they are settling, are important factors in predicting whether they will increase violent crime rates. Most studies show that migrants from Africa, the Middle East, and Central Asia are more likely to be violent criminals than natives in their receiving countries, while migrants from Western and East Asian countries generally have lower rates of violent crime convictions than do natives. Migrants from Somalia, Iraq, and Afghanistan can be as much as nine times more likely to commit a violent crime in Scandinavian countries; and even after adjusting for their age and sex (they are overwhelmingly young and male), still commit violent crimes at multiples of natives. See for instance Torbjørn Skardhamar, Mikko Aaltonen, and Martti Lehti, "Immigrant Crime in Norway and Finland," *Journal of Scandinavian Studies in Criminology and Crime Prevention* 15, no. 2 (2014) (http://dx.doi.org/10.1080/14043858.2014.926062); Göran Adamson, "Migrants and Crime in Sweden in the Twenty-First Century," *Society* 57 (2020): 9–21 (https://doi.org/10.1007/s12115-019-00436-8).

2   Even the pro-migration CATO Institute admits that migration increases housing costs, particularly for poorer natives who rent. Jacob L. Vigdor, "Immigration, Housing Markets, and Community Vitality," *Cato Journal* (Fall 2017) (https://www.cato.org/cato-journal/fall-2017/immigration-housing-markets-community-vitality). For a discussion of how social housing is being set aside for migrants at the expense of natives, see "Mass Migration Deepens the Housing Crisis," *Migration Watch* UK (February 16, 2024) (https://www.migrationwatchuk.org/news/2024/02/16/mass-migration-deepens-the-housing-crisis). For helpful recent discussions with links to studies, see: Paul Kupiec, "The Migrant and Housing Crises are Colliding with Predictable Results," *The Hill* (October 10, 2023) (https://thehill.com/opinion/immigration/4238426-the-migrant-and-housing-crises-are-colliding-with-predictable-results/); Sarah Bedford, "Fact Check: Does Immigration Increase Housing Costs?" *Washington Examiner* (May 24, 2023) (https://www.washingtonexaminer.com/news/2569511/fact-check-does-immigration-increase-housing-costs/).

3   For instance, Michael Huemer's home city of Denver, 40,000 new migrants in the last year is predicted to cost the city $180 million by the end of 2024, and is resulting in cuts to services already. Katie Parkins, "Denver Mayor Announces Reduction in DMV and Parks & Rec. to Offset Migrant Costs," *Denver 7 ABC* (February 9, 2024) (https://www.denver7.com/news/front-range/denver/denver-mayor-announces-reduction-in-dmv-and-parks-rec-after-failure-of-bipartisan-congress-immigration-bill).

4   For instance, in Michael Huemer's home city of Denver, hospital administrators consider their systems "overwhelmed" by migrants needing care: Claire Lavezzorio, "Denver Health Says Migrant Surge Causing Strain on Hospital, More Funding Needed," *Denver 7 ABC* (December 17, 2023) (https://www.denver7.com/news/local-news/denver-health-says-migrant-surge-causing-strain-on-hospital-more-funding-needed).

5   It is hard to measure "social discord," but headlines and college controversies seem to be increasingly about ethnic grievances. One underlying factor is decreased social trust brought about by mass migration (again, certain sorts of migrants decrease social trust more than others). See Peter Thisted Dinesen, Merlin Schaeffer, and Kim Mannemar Sønderskov, "Ethnic Diversity and Social Trust: A Narrative and Meta-Analytical Review," *Annual Review of Political Science* 23, no. 1 (2020): 441–65; Lauren McLaren, "Immigration, Ethnic Diversity, and Inequality," in *Handbook of Political Trust*, ed. Sonja Zmerli and Tom W. G. van der Meer (Cheltenham: Edward Elgar, 2017), 316–37.

6   Consider the massive Muslim protests and demonstrations in Europe, inter-migrant hostilities (e.g., Hindus vs. Muslims in Western countries), and, more recently, hostilities between supporters of Israel and Palestine across the West. Jessica Murray, Aina J. Khan, and Rajeev Syal, "'It Feels Like People Want to Fight': How Communal Unrest Flared in Leicester," *The Guardian* (September 23, 2024) (https://www.theguardian.com/uk-news/2022/sep/23/how-communal-unrest-flared-leicester-muslim-hindu-tensions).

7 On this well-documented phenomenon, see essays collected at International Migration Research Network's *Migration Hub* under "Extremism and Migration" (https://migrationresearch.com/taxonomies/topics-migration-consequences-for-migrants-sending-and-receiving-countries-legal-political-consequences-extremism-and-migration).

8 As J. S. Mill notes in Ch. 16 of *Representative Government*, authoritarian measures are often necessary to quell ethnic conflict and present a reason against mass migration (https://oll.libertyfund.org/titles/mill-the-collected-works-of-john-stuart-mill-volume-xix-essays-on-politics-and-society-part-2). In Europe, we see greater speech restrictions after the onset of their migrant crises. Support for First Amendment rights in the United States is declining in large part because it protects racially offensive speech. "Hate Speech Laws in the United Kingdom," *Wikipedia* (https://en.wikipedia.org/wiki/Hate_speech_laws_in_the_United_Kingdom, accessed March 16, 2024); Jacob Mchangama, "Evidence Is Growing That Free Speech Is Declining," *Foreign Policy* (December 12, 2023) (https://foreignpolicy.com/2023/12/04/evidence-is-growing-that-free-speech-is-declining/).

9 Michael Huemer, "Is There a Right to Immigrate?" *Social Theory and Practice* 36, no. 3 (2010): 429–61.

10 Inter alia, Joseph Carens, "Aliens and Citizens: The Case for Open Borders," *Review of Politics* 49 (1987): 251–73; Bas van der Vossen and Jason Brennan, *In Defense of Openness* (Oxford: Oxford University Press, 2018); Christopher Freiman and Javier Hildago, "Liberalism or Immigration Restrictions, But Not Both," *Journal of Ethics and Social Philosophy* 10, no. 2 (2016); Bryan Caplan's various work on the topic and the essays at https://openborders.info/.

11 The term "open residence" was suggested to me by Tom Metcalf.

12 Huemer, "Is There a Right," 430.

13 In a later passage, Huemer criticizes as coercive having "armed guards hired to patrol the borders . . . " (Huemer, "Is There a Right," 434).

14 Chris Freiman, "Open Borders, Poverty, and Universal Basic Income," Interview by Dave Rubin on *Rubin Report* (Jun 7, 2018, quotation marks and emphasis added) (https://youtu.be/tNxATohmZpo).

15 Christopher Freiman, "A Defense of Open Borders," in *The Palgrave Handbook of Philosophy and Public Policy*, ed. David Boonin (New York: Palgrave, 2018), 161–2 (emphasis in original).

16 Bryan Caplan and Zach Weinersmith, *Open Borders: The Science and Ethics of Immigration* (New York: First Second, 2019). Perhaps the best rebuttal to this claim that focuses only on wealth is by Caplan's colleague Garett Jones, *The Culture Transplant* (Stanford: Stanford University Press, 2022).

17 I'll alternate between "citizen" and "co-national," although these two are importantly different and would need to be distinguished in longer discussions. It's hard to state this principle: basically, it asks us to treat "outsiders" as if they were "insiders"—a distinction LOBOTs struggle with.

18 "For (Some) Immigration Restrictions," and "Response to Peter Jaworski," in *Ethics: Left and Right*, ed. Bob Fischer (New York: Oxford University Press, 2019), 191–8.

19 Peter Jaworski, "Markets Without Limits," in *Ethics: Left and Right*, ed. Fischer, 183–90.

20 Peter Jaworski, "Reply to Joshi," in *Ethics: Left and Right*, ed. Fischer, 201.
21 van der Vossen and Brennan, *In Dense of Openness*, 25–6.
22 6:20ff in Jason Brennan, "Lecture 9: Immigration Rights," *Libertarianism.org* (https://www.libertarianism.org/guides/lectures/immigration-rights) (my emphasis).
23 Uwe Steinhoff, *Freedom, Culture, and the Right to Exclude* (London: Routledge, 2022).
24 See Huemer's discussion of why nations should not be analogized to clubs in "Is There a Right," 445–8.
25 Michael Huemer, *The Problem of Political Authority* (New York: Palgrave, 2013).
26 Those who, like Raphael Nawrotski, appear to be actually quite statist but support open borders for other reasons, are being somewhat opportunistic when they appeal to LOBOT rationales such as Huemer's, which rely on premises statists are unlikely to accept. See Raphael Nawrotzki, "Climate Migration and Moral Responsibility," *Ethics, Policy & Environment* 17, no. 1 (2014): 69–87 (https://doi.org/10.1080/21550085.2014.885173).
27 Brennan similarly describes the Marvin case to be about Sam's preventing Marvin's "trade with a willing partner" at 3:30ff of "Lecture 9." Christopher Wellman ("Immigration and Freedom of Association," *Ethics* 119, no. 1 (2008): 109–a41 (https://doi.org/10.1086/592311.2008), notes (130ff) that libertarian open borders advocacy rests on "property rights" and "freedom of movement" rationales, and argues against both justifying open borders. I don't focus on the former, but dwell on arguments based on productivity for the poor, free movement, and migrant-citizen symmetry. Wellman also observes that the assumption that private firms and individuals have a right to invite whom they please to better transact with them more or less assumes anarchism, which is a main point of this section.
28 Nothing in the Marvin case would justify Marvin's entry into the marketplace if the "marketplace" (in a nonmaterial sense of mere opportunity to trade) were to come *to* Marvin—if, say, someone left a rich country and traded with Marvin in his impoverished homeland. This possibility raises the question of free trade, but not unrestricted migration.
29 "How does all this relate to U.S. immigration policy? The role of Marvin is played by those potential immigrants who seek escape from *oppression* or economic hardship" (Huemer, "Is There a Right," 423, emphasis added). Nothing in the Marvin case justifies being sheltered by the marketplace.
30 Todd Bensman, "Biden Admin. Sends Millions to Religious Nonprofits Facilitating Mass Illegal Migration," *Center for Immigration Studies* (January 30, 2024) (https://cis.org/Bensman/Biden-Admin-Sends-Millions-Religious-Nonprofits-Facilitating-Mass-Illegal-Migration).
31 Considerations such as this prompt Caplan to say that Israel, for instance, shouldn't have open borders, since so many people hostile to Jewish Israelis would migrate there to undermine or even kill Israelis. Of course, the same can be said of Christian or liberal Americans, Britons, and so on. See "Would Bryan Caplan Let in Terrorists?" *Aporia Podcast* (January 2024) (https://youtu.be/7k2nkdG_pb4?si=-CrZK58DReBbMO_1).
32 Migrant-citizen symmetry would seem to militate against such discrimination. Again, the reader should note that migrant-citizen symmetry seems to matter for LOBOTs

when it works in favor of migration, but LOBOTs will abandon it with ease if it tells against migration.

33 Huemer, "Is There a Right," 142ff.

34 Ibid., 144.

35 In reality, the political prize would be controlling the immigration bureaucracy that makes these calls.

36 Huemer, "Is There a Right," 449ff. See Rafael De Clercq, "Huemer on Immigration and the Preservation of Culture," *Philosophia* 45 (2017): 1091–8.

37 Michael Huemer, "The Right to Move versus the Right to Exclude: A Principled Defense of Open Borders," unpublished manuscript (https://philarchive.org/archive/HUETRT).

Responses

Response to Huemer on Open Borders

Daniel Demetriou

Study Questions

1. What reasons does Demetriou give for why the second premise of Huemer's argument is false?
2. According to Demetriou, what are the many costs of open borders?
3. Why are the costs of open borders ultimately irrelevant? What *is* relevant?

I thank Michael Huemer for engaging in this debate with me. His "core argument" for open borders (or at least what I would call "open residence") goes as so:

(1) Harmful coercion is prima facie wrong.

(2) Immigration restrictions are harmful and coercive.

(3) So, immigration restrictions are prima facie wrong.

Huemer defends this core argument in Part I of his essay. The rest of his essay defends "relatively open borders" for many countries—and the United States by name—in real-world circumstances.

Contra Huemer's Part I

Is (2) true? Huemer thinks that barring Marvin from entering your kitchen uninvited would not be even prima facie wrong because refusing to benefit someone doesn't harm them.[1] So there must be some disanalogy between your government's stopping Marvin at the border and your stopping him at your kitchen door. The difference for Huemer is that, unlike the relationship between you and your kitchen, there is no (what I'll call) *sovereignty relation* between your government and your nation's territory.[2] Huemer rejects the idea that a people can be sovereign over their territory because he is an extreme libertarian/anarcho-capitalist.[3] If his assumption is wrong, then there are times when a government may exclude migrants just as there are times when you can exclude uninvited guests.

But what if migrants *are* invited? Suppose you are housemates with soft-hearted but soft-headed Sally, who invites a homeless family to camp out in your living room. Or opportunistic Ollie, who invites in some sketchy dude to work for him in your basement. Or subversive Sam, who wants to sabotage your home and so sublets his closet to someone with obnoxious values, manners, and habits. Such actions would occasion a serious household conversation and may require someone moving out if rules can't be agreed upon. Likewise, unless you're an extreme libertarian, you not only believe that a nation is sovereign over its territory, but that a good government may exclude migrants even if they have been invited by some nationals. For some of our compatriots are imprudent, selfish, or subversive, and would impose immoral or unsustainable negative externalities on their fellows if given the chance, and this is why normal people don't think individuals should be allowed—even on their own property—to shelter fugitives, house hostile forces, or pollute in certain ways.

So whether the migrants in question are invited or not, what needs to be determined is whether parallel externalities would be true of them. And that's what Huemer is addressing in Part II of his main essay.

The Many Costs of Open Borders

Economic Competition

There is a body of literature that argues that mass migration is economically beneficial except for young and low-skilled natives. This research usually ignores certain important factors such as the long-term economic costs of political instability resulting from mass migration or increased housing costs (economists urge us to just build more housing—we'll discuss this in a moment).[4] On this question, I think natives should prioritize their low-skilled and younger compatriots over foreigners. My grandparents came to this country in the 1910s mostly because manufacturing executives preferred hiring cheaper Eastern and Southern European laborers over Black Americans and more expensive native whites. It seems to me those industrialists should have been forced to put their fellow Americans first, even if that meant slowing down American industrialization.[5] At this point, economists will make glib replies about using the extra productivity from mass migration to retrain poor natives or simply give them handouts. These don't seem to be materializing: Americans with lower cognitive capacities simply cannot "learn to code," and automation will only make the jobs they can do even more scarce (imagine what self-driving cars will do to rideshare and trucking employment). And as far as handouts go, even if natives received them, the result would likely be moral dissipation, boredom, and loss of self-respect.[6]

Fiscal Burdens

Mass migration is particularly costly when low-skilled migrants enter receiving countries with generous welfare benefits (notably, the Marvins of the world are attracted to "marketplaces" with the most generous welfare programs).[7] For instance, half of London's social housing units are occupied by migrants,[8] and 70 percent of the UK's immigrants from Somalia use social housing.[9]

Huemer's solution is simple: exclude migrants from social services. However, these services are unlikely to be withheld for long. First, because many natives will find it unbearable to let sick migrants die from lack of medical care, freeze for lack of housing, or remain uneducated from lack of schooling. Second, because bureaucrats running these programs want to expand their reach and thus will successfully agitate to extend benefits to migrants. Third, because welfare programs will become more, not less, popular as migrants from the third world stream in and exert political influence. And even if natives did adopt this measure, they would find themselves faced with a sizable resentful underclass who will, unless brutally cowed, eventually rise up and force wealthier natives to create costly redistributive programs (or worse) through violence.

Public Goods

These considerations also pertain to non-excludable "public goods." Will migrants tend to riot or commit more crime? Depending on where they come from, yes,[10] and natives will pay for the increased policing, jailing, and counterterrorism measures. Social capital will decrease as public areas become less safe and pleasant. Will the arrival of tens of millions of migrants increase your housing costs and disfigure your nation's countryside with massive and ugly tenements?[11] Affordable housing for your children, uncrowded spaces, natural beauty, and bucolic farms are also public goods, and mass migration destroys these, too.

Culture

Huemer, perhaps guided by citizen-migrant symmetry thinking, seems to think that natives have no more right to complain about cultural change due to mass migration than they would to endogenous cultural change adopted by their native fellows.[12] Huemer also focuses on the United States when discussing the cultural impacts of mass migration. But no other receiving country is as large or as culturally influential as America is. Small countries like Norway, Sweden, Denmark, and Canada would undoubtedly lose their national characters under open borders. And even American culture has changed substantially due to every successive wave of mass migration. For instance, American traditions, values, and cultural references were forever changed by the mass migrations of 1880–1920 (if you don't believe me, take a look at the McGuffey Reader,[13] a textbook for nineteenth-century American children). Just as few Catholic,

Orthodox, or Jewish migrants became Protestants in the twentieth century, few Muslim or Hindu migrants will become Christian in the twenty-first.

Mass migration to the West means that its social, political, and legal character will grow more global in nature: lower in average human capital; more authoritarian, corrupt, sectarian, polygamist, and socialist; less egalitarian, Christian, trusting, and trustworthy.[14] So-called "assimilation" will amount to change for both migrants *and* natives: a "new normal" that the natives usually don't like, and one which is arguably worse and certainly less distinctive than what they had previously. Migrants, who cannot appreciate what was lost and tend to be highly ethnocentric, usually assume they improved the place. Natives will usually remember with nostalgia the days before their arrival.

Subversion and Terrorism

LOBOTs such as Huemer and Bryan Caplan tell us that they are against open borders for Israel, insofar as millions of people would like to migrate there to destroy it from within. But Israel is not alone in this regard: many countries, including the United States, are also widely hated. Even countries without a history of colonialism are not immune to being resented by migrants they played no role in immiserating.[15] As 9/11 proved, it doesn't take many conspiring foreigners to permanently wound even a large, powerful country.

Conclusion: Costs Are Ultimately Irrelevant

Quite apart from the negative effects of mass migration on the lasting prosperity, safety, innovativeness, civility, and indeed civilization in the world's best countries, open borders is an ideology of subversion in the mouths of your enemies and betrayal in the mouths of your comrades. For *even if* some territory your nation currently controls hypothetically would be "improved" by mass migration to it, this would still result in the loss of your homeland and—barring the creation of a caste or other segregating strategy for them—the extinction of your people. Unfortunately, not everyone is part of a nation. And sadly, not every nation is sovereign over its own land. But let no one fortunate enough to be part of a people, no matter how humble, in a possession of a land, no matter how meager, be mesmerized into giving up either without a fight. Your country and your nation's institutions do not belong to the world's economic or cognitive elite. Or the globe's hungriest and most ambitious. Or foreign hordes of wretched refuse yearning for what's free. It is your homeland, *your* refuge in a cruel and uncaring world, the only country where *you* should be advantaged over others, a nursery for *your* people's children, and an inheritance to be passed on to *them*. All else is beside the point.

Notes

1 But it seems to me you *do* harm Marvin even in the kitchen case, although it's perfectly permissible to exclude him. In contrast, Huemer appears to be using "harm" in a moralized sense according to which an action isn't harming someone if it's prima facie permissible. On that understanding of "harm," I deny that, in most circumstances, barring migrants harms them, since it's *also* prima facie permissible to do so.

2 Maybe a polity's government isn't itself sovereign over its territory, true (but note that, e.g., the English sovereign legally owns all the land in England). Even so, just as you may hire a security guard to protect your kitchen, the government of a nation may be understood as hired to protect the people's territory.

3 Michael Huemer, *Problem of Political Authority* (New York: Palgrave, 2013). Huemer will argue that the people don't "own" their country. I actually agree that neither the government nor even the people of a nation own the territory of the said nation or even its public lands. But owning isn't the only way to be sovereign over something: it's commonsensical to think a nation (people), if it's lucky enough to have its own country (land, territory), is sovereign over it even though they don't "own" it. However, for a libertarian yet restrictionist discussion partially based on collective ownership of a nation's public property, see Stephen Kershnar, "Immigration and Collective Property," *Analitica* 2 (2022): 12–41.

4 Bryan Caplan and Ady Branzei, *Build, Baby, Build: The Science and Ethics of Housing Regulation* (Washington, DC: Cato Institute, 2024).

5 Yes, I'm saying my Greek grandparents should not have been allowed into the United States. For a discussion of the anti-Black nature of the 1880s–1920s wave of European migration, see Robert Mallory, "'Cast Down Your Bucket Where You Are': Black Americans on Immigration," *Center for Immigration Studies* (June 1, 1996) (https://cis.org/Report/Cast-Down-Your-Bucket-Where-You-Are-Black-Americans-Immigration). For an economic analysis discussing the concern, see, for example, Charles Hirschman and Elizabeth Mogford, "Immigration and the American Industrial Revolution from 1880 to 1920," *Social Science Research* 38, no. 4 (2009): 897–920 (https://doi.org/10.1016/j.ssresearch.2009.04.001).

6 There are polities where an underclass of foreign laborers, bereft of political rights, do all the work for natives who, despite enjoying lives of leisure, produce remarkably little literature, art, or technology—a repellent prospect for Westerners.

7 The average asylum migrant costs the Dutch about a half million euros, for instance; see Jan H. van de Beek et al., "Borderless Welfare State: The Consequences of Immigration for Public Finances" (Zeist, Netherlands: Demo-Demo, 2024) (https://demo-demo.nl/wp-content/uploads/2023/06/Borderless_Welfare_State-2.pdf).

8 Will Grimond, "Most Social Housing Residents in London were Born in the UK," *PA Media Blog* (December 18, 2023) (https://pa.media/blogs/fact-check/most-social-housing-residents-in-london-were-born-in-the-uk/).

9 Neil O'Brien, "It's Reasonable to Give British People Greater Priority for Social Housing," *Neil's Substack* (January 30, 2024) (https://www.neilobrien.co.uk/p/its-reasonable-to-give-british-people).

10 Even adjusting for age and sex, migrants from the Middle East, Africa, and Central Asia are multiple times more likely to be convicted of a violent crime; see, for example, "Immigrants in Denmark 2021," *Statistics Denmark* (December 9, 2021) (https://www.dst.dk/Site/Dst/Udgivelser/GetPubFile.aspx?id=34714&sid=indv2021).

11 For example, see links in "Save Our Green Space By Restoring Sense To Immigration Policy," *Migration Watch UK* (March 12, 2021) (https://www.migrationwatchuk.org/news/2021/03/12/save-our-green-space-by-restoring-sense-to-immigration-policy).

12 See pp. 449–50 of Michael Huemer, "Is There a Right to Immigrate?" *Social Theory and Practice* 36, no. 3 (2010): 429–61. For longer discussions of a right to exclude migrants for the sake of cultural preservation, see, for example, Rafael De Clercq, "Huemer on Immigration and the Preservation of Culture," *Philosophia* 45 (2017): 1091–8; Uwe Steinhoff, *Freedom, Culture, and the Right to Exclude* (London: Routledge, 2022).

13 See https://www.gutenberg.org/files/16751/16751-pdf.pdf.

14 For a defense of some of these claims see Garett Jones, *The Culture Transplant* (Stanford: Stanford University Press, 2022).

15 Felicity Capon, "Norway Seeks to Send Hate Preacher Into 'Internal Exile,'" *Newsweek* (February 18, 2015) (https://www.newsweek.com/norway-agonises-over-future-radical-cleric-307645).

Response to Demetriou on Open Borders

Michael Huemer

Study Questions

1. How does Huemer respond to Demetriou's claim that open residence would entail an enormous bureaucracy?
2. In what way does Demetriou misconstrue Huemer's argument?
3. Why does Huemer think that Demetriou's analogy of the business owner is flawed?
4. How does Huemer respond to Demetriou's concerns over demographic exclusions?

I would like to thank Dan Demetriou for his interesting and challenging discussion. Each of us wrote our opening statements before reading the other's, so there may be some disconnect between them. The first thing to clarify is my thesis. Demetriou correctly surmises that my argument in earlier work was meant to support "open residence," rather than "open access." Similarly, in this debate, I do not address open access; I intend only to defend (relatively) open residence.

Second, we should distinguish three targets of Demetriou's critiques:

a. My main argument in this volume, which uses the "Starving Marvin" example to suggest that immigration restrictions violate potential immigrants' prima facie right against harmful coercion.

b. Other arguments for "open borders" that might appear elsewhere, for example, one based on a general "migrant-citizen symmetry" principle.

c. The broader libertarian philosophy advanced in other work (by myself or others), including such ideas as skepticism about political authority.

I take myself here to be responsible only for defending (a). I do not have space to discuss (b) or (c).

What position is Demetriou responsible for defending? What alternative policy are we to compare to the "open residence" regime? I take Demetriou's view to be either that we should allow *no* immigration at all, or that we should continue something like the status quo, in which many aspiring immigrants are admitted but most are turned away. There are some indications that Demetriou favors the former option (see below).

I have space only to address four main arguments.

I. Bureaucratic Costs

Demetriou suggests that a regime of open residence without open access would entail "unprecedented border protections" and "an enormous bureaucracy" (p. 266). He lists several practical questions that would arise. Some of these leave a puzzle as to what Demetriou is defending. For example, he asks, "What sort of walls, wire fences, armed boats, and so on, are we willing to build and maintain to facilitate open residence without open access?" (p. 272). Presumably, Demetriou favors *at least* as many walls, and so on, as any LOBOT, so the cost of such security measures is no reason to favor his view over ours. Nor are these measures *unprecedented*; they are the status quo. There are no *added* fencing or similar costs introduced merely by *allowing more people in*.

Some of the costs that Demetriou lists could be obviated by a policy of complete exclusion—if the state automatically excludes *all* migrants, then we won't need a bureaucracy to vet migrants. Perhaps that is Demetriou's proposal.

One reason why the United States has not adopted this position is that some people around the world are fleeing terrible oppression, up to and including genocide. In 1939, the MS *St. Louis*, carrying over 900 Jewish refugees fleeing Nazi Germany, attempted to land in Cuba, then the United States, then Canada; no one wanted the Jews. The captain was forced to return to Europe, where 254 of those refugees were ultimately murdered during the Holocaust.[1] This sort of story is one reason why the United States and most of the world have signed the UN Protocol Relating to the Status of Refugees, which grants the right to asylum to refugees with a well-founded fear of persecution in their home country. This entails some cost for vetting refugees, but that cost is justified to prevent terrible injustices.

Perhaps Demetriou would say that the costs of evaluating immigrant applications will *increase* if the standards for admission drop, because more people will start coming. I think this is unlikely to be a major problem. The United States admits close to a million legal immigrants a year.[2] This is probably already enough to induce most of those who want to migrate to give it a try. The current US Immigration and Customs Enforcement budget is about $8 billion, which is about 0.1 percent of the federal budget.[3] So the added administrative costs due to a liberalization of immigration policy would be unlikely to break the bank. If somehow the government found it unaffordable, they could defray the costs through application fees or increased taxes on successful immigrants.

II. My Marketplace Analogy

In the Starving Marvin example, I imagine Marvin traveling toward a marketplace to buy food. Demetriou objects to the analogy, stating that he views countries rather as *homelands* than as marketplaces. I do not see why a homeland cannot also be a marketplace.

More importantly, this objection misconstrues the argument. This was my central argument:

(1) Harmful coercion is prima facie wrong.

(2) Immigration restrictions are harmful and coercive.

(3) So, immigration restrictions are prima facie wrong.

The role of Starving Marvin is to illustrate premises (1) and (2). The marketplace just serves as a (morally acceptable) way that Marvin would obtain food if no one interferes.

The same point applies to any other permissible way that Marvin might attempt to obtain food. Suppose Sam and Marvin live in a world where petitionary prayer is extremely effective. Marvin is about to pray to God, which would get him some manna from heaven to feed himself. Sam forcibly stops Marvin from praying, with the result that Marvin starves. Here, Sam acts wrongly by violating Marvin's prima facie right against harmful coercion.

In my main essay, I imagined Marvin obtaining food from a marketplace, rather than God, because this is most similar to how immigrants obtain money in the United States—through voluntary trade with other people. But this does not mean that the argument contains the nebulous claim "countries are marketplaces, rather than homelands," any more than it would contain the claim that countries are gods if I had chosen that illustration.

III. Demetriou's Analogy

Demetriou mentions that the owner of a business (including, say, a shopping mall) may exclude people from his business at will. Demetriou suggests that this marketplace analogy supports the right of countries to exclude immigrants at will.

I think this analogy is inapt. The reason why a business owner may exclude people from the business is that he *owns* the business. To draw the analogy to immigration restriction, one must claim that the government *owns the country*—then the government could permissibly exclude people from the country at will. But no one other than totalitarians thinks that the government is entitled to act like the owner of the country. Whatever your theory of authority is, you probably think the state's authority is *much* more limited than that.

For example, Dan Demetriou has a house. Because he owns it, he could decide that anyone using his house must agree to cut off their left hand, decline to vote if female, and never criticize Dan's political views. But the government may not do the analogous things. It may not declare that residents of the nation must cut off their left hands, refrain from voting if female, or refrain from criticizing the government's views. It is not only libertarians who think these things would overstep the state's authority; practically everyone (except totalitarians) agrees. So, we do not view the government as an owner of the country.

IV. Demographic Exclusions

May the state exclude migrants on demographic grounds—for example, bar young males from Muslim-majority countries from entering the United States, on the grounds that they are statistically more likely to commit terrorist attacks? I don't know. But I think that this policy would be *better* than a regime of tight, across-the-board restrictions. In other words, we *shouldn't* prohibit or severely limit immigration from *all* groups merely to prevent terrorist attacks, given that we have the option to only exclude migrants from high-risk groups.

Demetriou demurs. He suggests that such policies would lead to a "cynical and racially loaded" politics, in which our leaders abandoned "even an attempt at persuading our fellows to change their views" (p. 274), in favor of just trying to game the immigration system. I don't share his assessment, for three reasons:

1. It's been tried. Until 1965, the United States assigned immigration quotas to particular nations, with some nations having much higher quotas than others.[4] This did not corrupt our politics as Demetriou describes.

2. Congress already has this power. If they were to pass a law greatly increasing immigration quotas for all groups *other than* young men from Muslim countries, that would not give them any additional power to make cynical calculations that they don't already have.

3. There is, again, a keyhole solution: Grant legal residency without the right to vote. This is already the situation of millions of green card holders in the United States, and no one worries about this.

Why might it make sense to deny voting rights to immigrants but not to native-born citizens? Well, exactly the arguments that Demetriou gave. Demetriou warns that our democracy could be irreparably harmed by importing new voters, but he does not claim that our democracy would be harmed by allowing native-born citizens to continue to vote. If he is right, then it makes sense to continue to allow native-born citizens to vote, while denying the vote to immigrants. This addresses the problem much less harmfully than excluding the immigrants entirely, so exclusion can't be the right policy.

Notes

1 Wikipedia, "MS *St. Louis*," (https://en.wikipedia.org/wiki/MS_St._Louis, accessed April 14, 2024). The Jews wound up settling in the UK, Belgium, France, and the Netherlands, but three of those countries were then overtaken by the Nazis.
2 Statista, "Number of Persons Obtaining Legal Permanent Resident Status in the United States from FY 1820 to FY 2022" (https://www.statista.com/statistics/199958/number-of-green-cards-in-the-united-states/, accessed April 14, 2024).
3 Wikipedia, "U.S. Immigration and Customs Enforcement" (https://en.wikipedia.org/wiki/U.S._Immigration_and_Customs_Enforcement, accessed April 14, 2024).
4 Mark Hugo Lopez, Jeffrey Passel, and Molly Rohal, *Modern Immigration Wave Brings 59 Million to U.S., Driving Population Growth and Change Through 2065* (Pew Research Center, 2015), 18 (https://www.pewresearch.org/wp-content/uploads/sites/5/2015/09/2015-09-28_modern-immigration-wave_REPORT.pdf, accessed April 14, 2024).

Questions for Reflection

1) Which major reason for immigration restrictions do you think is the most weighty? How would you respond to Huemer's criticism of this reason?
2) How persuasive is the Starving Marvin scenario? Why?
3) Can a people or government own (be sovereign over) its territory? Why?

For Further Reading

Caplan, Bryan, and Zach Weinersmith. *Open Borders: The Science and Ethics of Immigration*. First Second, 2019.

Jones, Reece, ed. *Open Borders: In Defense of Free Movement.* The University of Georgia Press, 2019.

Miller, David. *Strangers in Our Midst: The Political Philosophy of Immigration.* Harvard University Press, 2018.

Simon, Julian. *The Economic Consequences of Immigration.* Blackwell, 1989.

Steinhoff, Uwe. *Freedom, Culture, and the Right to Exclude: On the Permissibility and Necessity of Immigration Restrictions.* Routledge, 2022.

Wellman, Christopher Heath, and Phillip Cole. *Debating the Ethics of Immigration: Is There a Right to Exclude?* Oxford University Press, 2011.

9

Gun Control

There Is No Right to Own a Gun for Self-Defense

Nicholas Dixon

> **Study Questions**
>
> 1. What is Dixon's initial utilitarian argument for gun control? What evidence does he provide in support of this argument?
> 2. How does Dixon establish a causal link between gun prevalence and homicide rates?
> 3. What is Huemer's argument against gun control? How does Dixon respond to that argument?
> 4. According to Dixon, in what way (contra Huemer and others) is the right to own a gun narrowly limited?
> 5. How, according to Dixon, do the rights of victims of gun violence undermine the case for gun ownership for self-defense?
> 6. Why does Dixon think that gun control would not violate the right of self-defense even for people who are at high risk of being victimized?
> 7. In what way does the case for gun rights prove too much?

Even strong gun rights advocates do not propose unlimited access to every kind of firearm, and they typically support restrictions based on such things as criminal convictions and mental illness.[1] They favor, that is, what I call *minimal* gun control. The debate over guns is primarily over access to firearms suited to personal self-defense, especially handguns. Gun rights advocates defend the right of mentally sound and law-abiding adults to have access to such weapons, while proponents of gun control would impose limits even in the case of such weapons and such people. The most extreme type of restriction, which I call *strict* gun control, is prohibition of public ownership of a class of firearms, which I have proposed for handguns[2] in the United States,[3] or of firearms in general, which is consistent with Jeff McMahan's expressed views.[4] Others have proposed more *moderate* gun control that still goes well beyond the restrictions currently in place in the United States. They include David DeGrazia who advocates, among other restrictions, that handguns be made a controlled weapon that is available only to those able to make a case for a special need for such protection;[5] and Hugh LaFollette, who proposes that strict liability be placed on the original owner for any crime committed with a firearm.[6] I will use "gun control" to refer to both moderate and strict forms, both of which go far beyond those supported by gun rights advocates and the status quo in the United States. The assertion of a right to own guns arises primarily as a response to arguments for gun control, one of which I briefly summarize in the next section.

I. The Initial Case for Gun Control

The case for moderate or strict gun control begins with a utilitarian argument that depends on the belief that the prevalence of guns is a major determinant of violent crime, especially homicide. The data are most striking in the case of the United States, which is why I and other advocates of gun control have focused primarily on this country. Homicide is the most serious of violent crimes, and in the United States in 2022, at least 77 percent of the 19,200 murders were committed with guns, most of which were handguns.[7] If it were not for the connection between guns and homicide and other violent crimes, the case for gun control would disappear.[8]

The most telling evidence arises from cross-sectional comparisons between the United States and similar countries with regard to gun ownership and homicide rates. David Hemenway wrote or co-wrote a series of studies that compare gun ownership, gun homicide, and overall homicide in the United States and other countries that are affluent and have a population of over one million.[9] These countries are all stable democracies with developed economies that are unlikely to have major sociopolitical differences *other than gun prevalence* that would explain the vast disparity between them and the United States. The United States has a massively higher number of privately owned guns per 100,000 people than other countries. Its gun ownership rate is 2.28 times as high as the second-placed country, Yemen, at least 3 times as high as all other countries with a population of over one million, and at least 10 times as high as the average of all countries.[10] In 2015, the United States had an overall homicide rate that is 7.5 times higher than the rate in twenty-eight other affluent, populous countries, fueled in large part by a firearm homicide rate that is 24.9 times higher.[11] These results show a huge, enduring disparity between the United States and other developed countries with regard to both firearms ownership and overall homicide rates.

Of course, correlation does not prove causation in the absence of a plausible causal theory. But precisely such a simple causal theory is readily available. Guns, especially easily concealable handguns, are a far more efficient means of killing people than knives, blunt objects, or unarmed assaults. Assuming murderous intent to be roughly evenly distributed among nations, we would expect the homicide rate to be higher when by far the most efficient method of killing is available in far greater numbers. The non-gun homicide rate in the United States is only 2.6 times as high as in the comparison countries,[12] indicating that it is the presence of guns that is the major contributor to the enormous disparity in overall homicide rates between the United States and the other countries. Mill's *method of difference* indicates the following reasoning when comparing the United States with other countries: since an extremely high homicide rate occurs in the presence of an extremely high gun ownership rate (United States), but not in the absence of extremely high gun ownership (the comparison countries), the United States' very high gun ownership rate is likely a cause of its very high homicide rate. Moreover, Grinshteyn and Hemenway's study supports yet another causal argument based on data comparing states *within* the United States with regard to gun ownership and homicide. The overall homicide rate in high, medium, and low gun ownership states is 7.8, 5.5, and 3.3 per 100,000, respectively.[13] Mill's method of *concomitant variation*,[14] which is applicable when the amount of a putative cause varies proportionately with the amount of the event whose cause we are seeking, entails that gun ownership within the United States is a likely cause of homicide.[15] This data and this sketch of a causal theory support a strong presumptive argument that the huge number of guns in private hands is a significant cause of the extraordinarily high homicide rate in the United States. Moderate and strict gun control is based on a simple application of Mill's Harm Principle. Reducing the number of guns, even to the extent of prohibiting certain types of weapons, is justified in order to prevent the large number of homicides that are attributable to the prevalence of guns.[16]

Gun rights advocates strongly oppose these causal claims. However, they do not typically rest their case on empirical claims that guns do not increase homicide. Instead, they insist on the right to own guns *even if strict gun control did indeed reduce homicide*. It is to this rights-based argument that the rest of this chapter is devoted.

II. The Alleged Right to Own Guns for Self-Defense

We have a prima facie right to engage in any activity that we choose to do and does not cause undue harm to others. If society wants to restrict an activity, it carries the burden of proof of showing how it harms others. The burden of proof is especially stringent in the case of activities that we deem to be exercises of *fundamental* rights, possession of which is essential to a good life. Widely recognized fundamental negative rights include the right to life, freedom of expression, and freedom of religion. Negative rights protect our liberty, even when restricting it would promote the common good—as Dworkin claimed, rights *trump* utility.[17] Two common reasons for owning guns—target shooting and collecting them—are not a plausible basis for a fundamental right to own guns. Neither use is essential to a good life, as is illustrated by the vast number of people who have splendid lives without ever using a gun. By far the most plausible case for a right to own guns, and the one on which most gun rights advocates have focused, is based on self-defense.[18] The right to self-defense is derived from the unquestioned fundamental negative rights to life and freedom from assault. While many methods of self-defense exist that do not involve guns, and while we can usually avoid death and injury without any need at all for self-defense, supporters of gun rights typically base their case on situations where a gun is purportedly the only effective method of self-defense.

Michael Huemer has been a clear and articulate defender of the deontological case against gun control, based on the right to self-defense,[19] and this is why I devote the lion's share of this chapter to evaluating his views. Even if moderate or strict gun control significantly reduces overall homicide, he argues, it is impermissible because it will lead to the death or injury of some people who could have protected themselves had they had access to a gun. In such cases, Huemer claims, the government is morally equivalent to an intruder who takes away a homeowner's gun to prevent her from using it to protect herself against his fellow intruder.[20] While the government's goal of reducing homicide is noble, it may not do so at the expense of sacrificing the lives of people who are denied the most effective means of self-defense. We may not violate the rights of individuals in order to promote the common good.

Jeff McMahan[21] and I[22] each independently came up with a similar response to Huemer. If the empirical claims that underlie the case for gun control are correct, such control will substantially reduce the amount of homicide and violent crime. Self-defense is not an end in itself. It is, rather, a derivative right that is based on the fundamental right to life and safety. People in general, including those who desire to protect themselves with guns, will be safer and less likely to be murdered in a society with moderate or strict gun control. And all murders, whether or not the victim is a person prevented by gun control from owning a firearm, are violations of the right to life. Even those people who are unfortunate enough to be victimized as a result of being prevented from protecting themselves by gun control were made safer in advance by these very laws, since the probability of being harmed by abuse of guns is far greater than that of being victimized as a result of being disarmed by strict gun control. That the United States' vast arsenal of guns does not make us safer is evidenced by its far greater homicide rate than that in comparable countries with far fewer firearms. The right to self-defense is not violated by gun control, which better achieves the fundamental rights to life and safety that are the raison d'être of the right to self-defense. To insist that we have a right to use guns in self-defense, even though the permissive gun laws that are necessary to make this possible actually make us *less* safe, is to misconstrue the *instrumental* value of self-defense in general and guns in particular as *intrinsic* value. While invoking rights normally sidesteps utilitarian arguments and takes certain policies off the table, even if they maximize the common good, this is not the case when it comes to the self-defense objection to gun control. Given that self-defense is aimed at the *state* of being safe, we cannot separate the morality of permitting people to have guns for self-defense from the question of whether doing so actually *achieves* this state. The claim that strict gun control violates the right to self-defense is vacuous if, as I have claimed, it makes us safer than permissive gun laws. There is, therefore, no general right to own a gun for the purpose of self-defense.

Gun rights advocates have responded to McMahan and me by making a distinction between *overall* safety and the safety of *certain individuals*. While each person may be made statistically safer by gun control, some people *will in fact* die as a result of being unable to defend themselves with firearms. Even if we granted that gun control would prevent the violation of the right to life and safety of huge numbers of potential victims of gun crime, Huemer argues, this would not justify the violation of a gun owner who is made defenseless by gun control. Huemer asserts that "it is normally wrong to violate a person's rights, even if doing so prevents someone else from violating even more persons' rights."[23] He characterizes my argument as a "consequentialism of rights" and states that "this is not how rights work."[24] Even if we admit that government has a duty to protect its citizens from harm, which is the goal of strict gun control,

> on a deontological ethic agents are morally responsible first for ensuring that their own actions do not violate rights. It is only *within that constraint* that agents may then have duties to prevent other agents from violating rights.[25]

The remainder of this chapter is a response to Huemer's and other arguments for the right to own guns.

III. The Need to Recognize Limits on Rights

Moral and legal rights in general are subject to constraint by other moral considerations. Take, for example, freedom of expression, a fundamental right that we jealously protect, even though we recognize certain exceptions, such as libel and incitement to crime, in which restrictions are justified.[26] The ground for such exceptions is that the harm caused by allowing free expression in these instances is substantial, while the harm of suppressing speech in such cases is trivial. In such cases, we should not say that the right to free expression is overridden by the rights of the victims of abuses of free speech. There is no right to commit libel or incite crime in the first place. The right to free speech is circumscribed by the need to avoid violating other people. My claim in this chapter is precisely that the right to self-defense, from which the right to own a gun is derived, is limited in a similar way. Given the enormous harm to society that arises from permissive gun laws, gun control does not violate the right to self-defense because this right does not entail the right to own a gun.

We should remember, moreover, that any right to use a gun for self-defense is narrowly limited by several circumstances. It is subject to the *necessity condition*, in that we may only use guns to defend ourselves when no nonviolent or less violent means are available. Most people manage to avoid being assaulted by using such measures as locking doors, obtaining restraining orders, avoiding dangerous situations, calling the police, reasoning with the assailant, running away, yelling for help, or using other weapons like pepper spray. It is only when such methods are not sufficient to protect ourselves that we may justifiably use a gun. Another factual assumption that underlies the putative right to own a gun for self-defense is that guns actually make us safer, which I have challenged above. Moreover, not only is society at large endangered by the prevalence of guns (especially handguns), but even the individuals who own them may be putting themselves at greater risk. Households with guns create a markedly greater risk of homicide than those without guns.[27] The extremely high homicide rate in the United States as compared with similar countries indicates that aggressive abuses of guns far outweigh their legitimate uses in self-defense. Any right to own a gun for self-defense is severely limited by these considerations.

IV. Rights of Victims of Gun Crime and Government's Duty to Protect Them

Some gun rights defenders do not discuss the rights of victims of gun crime and instead focus only on the right to self-defense of gun owners. In their view, if guns are an effective method of self-defense, we have a right to own them

> so long as the firearms in question can be reasonably considered to be an effective means for individuals to defend themselves against attackers intent on serious or lethal harm.[28]
>
> What justifies the right to own guns is not the risk of unjust attack (which, for most people, is very low), but the effectiveness they contribute in fending off unjust attacks when they do happen to occur.[29]

But it is implausible to exclude from consideration the catastrophic effects of widespread gun ownership on violent crime in the United States, as described in Section I above. Moreover, the gun control debate is not merely a conflict between the rights of gun owners and the utilitarian need to promote public safety. It is, additionally, a conflict between the putative right to own a gun for self-defense and the right of people to be free from violence committed with guns.

Huemer does not deny the right to life and safety of all victims of gun crime, whether or not they own guns. However, as we saw, he rejects as a "utilitarianism of rights" my argument that gun control is justified because permissive gun laws result in far more rights violations than gun control. He claims that our primary obligation is to avoid acting to violate others' rights, and that any duty to prevent other people from violating rights is secondary to this first duty. He asserts that enacting strict gun control, while it is designed to fulfill the second duty, is illicit because it infringes the first duty by violating gun users' right to self-defense. If permissive gun laws do indeed lead to more homicide and violence, on Huemer's view, the blame belongs to the assailants who use their weapons.[30] Huemer acknowledges that government does have a positive duty to protect the rights of its citizens, which is wise in view of many times governments have been criticized for a failure to do so (e.g., inadequate pollution controls, insufficient measures to prevent the spread of Covid). The problem is that he does not give this duty enough weight.

No good reason exists for the moral asymmetry that gun rights advocates assert when they prioritize the rights of gun owners over those of citizens in general. The fact that gun control is an act, whereas a lack of gun control is an omission, is not enough to justify this asymmetry, given that we *do* hold governments accountable for culpable omissions. This governmental duty exists, even when the wrongdoing of gun violence is inflicted by one citizen on another. DeGrazia asserts a positive duty on the part of government to protect citizens' right not to be shot and to a safe environment.[31] Similarly, Chetan Cetty argues that any wrongness of gun control results from its "enabling wrongdoing" function, not from violating the right to self-defense. And permissive gun laws also enable wrongdoing by armed aggressors.

> [T]he state wrongs just as much when it allows guns to be used to victimize innocent people as when it takes away guns. In either case, it is an accomplice to the serious wrongdoing that foreseeably follows.[32]

If, as I have argued, far more wrongdoing results from the misuse of firearms than is caused by disarming innocent people, permissive gun laws are a more serious wrong.[33]

My position is not, therefore, a "utilitarianism of rights." Instead, the case for gun control is based on weighing the rights of gun owners against the rights of victims of gun crime, and the government's duty to prevent wrongdoing. Given that the permissive gun laws that are required to allow people to use guns in self-defense create the certainty of enormous amounts of wrongdoing and rights violations, gun owners' rights are not sacrificed for the common good—there is no right to own a gun for self-defense in the first place.[34]

V. People at Special Risk of Harm Do Not Ground a Right to Own Guns

In response to my assertion that gun control makes even gun owners safer, Huemer claims that we can after all identify certain individuals as being at especially high risk of being victimized in the event of strict gun control. Take, for example, a woman who is at risk from her abusive, physically stronger ex-husband, or a person who has to walk home at night through a neighborhood that is rife with gang violence. In the case of these and other similarly situated people, Huemer claims, we can know with a high degree of probability that a gun is their best form of protection and that they will be made less safe by gun control. Such people will be sacrificed in the attempt to reduce the overall homicide rate (and hence to reduce the overall number of rights violations), which is precisely what deontology prohibits.[35]

However, like the "assailant's accomplice" analogy, this argument considers only the negative effects of strict gun control. As McMahan says, a more accurate analogy would involve "a situation in which a third party disarms both the aggressor and the potential victim and provides protection for the victim."[36] The biggest threat to abused spouses and inhabitants of high-crime areas comes from assailants who are themselves armed, which is less likely to be the case if gun control is enacted. These potential assailants include not only the ex-spouse and the neighborhood gangs but armed wrongdoers in general. While no doubt exists that some people are objectively more at risk of assault than others, it is not clear that the balance of positive and negative effects of gun control will result in their becoming more at risk for assault. Huemer asks us to assume that the woman has a 20 percent chance of being murdered or injured by her ex-spouse, which is far greater than the average risk of being a victim of gun crime.[37] But this speculative percentage is not enough to support the assertion that people in this and similar situations are made less safe by gun control. Gun control need not occur in isolation; on the contrary, it would be wise to accompany it with concerted efforts to combat spousal violence, enforce restraining orders, and increase policing in gang-dominated areas. Given the availability of these alternative measures to protect people who are currently at higher risk of victimization, as well as the violence-reducing effects of gun control, Huemer's claim that this policy endangers specifiable individuals remains questionable.

Even if we assume for the sake of argument that Huemer is correct that we can specify which people will be rendered less safe by gun control, this still does not establish his view that gun control violates the right to self-defense. Because it does not show that a *general* right to own guns for self-defense exists, the most it might establish is that gun *prohibition* (strict gun control) is wrong. It would not count against the moderate gun control that David DeGrazia has proposed, according to which guns are generally prohibited, with exceptions granted to precisely those people who can establish a special need to own them for self-defense.[38] However, my contention is that strict gun control—a ban on handguns and semi- and fully automatic weapons— would be a better policy.

I suspect that the attempt to specify which individuals are put at risk by gun prohibition may well be futile. I have already described difficulties in knowing whether, even in the case of the vulnerable people that Huemer describes, the violence-reducing effect of prohibition will be outweighed by eliminating the possibility of using guns for self-defense. Moreover, Dustin Crummett and Philip Swenson describe further epistemological barriers to specifying which people have a special need to own guns for self-defense. For example, people may overestimate the danger they face, or they may deliberately exaggerate the danger in order to qualify for the exemption that permits them to own a gun. If indeed the government cannot know which people will end up being harmed as a result of handgun prohibition, and if this prohibition will indeed reduce the amount of homicide and violent crime, then "each person's chance of survival is maximized by taking the paradigmatically consequentialist course of action."[39] Even in the case of such at-risk people, then, gun control does not violate the right to self-defense.

Furthermore, granting residents of dangerous neighborhoods an exception to a general prohibition on firearms may be self-defeating. The main danger that residents of crime-ridden areas face is precisely gun crime. Aside from those who are disqualified because of factors like a record of felonies or mental illness, it would be hard to deny any resident of such neighborhoods legal access to guns, and any denials would likely provoke legal challenges. Some would sincerely believe that they need firearms for self-defense, but others would lie in order to obtain weapons to use in crime. The result would be that dangerous neighborhoods would remain locked, as they already are today with our permissive gun laws, in a chronic spiral of ever higher gun ownership and persistently high levels of violent crime. More generally, while a strong case exists for continuing to make guns available for specific professions, such as police and security guards, the more exceptions that we make to gun prohibition, the more risk exists of criminal misuse of firearms, due to the ever-increasing pool of weapons available for theft, illegal transfers, and straw and fraudulent purchases. This is why in an earlier article I criticized the Brady Bill, which bars felons and people with documented mental illness from owning guns, as not going far enough to stem the daily carnage of gun violence in the United States.[40] While I welcome DeGrazia's proposal for moderate gun control as a clear improvement on the status quo, I contend that strict control, in the form of a general prohibition on handguns, automatic, and semi-automatic firearms, is needed to better protect, not only society at large but also even those individuals whom Huemer claims are endangered by denying them access to guns. In sum, appealing to the case of people who are at high risk of being subjected to violence does not give good reason for a right to own guns.

VI. The Case for Gun Rights Proves Too Much

If gun rights advocates insist on the right to have guns for self-defense, on the grounds that some people will be rendered defenseless by strict gun control, doesn't their reasoning also entail that (a much smaller group of) people will also have a right to own military-style weapons, such as hand grenades, anti-tank guns, and rocket launchers? Take, for instance, an innocent person (perhaps a suspected informant) who is targeted by a heavily armed paramilitary drug gang of the type portrayed in the TV series, *Breaking Bad*. When that person sees the drug dealers' vehicle convoy heading up his long driveway, using a missile launcher to detonate the cars may well be his best bet to save his life before the murderous drug gang members exit their vehicles with their automatic weapons. Similarly, lobbing a hand grenade might be a person's best bet for survival when cornered by a group of murderous thugs. Yet allowing ordinary citizens to own such military-style weapons seems absurd, because of the catastrophic harm that could be inflicted on society by miscreants who have access to these weapons.

Samuel Wheeler III, to his credit, faces up to this reductio ad absurdum argument, which he classifies instead as a *sorites*. He responds that in modern societies the need for such weapons is negligible and is outweighed by the risks that such weapons create for other people.[41] Similarly, Deane-Peter Baker asserts that, in a functioning democracy, citizens cede to the government sole use of the military-grade weapons that are needed to protect a country against external invaders, while retaining the right to own personal weapons like handguns and rifles to protect themselves against aggressors within their country.[42] Huemer too argues that his case for the right to own guns for self-defense applies only to firearms like handguns and not to military-grade weapons, on the grounds that the harm of their ownership by the public would vastly outweigh the rare instances where they would be needed for justified self-defense.[43] This reasoning is cogent, but it is also fatal for the gun rights view. This is because the ground for maintaining the ban on military weaponry is at least partly utilitarian, since it cites the enormous harmful consequences for society of their availability. Once utilitarian considerations enter the discussion, this lends credence to the original case for strict gun control, for personal firearms as well as military equipment, precisely because it helps reduce the carnage caused every day in the United States by the easy availability of weapons like handguns.

It is inconsistent to adopt an absolutist stance in the case of handguns, insisting that strict gun control is wrong if it prevents a single person from using their weapon to save their life, while citing the rarity of needing military-grade weapons, and the extreme danger they would pose to society, as a reason against allowing the public to own them. After all, in my *Breaking Bad*-inspired scenario, a person would *ex hypothesi* die as a result of not having access to a handheld rocket launcher. On Huemer's own argument, to insist that we need to ban such military weapons in order to prevent the devastation that they would cause would be an unjust "utilitarianism of rights." Gun rights advocates can't have it both ways. Either they admit that preventing homicide (which is itself a violation of victims' right to life) is a legitimate reason for control of both handheld missile launchers *and* handguns, or they must concede that the absolutist stance that they apply to handguns also entails a right to own military-style weapons. Since it entails a right to own military-grade weaponry, the gun rights view has been reduced to absurdity.

Conclusion

If the causal claims presented in Section I are sound, and permissive gun laws actually make society *less* safe, no right exists to own a gun for self-defense. Gun control does not sacrifice the self-defense rights of gun owners, or any subset of them, in order to promote the common good. Instead, it is needed to better protect the right to life and safety of all citizens. No good reasons exist to protect the freedom to use one particular means of self-defense when granting that freedom will predictably result in even more wrongdoing and rights violations. Just as we currently restrict private ownership of military-grade weapons because of the enormous danger that they pose to innocent people, we should enact at least moderate or, preferably, strict control over handguns and automatic weapons because of the extraordinarily high number of murders and injuries they cause every day in the United States.

Notes

1 See, for example, C'Zar Bernstein, Timothy Hsiao, and Matt Palumbo, "The Moral Right to Keep and Bear Firearms," *Public Affairs Quarterly* 29, no. 4 (2015): 345–63.

2 I also favor banning semi and fully automatic firearms of any size, but I have not argued for restrictions on single-shot rifles and shotguns, which are used far less often in crimes. In this and my other writings, I have focused on handguns because they are the firearms most in contention in the gun control debate, since even some gun rights advocates support more stringent restrictions on automatic weapons.

3 Nicholas Dixon, "Why We Should Ban Handguns in the United States," *Saint Louis University Public Law Review* 12 (1993): 243–83; Nicholas Dixon, "Handguns, Violent Crime, and Self-Defense," *International Journal of Applied Philosophy* 13, no. 2 (1999): 239–60; and Nicholas Dixon, "Handguns, Philosophers, and the Right to Self-Defense," *International Journal of Applied Philosophy* 25, no. 2 (2011): 151–70.

4 Jeff McMahan, "Why Gun 'Control' is Not Enough," *New York Times* (December 19, 2012); and Jeff McMahan, "A Challenge to Gun Rights," *Practical Ethics* online forum (April 17, 2015) (http://blog.practicalethics.ox.ac.uk/2015/04/a-challenge-to-gun-rights/).

5 David DeGrazia, "Handguns, Moral Rights, and Physical Security," *Journal of Moral Philosophy* 13, no. 1 (2016): 56–76; and David DeGrazia, "Part II: The Case in Favor," in David DeGrazia and Lester Hunt, *Debating Gun Control: How Much Regulation Do We Need?* (New York: Oxford University Press, 2016), 119–254.

6 Hugh LaFollette, "Gun Control," *Ethics* 110, no. 2 (2000): 263–81; and *In Defense of Gun Control* (Oxford: Oxford University Press, 2018).

7 Federal Bureau of Investigation, *Crime Data Explorer* (2023).

8 For example, the claim that guns are *inherently* evil regardless of their consequences and that the government can restrict them on the grounds of this alleged inherent evil seems laughably weak.

9 David Hemenway and Matthew Miller, "Firearm Availability and Homicide Rates across 26 High-Income Countries," *The Journal of Trauma: Injury, Infection, and Critical Care* 49, no. 6 (2000): 985–8; Erin Grinshteyn and David Hemenway, "Violent Death Rates: The US Compared with Other High-income OECD Countries, 2010," *The American Journal of Medicine* 129, no. 3 (2016): 266–73; and Erin Grinshteyn and

David Hemenway, "Violent Death Rates in the U.S. Compared to Those of Other High-Income Countries, 2015," *Preventive Medicine* 123 (2019): 20–6.

10 Small Arms Survey, *Civilian Firearms Holdings, 2017* (2018).

11 Grinshteyn and Hemenway, "Violent Death Rates in the U.S. Compared to Those of Other High-Income Countries, 2015."

12 Ibid.

13 Ibid., 25. For more evidence of the negative effect of permissive gun laws within the United States, see John Donahue, "The Swerve to 'Guns Everywhere': A Legal and Empirical Evaluation," *Law and Contemporary Problems* 83, no. 3 (2020): 117–36.

14 For more depth on Mill's methods of difference and concomitant variation, see Christopher Macleod, "John Stuart Mill," in *The Stanford Encyclopedia of Philosophy* (Summer 2020 Edition), ed. Edward N. Zalta (2020), section 3.3.

15 Three earlier studies, which compared not only the United States with other countries but also the other countries with one another, also offer strong support for my causal hypothesis. They concluded that the correlation between gun ownership and overall homicide is between .54 and .746, where 1.0 is a perfect correlation, with a probability between 0 and 0.05 that the correlation is due to chance. See Martin Killias, "International Correlations between Gun Ownership and Rates of Homicide and Suicide," *Canadian Medical Association Journal* 148, no. 10 (1993): 1721–5; Martin Killias, "Gun Ownership, Suicide and Homicide," in *Understanding Crime, Experiences of Crime and Crime Control*, ed. A. Alvazzi del Frate, U. Zvekic, and J. J. M. vanDilk (Rome: UNICRI, 1993), 289–303; and Martin Killias, John van Kesteren, and Martin Rindlisbacher, "Guns, Violent Crime, and Suicide in 21 Countries," *Canadian Journal of Criminology* 43, no. 4 (2001): 429–48.

16 Developing this utilitarian argument requires more depth than is possible in the current paper. For example, I need to rule out two alternative explanations of the data: (1) the high gun ownership rate in the United States is a consequence, rather than a cause, of its high homicide rate; and (2) both the high gun ownership in the United States and its high homicide rate are caused by a third factor. This is a task that I take on elsewhere. See Dixon, "Handguns, Philosophers, and the Right to Self-Defense," 153. Moreover, I need to address concerns about the effectiveness of such restrictions. Will criminals simply substitute other weapons for guns? Will restrictions make law-abiding citizens vulnerable to criminals who are unlikely to obey any new gun laws? I raise and respond to these and related objections in Dixon, "Why We Should Ban Handguns in the United States," 264–72; and "Handguns, Violent Crime, and Self-Defense," 244–8.

17 Ronald Dworkin, *Taking Rights Seriously* (Cambridge, MA: Harvard University Press, 1977), xi.

18 A completely different rationale for the putative right to own guns is to act as a deterrent to governmental tyranny. See Samuel Wheeler III, "Arms as Insurance," *Public Affairs Quarterly* 13, no. 2 (1999): 111–29. Limitations of space prevent me from discussing this interesting argument in this brief essay.

19 See Michael Huemer, "Is There a Right to Own a Gun?" *Social Theory and Practice* 29, no. 2 (2003): 297–324; and "Gun Rights as Deontic Constraints," *Social Theory and Practice* 45, no. 4 (2019): 601–12.

20 Huemer, "Is There a Right to Own a Gun?" 306–9.

21. McMahan, "Why Gun 'Control' Is Not Enough."
22. Dixon, "Handguns, Philosophers, and the Right to Self-Defense," 160–2.
23. Huemer, "Gun Rights as Deontic Constraints," 604.
24. Ibid., 606.
25. Ibid.
26. Joel Feinberg, "Limits to the Free Expression of Opinion," in Joel Feinberg, *Freedom and Fulfillment* (Princeton: Princeton University Press, 1994), 124–51.
27. Arthur Kellermann, Frederick Rivara, Norman Rushforth, Joyce Banton, Donald Reay, Jerry Francisco, Ana Locci, Janice Prodzinski, Bela Hackman, and Grant Somes, "Gun Ownership as a Risk Factor for Homicide in the Home," *New England Journal of Medicine* 329 (1993): 1084–91. Kellerman, et al's study has been criticized for exaggerating the risks of keeping guns in the home. Using their data, and excluding firearm suicides, I recalculated the ratio of homicides and accidental deaths over defensive killings as 2.94:1, which still indicates the peril of keeping guns at home. See Dixon, "Why We Should Ban Handguns in the United States," 276–7.
28. Deane-Peter Baker, "Gun Bans, Risk, and Self-Defense," *International Journal of Applied Philosophy* 28, no. 2 (2014): 236.
29. Timothy Hsiao, "Against Gun Bans and Restrictive Licensing," *Essays in Philosophy* 16, no. 2 (2015): 183.
30. Huemer, "Gun Rights as Deontic Constraints," 606–7.
31. DeGrazia, "Part II: The Case in Favor," 214–26. For more depth on the claim that a central positive duty of government is to act to protect people's rights, including the right to be free from gun violence, see Howard Ponzer, "Limited Government and Gun Control," *Essays in Philosophy* 16 (2015): 211–16.
32. Chetan Cetty, "Self-Defense, Claim-Rights, and Guns," *Philosophical Forum* 55, no. 1 (2024): 43.
33. Cetty defends the more radical view that there is no claim-right to self-defense in general. I have much sympathy with his view, especially his change in the terms of the debate from the right to self-defense to the more fundamental duty to avoid enabling wrongdoing (which is itself based on the right to life and freedom from assault). However, in this chapter, I defend the less contentious view that, even if there is a general claim-right to self-defense, it does not entail a right to own a gun.
34. Moreover, the gun rights view is itself vulnerable to the charge of (by omission) violating the rights of victims of gun crime in the name of protecting the putative right to own guns in self-defense.
35. Huemer, "Gun Rights as Deontic Constraints," 607–9.
36. McMahan, "A Challenge to Gun Rights."
37. Huemer, "Gun Rights as Deontic Constraints," 608.
38. DeGrazia, "Part II: The Case in Favor," 247–8.
39. Dustin Crummett and Philip Swenson, "Gun Control, the Right to Self-Defense, and Reasonable Beneficence to All," *Ergo* 6, no. 36 (2019): 1046. Space constraints do not permit giving Crummett and Swenson's argument, which is based on an elaborate series of thought experiments adapted from Caspar Hare involving saving lives by pushing suitcases containing people onto a trolley track, the attention that it

40 Dixon, "Handguns, Violent Crime, and Self-Defense," 243–4.
41 Wheeler III, "Arms as Insurance," 438–41.
42 Baker, "Gun Bans, Risk, and Self-Defense," 41–3.
43 Huemer, "Is There a Right to Own a Gun?," 323.

The Right to Bear Arms

Benjamin L. Mabry

Study Questions

1. What is Mabry's understanding of society?
2. How does Mabry understand the nature of crime and tyranny? How do they relate to justice and injustice?
3. According to Mabry, what does it mean for a thing to be real? In light of this, what does it mean to be a citizen?
4. Why does being a citizen imply that private arms are part of a free and equal society?
5. Why is the person being assaulted the only competent judge of what means may be used in self-defense?
6. What is Scheler's "Call of the Hour"? What quandary faces people in this hour when the government denies them the right to bear arms?
7. What objection to granting citizens the use of armed force does Mabry address? How does he respond to it?

The Right to Bear Arms derives from the question of what it means to be a free and equal citizen. This essay will show that the denial of civilian weapons is incompatible with an equal and democratic society. In short, I argue that (1) a free citizen is essentially one who resists acts making one unfree, (2) philosophers and lawyers are incompetent to judge the means to this end, and (3) arguments about costs and benefits of civil rights like the Right to Bear Arms might rationalize their usefulness or danger but are irrelevant to ethics.

As Eric Voegelin pointed out in his *New Science of Politics*, neglect of the sciences of first principles reduces political philosophy to a mere clash of opinions. Ethics is not theoretical principles of pure logic or abstract speculation on equity, but a practice of actual human life. For ethics to be meaningful, we must first know what a human being is. Who is the subject of ethics? Investigating the ethics of civil rights narrows that category even further. What is a citizen within society? As his student, Ellis Sandoz, would specify almost forty years later, in *A Government of Laws*, all questions of justice and social order begin with "who it is that will occupy this habitation."[1]

Phenomenology is a science that seeks to bypass cultural and ideological presuppositions and discover the experience itself under investigation. It begins by asking what "that" is without recourse to existing theories or assumptions. Though methods may differ between philosophers, phenomenologists agree that modern political discourse contains many "empty" symbols: words whose meanings are unclear or opaque. For example, debates over human rights that use "social contract" symbols ultimately degrade into an exchange of mutually unintelligible slogans because the concept of social contract is inherently unclear and subject to multiple culturally contingent interpretations. The goal of phenomenologists is to "reduce" phenomena down to unambiguous "univocal" symbols whose meanings are directly connected to the experience of something real. For example, rather than speak of "social contracts," the philosopher Max Scheler differentiates the various basic types of social and political interactions that people can have with one another and how we experience each one in practical life. In this essay, I will use these tools to explore how human beings experience social life, freedom, and self-defense. From these investigations, I hope to show that being armed essentially belongs to free and equal citizens of a society. Arms are a part of being free, and deprivation of arms necessarily precludes free and equal citizenship.

What Is a Society of Free and Equal Citizens?

It is an error to treat society like a physical object in the natural sciences, as do many philosophers. When humans experience society, we experience it through actions we undertake which have other people as intentional objects. All social acts are grounded in a way of experiencing the other person that Alfred Schutz calls the "we-relationship." This we-relationship is a mirroring of one person seeing another see himself. It constitutes a reflecting consciousness of the other as a person. In politics, this mirroring effect is demonstrated in how each person is simultaneously recognized as both actor and object of politics.[2] To be human in politics means to both participate in and be subject to law and political order.

Society is distinguished from community by the lack of shared folkways, customs, beliefs, and values that define the meaning of social relations. One does not need to know another's lifestyle or customs to interact socially with them. For example, one relates to the person behind the desk in an explicit understanding of the meanings of "clerk" and "customer." The signs indicating where one should stand and how one should proceed transcend any one community. Participants in society are originally equal because society reflects a myriad of one-on-one, transactional relationships. Because society is not a real object, but a symbol for a type of action, philosopher Max Scheler describes society as flickering in and out of existence at every moment. He uses the example of Robinson Crusoe to show that people experience society even when alone, in the norms and behaviors that demonstrate the possibility of reciprocal social behaviors.[3]

Freedom and equality form an experiential whole. They are not subject to being treated abstractly, because abstract freedom without purpose is meaningless. Freedom only possesses meaning as freedom *for something*, namely the social life of equals. Outside of social life, these notions are at best vain and empty words, and at worst are partisan anti-concepts used to stifle rather than provoke discussion.[4] For the alien among strangers, the hermit, or the soldier in battle, these notions correspond to nothing in reality. They are symbols representing how a citizen experiences social life.

What Is Crime and Tyranny?

The feeling of injustice is a privative feeling occurring when the sense of social order we already feel in our day-to-day life is suspended. Natural Right theories erroneously assume the ability to derive universal positive justice from a given negative injustice. For example, the reasonable desire to not be killed leads nearly everyone to agree that a Natural Right to Life exists. However, other than the negative desire to not be killed, it is impossible to agree on the scope and limits of the Right to Life in practical cases. What seems to be common sense is in fact one of the most contentious issues in political life, bearing on topics as diverse as abortion and the death penalty.

This problem is not new to philosophy; attempts to deal with the issue of deriving positive truths from negative experiences emerge at the very beginning of Greek thought. The experience of justice first appears conceptually in philosophers who differentiate original justice (*dike*) from its man-made approximation in law (*nomos*), especially in the works of Anaximander and Parmenides. *Nomos* is a practical effort to cope with the experience of injustice (*adikia*). *Dike* is an interpretation derived from our actually lived experience of *adikia*. We personally experience injustice in practical life, in the sense that nobody, at no time and in no culture, ought to do that to me. Positive justice, however, is a culturally relative concept we construct after experiencing injustice.[5]

Crime is an injustice we experience as resistance to the resumption of social relations. When we are alone, society exists as something that is not yet here, but could be. In crime, society cannot exist because the criminal prevents we-relationships from occurring. In being alone, we experience a space that could be filled by another person. As a victim of crime, that space is filled by an injustice (*adikia*) that resists any attempt to displace it.

Even criminals experience crime as a violation of the normativity of law. One who experiences this normativity is morally outraged if he is beaten, robbed, or assaulted. This does not mean that he knows or comprehends the law but that he acts in life as if he expects others to abide by it. It is violated when the criminal experiences this but still chooses to do it to others. He does not necessarily consciously grasp his own hypocrisy but displays it in practical behaviors.

These norms are not derived from any knowledge of the law but are immediately intuitively given in lived participation in both community and society.[6] Foundational experience of political order is not found in derivative legal symbols, but in the solidarity and abiding between fellow citizens that goes unnoticed in everyday life. We suddenly become aware of social normativity when it ceases to exist, like a fish being taken out of water. We feel criminal assault because criminal acts resist our attempts to restore the pre-criminal state of affairs.[7] Crime, therefore, is not something that must be proven but is immediately present to us in perception. Law, as *nomos*, is derivative and secondary. It is a way we cope with immediately experienced crime.

Lastly, tyranny is not distinct from crime, but both are names for the same experience of the forceful suspension of society. The interrelation of these concepts can be witnessed in the overlap and collaboration between tyrannical elites and criminal rabble within corrupt regimes, from Plato's *Republic* to modern-day totalitarianism.[8] Crime is petty tyranny, and the tyrant is merely another criminal.

Being a Citizen Demands a Will to Be Free and Equal

All real existence is a resistance to penetration by a respective not-itself. Let me explain this principle: a thing is real if it resists becoming what it is not. A wall resists penetration in a very literal sense by physically obstructing motion. A person exists by not being someone else but being a unique personality. When a person fails to resist becoming something they are not, this is the basis of a psychological illness. Likewise, when a wall fails to resist being penetrated, it is destroyed. That which is real is defined by its integrity, this resistance to actions that seek to turn it into something else. This distinguishes reality from fantasy. A fantasy object changes into something else merely by the wish of the person imagining it. *Being a citizen*, if it is real, must essentially be a resistance to being "what-a-citizen-is-not." In this section, it will be shown, based on our prior investigation, that private arms are part of the structure of a society of free and equal citizens.

Being a citizen is grounded in the will to be a free participant in society. A mere wish, an idle fancy, does not rise to the standard of an act of willing. Willing becomes more than mere wishing through an intention to act, which Scheler calls willing-to-do. Willing-to-do is a will to both the end and the means to that end. A person who imagines himself losing weight merely fantasizes about fitness. The one who actualizes this by going to the gym possesses a will-to-be fit. Likewise, a person who does not will-to-be a citizen is, in practice, merely a subject because he or she is unwilling to undertake the actions involved. Anything less is a mere wish to be free, a fantasy of citizenship, because it demonstrates a lack of the will to actualize the means to the end of citizenship.[9]

I will simply assume here that being a citizen is good, and better than being a subject, an assumption we find in Plato, Aristotle, Cicero, and many other classical writers. That which causes one to cease to be a citizen and to become a subject is necessarily evil. When a will to do good is opposed by a force that seeks to nullify the good, the ethical response is a form of moral defiance: a resistance against evil by an ethical person. The form of moral defiance is relative to the situation and context but must be an actual will-to-be a real resistance. Any moral defiance that limits its response to an arbitrary proportionality of force reveals itself as an illusory resistance because it is not actually willing to resist evil. A small woman who is attacked by a large, unarmed man is not "disproportionate" when she draws a firearm simply because her assailant lacks one. To choose to submit to evil because the means of resistance cross some arbitrary line is not an ethical choice but an absence of the will-to-be good in favor of a will-to-do that arbitrary principle. That she ought not be attacked is the ethical consideration, and that she therefore ought to resist determines the permissible means.

This is why a duty to permit evil, even to oneself, is impossible. The claim that resisting evil with violence "returns evil for evil" is a falsehood because it conflates evil with pain. One can suffer pain on behalf of a higher good beyond mere sensation, but suffering evil can never be for a higher good, since evil is the negation of good. The attempt to find value in suffering evil comes from two sources, psychological and religious. The pneumopathological[10] condition of *ressentiment* elevates the suffering of evil to a virtue in order to demean and degrade the good. *Ressentiment* is a disease of the spirit that causes the individual to displace negative, self-directed emotions like envy by hating and denigrating innocent bystanders. People suffering this condition commonly hate attractive people because of their own romantic failures or hate members of another race or ethnicity because they secretly envy them. Many political ideologies, like communism, are rooted in a *ressentiment* that dysfunctional people feel at seeing others living well. They inwardly celebrate the degradation of citizens at the hands of criminals while outwardly rationalizing crime as somehow justified by lurid ideological, imaginary injustices. On the other side, transcendent arguments about the virtue of suffering evil deal with a kind of sacred value that transcends existence, negates evil itself, and therefore regards no evil as occurring at all. This, however, is beyond ethics and is more properly a question of theology.[11]

Indeterminability of the Limits of Resistance

If we begin from the first principles of existence, any ethical limits of resistance to crime must be grounded in the existence of the citizen. For this reason, the question of what kind of means are necessary to a citizen's defense is indeterminable at the abstract level. For example, the extent to which lesser force can be substituted for lethal force is a practical, not ethical question. As Scheler writes, "Every moment of life in the development of an individual represents at the same time a possibility for the individual to know unique values and their interconnections, and, in accordance with these, the necessitation of moral tasks and actions that can never be repeated."[12] The scientific ethicist does not judge inductively on the basis of material facts and cannot say with certainty what would have sufficed to resist an aggressor. The only possible judge of this matter is the person being assaulted, who lived in the experience itself and alone has the capacity to judge in the moment of crisis.

Scheler gives us the principle that people grasp their situations only in the moment and confuse themselves by overthinking. This "reckoning with" is comparable to Heidegger's description of "coping" as the predominant mode of interacting with reality. Identification of a situation as an existential conflict belongs to this mode of reasoning; excessive theory creates pathological inabilities to deal with reality which Scheler labels "hesitation." The clearest understanding arises in the "Call of the Hour," in which intuition of the problem and required solution emerge coincidentally in consciousness.[13] A clear mind understands and acts immediately, but the mind clouded by excessive theory "hesitates" and cannot act decisively in a moment of crisis.

This is not to say that lethal force is always mandatory in moral defiance. The purpose of willing is to sustain a particular state, such as being a citizen, and not any particular means to that end. Moral defiance only demands that evil's resistance be overcome. In other words, it is only in the particular resistance of the assailant and the context of the victim that any particular means of defense become an individual moral duty. Moral defiance cannot be used to justify the use of violence against actions in which no coercive resistance is placed on the will of the victim. The resistance of an insult is nil since there is no contest between the will of the assailant and the will of the victim. What distinguishes justifiable homicide from revenge is the character of resisting evil in-the-moment.[14] However, a government policy that deliberately undermines the practical ability of citizens to practice moral defiance of evil is a collaboration with evil. If the existence of a good is good, the nonexistence of good is necessarily bad. A person who wills but is overcome is not ethically equivalent to one who does not will. A government that denies its citizens the means of resistance and creates a situation where a citizen is overcome by the wicked is objectively on the side of evil.

For this reason, a victim of crime has no uncertainty about the justice of the situation, nor is there any reason to establish, in the moment of the crime, the exact principles of law being violated or the proportionality of the response. These are irrelevant in the moment of criminal action, whose essence is not the violation of some statute or another, but of the violation of the very fabric of social relations. The justice of the instance of criminal action lies in the restoration of social order, while questions of desert or legal procedure only address the aftermath. The first step to healing any wound is to stem the bleeding, by any means necessary.

Distinction of Legal versus Ethical Resistance

To summarize, the original philosophical differentiation between *nomos* and *dike* establishes a distinction between the legal and ethical, as well as a strong critique of the excessive claims that the law makes on human action. Law is a social construct in response to the experience of *adikia*, or injustice, and which arises only in the absence of common feeling among members of society. In other words, law becomes necessary when we interact with people outside of our lived communities and who do injustice to us while rejecting our customary moral principles. Within a community of shared values, injustice is handled informally through social norms and community opinion. This is not possible in a society, as defined above.

In legal theory, jurisprudence is the creation of abstract "cases" or categories which are assigned to a legal precedent. Practical human actions are abstracted down to types which have explicit legal meanings (e.g., murder, theft, charity, etc.). The degree to which the meaning of an action depends on the particularities of persons and events is directly inverse to the clarity that jurisprudential symbols bring to bear on the subject. Essentially, the more that a situation's meaning is dependent on context, the less useful those legal categories become.

In a society, jurisprudence defines the rules of social interaction because society is inclusive of persons across cultures and beliefs. However, in practice, every society overlaps with a set of discrete communities who lend a cultural texture and interpretation to that society and its rules. Because jurisprudence is a "blunt force" tool that disregards contexts and meanings of actions, the less that social order relies on jurisprudence and the more it relies on intra-community mediation of conflicts, the healthier the society. For this reason, just systems of law interfere only when absolutely necessary to preserve social order. This is why Voegelin argued that the origin of totalitarian "closed systems" of law, in which laws defined all aspects of social life, was the product of atomized societies lacking any shared community life. It is only within this life-in-common that citizenship is possible.[15]

The inadequacy of law to judge situational context is best demonstrated in the problem of armed self-defense. Events can only be experienced in their occurrence, so courts must rely on representations of those events from the flawed perspective of witnesses or partial physical evidence. No judge can grasp a criminal encounter through the same eyes as the participants, to "reckon with" the event, in Scheler's language. What is given in court testimony is therefore a rationalization for the act and not its necessitation. Witnesses can explain why they acted in such a way, but never convey the reality of the situation itself. This is why most jurisdictions of American law only require a "reasonable person" standard to justify acts of lethal self-defense and why "duty to retreat" laws are ethically incoherent. A judgment of the state that retreat is always the best option in a confrontation is entirely arbitrary.

Arguments about what an assailant "deserves" confuse the burden that a negative action places on society and the in-the-moment moral defiance of an evil act. Actions that harm society can be measured and punished by law, but moral defiance is solely determined by the contest between good and evil wills. When one is being beaten, it is both indeterminable and irrelevant in the moment if the criminal is in the process of committing battery, attempted murder, or murder. The moral obligation is simply to stop the beating. Judicial authorities only arrive after civil order is restored, making a post-hoc determination of the burden this act placed on the public. Legal punishment is entirely distinct and incommensurate to in-the-moment resistance of the victim to the assault.

The myth of nonviolent civil disobedience, namely that it can substitute for an armed citizenry as a means by which democratic citizens can resist government injustice, is based on a deep misunderstanding of elite theory. As Robert Dahl shows in his famous study of the Birmingham bus boycott, nonviolent civil disobedience relies on persuading an already sympathetic faction of political elites that they have sufficient public backing to act, presupposing that the political elites of a society are primarily loyal to their constituents and not to their class interests. The size and strength of a nonviolent resistance movement only indicates the size and strength of elite support for that movement and not popular support. This means that nonviolence is absurd when the collective class interests of the elite override their loyalty to their formal constituencies, as described by elite theorists like C. Wright Mills and James Burnham. When elite interest is opposed to the interests of the general public, the barrier to government abuse is solely that the potential costs are significantly greater than the benefits accrued to the elite class. When elites block off avenues of political change, citizens being dangerous becomes the only check on tyranny. Trying to define democracy as a "special case" is absurd; the means by which elites are chosen has practical import but is ethically irrelevant. As Aristotle argued, the good or evil of government depends on the moral tenor of its practitioners, not its procedures.

Murder, Killing, and Death

Philosophical ethics is not concerned with adjudicating the particular factual case of when a homicide is justifiable, only clarifying the structure of assessment. In other words, ethics can tell us what murder is essentially, but not which criteria should be used by discrete societies to adjudicate murder cases. Ethics distinguishes between those societies that establish an authentic moral code and those that justify immorality. For example, ethical reasoning distinguishes between a rule that rationalizes revenge and one that permits killing to protect a higher good. As mentioned before, Scheler draws that line on the basis of active violence. There is no possible "we-relationship," and so no possible society, with the opposing soldier who presents as an anonymous enemy force.[16]

Friedrich Nietzsche's "promise-making creature" demonstrates the way our use of language defines our social life. A promise-making creature relates to other beings by telling them who he is. We only really know others in the words and actions they direct toward us which convey their true selves. Such a being places its entire being as collateral in promising; the social meaning of one's life is dependent on whether one keeps or breaks those promises.[17] Frederic Maitland, for example, found the origin of felony in broken promises to the community, which is why felony permanently severs the bonds between the felon and all other human beings.

The full meaning of life is intuited in the insight that there is no greater celebration of the value of life than one who courageously lays life down for something worthy, fulfilling that promise. Survivor's guilt, for example, manifests the givenness of values higher than mere continued life. It is the intuition that one could have done something better but did not in order to save oneself. Whether or not it is practically justified for a person to feel guilty for their actions under the threat of death, the proof of the existence of higher ideals manifests itself in this feeling.

It is in these moments that our promises place our entire existence on the betting table. A person can say that they are noble, honorable, or courageous, but these claims are tested by circumstances which may involve death. Only death can determine what type of being we are, through demanding we fulfill our promise to be who we are. The one who says that they are a free and equal citizen, but shirks from practical actualization of this, is a liar. Scheler's "Call of the Hour" is the moment in which one's entire being hangs in the balance, and this choice defines the person forever. It only takes one act to undo a life; one will always be the person who made that choice. The criminal's act is a revelation of who they are. When the criminal breaks his promise and reveals himself as an enemy force, the force invoked compels a revelation in response. To do nothing in response is to reveal that one's will to be a free citizen is not real and is a mere fancy of liberty.

For this reason, denial to citizens of the most efficacious means of personal defense places the best and most moral people in a quandary, where they must choose between not being a free and equal citizen or authentic death. We've demonstrated that the state is incompetent to judge this moment. The only political question at hand is whether the state will permit free and equal citizens to preserve themselves or collaborate with crime and tyranny.

Value Deception and the Legitimate Role of Law

A common objection to granting discretion to ordinary citizens to use armed force is that it will be abused to disguise murder as self-defense. This is an overblown concern. In fact, the very existence of government assumes the goodness of the vast majority. Without a critical mass of good people, no government whatsoever is sustainable. The proper response is the old Ciceronian legal maxim, that we must not make laws on the basis of exceptions or abuses.[18] The argument that rights may be abused in democracy is not an argument against rights but against the corruption of a justice system that places ideology and partisanship ahead of right.

Nonetheless, the possibility of deception, either conscious or subconscious, remains a reality. In this lies the legitimate role of the law, not in restricting the means to defense but judging when the rationale for armed force was falsified. As mentioned before, judicial determinations logically can't determine necessity but can judge rationales. When the criminal disguises himself as a victim, either deliberately or through ideological self-deception, legal proceedings are justified in reproducing the act to detect inconsistencies indicating deception.

When a society overlies a set of overlapping living-communities, this problem is negligible because the common ground between those worldviews provides a basis for shared objective justice. It is only in the absence of *any* lived unity among participants in society that justice becomes an object of competition among political factions. Abolishing the right to bear arms is no solution because violence is inherent in the disorder of corrupt societies where people no longer feel a sense of solidarity for one another. Society itself becomes a moral atrocity, of which murder is merely one of many manifestations.

In such a case, then, would banning arms be justified as a way to minimize the evils of a disordered society? Morally unnecessary regulation, even if the goal is good, is evil because it tends to bring about the evil that it sought to avoid. Illegitimate commands incite legitimate feelings of injustice in good citizens. The Kantian notion that all good must be commanded and all evil forbidden possesses this fundamental contradiction: that a good must simultaneously be commanded by authority as well as freely willed by moral persons. The good person, who would have otherwise done good intuitively, is now made aware of an evil which never would have come to mind, now morally re-formed as justified resistance against an illegitimate command.[19] The very act that the law sought to prevent becomes a symbol of liberty because the lawmaking authority has delegitimized itself. The real cause of gun culture in the United States, for example, is a response by free citizens to the irrational and unjust impositions of the anti-gun lobby. The AR-15 was a boutique weapon until anti-gun lobbyists made it the very symbol of resistance against tyranny. Thus, the result of unjust political action against gun owners was the proliferation of more powerful guns.

One can never derive justice from political utility. A politically necessary unjust and unethical government is still a tyranny. Even if it should be proven that the very existence of society required the loss of freedom and equality, including the right to bear arms, this political order is ethically wrong. The relevant question then becomes how free and equal citizens can exist under a tyranny, and whether a human being can remain human under the conditions of an evil society.

Conclusion

As we've demonstrated, being a citizen involves the will to remain free and equal in a society. This necessarily includes a will to resist those who would violently abolish society: criminals and tyrants. Government and philosophy are incompetent to determine the limits to this resistance abstractly, which can only be determined in the immediate moment of action, the "Call of the Hour." Misrepresentations of the meaning of the concepts of life, law, and utility only muddle a very simple question: What is more appropriate for a free and equal citizen—to be armed or to be unarmed? In *The Gulag Archipelago*, Solzhenitsyn recounts the story of Aleksandr Zakharov, who killed a man in order to avoid being beaten to death. The Soviet Criminal Code Article 139 set such strict limits on self-defense that Zakharov was convicted of murder. The prosecutor told him that he had a duty to flee, regardless of the fact that his assailant was preventing it. Are our governments no better than this Soviet prosecutor? With Solzhenitsyn, let it be asked again, "So tell me, *who* creates hoodlums?!"[20]

Notes

1. Eric Voegelin, *The New Science of Politics* (Chicago: University of Chicago [1952] 1987), 12; Ellis Sandoz, *A Government of Laws* (Columbia and London, 2001), 1.

2. Alfred Schutz, *The Phenomenology of the Social World* (Evanston: Northwestern University Press, 1967), 157. See also Max Scheler, *The Nature of Sympathy* (London and New York: Routledge, 2008), 246; and Max Scheler, *Formalism in Ethics and the Non-Formal Ethics of Values* (Evanston: Northwestern University Press, 1973), 480; and Voegelin, *The New Science*, 27.

3. Manfred S. Frings, *The Mind of Max Scheler* (Milwaukee: Marquette University Press, 1997), 178. See also Eric Voegelin, *Anamnesis: On the Theory of History and Politics* (Columbia and London: University of Missouri, 2002), 342; *The New Science*, Ch. 1; and Scheler, *Formalism*, 529.

4. This principle has been described by countless philosophers in countless ways, but perhaps most strikingly in Edward S. Corwin's statement that the US Constitution is the manifestation of the American spirit of liberty first, and a legal document only by extension (See Edward S. Corwin, *The "Higher Law" Background of American Constitutional Law* [Indianapolis: Liberty Fund, 1955], 4; also Sandoz, *A Government of Laws*, 15).

5. In technical terms, the science of justice is necessarily a *via negativa*, a negative science, based on Anaximander's identification of *adikia* as primary and *dike* as derivative (See Martin Heidegger, *The Beginnings of Western Philosophy: Interpretation of Anaximander and Parmenides* [Bloomington: Indiana University Press, 2015], 19; Eric Voegelin, *Order and History, Volume 2: The World of the Polis* [Baton Rouge: University of Missouri, 1957], 79; *Anamnesis*, 343; *The New Science*, 28; and Frings, *The Mind of Max Scheler*, 34).

6. Scheler, *Formalism*, 142.
7. Ibid., 512.
8. Eric Voegelin, *Hitler and the Germans* (Columbia and London: University of Missouri, 2003), §8.
9. Max Scheler, *Selected Philosophical Essays* (Evanston: Northwestern University Press, 1973), 319. See also, Scheler, *Formalism*, 121.
10. Eric Voegelin's term for a malformed value structure, comparable to Blaise Pascal's "*désordre du coeur*." For examples of how ideological pneumopathologies justify criminal behaviors and revel in the suffering of ordinary people, see Voegelin, *Hitler and the Germans*.
11. For example, the principle of transformative love in the Christian faith does not make good out of suffering evil but expresses love of such a height that it is entirely indifferent to the earthly scale of values. Attempts to reduce the transcendent values of divine faith down to the level of earthly moral systems result in absurdity. "Turning the other cheek" as an intramundane ethical command merely invites further aggression and perpetuates evil. This immanentization of Christian ethics lay at the root of Nietzsche's correct identification of ressentiment as the source of mundane bourgeois religiosity. See the conversation on this topic in St. Augustine's *De Libero Arbitrio* Book 1.
12. Scheler, *Formalism*, 493.
13. Frings, *The Mind of Max Scheler*, 67. See also, Scheler, *Selected Essays*, 57.
14. Scheler argues that the death penalty is revenge and murder because the state has chosen to preclude the possibility of repentance and forgiveness. Homicide is only ethically possible when social reconciliation is made impossible by the presence of violence, such as in combat (see Scheler, *Formalism*, 361).
15. Voegelin, *Hitler and the Germans*, §41.
16. Part of the horror of war is when the phenomenon of personhood reappears suddenly in the face of what was previously an anonymous enemy force. Examples of this phenomenon can be found in memoirs and novels by authors like Remarque and Jünger (See Frings, *The Mind of Max Scheler*, 48; and Scheler, *Formalism*, 313).
17. Scheler, *Formalism*, 481.
18. Voegelin, *The New Science*, Ch. 6. See also, Sandoz, *A Government of Laws*, Chs. 1 and 4.
19. Scheler, *Formalism*, 214.
20. Aleksandr Solzhenitsyn, *The Gulag Archipelago, Volume 2: An Experiment in Literary Investigation* (New York: Harper, 2020), 431.

Responses

Response to Dixon on Gun Control

Benjamin L. Mabry

Study Questions

1. What ungrounded value judgments does Mabry think Dixon makes? What problems does this entail?
2. What causal model does Dixon utilize? Why does Mabry reject this model?
3. Why does Mabry think that Dixon's view of rights is problematic?
4. How does Mabry's argument avoid "rights jargon"? Why is this important?

Max Weber's "ethic of responsibility" is an attempt to get at value-free cause-effect relationships in public policy through empirical methods. Dixon's work illustrates this ethic, as does much of modern social science culture, and this response will explore three flaws in this approach. These include: (1) the presumption of ungrounded value judgments, (2) inadequate theorization of causality, and (3) the use of hollow jargon regarding rights, lacking any correspondence to real phenomena.

Ungrounded Value Judgments

Empirical methods are an ideological conceit that begs the question of social scientific investigations. Eric Voegelin, following in the footsteps of Edmund Husserl, asserts that "empirical" is a hollow concept that merely indicates the negation of value judgments, rather than indicating real phenomena. One way that empiricists deal with values is to treat all values as absolutely relative, which results in a science of "worthless trash collecting," in Voegelin's words. These studies bombard the reader with irrelevant, untheorized factoids; the suicide rate involving firearms, for example, does not raise a justice claim and is therefore ethically irrelevant.

The other approach is to negate values in such a way as to open a gap for uncritical opinions and methodological biases to insinuate themselves through culturally contingent assumptions about human order.¹ Dixon's work demonstrates this second tendency in the way that he substitutes the value judgment of safety in place of justice as the ordering principle of social life. This substitution does not derive from detailed analysis of what society *is*, nor from an axiological analysis of the relative priority of justice to safety, but reflects an axiological bias toward ideological "safety-ism" derived from his choice of methodology. All Utilitarian methodologies neglect justice and assume safety-ist values due to their inability to even conceptualize a good other than a thing's utility. What is the good of a useful object? A useful object's value is in production and durability, and so its ethical principles are productivity and safety. These value structures make empiricism a valid methodology for thing-relationships like machines or organisms but fail to adequately describe the values appropriate to the kind of entity who thinks, cares, and acts in an ethical manner. Conceptualizing persons as work-things in utilitarian methodologies results in the stealth ingress of therapeutics, an approach to ethics which reduces humans to their thing-like, tool-like, and medical characteristics, with the goal of making people more productive and secure. Therapeutics is such a dangerous bias because it obscures the very possibility of values relating to personal, intellectual, moral, or spiritual existence, closing off the possibility of even asking those questions. It is an inherently authoritarian and technocratic approach to ethics which abandons philosophy as the universal human science in its quest to emulate the pretensions of medical expertise.[2]

Inadequate Causal Models

The lynchpin of Dixon's argument, as he admits, is the assumption that a direct causal line may be drawn between the proliferation of guns and homicide. However, all empirical approaches to social science beg the question being studied by preemptively excluding all possible causes except those pre-selected through the choice of methodology. This is why it is pointless to fling contrary empirical models back and forth by citing alternative gun studies by Lott or others. These kinds of studies tell us, via their methodologies, what researchers presumptively blame for homicide but are inadequate to show objective causation.[3] Even the explicitly empiricist US National Research Council report, *Firearms and Violence*, admitted that no empirical framework can adequately analyze the cause of gun violence, due to intractable problems with equivocal and politically defined variables.[4]

Empirical causal models are built on a flawed model of causation, substituting function for essence. As Hannah Arendt points out, functionalism mistakes reality for a machine, reducing all reality to process and envisioning social conditions as inputs to be engineered toward product-ends.[5] Like children banging on keyboards, functionalism attempts to luck into outcomes without knowing what, in fact, this thing they are manipulating actually is. Specifically, Dixon conflates the *occasion* of gun violence with the *cause* of gun violence. Causation is defined by the identification of an essential characteristic in the cause that necessitates the effect. For example, a golf course is the occasion for playing golf, but the cause of playing golf is the golfer's will-to-play.[6] That the existence of more golf courses occasions an increase in playing golf is causally irrelevant. Nothing in the essence or existence of the golf course compels play but merely occasions the actual cause. Mill's methodologies as cited in Dixon's article only obscure causal understanding by neglecting this distinction. If a criminal breaks into a house, steals a gun, and later uses the stolen gun to kill, do we seriously believe that the homeowner caused the homicide by owning a gun?

Hollow "Rights"

It is a principle of logic, dating to Aristotle, that no science can exist which deals entirely in contingent objects. If rights exist, they must be grounded in ontological relations with philosophically defined subjects, or else they are baseless assertions. In other words, one must be able to give a univocal definition of the essential subject while demonstrating that it is strictly necessary that such a right belong to that subject by virtue of its essence. Dixon's treatment of rights falls victim to this problem because he fails to define what a right is, drawing false conclusions from equivocal, arbitrary meanings that have accrued to the term over the last four centuries.[7]

Empirical attitudes see all objects "at hand," as manipulable tools, without understanding what they *are*. Just as aesthetics only gives us objects as images, utilitarianism only gives them as tools. These methodologies reduce people, ideas, and phenomena to useful metrics when they operationalize variables by abstracting from individual instances and universal concepts on the basis of attributes inessential to both, relating solely to the intentions or worldview of researchers. For example, researchers use a seven-point scale to represent political ideas from liberal to conservative. This scale abstracts away from real beliefs in order to assign an arbitrary number to individuals, not because it reflects reality but because the scale is useful to the scientist. Empirical variables are not real objects, but irreal representations inadequately constructed (in Husserl's words, *substructed*) for the agenda or convenience of the researcher, and therefore bear a mediate relationship to reality, or even become a game no more scientific than chess or cards.[8]

For example, Dixon's theoretical assertion of a thing-like "right to life" quickly equivocates into a right to safety, demonstrating an ideological presupposition that the meaning of life can be reduced to nothing more than its thing-ness, namely its biological continuation which is empirically substructed into aggregate homicide data. Dixon jumps between disparate levels of analysis in his arguments (from individual to collective) and between natural or empirical meanings of key terms like "life." Like a game of Three-Word Monte, whatever *meaning* is intended by the author in any given moment shuffles between these concepts like the Queen card, leaving us to fear that what is actually intended lies up the author's sleeve.[9]

Dixon's substruction of the ethical problem is found in the aggregate analyses of gun crimes that distort reality by burying the meaningful (reality-connected) justice-implicating incidents beneath masses of meaningless (detached from reality), untheorized data points.[10] For example, what justice question is raised when two criminals shoot one another? How can these incidents be compared to cold-blooded murder? Grouping together shootings with different moral meanings under the heading "homicide" obscures the moral valence of real-world events and equivocates between moral and immoral shootings. Aggregating real life into hollow datasets reduces away these ethical considerations, and as such removes our ability to address the reality of gun crime because of the inadequacy of aggregation as a method of analyzing multiple individuals. The *con*struction of data in this way *sub*tracts meanings vital to an adequate analysis of justice.[11]

Apart from the inability to avoid terminology like the "right to bear arms," my argument avoided rights-related jargon for this very reason and focused on existential justice. Rights jargon has become equivocal in meaning, as evidenced by Dixon's inconsistency between an individual or collective right, as well as the multiple thing-like meanings simultaneously applied to "life," including biological function, arbitrary safety statistics, and self-defense; interestingly, meanings of life derived from the ways that people choose to live their lives and imbue those lives with purpose were not included. When people make a judgment that justice, honor, dignity, or liberty has a higher value than life, they are defining the meaning of any right to life in their lived actions. To be meaningful, any person-value (like a right) must be immediately rooted in the univocal *existence* of an actual person, lest the notion devolve into mere signs pointing to signs that ultimately represent nothing but contingent preferences. The meaning of "right" exists in the way actual persons practice the essentials of their life and not some conceptual calculus of unactualized ideas justified by the hypothetical symmetry of intellectual systems-building.[12]

Denying justice dehumanizes a real person, requiring moral defiance by an ethical actor. In contrast, safetyism merely represents a conceptual bias for hypothetical low-risk environments because it has no grounding in what human beings are and its deprivation does not justify resistance. A finding of aggregate reduction in risk bears no necessary relationship to any person's life circumstances. Who would be so absurd (or immoral) as to be willing to fight or even kill on behalf of marginal increases in safety statistics? If it's not worth defending, is it even a right, or merely just a preference? If a preference, should we not also ask whose interests it serves?

Dixon's final argument regarding rocket-propelled grenades requires a return to that old Ciceronian maxim cited in my original article: *de minimis non curat lex*.[13] Formal principles of justice become absurd in extreme cases and disordered societies because laws only apply to normal cases. Without social order, justice cannot exist; in such a condition, the first principle of justice is the restoration of order by any means necessary. As Abraham Lincoln put it in his first inaugural address, the Executive is empowered to do what must be done in such circumstances without regard for strict lawfulness. If Dixon's claim is that America is that far gone, then he should defend it in another essay.

Notes

1 Edmund Husserl, *The Essential Husserl* (Bloomington: Indiana University Press, 1999), 25; Max Scheler, *Formalism in Ethics and the Non-Formal Ethics of Values* (Evanston: Northwestern University Press, 1973), 308; Alfred Schutz, *The Phenomenology of the Social World* (Evanston: Northwestern University Press, 1967), 7; Eric Voegelin, *The New Science of Politics* (Chicago: University of Chicago Press, [1952] 1987), 12.

2 Scheler, Arendt, and Voegelin all identify the link between positivism and therapeutic "safety-ism" as an axiological bias. For therapeutics as an ideological bias, see Paul Gottfried, *After Liberalism: Mass Democracy in the Managerial State* (Princeton: Princeton University Press, 1999) and *Multiculturalism and the Politics of Guilt: Toward a Secular Theocracy* (Columbia: University of Missouri Press, 2002).

3 Scheler, *Formalism in Ethics*, 178, 301.

4 Charles F. Wellford, John V. Pepper, and Carol V. Petrie, *Firearms and Violence* (Washington, DC: The National Academies Press, 2005).

5 Arendt, *Between Past and Future* (New York: Penguin Books, 2006), 60; Scheler, *Formalism in Ethics*, 49; Schutz, *The Phenomenology of the Social World*, 18; Voegelin, *From Enlightenment to Revolution* (Durham: Duke University Press, 1975), 27.

6 Scheler, *Formalism in Ethics*, 29, 72, 124, 265.

7 Sandoz, *A Government of Laws* (Columbia and London: University of Missouri Press, 2001), 79; Voegelin, *Anamnesis* (Columbia and London: University of Missouri Press, 2002), 341, 385; *From Enlightenment to Revolution*, 21.

8 Arendt, *Past and Future*, 59, 212, 263; Husserl, *Essentials*, 60, 116, 287, 314, 349; Scheler, *Formalism in Ethics*, 67, 86, 139, 302; Schutz, *Phenomenology of the Social World*, 76; Voegelin, *Anamnesis*, 359; *From Enlightenment to Revolution*, 238.

9 Husserl, *Essentials*, 262; Scheler, *Formalism in Ethics*, 184; Voegelin, *Anamnesis*, 375.

10 Scheler, *Formalism in Ethics*, 46, 103, 316; Schutz, *Phenomenology of the Social World*, 165, 183, 200; Voegelin, *From Enlightenment to Revolution*, 92.

11 For more information, see the introduction of Voegelin's *New Science of Politics* for his critique of Max Weber and methodology as the "Procrustean Bed" of science.

12 Arendt, *Past and Future*, 266; Scheler, *Formalism in Ethics*, 52, 100, 154; Voegelin, *Anamnesis*, 367.

13 Translated loosely, it means that laws are not meant to account for exceptional or rare circumstances.

Respone to Mabry on Gun Control

Nicholas Dixon

Study Questions

1. What problems does Dixon find with Mabry's view that citizens have a duty of forceful resistance to threats to their freedom?
2. According to Dixon, why does Mabry fail to offer a good reason to think that self-defense entails a right to own guns?
3. What mistake does Dixon think Mabry makes by focusing mostly on the value of guns in preventing crime?
4. Why does Dixon believe that an armed citizenry is not justified to prevent tyranny?

Professor Mabry has broadened the debate over gun rights in two ways. First, he has made extensive reference to twentieth-century phenomenologists, especially Voegelin and Scheler, whose work has not, to my knowledge, been cited before in the philosophical literature on gun control. Second, he has put the gun control debate in the context of foundational issues in political philosophy about the role of government vis-à-vis respecting individual rights. His central claim is that being a free and equal citizen requires that we have access to guns to protect ourselves against both fellow citizens and governments that threaten our freedom. While he has made a valuable contribution that furthers this debate, I will argue that he is no more successful in establishing a right to own guns than more familiar arguments based on the right to self-defense.

A Duty of Forceful Resistance?

Mabry asserts that genuine citizens actively resist any attempts to violate their freedom and equality. The failure to do so is a sign that a person suffers from "psychological illness" and is "merely a subject because he or she is unwilling to undertake the actions involved [in being a genuine citizen.]" (p. 306). Putting aside the concern that Mabry's view excludes large groups of people from genuine citizenship,[1] Mabry insists that able-bodied neurotypical adults have a duty of forceful resistance to threats. He states "[a]ny moral defiance that limits its response to an arbitrary proportionality of force reveals itself as an illusory resistance, because it is not actually willing to resist evil" (p. 307). He recognizes that we may not use force in response to trivial threats, like insults, because "no coercive resistance is placed on the will of the victim" (p. 308). One hopes that he does not regard the existence of threats to our will as *sufficient* to justify violent responses, since even embezzlement and identity theft clearly violate our will. Violence is surely only justified in order to prevent *physical harm*. But this is precisely the kind of discussion of proportionality that Mabry is at pains to sidestep, as shown by his dismissive epithet "*arbitrary* proportionality of force."

I suggest that it is not at all arbitrary to impose not only proportionality but also *necessity* as restrictions on when we may justifiably use force, typically in the context of self-defense. We may only use violence when it is *the only way* to protect ourselves or others (necessity), and when the violence is *not excessive* given the amount of harm that is threatened (proportionality). For example, shooting someone to prevent them from touching our shoulder would be both unnecessary and disproportionate. Now Mabry is correct when he asserts that we need to look at the context of each individual instance of self-defense to determine its justifiability, but this does not entail his claim that "[t]he only possible judge of this matter is the person being assaulted" (p. 308). This would be a purely subjective standard for justified self-defense that would exculpate *all* acts of self-defense, however excessive. Mabry himself points out that courts use a "reasonable person" standard to determine whether violence was justified, but this is an *objective* standard based on applying the principles of necessity and proportionality.

A Right to Guns for Self-Defense?

Curiously, Mabry devotes very little attention to defending the crucial step of his argument—how, that is, the general right to defend ourselves against violations of our freedom entails the right to own guns. The closest he gets to filling in this gap is to refer to guns as "the most efficacious means of personal defense" (p. 311). But using the most efficacious means is *not* justified when it is disproportionate and unnecessary, because we can protect ourselves with less violent or nonviolent means. In the vast majority of cases, we do not need guns to prevent violations of our rights, whether the threats be to our property or our person. We can report crimes to the police, call the police if crimes are imminent, walk away from or reason with the assailant, yell for help, take shelter in our homes, lock our doors, or use nonlethal methods of self-defense like pepper spray. Mabry's view that we have an unlimited right to violence, including using guns, to defend our freedom would be easier to defend if we lived in a state of nature, where there is no government to protect us against harm. In a functioning democracy, however, we have extensive governmental protections that make it much harder to justify using guns to defend ourselves.

Most defenders of gun rights take a different path from Mabry's. Rather than proposing a right to forceful self-defense that is unrestrained by requirements of necessity and proportionality, they point to situations where using a gun really would be the only way to protect ourselves. In view of such cases, Michael Huemer asserts that gun bans would violate the right to self-defense of the unfortunate victim of aggression.[2] My own essay in this volume is largely devoted to responding to Huemer. My response begins with the data that the United States, which has far more liberal gun laws and far higher gun ownership than twenty-eight other large, affluent democracies, has a homicide rate (most of which are committed with guns) that is a shocking 7.5 times higher than that in the other countries.[3] The United States is therefore an ongoing experiment showing that the permissive gun laws that allow people to own guns for self-defense actually make us *less* safe.

Guns for Preventing Crime?

Mabry considers the objection that allowing citizens the right to use violence in self-defense might be abused by those who disguise outright murder by falsely claiming that they were being assaulted. He replies, plausibly enough, that our courts are well able to distinguish between justified and spurious self-defense.[4] Far more important, however, is the staggering amount of violent gun crime in the United States that involves no deceptive claims of self-defense.

Similar to Huemer and other gun rights advocates, Mabry tries to divert attention from the crimes committed with guns and to focus only on their value as a means of *preventing* crimes. He states, "arguments about costs and benefits of civil rights like the Right to Bear Arms might rationalize their usefulness or danger but are irrelevant to ethics" (p. 303). But it is gratuitous to dismiss the catastrophic consequences of the United States' high gun ownership rate as being morally irrelevant. Mabry and other gun rights advocates are correct to insist on the right to life of those who want to use guns to protect themselves. However, each person killed by criminal uses of guns also possesses a right to life. Given the evidence that permissive gun laws lead to far greater homicide rates, the very same premise that Mabry uses—the need to protect people's freedom from violence—actually supports gun *restrictions*, not the right to own them.

Guns for Resisting Tyranny?

Criminals are not the only threats to our freedom and equality. Mabry also identifies tyrannical government as a threat, and he presents this as another ground for the right to own guns. We should first notice that we cannot in the current debate use the imposition of gun control as a reason for deeming a government to be tyrannical. After all, this would only be the case if there is a right to own guns, but whether such a right exists is precisely the point in question. The idea that an armed populace helps reduce the risk of governmental tyranny is well-known.[5] Mabry's own defense of this argument refers to the alleged inefficacy of nonviolent civil disobedience. He asserts that when, in contrast with the Birmingham bus boycotts, the interests of "political elites" are opposed to those of dissenters, the only deterrent to governmental tyranny is an armed citizenry (p. 310). I would respond that an armed citizenry is neither necessary nor sufficient to prevent governments from violating citizens' rights. United States and world history are replete with instances of nonviolent protests that were successful in changing unjust laws. Notwithstanding Mabry's claims about the Birmingham bus boycott, the US Civil Rights Movement was so successful precisely because its participants were nonviolent and *persuaded* the US public and government by advancing irrefutable moral arguments. No guns were needed. The fall of the Berlin Wall was a peaceful, spontaneous outbreak of civil disobedience that precipitated not only the reunification of Germany, but the breakup of the entire Soviet Union. Again, no guns were needed. In contrast, the violent insurrection of January 2021 at the US Capitol would have been truly catastrophic had the protestors been armed. As it was, the insurrection did *not* prevent governmental tyranny. It was itself an attempt to overturn the results of a democratic election and effectively plunge the country into anarchy.

In sum, the right of citizens to be free from harm from other individuals and from the government is better protected by strict gun control. The proliferation of guns gives us the worst of both worlds—it is not needed to prevent government from violating rights, and it makes us far more vulnerable to violent crime at the hands of fellow citizens.

Notes

1. Mabry's view appears to have the implausible implication that people unable to resist violations, such as young children and people with severe cognitive disabilities, are not true citizens and have less value than people who do actively resist threats to their freedom.
2. See Michael Huemer, "Is There a Right to Own a Gun?" *Social Theory and Practice* 29, no. 2 (2003): 297–324; and "Gun Rights as Deontic Constraints," *Social Theory and Practice* 45, no. 4 (2019): 601–12.
3. Erin Grinshteyn and David Hemenway, "Violent Death Rates in the U.S. Compared to Those of Other High-Income Countries, 2015," *Preventive Medicine* 123 (2019): 20–6.
4. Incidentally, such judgments are based on applying the necessity and proportionality restrictions, yet Mabry (p. 312) claims that "judicial determinations logically can't determine necessity."
5. See, for example, Samuel Wheeler III, "Arms as Insurance," *Public Affairs Quarterly* 13, no. 2 (1999): 111–29.

Questions for Reflection

1. Do you think Dixon has successfully rebutted the argument that gun control would prevent people from adequately defending themselves? Why?
2. Is Mabry correct that justice always trumps concerns about public safety? Why?

3. What views on the nature and purpose of government may be presupposed by Dixon's and Mabry's differing perspectives on gun control? Which view of government do you think is better? Why?

For Further Reading

Bernstein, C'Zar, Timothy Hsiao, and Matt Palumbo. "The Moral Right to Keep and Bear Firearms." *Public Affairs Quarterly* 29, no. 4 (2015): 345–63.

DeGrazia, David, and Lester Hunt. *Debating Gun Control: How Much Regulation Do We Need?* Oxford University Press, 2016.

Dixon, Nicholas. "Handguns, Philosophers, and the Right to Self-Defense." *International Journal of Applied Philosophy* 25, no. 2 (2011): 151–70.

Halbrook, Stephen. *The Right to Bear Arms: A Constitutional Right of the People or a Privilege of the Ruling Class?* Bombardier Books, 2021.

Lott, Jr., John R. *More Guns, Less Crime: Understanding Crime and Gun-Control Laws*, 3rd ed. University of Chicago Press, 2010.

Spitzer, Robert. *The Politics of Gun Control*, 9th ed. Routledge, 2024.

Wellford, Charles F., et al. *Firearms and Violence*. The National Academies Press, 2005.

10

War and Peace

War Can Be Morally Justified

Steven B. Cowan

Study Questions

1. What are the three viewpoints on war? Which view does Cowan defend?
2. What is a natural right? Why does Cowan think that we have a natural right to self-defense?
3. According to Cowan, why does government exist? What does this imply about war?
4. What objection to the possibility of a just war does Cowan consider? How does he respond to it?
5. What are the *Jus ad Bellum* criteria for a just war?
6. What are the *Jus in Bello* criteria for a just war?
7. What are the *Jus post Bellum* criteria for a just war?

As I write these words, Israel is (hopefully) winding down a bloody war against the terrorist organizations Hamas and Hezbollah. This war threatened (and may still threaten) to expand into a major regional conflict perhaps involving my own country, the United States of America. Also, the nation of Ukraine continues to fight for its national survival against Russia. And the People's Republic of China seems poised to mount a massive invasion of its island neighbor, Taiwan. War, and the threat of war, seems to be an ever-present reality in the world and always has been throughout recorded history.

No one doubts that war is a terrible and tragic evil. The violence of war results in untold destruction and misery. So, the question naturally arises: *Can war ever be morally justified?* In the history of ethical reflection on this question, three general answers have been given. First is the answer provided by *realism* (or *amoralism*): war can be justified for any reason that serves the interests of a given state. For the realist, the question of war is not subject to moral evaluation; rather, war is simply a matter of political expediency.

Second, at the opposite end of the moral spectrum, is *pacifism*. For the pacifist, war can never be morally justified—or for any other reason for that matter. There are different types of pacifism, and different rationales given for each, but the basic idea behind them all is that the deadly violence entailed by war is morally prohibited.

Third is the *Just War Theory*, which holds that war is morally justifiable under certain conditions. Just War theorists thus seek to capture the middle ground between realism and pacifism. War should not be waged for just any reason; it is subject to moral constraints contrary to the stance of the realists. But, against the pacifists, Just War theorists insist that war is sometimes the only right option in the face of unjust aggression.

In this essay, I will defend the Just War Theory (JWT). I will have very little to say with regard to realism. It seems evident that realism can only be defended on an ethical theory that subordinates moral considerations to political ones—for example, some version of moral conventionalism. But this seems to put things precisely backward. If, as I argue below, people have natural rights, then the very existence of any political authority requires a moral justification. It follows that the state, and any state policy (including war policy), is subject to moral evaluation.

A Case for Morally Justified War

The case for JWT that I will make may be summarized formally as follows:

(1) Every person has natural rights (e.g., life, liberty, pursuit of happiness).

(2) Government exists to secure our natural rights.

(3) If the government exists to secure our natural rights, then the government is obligated (under certain conditions) to use deadly force against threats to our natural rights.

(4) Our natural rights are threatened (made unsecure) by unjust foreign aggression.

(5) Therefore, the government is obligated (under certain conditions) to use deadly force against unjust foreign aggression.

In what follows in this section, I will explain and defend the premises of this argument.

The Natural Right to Self-Defense

I will take it as relatively uncontroversial that persons—human beings and any other rational creatures that may exist—have *natural rights*. A right, roughly, is something that a person is entitled to; something that others are obligated to acknowledge and respect. More formally,[1]

> S has a *right* to φ if and only if S is entitled to φ.

If S is entitled to φ, then, by the nature of the case, other people are obligated not to infringe S's entitlement to φ. So, for example, if a person, Sally, has a right to life, then others are morally obligated to respect Sally's life by not unjustly taking her life or irresponsibly endangering it.

To say that a right is a *natural* right means that people have it simply in virtue of *being persons*. There are other kinds of rights that people have that are not theirs simply because they are persons. For example, people in the United States (and other democracies and republics) have the right to vote. But this right is a *political* right, not a natural right. Voting is a right bestowed on people (by society or the government) who live under certain political systems. So, some rights, like the right to vote, are *conditional* on external circumstances. By contrast, natural rights are intrinsic to persons; they belong to people just because they are people. Put another way, it is the nature of persons that they have certain natural rights. Notice how this is described in the American *Declaration of Independence*:

> We hold these truths to be self-evident, that all men are created equal, that *they are endowed by their Creator with certain unalienable Rights, that among these are Life, Liberty and the pursuit of Happiness.*—That to secure these rights, Governments are instituted among Men, deriving their just powers from the consent of the governed.

The *Declaration of Independence* states that all human beings have certain rights—unalienable[2] rights—that are theirs because God endowed them with those rights when he created them. This is simply another way of saying that people have natural rights—albeit stipulating that the ground and source of those rights is God. While I think that our natural rights do indeed come from God, that point is not necessary for my argument.[3] All that matters is that we actually have natural rights, whatever their source.

Now one of the natural rights that people possess is the right to *self-defense*. This right is grounded in the more fundamental right to life. Human life is sacred. And because human life is sacred, every person is entitled to his life—his life belongs to him, and he has the right to keep it. It is morally wrong, therefore, to take another person's life without a just cause. It follows from this fundamental right to life that a person has the right to defend his life against unjust threats to his life. If, for example, someone breaks into my home and attempts to kill me, my right to life makes it permissible for me to defend myself against the attacker. If this were not so, then saying that I have a right to life would be meaningless.

Moreover, this right to self-defense entails that it is permissible for a person to use whatever force is necessary to prevent his life from being taken (or even seriously harmed). This includes, of course, the use of *deadly* force if that degree of force is (reasonably thought to be) necessary to save one's life. (In the next major section, I will respond to the objection that using deadly force against an attacker wrongly infringes on *his* right to life.)

Therefore, as premise (1) of the argument above states, *every person has natural rights*. And one of those natural rights is the right to self-defense.

The Government's Obligation to Secure Natural Rights

Premise (2) of the argument states that the very reason we have government in the first place is *to secure our natural rights*.[4] As the *Declaration of Independence* puts it, "Governments are instituted among Men" in order "to secure these rights." According to the social contract theory of government on which the Declaration is based, human beings create civil government because, in the "state of nature" (i.e., the condition in which no government exists), they have no sure way to secure their natural rights against the threats of those who don't care about the rights of others. The philosopher Thomas Hobbes explained it well: in the state of nature, human life would be "solitary, poor, nasty, brutish, and short."[5] So, human beings consent to create civil government in order to avoid the dangers posed by the state of nature.

By thus establishing civil government, the people transfer to the civil authority certain liberties or powers by which it can carry out its rights-securing function. For example, given that we all have a right to life, we delegate to the civil authority the power to secure that right—in other words, the power to protect our lives from unjust harm. And since we naturally have the right to use deadly force in self-defense (see above), we thus delegate to the civil authority the right to use deadly force (if necessary) to protect our lives from unjust threats. We also give the government the power to secure other natural rights that we have, such as the right to liberty and private property, and to use an appropriate level of force to do so.

Now, since government is created to secure our natural rights, and we delegate to it the power needed to do so, we rightly expect the civil authority to exercise those powers as appropriate. For example, if I am accosted by a mugger on the street, I (we) rightly expect the police to intervene to stop the mugger from taking my wallet—or at least apprehend the mugger later and return my wallet to me. All this to say that the government has an *obligation* to use coercive force when necessary to protect our natural rights. And there are contexts and conditions under which the force it uses is *deadly force*. That is, since I have the right to use deadly force when necessary to protect my life from others, and since I (under the social contract theory of government) have delegated to the state the right and power to secure my right to life, *the state has an obligation to use deadly force when necessary to protect my life from others* (Premise [3]).

War and Our Natural Rights

Premise (4) of the argument should be obvious. The unjust aggression of a foreign power clearly poses a serious threat to, even a direct infringement of, a people's natural rights. When one nation attacks another nation, the citizens of the attacked nation are endangered if not killed. They are subject to potential oppression and/or enslavement. Their property and their livelihoods are subject to damage and theft. Clearly, then, foreign aggression makes our natural rights unsecure.

Given our case for the right to self-defense, the people of a nation unjustly attacked by a foreign power have the right to defend themselves with deadly force. And since such people have delegated to their own government the obligation to secure their natural rights, it follows that (5) their government *has the obligation (under certain conditions) to use deadly force against unjust foreign aggression.* This means war.

A Pacifist Objection

I will have the opportunity later (in my response essay to Timothy Erdel) to offer criticisms of pacifism. Here in my main essay, I will only respond to one specific objection pacifists might raise to what I have argued so far. In the form of a question, the objection is: *Does using deadly force in self-defense violate an attacker's right to life?* Some pacifists might agree that human beings have a natural right to self-defense, but object that this right falls short of granting license to use deadly force. One reason to think so is that an attacker also has a right to life, and using deadly force in self-defense potentially violates his right to life just as much as his attack on my life violates my right to life. So, the pacifist argues, using deadly force in self-defense is morally prohibited.

This objection fails to make a distinction that seems intuitively obvious to most of us, namely, the distinction between *killing and murder*, or between just and unjust homicide. *Murder* is defined as the *unjust* taking of a human life—intentionally taking the life of another person without a just cause (e.g., for revenge, jealousy, or spite). *Killing* per se is not identical to murder. For example, I may kill another person accidentally. In that case, I have clearly not committed murder. So, obviously, there is a difference between killing and murder. But there seem to be other cases of killing that are not cases of murder. As noted above, my right to life is meaningless if it does not include the right to self-defense—that is, the right to prevent someone else from violating my right to life. But what if, in a particular case, the only way to prevent someone else from violating my right to life is to use deadly force and kill the attacker? To be sure, my act of self-defense *kills* the attacker, but have I *murdered* him? Have I taken his life *unjustly*? Surely not. We might even say, in such a case, that a violent aggressor has *forfeited* his own right to life by intentionally acting to unjustly violate another person's right to life.

The above considerations highlight the fact that the moral assessment of human action—including acts of killing—is deeply rooted in the notion of *intention*. Indeed, it is different intentions that are the basis for the distinction between killing and murder. When a murderer (or would-be murderer) uses violence, his intention is to kill. When a person acts in self-defense, however, his intention is not necessarily to harm or kill the attacker (though this may be the result), but simply to prevent his being harmed or killed by the aggressor. So, even if I use deadly force in self-defense (say, by shooting the attacker with a gun), I would be perfectly happy if the attacker survived so long as his attack against me is thwarted. This difference in intent helps explain why murder is wrong but killing sometimes isn't.

The Criteria for Morally Justified War

I have argued that war can be morally justified *under certain conditions*. But what are those conditions? The Just War Tradition, over the course of more than 2,000 years, has developed and defended a set of criteria for assessing and assuring the morality of any given war. Those criteria may be divided into three categories:

A. *Jus ad Bellum* ("justice to war"). These are those conditions that must be met in order to morally justify going to war at all.

B. *Jus in Bello* ("justice in war"). Granting that going to war is morally permissible, the *jus in bello* set the conditions for the just *conduct* of war.

C. *Jus post Bellum* ("justice after war"). These are the conditions for establishing and maintaining a just peace once hostilities have ceased.

In what follows, I delineate and explain the various criteria under each category.

Jus ad Bellum

Since war is not always morally permissible, when the leaders of a nation contemplate the permissibility and prospects of going to war, there are five criteria that must be addressed.

1. *Just Cause.* The first and most fundamental question that must be asked regarding the justice of going to war is the question of the war's rationale or cause. That is, for what *cause* is a war to be fought? Though Just War theorists differ on some details, the tradition recognizes three just causes:

a. *Defense against foreign aggression.* This is the most straightforward and obvious justification for war. Given the defense of the morality of war provided above, if a nation is unjustly attacked by a foreign power, then the government of that nation has the right and obligation (all other things being equal) to wage war in defense of its citizens and their natural rights. This includes the right to carry out *preemptive strikes* in the face of an imminent attack.[6] It would be foolish in the extreme (especially given the lethality of modern weapons) to allow the enemy to strike first if one has reliable intelligence that they are about to attack.

b. *Intervention to aid another nation being unjustly attacked.* While the moral justness of war is primarily grounded in the right to self-defense, there are other moral considerations that allow us to extend the just-cause criterion beyond the defense of one's own nation. Consider, for example, the fact that a violent home invader may not threaten me directly but may threaten my family. It would be morally repugnant for me to stand by and allow my family members to be harmed if I have the means to intervene on their behalf. I have, we might say, a covenantal obligation to protect my family from violent harm. This obligation justifies my use of deadly force against their attacker as surely as the right to self-defense justifies my use of deadly force. Likewise, nations may enter into covenants (treaties or alliances) that obligate them to mutual defense against unjust aggressors. Moreover, consider a situation in which I witness an innocent person (not a family member) being violently attacked on the street. If I have the means to come to her aid with little or no risk to myself, then doesn't brotherly love obligate me to do so? Our moral disgust at those who stand idly by and do nothing when others are victimized by violence suggests strongly that we *are* so obligated. What is true of individuals is likewise true of nations. If a weak nation is unjustly attacked by a stronger one, and the weaker nation asks our nation for help (even though we have no defense treaty with them), and we have the capability to intervene, then (all other things being equal) brotherly love dictates that we not stand idly by.

c. *Prevention of a future unjust attack.* Though more controversial than the causes mentioned so far, the so-called "Preventive War" is also morally justifiable under limited conditions.[7] A preventive war involves an attack against another nation in anticipation of a distant future threat. It differs markedly from a preemptive strike (see above) in that the threat of enemy attack is not imminent or certain. Yet it is arguable that preventive war is justifiable under two strict conditions: (1) The other nation either has or is in the process of developing the capacity for weapons of mass destruction (WMDs), and (2) the other nation has threatened to use WMDs against one's nation. Given the horrific destructive power of WMDs, it seems to me that no nation can afford to wait until an attack with WMDs actually takes place or becomes imminent.

2. *Just Intent.* As noted earlier, intention is morally significant. Even given a just cause for war, the intention of those authorizing the use of military force must be virtuous. Fighting for revenge, greed, or racial or religious hatred does not constitute a virtuous motive. Neither does the lust for power or a desire for territorial expansion. The consensus of the Just War Tradition is that the only just intent is to *establish a just peace*. A *just* peace is more than the mere absence of conflict; it is a peace *with justice*—a peace that brings about a just resolution to the unjust aggression that caused the war. This will include, of course, the cessation of hostilities (peace) by removing or disarming the aggressing forces, but may also include such things as the return of conquered territory, reparations for damages and loss of life, the punishment of war criminals, and so on. So, if the intent of those contemplating war is to bring about such a just peace, then the war (all other things being equal) is just.

3. *Legitimate Authority.* Not just anyone can declare a state of war. As Thomas Aquinas wrote, "It is not the business of a private person to declare war."[8] It is the *vigilante* who "takes the law into his own hands." Just war thinking forbids vigilantism. For war to be just, the war must be authorized by a legitimate civil authority. Since the government, as noted above, exists to protect the natural rights of its citizens, the exclusive responsibility for declaring war naturally falls to the government. Different governmental systems will invest such authority in different individuals, of course. In the United States, according to its *Constitution*, Congress alone possesses the power to declare war.[9]

4. *Last Resort.* If war can be averted, stopped, and/or redressed through diplomatic means, then justice requires that those diplomatic means be employed. The bloodshed and destruction that warfare inevitably involves should be the "last resort." This criterion should not be misunderstood to necessarily mean, however, that every conceivable diplomatic alternative to war should be exhausted before war is justified. David Corey and Daryl Charles aptly qualify this criterion:

> [W]ars are unjust as long as some solution short of war, a solution with reasonable likelihood of success, remains to be tried. Reasonable likelihood of success [is] the essential qualification; without it the thought becomes absurd. All wars, after all, can be postponed indefinitely, and villains can be

allowed to harm innocent people unopposed. But at a certain point, when all reasonable alternatives have been tried, the failure to respond becomes itself incompatible with the just war tradition properly understood, a tradition which maintains that acts of aggression can and sometimes should be resisted by a judicious use of force.[10]

Without this qualification, "last resort" becomes appeasement—and appeasement is antithetical to justice.

5. *Likelihood of Success*. Star Trek fans (and others) have heard the expression, "Resistance is futile." When that is known, or reasonably expected, to be true, then war is unjustified. The reason is simple. Even if a nation has a just cause and a just intent in the face of an unjust aggression by another nation, without a reasonable hope of success, resisting the attack will result in loss of life and property to no good purpose. So, even an otherwise just war may be fought only if the legitimate authorities judge that there is a reasonable likelihood of success.

Jus in Bello

It matters morally *how* one fights a war. Not just anything goes. So, in addition to addressing the *jus ad bellum* criteria discussed above, a nation at war must also adhere to the following principles for the just *conduct* of war.

1. *Proportionality*. Given that war is, at best, an unfortunate moral necessity, and given that war involves the use of deadly force that sometimes affects even the innocent (see below), a nation should use no more force than is necessary to achieve the goal of securing a just and lasting peace. This proportionate use of force requires judiciousness in the employment of both weapons and tactics. Regarding weapons, the idea is that one does not use a bomb when a bullet will do the job. Likewise, regarding tactics, proportionality forbids "burning down the barn to roast the pig."[11] Thus, for example, a "scorched earth policy" that seeks to completely destroy an enemy country is morally unjustified.

2. *Discrimination*. The just conduct of a war requires discriminating between legitimate and illegitimate targets. Such discrimination presupposes *noncombatant immunity*. Combatants are those who are directly involved in military combat (soldiers, navy sailors, etc.) or those closely supporting combat. *Non*combatants—those who are justly immune to military attack—include most civilians,[12] but also some who may wear military uniforms such as medical personnel, chaplains, and prisoners of war. Such noncombatants

may not be intentionally targeted for attack or placed in harm's way. A key word here, of course, is "intentionally." It is impossible to guarantee that noncombatants will not be harmed or killed in war *unintentionally*. Justice in war is not thereby violated as long as reasonable precautions have been taken to prevent such "collateral damage."

Jus Post Bellum

Once the objectives of a just war have been achieved and hostilities have ceased, consideration must be made of what justice requires *after* the war. Generally speaking, *jus post bellum* demands the realization of the just intent (see above): the establishment of a just and lasting peace. This will, undoubtedly, involve a measure of nation-building in the defeated nation by the victorious nation and the wider international community. Such nation-building may (sometimes) be likened to "radical surgery" according to Brian Orend.[13] A nation whose regime was willing to engage in unjust aggression must be morally rehabilitated. Also, the ravages of war on the defeated nation's infrastructure will necessitate that the victorious nation help to establish and maintain a stable civil order.

Moreover, because the defeated nation engaged in an unjust aggression, justice will demand that:

1. *The defeated aggressor make reparations for loss of life and property by the attacked victor nation.*
2. *Any territory conquered by the aggressor nation be returned to the attacked nation.*
3. *There is repatriation of all prisoners from both sides of the conflict.*
4. *Those responsible for initiating the war and any war criminals are fairly tried and appropriately punished.*[14]

Notwithstanding these practical and moral necessities, the *jus post bellum* requires that the victorious nation will:

5. *Respect the natural rights of the defeated nation's citizens.* Enslaving, exploiting, or otherwise harming them is morally forbidden. Their property rights and natural liberties are not to be infringed.
6. *Recognize the territorial and political integrity of the defeated nation.* Conquest, territorial annexation, or permanent occupation can never be a just intent. The integrity of the defeated nation *qua* nation is to be maintained as far as feasible.

Conclusion

The tragic horror of war cannot be overstated. And yet, as I have argued, justice sometimes dictates that we endure the horror. The alternative—injustice and even worse horrors—cannot and should not be endured. When evil men attack the innocent, good men are obliged to rise up in their defense. The Just War Theory shows good men the conditions under which war may be justly waged.

I am under no illusions, of course, about the difficulty of fighting a truly just war. There have been wars in the past in which neither side could honestly claim a just cause. A just intent is rarer still. And even when nations fully satisfy the *jus ad bellum*, the conduct of the war (*jus in bello*) and/or the aftermath of the war (*jus post bellum*), more often than not, fall egregiously short of just ideals. But this is no reason to give in to the naïve lure of pacifism. Acknowledging the shortcomings of those who have fought wars in the past should, rather, move the better angels of our nature to fight more justly.

Notes

1. For more on the nature of rights, see Leif Wenar, "Rights," in *The Stanford Encyclopedia of Philosophy* (2020), ed. Edward N. Zalta and Uri Nodelman (https://plato.stanford.edu/entries/rights/#AnalRigh).
2. "Unalienable" means "not able to be taken away or denied."
3. I think that our natural rights find their ground and source in God because I think that *all* objective moral value and obligation is grounded in God. In other words, if God does not exist, then no objective moral values and obligations would exist. Apart from the existence of an omnibenevolent God, we are left, at best, with moral relativism and, at worst, moral nihilism. For defenses of the view that God is the necessary ground of morality, see Mark Linville, "The Moral Argument," in *The Blackwell Companion to Natural Theology*, 391–448, Malden, MA: Wiley-Blackwell, 2012; Steven B. Cowan, "The Question of Moral Values," in *The Big Argument: Does God Exist?* ed. John Ashton and Michael Wesacott (Green Forest: Master Books, 2005), 165–77; and Matthew Flannagan, "Morality Depends on God," in *Problems in Value Theory: An Introduction to Contemporary Debates*, ed. Steven B. Cowan (London: Bloomsbury, 2020), 93–105.
4. I do not intend to claim here that securing our natural rights is the only legitimate function of government (though I am sympathetic to this view). I only claim that this is the *minimal* function of government.
5. Thomas Hobbes, *Leviathan*, XIII.
6. As Israel famously did in the *Six-Day War* (1967).
7. For arguments against preventive war from within the Just War Tradition, see J. Daryl Charles and Timothy J. Demy, *War, Peace, and Christianity: Questions and Answers*

from a Just-War Perspective (Wheaton: Crossway, 2010), 216–20; and Paul Ramsey, *The Just War: Force and Political Responsibility* (New York: Scribner's, 1968), 68.

8   Aquinas, *Summa Theologica* II-II Q.40.
9   See *U.S. Constitution*, Article I, Section 8, Clause 11.
10 David D. Corey and J. Daryl Charles, *The Just War Tradition: An Introduction* (Wilmington: ISI Books, 2012), 9–10.
11 I'm indebted to Scott Rae for this expression (see *Moral Choices: An Introduction to Ethics*, 3rd ed. [Grand Rapids: Zondervan, 2009], 316).
12 *Some* civilians may rightly be classified as combatants and thus not recognized as having noncombatant immunity. For example, those employed in munitions factories and merchant marines transporting weapons and military supplies to the battlefield. For more on classifying noncombatants and combatants, see Robert Phillips, *War and Justice* (Norman: University of Oklahoma Press, 1984). In this book, Phillips states the following helpful principle: "Generally speaking, classes of people engaged in occupations which they would perform whether or not a war were taking place, or services rendered to combatants both in war and out, are considered immune."
13 Brian Orend, *Michael Walzer on War and Justice* (Cardiff: University of Wales Press, 2000), 139.
14 Some Just War theorists hold that, in order to ensure fairness, this requirement should be carried out by neutral third parties.

Pacifism and Peacemaking

Timothy Paul Erdel

Study Questions

1. What are some core convictions shared by most pacifists? Who are the most consistent pacifists? Why?
2. What "daring imaginations" do pacifists have that proponents of war lack?
3. What three moral convictions about killing characterize pacifists? How does military training, according to Erdel, illustrate the third one?
4. What facts are pacifists willing to face that proponents of war are not?
5. What does Erdel mean by pacifists having "the courage to fail"?

People want peace. The question is, how should we seek peace in a world filled with powerful people bent on brutal conquest or ruthless revenge? In the twentieth century, whole cultures still pursued vicious evils ranging from headhunting to genocide. The Second World War alone cost over 50,000,000 lives. Nuclear weapons threatened global annihilation.[1] Today, in a new millennium, multiple savage wars continue unabated. Is lethal force sometimes necessary to stop murderous violence and secure peace?

There are many kinds of pacifism—too many to delineate here, still less to describe them each in detail. There are over two dozen types of *religious* pacifism alone.[2] Some pacifists reject all forms of violence, including psychological ones. Some are against any use of physical force, especially if it might prove lethal. Some allow for deadly force in police work, but not in warfare, saying wars inevitably introduce a completely different dimension of violence. Some people who are otherwise very dismissive of pacifism are nuclear pacifists.[3] Contingent pacifists (or practical pacifists) doubt that there has ever been a genuinely just war, nor could there be one right now; but they still grant that a Just War might be a theoretical possibility in some future setting given all the right conditions.[4] And so forth. There are also numerous proposals and strategies to achieve peaceful ends by peaceful means. Most pacifists do believe in force: "Moral force, the force of organized resistance to violence, the force of sharing wealth, and the force of dialogue, compromise and negotiation."[5]

Many pacifists (but not all) share core common convictions. Here are some of them. Human life is extremely valuable, even sacred. Killing human beings is wrong. Killing to end violence merely compounds that violence. There are better ways, nonviolent ones, to thwart violence and engage in peacemaking. Far more innocent people, whether civilians or soldiers, die when we try to end war with violence than if we pursued peace by nonviolent means. Even if pacifism leads to death, it is better to suffer and die than to become a killer.

Many pacifists are concerned with any threats to human life, sometimes referred to as "completely pro-life" pacifists. It is important to remember that wars are neither the only violent nor the most imminent threat to human life. In recent years, many times more people have been killed by medically induced abortions than by any other means—globally, 56,000,000 or more per year. This annual number is comparable to all the deaths in the Second World War. A majority are female fetuses, a deliberate choice that is sometimes called "gendercide," since females are devalued in some major cultures. Other causes of death include communicable diseases and malnutrition (10,000,000 or more a year, with a spike from Covid); the effects of smoking tobacco (8,000,000 or more); alcoholism (2,800,000 or more); traffic accidents (1,350,000 or so, roughly half due to intoxication); suicides (over 750,000); lethal violence, including wars (over 500,000); and opioids and illegal drugs (250,000 or so).[6]

Other pacifists focus on violence against women, the poor, or oppressed minorities, often emphasizing that violence may be structural as well as personal, or less than lethal yet still very damaging. Nevertheless, this discussion will focus on the pacifist opposition to military conflict since it is being paired with a chapter on Just War Theory. It does not consider other wide-ranging concerns for flourishing human lives shared by many pacifists.

Aristotle suggests we teach by half-truths. So, I will proceed with an oversimplification. There are at least four basic approaches to war—*militarism* (a belliciste or warmonger, the pursuit of power by means of war), *Just War Theory* (trying to keep any obligatory warfare within just boundaries), and *pacifism* (opposition to all war and the use of violence). Each of these first three basic stances has many gradations and variations. A fourth view, *moral realism* about war, sees war as a terrible but unavoidable alternative in a morally complex world ("War is hell!"). Moral realists oppose militarism, flatly deny that war and justice are compatible, yet also reject pacifism as a response to militarism.[7]

It is beyond the scope of this essay to describe, to explain, or to defend all the major forms of pacifism, still less to speak to all the possible perils from militarism or to respond to all the thoughtful arguments from Just War theorists or moral realists. Nor do I propose to account for the inconsistencies of people who claim to hold one position or another but fail to live up to their stances. Very few persons—none in my experience—are wholly consistent in all they say and do.

The most consistent pacifists tend to come from religious communities, often because they view all human life as in some sense sacred, whether Hindus, Jains, Buddhists, Christians,[8] Bahai, or the like. No religious body on the continent of Europe had a higher percentage of consistent pacifists during the Second World War than the Jehovah's Witnesses, and many died in Nazi concentration camps for their convictions.[9] But one need not be religious to be a pacifist, and some very ardent pacifists have been secular atheists or agnostics, though still deeply committed to the inherent dignity and value of human life, as well as opposed to the follies of warfare.

Nor is adherence to a particular religion a guarantee that one will be a pacifist. Mahatma Gandhi suffered repeatedly at the hands of nominal Christians during his nonviolent campaigns against British colonialism and was ultimately killed by a *fellow Hindu* for his attempt to deal fairly and justly with Muslims. Peacemaking, Jesus warned his followers in the Beatitudes, may lead to persecution. Muhammad Anwar el-Sadat (Egyptian president, *killed by militant Muslims*) and Yitzhak Rabin (Israeli prime minister, *killed by a rabidly conservative Jew*) are just a few in a long line of public leaders who have been assassinated for their efforts to bring peace. Notice that the opposition to peacemaking may come from within the same broader ethnic or religious community that gave rise to it, and coreligionists may become the assassins.

Some religious movements have, at least at times, even promoted violence. Islamic Jihad (in its more extreme literal forms) and the Christian Crusades come to mind. Sometimes religious impulses intermingle with nationalistic or other more secular ones that lead to deadly warfare. Examples might be the Papal Doctrine of Discovery or Protestant notions of Manifest Destiny that underlay brutal campaigns against Indigenous or tribal peoples.[10] Even the "Little House" children's book series repeats the hideous cliché, "The only good Indian is a dead Indian."

In what follows, we will explore four things that characterize many pacifists, whatever their specific motivations to pacifism. They are daring imaginations, strong moral convictions, the willingness to face facts, and the courage to fail.

Daring Imaginations

It makes all the difference how we see the world (our "worldview"), what kinds of social imaginations we have (our "social imaginaries"). For example, the United States currently experiences over 40,000 gun deaths a year (the simple majority are suicides). The people of contemporary Japan generally consider it a bad year if there are as many as a *dozen* gun deaths in a year. Since private gun ownership is legal in Japan, though bounded by rigorous requirements and restrictions, what is it in respective Japanese and US cultures that would account for such vastly different outcomes with respect to gun deaths? Is it just different degrees and measures of gun control? Less than a century ago, Japan was a militaristic society that lauded its violent warriors.[11] What has changed? Why do Canadians own more guns per capita than do US citizens yet experience significantly fewer gun deaths per capita than the United States?

When many of the headhunting, cannibalistic Sawi (Indonesia), or the head-*shrinking* Shuar and Achuar (Ecuador), or the terrifying Yanomami (Brazil and Venezuela), or the deadly Huaorani/Waodani (Ecuador) made dramatic changes from tribal cultures centered on violence to embrace radically new lifestyles promoting peace, what profound transformations occurred in their social imaginaries that allowed them to abandon untold generations of vicious warfare and revenge killings?[12]

Radical shifts in values and worldview may come about because of religious conversions, as has happened with some of the tribal peoples just named above. Or they may come from revulsion against the horrors of warfare, as apparently happened with the ancient military leader, King Ashoka the Cruel (*c.* 304–232 BCE)—among the first of many warriors down through history to turn from violence—regretting his own former savagery on the battlefield.[13]

One need not be a Christian (King Ashoka became a Buddhist), nor even particularly religious, however, to become an ardent pacifist or to see through the false claims that the latest conflict is "necessary." Lord Bertrand Russell, the Nobel Prize-winning, sexually profligate, self-proclaimed atheist, wrote against Great Britain's participation in the First World War, suffering the loss of an academic post at Trinity College, Cambridge, as well as spending time in prison for doing so. He was labeled a traitor when he infamously argued that it would be better for England to surrender unilaterally to Germany and suffer the humiliation of defeat and occupation than to see millions of lives needlessly destroyed in the horrific quagmire of trench warfare. He was convinced English culture would prevail in the end, though enriched by the German language and *Kultur*, just as the English culture had previously survived despite the Norman Conquest and the imposition of French rule. English life today is better for its having absorbed infusions from the French language and customs, without being swallowed up by them in the long run.[14]

British leaders could not tolerate Russell, a world-class logician, mathematician, and philosopher, because his *imagination* was too threatening to them. They didn't want people in Great Britain to even *imagine* that surrender to the Germans, with all its dire consequences, might still be a far better course of action than continuing the grim slaughter of millions.

People who see war as inevitable, or even as obligatory, fail to *imagine* that there are other, better alternatives. They cannot *imagine* a United States without its vast array of armed forces or the "special operations" of the CIA. When President José Figueres Ferrer disbanded the army of Costa Rica on December 1, 1948, some derided his action as suicidal. But his vision of directing national resources toward domestic needs rather than to the military has led to interesting results. Costa Rica is generally among the wealthier (per capita) and is the most peaceful and stable country in Latin America. Meanwhile, its heavily militarized neighbors have seen tens or even hundreds of thousands of their citizens killed by recurring armed violence, often with the complicity of the very forces that are purportedly there to protect them. Several nearby countries now lead the world in per capita gun deaths and do so by wide margins.

Who would have *imagined* that some of the most profound social and political changes in the twentieth century would come about through persistent but nonviolent protests led by persons such as Mahatma Gandhi or The Rev. Dr. Martin Luther King, Jr.? James Billington, former Librarian of Congress, vividly describes the nonviolent protests and religious prayers of the *babushkas* (Russian grandmothers) that led directly to the fall of the Soviet Regime in Moscow.[15] The twenty-first century dawned with the courageous Women of Liberia Mass Action for Peace, who brought Christian and Muslim women together to halt a bloody civil war.[16] There is now an impressive catalog of negotiations and nonviolent protests that have ended colonial rule, slavery, long-standing dictatorships, economic oppression, civil wars, and other evils in various locales around the globe.[17] But most responses to violence are violent because people and their leaders cannot *imagine* anything otherwise. They cannot *imagine* concerted, calculated, courageous, yet deliberately peaceful responses to violence, nor that such daring, risk-filled actions might prove more successful in sparing lives and civilized society than violent ones.

Another failure of imagination is our inability to conceive of justice as anything other than some form of fairness or equality. While there are various accounts of justice going back to the ancient Greeks, most that do not root "justice" in raw political power assume that fairness is at the core of justice. People with very different opinions about justice—whether referencing retributive, distributive, commutative, or restorative justice—are frequently just arguing about what is most fair, what would make things equal, what would restore balance. The most common symbol of justice in our society is of a blindfolded woman holding a perfectly balanced pair of scales.

Jesus and the teachings of the Bible suggest that there is yet another, more important kind of justice, one that is decidedly *un*fair and *un*balanced, because it tilts radically toward mercy and grace, granting people goodness and forgiveness they do NOT deserve. That is why Jesus can tell his followers to love and forgive their enemies.

For example, what would the term "just war" mean if justice were defined the way Jesus defines justice (δικαιοσύνη) in the Sermon on the Mount?[18]

Strong Moral Convictions

Pacifists give many reasons to oppose warfare. They include environmental degradation, economic catastrophes, chaotic upheavals, massive migrations, cultural annihilation, enduring hatreds, and a myriad more terrible consequences of war. There is an old saying, "War is like fire. You cannot 'win' a fire because fire is destruction."

The main reason many pacifists oppose war, however, is because war kills so many people, the vast majority of whom are wholly innocent with respect to the war. The First World War veteran Henry John "Harry" Patch (1898–2009), who became a legend as Britain's "Last Fighting Tommy," also became an ardent pacifist who famously said, "War is organized murder and nothing else." Pacifists frequently hold to one or more of the following three moral convictions about killing human beings. They reflect three common approaches to morality: deontological (rule-driven), consequentialist (often utilitarian), and virtue ethics (focus on character).

1. Killing human beings, especially innocent human beings, is inherently wrong. There are moral rules against killing innocent human beings in all major cultures. Pacifists reject the claim that wars provide an adequate moral exception to allow for killing.

2. Attempts to stop killing by killing in warfare inevitably make matters worse, if only because so many persons killed in wars are innocent women and children. Even if most persons killed in warfare were soldiers in uniform, which is almost never the case, most soldiers in most armies are conscripted against their will, sometimes at pain of death. (The contemporary US volunteer army is something of a historical anomaly.) So not only is killing morally wrong, but the number of killings committed is compounded by warfare, worsening the consequences.

3. Killing other human beings changes the killer profoundly. Potentially virtuous persons become profoundly vicious. Persons who realize what they have done and how they have changed frequently wrestle with mental and moral anguish the rest of their lives, if they don't commit suicide, which an increasingly high percentage now do.

Pacifists generally agree that they should not kill human beings. Many, including Bertrand Russell, have called for the love of enemies too. What we now know about forms of military training necessary to prepare soldiers to kill consistently and efficiently in warfare does not mesh well with such values. David Grossman, a foremost US Army psychologist (self-described "killologist") and former Army Ranger, delineates the way military recruits are now trained to kill. The recruits are, among other matters:

(1) deliberately brutalized and desensitized, (2) conditioned to violence itself, (3) further conditioned to respond reflexively with deadly violence, and (4) subjected to violent role models—all to overcome their strong, natural aversion to killing other human beings.[19] Here is a patriotic young man from Colorado named Kevin describing his initiation to West Point.

> I was whisked into a world of chaos and violence unofficially known as "beast barracks." I expected the shouting, the physical punishment, the psychological gamesmanship. What I did not expect, however, was the immediate, constant, and gratuitous emphasis on rape, human mutilation, and death. I will never forget the horror I felt as I stood in a dark hall, watching video images of killing while fourteen hundred other recruits, heads freshly shaved and wearing grey, shouted "kill, kill, kill" to the beat of hard-rock music. I was trained to be a killer. Soon I would be capable of ripping the enemy's heart out of his chest and eating it because I was ordered to do so.[20]

It is not easy to train reliable killers who retain their humanity.

A pattern of more US military deaths by suicide after the war than were killed in combat itself began with the Korean War. Over four times as many veterans of the US "Global War on Terror" have committed suicide after their return from service than died in battle. This is an astounding percentage. There are presumably many reasons for the depressive states that lead to suicide among former soldiers, including Post-traumatic Stress Disorder (PTSD) and Traumatic Brain Injury (TBI), but there is now a growing awareness that veterans may also have difficulty coping with the moral damage done to them. As soldiers realize that their naïve, well-intentioned attempts to defend their country and fight in a "just war" led instead to ruthless moral perversities, memories of those deeds overwhelm them with a psychologically destabilizing guilt.[21]

There is also a lack of moral seriousness in the contemporary military ethos that belies the claim of respect for human lives. There is very little in the embedded military practices to indicate how serious taking the life of an enemy soldier or an innocent civilian is, as compared to mourning the death of a comrade in arms. Following the Battle of Hastings, knights were expected to do a year of penance for each person they killed.[22] As we move from hand-to-hand combat toward technologies that offer faceless, nameless killings at a distance, there is very little to underscore the humanity of the deceased. While the trauma and suicides of returning veterans are well documented, the moral gravity of their deeds when killing others is mostly ignored.

The Willingness to Face the Facts

One of the commonest criticisms of pacifism is that pacifists are hopelessly unrealistic. On the contrary, the suggestion here is that it is pacifists who face the brutal facts of war and therefore reject participation in warfare as morally wrong.[23]

Those who suffer and die in war are rarely the culprits who provide the "justifying cause" for warfare. No Iraqis were among the twenty-six terrorists who carried out the attacks on 9/11, but the United States invaded Iraq as part of its larger "Global War on Terror." Hundreds of thousands of Iraqis died. Far more were wounded or had their lives upended permanently. Neither were any of the 9/11 terrorists from Afghanistan. But the United States invaded Afghanistan with even more devastating results; still more civilians were killed. This is the norm in war, not the exception. Colossal "collateral damage" (the killing of innocents) is the rule. How many of the over 50,000,000 who died in the Second World War caused the war or were responsible for it? Retribution is presumably the lowest form of justice. Some moral theorists challenge whether retribution is ever just. But even if retributive justice is thoroughly moral, war does not produce just retribution. It is far too indiscriminate. Human warfare is by nature unjust.

Fierce armed resistance to overwhelming evil is not necessarily more effective in saving innocent lives than determined nonviolent resistance. Consider the following case study, contrasting Denmark and Greece during the Second World War. The German military invaded and overran Denmark on April 9, 1940. The Danish government, which had tried to remain neutral in the first year of the war, surrendered in a matter of hours. Nevertheless, when the Nazis later tried to round up Jews for deportation to death camps, Danes worked swiftly to save Jews by hiding them or smuggling them out of the country. While 102 Danish Jews died in the *Shoah*, they were by far the fewest Jewish deaths of any Nazi-occupied country in Europe. Far less than in tiny Luxembourg. By some estimates, over 97 percent of Danish Jews survived.[24]

By way of contrast, Greece, another relatively small, poorly armed country, fought fiercely, first against the Italian Fascists, whom they thwarted against all odds, and then against the German Nazis, who overpowered them. Greeks suffered over 400,000 casualties during the Second World War. But their sacrifices neither spared their nation from German occupation nor saved the Greek Jews targeted by the Nazis for elimination. Somewhere between 84 and 87 percent of Greek Jews died in the Holocaust, one of the highest percentages in Europe.

Building up a military for purely "defensive" purposes greatly increases the odds that it will sometimes be used for other purposes. When trillions of dollars are invested in military infrastructure, when a single country maintains 800 or more military bases overseas in the name of "national defense," then the repeated temptations to employ such extensive military capabilities are likely to override both common sense and the strict stipulations of Just War Theory, which requires a just cause for going to war (and then as a last resort), just means in the conduct of war (sparing innocent lives), and just consequences (avoiding undue retribution and helping rebuild society).[25] Militarism and moral realism become the de facto modes of operation, whatever the initial or stated intentions in creating a massive military-industrial-political complex.[26] Today, it is also a military-industrial-entertainment complex, with simulated warfare in video games preparing young teens for the military.[27] Where are the pacifist games?

Most of the goods that are claimed as reasons for participating in wars have, in fact, been achieved in other contexts by nonviolent means. The twentieth century may have been a century of unprecedented warfare, but it was also a century in which there were unprecedented achievements by nonviolent means.[28]

It is possible for communities committed to peace to live peaceably over the centuries, refusing to participate in warfare. Some Christian communities have been marked by pacifism since their inception. Hutterites, for example, who have lived in communities where material goods are held in common since the time of the Reformation, have an extraordinary history of consistent pacifism. Two Hutterites were killed in the United States during the First World War, when they were forcibly conscripted but refused to wear military uniforms.[29] Other Hutterites still refused to don uniforms or fight.[30] The French village of Le Chambon quietly, effectively, defied the Holocaust.[31] Persons who are pacifists, not just in theory or in their imaginaries, but in their daily lifestyles, are the ones most likely to consistently live out their pacifist commitments.[32] They exhibit the courage and other qualities that are frequently labeled "martial virtues," as if they were restricted to soldiers.

It is also possible for persons who have committed unspeakably violent atrocities to confess their deeds, to face victims whom they have so badly abused, and to recognize the horrible truths about their own brutality and its consequences. There are multiple emerging strategies not just to avoid war or to live in peace, but to bring healing and restoration to deeply aggrieved and divided peoples through "Truth Commissions" and other forms of transitional justice.[33] There is also now a growing catalog of moving stories about gracious forgiveness, reconciliation, and hope that defy ordinary human expectations.[34]

Conclusion: The Courage to Fail

Assume for the moment that consistent pacifists still experience "failures," even when their recommendations are properly implemented. Jesus warned long ago in the Sermon on the Mount, where he calls his followers to love their enemies, that peacemakers would be persecuted for their just lives. Notable peacemakers have frequently been assassinated. Thousands of ordinary people down through history have been imprisoned, tortured, and died rather than take up the sword.[35]

Are the "successes" of warfare any better than the "failures" of pacifism? What counts as a "success" or "failure" probably turns more on one's worldview and moral values than on just counting how many people died or whether a war was "won" or lost by this means or that. In the end, warriors are willing to kill to achieve their goals (even if their stated goal is the apparently noble one of stopping the unjust killings done by others), while pacifists are not.

Notes

1. See, e.g., Bertrand Russell, *Common Sense and Nuclear Warfare* (New York: Simon & Schuster, 1959), and Bertrand Russell, *Bertrand Russell Speaks His Mind*, with Woodrow Wyatt, interviewer (Cleveland: The World Publishing Co., 1960), 151–62.

2. See John Howard Yoder, *Nevertheless: The Varieties and Shortcomings of Religious Pacifism*, 2nd ed. (Scottdale: Herald Press, 1992); David C. Cramer and Myles Werntz, *A Field Guide to Christian Nonviolence: Key Thinkers, Activists, and Movements for the Gospel of Peace* (Grand Rapids: Baker Academic, 2022).

3. See, e.g., G. E. M. (Gertrude Elizabeth Margaret) Anscombe, *Mr. Truman's Degree* (Oxford: by the author, 1958), pamphlet.

4. Larry May, *Contingent Pacifism: Revisiting Just War Theory* (Cambridge: Cambridge University Press, 2015); cf. Jenny Teichman, in *Pacifism and the Just War: A Study in Applied Philosophy* (Oxford: Blackwell, 1986); James Sterba, "Reconciling Pacifists and Just War Theorists," *Social Theory and Practice* 18, no. 1 (Spring 1992): 21–38; John Howard Yoder, *When War Is Unjust: Being Honest in Just-War Thinking*, 2nd ed. (Maryknoll: Orbis Books, 1996).

5. Colman McCarthy, *I'd Rather Teach Peace* (Maryknoll: Orbis Books, 2002), viii.

6. See "What's Killing Us?" *Mission Frontiers* [theme issue: "Making a Killing"] (September/October 2019), 12–17, pdf posted September 1, 2019 (https://www.missionfrontiers.org/pdfs/MF41-5_WEB_p_12-17.pdf, accessed January 5, 2024); and "Gendercide" [theme issue], *Mission Frontiers* (September–October 2017), 1–34, pdf posted September 1, 2017 (https://www.missionfrontiers.org/issue/archive/gendercide, accessed January 15, 2024). The first eight of eleven pieces in the issue deal with gendercide, especially as practiced in China and India.

    The figures in the above articles come from a variety of internationally recognized databases. The exact numbers obviously vary from year to year, but the general figures given in the text of this chapter are reasonable approximations for recent years.

7. Seth Lazar, "War," in *The Stanford Encyclopedia of Philosophy* (Spring 2020 Edition), ed. Edward N. Zalta (https://plato.stanford.edu/archives/spr2020/entries/war/, accessed January 5, 2024); and Alexander Moseley, "Just War Theory," in *The Internet Encyclopedia of Philosophy* (https://iep.utm.edu/justwar/, accessed January 5, 2024). The editorial policy of the *Internet Encyclopedia of Philosophy* is to not give the dates the articles were posted, but references in the article suggest sometime during or after 2007.

8. Cf. Willard M. Swartley, *Covenant of Peace: The Missing Piece in New Testament Theology and Ethics* (Grand Rapids: William B. Eerdmans Publishing Co., 2006), and John D. Roth, *Choosing against War: A Christian View: "Love Is Stronger Than Our Fears"* (Intercourse: Good Books, 2002).

9. For a fuller discussion of global pacifism in the first half of the twentieth century, see Timothy Paul Erdel, "Pacifism and Non-violent Resistance," in *The History of Evil in the Early Twentieth Century: 1900–1950 CE*, ed. Victoria S. Harrison, Chad Meister, and Charles Taliaferro, vol. 5 of *The History of Evil*, series ed. Chad Meister and Charles Taliaferro, 6 vols. (London: Routledge, 2017), 5:163–83.

10   See, e.g., Mark Charles and Soong-Chan Rah, *Unsettling Truths: The Ongoing, Dehumanizing Legacy of the Doctrine of Discovery* (Downers Grove: InterVarsity Press, 2019). Cf. Jonathan Lear, *Radical Hope: Ethics in the Face of Cultural Devastation* (Cambridge, MA: Harvard University Press, 2006).

11   Bryan Mark Rigg, *Japan's Holocaust: History of Imperial Japan's Mass Murder and Rape during World War II*, with a Foreword by Andrew Roberts (New York and Nashville: Knox Press, Simon & Schuster, 2024).

12   Don Richardson, *Peace Child*, 4th ed. (Ventura: Regal Books, 2005); Frank Drown and Marie Drown, *Mission to the Headhunters: How God's Forgiveness Transformed Tribal Enemies*, 2nd ed. (Fearn, Scotland: Christian Focus Publications, 2002); Mark A. Ritchie, *Spirit of the Rainforest: A Yanomamö Shaman's Story*, 2nd ed. (Chicago: Island Lake Press, 2000); and Kathryn T. Long, *God in the Rainforest: A Tale of Martyrdom and Redemption in Amazonian Ecuador* (New York: Oxford University Press, 2019). Cf. Timothy Paul Erdel, "The Great Commission and God's Righteous Kingdom," *Mission Focus: Annual Review* 16 (2008): 93–115.

13   Cf. Patrick Olivelle, *Ashoka: Portrait of a Philosopher King* (New Haven: Yale University Press, 2023).

14   Bertrand Russell, *Justice in War-Time* (Chicago: The Open Court Publishing Co., 1916), 40–50. For a more extended analysis of Russell on war, see Timothy Paul Erdel, "Where Russell Was Right and Lewis Was Wrong on War," paper presented at the Evangelical Philosophical Society Annual Meeting, San Antonio, Texas, November 15, 2023, printout (photocopied), available from the author or through The Marion E. Wade Center, Wheaton College, Wheaton, IL.

15   James Billington, "The Religious Dimension of Post-Modern Change," in *Summary of Proceedings: Fifty-second Annual Conference of the American Theological Library Association*, ed. Margret Tacke (Evanston: ATLA, 1998), 149–58.

16   See the 2008 documentary film, *Pray the Devil Back to Hell*, dir. Gini Reticker and produced by Abigail Disney.

17   E.g., see Erica Chenoweth and Maria J. Stephan, *Why Civil Resistance Works: The Strategic Logic of Nonviolent Conflict* (New York: Columbia University Press, 2011).

18   See Timothy Paul Erdel, "Four or More Forms of Biblical Justice," *Africanus Journal* 16, no. 1 (April 2024): 9–24; cf. Timothy Paul Erdel, "Holiness among the Mennonites," *Reflections* [theme issue: "An Anabaptist-Holiness Synthesis"] 10, no. 1–2 (Spring and Fall 2008): 5–42.

19   See David Grossman, *On Killing: The Psychological Cost of Learning to Kill in War and Society*, rev. and updated ed. (New York: Back Bay Books, 2009).

20   See McCarthy, *Teach Peace*, 66.

21   See Robert Emmet Meagher, *Killing from the Inside Out: Moral Injury and Just War*, with a Foreword by Stanley Hauerwas and an Afterword by Jonathan Shay (Eugene: Cascade Books, 2014), and Nancy Sherman, *Afterwar: Healing the Moral Wounds of Our Soldiers* (New York: Oxford University Press, 2015); cf. Phil Klay, *Uncertain Ground: Citizenship in an Age of Endless Invisible War* (New York: Penguin Press, 2022), and Phil Klay, *Redeployment* (New York: The Penguin Press, 2014).

22   See Bernard J. Verkamp, "Moral Treatment of Returning Warriors in the Early Middle Ages," *Journal of Religious Ethics* 16, no. 2 (Fall 1988): 223–49, see especially 224–5.

23 Cf. Chris Hedges, *What Every Person Should Know about War* (New York: Free Press, 2003).

24 See Chris Webb, with the Holocaust Education & Archive Research Team, "The Fate of the Jews of Denmark," *Holocaust Research Project* (https://web.archive.org/web/20080513043200/http://www.holocaustresearchproject.net/nazioccupation/danishjews.html, accessed January 15, 2024).

25 For some basic works on Just War Theory that grapple seriously with both its strengths and limitations, see David Rodin, *War and Self-Defense* (Oxford: Oxford University Press, 2002); Oliver O'Donovan, *The Just War Revisited*, Current Issues in Theology, gen. ed., Iain Torrance, vol. 2 (Cambridge: Cambridge University Press, 2003); and Mark Evans, ed., *Just War Theory: A Reappraisal* (Edinburgh: Edinburgh University Press; New York: Palgrave Macmillan, 2005). See also the sources in note 4 above. For my own reservations about Just War Theory, see Timothy Paul Erdel, "Is 'Just War' Still an Oxymoron?" *Criswell Theological Review*, n.s. 4, no. 2 (Spring 2007): 53–76.

26 President Dwight David Eisenhower warned the American people about the dangers of a "military-industrial complex." See the "Farewell Address by President Dwight D. Eisenhower, January 17, 1961," Final TV Talk 1/17/61 (1), Box 38, Speech Series, Papers of Dwight D. Eisenhower as President, 1953–61, Eisenhower Library, National Archives and Records Administration. An earlier draft apparently used the phrase, "military-industrial-political complex," but advisors convinced Eisenhower to remove the warning about the "political" dimension (US Congress).

27 See, e.g., Rosa Schwartzburg, "The US Military Is Embedded in the Gaming World: Its Target: Teen Recruits," *The Guardian* (February 14, 2024) (https://www.theguardian.com/us-news/2024/feb/14/us-military-recruiting-video-games-targeting-teenagers, accessed February 25, 2024); and Judy Woodruff with John Yang, Henry Brannan, Maea Lenei Buhre, and Dan Sagalyn, "US Focuses Recruiting Efforts on Video Playing Teenagers" [transcript and audio], *PBS News Hour* (September 1, 2022) (https://www.pbs.org/newshour/show/u-s-military-focuses-recruiting-efforts-on-video-game-playing-teenagers, accessed February 25, 2024).

28 See, e.g., the preliminary list (by decade via hyperlinks) "Peace Events of the 20th and 21st Centuries," Global Peacebuilding Center, United States Institute of Peace (https://www.usip.org/sites/default/files/2017-01/Peace%20Events%20of%20the%2020th%20and%2021st%20Centuries.pdf, accessed February 24, 2024). Cf. Peter Ackerman and Jack Duvall, *A Force More Powerful: A Century of Nonviolent Conflict* (New York: St. Martin's Press, 2000), and the companion PBS documentary series from 2000, *A Force More Powerful*, dir. Steve York (available free online at multiple sites).

29 See Duane C. S. Stoltzfus, "Armed with Prayer in Alcatraz Dungeon: The Wartime Experiences of Four Hutterite C.O.s in Their Own Words," *Mennonite Quarterly Review* 85 (April 2011): 259–92; and Duane C. S. Stoltzfus, *Pacifists in Chains: The Persecution of Hutterites During the Great War*, Young Center Books in Anabaptist & Pietist Studies, series ed. Donald B. Kraybill (Baltimore: The Johns Hopkins University Press, 2013).

30 The United States was far less punitive than some European countries during the First World War, but it still sentenced seventeen conscientious objectors to death and 142 more to life in prison—though all the sentences were ultimately commuted after

the war. See Peter Brock and Nigel Young, *Pacifism in the Twentieth Century*, 2nd ed. (Syracuse: Syracuse University Press with the University of Toronto Press, 1999), 57.

31 Philip P. Hallie, *Lest Innocent Blood Be Shed: The Story of the Village of Le Chambon and How Goodness Happened There* (New York: HarperCollins, 1994); cf. André Trocmé, *Jesus and the Nonviolent Revolution*, ed. Charles E. Moore, 2nd ed. (Walden: Plough, 2003).

32 Cf., e.g., Donald B. Kraybill, Steven M. Nolt, and David Weaver Zercher, *Amish Grace: How Forgiveness Transcended Tragedy* (San Francisco: Jossey-Bass, 2007).

33 On the basic elements of transitional justice, see "What Is Transitional Justice?" in *ICTJ: Justice, Truth, Dignity* [web site] (New York: International Center for Transitional Justice, 2021) (https://www.ictj.org/about/transitional-justice, accessed June 23, 2021), and "United Nations and the Rule of Law: Transitional Justice" (The United Nations, 2021) (https://un.org/ruleoflaw/thematic-areas/international-laws-courts-tribunals/transitional-justice/, accessed June 23, 2021).

34 There are stories of incredible forgiveness and grace from Rwanda, from South Africa, from the Amish at West Nickel Mines School in Pennsylvania, or from the Black parishioners' response to Dylann Roof, following his willful, unrepentant shooting and killing of nine persons ("the Emanuel Nine") at prayer at "Mother" Emanuel African Methodist Episcopal Church in Charleston, South Carolina, and more; but space does not allow us to document them all here. Or consider the case of Ruby Bridges during the Civil Rights movement, see Robert Coles, "The Inexplicable Prayers of Ruby Bridges: A Harvard Psychiatrist Is Mystified by a Six-Year-Old's Faith," *Christianity Today* 29, no. 11 (August 9, 1985): 17–20; and Robert Coles, *The Spiritual Life of Children*, The Inner Lives of Children, vol. 3 (Boston: Houghton Mifflin Co., 1990), or the courage and grace shown by certain Allied prisoners of war in the Valley of the River Kwai during the Second World War, who were determined to respond to their Japanese captors (and the Korean guards they employed) with the love of Jesus Christ as taught in the Sermon on the Mount (see Ernest Gordon, *Through the Valley of the Kwai* [New York: Harper & Bros., 1962]). Ultimately, these examples of extraordinary forgiveness and the love of one's enemies reflect the spirit of Jesus at his crucifixion ("Father, forgive them, for they do not know what they are doing"—*Luke* 23:34a) and of the martyr Stephen at his stoning ("Lord, do not hold this sin against them"—*Acts* 7:60).

I do not mean, by this focus on utterly gracious, preemptive forgiveness, to undercut the need for genuine repentance, including reparations. William J. Abraham (1947–2021) makes a good case that the failure to expect true repentance, including reparations, may cheapen and undercut the meaning of forgiveness and grace. See William J. Abraham, *Shaking Hands with the Devil: The Intersection of Terrorism and Theology* (Dallas: Highland Loch Press, 2013), 150. I last spoke with Billy on August 11, 2015.

35 Cf., e.g., Thieleman J. van Braght, *The Bloody Theater or the Martyrs Mirror of Defenseless Christians: Who Baptized Only upon Confession of Faith, and Who Suffered and Died for the Testimony of Jesus, Their Saviour, from the Time of Christ to the Year A.D. 1660: Compiled from Various Authentic Chronicles, Memorials, and Testimonies*, trans. Joseph F. Sohm, 2nd English ed. (Scottdale: Herald Press, [1660] 1950).

Responses

Response to Cowan on War and Peace

Timothy Paul Erdel

Study Questions

1. What is the "one overriding problem" Erdel sees in Cowan's defense of just war?
2. What two additional worries does Erdel have with the Just War Theory?
3. Why does Erdel think that the pacifist option is not as "hopelessly idealistic" as the Just War Theory?

There is much to commend in Steven Cowan's essay, "War Can Be Morally Justified." He recognizes that "war is a terrible and tragic evil." He believes, with good reasons, that persons possess natural rights. He thinks that it is the duty of good governments to secure and uphold those rights, especially what is presumably the most basic right, the right to life. He asserts that to do so may require force, even deadly force, especially when citizens are threatened by unjust foreign aggressors.[1]

Cowan would not rush to war. War is terrible. He would only do so under strict conditions that guarantee justice. (1) The war has a just cause. (2) The war is conducted by just means. (3) The war will bring just results. There are subsidiary rules to these three main ones, to make sure persons going to war are not deceived, but that the war they engage in is a truly just one.

Justice is a primary consideration in virtually all ethical discussions, and it is central to the teachings of the world's great religions. I contend that Christianity places a unique emphasis on justice, but if someone disagrees and says other religions or worldviews are more concerned about justice, that still underscores, prima facie, the importance of justice.[2] So, the emphasis on justice in war is a good one.

The basic question seems to be, "Can war be morally justified, that is, can a war motivated by a just cause be fought in a manner that both maintains and ultimately brings about genuine justice?" Sadly, I think not. There are many reasons why this is so. I once tried to articulate fourteen objections to the notion of a Just War in a public debate.[3] In this response, I want to focus on one overriding problem, given the case that Cowan has made, then suggest a few further reservations concerning his argument.

Killing More Innocent People

If the motivating purpose of war is to preserve innocent human lives in the name of justice, then there is an immediate conundrum. The long, sorry history of warfare teaches us just the opposite. Wars *inevitably* compound the loss of innocent human lives and generally do so exponentially. So, the justification for fighting a "just war" is undermined by the fact that what happens is just the opposite of what the stated purpose is for fighting that war: preserving innocent lives.

Note an important distinction between *necessity* and *inevitability*. If I am an excellent free throw shooter, it is not *necessary* that I miss any given free throw. But I will *inevitably* miss at some point. It may be that in some possible world, killing innocent people in a war is not a logical, moral, or material necessity. But in the whole of human history, I know of no conflict large enough to qualify as a war in which innocent persons did not die, usually civilians, often women and children. It is not uncommon for the number of innocent civilians who die to exceed the number of soldiers killed. But even if far more soldiers die than civilians, it is not always clear that the soldiers have done anything that deserves their deaths, either, other than put on a uniform. Many soldiers in most wars are conscripts, often against their will. As the saying goes, soldiers have mothers too. Even if killing innocent people were not necessary to the conduct of war, it seems to be the inevitable result of warfare.

I am not talking about the deliberate, mass killings of civilians, such as the ruthless slaughter of Chinese by the Japanese in what is known as "The Rape of Nanking," nor the Nazi attempts to exterminate Jews and other "undesirables," nor the deliberate firebombing of German and Japanese cities by the Allies toward the end of the Second World War,[4] nor the dropping of nuclear bombs on Hiroshima and Nagasaki, none of which would be allowed by strict adherence to standard rules for a just war. Targeting innocent civilians is evil. Rather, even when great care is taken to avoid civilian casualties, civilians become the unintended victims of violence. On November 15, 2006, when James Turner Johnson, the widely published Just War theorist, pointed out to me that the United States and its allies were trying to minimize civilian casualties during the war in Iraq by their employment of so-called "smart weapons," I immediately reminded him that those civilian casualties had already exceeded 100,000, drawing on figures just published in the *Lancet*.[5] That is just the nature of warfare, however well intentioned.

Additional Worries

I have another, more amorphous worry about Cowan's argument. Sometimes formal arguments fail because the universe is complicated. Untold generations of geometry students learned that no triangle could have more than one right angle. Euclidean geometry provides an absolute proof that this is so. But the real world is not restricted by the axioms and proofs of Euclidean geometry. The realization that there are triangles with three right angles helped make spaceflight possible. If wars were fought in tiny, well-ordered universes with fixed variables, then we might be able to control them and ensure that justice prevails from start to finish (and beyond). But wars are not board or video games, however elaborate. Wars are endlessly messy and complex, and it is their nature that we can neither control all the variables at work nor predict all the consequences of our actions. By their very nature, wars do not fit the neat rules set out by well-meaning Just War theorists. If only wars were as tidy as the narrow confines of Euclidean geometry or of war games, then I might find the arguments in favor of Just War Theory more persuasive. But wars rapidly burst any such boundaries. Again, that is their nature.

I have a related worry, also pragmatic. It is not just the obvious and frequent one where politicians invoke the notion of a "just war" when the war in view actually fails multiple criteria for a just war. Rather, my concern is that once well-motivated persons engage in warfare, however just the initial cause and however sincere their desire to maintain Just War standards, human limitations (even apart from temptations to deviate from strict Just War criteria) mean that even the best of efforts will not suffice to maintain the requirements of a just war to the very end.

Conclusion

Nevertheless, I want to salute Cowan for defending Just War Theory. If a war ever did stay within the tight boundaries of Just War Theory, I suspect the result would approach a form of limited pacifism.

The pacifist option might seem at first glance to be even more hopelessly idealistic than Just War Theory. But honest pacifists hold no illusions about what their position entails. It may well lead to tragic misunderstandings, to endless mockery, to severe penalties, to harsh punishments, to open persecution, or even to martyrdom. But the refusal to use deadly force means pacifists do not add to the killings; they have even, in some cases, thereby stopped the cycle of killings. Pacifists have also, in a surprising number of instances, been able to thwart large-scale threats of violence or to enact social changes that many others wrongly assumed could only have been achieved through violence. But the "successes" of pacifism over the past century or more are stories for another time.

Notes

1 There seems to be a "worst case scenario" implicit assumption in this point about unjust foreign aggression, as if defeat would inevitably lead to genocidal massacres or the loss of all natural (or political) rights. To the contrary, immediate surrender might

lessen or stop further killings; moreover, as Bertrand Russell noted, in some historical cases, conquest by foreigners has even improved the lives of local citizens.

2 Cf. Timothy Paul Erdel, "Four or More Forms of Biblical Justice," *Africanus Journal* 16, no. 1 (April 2024): 9–24.

3 Timothy Paul Erdel, "Is Just War Still an Oxymoron?" *Criswell Theological Review*, n.s., 4, no. 2 (Spring 2007): 53–76.

4 The Allies even *deliberately dropped bombs on hundreds of thousands of innocent French civilian allies*, doing so for "strategic" reasons that later proved misguided! Well over 60,000 died. See, e.g., Henri Amouroux, *La Grande Histoire des Français sous l' Occupation*, 10 vols. (Paris: R. Laffont, 1976–93), passim.

5 The total number of "excess deaths" in Iraq during the period leading up to October 2006 may have surpassed 900,000 according to the article I was referencing, but I was trying to use lower numbers that would not be controversial yet would still make my point. Prof. Johnson did not challenge my claim. (Cf. L. Roberts, R. Laña, R. Garfield, J. Khudhairi, and G. Burnham, "Mortality before and after the 2003 Invasion of Iraq: Cluster Sample Survey," *The Lancet* 364, no. 9448 [2006]: 1857–64.) Much back-and-forth debate about the validity of the methods employed and the reliability of the reported results ensued upon the publication of this article, but I still think the very low-end-of-the-scale figures I used in countering Prof. Johnson are readily justified.

Response to Erdel on War and Peace

Steven B. Cowan

Study Questions

1. How does Cowan respond to Erdel's charge that non-pacifists have a lack of imagination?
2. Why does Cowan think that Erdel's three moral convictions are, at best, only generalizations?
3. How does Cowan address Erdel's concerns about the deaths of noncombatants in war?
4. What evidence does Cowan offer for his claim that Jesus was not a pacifist?

Timothy Erdel offers a strong and appealing case for pacifism. He rightly underscores the horrors of war, especially the fact that civilians tend to bear the brunt of suffering that results from it. He is also correct to emphasize the desirability of pursuing nonviolent means of responding to military aggression. Nevertheless, I do not find his defense of pacifism convincing for reasons that I will explain below.

No Lack of Imagination

Erdel puts a lot of weight on the pacifists' powers of imagination. They are able, like Lord Russell, to imagine scenarios in which a nonviolent response—even capitulation—to unjust foreign aggression leads (eventually) to a more favorable outcome than would military resistance. Indeed, non-pacifists apparently suffer from a *lack* of imagination: they "fail to *imagine* that there are other, better alternatives" to war; they "cannot *imagine* . . . deliberately peaceful responses to violence" (p. 340, emphasis original).

The problem, however, is not that Just War advocates such as myself cannot imagine Erdel's pacifist scenarios, but it's that we can imagine *other* things, too—horrible things that could result from a failure to wage war in response to unjust aggression. Russell painted a rosy picture of what could have happened if Britain had surrendered to Germany in the First World War—Britain and its culture might even have been better off in the long run. Perhaps. But the Germany of the early twentieth century was very different from how it was later under the Nazi regime. Were Poland, France, Belgium, and so on, better off under that genocidal tyranny? Would Britain have been? And could anyone seriously doubt that, if the Allies had refused to resist the Nazis, we would all still be their slaves today? Would any Jews have survived the Final Solution? If anyone lacks imagination, it is the pacifists: they fail to imagine what evil men can do (and *have* done). Or, put positively, they fantasize that men are better than they are.

But whether or not surrendering to an unjust aggressor has such horrific consequences, the Just War advocate also "imagines" that such nonresistance is positively *unjust* because it allows an injustice to go unchallenged and unchecked. As I argued in my main essay, the citizens of a nation rightly expect their government to defend their natural rights (to liberty, property, etc.) against violations. That's why governments exist in the first place. The pacifist, it would seem, recommends peace at any cost without regard to matters of justice. But peace without justice is no real peace.[1]

At this point, though, Erdel would again claim a lack of imagination on my part, namely an "inability to conceive of justice as anything other than some form of fairness or equality" (Ibid). He recommends instead a view of "justice" rooted in the teachings of Jesus that "tilts radically toward mercy and grace." Here I plead "guilty as charged." I take "justice" to simply *mean* "getting what one deserves" (i.e., fairness or equality under the moral law).[2] However one interprets Jesus' ethic in the Sermon on the Mount (Erdel gets it wrong—see below), he is not talking about justice.[3] Mercy and grace are different concepts.

Faulty Moral "Convictions"

Erdel grounds his pacifism in three moral convictions: (1) Killing human beings is inherently wrong, (2) Attempts to stop killing by killing in warfare inevitably make matters worse, and (3) Killing other human beings changes the killer profoundly (for the worse). But these alleged moral convictions are, at best, only half-truths or generally (but not always) true.

Concerning (1), it is more accurate to say that killing human beings, even innocent human beings, is *generally* wrong. Erdel cites the fact that all major cultures have moral rules against killing innocent human beings. Yet, he fails to note that these same cultures allow for exceptions to these rules, that is, *justifiable* homicides, even of innocent people. Most pro-lifers, for example, grant that abortion is permissible to save the mother's life.

The only example Erdel gives of (2) concerns the fact that war compounds the number of people killed, especially innocent women and children. Apparently, what Erdel means is that fewer people will be killed if the nation that is unjustly attacked surrenders rather than fights back. While that may be true in some cases, it is surely false in others. Consider cases in which war is waged in order to prevent or stop a genocide (as in Bosnia-Herzegovina in the 1990s), or to put an end to piracy (as the US Navy did with the Barbary pirates in the early nineteenth century). More generally, is it appropriate to think that the Allies "made matters worse" by fighting the Axis powers in the Second World War? Simply worse in the number of people killed? That in itself is questionable (the Nazis and Japanese slaughtered millions of people who were *not* waging war against them, people they had conquered), but things can be better or worse in other ways besides counting the number of people killed. It's safe to say that most historians and ethicists think that the world is better off than it would have been given that the Allies waged war against the Axis.

Regarding (3), Erdel claims that killing makes "potentially virtuous persons become profoundly vicious" (p. 341). However, the vast majority of soldiers who kill in combat do not become "profoundly vicious" (which I take to mean that they become either indifferent or amenable to killing). I think Erdel knows this, which is why he immediately turns to the emotional anguish that many soldiers experience as a result of killing. In either case, Erdel's claims are greatly exaggerated. Most soldiers who kill in war do not become vicious,[4] and most do not suffer emotional anguish.[5]

A more important point to be made when it comes to virtue ethics, however, is that it is *pacifism*, not killing in war or self-defense, that engenders vice. A person who can stand idly by while evil men attack an innocent person is not acting out of virtue. Indeed, I submit that this is why most soldiers who kill in war, motivated by a just cause, do not develop or exhibit vicious characters or suffer mental anguish. Rather, they rightly see their actions as virtuous and noble.

Facing the Right Facts

As stated earlier, Erdel is right to point out that innocent noncombatants usually bear the brunt of the suffering and death that war involves. This is why the Just War Tradition requires strict adherence to the *jus in bello* criterion of discrimination. The fact that there have been wars in which this principle has been violated or inadequately followed is no argument against the moral justifiability of war; it is only an argument for greater and more consistent discrimination.

But Erdel claims that war is "far too indiscriminate" and "is by nature unjust" because most people killed in war are innocent civilians (p. 343). His evidence for this claim includes the fact that the fifty million people killed in the Second World War were mostly civilians who were not responsible for the war. Yet, Erdel fails to mention that almost all of these innocent civilians were killed by the Axis powers—the unjust aggressors; and the majority of those were not killed in combat as "collateral damage" but were intentionally massacred. These people would have been killed even if the Allies had followed the pacifist program.[6]

Erdel also correctly notes that "[m]ost of the goods that are claimed as reasons for participating in wars have in fact been achieved in other contexts by non-violent means" (p. 344). But this point is consistent with Just War thinking, which recognizes that war is not always the right (or first) response to foreign threats. The criterion of last resort demands that war be waged only when nonviolent means of redress have failed.

Jesus Was No Pacifist

Like many religious pacifists, Erdel points to the teachings of Jesus to justify his position. However, there are several reasons to doubt that Jesus was a pacifist or that he called his followers to strict nonviolence. First, Jesus himself acted in a very non-pacifist way when he violently chased the money changers out of the temple in Jerusalem (Mk 11:15-16; Jn 2:13-17). Second, Jesus apparently commanded his disciples to purchase swords ostensibly for the purpose of self-defense (Lk. 22:35-38).[7]

Third, the New Testament texts that pacifists quote in support of pacifism are almost certainly misinterpreted. The most oft-cited text reads:

> You have heard that it was said, "An eye for an eye, and a tooth for a tooth." But I say to you, do not resist an evil person; but whoever slaps you on your right cheek, turn the other to him also. (Mt. 5:38-39, LSB)

According to pacifists, Jesus abrogates the Old Testament *lex talionis* ("eye-for-eye" principle) and replaces it with an ethic of nonviolence. But it is telling that the example Jesus uses involves a slap on the face—an insult. If he truly wanted to rule out the use of violence in self-defense and war, he more likely would have said, "If someone tries to kill you or seriously injure you, do not resist him." Moreover, as Charles and Demy argue, Jesus' instructions have to do with "the realm of personal injury, not state policy."[8] In other words, Jesus forbade his followers from seeking revenge for personal insults and minor injuries but left it open to the state to enforce the *lex talionis*.[9]

Notes

1 On the relationship between peace and justice, see J. Daryl Charles and Timothy J. Demy, *War, Peace, and Christianity: Questions and Answers from a Just-War Perspective* (Wheaton: Crossway, 2010), 280–3.

2 See Ibid., 281–2; and Eric Patterson, "A Just War View: Christian Approaches to War, Peace, and Security," in *War, Peace, and Violence: Four Christian Views*, ed. Paul Copan (Downers Grove: InterVarsity, 2022), 15–16.

3 Jesus does use the Greek word δικαιοσύνη (*dikaiosune*), in the Sermon on the Mount (cf. Mt. 5:6, 20; 6:33), which is often translated as "righteousness" or "justice." But his use of the word must be interpreted in context. It seems evident that Jesus uses the word here not as equivalent to our concept of justice, and certainly not so as to equate it with mercy. Rather, as indicated in *Strong's Concordance*, it is used more broadly to mean "*what is deemed right by the Lord* (after His examination), i.e. what is *approved in His eyes*" (https://biblehub.com/greek/1343.htm). As Charles Quarles explains, "In the Gospel of Matthew, the term 'righteousness' [i.e., *dikaiosune*] normally refers to actual personal righteousness that results from one's personal relationship with God" (see his *Sermon on the Mount: Restoring Christ's Message to the Modern Church* [Nashville: B&H, 2011], 60). As such, Jesus is not using the term to introduce a new concept of justice, but he is describing the kind of person one must be in order to have God's approval—a person who, in addition to caring about justice, is *also* characterized by mercy and grace.

4 Erdel's example of the experience of Kevin, the West Point cadet, is by no means typical of the training that most soldiers receive. More typical is training in the criteria of the Just War Tradition.

5 See Blair E. Wisco, et al., "Posttraumatic Stress Disorder in the US Veteran Population: Results From the National Health and Resilience in Veterans Study," *NIH National Library of Medicine* (https://pmc.ncbi.nlm.nih.gov/articles/PMC9040390/). According to this study, about 8 percent of US veterans suffer from PTSD. Interestingly, most of these suffer PTSD *not* as a result of having killed but from being placed in other traumatic situations such as being in danger (i.e., being attacked by the enemy and thus in fear of their own lives). Also, a recent study involving soldiers who actually killed in combat shows that context matters when it comes to soldiers' mental health. That is, "where combat was expected and rules of engagement were clear," the study "showed no long-term psychological harm from killing" (Nancy Bazilchuk, "Killing in Combat Doesn't Always Harm Soldiers' Mental Health," *NeuroscienceNews.com* (https://neurosciencenews.com/combat-mental-health-psychology-28517/#:~:text=The%20study%20suggests%20that%20alignment%20between%20mission%20 expectations%2C,health%20negatively%20when%20mission%20expectations%20didn't%20justify%20it).

6 Erdel offers a peculiar "case study" to demonstrate the superiority of the pacifist approach to military aggression. He contrasts the responses to Nazi invasion by Denmark and Greece, the former immediately surrendering and the latter resisting fiercely until overwhelmed. The result was that 97 percent of the Jews in Denmark survived the Nazi Holocaust, while 87 percent of the Jews in Greece were killed. This seems like a perfect example of the *non causa pro causa* fallacy. Why think that there is any connection between the "pacifist" response of the Danes and the survival of

the Jews in Denmark? Isn't it more likely that it was simply the greater efforts of the Danes in hiding and smuggling the Jews, something that might have been the case even if the Danes had resisted the Nazis like the Greeks?

7 See the excellent article on this text by Timothy Hsiao, "Does Jesus Endorse Armed Self-Defense in Luke 22:36?" *Evangelical Quarterly* 92 (2021): 351–66 (https://firearmsresearchcenter.org/wp-content/uploads/2025/03/2021-Does-Jesus-Endorse-Armed-Self-Defense.pdf). Hsiao argues that Jesus endorsed the carrying of weapons for personal protection and responds to pacifist objections to this interpretation.

8 Charles and Demy, *War, Peace, and Christianity*, 251–4.

9 Relevantly, the Apostle Paul clearly interprets Jesus this way. In Romans 12, like Jesus, he enjoins Christians to "bless those who persecute you; bless, and do not curse. . . . Never paying back evil for evil to anyone, . . . never taking your own revenge, beloved—instead leave room for the wrath *of God*" (vv. 14–19). But then in Romans 13, he asserts that the civil government "does not bear the sword in vain, for it is a minister of God, an avenger who brings wrath on the one who practices evil" (v. 4).

Questions for Reflection

1. Cowan argues that addressing the injustice of foreign aggression is more important than the potential horrific consequences of resistance. Is he right? Why?

2. Erdel is much concerned about the effects of war on the civilian population. But what if the civilians *want* their government to wage war in their defense? Would this make a moral difference? Why?

3. Do you see problems with any of the criteria for a just war? Why?

For Further Reading

Copan, Paul, ed. *War, Peace, and Violence: Four Christian Views*. InterVarsity, 2022.
Corey, David D., and J. Daryl Charles. *The Just War Tradition: An Introduction*. ISI Books, 2012.
Evans, Mark A. *Just War Theory: A Reappraisal*. Edinburgh University Press, 2005.
Holmes, Robert L. *Pacifism: A Philosophy of Nonviolence*. Bloomsbury, 2016.
Patterson, Eric. *Just War Thinking: Morality and Pragmatism in the Struggle against Contemporary Threats*. Lexington Books, 2009.
Ramsey, Paul. *The Just War: Force and Political Responsibility*. Scribner's, 1968.
Yoder, John Howard. *The War of the Lamb: The Ethics of Nonviolence and Peacemaking*. Brazos Press, 2009.

11

Reparations

For Reparations for Past Injustices

Federico Lenzerini

> **Study Questions**
>
> 1. Why are reparations essential to upholding human rights?
> 2. What two arguments against reparations for past injustices does Lenzerini discuss? How does he rebut them?
> 3. How does Lenzerini respond to the "intertemporal law" claim that legal questions must be evaluated on the basis of the law in force at the time when a given behavior was done?
> 4. How does Lenzerini justify making reparations to contemporary Indigenous peoples?
> 5. How does Lenzerini justify making reparations to descendants of former slaves?

I. Reparations as Essential Requirement for Ensuring Effectiveness of Human Rights

Back in 1961, Justice Guha Roy, former judge of the High Court of Calcutta, in India, wrote, "[t]hat a wrong done to an individual must be redressed by the offender himself or by someone else against whom the sanction of the community may be directed is one of those timeless axioms of justice without which social life is unthinkable."[1] In equivalent terms, today one basic principle constantly expressed in the judgments of the Inter-American Court of Human Rights is the one according to which "any violation of an international obligation that has caused harm entails the obligation to repair this adequately . . . this . . . reflects a customary norm that constitutes one of the fundamental principles of contemporary international law on State responsibility."[2] A right to redress for the wrongs suffered is indeed inherent in human (individual and collective) rights. In fact, human rights can only fulfill their very purpose of efficiently protecting the human person and her inherent dignity if their effectiveness is guaranteed. Merely recognizing human rights on paper would be ineffective if this recognition is not complemented by the opportune institutions and means to guarantee their enforcement in case of breach. Reparation plays a decisive role in this respect, as it represents the tool through which the state of things preexisting the breach—the good order of life broken by the wrong—can be brought back home, at least to the extent possible. In other words, reparations may have the power (although not in all circumstances) to bring the victim of the wrong back to the situation existing before her/his rights were unjustly infringed. Hence, effective enjoyment of human rights cannot prescind from reparations.

II. Ethics of Reparations for Past Injustices

Aristotle considered reparative (*rectius*: corrective) justice as the reestablishment of a moral state of equality breached by a wrong.[3] The idea of corrective justice can be summarized with the assumption that, "if one agent has wrongfully harmed another, then the perpetrator has a prima facie moral obligation to repair, so far as possible, the damage to the victim."[4] "The moral balance can only be restored [by taking] from the perpetrators what they unjustly acquired and [giving] to the victims what they lost. In cases where restoration of lost possessions is impossible, then reparative justice demands that the perpetrators compensate their victims by an amount equal to the value of what was lost (and perhaps also compensate them for other harms resulting from the wrong)."[5] Consistent with this perspective, the starting point of my case is that a sound ethical basis exists supporting the rightfulness and worthiness of reparations for past injustices. However, several arguments have been raised—and are currently being used by some scholars—to challenge and disprove this position. Among those arguments, in my opinion, two of them are particularly relevant for the present investigation; in this section, I will try to expose and rebut them.

First, it has been claimed that "reparations schemes are justified on the basis of backward-looking reasons—remediation of, or compensation for, past injustices—rather than on the basis of forward-looking reasons—increasing utility, deterring future wrongdoing, or promoting distributive justice."[6] In reality, as held by Roy Brooks, reparations "are more usually justified on stronger, forward-looking grounds of restorative justice, specifically reconciliation and redemption [. . .] They are, indeed, a redemptive response to an atrocity . . . [signaling] the perpetrators' readiness to imbibe a spirit of heightened morality, identity, egalitarianism, and restorative justice."[7] In fact, reparations are usually aimed at healing wounds which—while they were primarily carried on the bodies of those who directly suffered the effects of a wrong—usually influence the good order of social relations within a society, through producing grounds for hatred and clashes, and polluting human interactions. Through removing such grounds, it is possible to place the bases for reconciling the different communities living in the same society (even the perpetrators and the victims of an injustice) and, consequently, to promote a more serene future and pursue tolerance and mutual understanding. The capacity of reparations to play this role confirms and reinforces their ethical legitimacy.

Second, perplexities have been raised on account of two elements allegedly inherent in the reparation discourse. According to this view, reparations would often be hardly practicable and ethically inappropriate because "(1) justice permits reparations only where compensation is paid to actual victims of wrongdoing (as opposed to say, nonvictim members of the same racial group), *and* (2) justice permits the payment to be extracted in part from those who did not themselves wrong anyone, through taxes or other mechanisms."[8] Reversing the order of the two arguments, in my view, under an ethical perspective, the second is easily rebuttable. In fact, reparations have the purpose to heal a wound of the whole society, determined by a wrong that has broken the social order of the human group concerned. Reparations aim to remove this fracture. It follows that paying taxes for financing reparation processes is perfectly coherent with the solidaristic function mainly pursued by taxes themselves. In the end, as has been efficaciously expressed, "[p]aying tax is the glue in the social contract."[9]

As regards the first postulation, it appears to recall the Aristotelian theory of corrective justice, according to which a duty to repair only subsists if both the person (or other entity) responsible for the wrong and the victim still exist; this requirement would impose "a time limit on . . . [the ethical justification of] redressing historical wrongs: the duty of repair ends once the wrongdoer or the victim ceases to exist."[10] This aspect may actually appear as seriously threatening the ethical legitimacy of reparations, and must therefore be addressed very seriously. It, in fact, menaces the moral validity of reparations for past injustices through supporting the claim that today there is no direct harm, as, contextualizing the argument in the case of slavery, "[t]here are no slaves alive today who can bring suit, and there are no slave-owners who can be sued."[11] Hence, the existence requirement needs to be considered as regards both the author of the wrong and the victim. With respect to the former, clearly, it would be against the basic postulates of justice to exact reparations from a person or other entity who/which cannot be considered—to any extent—responsible for the wrong. It is also evident that, for most cases of past injustices for which reparation is claimed, the individuals who *materially* committed the wrong do not exist any longer. At the same time, it is equally true that, in most instances, the past injustices for which reparation is usually claimed were perpetrated by somebody who—even when he/she was not a state agent—was acting with, *as a minimum*, the acquiescence of the state and/or its organs or agents. This acquiescence usually took the form of a normative and/or social or political background in the context of which the behavior determining the wrong was allowed or, at least, tolerated by the government. It follows that the state can usually be considered, if not the direct wrongdoer, at least an accomplice of the latter, hence bearing responsibility for the injustice. In fact, "[a] government that sponsored or permitted slavery, the slave trade, or other severe racist practices should not . . . be allowed to avoid responsibility simply because of the passage of time."[12] Not to mention that the state concerned may have accrued benefits "from . . . slavery or abusive colonialism . . . that presumably helped to jumpstart [its] industrialization and thus continue to the present."[13] This conclusion could only be contested if, at some point in the time passed between the perpetration of the wrong and the claim of reparations, the state concerned would have been subjected to such a drastic political transformation that the state existing at the moment of the claim could not be considered the same (in terms of international subjectivity) as the one existing at the time of the perpetration of the injustice. In this case, in fact, there would not be any continuity between the state responsible for the wrong and the one in front of which redress would be claimed, or, in other words, the legal subject (under international law) responsible for the wrong would not be the same as the one which should grant the reparations claimed. Even in this case, however—for how controversial this assumption may be—one might reasonably assert that the "new" state would continue to hold responsibility for the wrongs committed by the "old" one, for the reason that the two subjects are in any case tied by an element of continuity in regulating and managing the social existence of the human group subjected to their authority, the social and cultural identity of which remains the same. In any event, this aspect does not necessarily need to be accurately clarified for the purposes of the present chapter, as in virtually all cases of reparatory claims included in the scope of this writing, no changes have occurred in the identity of the states concerned from the time of the injustices to that of the claims.

Concerning the existence requirement applied to the victim, interpreting this term as referring only to the person(s) *directly* affected by the wrong clearly has an ontological flaw. In the context of (both national and international) human rights law, it is uniformly and indisputably accepted that a victim of a wrong can also be somebody *indirectly* affected by the latter, like the relatives or the heirs of the direct victim, even those belonging to future generations. The only condition that must be fulfilled is that the beneficiaries of reparations are somehow negatively affected by the effects of the wrong. Scholars have tried to justify this conclusion on the basis of different arguments, including the interest of the direct victim, which would continue to exist after his/her passing, to "the well-being of the remaining family members that they knew while they were alive,"[14] or the extension of the definition of "victim" to "descendants of direct victims as victims of the injustice"—either "because the suffering of their forebears left the forebears less able to support their descendants materially and emotionally," or "because the injustice deprived them of their inheritance rights."[15] In reality, adopting a down-to-earth approach, my position appears better grounded on the basis of the assumption that, since the main purpose of reparations is to redress an unjust pain or suffering as determined by an injustice, indirect victims are entitled to such a redress if and to the extent that the tort has caused pain or suffering to them, in addition to the direct victim. This also presupposes the existence of a limit to the ethical legitimacy of reparations for past injustices, that is, that they are no longer due when nobody exists anymore who perceives—to whatever extent—the effects of the wrong.

A related issue is connected to the aspect of *intertemporal law*, a legal principle according to which a legal question has to be evaluated on the basis of the law in force at the time when it arose, implying that a given behavior should be considered a wrong only if and to the extent that it was considered illegal at the time when it was held. This requirement does not, prima facie, appear to be fulfilled for most cases of reparatory claims for past injustices. In particular, as regards reparations for slavery and slave trade, the principle of intertemporal law—if rigidly applied—would render the viability of such reparations impossible, because up to the early nineteenth-century slavery and the traffic in slaves were *not* prohibited by either international law or most domestic legal regimes, including in the United States (where slavery was abolished by the 13th Amendment to the Constitution in 1865).[16]

Other arguments have been used to deny the ethical legitimacy of reparations for past wrongs. For instance, referring to the case of slavery, one author has claimed that "[r]eparationists refuse to acknowledge that slavery had a negative impact on everyone. Reparations advocates will give short shrift to white poverty, perhaps even denying that slavery was meant to, and in fact did, impoverish the masses of white people as much as it did the Blacks."[17] This would make reparations not only inappropriate—as no members of the society would have been affected by the wrong more than the generality—but also potentially harmful. It appears, however, that arguments of this kind are clearly denied not only by historical evidence but also by the social reality of contemporary times.

In the next sections, I will defend the ethical legitimacy of two specific instances of reparatory claims for past wrongs: reparations for the torts suffered by Indigenous peoples and reparations for slavery and slave trade. I will do so by addressing the two aspects concerning, respectively, the requirement that somebody still exists who suffers the effects of a past wrong and the principle of intertemporal law. In doing this, I will establish a clear link between ethics and law, basing my ethical evaluations on whether the two aspects described—which are of both legal and ethical character—are fulfilled. In the end, a sort of *circular* relationship exists between ethics and law, in the sense that ethics must infuse law to ensure its fairness and justice, and, at the same time, one of the main purposes of law must always be to realize the ethical values of the society within which it is applied. As noted above, the two aspects that I am going to use as *parameters* for establishing the ethical legitimacy of reparations for past wrongs are related to one another, especially with regard to the conditions to be fulfilled for satisfying them.

III. Reparations for Past Wrongs Suffered by Indigenous Peoples

For Indigenous peoples, reparations for past wrongs represent an indispensable condition for their cultural—in some cases even physical—survival. Their holistic understanding of life (mainly based on spiritual values and beliefs) requires that all elements of existence, both animate and inanimate, both visible and invisible, retain their place in the circle of life, according to a precise social order, shaped by the intersections existing between all cultural values modeling the specific identity and uniqueness of each Indigenous community. When this order is broken, due to an injustice suffered by the community or its members, a deep wound is usually opened which will continue to exist for many generations, and which can only be healed through removing the effects produced by the wrong, by means of the planning and execution of appropriate reparatory programs decided in conjunction with the community concerned. This holds true, in particular, when an Indigenous community is relocated from, or in any other way deprived of, its traditional lands, territories, and/or resources.[18] It follows that the ethical legitimacy of reparations for past wrongs suffered by Indigenous peoples cannot be reasonably contested.

The two problems raised at the end of the previous section can, in fact, be easily fixed. Indeed, the intergenerational transmission of the effects of the wrongs suffered by Indigenous peoples in the past fully satisfies the "victim's existence requirement," as all members of the community concerned usually continue to suffer such effects for many generations, even centuries after the perpetration of the injustice, if the latter is not adequately redressed. Simultaneously, the same factual reality also allows for surmounting the aspect of intertemporal law, for the reason that the perpetuation of the effects produced by the past injustice makes the latter a *continuing violation* of the human rights of the community concerned and/or of its members. In fact, where a wrong has not been properly redressed, "the victim's continued suffering would amount to a continuing harm,"[19] making it enforceable based on the legal rules in force at the time when the reparatory claim is advanced.[20]

IV. Reparations for Slavery and Slave Trade

The debate concerning the ethical legitimacy of reparations for slavery and slave trade has been developed for many years by legal philosophers, particularly in the United States, where it has also been referred to as "reparations for Black slavery," "reparations for African Americans," or "Black reparations." This debate is characterized by the theorization of conflicting views, most of which appear reasonably grounded if considered on the basis of different perspectives. The present assessment will be limited to an investigation of the case of reparations for individuals or groups of individuals, while it will not cover reparatory claims advanced by African countries for the damages suffered in consequence of slave trade. My approach will be the same as that adopted in the previous section, based on an attempt to untangle the two issues of victim existence and intertemporal law.

The ethical legitimacy of reparations for slavery and slave trade is frequently based on the principle of corrective justice, according to the terms explained in Section II above. According to Thomas McCarthy,

> [i]t is not difficult to sketch, at least in broad outline, how a moral-political case for reparations for slavery might be constructed from this [principle] within a liberal framework. Political justice is here rooted in impartiality or fairness, which requires equal respect for each person, equal rights and liberties for all, equal treatment under the law, and equal consideration of the interests of all. There is no question that these were denied, under law, to slaves and their descendants at least into the 1960s. And there is a convincing case to be made for the continuing effects of these past injustices in the present inequalities of income, wealth, housing, health care, social standing, education, employment, and other opportunities that characterize the situation of African Americans in the United States. Correcting this legacy of past injustice, making these wrongs right . . . seems clearly to be a moral-political requirement of justice as fairness.[21]

This argument may be used to bypass the obstacle potentially posed by the principle of intertemporal law, postulating (albeit through an extensive interpretation of the concept) the existence of a continuity in the effects of the wrong, similarly to what I have assumed regarding the case of reparations for Indigenous peoples for past injustices. It does not fix, however, the requirement of the victim's existence. This condition may appear particularly hard to satisfy, not only for the long time passed since the perpetration of the wrong, but also for the fact that "[h]istorical injustice not only determines people's fate, it also determines their very existence";[22] consequently, "how can one claim compensation for historical injustice, without which one would not even have existed?"[23] One solution that has been proposed to overcome the complexities posed by the victim's existence requirement rests in the "chains of duties of care that connect the subsequent generations," explained by Marc Loth as a duty of the author of the wrong to compensate not only its *direct* victim, but also the latter's "children for failing to compensate the parents if and when they had a duty to take care of their children."[24] This solution would allow "claims of an unlimited number of subsequent generations, on condition they are able to prove that they have suffered damage as a result of the non-compliance of the elderly duty of care."[25] Another possible way out of this problem would be represented by the theory of "cross-generational duties of care" existing within the family, envisaged by John Rawls as a duty of each person to "take care about the well-being of some of those in the next generation, it being presumed that their concern is for different individuals in each case. Moreover, for anyone in the next generation, there is someone who cares about him in the present generation."[26] The fact of being the addressees of this care would entitle the heirs of direct victims of the wrong to be the beneficiaries of reparations for the torts suffered by their predecessors.

In my modest opinion, whatever philosophical theory should be considered as the most plausible, the decisive aspect for attributing to somebody the status of *indirect* victim—hence of person entitled to reparations for past wrongs suffered by a person with whom one is tied—is the existence of an effective perception by the person(s) concerned of a current, *real, and genuine feeling of suffering or anguish* determined by the past injustice. The actual existence of such a feeling in members of current generations of successors of the direct victims of slavery and slave trade is not really difficult to identify. There are many different reasons which can induce in a person a perception of moral anguish. Certainly, the successors of slaves living today cannot directly perceive—in addition to the whiplashes and other brutal physical violence—the constant humiliation, mortification, and commodification of their enslaved predecessors, but they can anyway feel certain forms of sorrow. This sorrow can be determined, in particular, by the outrage that slavery and slave trade have caused to the cultural and ethnic identity of the persons concerned, or to their sense of belonging to the racial group targeted by slavers and slave traders. Or it can be the result of the inability, by the successors of the direct victims, to come to terms with the events that affected their cultural or familial lineage in the past. Even the feelings of injustice and inequality transmitted by past wrongs to present generations can produce a sentiment of grief entitling the persons feeling such grief and maintaining some ties with those directly affected by the wrongs to be adequately redressed.

A related aspect is represented by the *collective* implications that the brutality of slavery and slave trade have transmitted to contemporary generations. It is even possible to assert that the passing of time has led to a sort of depersonalization of the identity of the victims of slavery and slave trade, in the sense that individual victims have today been replaced by an entire racial group sensing the prevarications suffered by its past members as an offense against the community as a whole, in consideration of the fact that the victims of slavery and slave trade were exactly selected on the basis of their belonging to that group. Actually, until the effects produced by slavery and slave trade are appropriately healed, they will continue to be considered, within society, as a wound breaking the social equilibrium and creating an imbalance in the social position occupied by the different components of society itself, with one specific group (the successors of the slaves) perceiving a (sometimes creeping but always tangible) sense of injustice and inequality which has not yet properly been eradicated, based on the awareness that "present-day inequality is the result of past injustice."[27] It follows that reparations attain the role of re-equilibrating a fair social order within society, through removing the reasons leading the successors of the victims of slavery and slave trade to continue to perceive the effects of the wrongs suffered by their predecessors. In fact, "[i]t is only the demanding and payment of reparations to the [successors of the victims that allows them to] consider themselves equal and be actually equal to the rest of [the society]."[28] Under this perspective, taking into account the role they should accomplish, reparations should not primarily take the form of pecuniary compensation (unless specific successors of the direct victims are identifiable who, for whatever reason, have suffered a definite and recognizable economic loss in consequence of the wrongs concerned), but rather that of *symbolic* redress, including, for example, formal apology, recognition of the wrong, building of monuments, development of social programs aimed at removing the persisting effects of the wrong, and so on.

There is another, more pragmatic, argument that can be used to defend the ethical legitimacy of reparations for slavery and slave trade according to a collective perspective, based on the fact that the perpetration of such forms of prevarication by a section of the community over another created a situation of notable economic advantage in favor of the former—through unjust enrichment[29]—to the detriment of the latter. Such an economic imbalance was so huge that, in general, it has not been re-equilibrated with the passing of time, to the point that it has been transmitted to current generations in the form of economic privileges enjoyed by the successors of the perpetrators, while the successors of the victims continue, in general, to suffer the negative economic repercussions of slavery and slave trade. To use the words of Katrina Forrester (who, on her turn, refers to the work of Bernard Boxill), the right of the victims' community to receive reparations

> depended "precisely on the fact that such people have been reduced to their present condition by a history of injustice". Slaves, for instance, had "an indisputable moral right to the products of their labor", a right they conferred to their descendants just as the slave masters passed the expropriated product to theirs, meaning that "the descendants of slave masters are in possession of wealth to which the descendants of slaves have rights."[30]

Put in different, but equivalent, terms, taking as an example the specific case of the United States, reparations have the power to "either directly or indirectly modify the economic injustices that continue to face African Americans in their adopted nation (America)."[31] This entitles the whole community of the successors of the victims to receive reparations. According to a number of scholars, the costs of such reparations should be borne by the community of the perpetrators' heirs.[32] In my opinion, however, consistent with the position assumed in Section II above, such costs should be assumed by the state, as the heirs of the perpetrators cannot—both morally and legally—be considered responsible for the wrongs committed by their ancestors (even though they may have inherited some benefits accruing from such wrongs).

There are, of course, practical difficulties in properly identifying the exact composition of the communities of, respectively, the perpetrators' and the victims' successors. Among other things, this identification would be notably complicated by "[i]ntermarriage between historical slave-holding and non-slave-holding families, as well as enslaved families."[33] Even more challenging is the consideration that "what requires reparation is not merely slavery but a history of closely related wrongs: wrongs that were not merely a matter of some families oppressing others, but involved the operation of legal, social and political institutions that over many generations supported slavery or abetted or ignored oppression of [victims]."[34] This reinforces the assumption that—provided that in concrete terms it is possible to identify with reasonable accuracy those entitled to receive reparations—the costs of the latter should be borne by civil society, including, as noted in Section II above, by taxpayers, consistent with the solidaristic function pursued by taxes. It is also opportune to clarify that, to the extent that the ethical legitimacy of reparations is based on the perspective of unjust enrichment, in principle, reparations should primarily take the form of economic compensation, as they are aimed at restoring the economic loss inherited by the victims' successors because of slavery and slave trade. However, this compensation should not necessarily consist of a reimbursement in favor of the individual heirs of the victims, but rather—in light of its collective function—of programs financing the social growth of the affected community as a whole, through, for example, "investment in education, housing, health care, or job training."[35] This is consistent with the assumption that, "[b]y looking at the reparations campaign in the United States as a social movement, we discover that it was never entirely, or even primarily, about the money. The demand for reparations was about social justice, reconciliation, reconstructing the internal life of black America, eliminating institutional racism."[36]

While the arguments just described may provide strong legitimization of the ethical legitimacy of reparations for slavery and slave trade, it is worth reiterating that the decisive requirement that must be satisfied to remove any argumentative objection against the above legitimacy is that the detrimental effects of slavery and slave trade must continue to be perceived today by the potential beneficiaries of reparations. Otherwise, for instance, the objection advanced by the supporters of the so-called "redundancy thesis"—according to which, in simplified terms, if the problem is that of inequality, it is not strictly necessary to advocate the need for reparations to fix it[37]—could hardly be rebutted. Conversely, no attempt to achieve effective equality and reconciliation between the different sectors of society could succeed if the wounds produced by a past injustice remain open, which is actually the case of the effects produced by slavery and slave trade, especially in the United States. In fact, "there cannot be true reconciliation where there is not a genuine attempt to rectify wrongdoing."[38]

Conclusion

According to John Locke, the denial of a person's right to reparation is equivalent to a refusal to recognize her full moral status.[39] As noted by Kyla Jermin, "[s]lavery is not a closed chapter of American history. While the practice itself no longer remains, its aftershocks are still present in society";[40] "[r]egardless of how one personally feels about the subject, there is no denying that a crime was committed—and is still being committed—and that there is" a demand for reparation.[41] In fact, "in most cases of plausible reparation claims, many generations of people have suffered needlessly under the yoke of subjugation and now languish in penury . . . [hence,] offering some reparation can be an important step toward satisfying the demands of justice and helping people overcome the hardship that is significantly the result of their oppression."[42] This makes it absolutely possible to base contemporary reparatory claims—both for past wrongs suffered by Indigenous peoples and for slavery and slave trade, among other cases—on the prejudicial effects they *continue to produce today*, attributing the status of *continuing violations* to said wrongs and, consequently, presupposing a duty—*rectius*: an obligation, of both legal and moral character—to guarantee reparations in favor of those who continue to feel such prejudicial effects on their skin and, especially, inside their soul. This reality allows us to contextually overcome the two main potential obstacles to the affirmation of the ethical (and legal) legitimacy of reparations for past wrongs, including for slavery and slave trade, that is, the issue of victims' existence and the principle of intertemporal law. Consequently, such ethical legitimacy cannot be reasonably refuted.

Notes

1. S. N. Guha Roy, "Is the Law of Responsibility of States for Injuries to Aliens a Part of Universal International Law?" *American Journal of International Law* 55 (1961): 863.
2. See, among others, *Case of Velásquez Rodríguez v. Honduras*, Reparations and costs, Series C No. 7, Judgment of July 21, 1989, paras. 25–7; *Case of the Indigenous Communities of the Lhaka Honhat (Our Land) Association v. Argentina*, Merits, reparations and costs, Series C No. 400, Judgment of February 6, 2020, para. 306.
3. See *The Ethics of Aristotle*, trans. J. K. Thomson (Harmondsworth: Penguin, 1955) 148.
4. See Thomas McCarthy, "Coming to Terms with Our Past, Part II: On the Morality and Politics of Reparations for Slavery," *Political Theory* 32 (2004): 750, 752.
5. See Janna Thompson, "Memory and the Ethics of Reparation" (2005), 2 (https://glc.yale.edu/sites/default/files/files/justice/thompson.pdf, accessed March 4, 2024).
6. See Eric A. Posner and Adrian Vermeule, "Reparations for Slavery and Other Historical Injustices," *Columbia Law Review* 103 (2003): 689, 692.
7. Roy L. Brooks, "Getting Reparations for Slavery Right—Response to Posner and Vermeule," *Notre Dame Law Review* 80 (2004): 251, 255.
8. See Posner and Vermeule, "Reparations for Slavery and Other Historical Injustices," 693.
9. See Alex Cobham, "The Pandemic has Exposed the Costs of Tax Injustice—Now is the Time to Make It Right," International Monetary Fund (March 2022) (https://www.imf.org/en/Publications/fandd/issues/2022/03/Taxing-for-a-new-social-contract-Cobham, accessed March 6, 2024).
10. See Katrina M. Wyman, "Is There a Moral Justification for Redressing Historical Injustices?" *Vanderbilt Law Review* 61 (2008): 127, 150.
11. See Gregory Kane, "Why the Reparations Movement Should Fail," *University of Maryland Law Journal of Race, Religion, Gender and Class* 3 (2003): 189, 198.
12. See Human Rights Watch, "An Approach to Reparations" (July 19, 2001), 6 (https://www.hrw.org/news/2001/07/19/approach-reparations (accessed March 12, 2024).
13. Ibid.

14 See Michael Ridge, "Giving the Dead Their Due," *Ethics* 114 (2003): 38, 42–5, 52; Wyman, "Is There a Moral Justification for Redressing Historical Injustices?" 154.

15 See Wyman, "Is There a Moral Justification for Redressing Historical Injustices?" 155.

16 See Max du Plessis, "Historical Injustice and International Law: An Exploratory Discussion of Reparation for Slavery," *Human Rights Quarterly* 25 (2003): 624, 634–5.

17 See Kane, "Why the Reparations Movement Should Fail," 199.

18 Generally, on reparations for Indigenous peoples, see *Reparations for Indigenous Peoples: International and Comparative Perspectives*, ed. Federico Lenzerini (Oxford: Oxford University Press, 2008); Federico Lenzerini, "Reparations, Restitution, and Redress: Articles 8(2), 11(2), 20(2), and 28," in *The UN Declaration on the Rights of Indigenous Peoples. A Commentary*, ed. Jessie Hohmann and Marc Weller (Oxford: Oxford University Press, 2018), 573.

19 See McCarthy, "Coming to Terms with Our Past," 752.

20 See Lenzerini, "Reparations, Restitution, and Redress," 590–1.

21 See McCarthy, "Coming to Terms with Our Past," 753.

22 See Marc Loth, "How does Tort Law deal with Historical Injustice? On Slavery Reparations, Post-Colonial Redress, and the Legitimations of Tort Law," *Journal of European Tort Law* 11 (2020): 181, 193.

23 Ibid.

24 Ibid.

25 Ibid.

26 See John Rawls, *A Theory of Justice* (Cambridge, MA: Harvard University Press, 1971), 128–9.

27 See Andrew Valls, *Rethinking Racial Justice* (Oxford: Oxford University Press, 2018), 119.

28 See Jason L. Moulenbelt, *A Study in the Morality of the African American Reparation* (Western Michigan University, Graduate College, Master Thesis 4-2002), 52, (https://scholarworks.wmich.edu/cgi/viewcontent.cgi?article=5199&context=masters_theses, accessed March 12, 2024).

29 See, among others, Dennis Klimchuk, "Unjust Enrichment and Reparations for Slavery," *Boston University Law Review* 84 (2004): 1257.

30 See Katrina Forrester, "Reparations, History and the Origins of Global Justice," in *Empire, Race and Global Justice*, ed. Duncan Bell (Cambridge: Cambridge University Press, 2019), 1, 39 (footnotes omitted), quoting Bernard Boxill, "The Morality of Reparation," *Social Theory and Practice* 2 (1972): 113, 117–21.

31 See A. B. Assensoh and Yvette M. Alex-Assensoh, "The Political Economy of Land and Reparations: The Case of Reparations for African Americans in the 21st Century," *American Journal of Economics and Sociology* 80 (2021): 699.

32 See, e.g., Boxill, "The Morality of Reparation," 120–1; Moulenbelt, *A Study in the Morality of the African American Reparation*, 52.

33 See Thomas J. Grennes, "Considering the Case for Slavery Reparations," *Regulation* (Winter 2022–2023): 20, 23.

34 See Thompson, "Memory and the Ethics of Reparation," 16.

35 See Human Rights Watch, "An Approach to Reparations," 4.
36 See Robin D. G. Kelley, *Freedom Dreams: The Black Radical Imagination* (Boston: Beacon Press, 2002), 114.
37 On this issue, see Megan Blomfield, "Reparations and Egalitarianism," *Ethical Theory and Moral Practice* 24 (2021): 1177, 1182.
38 See Howard McGary, "Reconciliation and Reparations," *Metaphilosophy* 41 (2010): 546, 555.
39 See John Locke, *The Second Treatise of Government*, ed. Thomas P. Peardon (New York: The Liberal Arts Press, 1968), 7–9.
40 See Kyla A. Jermin, "The Ethics of Reparations for Slavery," Ursinus College, Philosophy Summer Fellows (2016), 6 (https://digitalcommons.ursinus.edu/phil_sum /6, accessed March 12, 2024).
41 Ibid., 42.
42 See Andrew I. Cohen, "Compensation for Historic Injustices: Completing the Boxill and Sher Argument," *Philosophy & Public Affairs* 37 (2009): 81, 102.

The Case Against Slavery Reparations

Andrew Bernstein

Study Questions

1. What does Bernstein consider the false premise on which slavery reparations rest?
2. What absurdities does Bernstein believe follow from racial moral responsibility?
3. How does Bernstein respond to the charge that he has made a straw man of the reparations argument?
4. What concerns does Bernstein have about the question of who decides who pays?
5. How does Bernstein answer the claim that white Americans benefited and continue to benefit from Black slavery?
6. Why does Bernstein think that reparations will not really benefit Black Americans? What will benefit them?

On December 7, 1993, a Black Jamaican immigrant named Colin Ferguson boarded a Long Island Railroad train at Garden City and opened fire on white passengers, murdering six of them and wounding numerous others. At his subsequent trial, it came out that he was an inveterate hater of white people.

Today, some thirty-two years later, my Black college students are unfailingly good kids, hardworkers who pursue an education honestly. Many of them are roughly twenty years old, born in 2004 or 2005. If I were to proclaim that they are morally responsible for the Colin Ferguson atrocity and therefore owe restitution to the victims' families and, perhaps, to whites generally, rational people would be nonplussed. "Dr. Bernstein," they would say, "an adult individual is responsible for his/her actions and, perhaps, for the actions of his underage children. He is not responsible for the actions of another, a person he never met and whose murderous crimes took place before he was born."

"Nevertheless," I respond, "they're the same race and, by God, any person is responsible for the actions of other members of his race."

My most rational critics would reply: "No, moral responsibility requires choice. If a student of race x in your class cheats on the midterm exam, he is responsible for it. The other students of race x in the class, who did their own work, and who neither aided nor abetted the cheater, are not responsible for the malfeasance."

They are correct. Moral responsibility is individual, not collective. It is volitional, not deterministic. One cannot be born with the moral turpitude of one's ancestors hardwired into one's character. Put simply, moral responsibility is based on an individual's choices, not on one's racial membership.

It should be clear how this principle applies to the issue of slavery reparations. The culprits responsible for US slavery are long gone. The victims are similarly long gone. If the year were, say, 1870, and former slave owners and slave traders still lived, then restitution by the guilty to the innocent victims would be appropriate, indeed morally obligatory. For an individual is responsible for their actions and, to the best of their ability, must make amends for the misery they have inflicted on innocent others. But 1870 is long gone; so are those responsible for inflicting the misery, as are those who bore the brunt of it.

The False Premise of Racial Moral Responsibility

The argument for slavery reparations ignores these inconvenient truths. It rests on the pernicious and egregiously false premise of racial moral responsibility. Let's briefly explore the logical consequences of such a collectivist idea. Let's say, as a thought experiment, that I accepted this notion and then applied rigorous logic to think out its results.

The Irrationality of Reparations

Under this assumption, I realize that I, a white man, am morally responsible for the crime of Black US slavery and must make restitution. That my family was not even in the country when these atrocities were perpetrated and arrived as immigrants only some forty years after they ended, and that I was born many decades after these events . . . all of this is irrelevant. I am morally responsible.

This is a depressing truth. But then another truth occurs to me: Aristotle, Newton, Shakespeare, Beethoven, Edison, and many other heroes were also white men. Their achievements redound immensely to the advancement of human life. If I am responsible for the crimes of my racial ancestors, surely, I am likewise responsible for their life-giving achievements. After all, moral responsibility involves virtuous as well as vicious actions. If a student chooses to cheat on an exam, he is morally blameworthy; if he chooses to work honestly, he is morally praiseworthy. It is only because working honestly is morally right that cheating is morally wrong. Good and evil are correlative concepts. There cannot be one type of judgment in the absence of the other. Logically, there is no escape from this.

Now, I am happy. For the accomplishments of my racial ancestors have conferred enormous benefit on millions of non-whites. Advances in agricultural science and technology, antibiotics and other medical breakthroughs, electric light, the automobile, the airplane, the field of architecture, the construction of houses and cities, the mass production of inexpensive oil and steel, the novels, the dramas, the symphonies, songs, and sonatas, the advances in philosophy and logic, the scientific theories, and a great deal more—much of it was created by white men and women.

Henry Ford, the Wright brothers, John D. Rockefeller, Andrew Carnegie, Victor Hugo, Ayn Rand, Frédéric Chopin, Albert Einstein, the geniuses named above—especially Aristotle—and many others contributed monumentally to the furthering of human life. Don't non-whites owe me restitution for these fulsome benefits? We must impose a "gratitude tax" on non-whites to pay back white men for the immense benefits we have conferred on their lives. Yay! I get my reparation dollars—and my pride—back. I do my happy dance.

But then another thought occurs to me. All white people, including me, benefit deeply from the accomplishments of numerous Black geniuses. We benefit from the agricultural advances of George Washington Carver, from the brilliant jazz compositions of Duke Ellington; we are inspired by the extraordinary rags-to-riches story of Sarah Breedlove/Madam C. J. Walker, history's first self-made female millionaire; we are intellectually enlightened and emotionally moved by the novels of Zora Neale Hurston; we gain from the brilliant books on economics and social theory by the immortal Thomas Sowell; from the pioneering work in children's brain surgery by Dr. Ben Carson; by the superlative work of Denzel Washington, perhaps this generation's finest actor; and from the creative work of many others. Because all Blacks are responsible for these achievements, I am morally obliged to pay my reparations dollars right back to them.

But then, the creative work of Bill Gates, Steve Jobs, Jeff Bezos, Elon Musk, and other recent/current entrepreneurs greatly benefits non-whites; therefore, as a white man, I must receive the money back. Such examples can be endlessly extended and, on the premise of racial moral responsibility, the related arguments constitute sound reasoning.

Slavery Not the Only Crime

Further instances come to mind: violent crimes perpetrated by members of one race against members of another have long occurred and continue. We must factor these into our racial calculus and determine the degree of culpability shared by members of the perpetrator's racial group and the restitution to be made to ethnic compatriots of the victims. For example, slavery was hardly the only crime perpetrated by whites against Black Americans. Countless numbers of possibly innocent Blacks were never allowed to go to trial because they were brutally lynched by violent white mobs. One such case was that of Mary Turner in 1918, Georgia. She was eight months pregnant and vowed to bring legal justice to the white men who had killed her innocent husband. The mob stripped her, hung her upside down from a tree, doused her in gasoline, and burned her alive. A white man ripped open her belly with a knife, the infant fell out, and the mob stomped him to death. Incredibly, the *Atlanta Constitution* reported on this horror with sympathy for the perpetrators, not for the victim. Its story was sub-headlined, "Fury of People is Unrestrained." Its reporter blandly wrote that Mary Turner "made unwise remarks . . . the people were angered by her remarks, as well as her attitude."[1] No members of the lynch mob were legally punished. Ghastly as this was, Mary Turner's story is hardly unique. The archivists at Tuskegee Institute in Alabama kept newspaper and magazine stories of numerous Black victims. Between 1882 and 1962, 3,417 Blacks were lynched *with public knowledge*, largely in the Jim Crow South. God alone knows how many Blacks were murdered privately by whites with no publicity.[2]

Nor were lynchings the sole atrocity perpetrated on innocent Blacks. White race riots were also terribly destructive. One heinous example was the Tulsa murder spree in 1921. An innocuous occurrence between a Black youth and a white woman led to a call for lynching the young Black man, who had been arrested and was protected by the authorities. The lynch mob was rebuffed in its attempt to kill the youth and turned its violence against Blacks in general. Greenwood was a prosperous Black neighborhood, home to many businesses, newspaper offices, schools, banks, churches, doctors' offices, a hospital, a library, and so forth. The white mob invaded it; Blacks fought to defend their homes, businesses, and families; the battle raged over two days, and in the end, Greenwood was burned to the ground, more than 1,000 homes and businesses were destroyed, and anywhere from 50 to 300 people were killed, most of them Black. None of the white perpetrators were punished, and no reparations to the innocent Black victims were paid.[3]

These specific crimes and other similar ones were committed over a century ago. All of the adult perpetrators are gone. But that doesn't matter, because members of the same race still live and, on the premise of racial moral responsibility, can be held accountable. In our day, violent white supremacists such as Dylann Roof, Peyton Gendron, and others murder innocent Black victims. These ignorant thugs most likely have no resources with which to pay restitution to the family members of the victims. But what does that matter? There are some 234 million white Americans. The overwhelming majority of them are neither white supremacists nor violent criminals, but, because they share the same skin color as the perpetrators, they can be properly forced to pay reparations.

Should Whites Receive Reparations, Too?

Furthermore, there is no reason to hold that racial moral responsibility moves solely in one direction. The same principle must hold for crimes committed against members of another race by Blacks, Asians, Latinos, and biracial individuals. Today, the rate of Black-on-white violent crime, including homicide, is substantially higher than the rate of white-on-Black violence. Perhaps the Black murderers (like Colin Ferguson) are incarcerated and have no means to pay restitution to family members and loved ones of the victims. But the same moral principle applies: there are more than forty million Black Americans; although the vast majority are honest, productive individuals who commit no violent crimes, their racial identity makes them morally responsible for those Blacks who do; they must be forced to pay reparations.

The Worldwide Calculus

While we are about this, it is logically and morally incumbent to extend our racial calculus worldwide. If moral responsibility is collective, not individual—and wrought by biological inheritance, not volitional choice—then the principle applies equally to every form of crime perpetrated by a nation, tribe, and/or ethnic group against a rival collective. For example, in 1915 during the First World War, the Ottoman Turks perpetrated the horrific Armenian Genocide, murdering between 1 and 1.5 million innocent Armenian civilians.[4] To this day, the Turkish regime denies the atrocity. In reality, it is long past time for the Turkish regime to acknowledge this bitter truth and express sincere contrition. What about reparations? On this theory, every last individual of Turkish descent must be held to account. What if a given Turkish family was overseas at the time and took no part in the massive crime? No matter. What if individual Turks vehemently opposed the massacre and risked their lives to save innocent Armenians, the way Oskar Schindler, Irina Sendler, Raoul Wallenberg, and other Christian heroes did to save Jews from the Nazis? It changes nothing. Now, more than a century and five generations later, are the great, great, great grandchildren, born some eighty to ninety years subsequent to these horrific events, to be held responsible for them? On this theory, indeed they are—and they must pay reparations not even to the victimized survivors, who are long gone, but to descendants five generations removed, who, thankfully, were not forced to live through this massive atrocity. It is true that many Armenians had lands stolen from them, which could be returned. But to whom—and by whom? The original owners are long gone, and the land in question may have been in the possession of the present occupant's family for generations. Is it morally right to penalize the innocent descendants of criminals, who themselves may well be honest individuals, to restitute land to the descendants of the victims? Another way to ask this question is: How many centuries must pass and how many generations occupy the land before a statute of limitations applies that nullifies a legitimate call for reparations? On a racial theory of moral responsibility, consistently applied, no amount of either will suffice.

How Far Back?

This theory compels us to raise a somewhat bizarre question: How far back, over how many centuries and generations, must we look before we come to a terminus of a contemporary racial group's moral responsibility for the crimes perpetrated by its ancestors? Indeed, is there any terminus—or does our responsibility extend all the way back to the impenetrable mists of prehistory? *How far back*? It is a legitimate question. For example, long ago on the North American continent, in the centuries before the arrival of Europeans, the Iroquois tribe conducted genocidal warfare against the Algonquin.[5] Surely, descendants of the Iroquois owe reparations to descendants of Algonquin survivors. In the western part of what became the United States, the Comanche were notoriously brutal to other tribes.[6] Similarly, their descendants owe restitution to the descendants of their tribal victims. In Asia in the thirteenth century, it is believed that Genghis Khan was responsible for slaughtering thirty million individuals in China alone[7]—so contemporary Mongolians are definitely responsible for reparations to descendants of his victims. In the Mediterranean region, the Barbary pirates, North African Islamic corsairs who were satraps to the Sultan of the Ottoman Empire, enslaved roughly 1 million to 1.25 million white European Christians during the early centuries of the modern era—and under horrific conditions.[8] Clearly, North Africans today owe restitution to white people. One final example of many that could be adduced: powerful African tribes conquered and enslaved members of weaker tribes; they held some in bondage themselves and sold others to European slave traders.[9] Descendants of these tribes owe restitution to descendants of the conquered tribes. And the beat goes on . . . endlessly.

In the relentless warfare of mankind's history, there is literally not a square inch of real estate anywhere on this earth that has not been conquered, reconquered, and conquered again. Slavery has existed all over the world throughout all of history, brutal subjugation, mass rape, and pandemic slaughter . . . such horrors, tragically, have too often been the norm in human life. If the descendants of one tribe owe restitution to the descendants of another group brutalized by their ancestors, how would we determine who owes what to whom . . . and how much? Every group in history has been oppressed at some point by somebody and has legitimate grievances that can be raised, some more recent than the end of slavery in the United States, and some further back in the past. One notorious example occurred during the Second World War: when Germany conquered large parts of Russia, the Nazis murdered countless innocent Russian civilians. Similarly, when the Russians conquered large parts of

Germany later in the war, Soviet troops perpetrated massive rape and brutalization of the German civilian population. How would we sort out and comprehend such a massive cluster of crimes and counter-crimes? How could we adjudicate such a welter of resulting claims and counterclaims? How would we know which Germans owed what to which Russians—and vice versa? The simple answer is: we could not.

Regarding racial moral responsibility: the irrationality of the premise leads logically to such unanswerable conundrums.

A Straw Man?

Critics might accuse me of setting up a straw man argument, that is, of so exaggerating or distorting the case for slavery reparations as to make it grotesquely illogical and utterly impracticable. In reality, my critics might add, we do not claim that all white Americans owe restitution to all Black Americans. We maintain only the narrower claim that the descendants of white slave owners owe reparations to the descendants of Black slaves. My response is that there is still both a moral and a practical problem with this proposal. The moral difficulty is that 160 years after the fact, we have neither the victimizing nor the victimized parties. Should we punish one group, eight generations later, because their distant ancestors perpetrated heinous crimes? And should we reward one group because deep in the past their family members were brutally persecuted? What if, in subsequent generations, the slave owner's progeny became active opponents of Jim Crow laws, the Ku Klux Klan, the persecution and lynching of Blacks? Does that matter? Is it sufficient to partially mitigate the present descendant's culpability? And what if, among the more recent ancestors of a present-day descendant of slaves, we find a murderous criminal? Will that matter? Is it enough to offset the present descendant's status as unrelieved victim? The moral problems are endless.

Further, the practical difficulty is manifest. How do we discern, through the fog of time, the legal status of a current individual's ancestors of 150 or 200 or 300 years ago? The problem is especially acute regarding the relatively small number of white slave owners. How do we identify them? Do we comb through every legal document we can find of every white person in America? Or of every white Southerner? The task is akin to a Herculean labor. Who will do it? Who gets to spend years of their lives sifting through archives, searching for ghosts of the past—for slave owners and for the marriage and birth records of their descendants? And what of the *Black* slave owners of the antebellum South? There were some. Do their progeny pay reparations to the descendants of slaves—or is discharging that burden solely the responsibility of whites? And what if some of the Black slave descendants are today affluent or rich, and some of the white progeny of slave owners are poor? Does this matter? Is there some financial cutoff point below or above which one is absolved of guilt or restrained from gaining reward?

The Significance of the Civil War

Further, it could certainly be argued that white Americans have already paid reparations for slavery . . . paid in blood. The long-held estimate of Union dead in the Civil War was some 360,000 (calculated upward in recent years). The South seceded over slavery, the North went to war over secession, but Union victory on the battlefield enabled President Lincoln and a Republican Congress to pass the 13th Amendment ending slavery in this country. Human slavery has been an ages-old, worldwide horror—and still is in Sudan, North Korea, China, and elsewhere. But how many nations have fought the bloodiest war in their history, resulting in their ability to terminate slavery? Very few. That many whites continued to brutally oppress Black Americans is a sad truth of US history. But it must also be acknowledged that the bloodshed to terminate human slavery in this country is a much higher cost than can be paid in money.

What about Biracial Americans?

Another interesting conundrum involves biracial Americans, for example, the super-wealthy New York Yankees slugger, Giancarlo Stanton, whose father is white and whose mother is Black. Does the white part of Stanton pay reparations to the Black part of him? Does he owe money to his mother but is owed money by his father? Should the white half of him pay reparations to Black Americans while the Black half receives reparations from white Americans? Even the wisdom of Solomon would prove insufficient to deduce rationally just answers to these questions.

Who Decides Who Pays?

A further question is: Who decides who pays and who is paid? Because reparations are a Marxist program of coercively redistributing income, the federal government will presumably appoint a committee to study the issue and make recommendations. They name it the Slavery Reparations Commission. Who are the members of the commission—and who heads it? For example, should Ibram X. Kendi be a member—or even head—of the commission? Certainly, the commission members must be theoretical supporters of race-based, coercive redistribution of wealth—and Kendi is a prominent spokesman for that theory. He supports a federal bureau of anti-racism that will redistribute wealth, ensuring financial equity to all racial groups; a massive theft and redistribution of wealth that must occur regardless of whether or not specific inequalities are caused by racial discrimination. He also desires the government to monitor and restrict the speech of those who criticize these programs.[10] Kendi (or one of his ilk) is a logical choice to head the commission. The programs he advocates compose a totalitarian state, specifically Communism, and slavery reparations are a step down that path, an exquisitely irrational policy of massive governmental theft, composing a sort of halfway house of semi-socialism on the road to a full coercive redistribution of income.

The Economic Difference between Slavery and Freedom

My critics will respond: "But white Americans benefited from black slavery—and still do." However, this claim is egregiously false. Let's go back in time and then push our analysis forward. The slave-holding South was far poorer than the freer North. One reason, although not the only one, is that slavery is not a viable economic system; hiring free laborers is much more profitable. Slavery is expensive: slaves must be bought, fed, housed, clothed, and medically cared for. They are motivated to do only as much work as necessary to avoid the lash and no more. Fences must be built to herd them in and/or slave patrols deployed to hunt down fugitives. Militias must be maintained to guard against such slave uprisings as those of Gabriel Prosser, Denmark Vesey, and Nat Turner—and against raids by such fervent abolitionists as John Brown. Indeed, abolitionism must be fought tooth and nail—and slave states resorted to opening mail to remove offending anti-slavery literature.

Hiring free laborers obviates all of this, and such workers can be motivated to increased productivity by offering higher wages. Adam Smith explained this a long time ago: slavery is not about profits—it is about power, it is about domination over others.[11] Everybody, including plantation owners, would profit by ending (or never beginning) slavery. All of the labor, time, and wealth invested in trading for slaves with African tribal chiefs, building ships for the slave trade, manning those vessels, forming patrols to hunt fugitives, maintaining armed militias, combating abolitionism, and fighting a bloody war against the North—all of it could be deployed in productive work, in building and constructing, rather than in initiating force against innocent victims. The South would have been more productive and more profitable. But power-lust and brute force are seductive lures—and often lead men to act against their rational self-interest.

Related, slave drivers have a vested interest in keeping slaves uneducated and ignorant, and in many slave states, it was illegal to educate slaves; for educated men are far more likely to recognize the inalienable moral right of each individual to liberty. Note that Prosser, Vesey, and Turner were all educated men who taught their compatriots the principles of the American Revolution.[12] But Ayn Rand demonstrated brilliantly in *Atlas Shrugged* that the mind, not whip-driven slave labor, is mankind's survival instrument.[13] It is human intelligence that has created the life-giving advances in the arts, in philosophy and logic, in science and technology. If slaves were free, some percentage of them would pursue education. Some would become teachers, professors, doctors, lawyers, entrepreneurs, writers, artists, and so forth, creating vast human capital enriching American society. The economic difference between slavery and freedom can be summed up in the microcosm, in the life of George Washington Carver: think of the difference in productive output between Carver the enslaved field hand and Carver the agricultural scientist whose innovations substantially improved crop yields for Southern farmers, white and Black. Economically, there is no comparison between freedom and slavery.

If further evidence of this point is necessary, we can examine such Communist countries as the former Soviet Union, China, and North Korea, all of which employ(ed) massive slave labor, and all of which were desperately poor, or, at the very least, substantially poorer than the freer capitalist or semi-capitalist nations.

White Americans have greatly benefited from the creative work of George Washington Carver and other Black geniuses. But nobody benefits from slavery. The foregone benefits of the brutal system vastly outweigh its relatively meager productivity.

Benefiting Black Americans

In addition to the moral difficulties, there is the practical point that reparations will bring few or no benefits to Black Americans. There are roughly 41.5 million Black Americans. If, for example, the federal government shelled out $1,000.00 per capita, the cost runs to $41.5 billion. If it paid $2,000.00 per head, the cost is doubled to $83 billion, and so forth. That is a lot of money. But what will $1,000.00 or $2,000.00 do for individual Black Americans? It will buy groceries for perhaps a few weeks, or maybe serve as a down payment on a car—but then what? People are back to whatever their lives were before.

What will have deep, long-lasting benefits for Black Americans? Two things: (1) a politics of individual rights with its attendant code of color-blind individualism, and (2) a culture of reason and education. Let's examine these one at a time.

Color-Blind Individualism

All human beings must learn that race means nothing important about a person. Character is everything. It is appropriate to judge an individual by reference to the moral choices he/she makes, not by reference to the racial group he happens to be born into; by examining what is in his volitional control, not in accordance with what is not. In logic, this is the only panacea for racism in any of its hideous iterations; this is the sole antidote for racial discrimination of any and all types. Every human being on earth will benefit from this realization; first and foremost, it aids members of historically oppressed minorities. Some individuals in contemporary America repudiate color-blind individualism as a "micro-aggression." But the truth is that anyone who rejects the only logical cure for this social ill forfeits any right to consider himself a foe of racism.

A Culture of Reason

In the antebellum South, many slave owners prohibited their slaves from gaining an education. And today, the government school system is largely a wasteland, and perhaps worst of all in many Black urban areas.[14] Especially harmful is the physicalistic, anti-intellectual subculture embraced by many young urban Black men, a set of ideas that too often leads to rejection of education, and to drug use, crime, drug gangs and trafficking, and hideously internecine violent crime. Entire books may be written on how to resolve such seemingly intractable dilemmas. But one important virtue can be enacted by all families. Reading is the single most important cognitive skill. Once a child learns how to read, the entire world of knowledge is open to him, and he then possesses the ability to be a lifelong learner. It is very easy to teach a motivated child how to read. The first step is to let a very young child pick out a book(s) that looks interesting to him, whether in a bookstore, at a library, or on Amazon. Then Mom (or Dad or Grandma) reads to him. The child thereby learns that books are fun, that there are all kinds of interesting things to read about. He is motivated to learn to read. By the age of four, most children are able to learn to read, to match the verbal symbols they already know with the literary symbols on the written page. The parent employs systematic phonics, teaching the child the sound of each letter in the alphabet and of the combination of sounds. The child can then sound out the overwhelming preponderance (some 87 percent) of the words in the English language and is well on his way to becoming an accomplished reader. Will a strong reading ability cure all the woes of a failed school system and of the appeal of criminal gangs? It will not. But it is a good start to valuing education and to respecting the characteristic most distinctively human: our minds.

Reparations Must Be Dismissed by All Honest Persons

Morally, the idea of slavery reparations rests on the reprehensible claim of racial—rather than individual—responsibility. Economically, it rests on the false premise that white Americans, or anybody, profits from slavery. The theory is both false and despicable—and, as such, must be dismissed by all honest persons.

Ayn Rand has shown us what will benefit Black, as well as all other Americans: a culture that celebrates the mind, and a politics that upholds inalienable individual rights. When this occurs in American culture, and especially in Black urban neighborhoods, we will witness a Renaissance, an outpouring of creative minds—Black, Asian, white, Latino, and biracial—whose achievements in every intellectual field will redound to the betterment of all human lives, as have the advances wrought by the towering geniuses briefly mentioned above.

Notes

1 Philip Dray, *At the Hands of Persons Unknown* (New York: The Modern Library, 2003), 245–6.
2 Ibid., vii–viii.

3. Scott Ellsworth, "Tulsa Race Massacre," in *The Encyclopedia of Oklahoma History and Culture* (https://www.okhistory.org/publications/enc/entry?entry=TU013, accessed June 10, 2024).

4. Vahakn Dadrian's *The History of the Armenian Genocide* is the definitive examination of this atrocity (New York: Berghahn Books, 1995), *passim*. See also, Andrew Bernstein, "Lessons of the Armenian Genocide," *The Objective Standard* 10, no. 2 (Summer 2015): 48–57.

5. Clark Wissler, *Indians of the United States* (New York: Doubleday, 1940), 69–70, 127–32.

6. Jeff Fynn-Paul, *Not Stolen: The Truth About European Colonialism in the New World* (New York: Bombardier Books, 2023), 188.

7. Matthew White, *Atrocities* (New York: W. W. Norton & Company, 2012), 123.

8. Giles Milton, *White Gold: The Extraordinary Story of Thomas Pellew and Islam's One Million White Slaves* (New York: Farrar, Strauss and Giroux, 2001), 1–50 and *passim*. Robert Davis, *Christian Slaves, Muslim Masters: White Slavery in the Mediterranean, the Barbary Coast, and Italy, 1500–1800* (New York: Palgrave Macmillan, 2003), *passim*.

9. Thomas Sowell, *Race and Culture* (New York: Basic Books, 1994), 194–5. See also, David Smith, "African Chiefs Urged to Apologize for Slave Trade," *The Guardian* (November 18, 2009) (https://www.theguardian.com/world/2009/nov/18/africans-apologise-slave-trade, accessed March 14, 2024).

10. Ibram X. Kendi, "Pass an Anti-Racist Constitutional Amendment," *Politico* (2019). Quoted in James Lindsay, *Race Marxism* (Orlando: New Discourses, 2022), 73.

11. Barry Weingast, "Adam Smith's Theory of the Persistence of Slavery and its Abolition in Western Europe" (https://web.stanford.edu/group/mcnollgast/cgi-bin/wordpress/wp-content/uploads/2013/10/asms-theory-of-sy.15.0725.print-version.pdf, accessed March 9, 2021).

12. Andrew Bernstein, "Black Slaves Who Could Have Been American Founders," *The Objective Standard* 10, no. 4 (Winter 2015–2016): 40–6.

13. Ayn Rand, *Atlas Shrugged* (New York: Random House, 1957).

14. Andrew Bernstein, *Why Johnny Still Can't Read or Write or Understand Math* (New York: Bombardier Books, 2022).

Responses

Response to Lenzerini on Reparations

Andrew Bernstein

> **Study Questions**
>
> 1. What does Bernstein think is the major error in Lenzerini's argument? How does his point apply to the question of reparations?
> 2. What does Bernstein mean by "the moral is the practical," and what does this have to do with reparations?
> 3. According to Bernstein, what will be the deleterious consequences of reparations?

Professor Lenzerini makes a case for slavery reparations. However, I think his argument fails at several key points.

The Moral Is the Practical

The major but not the only error in Lenzerini's argument is his willingness to egregiously violate individual rights. He speaks of "human rights" but never of individual rights. He writes: "A right to redress for the wrongs suffered is indeed inherent in human rights" (pp. 358–59). But there are no human rights in the absence of individual rights. An individual human being has an inalienable right to life, liberty, and the pursuit of happiness, as Thomas Jefferson so eloquently stated. This principle is a requirement of human life and flourishing. If an individual does not possess such rights, then no moral principle constrains either a private criminal from shoving a knife into the heart of an innocent victim or a Communist or National Socialist murder state from annihilating millions of individual human beings whose sole "crime" was being members of a class or race demonized by the butchers-in-chief. In the United States, coercive slavery reparations will be a crime of massive theft perpetrated against millions of honest individuals innocent of imposing a system of slavery abolished 160 years ago.

Related, the moral is the practical and the immoral is the impractical. For example, if we respect and protect individual rights, as we should, then the independent thinkers in any and every society are free to develop and promote new ideas in all fields, regardless of whether they clash with the political or religious authority. Progress regarding every endeavor results, substantially enriching human life in literature and the arts, in philosophy, in theoretical and applied science, in technology, in medicine, in law, and in every other rational discipline. But if we abrogate individual rights, then no moral principle restrains the State or church from suppressing free thinkers whose novel ideas clash with established orthodoxy. Morally and legally empowering the State to rob innocent individuals to finance reparations for a massive crime abolished long ago—or any other vicious scheme to redistribute wealth that the State might hatch—transforms the State from a protector of individual rights to a violator of them, the most powerful and thereby the most dangerous violator of them all.

After all, if an individual has no right to his own wealth, then what right has he to his own thinking? A human being is a composite of mind and body—there is no separating them in fact. He earns wealth by means of his thinking and physical effort: if he has no right to the wealth he has earned via his thinking, then what right has he to the thinking that created it? If we deny the effect, we vitiate the cause. And what does the Robber State do to its private citizens who vociferously protest its larcenous activities? There may be a time lag in a coercive government moving from violating its citizens' right to their own wealth to violating their right to their own thinking, but if the principle of individual rights is neither implemented nor restored, a time lag is all that it is. Witness, for example, in the United States, the move from a coercively redistributive state toward censorship: the Twitter files showed government agencies "coaching" privately owned social media platforms regarding whose thinking could be articulated on those platforms and whose could not. Predictably, those whose thinking agreed with government pronouncements and policy could be heard—and those who disagreed were silenced.[1] Perhaps even more baleful was the mercifully short-lived Disinformation Governance Board at the Department of Homeland Security—*a law enforcement agency*—a step toward the government arrogating to itself the power to determine truth and falsity.[2] Recall also the ominous words of Jacinda Ardern, then prime minister of New Zealand during the pandemic: "We [the government] will continue to be your single source of truth. . . . Unless you hear it from us it is not the truth."[3] Serious students of George Orwell recognize an incipient Ministry of Truth when they see one—and are properly terrified by it. The moral principle of individual rights, widely understood and upheld in a nation and embedded in its written Constitution, is the strongest bulwark against tyranny.

The Bad Consequences of Reparations

Because slavery reparations is an immoral policy, it will have deleterious consequences. First, *what good will it do?* The government will extort billions of dollars to give each Black American, on average, several thousand dollars. When this small amount is spent, let's say to buy a family several months of groceries, what then? It's back to business as usual—except for the residual harm too easily overlooked. Frederic Bastiat, the great liberal economic writer, warned us brilliantly, in his essay, "That Which Is Seen, and That Which Is Not Seen," to identify all consequences of a public policy on all people, not merely some consequences on some people. Millions of honest people, innocent of all blame for slavery, will understandably be resentful at being coerced into a policy that they properly recognize as madness. Will such resentment contribute to a resurgence of the racism that has tormented America—and all of humanity—throughout history? Perhaps so. But more pernicious will be the belief that we have now, to a degree, succored the victims. We will not have done so.

We may become even less cognizant, if that is possible, of what will, in fact, benefit Black Americans (and members of oppressed races, tribes, and ethnic groups worldwide): the principle of color-blind or race-blind individualism. The principle, stated simply, is that *character* matters, race does not. The principle is right and just and true, because it counsels us to judge individuals on their moral choices rather than on the tribe or ethnic group into which they happen to be born, on what is in their volitional control rather than on what is not. The salutary consequences are that we will stop judging human beings on their race, that is, on a trivial and unchosen characteristic of theirs. All human beings will thereby benefit; first, foremost, and always those members of historically oppressed racial or ethnic groups. Once again, the moral is the practical; the immoral is the impractical. There are people who regard support for color-blind individualism as a "micro-aggression." The answer to such a claim is that we can end racism in any form solely by recognizing that race does not matter. In logic, color-blind individualism is the only panacea for racism. To reject it is to sustain racism's ghastly existence.

Further, Professor Lenzerini seems to think, as do many people, that slavery contributed to industrialization and wealth creation in the West, including in the United States. He writes: "Not to mention that the state concerned may have accrued benefits 'from . . . slavery or abusive colonialism . . . that presumably helped to jumpstart [its] industrialization and thus continue to the present'" (p. 361). He qualifies the claim with a "may have." He is wise to do so because the primitive institution of slavery hinders industrialization and wealth creation; it does not advance it.

For example, the Soviet Union deployed widespread slave labor but relied heavily on aid from the United States and other semi-capitalist nations to achieve whatever degree of industrialization it did—and despite massive Western aid, it still collapsed in abysmal poverty.[4] China under Mao also suffered extensive slavery and remained poorer even than the Soviet Union. Today, North Korea enslaves a staggering 10 percent of its population and is utterly destitute.[5] In the United States, the slave South was substantially poorer than the freer North, and the American Industrial Revolution took place in the section of greater liberty. Great Britain's Industrial Revolution was initiated in the late eighteenth century at the same time that the British birthed humanity's first abolitionist movement.

What explains all of this? Industrialization depends on advances in science and technology. As with progress in the arts, philosophy, medicine, and other intellectual disciplines, this requires human mind power at work. But the creative mind must be free, not enslaved or suppressed under totalitarian regimes. For example, the British and, later, the American Industrial Revolutions occurred because the relative freedom of those societies liberated such productive geniuses as James Watt, Matthew Boulton, the other great minds of the Lunar Society of Birmingham, Thomas Edison, the Wright brothers, Henry Ford, Andrew Carnegie, and so forth. The principle of individual rights, to the extent it is adopted, liberates the great thinkers in any society to create both intellectual and material wealth. This wealth creation already benefits many Black Americans; a readoption of the principle of individual rights in America, with its corollary of color-blind individualism, will benefit Black Americans much more than slavery reparations will.

Once again, as always, the moral is the practical.

Notes

1 Jesse O'Neill, "Biden Admin Pushed to Bar Twitter Users for COVID 'Disinformation,' Files Show," *New York Post* (December 26, 2022) (https://nypost.com/2022/12/26/biden-admin-pushed-to-ban-twitter-users-for-covid-disinformation/, accessed August 9, 2024).

2 Jill Goldenziel, "The Disinformation Governance Board Is Dead. Here's the Right Way to Fight Disinformation," *Forbes* (May 18, 2022) (https://www.forbes.com/sites/jillgoldenziel/2022/05/18/the-disinformation-governance-board-is-dead-heres-the-right-way-to-fight-disinformation/, accessed August 9, 2024).

3 "Government is Not the Divine Source of Truth," *Spectator Australia* (July 26, 2022) (https://www.spectator.com.au/2022/07/government-is-not-the-divine-source-of-truth/, accessed August 1, 2024).

4 Antony Sutton, *Western Technology and Soviet Economic Development*, 3 vols (Palo Alto: Hoover Institute Press, 1968, 1971, 1973).

5 "Modern Slavery in North Korea: Global Slavery Index 2023 Country Snapshot" (https://cdn.walkfree.org/content/uploads/2023/09/27164815/GSI-Snapshot-North-Korea.pdf, accessed August 2, 2024).

Response to Bernstein on Reparations

Federico Lenzerini

Study Questions

1. What two conditions does Lenzerini say must be satisfied in order to justify slavery reparations?
2. According to Lenzerini, how do slavery reparations meet the first condition? How do they meet the second condition?
3. Why do reparations for slavery and slave trade need not be conceived in economic terms? How does this point allow Lenzerini to diffuse some of Bernstein's concerns?

If it is true that all kinds of opinions and views are inherently relative and questionable, this is all the more true when it comes to ethical (or moral) views. Depending on the perspectives, arguments used to support opposite ideas may appear equally valuable and convincing. This is why I much appreciate the arguments used by Bernstein to refute the morality of slavery reparations, and I actually agree with many of them. At the same time, however, I do not agree with his main standpoint, postulating the lack of a sound moral basis justifying reparations for slavery and slave trade.

At the beginning of his brilliant essay, Bernstein argues that "[o]ne cannot be born with the moral turpitude of one's ancestors hardwired into one's character. Put simply, moral responsibility is based on an individual's choices, not on one's racial membership" (p. 371). I could not agree more. Obviously, the assumption that innocent descendants of perpetrators should not be considered responsible to pay reparations for the crimes committed by their ancestors appears objectively indisputable. This notwithstanding, in my modest opinion, the ethical legitimacy of reparations for slavery and slave trade can still be convincingly defended, on the condition that two requirements are satisfied. The first of these requirements is that somebody must exist who still suffers—albeit indirectly—the detrimental effects originally produced by slavery and slave trade. The second requirement, which is interconnected with the first, consists in the condition that the obstacle posed to the legal (and, *a fortiori*, ethical) legitimacy of reparations by the principle of *intertemporal law* can be overcome.

As regards the first requirement, damages arising from slavery and slave trade suffered by people living today need not necessarily be of an economic nature. Indeed, empirical evidence shows that many persons exist today who continue to perceive a current, real, and genuine feeling of suffering or anguish determined by the past injustices produced by slavery and slave trade. This feeling can be determined, for instance, by the outrage that slavery and slave trade have caused to the cultural and ethnic identity of the persons concerned, or to their sense of belonging to the racial group targeted by slavers and slave traders; or, for example, it can arise from a sense of injustice and inequality transmitted by past wrongs to present generations, or even from the economic or (especially) social imbalance between different sectors of the society that was produced by slavery and slave trade and that has been perpetuated up to present days. These circumstances can produce sentiments of grief, establishing an evident and *tangible* tie between the persons concerned (living today) and those who, in the past, were directly affected by the wrongs produced by slavery and slave trade, attributing to the former a right to be adequately redressed for the effects of such wrongs they continue to perceive. Put in different, but equivalent, terms, reparations have the power to "either directly or indirectly modify the . . . injustices that continue to face African Americans in their adopted nation (America)."[1]

With respect to the second requirement, intertemporal law is a legal principle according to which a legal question must be evaluated on the basis of the law in force at the time when it arose, implying that a given behavior should be deemed wrong only if and to the extent that it was considered illegal at the time when it was done. This requirement would apparently negate the legitimacy of any reparations claims for the wrongs produced by slavery and slave trade. In fact, up to the early nineteenth century, those practices were *not* prohibited by either international law or by domestic law in the United States, where slavery was abolished by the 13th Amendment to the Constitution in 1865. However, considering what I just wrote regarding the effects that slavery and slave trade continue to produce today on a significant number of persons, this apparent obstacle is overcome by the existence of a continuity in the effects of the wrongs originally produced by slavery and slave trade, which continue to project their consequences on the contemporary society. In fact, "there is a convincing case to be made for the continuing effects of these past injustices in the present inequalities of income, wealth, housing, health care, social standing, education, employment, and other opportunities that characterize the situation of African Americans in the United States."[2] This is the reason why I respectfully disagree with Bernstein when he claims that it "is egregiously false" that "white Americans benefited from black slavery—and still do" (p. 378). Indeed, it clearly appears that slavery and slave trade have generated social and cultural disparities—putting, in general, the descendants of slave owners in a position of social advantage—whose effects have been perpetuated to present times.

That said, I wish to elaborate on the fact that the question of reparations for slavery and slave trade must not necessarily be conceived in economic terms. On the contrary, it is clear how the economic aspect is not the preponderant one. Reparations for past injustices may take many different forms, depending on what is perceived by the victims as necessary to effectively restore the torts they have suffered, which is different and unique in each instance of past wrongs. In the case of slavery and slave trade, the main purpose of reparations should be to restore the social and cultural disequilibrium determined by the wrong, or—which is the same—to reestablish the social order broken by the latter. It follows that, in principle, reparations should not take the form of financial compensation (unless specific successors of the direct victims are identifiable who, for whatever reason, have suffered a definite and recognizable economic loss in consequence of the wrongs concerned), but rather that of *symbolic* redress, including, for example, formal apology, recognition of the wrong, building of monuments, development of social programs aimed at removing the persisting effects of the wrong, and so on, with the ultimate purpose of eliminating the social inequalities and the sense of injustice transmitted by slavery and slave trade to present generations. Consequently, the costs of reparations for slavery and slave trade should not be borne by the individual descendants of perpetrators, but rather by the society as a whole (namely, the state, including through taxes, consistent with their solidaristic function), exactly for the reason that reparations would have the (solidaristic) purpose of healing a wound of the whole society, determined by a wrong that has broken its social order. In this context, reparations would attain a predominantly *collective* connotation. Consistently, I disagree with the assumption by Bernstein that "[m]oral responsibility is individual, not collective" (p. 371). It actually depends on the specific circumstances characterizing a given case of past wrongs. For instance, today, both at the international and domestic level, the idea has consolidated according to which Indigenous peoples are entitled to reparations from the whole society of the state where they live, because the torts they have suffered in the past were perpetrated with, as a minimum, the acquiescence of the state and/or its organs or agents (exactly like in the case of slavery and slave trade).

Conceived in the way just described, the discourse of reparations for slavery and slave trade—in addition to validating the ethical legitimacy of such reparations—makes them consistent with the Aristotelian theory of corrective justice, conceived as the reestablishment of a moral state of equality breached by a wrong.[3] Furthermore, it allows to defuse a number of issues, including some raised by Bernstein in his essay. Such issues include, for instance, whether or not slavery is/was economically advantageous, or whether or not the whole national society or part of it benefited from slavery, as well as the problems related to the identification of "white slave owners" or to the possibility that "some of the black slave descendants are today affluent or rich—and some of the white progeny of slave owners are poor." It would also neutralize the significance of the question "how far back?," as the ethical legitimacy of reparations for slavery and slave trade would not depend on considerations of temporal character, but on the fact of whether a connection still exists between the wrongs produced by such practices and people living today.

In his excellent essay, Bernstein refers to Ayn Rand as holding that "what will benefit black, as well as all other Americans" is "[a] culture that celebrates the mind, and a politics that upholds inalienable . . . rights" (p. 380). Essentially, the main purpose of reparations for slavery and slave trade should exactly be that of recognizing that those practices seriously denied people their inalienable human rights and, more generally, broke the positive values on which a fair and ethically just society is grounded, as well as that of putting in place appropriate social measures aimed at promoting such rights and values, through removing the social and cultural inequities that were originally determined by said practices and that have been passed down to contemporary generations.

Notes

1. See A. B. Assensoh and Yvette M. Alex-Assensoh, "The Political Economy of Land and Reparations: The Case of Reparations for African Americans in the 21st Century," *American Journal of Economics and Sociology* 80 (2021): 699.
2. See Thomas McCarthy, "Coming to Terms with Our Past, Part II: On the Morality and Politics of Reparations for Slavery," *Political Theory* 32 (2004): 750, 753.
3. See *The Ethics of Aristotle*, trans. J. K. Thomson (Harmondsworth: Penguin, 1955), 148.

Questions for Reflection

1. Do you think that Lenzerini has successfully addressed Bernstein's charge that slavery reparations would be a violation of individual rights? Why?

2. Lenzerini makes much in his case for reparations of conditions that exist in the present rather than the past (e.g., the emotional anguish experienced by people today because of past injustices). How, if at all, could Bernstein address this concern?

3. How might the process for determining eligibility for reparations work? What ethical issues might arise in implementing the process?

For Further Reading

Darity, Jr., William A., and Kirsten Mullen. *From Here to Equality: Reparations for Black Americans in the Twenty-First Century*, 2nd ed. University of North Carolina Press, 2022.

Epstein, Richard A. "The Case against Black Reparations." *Boston University Law Review* 84 (2004): 1177.

Kane, Gregory. "Why the Reparations Movement Should Fail." *University of Maryland Law Journal of Race, Religion, Gender, and Class* 189 (2003), 189–208.

Lenzerini, Federico. *Reparations for Indigenous Peoples: International and Comparative Perspectives*. Oxford University Press, 2008.

Sowell, Thomas. *Discrimination and Disparities*. Hachette, 2019.

Turner, Robert. *Creating a Culture of Repair: Taking Action on the Road to Reparations*. Westminster John Knox Press, 2024.

12

Free Speech

Free Speech Absolutism

Onkar Ghate

> **Study Questions**
>
> 1. How does the American view of the individual's relation to the government differ from the view of previous forms of government?
> 2. How does Ghate compare and contrast freedom of speech in collectivist forms of government versus the new, American form of government?
> 3. What connection does Ghate make between free speech and pursuing the true and the good?
> 4. According to Ghate, what does the right to free speech mean and what does it protect?
> 5. How does Ghate show that exercising *any* right can affect other people without providing grounds to abridge it? What application of this general point does he make to hate speech?
> 6. What kinds of speech does the right to free speech not protect? Why?

With the exception of the United States, hate speech laws prevail throughout the Westernized world. In my native country, Canada, for example, "Everyone who, by communicating statements, other than in private conversation, wilfully promotes hatred against any identifiable group is guilty of (a) an indictable offence and is liable to imprisonment for a term not exceeding two years; or (b) an offence punishable on summary conviction."[1] Canadian law puts special emphasis on denial of the Holocaust: "Everyone who, by communicating statements, other than in private conversation, wilfully promotes antisemitism by condoning, denying or downplaying the Holocaust

(a) is guilty of an indictable offence and liable to imprisonment for a term not exceeding two years; or (b) is guilty of an offence punishable on summary conviction."[2]

As these sections of Canadian law should make clear, what is being legally prohibited is *speech*. The government has the power to *censor* the expression of certain ideas or viewpoints. In the United States, by virtue of the First Amendment, hate speech laws such as these would (or at least should) be declared unconstitutional. "Congress shall make no law," the First Amendment reads in part, "abridging the freedom of speech, or of the press."[3] No matter how irrational or abhorrent the content of a person's speech, no law means no law.

The US Constitution, in other words, deprives the government of the power to censor; it treats the right to freedom of speech as absolute, permitting no legal abridgement, no carving out of exceptions. This, I will argue, is the correct approach to freedom of speech. Or at least *if* the fundamentally new form of government that the Declaration of Independence and the US Constitution brought into existence is the correct form of government, which I believe it is, then freedom of speech should be regarded as an individual, absolute, inviolable right.

The New, American Form of Government

The radicalism of the American Revolution consists in rooting proper government, not in the theories of collectivism but of *individualism*. Previous forms of government regarded the individual as subordinate to the state and its goals or ends. The individual was a *subject*, the quasi property or possession of the nation as a whole and its representatives or spokesmen, be it the king or the pope or the aristocracy or the majority, who were responsible for upholding the collective will. On this conception of government, a collective good—the glory of our nation, the propagation of our religion, the advancement of the public interest—transcends the interests and life of the individual. The individual is subordinate to this collectivist goal, a mere means to an end.

In principle, though certainly not in full practice given the continuation of slavery, the Declaration and Constitution broke with this long-standing view. The individual was no longer viewed as subordinate to some higher goal or end embodied by the state. The individual *was the end*, the state the means. That the individual has a right to the pursuit of her own happiness, a moral right to live her own life, preexists government.[4] Government, properly, is created solely to secure and protect these rights: a proper government protects the freedom of every individual to pursue her own happiness. On this new conception of government, we as individuals are no longer subjects but *citizens*. As citizens, we are not subordinate to government; government is subordinate to each of us. As the Declaration famously states these points,

> We hold these truths to be self-evident, that all men are created equal, that they are endowed by their Creator with certain unalienable Rights, that among these are Life,

Liberty and the pursuit of Happiness.—That to secure these rights, Governments are instituted among Men, deriving their just powers from the consent of the governed,—That whenever any Form of Government becomes destructive of these ends, it is the Right of the People to alter or to abolish it, and to institute new Government.[5]

Thus, representative, constitutionally limited government came into existence. The government is the representative of the individual: each individual delegates to government the power to secure and protect her rights, her legitimate freedom of action. *That is the only enforcement power she can delegate to government.* And that delegation establishes the only legitimate function of government: to secure and protect the rights of *each and every individual* within its jurisdiction, including, as the First Amendment makes clear, the right to freedom of speech.

Freedom of Speech under Collectivist Forms of Government

Under collectivist forms of government, the ruling authorities have the power to censor the speech of individuals in order to further the specific collectivist goal that the state is thought to embody or secure. If, for instance, the glory of our nation or the propagation of our religion is thought best served by silencing a particular individual, the authorities lawfully can silence that individual. The church's censoring of Galileo by the charge of heresy to prevent him from expounding the heliocentric theory of the solar system is an important historical case in point, one with which the creators of America's new form of government were certainly familiar.[6]

Today, we can see this same collectivist approach in Canadian hate speech laws. At first glance, Canada seems to recognize the individual's absolute right to freedom of expression in terms similar to those of the First Amendment. Section 2 of the *Canadian Charter of Rights and Freedoms* states that "Everyone has the following fundamental freedoms: (a) freedom of conscience and religion; (b) freedom of thought, belief, opinion and expression, including freedom of the press and other media of communication; (c) freedom of peaceful assembly; and (d) freedom of association."[7]

But in reality, these supposed guarantees of the individual's freedom of thought and expression are not held by *right*. They are held by *permission* of the government, as the enforcer of a collectivist goal, in this case, the public interest. Section 1 of the *Charter* states that "The *Canadian Charter of Rights and Freedoms* guarantees the rights and freedoms set out in it subject only to such reasonable limits prescribed by law as can be demonstrably justified in a free and democratic society."[8] In terms of freedom of thought and expression, this means that so long as the individual exercises his thought and expression in a way that the government deems to be in the public interest, the government *permits* the individual to do so. But if he exercises his thought and expression in a way that is deemed to harm the public interest, the government can censor him. This is precisely what the Canadian hate speech laws do: they outlaw the expression of certain content when expression of that content is deemed incompatible with the so-called public interest.[9]

Just as the Canadian government can censor speech, it can *permit speech with the very same content* when it deems that speech to be in the public interest. A valid defense against the charge of hate speech, as mentioned in an earlier endnote, is to show that one's "statements were relevant to any subject of *public interest* [emphasis mine], the discussion of which was for the *public benefit* [emphasis mine], and if on reasonable grounds he believed them to be true."

In Canada, as in other countries with hate speech laws, freedom of speech is not an absolute; it is not an individual right, but a permission granted by the state in the name of a collectivist goal, a permission that can be and sometimes is rescinded in the name of that collectivist goal.

Freedom of Speech under the New American Form of Government

The US approach is fundamentally different because it is individualistic, not collectivistic. Neither the Declaration nor the US Constitution charges the government with the task of advancing the public interest when the "public interest" is conceived to, at least sometimes, transcend the interests and rights of specific individuals. The task of the government is to secure the rights of each and every individual, not to abridge *any* individual's rights in the name of some collectivist goal or cause. And in the American approach, the rights to freedom of thought and speech are regarded as integral to the rights listed in the Declaration: the individual's rights to life and the pursuit of happiness. Why?

To *live* my own life and *pursue* my own happiness, I have to possess the freedom to chart and then travel my own course, to *figure out for myself* what is *true* and *good* and to then follow through on my convictions in action, all the while recognizing and respecting the same freedom of action of every other individual in my society. The authors of the Declaration and Constitution understood that the pursuit of happiness is a difficult endeavor, requiring careful thought and much effort on the part of each individual, but it's possible to a rational being who is left free to function as a rational being.

To figure out what I think is true and what I think is good *requires* that I'm free to examine any and every idea, argument, viewpoint, fact, potential lead, and alleged piece of evidence that to me seems relevant, and to express, listen, discuss, argue, and debate with whomever I judge it valuable to do so. The quest for the true and the good is difficult, and no doubt I'll make false starts and go down wrong alleys. In discussing with others, I'll find some of what they think and say helpful and illuminating, and some wrongheaded, irrational, even evil. *But these are precisely the judgments I must make for myself if I'm to grasp the true and the good.*

To cede to government the power to curtail the freedom of thought and expression, to allow government to declare some viewpoints heretical or inimical to the public interest, and so to declare certain books or ideas or arguments off limits to me, on penalty of fines or imprisonment or death, is to abandon my quest for the true and the good. Instead, government officials will decide for me what counts as viewpoints worth entertaining, arguments worth considering, or leads worth investigating—and I'll content myself with sifting through their blinkered view of reality. To accept such a predicament is to relinquish control of my life and happiness. How can I decide if Galileo's heliocentric theory or someone's denial of the Holocaust is well-reasoned or not, rational or perverse, without being able to read their books or listen to their claims?

It does not matter if the government censors viewpoints that are in fact true, like Galileo's, or false and abhorrent, like the denial of the Holocaust. If I cannot consider any and all viewpoints and arguments that I judge might have some bearing on the truth—even if I later come to think, as will often be the case, that some of these viewpoints are false and even corrupt—I cannot genuinely make up my mind. Instead, someone is trying to make up my mind for me.

To put the same point another way: if I don't yet know that denial of the Holocaust is false and perverse, I cannot permit government to declare that viewpoint off limits to me, to prevent me from even considering it; if I *know* that denial of the Holocaust is false and perverse, it's only because I was free to consider the matter.

This, in short, is the case for freedom of thought and expression on an individualist approach. If government is not the master but the servant of the individual, then it cannot possess the power to censor. As an individual, I don't have the right to tell other individuals what they can or cannot think or say or listen to, and so could not delegate enforcement of this right to government. And likewise, no other individual has the right to tell me what I can or cannot think or say or listen to, and so could not delegate enforcement of this right to government. In the individualist as against the collectivist approach, government does not have the power to censor any individual. As the First Amendment declares, freedom of speech is an absolute: a proper government must make no law abridging it.

What the Right to Freedom of Expression Means and Protects

I've now briefly discussed the individualist justification for the right to freedom of speech or freedom of expression.[10] Now let's consider in a bit more detail what the content of this right is, what the right encompasses, and what it does not.

The right to freedom of expression, like all rights, sanctions and protects an individual's freedom to take certain *actions*. As the philosopher Ayn Rand formulates the point in a seminal essay, "The concept of a 'right' pertains only to action—

specifically, to freedom of action. It means freedom from physical compulsion, coercion or interference by other men."[11] The right to property, for instance, "is not the right to an object, but to the action and the consequences of producing or earning that object. It is not a guarantee that a man will earn any property, but only a guarantee that he will own it if he earns it. It is the right to gain, to keep, to use and to dispose of material values."[12]

No right guarantees a specific outcome. Just as the right to property protects your freedom of action to, for instance, pan for gold on your land and to own any gold you discover, but does not guarantee that you will discover any gold—so the right to the pursuit of happiness protects your freedom of action to try to build a happy life, but doesn't guarantee that you will succeed. Similarly, the right to freedom of speech "does *not* mean that others must provide a man with a printing press, a publishing house, a newspaper, a theater or a television studio through which to express his views."[13] It sanctions and protects only a certain form of action: "the freedom to advocate one's views and to bear the possible consequences, including disagreement with others, opposition, unpopularity and lack of support."[14]

For something to be an individual right, it must be co-possible, which means every individual must enjoy the same freedom of action, and no individual can legitimately interfere with the sphere of action protected by another's right. Your rights entail that other people *refrain* from trespassing on your rights, just as their similar rights entail that you *refrain* from trespassing on their rights. But rights do not require that other people *perform* any particular action: that requires their voluntary, uncoerced *consent*.

The right to freedom of association, for example, means that you can try to associate with whomever you choose—and that other people can refuse to associate with you and go their separate way. The right to freedom of trade means that you can buy and sell with whomever you choose—and that other people can refuse to buy from you if, say, they think the price you're asking is too high, or refuse to sell to you if they think the price you're offering is too low. The same goes for freedom of speech. Important in understanding this right is understanding that "Freedom of speech includes the freedom not to agree, not to listen and not to support one's own antagonists."[15]

It is important to understand, in the context of hate speech laws and other proposed abridgments of the right to freedom of expression, that the exercise by an individual of *any* of her rights can and often will affect other people in ways they judge both positively and negatively. But neither are grounds to abridge the right—not so long as those other people retain the same rights, that is, the same freedom of action. This means in particular that the fact that one person's exercise of her rights "harms" (i.e., in some way negatively affects) another person is not sufficient grounds to outlaw the action.

For example, I may paint the front door of my house red, a color my neighbor dislikes, or plant a maple tree in my backyard, a type of tree that unfortunately evokes for my neighbor memories of home and a difficult childhood. But these negatives experienced by my neighbor, though real, don't give her veto power over the color I paint my front door or the trees I plant in my backyard, not so long as she retains the same freedom of action: she can paint her front door green and plant birch trees in her yard.

Or: I may open a new office building for a thousand employees, and the increased lunchtime foot traffic may help make nearby restaurants more profitable. But though this positive effect on the restaurants is real, it doesn't entitle me to veto their increased sales unless they share with me a portion of their increased profits. If I wanted to try to take advantage of the increase in foot traffic, I retain the same freedom of action as those restaurant owners: I could open and run my own restaurant.

Or: smartphone manufacturers like Apple may make the cameras on iPhones so good that most people stop buying film or digital cameras, and companies like Canon lose sales. But this negative, though real, does not give Canon veto power over the smartphones Apple can design and sell, not so long as Canon retains the same freedom of action: like Apple, Canon is free to try to design and sell its own smartphones.

The same goes for the right to freedom of expression. Consider first the commercial realm. If Apple advertises the cameras on its latest iPhones—a form of expression Apple of course regularly engages in—and those advertisements persuade customers to buy an iPhone over a Canon PowerShot camera, Apple's expression does result in a negative for Canon. But this negative does not give Canon the right to demand that Apple's advertising be silenced, not so long as Canon retains the same freedom of action: the freedom to advertise its own cameras and try to persuade people to buy them.

Consider now the intellectual and ideological realms. Atheists may persuade people to abandon their religion, and churches may see a drop in attendance. Though a real, negative effect, it does not give priests the right to demand that atheists be censored, not so long as the priests retain the same freedom of action, the freedom to try to persuade people that they should not abandon but embrace religion. Even if the priests are scandalized and upset by the atheists' views, which they regard as blasphemous, this does not give them the right to demand that atheists be silenced.

Or: a socialist or white nationalist may persuade people of their collectivistic doctrines, and in the process teach people to hate and despise large swaths of other people, be it profit-seeking businessmen in the case of socialism or darker-skinned individuals and immigrants in the case of white nationalism. This may lead to a social atmosphere that is less benevolent, less welcoming, less American, and to demands for the passage of anti-business or anti-immigration laws, which are certainly experienced as real negatives by the individuals being demeaned.[16] But in neither case do the opponents of socialism or of white nationalism have the right to demand that socialists or white nationalists be censored, not so long as they possess the same freedom of action: the opponents are free to try to persuade people of the irrationality of socialism and of white nationalism (and I hope they exercise this freedom).

It may surprise you that I list socialism as an irrational doctrine that foments hatred against innocent people, but that is part of the point. Though this is my actual evaluation of socialism, I'm not trying to convince you of the truth of that evaluation.[17] Rather, the example illustrates that *what constitutes irrational doctrines that foment unjust hatred against whole groups of people is a contentious matter.* As in today's world, historically this has been an issue over which there has been heated disagreement. Catholics have regarded Protestant doctrines in this way, and Protestants likewise have regarded Catholic doctrines in this way, similarly for Sunni and Shiite Muslims, for some Enlightenment thinkers toward Christian doctrines and for some Christians toward Enlightenment doctrines, for abolitionists toward proslavery doctrines and for enslavers toward abolitionist doctrines, for capitalists toward the doctrines of socialism and for socialists toward the doctrines of capitalism. Whose speech should hate speech laws ban—and by what right? These examples from history help showcase, from another angle, the danger of claiming that your neighbors have the right to veto your freedom of expression if they consider what you say irrational, hateful, or demonizing of large groups of people.

As an individual, the only right you possess to oppose expression which you regard as evil is to ignore the speaker and walk away or to engage in counterspeech. To the government we delegate the power to enforce our rights, but it is not within my rights to silence my neighbor, even when I abhor what she is saying, and it's not within her rights to silence me, even when she abhors what I'm saying. Just as her expression, however objectionable to me, does not interfere with or trespass on my freedom of action, so my expression, however objectionable to her, does not interfere with or trespass on her freedom of action.

What the Right to Freedom of Speech Does Not Protect

If the individual's right to freedom of expression is indeed a right, then, like all rights, it is absolute: it permits no breaches or exceptions. Many defenders of free speech deny this. They contend that the right to freedom of expression is compatible with some exceptions, such as legal prohibitions against threats, incitements to violence, and harassment. For the legitimacy of hate speech laws in particular, then, the question becomes whether or not they too should be considered allowable exceptions to the right to freedom of expression.

Nadine Strossen, for example, in her book *HATE: Why We Should Resist It with Free Speech, Not Censorship*, writes approvingly that

> government may punish speech when necessary to avert serious harm that cannot be averted through non-censorial measures—notably, law enforcement and counterspeech. Accordingly, government may punish "hate speech" (or speech conveying any other message) when, in context, it directly, demonstrably, and imminently causes certain specific, objectively ascertainable serious harms. The Supreme Court has identified several kinds of situations in which speech satisfies

this general emergency standard, specifying particular criteria for each. These criteria are appropriately strict, to circumscribe officials' opportunity to assert the potential harm as a pretext for suppressing speech merely because its message is disfavored, disturbing, or feared.[18]

She goes on to discuss, among a few others, such emergency exceptions as "True Threats," "Punishable Incitement," and "Harassment."[19]

But this conceptualization in terms of emergencies and exceptions is misguided. Many types of actions involve, or at least often involve, speech or other forms of expression and communication. This does not mean that all such actions are protected by the right to freedom of expression or that a legal system, in order to prohibit these actions, must carve out exceptions to the right to freedom of expression. Properly understood, threats, incitement, and harassment are not exceptions to the right to freedom of expression; they are actions that fall outside the protection of this right in the first place. Why? Because these acts are, in essence, *not acts of expression or communication to a willing audience, which is free to walk away (and engage in counterspeech), but acts of coercion, which seek to override other people's voluntary choices and consent.*

To see this, let's briefly consider the nature of threats, incitement, and harassment.

Threats

If I walk into a bank and declare, "This is a stick up. Hand over all your cash!"—and the police come to arrest me, it's absurd for me to protest that the police are interfering with my right to freedom of expression, since, after all, I was just having a conversation with the teller. Why is my protest absurd? Because I have introduced into the situation physical coercion. I have changed my relationship with the bank from the voluntary to the coercive. If, say, I don't like the interest rate the bank is offering, I'm free to go elsewhere; if the bank considers my initial deposit to be below its minimum threshold for that particular kind of savings account, it can refuse to open an account for me. Each of us is free to walk away if we don't consent to the particular terms the other is offering. But this is no longer true after my threat. The teller cannot just walk away—not without the worry that I might put a bullet in his back if he does.

It does not matter if I actually have a gun with me or not, or if I do, whether I intend to start shooting if the teller refuses my demand. As long as it is reasonable for the teller to think I might carry out my threat, his decision-making should no longer be seen as fully voluntary but as coerced, as occurring under physical duress. This is why such threats are prohibited by law. The verbal threat that I may resort to physical coercion if I don't get my way *is* the introduction of coercion into the relationship. It is my declaration that I will not let the other party walk away, that I will deny them that freedom of action, that is, deny them that right. The police do not have to wait until I start shooting before they arrest me.

The essence of a threat is that it is *not* an act of persuasion, rational or irrational, in which the other party is free to walk away if they disagree, but *an attempt to bypass the need for persuasion*. What a court must decide, therefore, is whether an actual threat has been made; if it decides that a threat has been made, there is no legitimate objection that prohibiting the threat violates the right to freedom of speech protected by the First Amendment.

Incitement

Perhaps the easiest way to grasp the essential nature of incitement is to see its similarity to plotting a crime, which properly is held to be an illegal activity on the part of the co-conspirators. Like many other forms of criminal activity, plotting a crime involves speech or expression. A crew of four who are planning to rob a bank will be communicating with one another. Which bank are they targeting? What kind of security system does it have? Where will they get the explosives to blast off the safe's door? Who will drive the getaway car? And how will they split the money afterward? This is what they are discussing. But for the law to treat the plotting of a crime as itself a crime is not an interference with the plotters' freedom of speech, for the same basic reason as in the case of threats: the plotters are introducing physical coercion into human affairs.

The plotters are not planning to make the bank an offer—"We want to buy all your deposits on hand for a thousand dollars, do you accept?"—an offer the bank is free to refuse. The plotters are planning to physically seize the bank's deposits without the bank's consent. In such a situation, the police do not have to wait until the plotters enter the bank, or blow off the safe's door, or start driving away with the money, before they can arrest the plotters. The attempt to rob the bank *begins* with the active plotting and becomes criminal at that point for *all* who are actively involved. Even if the mastermind of the plot plans to stay home and to send only his henchmen to enter the bank and seize the money, *all* are guilty of a crime.

Incitement can be regarded as *hatching a criminal plot in the moment*. It is more spontaneous, less considered or deliberative than, say, plotting to rob a bank, but no less criminal. For instance, if a group of people is protesting an election result outside a government building, and someone in the group starts to egg the crowd on, to declare that they will never get justice, that they will lose their country if they don't do something now, and that maybe they should take the law into their own hands, maybe some government officials need to be hanged, and these words help rile up the crowd, and the crowd storms into the government building, the person who helped rile up the crowd is guilty of incitement, *as if he helped plot the crime*. In other words, he is part of the action of breaking into the government building, even if he, like the mastermind who plotted a bank robbery, never entered the bank. Of course, the individuals breaking into the government building are also guilty of a crime, like the henchmen who break into the bank, but the point is that so is the inciter, who actively helped launch the action.

And again, the fact that the action of incitement, like the action of plotting, involves speech does not mean that in legally prohibiting it, the government is interfering with freedom of speech or carving out some exception to the right to freedom of speech. Just as plots to initiate the use of physical coercion are not essentially acts of expression, so inciting others to initiate the use of physical coercion is not essentially an act of expression. Both are attempts to coerce others, to bypass their voluntary participation and consent, and their freedom to walk away.

Harassment and Disturbances of the Peace

Like threats and incitement, certain forms of harassment and certain forms of disturbances of the peace are also often categorized as permissible exceptions to the right to freedom of speech, but should not be. If I follow a man or woman through the subway system of New York City, commenting on their appearance and attractiveness, or if every morning I ring the doorbells of all the houses on my street, trying to convince their occupants to convert to Christianity, I'm guilty of harassment. And it is not a legitimate defense for me to say that I'm expressing my views, so my action is protected by the First Amendment. Precisely because I am not allowing the other person to consent to the activity—to decide if they want to listen and engage or not—I cannot claim that my action is part of the freedom of action protected by the right to freedom of expression.

Similarly, if in the backyard of my house, I play my speaker system so loud that it disturbs my neighbors, I am guilty of disturbing the peace. The freedom of action encompassed by my freedom of speech never included the freedom to blare my speaker system outdoors at 110 decibels. Individual rights, as I indicated above, must be co-possible. I have the right to listen to what I want to listen to, but so do my neighbors. That in blaring my speaker system, I'm disturbing the peace really means that I'm depriving my neighbors of their freedom of action to decide what they want and don't want to listen to. My music is so loud that even if they don't want to listen to it, the sound nevertheless intrudes upon them. There is no right to trespass on the rights of others, in this case, on their right to freedom of expression. I never had the right to force my neighbors to listen to the music I like, and in prohibiting me from doing so, the government is not carving out an exception to freedom of expression but is rather protecting my neighbor's right to freedom of expression.

In short, threats, incitements, and verbal harassment and disturbances of the peace are not exceptions to the right to freedom of speech. They are not essentially acts of expression and should not be classified as such. If a legal system prohibits these actions—and when these actions are properly defined and delimited, it should—it is not carving out exceptions to freedom of expression.

Conclusion

The right to freedom of speech is an absolute. Any individual who values his own pursuit of the true and the good should claim the right to freedom of thought and to freedom of expression. She should never relinquish these rights, never cede to government the power to censor any form of expression, to infringe in any way on the individual's right to think and speak freely. But in embracing freedom of expression as an absolute, one is not thereby forced to tolerate threats, incitement, harassment, and the like as the supposed price one must pay for a free society, because such acts are not essentially expressive acts. They are acts that introduce physical coercion into human relationships, acts that seek to bypass other people's voluntary consent and participation, and the legal prohibition of these acts is compatible with, indeed often part of protecting, the right to freedom of expression.

Notes

1. Section 319(2) of the Criminal Code of Canada (https://laws-lois.justice.gc.ca/eng/acts/c-46/section-319.html). "Defences" against the charge of communicating any non-private statement that "willfully promotes hatred against any identifiable group" mentioned in the law include the following in Section 319(3): "(a) if he establishes that the statements communicated were true; (b) if, in good faith, the person expressed or attempted to establish by an argument an opinion on a religious subject or an opinion based on a belief in a religious text; (c) if the statements were relevant to any subject of public interest, the discussion of which was for the public benefit, and if on reasonable grounds he believed them to be true; or (d) if, in good faith, he intended to point out, for the purpose of removal, matters producing or tending to produce feelings of hatred toward an identifiable group in Canada."
2. Section 319(2.1) of the Criminal Code of Canada (https://laws-lois.justice.gc.ca/eng/acts/c-46/section-319.html).
3. See https://www.archives.gov/founding-docs/bill-of-rights-transcript.
4. Contrary to the Declaration, we need not, and for philosophic reasons I think should not, ground these preexisting moral rights in the alleged existence of a god or of some other supernatural phenomenon.
5. See https://www.archives.gov/founding-docs/declaration-transcript.
6. Here are two brief accounts of Galileo's conflict with the Inquisition: https://www.history.com/news/galileo-copernicus-earth-sun-heresy-church and https://newsroom.ucla.edu/releases/the-truth-about-galileo-and-his-conflict-with-the-catholic-church.
7. See https://laws-lois.justice.gc.ca/eng/const/page-12.html.
8. Ibid.
9. For more on why the "public interest" is a collectivist term and incompatible with the rights of the individual, see Ayn Rand, "The Pull Peddlers," in *Capitalism: The Unknown Ideal* (New York: New American Library, 1967) (https://courses.aynrand.org/works/the-pull-peddlers/).

10 "Expression" is the better term, encompassing as it does both verbal and nonverbal content, such as that of a symphony or ballet.
11 Ayn Rand, "Man's Rights," in *The Virtue of Selfishness* (New York: New American Library, 1964), 110 (https://courses.aynrand.org/works/mans-rights/).
12 Ibid., 110–11.
13 Ayn Rand, "Freedom of Speech," in *The Ayn Rand Column*, rev. 2nd ed. (New Milford: Second Renaissance Books, 1998), 71.
14 Rand, "Man's Rights," 114.
15 Ayn Rand, "The Fascist New Frontier," in *The Ayn Rand Column*, 106.
16 If anti-business or anti-immigration laws are actually passed in the United States, I contend that they should often be declared unconstitutional by the courts because the laws abridge the third fundamental right explicitly mentioned in the Declaration and featured prominently in the Fourteenth Amendment to the Constitution: the right to liberty. But that, of course, is an argument for another time.
17 But for a bit more on this evaluation of socialism, see the entry on socialism in *The Ayn Rand Lexicon* (New York: Penguin, 1998), 463–6 (https://courses.aynrand.org/lexicon/socialism/); and Rand's essay, "America's Persecuted Minority: Big Business," in *Capitalism: The Unknown Ideal*, 44–62.
18 Nadine Strossen, *HATE: Why We Should Resist It with Free Speech, Not Censorship* (Oxford: Oxford University Press, 2018), 59. As the title of her book should make clear, Strossen does not regard hate speech laws as legitimate exceptions to freedom of speech.
19 Ibid., 59–68.

There Should Be Legal Limits to Free Speech

Andrei Bespalov

Study Questions

1. What are the three criteria that must be met for an expression to count as hate speech? What paradigmatic example of hate speech does Bespalov give?
2. What is Bespalov's principled argument for hate speech laws?
3. What is the problem of drafting sufficiently precise hate speech laws? How does Bespalov address this problem?
4. What was Mary Kate McGowan's response to the argument that hate speech laws should not be implemented because they cannot change the discriminatory attitudes that underlie hate speech? What problems does her argument have?
5. How does Bespalov respond to the charge that hate speech laws are either useless or redundant?

Should law restrict freedom of speech? By posing this question, philosophers usually do not mean to ask whether or not we should be legally permitted to say publicly whatever we want. The answer to this broad question would be a rather obvious "No." There is widespread agreement that incitement of violence, fighting words, true threats, targeted harassment, libel, defamation, and false commercial advertising must be prosecuted by law.[1] These kinds of speech are clearly dangerous, and often they are actually harmful. Even in those legal regimes that protect freedom of expression most vigorously, speech may be legitimately restricted when it directly, demonstrably, and imminently causes specific objectively ascertainable serious harm.[2]

Genuine philosophical controversy arises with regard to the forms of expression whose harmfulness seems uncertain or insufficient to outweigh the potential downsides of legal censorship.[3] The three most controversial forms of expression in this context are hate speech, political fake news, and pornography. In this short paper, I will focus on hate speech only.[4]

Recent literature specifies three major criteria that an expression must meet in order for it to be an instance of hate speech.[5] First, the expression must target individuals on the basis of their socially salient group characteristics, such as race, ethnicity, religion, sexual orientation, and so on. Second, it must ascribe to all individuals who share this characteristic some undesirable qualities, such as being prone to criminality, intellectually deficient, or diseased. Third, it must label those individuals as appropriate objects of hostility and contempt, communicating thereby that their presence in society is unwelcome.

A paradigmatic example of hate speech is antisemitic discourse.[6] Its most grotesque myths can be traced back to the Middle Ages, when Jews were accused of murdering children for barbaric ritual purposes. A popular prejudice against Jewish people as greedy and treacherous had been established in Europe by the start of the modern era. The advent of global trade and capitalism brought the narrative of a worldwide Jewish conspiracy, which was epitomized in the infamous *Protocols of the Elders of Zion*. This fraudulent pamphlet, fabricated by the Russian Orthodox religious writer Sergei Nilus in 1903–5, became the groundwork for the German Nazi propaganda. The latter infused traditional antisemitic tropes with racist pseudoscientific theories and set the dissemination of hateful messages through mass media on an unprecedented scale. This massive production of hate culminated in the Holocaust—the extermination of six million European Jews by the Nazi regime and its collaborators during the Second World War. Blatant public expressions of hostility toward Jews as an ethnic and religious group are broadly condemned in today's liberal democracies, but antisemitic speech continues its presence on social media and niche communication platforms populated by racist hate groups.

So, should we legally prohibit hate speech? I will argue that we should. I will start with a principled argument showing that hate speech laws do not compromise the values associated with freedom of expression—on the contrary, they help to protect those values. However, the principled argument provides only a *pro tanto* reason for the legal censorship of hate speech. There are two practical concerns about the effectiveness of such censorship. First, can legal censorship tackle hate speech without doing too much "collateral damage" to the freedom of expression overall? Second, can legal censorship really contribute in any significant way to the dismantling of the identity-based social hierarchies that find their reflection in hate speech? I will address these concerns in the final sections of the essay, then I will summarize the all-things-considered case for hate speech laws in the Conclusion.

The Harm of Hate Speech

An argument for legal restrictions on hate speech must show that hate speech causes harm that is not outweighed by the benefits of not having those restrictions. As we will see, this task turns out to be easier than it may seem from the outset, because hate speech jeopardizes precisely those values that are protected by the right to free expression.

The most decisive recent criticism of hate speech comes from Jeremy Waldron, who interprets it as a form of group defamation. In this capacity, bigoted speech that ascribes repugnant characteristics to individuals on the basis of their group identity disfigures the social environment. The disfiguring effect consists in making it the case that "in the opinion of one group in the community, perhaps the majority, members of another group are not worthy of equal citizenship."[7] The erosion of civic equality affects both the way the general public sees the targeted group and the way the members of the targeted group see themselves. The latter lose the assurance of their civic dignity, that is, their status as "members of society in good standing."[8]

The assault on the civic dignity of individuals, especially of those who belong to a minority or a historically marginalized group, diminishes their capacity for equal democratic participation.[9] Even if the electoral votes of the individuals marginalized by hate speech continue to count for as much as the votes of other citizens, their voices in the process of democratic deliberation start to matter less than they should. The concerns of society's "deplorables" become too easily dismissed, and the general public starts to see their troubles as well-deserved. The inequality of real opportunity to influence public opinion threatens to establish the relations of domination of one part of the citizenry over the other.[10]

Political interests are not the only ones that are set back by hate speech. It creates a pervasive discriminatory environment, reducing all sorts of opportunities that would otherwise be available to its targets. This includes the opportunities for education and employment, as well as the opportunities for socialization in a broad sense, such as becoming a welcome member of a family, joining a nonprofit organization, or entering an informal community of neighbors. Assuming that an individual's autonomy admits of degrees relative to the range of available options, the harms that result from hate speech turn out to be "serious autonomy-undermining harms."[11]

Essentially, hate speech infringes on the very capacity of its targets to speak and be heard.[12] Open or only slightly covered expressions of hostility, toxic accusations of intellectual inferiority and moral corruption, humiliating labels and dehumanizing metaphors are fundamentally alienating. The first thing they purposefully destroy is the possibility of holding a dialogue on equal terms. Hate speakers do not consider themselves answerable to the targets of their invectives.[13] An antisemite does not think that he has to prove the truth of his favored conspiracy theory to Jews, for "of course, they will deny it!" Similarly, a racist does not think that the supremacy of the culture that she associates with her race can be meaningfully questioned by anyone. In her view, the very attempt at such questioning is a sign of either "immaturity" or "degeneracy," or both at the same time. The very absurdity and preposterousness of racist, sexist, or homophobic vitriol can leave its targets speechless, especially if they are not willing to throw away all vestiges of reason and respond in kind.

The silencing effect of hate speech reveals that, in fact, it has nothing to do with the free exchange in the marketplace of ideas, which, as John Stuart Mill has argued, is crucial for a successful pursuit of truth in a society.[14] It would take great irony, indeed, to talk of seeking truth through "free trade in ideas" in order to defend the right to engage in hate speech, which sells nothing but pernicious lies, ridiculous fiction, and stubborn prejudice.

To summarize, hate speech undermines those same values that freedom of expression is meant to protect, namely, equal opportunity for democratic participation,[15] freedom from domination,[16] autonomy,[17] unhindered rational communication, and the pursuit of truth.[18] Furthermore, insofar as hate speech has a silencing effect on its targets, it subverts the freedom of speech itself. Thus, a purely principled opposition to hate speech laws in the name of freedom, equality, and the pursuit of truth would be self-defeating.

However, the hostility of hate speech to the foundational values that liberal governments are supposed to protect is only a *pro tanto* reason for legal censorship. Even if there is a moral duty to refrain from engaging in hate speech, there may be all-things-considered reasons not to enforce this duty by the coercive power of the state. That is because the enforcement may result in an unacceptable "collateral damage" to free expression, and it may be useless for curbing the hostilities that manifest themselves in hate speech. I address these concerns below.

Can Hate Speech Censorship Be Sufficiently Precise?

If we resort to legal censorship, we want it to prevent and punish as many instances of hate speech as possible without silencing morally permissible expression. The problem is that it is not always easy to distinguish between genuine acts of hate speech and fierce but legitimate public criticism. The latter may offend its targets, and even intentionally so, without aiming to undermine their civic dignity. For example, long before the tragic war in Gaza that started from the terrorist attack on Israel by Hamas on the 7th of October in 2023, many people had denounced Israeli policies in Palestinian territories as "settler colonialism" and "apartheid."[19] Such language may certainly be taken on board by antisemites.[20] Yet, it is also easy to imagine how the criticism that uses this strong language may be dismissed from the outset as inherently antisemitic. As a result, laws against hate speech may become instrumental in the suppression of Israeli government critics at home and abroad.

To generalize, the slippery slopes in legislative and judicial reasoning that emerge due to the ambiguity of acts of expression may lead to excessive censorship of public discourse.[21] In particular, the apparently elusive line between genuinely hateful and "merely offensive" speech can be exploited by those agents within society, including the government, who are interested in shielding their social, cultural, or political agendas from public criticism. At the very least, the threat of legal sanctions, combined with the uncertainty about the criteria of their application, is likely to have a chilling effect on the public discussion of controversial topics.[22]

A usual response to this concern is that the uncertainty about the content and application of hate speech laws is not inevitable. These laws can be formulated precisely enough to prevent the officials from sliding down the argumentative slippery slopes, and the chilling effect can be mitigated by free speech provisos.[23] For example, the *UK Public Order Act* of 1986, as amended in 2006, 2008, and 2013, prohibits stirring up hatred against persons on the grounds of their race (including color, citizenship, ethnic and national origin), religion (including lack of religious belief), and sexual orientation. The list of protected characteristics does not include any indeterminate clauses, such as "and other group characteristics." This prevents the *Act* from being stretched onto other groups in addition to those that it enumerates explicitly. The *Act* also includes free speech clauses that are meant to prevent excessive censorship. One of those clauses warns that nothing in the *Act* should be understood "in a way which prohibits or restricts discussion, criticism or expressions of antipathy, dislike, ridicule, insult or abuse of particular religions or the beliefs or practices of their adherents" (29J). The other two clauses state that the criticism of sexual conduct and marriage, including the criticism which concerns the sex of the parties to marriage, "shall not be taken of itself to be threatening or intended to stir up hatred" (29JA).

Certainly, the free speech provisos that I have just cited make practical sense only if it is possible to distinguish between the "insult or abuse" of particular beliefs and practices on the one hand, and the "stirring up of hatred" toward their adherents on the other. Usually, the proponents of hate speech laws, and Waldron in particular, assume that "the basic distinction between an attack on a body of beliefs and an attack on the basic social standing and reputation of a group of people is clear."[24] I concede, however, that this distinction should not be taken for granted. Religious, moral, and philosophical beliefs that involve the basic definitions of good and evil, right and wrong, true and false may be crucial for people's personal and group identification. These are the beliefs around which people build their identities as Christians and Muslims, socialists and libertarians, or perhaps, if they dive deep into moral philosophy, as committed Kantians and utilitarians. It is very difficult to distinguish between irreverent criticisms of such beliefs and attacks on the dignity and reputation of those who embrace them.

One case has been particularly widely discussed in this context. It is the publication of a cartoon in the Danish newspaper *Jyllands-Posten* in 2005, which depicted Prophet Muhammad as a bearded man wearing a bomb on top of his turban.[25] Was the publication an act of hate speech against Muslims? Those who argue that it was, emphasize that the cartoon mocked the central figure in the Islamic faith. By doing so, it expressed profound disrespect for the foundational religious beliefs of Muslims that are essential to their religious identity. It is far from clear how public derision of the identity-forming beliefs of Muslims can avoid undermining their civic status in the Danish society.

Waldron's general response to such controversies is to lament what he calls "the tendency of identity politics" to present the criticism of a person's belief as an assault on that person. As he contends, this "makes it much harder for a society to be administered in the midst of difference and disagreement. Better to reserve the idea of 'an assault on me' for attacks on my person or attempts to denigrate or eliminate my social standing."[26] Admittedly, this suggestion sounds more like an attempt to wish away the problem than a genuine solution. It would certainly make the administration of religious difference and disagreement much easier if citizens did not identify themselves as Christians, Muslims, or atheistic nonbelievers. But the separation between persons' self-identification and their deeply held beliefs is not something that a liberal democratic society can reasonably expect from its citizens. The freedom to choose the way to identify oneself—be it on the basis of one's religious beliefs or otherwise—is part of the very basic freedom of thought, which liberal democracies are meant to respect and defend.

Waldron is not unaware of this conundrum. Therefore, his specific solution to the Danish cartoons case is not that Muslims should simply try to separate their personal identity from their faith in the Prophet. Instead, he argues that closer attention should be paid to the actual message the cartoons were meant to communicate. "They would come close to a libel on Muslims if they were calculated to suggest that most followers of Islam support political and religious violence."[27]

Indeed, the distinction between hate speech and legitimate criticism should not depend on whether or not a critical claim affects someone "personally." If criticism is directed at some foundational beliefs, powerful desires, or purposefully cultivated practices, it will most surely be taken "personally" by those who embrace them. Instead, we should check if the critics ascribe repugnant or dangerous beliefs, intentions, character traits, and behaviors to individuals in a sweeping and unsubstantiated manner, insensitive to what those individuals actually believe, say, and do. Similarly, we should check if criticized individuals are labeled as unwelcome without due consideration of how their words and actions really affect other members of society.

Some acts of expression, like the Danish cartoons, may be deliberately constructed in a way that allows them to evade unequivocal interpretation. In such cases, we can directly demand that the publishers explain the message they meant to communicate. If the message was "Muslims are terrorists" or, to put it more subtly, "It is hard to fight the impression that some integral aspects of the Islamic faith inevitably lead its adherents to condone terrorist action," then the publication was hateful. If the message was "This is what terrorists make of Islam" or "This is how an Islamophobic society sees Muslims," then the publication was a piece of legitimate criticism, which was not even aimed at the Muslim community.

Since the decisions about the genuine character of controversial claims require careful interpretation, they ought to be made on a case-by-case basis. The legislation may provide a general definition of hate speech and a list of group characteristics that must be protected from hateful attacks, but there are hardly any generic rules for determining whether or not a particular critical remark or discourse is hateful. This does not mean that the application of hate speech laws is inevitably arbitrary. Expressive acts may, indeed, be ambiguous, but that is why the legal verdicts on whether or not those acts are hateful must be made on the basis of how the speakers themselves would disambiguate their speech publicly, so that everyone interested could see what the controversial claims were aiming at.

This, by the way, addresses the concern that in today's intellectual climate, where open manifestations of hatred are beyond the pale, more subtle hate speech tends to be more influential. Allegedly, this fact makes hate speech legislation "endemically underinclusive."[28] However, requiring speakers to explain in plain terms the intended meaning of their controversial acts of expression tackles the problem. The controversial speakers will have to face sanctions for "stirring up hatred" if, and only if, they are unable to give a convincing, legitimate explanation of what they meant to say, and/or they are unwilling to publicly condemn the bigoted reading of their messages.

Finally, arbitrary judgment about controversial messages can be avoided by grounding the restrictions of hate speech in well-established liberal principles. One or another of those principles may be especially relevant for a particular case. For example, we may draw on the principle of separation of church and state to decide whether public denunciation of homosexuality on religious grounds should be prohibited. On the one hand, a secular government is meant to prevent any church from encroaching on the whole society. On the other hand, the government must not interfere with the churches' internal affairs. Accordingly, the claim "Homosexuals shall not be welcome in our society" must be legally censored, regardless of whether or not it is made on the grounds of a deeply held religious belief. But the claim "Homosexuals shall not be welcome in our church" must not be censored, regardless of how offensive it sounds.

To summarize, given that in every society it is usually well-known who is likely to be targeted by hate speech, drafting sufficiently precise hate speech laws is not impossible. Applying these laws to particular cases may be more challenging, due to the possible ambiguity of acts of expression. This task requires careful judgment on a case-by-case basis, but we should not exaggerate its complexity. We can always demand that controversial speakers explain their own messages and publicly condemn their hateful interpretations.

Do Hate Speech Laws Help to Dismantle Identity-Based Hierarchies?

Some opponents of legal censorship doubt that hate speech causally contributes to the creation and maintenance of racial, gendered, religious, and other identity-based hierarchies.[29] In their view, hate speech may well be just a downstream consequence, not the cause, of such hierarchies. If hate speech sounds threatening in real life, it is because it gets its potency "from the fact that it does reflect a deeper, sinister current of identity-oppressive intention."[30] What erodes individuals' assurance of their equal civic status is the existence of malevolent attitudes in society, not the act of bringing them into the open in hate speech. For the targets of hate speech, restricting it "will not alleviate the assurance-eroding knowledge that there are others in their wider political community who feel contempt and hostility towards them."[31] So, if hate speech legislation cannot change the discriminatory attitudes underpinning the identity-based social hierarchies, then there is no sufficient reason for implementing it, especially given the worry that hate speech laws are susceptible to abuse, which I discussed in the previous section.

One philosophically sophisticated reply to this concern has recently been developed by Mary Kate McGowan.[32] She neither defends nor challenges the view that hate speech *causes* harm by leading people to accept discriminatory beliefs and act upon them. Instead, McGowan argues that racist, sexist, and otherwise bigoted speech *constitutes* harm.[33] By using certain words and expressions or by making certain claims, a speaker changes the score of a conversation—namely, he enacts conversational norms according to which the words and expressions he uses and claims he makes are permissible. Through his utterances, the speaker engages in a conversation that is part of a broader social practice, and thereby, he enacts the norms of that social practice. Hate speech enacts the norms of conversation that allow speaking about the members of certain groups in degrading terms. Such norms, in their own turn, assume the permissibility of discriminatory attitudes and oppressive behavior toward the members of those groups, which is harmful.

McGowan's key example is a dialogue between two male colleagues in which one of them, named Steve, casually uses a degrading word to refer to a woman he dated the night before. His interlocutor, John, quickly tunes into this style of conversation.[34] As McGowan comments,

> Steve's utterance makes it permissible, in this immediate environment and at this time (here and now), to degrade women. By so doing, his utterance makes women

count as second-class citizens (locally and for the time being). . . . By altering the normative landscape of the workplace in these ways, Steve's utterance enacts norms that prescribe behaviors that oppress women. As such, his remark constitutes an act of oppression.[35]

McGowan's theory has been criticized for failing to distinguish clearly between the constitution of harm and the causal contribution to harm through speech. Also, the criticism goes, her theory does not explain exactly how a speaker can make something permissible by an utterance, if not by stating explicitly, "Let the act A be allowed as part of the practice P." As a result, the two main claims of McGowan's theory—first, that merely by making an utterance a speaker enacts a particular conversational norm, and second, that by enacting a conversational norm the speaker enacts a particular norm for a broader social practice—remain nothing more than stipulations, which are intuitively obscure, analytically unsubstantiated, and empirically unverified.[36]

Furthermore, even if we fully accept McGowan's idea that hate speech constitutes harm by changing what is considered permissible in a conversation, then, apparently, public counterspeech already constitutes a sufficient remedy.[37] No legal censorship is needed where citizens do not hesitate to challenge hate speakers. Counterspeech tackles the wrongdoing immediately by resisting (although not necessarily reversing[38]) the undesirable changes in conversational scores, and thereby, it cuts short the enactment of harmful social practices.

As it turns out, the opponents of hate speech laws might argue, legal censorship of hate speech is either useless or redundant. Censorship is useless insofar as it does not help to reduce the spread of discriminatory attitudes that make hate speech harmful. Censorship is redundant because, even if hate speech is somehow harmful in itself, it can be tackled by citizens' counterspeech in the public square.

In reply, I would argue that it is not necessary to provide any specific explanation of how hate speech produces its harmful effects in order to show that laws against it are useful. Regardless of how exactly hate speech is connected with discriminatory attitudes and social hierarchies, suffice it to say that degrading speech is part of degrading treatment. Being targeted by hate speech is what it means to be treated as a second-class citizen, alongside being denied access to opportunities and shunned by the members of privileged groups. This is fairly uncontroversial regardless of whether hate speech causes the formation of discriminatory attitudes and identity-based hierarchies, or merely expresses those attitudes, represents those hierarchies, or relates to them in some other way. Therefore, together with anti-discrimination laws, hate speech laws should be an integral part of the legislation against the establishment of identity-based social hierarchies.

Next, the criticism of hate speech laws on the grounds that they do not give enough assurance against the existence of discriminatory attitudes is misplaced. Although legal censorship performs a certain expressive function—it communicates that hate speech is not just problematic but clearly impermissible—changing discriminatory beliefs and attitudes is not what it is meant to do in the first place. The primary purpose of law is not expression or education, but deterrence, prevention, and retribution. Laws against theft may or may not change some individuals' beliefs about the moral permissibility of stealing other people's property, but their primary purpose is to deter potential thieves by the threat of punishment. Similarly, the primary purpose of hate speech laws is not to change people's racist, sexist, homophobic, and otherwise bigoted views. Instead, legal censorship is meant to deter bigots from expressing their views publicly and, if necessary, make sure that they are punished for doing so. The assurance that hate speech laws are meant to provide is not that there are no bigots in society, but that bigots will either not go public, or regret it if they do.

Focusing on the deterrence, prevention, and retribution purposes of legal censorship helps to see that it is not redundant even in the presence of robust counterspeech against hate in the public square. Counterspeech can be successful in deterrence, prevention, and retribution only if it subjects hate speakers to immense reputational costs. In order to shame bigots so strongly as to deter them from ever expressing their views publicly, it is not enough just to engage in a confrontational debate with them. One has to actually win the debate; otherwise, the confrontation may backfire. Perhaps even mere winning might be insufficient. One has to completely dominate the public debate with the hate speaker, so as to exclude any impression that there was something true to his words. Otherwise, it would not be unreasonable for your opponent and your audience to think that he could try to prove his point again next time. Furthermore, in order to incur significant reputational damage, the speaker must become widely known for his hate speech, which means that the message he tries to spread must be circulated widely. However, the wide circulation of their messages and public engagement is what hate speakers themselves actively seek. This is not surprising, given that hate speech is confrontational by its very nature—confrontation is what it sows, and through confrontation it spreads. So, it is highly unlikely that publicly confronting hate speech can do enough for its deterrence, prevention, and punishment.

To summarize, hate speech laws are neither useless nor redundant. Even if legal censorship does not eliminate discriminatory attitudes, it protects vulnerable citizens from the degrading treatment which they become subject to when those attitudes are expressed publicly. Some of the harmful effects of hate speech can be alleviated by publicly confronting it, but, given that, oftentimes, public confrontation is what hate speakers deliberately seek, counterspeech is not a sufficient solution. Shaming hate speakers is usually not enough to make them go silent.

Conclusion

I have argued that at least one controversial form of expression—namely, hate speech—should be legally restricted. Hate speech undermines the equal civic status of its targets. As a result, it wrongfully sets back their political interests, reduces their opportunities in society, and eventually has a silencing effect on them. Accordingly, hate speech is hostile to the values of equality, liberty, and toleration that are associated with freedom of expression. Ultimately, it is antithetical to the freedom of expression itself. This gives a *pro tanto* justification for hate speech laws.

I have addressed two major concerns regarding the practical desirability of introducing hate speech legislation. First, I have argued that, despite popular worries, hate speech laws can be formulated in a sufficiently precise way that is not conducive to excessive censorship of public discourse. Admittedly, due to the possible ambiguity of acts of expression, the proper application of hate speech laws in controversial cases requires significant interpretative efforts. Yet, these complexities do not entail arbitrary adjudication, because the decisions about censoring speakers can and should be made only after giving them the opportunity to publicly explain their controversial messages and thereby defend themselves against the accusations of stirring up hatred.

Second, I have argued that, even if legal censorship does not make hate speakers change their prejudiced attitudes and beliefs, it still plays an important role in protecting individuals from degrading treatment in the public square. By making it costly to publicly express one's bigotry, hate speech laws perform the deterrence, prevention, and retribution functions that cannot be adequately realized by means of public counterspeech.

Thus, legal censorship of hate speech is justified as a matter of principle, and it is not infeasible, nor is it useless or redundant as a matter of practice. Therefore, there should be legal limits to free speech.

Notes

1 Matthew H. Kramer, *Freedom of Expression as Self-Restraint* (Oxford: Oxford University Press, 2021), Ch. 3, Ch. 6: section 6.1.

2 Nadine Strossen, *Hate: Why We Should Resist It with Free Speech, Not Censorship* (Oxford: Oxford University Press, 2018), 60.

3 Jeffrey W. Howard, "Dangerous Speech," *Philosophy and Public Affairs* 47, no. 2 (2019): 208–54.

4 On fake news, see Étienne Brown, "Free Speech and the Legal Prohibition of Fake News," *Social Theory and Practice* 49, no. 1 (2023): 29–55; on pornography, see Rae Langton, *Sexual Solipsism: Philosophical Essays on Pornography and Objectification* (Oxford: Oxford University Press, 2009), Ch. 1.

5 See Andrew Walton, William Abel, Elizabeth Kahn, and Tom Parr, *Introducing Political Philosophy: A Policy-Driven Approach* (Oxford: Oxford University Press, 2021), 30; Jeffrey W. Howard, "Free Speech and Hate Speech," *Annual Review of Political Science* 22 (2019): 93–109, at 96; Bhikhu Parekh, "Hate Speech: Is There a Case for Banning?" *Public Policy Research* 12, no. 4 (2006): 213–23, at 214.

6 For a concise review of the main antisemitic tropes, see antisemitism.adl.org, *Antisemitism Uncovered: A Guide to Old Myths in a New Era* (https://antisemitism.adl.org/). For a detailed historical account, see Albert S. Lindemann and Richard S. Levy, eds., *Antisemitism: A History* (Oxford: Oxford University Press, 2010).

7 Jeremy Waldron, *The Harm in Hate Speech* (Cambridge, MA: Harvard University Press, 2014), 39.

8 See ibid., 47, 59–61, 81–9, 105, 138.

9 Alexander Brown, *Hate Speech Law: A Philosophical Examination* (London: Routledge, 2015), 194–201; Andrew Reid, "Does Regulating Hate Speech Undermine Democratic Legitimacy? A Cautious 'No'," *Res Publica* 26 (2020): 181–99.

10 Matteo Bonotti and Jonathan Seglow, "Freedom of Speech: A Relational Defence," *Philosophy and Social Criticism* 48, no. 4 (2022): 515–29.

11 Susan J. Brison, "The Autonomy Defence of Free Speech," *Ethics* 108, no. 2 (1998): 312–39, at 338.

12 Caroline West, "Words That Silence? Freedom of Expression and Racist Hate Speech," in *Speech and Harm: Controversies Over Free Speech*, ed. Ishani Maitra and Mary Kate McGowan (Oxford: Oxford University Press, 2012), 222–48.

13 Bonotti and Seglow, "Freedom of Speech: A Relational Defence," 521, 525–6.

14 John Stuart Mill, "On Liberty," in *Utilitarianism and On Liberty,* 2nd ed., edited with an introduction by Mary Warnock (Malden: Blackwell, 2003), 88–180, Ch. 2. Admittedly, Mill himself did not use the expression "marketplace of ideas" (see Jill Gordon, "John Stuart Mill and the 'Marketplace of Ideas'," *Social Theory and Practice* 23, no. 2 [1997]: 235–49).

15 Ronald Dworkin, "Foreword," in *Extreme Speech and Democracy*, ed. Ivan Hare and James Weinstein (Oxford: Oxford University Press, 2009), v–ix; James Weinstein, "Hate Speech Bans, Democracy, and Political Legitimacy," *Constitutional Commentary* 32 (2017): 526–83.

16 Bonotti and Seglow, "Freedom of Speech: A Relational Defence."

17 T. M. Scanlon, *The Difficulty of Tolerance: Essays in Political Philosophy* (Cambridge: Cambridge University Press, 2003), Chs. 3, 5.

18 Seana Valentine Shiffrin, *Speech Matters: On Lying, Morality, and the Law* (Princeton: Princeton University Press, 2014), Chs. 3, 4.

19 bdsmovement.net, *What Is BDS?* (https://bdsmovement.net/what-is-bds).

20 adl.org, *The Boycott, Divestment and Sanctions Campaign (BDS)* (https://www.adl.org/resources/glossary-term/boycott-divestment-and-sanctions-campaign-bds).

21 See several characteristic examples in Strossen, *Hate: Why We Should Resist It with Free Speech, Not Censorship*, 94–9.

22 Ibid., 99–100.

23 Alexander Brown and Adriana Sinclair, *The Politics of Hate Speech Laws* (London: Routledge, 2020), 229–30.

24 Waldron, *The Harm in Hate Speech*, 120.

25 Peter Jones, "Religious Belief and Freedom of Expression: Is Offensiveness Really the Issue?" *Res Publica* 17, no. 1 (2011): 75–90; Andrew F. March, "Speech and the Sacred: Does the Defense of Free Speech Rest on a Mistake about Religion?"

Political Theory 40, no. 3 (2012): 319–46; Matteo Bonotti and Jonathan Seglow, "Self-Respect, Domination and Religiously Offensive Speech," *Ethical Theory and Moral Practice* 22, no. 3 (2019): 589–605; Masooda Bano, "Caricaturing the Prophet: Pushing the Right to Free Speech Too Far?" *Philosophy and Social Criticism* 48, no. 4 (2022): 544–55; Daniel Gamper, "Cartoons Go Global: Provocation, Condemnation and the Possibility of Laughter," *Philosophy and Social Criticism* 48, no. 4 (2022): 530–43.

26 Waldron, *The Harm in Hate Speech*, 135.
27 Ibid., 125.
28 Strossen, *Hate: Why We Should Resist It with Free Speech, Not Censorship*, 141–3; also see Eric Heinze, *Hate Speech and Democratic Citizenship* (Oxford: Oxford University Press, 2016), 145–8.
29 See Matteo Bonotti and Jonathan Seglow, "Freedom of Expression," *Philosophy Compass* 16, no. 7 (2021): e12759, at 5.
30 Robert Mark Simpson, "Dignity, Harm, and Hate Speech," *Law and Philosophy* 32, no. 6 (2013): 701–28, at 724.
31 Ibid.
32 Mary Kate McGowan, *Just Words: On Speech and Hidden Harm* (Oxford: Oxford University Press, 2019). For alternative but closely related accounts of harm in hate speech, which are grounded in contemporary philosophy of language, see Ishani Maitra, "Subordinating Speech," in *Speech and Harm: Controversies Over Free Speech*, ed. Ishani Maitra and Mary Kate McGowan (Oxford: Oxford University Press, 2012), 94–120; Rae Langton, "The Authority of Hate Speech," in *Oxford Studies in Philosophy of Law*, ed. John Gardner, Leslie Green, and Brian Leiter, vol. 3 (Oxford: Oxford University Press, 2018), 123–52.
33 McGowan, *Just Words*, 23–4.
34 Ibid., 110.
35 Ibid., 112.
36 Uwe Steinhoff, "Really Just Words: Against McGowan's Arguments for Further Speech Regulation," *Philosophia* 50 (2022): 1455–77.
37 For an overview of work on counterspeech, see Bianca Cepollaro, Maxime Lepoutre, and Robert Mark Simpson, "Counterspeech," *Philosophy Compass* 18, no. 1 (2023): e12890.
38 See McGowan, *Just Words*, 118–20; Maxime Lepoutre, "Can 'More Speech' Counter Ignorant Speech?" *Journal of Ethics and Social Philosophy* 16, no. 3 (2019): 155–91, at 160–3.

Responses

Response to Ghate on Free Speech

Andrei Bespalov

Study Questions

1. How does Bespalov respond to Ghate's apparent assumption that public interest and individual freedom are necessarily opposed?
2. According to Bespalov, what negative effects of hate speech does Ghate gloss over?
3. Why does Bespalov think that hate speech laws do not undermine our epistemic autonomy to pursue the true and the good?
4. How does Bespalov respond to Ghate's argument that identifying genuine hate speech is too difficult?

Onkar Ghate and I agree that threats, incitement of violence, harassment, and disturbance of the peace are not protected by the right to free speech. I also agree with Ghate's explanation of why this is so—although these acts involve speech, they are not essentially "acts of expression or communication to a willing audience" (p. 398). What we disagree about is whether or not all acts of expression and communication should be free from government interference. I have argued that, at the very least, the government should ban hate speech. Ghate has argued that no speech should be legally banned no matter how abhorrent it is. In my response, I will address four points in Ghate's defense of free speech absolutism that I find either wrong or misleading.

Are Public Interest and Individual Freedom Necessarily Opposed?

The first point has to do with Ghate's initial framing of the problem. Ghate makes an uncontroversial claim that, in liberal democracies, freedom of speech is understood as a basic freedom of human individuals. He also rightly assumes that the state must pursue public, not private, interests. What I find problematic, though, is Ghate's assumption that public interest necessarily amounts to some communitarian goal that "the state is thought to embody or secure" (p. 392). In this perspective, any government limitation of freedom of speech has no other purpose but to maintain the ideology of the state or some other corporate body over the dissenting views of its individual members. Therefore, any government censorship belongs to the same kind of ideological censorship that the Catholic church employed against Galileo, whose heliocentric theory of the solar system sounded intolerably subversive of the church's epistemic authority.

I contend that drawing a necessary opposition between public interest and individual freedom is wrong. As Ghate himself points out, what distinguishes liberal democracies is precisely the fact that they do not serve any collective interests that go beyond or against the protection of the individual freedom of their citizens. The public interest of liberal democratic states is nothing else but equal protection of each citizen's rights and liberties. So, not all limitations of individual freedom by the government are necessarily aimed at some communitarian goal. A liberal democratic government may legitimately restrict a citizen's freedom in order to make it compatible with the same freedom of all other citizens. Accordingly, not all legal restrictions of speech are analogous to the ideological censorship that Galileo suffered from the narrow-minded, power-hungry Roman Inquisitors. The government may legitimately ban certain forms of speech if engaging in them infringes on other citizens' individual freedoms, including their freedom of speech.

What Are the **Real** *Negative Effects of Hate Speech?*

To be fair, Ghate later turns to argumentation having the purpose of making individual rights "co-possible," meaning that it must be possible for each citizen to enjoy her freedom of action without interfering with the freedom of action protected by another's right. Ghate argues that, although hate speech may set back some interests of its targets, this is insufficient to justify censorship, because the targets of hate speech are free to speak back. For example, white nationalist discourse in the public square "may lead to a social atmosphere that is less benevolent" and result in the passage of anti-immigration laws. Nevertheless, the opponents of white nationalism remain free to persuade everyone that it is irrational and challenge anti-immigration laws in court (p. 396 and note 16).

This brings us to the second problematic point in Ghate's argument. His description of the harms of hate speech glosses over its most significant negative effects. These include the assault on individuals' civic dignity, which wrongfully reduces their opportunities in society, and the silencing effect, which is antithetical to the ideal of equal freedom of speech for everyone. It is true, of course, that even the pervasive public presence of hate speech does not prevent its targets from raising their voices and fighting for their civic dignity. The problem is that hate speech makes this fight necessary in the first place. In other words, the problem with hate speech is not that it may deprive its targets of the capacity to speak publicly and participate in society. The problem is that it doesn't allow them to do so on equal terms with other citizens.

Free speech absolutists have to justify this inequality somehow. But how can one justify, for example, requiring individuals targeted by racist hate speech to prove that denying their status as members of society in good standing is irrational, while others, including the racist speakers, enjoy this status by default? Furthermore, consider the fact that to speak is to engage in a communicative relation—making an utterance that cannot be heard and understood adequately does not constitute speaking in the proper sense. Then how can one meaningfully say that the marginalized minorities retain their full freedom of speech, when hate speakers preemptively degrade the minorities' contributions to public discourse and effectively communicate the refusal to listen to them? Without addressing these questions, the account of hate speech becomes too limited. Reducing the discussion of the effects of hate speech to the mere fact that it may result in "a social atmosphere that is less benevolent" is misleading.

Is Epistemic Autonomy Undermined by Censorship?

Perhaps free speech absolutists might defend their position by insisting that, in their estimation, all the regrettable effects of hate speech are insufficient to justify censorship. That is because unimpeded access to all sorts of controversial ideas is necessary for us to freely form our conceptions of the true and the good. As Ghate puts it, for example, "how can I decide if . . . someone's denial of the Holocaust is well-reasoned or not, rational or perverse, without being able to read their books or listen to their claims?" (p. 394). Ghate's primary concern here is not our ability to acquire knowledge but our ability to do it freely. As I understand, he argues that our epistemic autonomy is inevitably undermined by censorship enforced by the state. This is the third problematic point in Ghate's argument.

I concede that, in order to be really free in acquiring knowledge of historical and natural scientific facts, one has to be allowed to consider all sorts of relevant information, including the most preposterous and abhorrent. But this does not entail permissiveness with regard to public circulation of hateful messages. Banning Holocaust denial is not the same as banning the public discussion of Holocaust denial. Proper hate speech laws do the former, not the latter, and therefore, they do not prevent anyone from knowing what Holocaust denial means and aims at. Proper hate speech laws do not censor speech topics; they censor speech types. Accordingly, a documentary exploring the history of Holocaust denialism may well be broadcast freely, but a documentary purporting to present "new evidence" that the Holocaust is a fabricated narrative should be banned. The former is informative and helpful for drawing important lessons regarding the ideological tensions in today's society; the latter is misleading, and it helps nothing except stirring up the hatred of Jews. Thus, it is simply wrong that free circulation of hate speech in the public square is necessary for our epistemic autonomy.

Is It Too Difficult to Identify Hate Speech?

Finally, Ghate notes that "what constitutes irrational doctrines that foment unjust hatred against whole groups of people is a contentious matter" (p. 397). As an example, he cites his own view of socialism as an irrational doctrine that foments unjust hatred of profit-seeking businesspeople. Ghate points out that many of his readers would be surprised by this view, suggesting, thereby, that they might be similarly surprised by how many philosophical and religious doctrines can become subject to censorship if we take for granted what the opponents of those doctrines say about them.

I agree that, over time, some widely contested doctrines, like socialism, became associated with diverse perspectives, including those that are radical and aggressive. For instance, bolshevism may well be characterized as a militant, "hateful" version of left-wing ideology that casts a dark shadow on the socialist ideal. However, alongside doctrines whose irrationality and hatefulness are contentious, there are racist, sexist, and fundamentalist doctrines that are clearly irrational and hateful. Some versions of anti-capitalism may sound unreasonable and aggressive, but no version of antisemitism sounds like a piece of rational and constructive critique. So, it is misleading to defend free speech absolutism by pointing at doctrines whose hatefulness is subject to controversy because these are not the doctrines that are targeted by hate speech laws in the first place. Speech can be ambiguous, and sometimes it may be difficult to determine if it is actually hateful. But the difficulty of identifying genuine instances of hate speech is not a sufficient reason to reject hate speech laws, especially given the fact that, sometimes, identifying hate speech is not difficult at all.

Conclusion

To summarize, not all legal censorship is antithetical to the protection of citizens' individual freedom. Also, allowing all kinds of public expression, including hate speech, is not necessary for our epistemic autonomy. In addition, the advocacy of free speech absolutism becomes misleading insofar as it underestimates the harmful effects of hate speech and overestimates the difficulty of identifying it.

Response to Bespalov on Free Speech

Onkar Ghate

Study Questions

1. How does Ghate respond to Bespalov's claim that hate speech laws are just another acceptable exception to the right to free speech?
2. According to Ghate, how does Bespalov conceive the function of government? Why does Ghate reject this view?
3. Why does Ghate think that Bespalov's position is contradictory?
4. What problem does Ghate see with Bespalov's criteria for identifying an instance of hate speech?

Andrei Bespalov argues for government's power to censor speech, presenting versions of some of the major positions I argued against in my essay. Bespalov holds that government censorship of so-called hate speech should be seen as just one more legitimate exception to freedom of speech. His argument proceeds from a collectivist approach to government. As such, he's prepared to make government the arbiter of truth and morality. By contrast, I argued that proper law does not carve out exceptions to freedom of speech, that the right to free speech must be rooted in an individualistic approach to government, and that no individual can delegate to government the coercive power to impose his conception of the true and the good on others. Let me expand briefly on these crucial differences in our positions.

Hate Speech Laws Are Not Just Another Exception to the Right to Free Speech

Bespalov begins by noting that there "is widespread agreement that incitement of violence, fighting words, true threats, targeted harassment, libel, defamation, and false commercial advertising must be prosecuted by law" (p. 403). The question he's addressing and answering in the affirmative is whether so-called hate speech should be added to this list of exceptions to free speech. The reason its addition is controversial and requires argument, he writes, is that hate speech, like "political fake news" and "pornography," is a form of "expression whose harmfulness seems uncertain or insufficient to outweigh the potential downsides of legal censorship" (Ibid).

Although there is widespread agreement that the law should curtail freedom of speech in various ways, I maintained in my essay that this common understanding is mistaken. Using threats, incitement, and harassment as examples, I argued that, properly defined, these actions should be illegal, but that in prohibiting them government is *not* abridging freedom of speech, *not banning speech based on its content*. The freedom of action secured by the right to free speech does not encompass those actions in the first place. When the creators of the First Amendment insisted that the right to free speech is absolute and that, therefore, government "shall make no law . . . abridging the freedom of speech," they were not declaring unconstitutional laws prohibiting threats or incitement.[1] For the details of my argument, refer back to my main essay.

Proper Government: Individualistic Not Collectivistic

More important than the issue of alleged exceptions to the right to free speech is the conception of government operative in Bespalov's argument. His essay contains no discussion of the rights of the individual, of their nature or content, no discussion of the Declaration of Independence's new conception of the proper function of government—"That to secure these rights, Governments are instituted among Men"—and no discussion of the idea that individuals can delegate to government only one basic power, the enforcement of their rights.[2] His essay contains but one mention (see the first paragraph) of a *right* to free expression. Instead, Bespalov conceives the function of government to be to prevent harms, when the harms being prevented allegedly outweigh any harms created by the prevention. This is the meaning of saying that governments should censor speech if its harmfulness is sufficient to "outweigh the potential downsides of legal censorship."

If we ask, "Who is the government preventing harm to?," the answer cannot be that it's preventing harm to each and every individual citizen, *because the individuals being censored are being harmed by the government, no longer free to express their views*. The government's basic goal, on Bespalov's view, is not individualistic but collectivistic. In the name of promoting the so-called public interest, government must reduce overall harms in society. If depriving some individuals of their rights—in the case of censorship, the right to free speech—will allegedly reduce overall harms in society, then government should deprive those individuals of their rights. If, writes Bespalov, journalists at one of Denmark's major newspapers, the *Jyllands-Posten*, published cartoons with the message that "'Muslims are terrorists' or, to put it more subtly, 'It is hard to fight the impression that some integral aspects of the Islamic faith inevitably lead its adherents to condone terrorist action,' then the publication was hateful" (p. 408)—and those journalists (presumably) should have been censored.[3]

By contrast, one motivation behind the First Amendment was to remove any possibility that government possesses the power to censor journalists. This difference in positions between the architects of the Constitution and Bespalov vividly illustrates the difference between the individualistic approach to government, which views the function of government as securing the rights of every individual, and the collectivistic approach rooted in the idea that government exists to promote the so-called public interest. Here is how Ayn Rand states the difference: "Since there is no such entity as *'the public,'* since the public is merely a number of individuals, the idea that 'the public interest' supersedes private interests and rights, can have but one meaning: that the interests and rights of some individuals take precedence over the interests and rights of others."[4]

Hate Speech Laws: Making Government the Arbiter of Truth and Morality

Bespalov contends that in advocating for government censorship of so-called hate speech, he's not destroying but preserving freedom: he's offering "a principled argument showing that hate speech laws do not compromise the values associated with freedom of expression—on the contrary, they help to protect those values" (p. 403). But his position amounts to the contradictory claim that it's necessary to abandon the principles of freedom in order to save them.

Any law that grants government the power to censor viewpoints and their advocates, such as censoring journalists who are extremely critical of a religion and its adherents, is incompatible with the values underlying free speech. This remains true even if the viewpoints being censored are irrational and evil. As I previously wrote, viewpoints like socialism and white nationalism "teach people to hate and despise large swaths of other people, be it profit-seeking businessmen in the case of socialism or darker skinned individuals and immigrants in the case of white nationalism" (p. 396). But this fact does not license the government of a free society to censor these viewpoints and their advocates. This is so in part because "*what constitutes irrational doctrines that foment unjust hatred against whole groups of people is a contentious matter*" (p. 397). Put differently, the issue of which doctrines are irrational and evil, and deserve to be boycotted and opposed, is a matter that individuals must think through for themselves. To grant government the power to decide which doctrines are irrational and evil, and then the power to coercively enforce its decision through censorship, is to make government the arbiter of truth and morality. No one who prizes their own freedom should yield to government such power.

To appreciate how far-reaching is the power that hate speech laws would grant to government, consider the three criteria Bespalov gives for identifying an instance of hate speech.

> Firstly, the expression must target individuals on the basis of their socially salient group characteristic, such as race, ethnicity, religion, sexual orientation, etc. Secondly, it must ascribe to all individuals who share this characteristic some undesirable qualities, such as being prone to criminality, intellectually deficient, or diseased. Thirdly, it must label those individuals as appropriate objects of hostility and contempt, communicating thereby that their presence in society is unwelcome. (p. 403)

This characterization encompasses socialism. Marxism as a theory, for instance, targets the bourgeoisie or capitalists as a class; that is, it targets individuals based on a "socially salient group characteristic." It ascribes to all these individuals "some undesirable qualities," such as a rapacious desire for extracting surplus value from exploited workers. And it teaches hostility toward capitalists, "communicating . . . that their presence in society is unwelcome." This is in part why Marxism maintains that a dictatorship of the proletariat is necessary. Is censoring the many advocates of Marxism, including many professors, compatible with a free society?

Or consider again the case of the *Jyllands-Posten*. Many thinkers who were part of the Enlightenment or who have been influenced by the Enlightenment maintain that when religion is taken seriously as the fundamental guide to all of human life, including political life, a deep connection develops between religion and coercion, including terrorism and torture. To many of these thinkers, centuries of religious wars, of inquisitions and forced conversions, were not accidents or aberrations. There was a grim logic to these developments. If expressing such a viewpoint, if maintaining, as Bespalov puts it, that there are "integral aspects of the Islamic faith," just as there are integral aspects of the Christian faith, that "inevitably [i.e., logically] lead its adherents to condone terrorist action" (p. 408) is to engage in hate speech, then many thinkers, past and present, have engaged in hate speech, myself included.

To proclaim that it is government's function to determine which philosophical position on the nature and consequences of religious faith is true, and to proclaim that government then has the power to censor dissenters, including journalists and other intellectuals, is to advocate for the opposite of a free society. This is the kind of society that did not separate church from state, the kind of society that the First Amendment was doing away with. Let us not take a step backward toward such a society, and certainly not in the name of freedom.[5]

Notes

1 See https://www.archives.gov/founding-docs/bill-of-rights-transcript.
2 See https://www.archives.gov/founding-docs/declaration-transcript.
3 For a firsthand account of the publication of the Danish cartoons and its aftermath, see Flemming Rose, *The Tyranny of Silence* (Washington, DC: Cato Institute Press, 2014).
4 Ayn Rand, "The Pull Peddlers," in *Capitalism: The Unknown Ideal* (New York: New American Library, 1967), 170 (https://courses.aynrand.org/works/the-pull-peddlers/).
5 On the separation of church and state, see Onkar Ghate, "A Wall of Separation Between Church and State: Understanding This Principle's Supporting Arguments and Far-reaching Implications," in *Foundations of a Free Society* (Pittsburgh: University of Pittsburgh Press, 2019) (https://newideal.aynrand.org/church-state-separation-a-principle-not-a-wall-part-1/; and https://newideal.aynrand.org/church-state-separation-a-principle-not-a-wall-part-2/).

Questions for Reflection

1. Do you agree with Ghate that threats, incitements, and harassments are not really forms of expression but acts of coercion? Why?

2. How might Bespalov respond to Ghate's charge that his view is contradictory?

3. How do modern challenges such as misinformation on social media complicate the debate over free speech? What solutions might be fair and effective?

For Further Reading

Brown, Alexander. *Hate Speech Law: A Philosophical Examination*. Routledge, 2015.

Maitra, Ishani, and Mary Kate McGowan. *Speech and Harm: Controversies Over Free Speech*. Oxford University Press, 2012.

Mchangama, Jacob. *Free Speech: A History from Socrates to Social Media*. Basic Books, 2022.

Strossen, Nadine. *Free Speech: What Everyone Needs to Know*. Oxford University Press, 2023.

Strossen, Nadine. *HATE: Why We Should Resist it With Free Speech, Not Censorship*. Oxford University Press, 2018.

Waldron, Jeremy. *The Harm in Hate Speech*. Harvard University Press, 2014.

13

Same-Sex Marriage

Against Same-Sex Marriage

James S. Spiegel

> **Study Questions**
>
> 1. What is the standard argument or rationale given for same-sex marriage? What critical assumption is made by this argument according to Spiegel?
> 2. Why does Spiegel think that laws that restrict marriage to the union of one man and one woman do *not* deny a right to homosexuals that is granted to heterosexuals?
> 3. How does Spiegel respond to the objection that his argument falsely assumes that same-sex desire is merely a matter of personal preference?
> 4. How does Spiegel respond to the argument that marriage is not an individual right but a *collective* right?
> 5. What is Spiegel's argument that same-sex marriage is unjust?
> 6. What objections to his argument that same-sex marriage is unjust does Spiegel consider? How does he respond to these objections?

Same-sex marriage (SSM) is a major contemporary issue, from the standpoints of both ethics and politics. While the *Obergefell* decision of 2015[1] has, at least temporarily, put the matter to rest from a federal legal standpoint, it has done nothing to settle the *moral* question about same-sex marriage. Is SSM morally legitimate? In this essay, I will affirm the negative position on this question, defending the traditional view of marriage which says that marriage ought only to be between one man and one woman.[2] The most common critiques of same-sex marriage are empirical in nature, focusing on alleged negative consequences of SSM.[3] These arguments appeal to such things as public health concerns,[4] harms to children,[5] harms to women,[6] hostility to religion,[7] the undermining of marital fidelity,[8] and corruption of the concept of marriage—the so-called "dilution problem."[9] Since these consequentialist arguments have been frequently deployed elsewhere, I will instead present a *deontological* case against SSM, focusing on two concerns at the core of the debate: equality and justice. First, I will disarm the SSM defense by critiquing what is widely acknowledged to be the central argument for SSM: the appeal to equal rights. Next, I will present an argument that shows why SSM is inherently unjust, and I will respond to some objections to my argument.

Same-Sex Marriage and Equal Rights

The standard rationale deployed in defense of SSM appeals to the moral ideal of equality. Ralph Wedgwood is typical in calling this the "fundamental argument" for SSM. According to Wedgwood, "the most plausible objection to laws that exclude same-sex couples from marrying is not that these laws violate a natural or pre-political right to marry, but that they deny a legal right to some that is *actually given* to *others*. That is, these laws conflict with the value of equality."[10] To further elucidate his point, he adds that "marriage seems to be one of the basic institutions of society. So, according to the principle of equality, everyone should have an equal right to participate in the institution: everyone should have an equal right to marry (unless an unequal arrangement has some uncontroversial and compelling justification)."[11] Andrew Koppelman, too, regards this appeal to equality as "the most powerful argument" for same-sex marriage, insisting that "Like things should be treated alike. Unless there is some salient moral difference between the two kinds of couple, they should be treated the same." After all, says Koppelman, "couples of both types are equally able to form households, care for each other, and create environments in which children can thrive."[12]

It is important to note that this equality argument advanced by Wedgewood, Koppelman, and many others[13] is essentially an argument from *justice*. The basic idea is that laws precluding same-sex marriage contradict the value of equality, and *therefore* such laws are unjust. But there is a critical assumption here that warrants addressing, specifically that traditional marriage laws (one man and one woman) constitute unequal treatment. I will argue that this assumption is false and that, therefore, traditional marriage laws are not unjust, at least as far as equality is concerned.

A common analogy used by defenders of SSM compares traditional marriage laws to previous laws that denied women the right to vote or laws that prevented Blacks from attending the same schools as white people. Such laws were rightly rejected as unjust because they denied Blacks and women basic rights that were enjoyed by white men. So, do laws that restrict marriage to the union of one man and one woman constitute unequal treatment in the same way? Specifically, do such traditional marriage laws deny a right to homosexuals that is granted to heterosexuals? No, they do not. These laws treat every adult equally, since they grant *all* adults, regardless of their sexual orientation, the right to marry a person of the opposite sex. And such laws deny *all* persons, again regardless of sexual orientation, the freedom to marry persons of the same sex. There is no unequal treatment here. For this simple reason, the argument from equality fails, as do analogies with classic cases of unjustly unequal treatment of Blacks and women in the contexts of suffrage and education. Richard McDonough summarizes the point by noting that under traditional marriage laws, "since no one has the right to marry persons of the same sex, [SSM defenders'] demand for the right to same-sex marriage is not analogous to the blacks demand for the right to study at the same schools as whites or a woman's demand for the right to vote."[14]

McDonough notes that defenders of SSM are likely to insist that the key difference here is that homosexuals do not *want* to marry a person of the opposite sex, and it is precisely this that makes traditional marriage laws somehow violative of the value of equality. But notice that this rationale crucially alters the nature of their argument, now making personal *preference* the pivot point for the right to marry. And to make personal preference or desire the decisive criterion for marriage rights entails the acceptance of many other marital arrangements, including polygamy, endogamy, pederasty, and bestiality. So, the appeal to desire not only fundamentally alters the equality argument but also leads to crippling complications in the case for SSM.

Here, SSM proponents are likely to push back on the idea that same-sex desire is a mere matter of personal preference. Thus, Andrew Lister argues as follows:

> For most people, sexual preference is not a matter of somewhat preferring one sex to the other while being able to enjoy both, but rather of being unable to form intimate, romantic attachments with one sex. If one believes that sexual preference is in this sense not simply a preference, and that it is for most an unchosen and unchangeable condition, then a gay person cannot honestly and fully marry someone of the opposite sex. From this perspective, the legal definition of marriage as opposite-sex only effectively prohibits gays from marrying much in the same way that prisoners were prohibited from marrying, in Missouri, prior to *Turner v. Salley*.[15]

There are problems with this argument. For starters, it is no less vulnerable to the *reductio* problem just noted, since it can as easily be deployed in defense of a wide variety of unconventional marriage arrangements. Many pederasts and polygamists have insisted that their preferences for children and multiple spouses are no less intense and exclusive than those who testify to exclusively homosexual desires. So are we, therefore, duty-bound in the interest of anti-discrimination to allow pederastic and polygamist marriage arrangements? Furthermore, even inveterate same-sex desires, which are "unchosen and unchangeable," do not prevent a person from acting on the right to a traditional marriage. As McDonough points out, "many homosexuals have married persons of the opposite sex, produced children, and, apparently, led stable, happy, and fulfilling lives."[16] Presumably, Lister would reject such marriages—

however demonstrably happy and fulfilled they might be—as not "full" or "honest." But such reasoning betrays a shallow and narrowly erotic concept of marriage. Many healthy, mature marriages are not primarily—nor even largely—erotic. Rather, they are a complex of moral, emotional, intellectual, and otherwise relational factors that combine to motivate a mutual commitment that goes well beyond sexual desire. And, it is important to note, this commitment is sufficient as a foundation for procreation and child-rearing, which are, of course, the most significant contributions that marital relationships provide society.

Reginald Williams offers an interesting alternative counter to this critique of the equality argument. He argues that "marriage is best seen, not as an *individual right* like free speech and voting rights, but as a *collective right*—i.e., a right that cannot be exercised by a single individual and thus properly belongs to a social unit that consists of more than one individual: namely, to couples."[17] He goes on to say that "the right to marry is akin to assembly rights, which are collective in the sense that they cannot be exercised by a single individual, since one cannot assemble by oneself."[18] Thus, Williams presses for a different way of categorizing the right to marriage, according to which the equality argument seems salvageable. For, given this way of understanding the right to marriage, traditional marriage laws do appear to treat heterosexual and homosexual *couples* differently, since such laws permit the former to marry while excluding the latter. And this apparently constitutes unjustly unequal treatment.

What are we to say to this? The first problem with Williams's argument is that while he perhaps shows that the right to marry *can be seen* as a collective right, he does not show why it *must* most fundamentally be viewed this way. In fact, there are strong reasons for rejecting his proposal and viewing marriage as an individual right. He compares the right to marry to the right to assemble, since both require a plurality of participants. But even in the case of assembly, the individual right is more fundamental. After all, there can be no assembly of a plurality of people without *individual* persons first choosing to assemble. And so it goes with marriage. Yes, it takes two persons to marry, but each must individually decide to enter into this contract. This shows that the individual right is logically prior to the collective right, whether in the case of marriage or assembly. And, to return to McDonough's main point, the right to choose to enter a traditional marriage is equally available to all individual adults, not just persons of a particular gender or sexual orientation.

Second, even if we concede Williams's point that marriage should be viewed as a collective right, this only leads to more problems—the same sorts of problems noted earlier that plague the desire criterion for marriage rights. Why restrict collective marriage rights to couples? After all, there are many more possible collectives besides couples. By Williams's logic, it is no less unequal treatment, and therefore presumably unjust, to prohibit marriages between three or more persons. Williams effectively ignores this concern, dismissing discussions of polygamy as a distraction into which "the same-sex marriage debate sometimes degenerates."[19] But given the nature of Williams's argument, the question of polygamy is no mere distraction but must be considered a legitimate alternative marital arrangement—or, rather, one of a whole *array* of marital arrangements. Indeed, his argument implies we should take all forms of polygamy no less seriously than the marriage of couples.

It is evident, then, that the equality argument fails to provide a compelling rationale for SSM. As we have seen, traditional marriage laws do not constitute unequal treatment, since they grant all adults the right to marry someone of the opposite sex. We have also seen that appeals to desire and collective rights as marriage criteria cannot salvage the argument from equality for SSM, as both have unacceptable implications. This naturally raises the question, what *is* a reasonable criterion for deciding what marriage arrangements should be legally sanctioned? Historically and trans-culturally, the criterion has been heterosexual coupling, because this union *alone* is the kind of union that is essentially procreative. Only the heterosexual union brings forth new human beings and is the reason why the human race has continued to exist for millennia. Thus, only the heterosexual union deserves that highest social sanction and honorific called "marriage." This fact is the basis of my next argument.

The Injustice of Same-Sex Marriage

Many defenders of traditional marriage focus on the essentially procreative nature of the heterosexual union. For example, Douglas Kmiec says that the state has a special interest in "both the encouragement of procreation and its responsible treatment by heterosexual couples."[20] And Maggie Gallagher writes,

> The reason the state is justified in "imposing" [traditional marriage] norms on people's intimate lives is that sex makes babies, societies need babies, and children deserve their own mothers and fathers. While marriage and children are optional for individuals, they are not for societies. Managing the sexually-based phenomenon known as "procreativity" is not optional, but essential if a civilization is to perpetuate itself over the long term.[21]

What Kmiec and Gallagher point to here is the fact that the state has an especially strong interest in procreation because without it, well, there would *be* no state. There would be no *people*. So, when we consider the goods that are important for a society to flourish, we cannot think of a good greater than the people themselves. And since it is through heterosexual union that all people come into existence, this essentially procreative union must, too, be regarded as a profoundly great social good deserving of the highest recognition by the state. Herein lies the deep injustice in the legal recognition of same-sex marriage. As George Dent puts it, "the corollary to recognition [is] that traditional child-bearing and child-rearing marriages [are] no longer . . . legally special. They [are] treated as no better than a gay partnership." And this, he notes, constitutes "the denial of a deserved accolade."[22]

This point regarding the special social value of the heterosexual union forms the basis of a strong argument for the injustice of same-sex marriage. The argument can be formalized as follows:

(1) Heterosexual union is the indispensable means by which humans come into existence and therefore has special social value (indeed, the greatest possible social value because it is the first precondition for the existence of society as well as its continuation).

(2) What has special value to human society deserves special social recognition and sanction.

(3) Civil ordinances which recognize same-sex marriage as comparable to heterosexual marriage constitute a rejection of the special value of heterosexual unions.

(4) To deny the special social value of what has special social value is unjust.

(5) Therefore, same-sex marriage is unjust.[23]

Now I would like to clarify a few points and respond to some objections. First, in this argument, I am assuming a very basic and uncontroversial conception of justice, namely that justice is, or at least fundamentally requires, *giving to each its due*. This basic idea underwrites all particular forms of justice and its specific applications in the public sphere, including commercial justice, retributive justice, and distributive justice. It is just this core idea of justice as giving to each its due that is the moral engine of my argument.

As for the argument itself, I want to make a disclaimer regarding the first premise, which asserts that heterosexual union is the indispensable means by which humans come into the world. Note that this does *not* entail that procreation is the sole or even primary purpose of heterosexual relations. Neither this premise nor any other part of the argument presupposes any concept of marital teleology. The first premise simply asserts an undeniable fact: that new humans come into this world only through heterosexual union, and this is a unique and incomparably great social good.

Here, one may object that the role of the heterosexual union in the propagation of the human species may be special to this point in history, but it need not remain so. Even now, *in vitro* fertilization makes heterosexual coitus unnecessary for reproduction. Perhaps reproductive technologies will even advance to the point that heterosexual union becomes virtually obsolete in procreation. In reply, I would note, first, that contemporary advances in reproductive technology have not changed the fact that heterosexual union is indispensable in human reproduction. Currently, *in vitro* fertilization enables human reproduction without a sex act, but this method is no less reliant upon the combination of male and female germ cells and thus is still heterosexual in essence. And the notion that one day there might be a means of genetically engineering a means of reproduction without the use of egg and sperm remains a mere theoretical possibility that might never be achievable in practice. Lastly, even if in the distant future such technology is achieved and heterosexual union becomes reproductively unnecessary, it would nonetheless remain that case that for millennia human civilization has been dependent upon this, so the profoundly special value of the heterosexual union will remain for as long as the human species lasts.

In light of the above, the critic may grant that heterosexual union is *necessary* for procreation but lodge another kind of complaint based on the fact that heterosexual union is not *sufficient* for procreation. Here I am referring to the fact that not all married heterosexual couples *can* procreate, whether due to advanced age, medical complications, or congenital defects. If such infertile couples are entitled to the public honorific of marriage, then why not allow homosexual couples to enjoy this same privilege? In response, I would note that traditional marriages that are infertile are nonetheless the *kind* of union that produces children. Or, as Robert George puts it, while such marriages are not reproductive in *effect*, they remain reproductive in *type*. George explains as follows: "Reproductive-type acts have unique meaning, value, and significance because they belong to the class of acts by which children come into being. More precisely, these acts have their unique meaning, value, and significance because they belong to the only class of acts by which children can come into being."[24] A related but distinct response to the objection is offered by George Dent, who appeals to the fact that marital arrangements serve the function of reinforcing social norms, and all heterosexual couples serve to uphold the heterosexual union as a social norm, thus encouraging others to follow this norm, which is immeasurably valuable to any society. He notes that "exceptions do not invalidate a norm or the necessity of norms. How some individuals make use of [traditional] marriage, either volitionally or as the result of some incapacity, does not determine the purpose of that institution. In that context, heterosexual sterility does not contradict that meaning of marriage in the same way same-sex marriage [does]."[25]

Now someone may respond that my argument insinuates that proponents of SSM aim to diminish or undermine heterosexual union and its social significance. And they may press the point that, appearances notwithstanding, defenders of SSM have no beef with traditional marriage and may applaud its procreational benefits as strongly as anyone else. So, critics of SSM are misguided in their efforts to give heterosexual couples the exclusive privilege to marry. In response, I would note that, however noble the motivations for SSM, allowing such marital arrangements is nonetheless a denial of the special social status of heterosexual union and is therefore unjust. Consider this analogy. The Purple Heart is a military decoration awarded to American military personnel who have been wounded or killed in battle. Suppose the US military decided to revise the criterion for this award such that anyone who serves in the armed forces, whether or not they have been wounded or killed, will be awarded the Purple Heart. And suppose that the motivation for so expanding recipient qualifications were very generous and noble, appealing to the fact that all military members deserve to be honored for their courage and commitment. Suppose further that proponents of this change insisted that they in no way intended to diminish the valor of those servicemen and women who have been killed or wounded in battle. What would be a reasonable response to such a revision? Surely, it would be that this defeats the purpose of the Purple Heart award, since it was devised as a way of honoring those who have made a *special* sacrifice for their country. Altering the criteria for the Purple Heart in this way would be unjust. And the fact that those who initiated the change had the best of intentions would not change this fact.

I provide this analogy merely to illustrate the point that the intentions of SSM proponents are irrelevant to the question of the justice of expanding marital arrangements in this way. Curiously, one critic of my argument, Alexander Bozzo, presses my analogy in an attempt to show that my argument depends upon "the contention that the *purpose* of marriage is the recognition of the special social value of heterosexual unions."[26] And, from here, he argues that, since I do not defend this claim, my argument begs the question. However, as I said above (and in my original essay), my argument assumes nothing about marital teleology. It simply assumes that heterosexual unions provide a unique and profound social good: *people*. No particular view about the purpose of marriage is necessary or assumed.

Bozzo offers another criticism that is more substantive, focusing on the second premise of my argument:

(2) What has special value to human society deserves special social recognition and sanction.

Bozzo begins his critique of this premise with an illustration about a person, Candice, who inadvertently saves the human race by flipping a light switch. Even though her action had immense social value, Candice doesn't deserve special social recognition because her intention was just to provide some additional reading light; she had no *intention* to save anyone. Bozzo compares this to heterosexual couples who procreate without any intention to provide a social good, and he says this shows that my second premise

> needs modification, for it does not take into account whether such acts are *intentional*; that is, whether they are done *for the sake of* the socially beneficial end. But this creates a problem for Spiegel's application of the premise to heterosexual unions. The problem of course is that heterosexual couples do not typically have children in order to furnish society with members. Rather, people have children, when they do so deliberately, because of the satisfaction that such children bring. Hence, heterosexual unions do not typically deserve special recognition.

Bozzo goes on to observe that "heterosexual acts, even ones that result in procreation, . . . are as ordinary as they come," and he proposes that what actually deserves special social recognition are "*deliberate and extraordinary act[s] of special social worth*."[27]

With this argument, Bozzo commits a basic logical error, specifically pertaining to his appeal to the concept of intentionality as a prerequisite for special social recognition. Certainly, when it comes to evaluations of individual acts, such as that of Candice in the light switch illustration, intentionality is a necessary condition for laudability and special recognition. But although this applies to individual persons, it doesn't apply to social *institutions*. To illustrate, consider an institution such as a hospital. Because of the many benefits provided by the hospital, it deserves honor and respect. And this would be the case even if very few people working there had laudable motives or even genuine concern for the health and well-being of those they served. The same is true of other institutions, from departments of the federal government to private businesses that serve a public good. The social goods they provide, and thus the recognition they deserve, are not contingent upon the properly aimed intentions of those who make up these institutions. In the same way, the institution of marriage serves a great public good (when involving heterosexual couples), irrespective of the intentions of those who participate in it.

Bozzo's argument, then, commits the logical *fallacy of division*, which is illicitly reasoning from a feature of a whole to its various parts. Specifically, he reasons that if a given institution (marriage) is laudable and deserving of special social recognition, then the various individuals participating in that institution (particular married couples) must exhibit the qualities that merit such laudability and social recognition. But, as we have seen, this is not true.[28]

Conclusion

I have presented a twofold argument in defense of the exclusivity of traditional marriage as one man and one woman. I argued, first, that traditional marriage laws are *not* unjust, at least so far as equality is concerned. Second, I argued that same-sex marriage *is* unjust. While justice concerns are but one dimension of an overall assessment of any moral issue, they nonetheless constitute an extremely important dimension of such an assessment. So, if my arguments are on the mark, then we have significant grounds for thinking that marriage should be exclusively reserved for heterosexual couples.

Notes

1 *Obergefell v. Hodges* 14-556 (2015).
2 I do not have space to present a full defense of the traditional view of marriage, as this would require not only a positive case for heterosexual monogamy but also a critique of other claimants to marital legitimacy, such as polygamy, endogamy, and pederasty. Since SSM is the primary challenger to the traditional view (evidenced,

obviously, by the fact that SSM now enjoys federal legal sanction in the United States, among many other countries), I will here focus my discussion on a critique of same-sex marriage.

3 For a general discussion of the negative consequences of same-sex marriage, see R. R. Reno, "Harms Done by Gay Marriage," *First Things* (November 2022) (https://www.firstthings.com/article/2022/11/harms-done-by-gay-marriage, accessed March 20, 2024).

4 See, for example, George W. Dent, Jr., "Defense of Traditional Marriage," *Journal of Law & Politics* 15, no. 4 (1999): 641–2; and Dale M. Schowengerdt, "Defending Marriage: A Litigation Strategy to Oppose Same-Sex 'Marriage'," *Regent University Law Review* 14, no. 2 (2001): 509–10.

5 For example, see George W. Dent, Jr., "Straight is Better: Why Law and Society May Justly Prefer Heterosexuality," *Texas Review of Law and Politics* 15 (2010): 371–87. Also, see Maggie Gallagher, "(How) Will Gay Marriage Weaken Marriage as a Social Institution: A Reply to Andrew Koppelman," *University of St. Thomas Law Journal* 2, no. 1 (2004): 49–51.

6 For example, see Dent, "Defense of Traditional Marriage," 627–8.

7 See, for example, Roger Severino, "Or for Poorer: How Same-Sex Marriage Threatens Religious Liberty," *Harvard Journal of Law and Public Policy* 30 (2006): 939–82; and Thomas M. Messner, "Same-Sex Marriage and the Threat to Religious Liberty," *Backgrounder* 2201 (October 2008): 1–23.

8 See, for example, Mollie Ziegler Hemingway, "Same Sex, Different Marriage," *Christianity Today* (May 10, 2010).

9 For example, see Kmiec, "The Procreative Argument for Proscribing Same-Sex Marriage," 661–4. Also, see Dent, "Defense of Traditional Marriage," 616–27.

10 Ralph Wedgwood, "The Fundamental Argument for Same-Sex Marriage," *The Journal of Political Philosophy* 7, no. 3 (1999): 225–42, at 240 (emphasis his).

11 Ibid., 240.

12 Andrew Koppelman, "The Decline and Fall of the Case Against Same-Sex Marriage," *University of St. Thomas Law Journal* 2, no. 1 (2014): 5–32, at 11, 14.

13 See, for example, Kory Schaff, "Equal Protection and Same-Sex Marriage," *Journal of Social Philosophy* 35, no. 1 (2004): 133–47, at 140–1.

14 Richard McDonough, "Is Same-Sex Marriage an Equal-Rights Issue?" *Public Affairs Quarterly* 19, no. 1 (2005): 51–63, at 52.

15 Andrew Lister, "How to Defend (Same-Sex) Marriage," *Polity* 37, no. 3 (2005): 415.

16 Ibid., 53.

17 Reginald Williams, "Same-Sex Marriage and Equality," *Ethical Theory and Moral Practice* 14 (2011): 589–95, at 590.

18 Ibid.

19 Ibid., 593.

20 Douglas W. Kmiec, "The Procreative Argument for Proscribing Same-Sex Marriage," *Hastings Constitutional Law Quarterly* 32, no. 1 (2004): 653–76, at 656.

21 Gallagher, "(How) Will Gay Marriage Weaken Marriage as a Social Institution," 52.

22 Dent, "Defense of Traditional Marriage," 617.

23 For my original presentation and defense of this argument, see James S. Spiegel, "Why Same-Sex Marriage is Unjust," *Think* 15 (2016): 81–9.
24 Robert P. George, "'Same Sex Marriage' and 'Moral Neutrality'," in *Homosexuality and American Public Life*, ed. Christopher Wolfe (Dallas: Spence Publishing, 1999), 144.
25 Dent, "Defense of Traditional Marriage," 602.
26 Alexander P. Bozzo, "Is Same-Sex Marriage Unjust?" *Think* 21 (2022): 5–17, at 11 (emphases his).
27 Ibid., 16 (emphasis his).
28 Bozzo's error is also evident in the fact that he equivocates between my use of the importantly *general* term "heterosexual union" and his own use of the plural "heterosexual *unions*." My argument crucially makes a claim about the special social significance of the heterosexual union as a kind or type, hence my use of the singular general term. Bozzo illicitly shifts the focus to particular heterosexual unions in order to enable his critique, which pivots on intentionality. In so doing, he distorts my argument.

A Case for Same-Sex Marriage

Christopher Arroyo

Study Questions

1. What lessons concerning "traditional marriage" does Arroyo draw from his survey of the history of marriage?
2. Why does Arroyo think there is no structural feature of the American legal system that entails limiting marriage to different-sex couples?
3. How does Arroyo characterize the nature of promises and why we have the convention of making promises? What does this have to do with marriage?
4. According to Arroyo, why is same-sex marriage a genuine human good?
5. How does Arroyo show that there are no relevant differences between same-sex and different-sex marriages with respect to whether they can form part of a flourishing human life?

It is safe to say that there remains plenty of work to do with respect to advocating for same-sex marriage. In most countries, same-sex marriage remains illegal, and around the world, homosexuality is still widely persecuted. For example, sixty-one countries belonging to the United Nations have statutes criminalizing consensual same-sex sexual acts, which means that approximately one-third of the world's population lives in places where engaging in same-sex sexual activity is punishable by law.[1] Even in countries such as the United States, where same-sex marriage enjoys widespread approval, there is reasonable worry that the Supreme Court is willing to overturn the federal law legalizing same-sex marriage.

This chapter lays out a modest though (I hope) compelling case for legalized same-sex marriage. In order to make this case as persuasively as I can, I need first to limit the scope of my argument by identifying some issues that space restrictions prevent me from discussing.

First, this paper focuses on the issue of legalized same-sex marriage as it pertains to the United States. I have chosen this focus because the United States is where I live, which makes it the society with which I am most familiar. Accordingly, the arguments I make in the paper with respect to same-sex marriage and the law presume the American legal system, which may make those arguments of limited use to people living in other nations.

Second, because I am writing with respect to an American context, and because I am trained as a philosopher, I am setting to one side theological arguments for same-sex marriage.[2] In this context, it is worth remembering that marriage originated as a secular institution.[3] Moreover, the United States is a nation whose constitution prohibits the establishment of a state religion, which entails a sharp separation between church and state. That separation rules out theological appeals when advocating for legislation and when making arguments in the public sphere.

Third, I am presuming that marriage is worthwhile. In other words, I shall consider neither the view that marriage is an unjust institution that should be abolished nor the view that marriage should be expanded beyond the limits of presumed romantic relationships.[4] It is not that I think that those positions have no merit. Rather, it is that the parameters of this discussion preclude me from responding directly to them.

Fourth, I cannot discuss the various ethical theories on which one might rely when arguing for same-sex marriage. For example, there are utilitarian arguments for same-sex marriage (i.e., arguments that look merely to the foreseen consequences of allowing same-sex marriage in order to show that, overall, they would be good) and deontological arguments in defense of same-sex marriage (i.e., arguments that focus on the way in which our allegedly universal moral obligations require us to allow same-sex marriage).[5] I approach the issue of same-sex marriage from what today is called "ethical naturalism," an approach I take because it captures what I think is true regarding human goodness. But it is also, coincidentally, the approach that is in the best position to argue with philosophical critics of same-sex marriage on their own terms, since many of these critics embrace a form of ethical naturalism.[6]

One final prefatory remark. For purposes of this paper, I am really arguing for two closely related but distinct claims. On the one hand, I show how legalized same-sex marriage is consistent with the constitutional principles of the American legal system as it currently exists. On the other hand, I explain why same-sex marriage is a genuine human good, which is just to say that marriage between same-sex couples is one of the many goods that people can (though need not) pursue as part of a flourishing human life.

I. Traditional Marriage? A Very Brief History of the Institution

One of the most challenging obstacles to persuading people that same-sex marriage should be legal is the presumption, which many people hold, that marriage is a universal human practice with an essence that has remained relatively unchanged throughout human history. This presumption, however, is plainly wrong. Elizabeth Brake eloquently summarizes the historical realities:

> In considering whether marriage has a fixed essence or definition, the historical and cross-cultural diversity of marital practices cannot be overstated. Structurally, it includes polygamy (both polyandry and polygyny) and polygynandry (multiple men with multiple women) as well as monogamy. Nomadic tribal bride exchange and arranged dynastic marriages must be set beside 1950s male-breadwinner unions and 1960s group marriages. In many cultures, extra-marital sex has been the norm—including communal sex, spouse-swapping, and sexual double-standards. Standards for divorce have ranged from a simple announcement (saying "I divorce you" three times) to a papal annulment or a British Act of Parliament. Some cultures have seen the ideal marital relationship as reserved, others as intimate and amorous; some have seen it as hierarchical, others as an equal partnership. Marriage includes passionate elopements as well as proxy marriages, in which Japanese or Korean picture brides, chosen by photograph, would marry proxies of their husbands in their home country, before immigrating to join their husbands. While most marriage institutions have been different-sex, marital or marriage-like same-sex relationships have been recognized. John Boswell documents same-sex unions in the Greco-Roman era and (controversially) in medieval Europe, Chinese historians report similar practices, and some Native American tribes, with fluid concepts of gender, allowed males to marry each other. Some rare societies have not been organized around sexual partners at all. In "husband-visitor societies" mother and child lived apart from the father or "husband." For instance, the Na, in China, had no marriage practice. Na women lived with their brothers; their male sexual partners were not integrated into the family.[7]

Most Americans are unaware of the preceding history of marriage and, instead, cling to a view of marriage that American historian Nancy F. Cott characterizes as entailing "lifelong faithful monogamy, formed by mutual consent of a man and woman, bearing the impress of Christian religion and the English common law in its expectations for the husband to be the family head and economic provider, his wife the dependent partner."[8] This conception of marriage often gets called "traditional marriage," a phrase that implies that it must be what most people most of the time have taken marriage to be. But "traditional marriage" is a relatively recent invention.

The prominent historian of marriage, Stephanie Coontz, argues that "traditional marriage," which she calls "the male-breadwinner conception of marriage," had its heyday in "the long decade of the 1950s, stretching from 1947 to the early 1960s in the United States."[9] A number of factors helped make the male-breadwinner conception of marriage the norm during that period of time, factors that include but are not limited to:

- the eighteenth-century invention of love-based conceptions of marriage in Europe and North America;
- the move in the late nineteenth century from a "calling culture" (in which young women invited young male suitors to their homes, where the courtship could be closely supervised by parents) to a "dating culture" (where young men courted young women out in public, away from the prying eyes of parents);
- the women's liberation movements of the 1920s;
- the economic boon and baby boom that followed the end of the Second World War;
- the invention and widespread purchase of electrically powered household appliances, which gave wives more free time to dote on their children and make themselves more attractive to their husbands; and
- the invention and proliferation of televisions in American households, since television programs and television advertising helped create and promulgate the norms of the male-breadwinning conception of marriage.

So-called "traditional marriage" is neither a universal institution nor a historical inevitability. Rather, like the other conceptions of marriage that Brake identifies, the male-breadwinner conception of marriage was born of particular economic and cultural forces that help explain how it came to be, and we are no more beholden to it than to any of the other versions of marriage that human beings have practiced.

Additionally, there are good reasons to think that the male-breadwinning conception of marriage should not serve as our paradigm of marriage. For example, Coontz reports that "in 1957, a study of a cross section of all social classes found that only 46 percent of U.S. married couples described themselves as 'very happy.'"[10] Though some husbands objected to the norms of male-breadwinning marriage as burdensome, the situation was particularly bad for wives and children. Women at the time were almost completely financially dependent on men, and it was legal to pay women less than men for doing the same work. Most states in the United States had "head and master laws," which legally empowered husbands to be the sole decision-makers in families. Domestic abuse of wives and children, including the sexual assault of daughters by their fathers, was a practice that was seldom discussed and, therefore, seldom addressed. Nowhere was it illegal for a husband to rape his wife.[11] Perhaps, then, it is time we abandoned the male-breadwinning conception of marriage as the ideal to which we turn when thinking about what marriage is, or should be.

II. What Makes a Marriage? Marriage Laws in the United States

Even if one recognizes the great diversity marriage has taken throughout human history, and even if one acknowledges the ways in which the male-breadwinner conception of marriage is flawed, one may nonetheless wonder whether there is not some structural feature of American law, some deep-rooted presumption in the US legal system, that entails limiting marriage to different-sex couples. If one looks at the requirements for marriage in the United States before same-sex marriage was made legal, however, one learns that there were surprisingly few. Though the federal government recognizes marriages, the term "marriage" does not appear in the United States Constitution. In the United States, in order for one individual to enter into a federally recognized marriage[12] with another individual, the following conditions must be met: (1) each individual must be of marital age; (2) each individual must consent to entering the marriage; (3) each individual must be unmarried. That's it. States are free to determine the particulars of marriage laws, so long as those laws do not violate the US Constitution. And each state is federally required to recognize marriages established in all the other states and US territories.

No doubt most Americans up until the twenty-first century would simply have presumed that marriage can only be between a woman and a man, but that presumption is unjustified in light of the history of marriage. Moreover, this presumption is not relevant to determining what the law requires or prohibits with respect to marriage. Actually, what is especially revealing about marriage laws in the United States is what they *did not* (and do not) require of married couples. In particular, US law did not (and still does not) require spouses (a) to procreate, (b) to engage in sexual activity, (c) to live in the same household, or (d) even to be in a romantic relationship. It is true that prior to the legalization of same-sex marriage in 2015, the majority of US states had laws on the books that restricted marriage to different-sex couples, but such a restriction was inconsistent with the other legal requirements for marriage in the United States. Actually, there were (and are) good reasons to include same-sex couples in the institution of marriage, quite apart from what the law requires or allows. In order to bring those reasons to light, I am going to shift from considering marriage as a legal institution to considering it as a human convention so that I can explain why same-sex marriage is a genuine human good that can form part of a flourishing human life.

III. Marriage, a Human Invention

Marriage is a contract between two people, a promise they make to each other that gives each spouse rights and responsibilities in virtue of being a partner in their marriage. At bottom, marriage is a convention, a practice that human beings invented. In order to see why same-sex marriage is a worthwhile practice for human beings to have, one needs to understand how marriage works. Of course, merely reciting wedding vows[13] is insufficient for making two people married; each person has to recite those vows sincerely and in the right context (e.g., in front of a judge who is officiating). Nonetheless, two people marry because they make a promise to each other in the vows they exchange. The power that those vows have depends on the more basic human convention of making promises to each other. But how does that convention work? How is it that two people in the right context sincerely saying to each other, "I take you as my lawful spouse, to have and to hold, from this day forward, for better, for worse, for richer, for poorer, in sickness, and in health, until death do us part, and I will love you and honor you all the days of my life," results in a marriage and all that it entails?

To answer that last question, one must realize that making promises is a human linguistic practice that rests on learning and following rules. The twentieth-century philosopher, Elizabeth Anscombe, explains how the convention of making promises works by drawing our attention to the linguistic practices on which the convention rests. According to Anscombe, our ability to make promises turns on our mastery of modal auxiliary verbs, that is to say, verbs that are used in conjunction with other verbs in order to express possibility and necessity. In her account of promises, Anscombe focuses on what she calls "stopping modals": auxiliary verbs such as "must," "shall," "should," and "have to." As Anscombe rightly notes, "It is part of human intelligence to be able to learn the responses to stopping modals without which they wouldn't exist as linguistic instruments and without which these things: rules, etiquette, rights, infringements, promises, pieties and impieties would not exist either."[14] Learning how to use stopping modals is just one of the skills human beings learn as part of learning a language. Moreover, sincerely saying, "I promise to X," or "I solemnly swear to Y" is not a matter of someone performing some private mental act that just happens to be accompanied by some verbal utterance. To make a promise is to participate in a public human institution, and we participate in human institutions by being initiated into them: we each learn how to promise because people teach us how to do it. Anscombe illustrates how we learn to promise by imagining that "Bump!" when uttered by someone, has the force of "I promise to . . ."

> Let us ask how this [use of "Bump!"] could be learnt as an utterance having something of the same force as "I promise to do so-and-so." It will be characteristic that the learner is induced to say "Bump! I will . . ." and is then told "Now you've got to do it" and is then *made* to do the thing or reproached if he does not, and that the theme of the reproach is not merely that he did not do it after it was required of him, but that he failed to do it after saying "Bump! I will." He also learns to extract the utterance from others in connection with what he wants them to do and to use their having made it as a weapon in making them do what they have said they

would, and as a ground of reproach if they do not. The one thing that gives "Bump" the significance of a promise is that the receiver *wants* the thing to be done.[15]

We learn how to use "I promise" (and other similar phrases) in just the ways in which one would learn how to use "Bump!" in Anscombe's example. That is, we learn how to promise by learning the rules (linguistic and otherwise) that govern the practice of making promises. Most importantly, we have the convention of making promises because making promises serves a genuine and important human need, namely, the need human beings have to get others to do things for them:

> What ways are there of getting human beings to do things? You can make a man fall over by pushing him; you cannot usefully make his hand write a letter or mix concrete by pushing. . . . You can order him to do what you want, and if you have authority he will perhaps obey you. Again, if you have power to hurt him or help him according as he disregards or obeys your orders, or if he loves you so as to accord with your requests, you have a way of getting him to do things. However, few people have authority over everyone they need to get to do things, and few people either have power to hurt or help others without damage to themselves or command affection from others to such an extent as to be able to get them to do the things they need others to do.[16]

Promising allows people to get others to do the things that they need others to do without resorting to violence or coercion, which is why promising is a human good. Were it not for promises (or some similar convention), people could not live together. We need the ability to make promises, to keep promises, and to hold others to their promises if we are to thrive as human beings.

IV. The Elephant in the Room: Same-Sex Sexual Relations and the Human Good of Same-Sex Marriage

One might object as follows: even if the ability to promise is a human good, and even if we acknowledge that different-sex marriage, as a kind of promise, is a human good that can be part of a flourishing human life, that does not mean that *same-sex* marriage is a human good that can be part of a flourishing human life. In other words, one might still wonder whether same-sex marriage is one of the goods that human beings can pursue and achieve while thriving as human beings. What I intend to establish in this section is that same-sex marriage is a genuine human good in that sense because there are no morally relevant differences between same-sex marriage and different-sex marriage; that is, on the presumption that different-sex marriages are a human good that can form part of a flourishing human life, same-sex marriages must be, too, since none of the differences that can obtain between a different-sex marriage and a same-sex marriage have anything to do with the goodness of marriage considered as a human practice.

The preceding claim may seem obviously false to some readers, since some readers may believe that the main purpose of marriage is entailed by the allegedly main purpose of human sexual activity, namely, procreation. On this view, same-sex marriage should be prohibited because same-sex sexual activity is intrinsically immoral. There are, however, compelling reasons to take issue with the view of same-sex sexual activity that motivates this objection to same-sex marriage.[17]

Throughout this chapter, I have written of "genuine human goods." In using that phrase, I am relying on the account of such goods that the twentieth-century philosopher, Philippa Foot, provides in her book, *Natural Goodness*.[18] Foot distinguishes *natural goodness* evaluations of living beings, which are evaluations of living beings on their own terms, from evaluations of *secondary goodness*, which are evaluations of living individuals with respect to the interests of members of another species. According to Foot, natural goodness "which is attributable only to living things themselves and to their parts, characteristics, and operations, is intrinsic or 'autonomous' goodness in that it depends directly on the relation of an individual to the 'life form' of its species."[19] An example of a natural goodness evaluation is, "This oak tree has good (strong) roots, which allow it to get the nutrients it needs." An example of an evaluation of secondary goodness is, "This oak tree has good (thick) branches, which allows those squirrels to build their nest."

When we make natural goodness evaluations of individual living beings, we rely on two kinds of judgments. The first kind of judgments are those we make about the individual being evaluated. These are judgments, for example, about *this* oak tree. The second kind of judgments are what Foot calls "natural history propositions." These are judgments we make about the life-form of the species we are evaluating. The life-form of the species picks out those features of the life of a species that the members of the species need in order to thrive *as members of that species*. For example, judgments about the life-form of oak trees have to do with what oak trees in general need if they are to flourish as oak trees (e.g., "Oak trees have deep, strong roots, which allow them to absorb water and nutrients from the soil").

There are a few features of natural history judgments that are worth emphasizing. First, natural history judgments are ones that rest on an empirical investigation of living species. For example, we can make true natural history judgments about oak trees only by studying oak trees. Second, natural history judgments pick out what *most* members of a species need in order to flourish as members of that species; they do not make pronouncements on what *all* members of the species have or do. For example, some oak trees have shallow, weak roots, but this acknowledgment does not detract from the fact that deep, strong roots are what oak trees need to flourish. Third, natural history judgments are teleological. That is, these kinds of judgments do not merely pick out statistical regularities. Instead, they identify what most members of a species *need* in order to thrive or flourish. Fourth, natural history judgments are ones we make about *this particular species*. If, for example, I want to make true natural history judgments about oak trees, then I need to examine oak trees and how they live. It does me no good to examine sequoias, palm trees, or rose bushes, since what I need in this circumstance is to discover the characteristics and activities that are particular to oak-tree life. Comparing oak trees to other species of plants in order to discover what is good for oak trees is like watching a game of ping pong in order to learn how to play baseball well.

Just as we are able to make natural goodness evaluations of oak trees and ostriches, we also can—and do—make natural goodness evaluations of human beings. The life-form of human beings is much more complex than the life-form of other living beings, which allows for innumerably more ways for human beings to be naturally good (or bad). For example, some people benefit from being married and having children, while others flourish while remaining single and childless. Despite the range of possibilities, the basic ingredients of natural goodness evaluations of human beings remain the same as in natural goodness evaluations of other living beings: in making these evaluations, we rely on judgments about the individual human being in question and natural history judgments about the life-form of human beings. If same-sex sexual activity is a natural human good, then when this or that human being (say, Miranda or Joel) engages in same-sex sexual activity, that person (all things being equal) can act well. In order to explain how, one needs to form some true natural history judgments about sexual activity and its roles in the human life-form.

It is tempting to think that *the* role of sexual activity in a flourishing human life is procreation, since human beings and lots of other species of animals reproduce sexually, but giving in to that temptation leads to a mistaken conception of human sexual activity. In determining which human needs are met by sexual activity, it is no help to generalize across species. The issue, after all, is to determine what is naturally good for human beings (not kangaroos or muskrats or whales). When one actually examines the roles of sexual activity in human beings and determines which needs sexual activity meets, one sees reproduction is but one of many such needs. And most of the needs that sexual activity meets have nothing to do with procreation. To list just a few, sexual activity helps people raise their self-esteem; it helps people learn about their sexual preferences; it is one of the ways that people reconcile; it expresses affection; and it relieves sexual tension and frustration. On the one hand, when it comes to its ability to meet each of those needs, there are no relevant differences between same-sex sexual activity and different-sex sexual activity. On the other hand, since procreation is but one possible purpose of different-sex sexual activity, and since sexual activity between women and men can be naturally good without being procreative, the sole difference between same-sex sexual activity and different-sex sexual activity is irrelevant to our moral evaluations of the latter. Accordingly, we have every reason to think that same-sex sexual activity is a genuine human good that can form part of a flourishing human life.

We fail to see the moral equivalence between different-sex and same-sex relationships when we fall into the error of thinking that human sexual activity has but one purpose, one role to play in the lives of human beings, namely, to help us reproduce. This error is in part the result of misunderstanding how to make natural goodness evaluations, and it is in part the result of failing to recognize the roles sexual activity plays in the lives of flourishing human beings. Similarly, the error of thinking that same-sex marriage is not a genuine human good is in part the result of failing to recognize how marriage works (what the convention entails), and it is in part the result of failing to recognize the various human needs that marriage meets. Those needs (e.g., the need for companionship, romantic friendship, and support, to name a few) do not pertain to human procreation, and different-sex couples need not procreate in order to be married. More importantly, people can (and do) procreate and raise their children well outside of the institution of marriage. All of these considerations, when taken together, lead to the conclusion that if different-sex marriage is a genuine human good, then same-sex marriage is, too.

Conclusion

Prohibiting same-sex marriages perpetrates an injustice against gay women and men because it prevents them from enjoying an important good and prevents straight women and men from acknowledging this good. What I have been arguing in this essay is that there are no relevant differences between same-sex and different-sex marriages with respect to whether these marriages can form part of a flourishing human life. Prohibiting same-sex marriages obscures that important fact, but allowing them expresses an esteem for same-sex romantic-sexual relationships by recognizing these relationships as good and legally permissible. The importance of such recognition cannot be overstated, given the persecution and oppression of gay women and gay men throughout the world.[20]

Notes

1 See https://database.ilga.org/criminalisation-consensual-same-sex-sexual-acts, accessed January 3, 2024.
2 For an account of how Christian sacramental practices came to inform secular marriage laws and norms, see John Witte, Jr., *From Sacrament to Contract: Marriage, Religion, and Law, Second Edition* (Louisville: Westminster John Knox Press, 2012).
3 Stephanie Coontz, *Marriage, A History: How Love Conquered Marriage* (New York: Penguin Books, 2006), 34–45.
4 For someone making a case against the institution of marriage, period, see Claudia Card, "Against Marriage and Motherhood," *Hypatia* 11, no. 3 (1996): 1–23. For

someone making a case for expanding marriage to a variety of caring relationships, see Elizabeth Brake, *Minimizing Marriage: Marriage, Morality, and the Law* (Oxford: Oxford University Press, 2012).

5 For an example of a defense of same-sex marriage that takes a utilitarian approach to the topic, see Jonathan Rausch's *Gay Marriage: Why It's Good for Gays, Good for Straights, and Good for America* (New York: Henry Holt and Company, 2004). For an example of a book that takes a deontological approach to the topic, see my *Kant's Ethics and the Same-Sex Marriage Debate: An Introduction* (Dordrecht: Springer, 2017).

6 Edward Feser is an example of someone who is an ethical naturalist who rejects same-sex marriage as immoral. Coincidentally, Feser is also a Catholic, but he contends that his version of ethical naturalism allows him to make arguments that are not theological in the sense in which I have defined the phrase "theological argument." See, for example, Edward Feser, "Teleology: A Shopper's Guide," *Philosophia Christi* 12, no. 1 (2010): 142–59.

7 Brake, *Minimizing Marriage*, 9. Brake's paragraph draws on three important studies: Coontz, *Marriage, A History*; Nancy F. Cott, *Public Vows: A History of Marriage and the Nation* (Cambridge, MA and London: Harvard University Press, 2000); and Helen Fisher, *Anatomy of Love: The Natural History of Monogamy, Adultery, and Divorce* (New York: W. W. Norton & Company, 1992).

8 Cott, *Public Vows: A History of Marriage and the Nation*, 3.

9 Coontz, *Marriage, A History*, 229.

10 Ibid., 237.

11 Ibid., 235–41. See also Stephanie Coontz, *The Way We Never Were: American Families and the Nostalgia Trap* (New York: Basic Books, 1992).

12 Even before same-sex marriage was made part of federal law in the United States, some states allowed same-sex couples to enter into civil unions. The main difference between such civil unions and marriages in the United States is that marriages are recognized and sanctioned by the federal government as entitling spouses to a host of rights and benefits, whereas civil unions have no such federal recognition.

13 Some theists (e.g., Catholics) would want to distinguish vows from ordinary promises, with the former being promises to God that carry special weight. I am not using "vow" in that specialized sense. Rather, I am using the term in its colloquial sense, where it is a synonym for "promise."

14 G. E. M. Anscombe, "Rules, Rights, and Promises," in *Midwest Studies in Philosophy, Volume III: Studies in Ethical Theory*, ed. Peter A. French, Theodore E. Uehling, Jr., and Howard K. Wettstein (Morris: University of Minnesota Press, 1978), 101.

15 G. E. M. Anscombe, "On Promising and Its Justice, and Whether it Need Be Respected *in Foro Interno*," in *Ethics, Religion, and Politics: Collected Philosophical Papers. Volume III* (Oxford: Basil Blackwell, 1981), 16.

16 Ibid., 18.

17 Here, coincidentally, is where Elizabeth Anscombe and I part ways; her Catholicism committed her to the view that homosexuality is intrinsically immoral.

18 Philippa Foot, *Natural Goodness* (Oxford: Oxford University Press, 2001). For an extended version of the argument of this section of the chapter, see my "Natural

Goodness, Sex, and the Perverted Faculty Argument," *Philosophy* 97, no. 1 (2022): 115–42.

19 Foot, *Natural Goodness*, 26–7.

20 I would like to thank Peter Costello, Brian Davies, Colin King, and Anne Ozar for helpful comments on earlier drafts of this chapter.

Responses

Response to Spiegel on Same-Sex Marriage

Christopher Arroyo

Study Questions

1. Why does Arroyo think that Spiegel's argument that traditional marriage laws do not treat homosexuals unequally is specious?
2. How does Arroyo respond to Spiegel's claim that heterosexual unions have a special value in virtue of being essentially procreative?
3. How does Arroyo respond to Spiegel's argument that legalized same-sex marriage is unjust because it undermines the special social recognition of different-sex marriage?

James Spiegel focuses his chapter on what he calls the *moral* question of same-sex marriage, namely, "Is [same-sex marriage] legitimate?" His view is that it is not, since he holds what he calls "the traditional view of marriage, which is the view that marriage ought only to be between one man and one woman" (p. 424). In my main essay, I have shown (1) that this "traditional" view of marriage is neither traditional nor without its problems, and (2) that marriage should not be restricted to different-sex couples. I shall not rehearse those arguments here. Instead, I want to focus on Spiegel's allegedly deontological[1] case against the legitimacy of same-sex marriage, a case that rests on two related claims: (1) that restricting marriage to different-sex couples is not unjust, and (2) that legalized same-sex marriage undermines the special recognition that should be reserved for marriages between different-sex couples, which (on his view) makes same-sex marriage unjust.

Equality and the Right to Marry

Spiegel correctly identifies arguments regarding the equal treatment of gay couples as central to defenses of same-sex marriage. In my chapter, I argue that there are no relevant differences between different-sex marriages and same-sex marriages that justify legalizing the former but not the latter. Spiegel, however, contends that such reasoning rests on an unjustified assumption:

> Specifically, do such traditional marriage laws deny a right to homosexuals that is granted to heterosexuals? No, they do not. These laws treat every adult equally, since they grant *all* adults, regardless of their sexual orientation, the right to marry a person of the opposite sex. And such laws deny *all* persons, again regardless of sexual orientation, the freedom to marry persons of the same sex. There is no unequal treatment here. (pp. 425-26)

The preceding argument may appear persuasive, but in reality, it is specious. First of all, to say that US federal marriage law prior to *Obergefell v. Hodges*[2] was not discriminatory because it gave everyone the right to marry someone of a different sex is sophistical. One might as well say that Jim Crow laws (state and local laws establishing racial segregation in the American South) were not unjust because they equally restricted Black people and white people to their own respective facilities. Or, better still, on Spiegel's line of reasoning, laws prohibiting interracial marriage are not discriminatory because the restrictions such laws place on whom one may marry apply equally to whites and non-whites.

Second, Spiegel's argument ignores the fact that providing gay people with the right to marry people of a different sex does not provide gay people with a genuine choice. People who get married typically do so because they are sexually attracted to each other and want to build a life together. A gay person, however, is no more capable of being sexually attracted to someone of a different sex than I am capable of wagging my arms and flying to the moon.[3] And that means that affording gay people the choice to marry persons of a sex different from themselves does not afford gay people a genuine choice at all.

Finally, Spiegel gets the facts wrong. Prior to *Obergefell v. Hodges*, United States federal marriage law did not grant each person the right to marry someone of a different sex than themselves; the law was not that restrictive. Rather, federal marriage law granted unmarried individuals of a certain age the right to marry a person of their choosing, so long as both parties consented to the marriage. Since being of marital age and consenting to the marriage were the only federal requirements, there is nothing about same-sex relationships that makes them incapable of meeting the bar for marriage in the United States. Therefore, contrary to what Spiegel claims, laws restricting marriage to different-sex couples are discriminatory and, therefore, unjust.

The Alleged Special Value of Different-Sex Marriage and the Alleged Injustice of Same-Sex Marriage

Spiegel, however, denies just that claim. That is, he asserts that there is at least one relevant difference between same-sex relationships and different-sex relationships.

Hence, the second main claim he makes in his essay, namely, that legalized same-sex marriage is unjust because it robs different-sex marriage of "the highest recognition of the state," thereby rendering different-sex marriage no longer "legally special" (p. 428). The basis for such recognition and special legal status, according to Spiegel, is "the essentially procreative nature of the heterosexual union" (Ibid). On this line of reasoning, "What has special value to human society deserves special social recognition and sanction," and "civil ordinances which recognize same-sex marriage as comparable to heterosexual marriage constitute a rejection of the special value of heterosexual unions" (p. 429). In short, according to Spiegel, heterosexual unions have a special value, and recognizing same-sex marriage undermines the recognition of this alleged special value.

Let me start with the claim that heterosexual unions have a special value in virtue of being essentially procreative. I should preface my critique by noting that Spiegel's use of the phrase "heterosexual union" is equivocal. Sometimes he uses it to refer to coitus; other times he uses the phrase as a synonym for "marriage." Insofar as "marriage" is not reducible to "coitus" (and *vice versa*), this equivocation undermines the soundness of his argument. But even if one ignores such equivocation, there are several other problems with his claim.

First, why should we think of coitus as *essentially* procreative?[4] Not every act of coitus results in procreation. Biologically speaking, there is a small window of time each month during which fertile women and fertile men can engage in coitus together and procreate. For example, if a fertile man and fertile woman engage in coitus each day of a given month, all but a handful of their sex acts shall have the potential to result in procreation, which hardly justifies calling coitus *essentially* procreative. Moreover, it is coitus, not marriage, that can lead to procreation. So, on Spiegel's argument, it would be coitus, not marriage, that is deserving of the highest recognition of the state.

Second, why single out coitus that results in procreation as deserving of special recognition? Spiegel argues that such "heterosexual unions" are necessary if human societies are to continue. But there are seemingly innumerable activities that are necessary for the perpetuation of human societies (e.g., securing sufficient food for members of society, educating members of society, creating and sharing stories). Why not say that these activities are also deserving of special recognition?

Third, people do not have to be married to each other in order to reproduce, nor do they have to be married to each other in order to raise children (and to raise them well). So, if there is a special value to procreating and raising children, that value is distinct from the value of different-sex marriage.

Fourth, the United States does not require married couples to procreate. In order for Spiegel's argument to have a chance at working, he would have to claim that we should, by law, require married couples to procreate. He does not make that argument in his chapter.

Finally, not every different-sex married couple procreates. Some choose not to. Others attempt to procreate but cannot, either because of bad luck or because one or both of the spouses is infertile. Spiegel acknowledges such cases of infertility and claims, with Robert George, that coitus between infertile people is still a "reproductive-type of act" (p. 430). But calling coitus between infertile people "a reproductive-type of act" cannot be correct. To call a sex act reproductive is to make a causal claim: *this* sex act did, or could have, resulted in procreation. Since no infertile person *can* reproduce, no sex act of such persons can sensibly be called "reproductive."[5]

What of Spiegel's claim that legalized same-sex marriage is unjust because it undermines the special social recognition of different-sex marriage? Here again, Spiegel is mistaken. Even if one grants that different-sex marriage is deserving of special legal recognition, legalizing same-sex marriage does nothing to undermine that recognition. One need only look to other forms of special recognition to see the truth of my claim. If, for example, two graduating seniors each earn the highest grade point average and are, therefore, each named valedictorian, the fact that there are two valedictorians does nothing to undermine or diminish the formal award of valedictorian or the sanction of academic achievement that it entails.

Conclusion

Why, then, does Spiegel think that legalized same-sex marriage undermines the social recognition of different-sex marriage? We get a glimpse at the answer to that question when he writes, "marital arrangements serve the function of reinforcing social norms, and all heterosexual couples serve to uphold the heterosexual union as a social norm, thus encouraging others to follow this norm, which is immeasurably valuable to any society" (Ibid). Although he never explicitly argues for it, I think the cornerstone of Spiegel's position is the view that same-sex sexual relationships are (to use his word) illegitimate. But, as I showed in the fourth section of my chapter, that view is groundless.

Notes

1 Although it is not consequential to my critique of Spiegel's position, I think his characterization of his own argument as deontological is unjustified. In moral philosophy, deontological arguments are ones that purport to show why one is required to perform (or required not to perform) some type of action on the grounds that the type of action in question is prescribed or prohibited by one's moral duties or moral obligations. Spiegel makes no such arguments in his chapter, and so I am unclear as to why he claims that his argument is deontological.
2 The 2015 US Supreme Court decision that legalized same-sex marriage for all US states and territories.
3 Thanks to Brian Davies for pointing this argument out to me.

4   It is only because I am a linguistic animal who has mastered a language that I can, for example, call my colleague a moron, but it would be wrong to conclude from that fact that speaking a language is essentially disparaging.

5   For a comprehensive critique of the view defended by Robert George, see Stephen Macedo, "Against the Old Sexual Morality of the New Natural Law," in *Natural Law, Liberalism, and Morality*, ed. Robert George (Oxford: Oxford University Press, 1996), 27–48.

Response to Arroyo on Same-Sex Marriage

James S. Spiegel

Study Questions

1. What does Spiegel say in defense of theological arguments in the public square?
2. According to Spiegel, what fallacies is Arroyo guilty of in his discussion of the history of marriage?
3. How does Spiegel respond to Arroyo's claim that marriage is a human invention?
4. How does Spiegel rebut Arroyo's claim that the procreative power of heterosexual marriage is irrelevant to assessing the goodness of marriage?

I appreciate Christopher Arroyo's effort to make a reasoned "case for same-sex marriage," but his reasoning is problematic at multiple levels. Most critically, his argument fails to recognize the significance of the fact that only heterosexual unions are procreative and, therefore, as a simple matter of justice, deserving of special social sanction which only the institution of marriage adequately provides. In what follows, I will highlight this point and several flaws in Arroyo's argument.

On Theological Arguments

Early in his essay, Arroyo states that "the United States is a nation whose constitution prohibits the establishment of a state religion, which entails a sharp separation between church and state. That separation rules out theological appeals when advocating for legislation and when making arguments in the public sphere" (p. 435). While this point is not central to Arroyo's argument, it is worth highlighting because it is such a common and egregious misconception. The Establishment Clause of the First Amendment prohibits the creation of an official or favored religion, but this does *not* entail the proscribing of theological arguments in the public square, as Arroyo maintains. Although Arroyo's assertion is, sadly, a popular one, many constitutional scholars have powerfully rebutted it.[1]

There is the further problem that such a view essentially condemns the approach of Martin Luther King and the entire basis of the Civil Rights Movement, as King's arguments for racial justice were often explicitly theological.[2] King understood, as we should, that debates about law and public policy are properly informed by all of the disciplines, including science, history, ethics, psychology, and, yes, theology. This is why theological arguments for exclusively heterosexual marriage *are* appropriate in the public square. While the arguments from justice and equality that I deploy in my chapter are not theological in nature,[3] these may be powerfully supplemented with theological arguments.[4]

On the History of Marriage

Arroyo sets the stage for his central claim by providing a "very brief history of the institution" of marriage, quoting Elizabeth Brake's survey of the many different forms that marriage has taken throughout history and across cultures, including polygamy, group marriage, same-sex marriage, and what Brake calls the "male-breadwinner" marriage model. This culminates in Arroyo's assertion that

> So-called "traditional marriage" is neither a universal institution nor a historical inevitability. Rather, like the other conceptions of marriage that Brake identifies, the male breadwinner conception of marriage was born of particular economic and cultural forces that help explain how it came to be, and we are no more beholden to it than to any of the other versions of marriage that human beings have practiced. (p. 437)

Note that here, as elsewhere in his chapter, Arroyo equates traditional, heterosexual marriage with the "1950s male-breadwinner model of marriage." This is a straw man denigration of heterosexual marriage, which actually allows for many different socioeconomic arrangements beyond that which was hegemonic in 1950s America. Elsewhere, Arroyo says, "there are good reasons to think that the male breadwinning conception of marriage should not serve as our paradigm of marriage," and a little later he concludes, "it is time we abandoned the male-breadwinning conception of marriage as the ideal to which we turn when thinking about what marriage is, or should be" (pp. 437-38). Again, note the repeated straw man conflation of heterosexual monogamous marriage with the pejorative "male breadwinner" model.

Second, Arroyo's reasoning commits a subtle but important fallacy. He reasons from the uncontroversial, obvious historical *fact* about the many forms that marital institutions have taken to the very controversial and far-from-obvious normative claim that we are not "beholden" to any particular form of marriage. But how does the historical plurality of marital arrangements imply anything about what we are "beholden"—by which Arroyo apparently means *obligated*—to practice? This normative claim requires an argument. Apparently, it is Arroyo's contention that it is because marriage is a mere human invention that there is nothing that obligates us to sanction one form of marriage over others.

Is Marriage a Human Invention?

According to Arroyo, "marriage is a convention, a practice that human beings invented" for the sake of achieving certain goods that contribute to a flourishing human life (p. 439). And since same-sex marriage is no less capable of supplying such goods, it is appropriate that same-sex couples should be allowed to marry. Arroyo writes,

> [T]here are no morally relevant differences between same-sex marriage and different-sex marriage; that is, on the presumption that different-sex marriages are a human good that can form part of a flourishing life, same-sex marriages must be, too, since none of the differences that can obtain between a different-sex marriage and a same-sex marriage have anything to do with the goodness of marriage considered as a human practice. (pp. 440-41)

There are problems with Arroyo's reasoning here. First, as to his crucial premise that marriage is a *human* invention, Arroyo simply *assumes* this to be the case. He never argues for or provides evidence, historical or otherwise, for this claim. But billions of devotees of Abrahamic religious traditions (Judaism, Christianity, and Islam) believe marriage was invented by our Creator for the sake of certain specified ends, and the conviction that marriage is divinely purposed is generally shared by practitioners of Hinduism, Sikhism, and other religious traditions, as well as many others who hold to a more philosophical theism. That Arroyo would so dogmatically dismiss the globally broad and historically long-standing affirmation of marriage as a divine institution is striking. Yet, in one sense, it is not surprising, since there is no evidence for the human-origin view, and abandoning this premise would cripple Arroyo's argument from the start.

Of course, even if marriage *is* a human invention, it doesn't follow from this that there are no absolute moral guidelines for how it should be practiced. Cars, computers, and medicine are human inventions as well, but our use of these things is nonetheless subject to moral standards. There are morally appropriate and inappropriate ways to behave while driving, sending emails, and using pharmaceuticals. So it goes for the institution of marriage.

The Key Difference between Heterosexual and Same-Sex Unions

To his credit, Arroyo appears to acknowledge this with his deployment of Philippa Foot's notion of "natural history judgments" when making evaluations of the human practice of marriage. It is in this context that he underscores the needs met by sexual activity which contribute to a flourishing life. Such needs, Arroyo says, include expressing affection, improving self-esteem, enabling reconciliation, and relieving sexual tension and frustration. In light of these goods, he asserts that "procreation is but one possible purpose of different-sex sexual activity, and since sexual activity between women and men can be naturally good without being procreative, the sole difference between same-sex sexual activity and different sex sexual activity is irrelevant to our evaluations of the latter" (p. 442).

But there *is* a very relevant difference between same-sex sexual activity and different-sex sexual activity, specifically that the latter is procreative in nature while the former is not. The fact that some heterosexual unions do not result in procreation is irrelevant here, since such unions are uniquely the *kind* of unions that produce new human beings. And as I show in my essay, this constitutes a profoundly special *value* of heterosexual unions—a value that is, in fact, incomparable since no other human needs can be met without it. Indeed, no humans can *exist at all* without it. So, when Arroyo says, "none of the differences that can obtain between a different-sex marriage and a same-sex marriage have anything to do with the goodness of marriage considered as a human practice" (pp. 440-41), he is quite mistaken. The procreative power of heterosexual union morally distinguishes traditional ("different sex") marriage from same-sex unions, and the failure to recognize this legally by allowing for same-sex marriages is profoundly unjust for this reason.

Notes

1 For some insightful discussions of this important point, see Michael J. Perry, *Love and Power: The Role of Religion and Morality in American Politics* (New York: Oxford University Press, 1991); Stephen L. Carter, *The Culture of Disbelief: How American Law and Politics Trivialize Religious Devotion* (New York: Anchor Books, 1994); and Francis J. Beckwith, *Taking Rites Seriously: Law, Politics, and the Reasonableness of Faith* (New York: Cambridge University Press, 2015).

2 For more on this, see my "Celebration and Betrayal: Martin Luther King's Case for Racial Justice and Our Current Dilemma," *Themelios* 45, no. 2 (August 2020): 260–76.

3 For different and more extensive nontheological defenses of traditional marriage, see Sherif Girgis, Ryan T. Anderson, and Robert P. George, *What is Marriage? Man and Woman: A Defense*, 2nd ed. (New York: Encounter Books, 2020); and Ryan T. Anderson, *Truth Overruled: The Future of Marriage and Religious Freedom* (Washington, DC: Regnery Books, 2015).

4 See, for example, Andreas J. Köstenberger and David W. Jones, *God, Marriage, and Family: Rebuilding the Biblical Foundation*, 2nd ed. (Wheaton: Crossway, 2010); and Darrin W. Snyder Belousek, *Marriage, Scripture, and the Church: Theological Discernment on the Question of Same-Sex Union* (Grand Rapids: Baker Books, 2021). And for a defense of the view that government should not be involved with marriage

at all, see Stephen L. Carter, "Defending Marriage: A Modest Proposal," *Howard Law Journal* 41, no. 2 (1998): 215–28.

Questions for Reflection

1. Is marriage a purely human invention or does it have a fixed essence? Why?
2. Who makes the better case, Spiegel or Arroyo, on whether traditional marriage laws treat homosexuals unfairly?
3. Would recognizing the legitimacy of same-sex marriage imply the legitimacy of other possible marital relationships, such as polygamy, group marriage, and so on? Why?

For Further Reading

Belousek, Darrin W. Snyder. *Marriage, Scripture, and the Church: Theological Discernment on the Question of Same-Sex Union*. Baker Books, 2021.

Brake, Elizabeth. *Minimizing Marriage: Marriage, Morality, and the Law*. Oxford University Press, 2012.

Coontz, Stephanie. *Marriage, A History: How Love Conquered Marriage*. Penguin Books, 2005.

Corvino, John, and Maggie Gallagher. *Debating Same-Sex Marriage (Point/Counterpoint)*. Oxford University Press, 2012.

Girgis, Sherif, Ryan T. Anderson, and Robert P. George. *What Is Marriage? Man and Woman: A Defense*. Encounter Books, 2020.

Issenberg, Sasha. *The Engagement: America's Quarter-Century Struggle Over Same-Sex Marriage*. Vintage Books, 2022.

14

Transgender Rights

The Case for Trans Rights

Jasper Heaton

> **Study Questions**
>
> 1. What does it mean for a person to be an "epistemic interdependent"? Why is this concept important to Heaton's defense of trans rights?
> 2. According to Heaton, why should trans people's self-identities be respected? How does this explain why it is so violating when other people deny our self-identities?
> 3. Under what conditions can it be ethical to dissent from a person's first-person authority over their self-identity? What is the role of the epistemic community in knowing when and how to apply these conditions?
> 4. What is the "dominant view of sex"? What narratives does this view create for trans people's self-identities?
> 5. Why does Heaton reject the dominant view of sex as false? What does this imply about the epistemic community trans and cis people share and whether trans people's first-person authority can be rightly challenged?
> 6. What is "hermeneutical virtue" and what does it mean to exercise it? What does this involve regarding trans people, according to Heaton?

In this chapter, I argue that trans people have a right to have their gender identities respected. Respect for people's self-identities is not in general an "anything goes" proposal, and it is possible to ethically dissent to people's self-identities. However, I argue that cis people do not meet the conditions that must be met for ethically dissenting to trans people's gender identities. I show that, in order to respect trans people's gender identities, cis people need to realize certain epistemic virtues toward trans people.

I. What Are We Arguing For?

What is *the case for trans rights* a case for? Transfeminists and other advocates for trans rights claim that trans people[1] should be "accepted" or "respected" as the genders they self-identify as. A minimal demand for someone to respect another person's self-identity as X is for them to assent or be disposed to assent to that person's self-identity, and to not dissent to them being X (e.g., by calling them "not-X").[2] To assent to, for example, a trans woman's identity, then, is to agree with her (or other people's) claim that she is a woman and to not call her a man or tell other people that she's a man. In this essay, though, I am interested in other, potentially more substantial demands of respect. In particular, I want to address the *epistemic* demands that the obligation to respect trans identities makes of individual people.

To be clear, I will not argue that respecting trans identities requires that people *believe* what trans people believe about themselves. But there are other important epistemic relationships we have with each other, beyond belief and disbelief, that must be maintained for our epistemic communities to function well. Human beings can be reasonably held to moral and ethical standards because we are *agents*—we have the capacity to choose our actions and to reflect on our motives and assess their outcomes. To respect a person's agency is to relate to them in this capacity, which involves holding them to moral standards. There are also obligations we can reasonably be held to given our capacity as *epistemic* agents, as creatures who not only know and believe things but who can assess and provide evidence to justify their beliefs, and make choices about the information they seek out, reveal, hide, and act on.

Some of our obligations as epistemic agents pertain to the way we are epistemically *interdependent* on each other. Several factors go into this, but there are three especially relevant ones that I want to highlight here:

i. We are finite creatures who can't experience everything, and we rely on other people to fill the gaps in our knowledge.

ii. We rely on testimony from other people to accurately report new information to us.

iii. Our own experiences are sometimes erroneous, and we rely on other people to calibrate with and correct us when we go wrong.

Interacting with people in these three ways is to treat them as *epistemic interdependent*, and treating people as epistemic interdependents is key to respecting them as epistemic agents.

Before getting into my arguments, I want to acknowledge that readers might wonder why I am focusing on such a seemingly narrow slice of the case for trans rights. Why not focus on, say, the principle that individuals have the right to act however they choose unless their actions cause harm to others, and point out that there is no evidence that trans people violate this principle? Or why not focus on trans people's right to access healthcare relating to transition, and point out that all evidence shows that trans healthcare is as safe and successful as other, less controversial procedures are?[3]

A persistent problem for transfeminists is that the case for trans rights has not been allowed to be a debate about autonomy, liberty, or even the potential harms of gender transition. The debate has been framed as a debate about the metaphysical nature of sex and gender, where the case for trans rights hangs on the question of whether trans people are "really" the genders they self-identify as. This has allowed opponents of trans rights to claim that the debate is settled by "common sense." This framing means trans people are dismissed as not being epistemic interdependents, trans people's claims about gender are seen as "obviously wrong," and trans people are not seen as contributing any new or useful information about sex or gender. The refusal to relate to trans people as epistemic interdependents is a vital part of how transphobia is perpetuated and maintained, and it is why the debate over trans rights persists.

In this chapter, I will make the following case for trans rights. Trans people should be respected as the genders they self-identify as. Fulfilling this obligation requires more than passing some laws and makes demands on individual people. People should assent to trans people's gender identities, though this obligation is not unqualified, and it is possible to ethically dissent to a trans person's gender identity. However, to ethically dissent to a trans person's self-identity—or to a person's self-identity in general—requires being in a relationship of epistemic interdependence with them, and cisgender[4] ("cis") people frequently fail to relate to trans people this way.

II. Ethical First-Person Authority

Transfeminists like myself think that trans people should be respected as the genders they self-identify as because trans people, like all people, have *first-person authority* (FPA) over their identities.[5] The basic idea is that the authority of FPA derives from the ethical badness of *not* respecting the way people identify themselves. Certainly, denying people's self-identities is frequently associated with egregious, psychologically, physically, and socially harmful outcomes; but in addition to these harms, it also violates what I will call people's right to *self-authorship*.

To author oneself is to express or put forward a version of oneself as some kind of person that other people can take up and interact with, and rely on in the future. Additionally, though, while self-authorship is a right, it is also a responsibility.[6] To be a person is to author oneself, and crucially, to be persons with others, we must author ourselves and say who we are so that other people can know who we are and can hold us accountable to who we say we are—and while this might sound lofty and abstract, the idea is relatively mundane.

Imagine you are at a party and the friend who drove you asks, "Do you want to go home?" and you say, "I'm not sure that I have the attitude of wanting to go home"—or perhaps you say, "I can inform you with certainty that the attitude of wanting to go home is among my mental states." In either case, you haven't answered your friend's question. They don't want a report of your mental states; they want you to make a *decision*. They want to know how they can interact with you, and to answer your friend, you must author a desire that they can then take up. Suppose you say, "Yes, I want to leave," but then you get another drink and settle back into the conversation you were having. This behavior does not match your answer, and you can be held accountable for this. Your friend might be irritated with you and refuse to drive you home in the future.

Suppose instead that you consistently leave parties early. Your friends will expect this of you and will treat you as that kind of person by, for example, no longer inviting you to late-night afterparties. If you complain that they never invite you to the late-night afterparties, they could point to your behavior and say they thought you didn't like late nights.

The fact that we are held to account in these ways helps explain why it is so violating when other people deny our ethical first-person authority. Imagine someone tells you that you want to go home, as in, they tell you what you are desiring. This is violating, even if their attribution is accurate. Perhaps you do feel like you want to go home, but you are fighting that feeling because you are worried your friends think you are boring because you always leave parties early. In fact, you leave early because you always start to feel shy, and by staying later at the party, you are trying to overcome your shyness because you don't want to be a shy person. By announcing to everyone at the party that you want to go home, by presuming they have the authority to tell everyone what your mental states are, this person is dragging you back to a version of yourself that you don't want to be. This is deeply unfair. It strips you of your ability to author yourself, and by forcing you into this earlier version of yourself, it erases your own reasons for acting, your feelings about your shyness, and your desire to change.

III. Ethically Rejecting Ethical FPA

If first-person authority is ethical, not epistemic, then where do the implications for trans people's epistemic rights come in? To answer this, we must first look at the limitations of ethical FPA and, in particular, why it does not provide an *unqualified* obligation to respect trans identities. The idea that, in general, it is *always* unethical to dissent to *any* claim that *any* person makes about their identity is implausible. But we have already seen that respecting a person's right to self-authorship does not mean uncritically assenting to anything they say about themselves; it means holding them accountable for who they say they are. Here, I want to detail four scenarios of holding people accountable for how they self-identify, where it can be ethical to dissent to their self-identities.

1. *Their self-identity violates the Harm Principle.* For example, I am under no obligation to respect a person's self-identity as a Nazi or accommodate their self-conception, for example, by maintaining a racially segregated environment. While this might harm the Nazi, it is justified harm because respecting them would cause more severe forms of harm to other people.

2. *Their self-identity is erroneous.* Crucially, not all errors are grounds for dissenting to a person's self-identity. For example, a person might self-identify as a painter despite having just started learning and still frequently making mistakes, but their mistakes do not justify denying their self-identity. However, suppose I sincerely self-identify as Lady Gaga's biggest fan, but I don't know her music and have never bought an album. Here, it can be ethical to dissent to my self-identity, because I seem to not understand what being the biggest fan implies.

3. *Their self-identity is insincere.* Suppose someone wrongs me and I confront them about it, and they say, "But I'm your friend! You should be more forgiving." However, suppose I have a good reason to think that they are insincere. Being a friend involves certain kinds of commitments, and this person's behavior has been incompatible with friendship; they aren't confused about what friendship involves; they just aren't really my friend.

4. *The person has diminished capacities of autonomy and agency.* A young child might wear a Spider-Man costume because they really identify with the character. A person with dementia might claim they are someone they are not. We can dissent to people's self-identities on the grounds that they do not have the capacity for taking responsibility for who they claim to be, though we might still "play along" and humor them.

Dissenting to people's self-identities is frequently discussed in connection with political oppression, and we will get to that shortly. But it is important to see also that the possibility of ethically dissenting to people's self-identities is crucial to why identifying oneself is a substantial, meaningful act. To self-identify as something *is* to say something about who you are and the commitments you hold. It is to say something about who you are or will be in the world with others. This is why we typically care when someone self-identifies as something. It is why self-identification is a significant act. But this is also why identifying oneself is a risky act.

Claiming to be something is not the same as being it. If you don't turn out to be the kind of person you claim to be, if people can't take you up as that kind of person in a reliable way, this is something you can be held to account for. If there were no possibility of ethical dissent to self-identity, then self-identity would be meaningless and insubstantial, as it wouldn't actually imply or commit to anything about what kind of person the self-identifier is.

The possibility of ethical dissent to self-identity is part of broader processes of identity creation and calibration. One of the central tasks of living is to understand ourselves. We must figure out what we feel, need, and want in order to lead successful lives and pursue healthy relationships. Fortunately, we don't have to start from scratch. We inherit a trove of concepts and other resources, from stories and media tropes to medical diagnoses, that provide blueprints of kinds of people and ways of living that we use to interpret who we are. For example, I can interpret myself as a *philosopher* because I can see that the mode of inquiry I enjoy, the sorts of topics I'm interested in, and the questions I like to ask fit with the description of that concept. Having the concept gave me a name for my preferences, and it also helped me accurately predict that I would enjoy doing a philosophy PhD.

But just as we have a finite and fallible view of the world, we also have a finite and fallible view of ourselves. My own biases can make me pay attention to some parts of myself over others, or distort my perception of my own behavior and motives. Perhaps I think I enjoy philosophy, but a less biased observer could see that I don't, that I get frustrated by philosophical puzzles, but that what I do enjoy is "sounding smart"—at which point, maybe I have some soul-searching to do. To understand myself, I rely on other people's experiences of me and they rely on me for the same.

For these processes to work, our epistemic communities must be well-functioning. Our knowledge about different kinds of people provides the standards we use to hold people's self-identities to account. But for the process of holding to account to work properly, the knowledge and standards that are being applied must be something that all parties, and especially the party being held to account, agree to—or at least, the standards must be such that all parties *should* rationally assent to them. For instance, in case 2 above, it would be irrational for the self-identified fan to reject the standards being applied to them—that is, they should accept that being the biggest fan *is* a matter of knowing the music and buying the albums. For this to be the case, though, the epistemic community shared by the parties to any such exchange needs to function properly and not have any issues that would undermine the rationality of accepting those standards. However, this is not the epistemic situation that trans people are in.

IV. Sex and the Power of Ignorance

I said at the outset that the debate about trans rights has been framed as a debate about the metaphysical reality of sex, and in this framing, trans people and advocates for trans rights are seen as making "obviously false" claims about trans people's genders that should not be respected or assented to. Going into more detail, trans people's claims about their genders are not just seen as false, they are seen as *unserious* and *inauthentic*. Trans people are frequently depicted either as liars or as deeply confused and delusional. These accusations make sense from the perspective of the dominant view of gender as sex. When someone says, "I'm a woman," they are typically understood to be saying they are female, that is, that they were born with a vagina, and their claim is accepted as true if they are female. When a trans woman says, "I'm a woman," this is what she is read as saying. Yet according to the dominant view, trans women are "really male"—why, then, would a male claim to be female?

Two options present themselves. If we presume that trans women know they are male and know what "woman" means, then their claims must be insincere—they can't be sincerely claiming to be female. They must be lying. On the other hand, if trans women really are sincere in their self-identities and really do mean to claim they are female, then they must be deeply confused about what "female" means or else be delusional about what their bodies are like. These narratives have serious practical and ethical implications for trans people. We saw earlier that we are not obligated to assent to the claims of liars or enable them to keep lying, and while delusional people might deserve our compassion and help, we should not provide them the means to persist in their delusions, and we are not obligated to assent to them any more than we must take seriously a child playing in a lab coat saying they're a doctor.

These narratives are based on this dominant view of sex. Yet this view of sex is, strictly speaking, false. This is not to say that "sex is not real." These arguments are well-rehearsed, and I will not reproduce them in full here.[7] Human sex characteristics are, of course, real, and there are real biological differences between people and other sorts of differences that are heavily influenced by which sex characteristics they exemplify. However, the dominant view describes a strict binary according to which everyone is either male or female, where males and females are sharply dichotomous categories that can be defined in terms of some feature all its members share and which all of the members of the other category lack. In reality, this is not the case, and human sex characteristics are exemplified in many more complex combinations than are described by this picture.

While a full account of this is beyond my scope, there are two key points to take in. First, while some bodies exhibit the features expected of the sex binary, the extent to which this is so is not a "natural fact" but a product of social forces. For one, there are billion-dollar industries, like make-up and cosmetic surgery, that deploy many effective strategies to make it more likely that people will choose to physically alter their bodies to appear more normative, more "manly" or "womanly," and nonconsensual surgeries are performed on very young infants to make their bodies more like what their parents expect of "little boys or girls." These practices are reinforced by deeply entrenched cultural notions about which combinations of sex characteristics are "normal" or "abnormal." Almost every story we see about humans presumes the sex binary and shows us an image of normative male and normative female bodies, and rarely are other body types featured. Because so many people choose to alter their bodies so that they appear like these normative types, and because other body types are so hidden from people's view, these notions of binary sex seem correct to most people—the binary concepts of *male* and *female* seem to accurately describe the world.

Second, the people with most control over the social forces that produce these ideas are cis people. Of course, not *all* cis people have had an equal hand in this. But cis people, more than any other group, are the ones with the power here. They have been the doctors, the scientists, and the researchers putting forward theories of sexed bodies. They have been in charge of decisions about which research projects get funded or which results get published. Crucially too, the concepts they've coined and the stories they've shared have all been apt to the things they experience, the situations they encounter, and the obstacles they face, and cis people have assumed that some bodies and some ways of experiencing one's body (specifically, their bodies and their experiences of their bodies) are normal, while other bodies and body experiences (specifically, those that are different from their bodies and body experiences) are abnormal.

This by itself would be a relatively innocuous fact. The concepts we coin should help us make sense of the world we find around us. If I live in a forest, I need concepts for all the plants and animals I encounter so that I can successfully navigate around them, avoid their dangers, and identify any potential benefits. If I find myself in a world filled with binary sexed bodies, then I need concepts to identify those bodies and to make predictions about them and their behavior; and if I do not find any other sorts of bodies in the world, and if I do not encounter people wanting to change their bodies from one type to another, then I do not need any concepts for those things.

The problem is that, as we've seen, no person's experiences exhaust reality, and some people might frequently experience things that other people go their whole lives without encountering. Thus, if some groups are excluded from the processes of coining our concepts and producing our knowledge, there will be gaps where concepts fail to describe parts of the world that some people typically experience. Trans people have been excluded in this way. Trans people have largely been excluded from the kinds of roles that would give them the opportunity to offer their insights and perspectives into the creation of our shared conceptual resources. Trans people have been the objects of scientific and medical studies, and cisgender scientists have observed their behavior and drawn conclusions based on their own experiences and biases. But trans people have not been allowed to create their own theories, publish books, or tell their own stories.[8] As a result, trans people haven't been able to fill in the parts of the world that cis people don't experience.

The result is that our concepts about the world are skewed—they are useful for identifying and understanding cis people's experiences, including their experiences of their bodies, but they are not so useful for making sense of the experiences that are typical for trans people. However, cis people are the ones who hold the power; they alone are in the positions to change and update our concepts. Yet, because our concepts do work for cis people, they see no reason to change them. The experiences that trans people are trying to report about are not experiences that cis people have, and because the sex-based view of gender is so well established in society, nothing trans people say and no evidence they present is able to counter it. Moreover, not only do cis people not share trans people's experiences, they presume that they already know everything they need to know, that trans people are either lying or are delusional, and that whatever they are saying about the errors of our concepts does not need to be taken seriously. This makes them feel justified in continuing to unjustly exclude trans people from the processes of creating and calibrating our concepts about sex and gender.[9]

The upshot of all this is that the epistemic community trans and cis people share is not well-functioning. It perpetuates ignorance about trans people's experiences and the realities of trans people's lives by unjustly excluding trans people from the processes through which our concepts are created and propagated. The sex-based view of gender that is used to hold trans people to account and deny their FPA is a product of this unjust, ignorance-maintaining system, and in this situation it would be irrational for trans people to assent to the standards used to hold them accountable—not only do trans people know what is said about them is false (more on this shortly), the fact of their unjust exclusion gives them reason to protest these standards. This also means that cis people are not in a position to ethically dissent to trans identities, at least not on this basis.

V. Epistemic and Hermeneutical Virtue

Everyone has the right to conceptual resources that enable them to interpret themselves and their experiences and to communicate about them with others, and in ideal epistemic communities, the conceptual resources should allow for this. But because some people have the power to skew these resources so that they only illuminate some parts of reality and obscure or even distort other parts of reality, other people do not have the concepts to interpret or communicate about their experiences of reality. Philosophers call this a situation of *hermeneutical injustices*. As we've seen, hermeneutical injustices create forms of ignorance that perpetuate social injustices. For instance, prior to coining the concept of *sexual harassment*, women who suffered sexual harassment were unable to name and identify their experiences of it, and instead, sexually harassing behavior was seen as a "joke" and "harmless" fun, which allowed the behavior to continue.[10] Similarly, the inability to see trans people as nothing but delusional liars prevents trans people from communicating the meaning or respectworthiness of their gender identities, which allows their identities to continue to be rejected. Thus, to combat these injustices, we must aim to combat the ignorance.

Of course, there will always be gaps in our knowledge, for again we are finite and fallible creatures. For our epistemic community to function well requires that those gaps not be the result of hermeneutical injustice and unjust epistemic marginalization. To reach this point—or even just to start moving toward it—requires that everyone in our epistemic community be related as epistemic interdependents. This includes trans people.

One might still think there is a reasonable question of how we are to do this. After all, sometimes people really do make outlandish, false, and insincere claims, and from the perspective of someone who believes in the dominant view of sex, trans people's claims do seem outlandish and obviously false—and what are we to do as individuals but evaluate things from our own perspectives and the information that's available, and judge the truth and plausibility of people's claims based on this? It seems that individual people are blameless for dissenting to trans identities—what other things should they be doing to avoid the problem I've described?

The answer is that people should exercise *hermeneutical virtue*. Hermeneutical virtue is an epistemic virtue, and epistemic virtues are virtues that pertain to the well-functioning of epistemic communities.[11] To exercise hermeneutical virtue is to practice epistemic interdependence in a way that is explicitly aware of the possibility or the presence of hermeneutical injustices, as per the three factors described in Section I. We can see what this involves regarding trans people. It requires cis people to acknowledge that trans people have experiences of their bodies, and of other parts of the world, that are very different from what cis people experience but that are just as real, meaningful, and motivating to them as cis people's experiences are to them. It requires cis people to have some humility, and to accept that their own perspectives are incomplete, and to even accept that some of their beliefs might be false, even when they seem obviously correct. For if some group(s) like trans people have been epistemically excluded, then cis people's beliefs have not been calibrated to all the relevant information. It requires cis people to listen to trans people with a presumption that there is something real that trans people are sincerely trying to communicate, even if what they are saying sounds strange or outlandish. It requires cis people to acknowledge that the reason trans people's claims might sound strange is not because trans people themselves are fools or liars, but because the cis people themselves might not yet have the tools to fully understand them.

Trans people already have tools for understanding our self-identities, and we hold each other to account for what we say about ourselves. Trans people do not evaluate each other on the basis of the mainstream view of sex because we know that our self-identities are not meant to communicate some fact about our sex as determined by our natal genitalia. We know we are not lying. Trans people know that self-identifying as a gender does not necessarily signal any desire to physically change their body, and we know that if a person does not "look like" the gender they identify as, this does not mean their self-identity is unserious. But even when, for example, trans women claim to be biologically female, their claims are intelligible within trans-inclusive communities because those communities deploy more sophisticated concepts of sex that do a better job of tracking the different combinations of sex characteristics and the way those characteristics can be changed. We are not confused or delusional in deploying these concepts. Rather, trans people and transfeminists are leveling a challenge to the dominant view of sex partly on the basis that it does not adequately describe reality.[12] And where cis people have failed to attend to the realities that trans people experience, trans people have been filling in those gaps and are now trying to offer our findings to everyone else.

Ultimately, if cis people want to have conversations about gender with trans people, if they want to talk about trans people's choices and behavior, and even if they want to be in a position to hold trans people to account for our self-identities, that is fine—cis people are welcome to come on board. But coming on board means exercising hermeneutical virtue. It means treating us as epistemic agents, as people who are able to tell our own stories and, moreover, who are able to tell you new things about the world that you might not have experienced before. It means picking up the tools that trans people are offering so that we may be understood and respected. Until cis people do that, they are in no position to dissent to trans people's self-identities.

Notes

1 In this chapter, "trans" or "transgender" refers to any person who does not identify with the gender they were assigned at birth. This includes trans men and trans women as well as non-binary people. Some people still distinguish between *transgender* people and *transsexuals*, but I will not touch on those debates here.
2 See Talia Bettcher, "Trans Identities and First-Person Authority," in *You've Changed: Sex Reassignment and Personal Identity*, ed. Laurie Shrage (Oxford: Oxford University Press, 2009), 98; Burkay Ozturk, "The Negotiative Theory of Gender Identity and the Limits of First-Person Authority," in *The Philosophy of Sex: Contemporary Readings, 8th Edition*, ed. Raja Halwani, Jacob M. Held, Natasha McKeever, and Alan G. Soble (Lanham: Rowman & Littlefield, 2022), 261.
3 See Taciana Silveira Passos, Marina Sá Teixeira, and Marcos Antonio Almeida-Santos, "Quality of Life after Gender Affirmation Surgery: A Systematic Review and Network Meta-analysis," *Sexuality Research and Social Policy* 17, no. 2 (2020): 252–62 (https://doi.org/10.1007/s13178-019-00394-0).
4 Cisgender people are people who identify with the gender they were assigned at birth.
5 Bettcher, "Trans Identities," 98; and Katharine Jenkins, "Towards an Account of Gender Identity," *Ergo* 5, no. 27 (2018): 713–44 (https://doi.org/10.3998/ergo.12405314.0005.027).
6 Bettcher, "Trans Identities," 102. See also Rowan Bell, "Gender Together: Identity, Community, and the Politics of Sincerity," *Blog of the APA* (January 11, 2023) (https://blog.apaonline.org/2023/01/11/gender-together-identity-community-and-the-politics-of-sincerity/).
7 See Laurie Shrage, "Sex and Miscibility," in *You've Changed: Sex Reassignment and Personal Identity*, ed. Laurie Shrage (Oxford: Oxford University Press, 2009), 175.
8 See Sandy Stone, "The Empire Strikes Back: A Posttranssexual Manifesto," in *The Transgender Studies Reader* (Routledge, 2013), 221, New York.

9 Gaile Pohlhaus, "Relational Knowing and Epistemic Injustice: Towards a Theory of Wilful Hermeneutical Ignorance," *Hypatia* 27, no. 4 (2012): 715 (https://doi.org/10.1111/j.1527-2001.2011.01222.x).
10 Miranda Fricker, *Epistemic Injustice: Power and the Ethics of Knowing* (Oxford: Oxford University Press), 149–52.
11 Ibid., 169–75.
12 And because it is a mechanism of transphobic oppression.

Against Transgender Rights

David S. Crawford

Study Questions

1. How do rights function in society? What implications does this have for the debate over transgender rights?
2. What different meanings does the term "transgender" have? What implications do the various views have regarding the self's relation to the body and the nature of gender transition?
3. According to Crawford, in what way do transgender assumptions lead to a fragmented view of the human person?
4. How is the fragmentation of the human person seen and better understood in the background concepts of "gender" and "gender identity"?
5. What logical and metaphysical problems does Crawford think result from transgenderism, especially as seen in recent legal decisions?

The debate over "transgender rights," like so many vital human conflicts today, typically plays out in clashes over individuals' and groups' competing interests. So, battles are fought over whether "transwomen" should compete in women's sports or use women's restrooms and locker rooms, whether schools can or must shield children's "identity" choices from parents, whether parents should be sanctioned if they refuse to accept the child's choice of name and pronouns, whether it is good medicine to prescribe hormonal treatments to children, and so on. These points of conflict certainly raise important issues of basic justice. However, their multiplicity suggests that something more is at stake than the parties' particular claims, that the arguments are proxies for deeper beliefs and assumptions that are difficult or impossible to articulate in the conventional modes of liberal public discourse. This tendency toward proxy arguments has consequences. While the conflicts concern fundamental questions of human nature and meaning, they are decided as matters of competing interests and rights.

This means that the deeper questions at stake are tacitly decided—indeed, decided for the whole of society—without ever having been openly or explicitly engaged.

This mismatch between what is really at stake and the way we tend to decide political conflicts serves as the wider background for what I have to say in these reflections. My goal is to offer a critique of "transgender rights" by unearthing the fundamental question of nature and meaning at stake: the ideology of "transgender rights" universalizes a fragmented understanding of human persons and communities, and in doing so brings harm to people, including those it purports to help, and the communities that make human society livable.

I. Some Preliminary Points

Of course, by "rights" we mean legal rights, so our discussion will necessarily dwell on the political and legal realm. Given this context, a few preliminary points seem appropriate.

First, my critique will be of a pervasive idea, not of persons. Many people suffer from conditions and circumstances warranting compassion rather than condemnation. Others have chosen to be part of a large, diverse, and currently chic movement and are happy and satisfied with their choices. Again, my point is not one of condemnation. Rather, my point is that all of us in modern, liberal societies have absorbed some stunningly bad ideas, and those bad ideas themselves can cause untold suffering for some and misguided beliefs, priorities, and choices in others. So, my opponent is never persons or groups but a culturally animating concept that is mediated by the transgender movement.

Second, the rights about which we are speaking are specifically "*transgender* rights." The language of rights evokes in our minds a historical arc encompassing the progress of civil rights for racial minorities and women. Claiming this mantle, of course, suggests that the category "transgender" is analogous to those others and that "transgender" therefore describes a historically definable and continuous minority with what would seem to be (if the analogy is to hold up) a naturally given attribute. It is sometimes difficult to distinguish in our minds the advent of "transgender rights" from this larger historical narrative of progress. The common charge that those who oppose "transgender rights" are on the "wrong side of history" suggests the claim's whiggish assumptions.[1] All persons, of course, should, and in worthwhile political regimes do, possess legal rights based on our shared humanity. However, "transgender rights" are accorded to persons specifically based on "identifying" as transgender, which depends on the correlative idea of "gender identity." As I will attempt to show, this last term is conceptually problematic, lacking a foundation in authentic human nature. If I am successful, then we should distinguish between the concept of "transgender rights" and the other, genuine achievements in civil rights.

Finally, we need to think about how rights function in society. Our tendency is to think of "rights" only as protections and empowerments for individuals or groups, and indeed, much of the rhetoric surrounding "transgender rights" reflects or assumes this limited viewpoint. The rhetoric of inclusion and choice, as pervasive today as the air we breathe, reflects this tendency. However, rights also necessarily impose constraints on others, and in doing so, they alter and shape action and speech. In addition, they highlight certain behaviors or groups as legal subjects to be protected or condemned. So, rights are not only protections and empowerments; they also imply a specific social and legal order and its coercive application of law.

As a part of civil law, then, rights profoundly shape our understanding of ourselves and of reality more broadly. The anthropologist Clifford Geertz long ago observed that law is "part of a distinct manner of imagining the real." Law offers "visions of community," he said, "not echoes of it."[2] More profoundly than we normally think, law tacitly conveys to us an understanding of who and what we are. So, while we might think that the conflict over bathrooms and swim teams is only another liberal struggle over competing interests, in fact, what is at stake is what society at large will be permitted to believe is real.

There is nothing novel in this claim. In fact, it is clearly viewed by transgender advocates as a feature and not a bug. When school districts and employers are required by law to treat their students and employees in accordance with reported "identity" rather than their bodily sex, these requirements prioritize "identity" over the fully human meaning and importance of the differences between men, women, boys, and girls visible in human sexual dimorphism. Some of the effects of this are obvious, such as the advantages of male bodies in athletic competition. But the implications run much deeper. Such laws channel the words and actions of bureaucrats, school officials, teachers, employers, employees, students, clients, customers, and so on, in accordance with this prioritization. Indeed, this channeling of word and action is nothing less than a sustained enforcement of thought, since the dissenter is confronted with a choice between the internal tension of dishonesty—the distance between what must be said and internal belief (I must say one thing, though my eyes and common sense tell me something else)—or gradual conformity to the new frame of mind. Of course, the latter will always be the long-term resolution of that dilemma, especially for children. This is why activists and politicians are so focused on education and children, and it is why dissenters find such legal constraints so totalitarian.

These implications are highly consequential in the formation of culture and in the social formation of persons and their communities. When a child's classmate goes from Johnny to Julie over the summer break, the event changes the child's understanding of what male and female mean, and therefore also of his mother and father, his brothers and sisters, as well as his growing conception of himself, his other friends, and his place in society and the world. The meaning of family is, in this way, changed universally, since its constituting relationships are made to appear contingent and even arbitrary. When women are forced to shower and dress in front of male bodies, the requirement alters how they can conceive themselves and their own bodies and, therefore, also their relationships with both men and each other, their parents, and their children. The sense of what it is to be a man or woman is therefore also changed universally. Again, these results are a goal rather than a side effect for gender advocates. Yet, we seldom ask in a serious way whether these changes are good for people or society.

Transgender advocates discount the importance of these human realities and the harm in their loss or suppression and paradoxically maximize in their place the significance of "gender non-conformity's" own alleged "erasure." The problem with the erasure claim is that it cuts the other way as well. It is increasingly difficult to think of ourselves as men or women simply because of *being* men or women in the organic wholeness of our sexually dimorphic selves.[3] Rather, our conceptual resources allow us only to think of ourselves on the basis of "identities" that *arbitrarily* relate to materialized bodies. The "experience" of the vast majority of people in our own day and throughout time, in other words, is rapidly being "erased."

II. The Ambiguities of "Transgender"

Now, anyone tasked with writing about "transgender rights" is immediately beset by the term's inherent ambiguity. "Transgender" can mean many things. In part, the term seems too narrow, since much of the debate revolves broadly around the "LGBTQ+" movement generally, of which "transgender" is purportedly only a part. If we nevertheless set aside "LGB" as involving "orientation" rather than "identity," the debate concerning "T" nevertheless bleeds into the wider and indefinite further set indicated by the "Q+." But even if we limit our scope to "transgender" more strictly— with its implied disjuncture between the natural sex of the human body and subjective "identity"—the internal composition of the disjuncture remains ambiguous.

For example, in both the popular and legal arenas, discourse about "transgender" often presupposes a tragic division within the individual between an inner subjective state—the "identity"—and the external sex of the body. Some speak, for example, of "the trauma of being cast" or "trapped in the wrong body."[4] "Identity" is in this case treated as an immutable and gendered essence living in tension with a merely external and personally indeterminate but nevertheless sexed body.[5] The rhetoric often states or suggests that "transition" is simply bringing the body into conformity with an individual's true, inner nature.

We see these assumptions in the idea that the "transgender man" *really is* a man and the "transgender woman" *really is* a woman, even though their bodies *really are* the opposite of their experienced identities. This suggestion begs the question of how a man who thinks he experiences the identity of a woman, for example, can know he really is experiencing the identity of a woman, rather than simply experiencing the identity of a man who *thinks* he is experiencing the identity of a woman. More fundamentally, the language and rhetoric of the debate often suggest the idea of an underlying personal truth or nature, a kind of gendered Cartesian ego or consciousness. Here, the disjuncture would imply the very anthropology ridiculed by Gilbert Ryle in 1949 as "the dogma of the Ghost in the Machine."[6]

A more sophisticated view, however, resists the "medicalization" of the disjuncture. This view implicitly denies that there is a particular way the body and identity *should* relate. Transgender would be more accurately described, then, as a lack of alignment between a socially constructed identity or gender and the social expectations for a materially sexed body. Therapeutic or surgical "transition" would then boil down to tailoring the body to fit those expectations. If so, then "reassignment" procedures would certainly fall under Judith Butler's censure of carving "gender regulations" into patients' flesh.[7] Of course, it is obvious that culture shapes sexuality in profound ways, but the claim here rejects sex's rootedness in nature altogether, suggesting that the relationship between bodily sexual dimorphism and the subject's identity is in fact arbitrary.

This last implication continues in a more direct way in the growing trend of rejecting the man-woman "binary" altogether.[8] This movement sometimes appears to be choice-driven, for example, in parents who raise their "children without imposed gender identities," reportedly for greater autonomy.[9] Here the body is externalized and instrumentalized to a certain idea of freedom, sometimes called "freedom of indifference," that views any sort of given order or natural direction as outside of and antagonistic to free acts or decisions.[10]

Finally, debate over "transgender rights" has been colored more broadly by the radicalized and politicized poststructuralist view, according to which "gender nonconformity" is treated as a form of protest or aggression toward society's expectations. Traditions, conventions, and nature are equally viewed as mere impositions of social power, similar to Adrienne Rich's "compulsory heterosexuality."[11] Sexual variance is said to have been pathologized as an expression of power.[12] Here we have come full circle: transgression of the binary is liberation, rather than a problem. While some feminists and others have employed a strong sense of the gender/sex distinction, others have criticized its residual essentialism. For some, *the body itself* is socially constructed—following the Foucauldian view, but qualified by Butler—because the understanding and experience of oneself as a subject and as a body is always already mediated by the dominant power structures of society.[13]

While the radicalized view has been profoundly influential, its obsessive concern with social power dissolves both embodied wholeness and the binary nature of human sexuality into a discourse about that power. The rejection of human nature as anything other than its expression presupposes (like the dualistic and more obviously fragmented versions it sometimes criticizes) the evacuation of the dimorphic body's fully human meaning and the centrality of the sexual complementarity of man and woman, as if the discussion of gender, sex, men, women, or even "non-binary" could possibly be intelligible without the primacy of the binary. In this sense, the poststructuralist version is merely the prolongation of the earlier fragmented understanding.

Philosophers, sexologists, psychologists, and gender theorists and activists have produced a massive literature and an impressive jargon concerning gender questions. But the assumptions and discourse that drive the debate are nevertheless an evolving swirl. Endemic to the swirl, however, is a conceptual fragmentation of the human person, in which personality is withdrawn from its organic links to the body, which is externalized, materialized, and instrumentalized to an expression—or, on the more transgressive side, a *propaganda*—of this falsely spiritualized and isolated self.

III. From Sex to Gender Identity

However we may resolve these cultural and conceptual ambiguities, the fragmentation implied by "transgender" can be seen in the background concepts of "gender" and "gender identity." The first of these terms was plucked from linguistics by the psychologist and sexologist John Money in the 1950s to aid in his study and clinical work on the rare set of conditions then grouped under the term "hermaphroditism" (but now known as "intersex").[14] For Money, "gender" was a distinct psychosocial determinant, which related in complex ways to the physiological aspect, "sex," which he further divided—morphological sex, gonadal sex, chromosomal sex, and so forth.[15] This division and then subdivision into further elements spawned an influential but ultimately problematic way of seeing sexuality: a sexed body, which was separated into parts and reduced to physiological functionality, set alongside the psychosocial element of "gender."

If Money provided for a certain integration of the physiological and psychosocial elements through his theory of neurological "mapping," the sex/gender distinction he had invented quickly hardened into a classic dualism in the hands of those who took it up thereafter.[16] Among the first of these was the famed psychoanalyst, Robert Stoller. Stoller's primary work in the 1960s was with "transsexuals." Given this context, Stoller brought the term "gender identity" to prominence, which he described as "the awareness 'I am a male' or 'I am a female.'"[17]

Paradoxically, the effect of this dualism, with its implicit devaluation of the body, has been to maximize the importance of "gender identity" for personal self-understanding and to vest it with an inviolable spiritual quality, an unchangeable center surrounded by a set of essentially plastic or alterable body parts. As an expert from the World Professional Association of Transgender Health put it, "attempts to change one's gender identity have been unsuccessful and in many cases were very harmful to the individual involved." Therefore, "whenever there is a lack of congruence among the various elements of sex, the goal of gender specialists is to bring the other elements of sex into conformity with one's gender identity, thus confirming the primacy of gender identity relative to the other aspects of sex."[18] "Transition" and "reassignment surgery" are therefore treated in essence as ways to "fix" an otherwise perfectly healthy body that does not fit an internal, subjective state.

According to this view, subjectivity itself appears to be integrated by "identity," while the sexually dimorphic body is implicitly placed outside of identity and reduced to the functional relations of its parts and aspects. Indeed, if "identity" (*identitas* = "sameness") refers to the distinctness and unity, or perhaps "self-sameness," of an individual, then the human subject appears to be unitary only by virtue of *not* being organically related to this fragmented and materialistic body.

Just as importantly, both Money and Stoller were concerned with what they considered disorders. Yet, their reconceptualization of sexuality presents us with a certain paradox. Already in their own work, this fragmented way of seeing persons, such that the whole is in effect reduced to its parts, rapidly expanded to become a lens for understanding human sexuality as such, even for those who do not experience nonalignment. In other words, a category originally intended to aid in understanding and remediating disorders or anomalous conditions became an indispensable conceptual tool for understanding the nature of sexuality universally. Both Money and Stoller acknowledged this seeming paradox. Indeed, Stoller characterized his patients as "natural experiments," by which we can gain a more exact understanding of the nature of human sexuality.[19] So, the ideas of "gender" and "gender identity" effectively viewed human sexuality in its very nature through a lens designed to understand aberration. If activists claim that centralizing the "binary" falsely pathologizes sexual variance, Money and Stoller in fact inaugurate a pathological understanding of sex in its very nature. In their hands, the conditions explaining transgender or intersex—that is, the fact of nonalignment of parts and aspects—have become the optic for saying what sex *is*.

We can now see more clearly what I mean by "fragmentation" and "arbitrary." The Money/Stoller optic assumes a principled *lack* of organic unicity or order between the sexually dimorphic body and the internal subjective state, and this lack of order—this arbitrariness—is taken as the universal character or truth of sex. In other words, we can understand "sex" by knowing that "identity" and the sexually dimorphic body are in principle independent aspects, that a woman, for example, who "identifies" as a woman does so because these aspects "align," rather than because she is an organically constituted whole. The relationship (and therefore what we mean by "sex") in that sense is essentially "fragmented" and "arbitrary," that is, "without order" (=*dis*-order, *pathological*), *even where there is "alignment."* As we shall see, this understanding of sex is logically and metaphysically fraught.[20]

For second-wave feminists who followed in the 1970s, the medical context was removed entirely, while the fragmentation of the human subject into sexed "biology" plus a gendered "identity" was further universalized, popularized, and politicized.[21] Hence, Gayle Rubin was able to dream of "an androgynous and genderless (though not sexless) society, in which one's sexual anatomy is irrelevant to who one is, what one does, and with whom one makes love."[22] Since then, "gender identity" has come to dominate discourse about human sexuality on the back of the developing but potent "LGBTQ+" movement. This conceptual framework now dominates public discourse and personal self-understanding alike, so that we no longer speak of the "sexes" but rather of "genders."

IV. Sexuality and Human Nature

The fragmentation inaugurated by Money and Stoller haunts the legal understanding of transgender rights to our day. Consider, for example, one US court's 2016 rejection of a school district's justifications for its sex-segregated bathrooms. The court tells us that the district's interpretation of "sex"

> assumes a student population composed of individuals of what has traditionally been understood as the usual "dichotomous occurrence" of male and female where the various indicators of sex all point in the same direction. It sheds little light on how exactly to determine "the character of being male and female" where those indicators diverge.[23]

The argument seeks to show the imprecision surrounding the concept "biological sex" and suggests a consequent ambiguity in the application of a sex-segregated bathroom policy. Like the reductive view inaugurated by Money, this argument relies on the fragmentation of sexuality into separate parts that may or may not "align." As in Money, the proof that sex really is, in fact, reducible to these components is shown by the existence of intersex and transgender individuals.

The problem here is how to understand what "sex" is for statutory purposes. But it is clearly obscurity, rather than precision, to define "dog," for example, as a set of organs, an amalgam of various types of tissues, a certain genetic configuration, or a constellation of organic compounds that may or may not work together properly. Here, it is likewise unhelpful—when the question is effectively "what is sex?"—to respond that sex is a set of elements that may "diverge." Yet the court implicitly does just that. The result is a profound relativizing of the idea that sex or even the sexually dimorphic body is intelligible at all.

Of course, we sometimes isolate components to understand how they may affect the whole, whether for scientific or therapeutic purposes. Indeed, this was the initial motivation of Money and Stoller. But to use the reduction to render the whole ambiguous or insubstantial, which is of course the very purpose of the court's argument, drains sex of its intelligibility. Each of the components is, in fact, only intelligible as a component of sex insofar as the individual person in his or her sexually dimorphic body is conceived as an organic whole, existing in a complementary and even constitutive relation to the opposite sex.[24] The whole is therefore prior logically and ontologically to its parts. For the parts to be parts, there must be a whole that makes them meaningful as parts, that, in other words, *allows them to be*. Likewise, "sex" (or the sexually dimorphic body, or the organic whole that is the human person) can only be understood by assuming the natural integration of its aspects or components. Money's reductive approach must be rejected when the question is, what do we mean by "sex"? Yet, like Money, the *Grimm* court treats sex as though the "whole" really is a set of parts, *even when they "all point in the same direction."*

The court also points to the possibility of individuals who have "undergone sex-reassignment surgery," "individuals born with X-X-Y sex chromosomes," and those "who [have] lost external genitalia in an accident" to argue that these possibilities make "biological sex" an ambiguous category.[25] The court does not tell us how this perplexity can be lessened by appeal to the infinite variation implied in the inherently ambiguous and subjectivist concept of "gender identity."[26] Indeed, the court's argument moves in the direction of eliminating sex-segregated facilities altogether, since logically the only criterion that matters after the ruling is "identity," while bodily sexual dimorphism falls away entirely (i.e., *all* who identify as a girl go to the girls' bathroom; *all* who identify as a boy go to the boys' bathroom). But of course, the inherently amorphous character of "gender identity" cannot in the long run support such a practice, so in fact the direction here is toward entirely androgynous facilities—for example bathrooms, locker rooms, or college dorms—since the court has effectively "erased" men, women, boys, and girls in favor of an infinite possible number of "identities."

But the argument is unconvincing for a more fundamental reason. The fragmentation of sexuality into parts that may or may not align loses sight of the nature of sexuality, and in doing so, it places that nature and anomalous occurrences on the same footing. This is the condition allowing the court to use those anomalous cases to undermine the intelligibility of sex, and it is the result of Money's and Stoller's pathologization of sex. The court sees variations in sexuality as equivalent instantiations. In this way, anomalous variants are given the same logical and ontological status or weight as the central case of human sexuality.

To continue the earlier dog analogy, the argument is a little like observing that, while dogs normally have four legs, some may be found to have three and others to have five (whether due to injury, disease, or birth defect), and then concluding that we must define "dog" as a three-to-five-legged animal. This would be a case of interpreting the meaning of "dog" through the lens of anomalous instantiations. Notice that three- and five-legged dogs are still dogs, although they may not be able to move about as dogs normally do. However, it would be absurd to define "dog" in terms of these instantiations. It would be, in effect, to pathologize our understanding of "dog."

Of course, the problematic nature of the court's argument is even more serious than my analogy suggests, because four-leggedness is not centrally defining for the intelligibility of "dog" in the way that sexual dimorphism (with its procreative potential) is for the concept of "sex."[27] The problem faced by the pathological view of the nature of sex is that to make sense even of the anomalies, there needs to be a central intelligibility or nature. But it is this central point of intelligibility or nature that is opposed. Lost to the judges, in other words, is an order by which we can make sense of the variants. Their argument is, in fact, illegitimate: it depends on (1) a conceptualization of sex as a set of variations, which themselves depend on the central idea of sex for their intelligibility as variants, and (2) simultaneously using the existence of those variants to undermine the central concept's intelligibility. For example, whatever we might make of the concept of "nonbinary," what we do know very certainly is that the idea depends on the more basic reality of "binary," which itself depends on the irreducible dimorphism of men and women. Without the prior concept of "binary," there simply cannot be a "nonbinary."

By shifting the center of sexuality away from the body and onto identity, then, the court is treating all the students (in fact, all of humanity) according to the constitution of sexuality inherent in the anomalous situations, particularly transgenderism. This treatment is implicit in the term "cis," which in effect designates a position on a spectrum defined by the possibility of "trans." The spectrum itself, of course, is predicated on the arbitrary relationship between identity and the body. In this sense, it treats "cis" as a variant of "trans."

This fragmentation and its inherent arbitrariness also stand behind the "conservative" US Supreme Court's 2020 decision in *Bostock*, which equated men who identify as women with actual women. If Title VII requires equal treatment in employment between men and women, the Court reasoned, treating a man and a woman who each "identify as a woman" differently is a type of sex discrimination. The argument depends on the idea that "identification as a woman" constitutes a shared characteristic. The reasoning assumes that "identity as a woman" is a univocal quality or subjective state that either a man or a woman might possess. "Equality" in this case, therefore, depends on an arbitrary relationship between identity and the sexually dimorphic body. Whatever we may think about employment discrimination in this case, the Court's solution is to reconceive sex universally. To treat the woman who identifies as a woman as equivalent to the man who identifies as a woman is to fragment the woman's sense of herself. It is, in fact, to fragment sexuality for the whole of society. There is no room here for the fact that simply *being* a woman—through the organic wholeness that constitutes a woman—implies an irreducible personal "self-sameness" simply on that basis, a basis impossible to find in a man.

This logic is carried further in a 2018 court decision, which ridiculed the "stereotype" that "sexual organs and gender identity ought to align."[28] If a woman could really have male sex organs, on what basis can we say that sex organs are truly "male" or "female"? This result is nothing less than the oblivion of sex altogether, its complete loss of intelligibility, an implication verified in the court's further claim that, like "religious identity," "gender identity" is "fluid" and "variable" since "both have a 'deeply personal, internal genesis *that lacks a fixed external referent.*'"[29]

Conclusion

I began by pointing out that rights are never simply protections and empowerments but that they always channel actions, language, and thought by force of law. They dictate what we are permitted to think far more pervasively than they protect and empower. I began by stipulating that all have basic rights rooted in our shared humanity, while distinguishing transgender rights as based on the false concept of "gender identity." Transgender rights are part of a larger cultural current that imposes a particular conceptual framework for human sexuality and, therefore, also for what it means to be human. The message is that persons lack integral wholeness and that the body is related arbitrarily to the interior subject and is somehow less than fully personal. These implications invite a forgetfulness of the tissue of organic ties of natural communities because they treat their constitutive relationships as also arbitrary and contingent. Yet, this tissue is fundamentally human, and a necessary ingredient of personal *identity*. The male and female bodies point to each other and can only have their meaning—precisely as male and female—in relation to each other. They also point to the child, and the child likewise points back to the parents. When we gaze in the mirror as we age, our parents peer back at us. This is a bracing vision, helping us to see our origins and the weight of mortality. The view of ourselves we see in our children is also a promise of a future beyond our own existences. Just as importantly, we see in these family relationships the organic ties we have with all others, since the tissue of relations extends indefinitely. Receiving life from a mother and father—even when the relationships are painful—means that we always bear within ourselves a visible and foundational likeness to others. It means that we bear society within ourselves. In this way, human communities point both to the past and the future as they reflect the connectedness of men, women, and children in the endless river of generations. The implicit denial of these organic relationships is a dangerous denial of our shared humanity.

Notes

1 See Herbert Butterfield's classic, *The Whig Interpretation of History* (New York: W. W. Norton & Company, 1965 [1st ed. 1931]), which criticizes ideological impositions on historical interpretation, especially those seeking to valorize a progressive movement toward a present or hoped-for ideal.

2 Clifford Geertz, *Local Knowledge* (New York: Basic Books, 1983), 173, 218, quoted in Fernanda Pirie, *The Anthropology of Law* (Oxford: Oxford University Press, 2013), 57.

3 Many philosophers have decried the modern conceptual fragmentation of wholes into their parts. Hans Jonas offers perhaps the most profound recuperation of the sense of organic wholeness necessary for the intelligibility of organisms and therefore of life (*bios*), beginning with the simplest organisms. See his *The Phenomenon of Life: Toward a Philosophical Biology* (Evanstan: Northwestern University Press, 1966).

4 S. Elizabeth Malloy, "What Best to Protect Transsexuals from Discrimination: Using Current Legislation or Adopting a New Judicial Framework," *Women's Rights Law Reporter* 32 (2010): 283–323, at 283, 286 (http://scholarship.law.uc.edu/fac_pubs/302, accessed July 27, 2024).

5   See e.g., *Equal Emp't Opportunity Comm'n v. R.G. &. G.R. Harris Funeral Homes, Inc.*, 884 F.3d 560, 568–9 (6th Cir. 2018).

6   Gilbert Ryle, *The Concept of Mind* (University of Chicago Press, 2000), 15–16.

7   Judith Butler, "Gender Regulations," in *Undoing Gender* (New York: Routledge, 2004), 40–56, at 53. Butler is speaking here of surgery on intersex patients, but her comment applies to our present context as well.

8   E.g., see Julie Compton, "Neither Male nor Female: Why Some Non-Binary People Are 'Microdosing' Hormones," NBC News (July 13, 2019) (https://www.nbcnews.com/feature/nbc-out/neither-male-nor-female-why-some-nonbinary-people-are-microdosing-n1028766, accessed July 27, 2024).

9   E.g., Nayanika Guha, "How to Raise Theybies: Children without Imposed Gender Identities," *Verywell Family* (September 19, 2022) (https://www.verywellfamily.com/how-to-raise-a-child-without-gender-6499907, accessed July 27, 2024).

10 Servais Pinckaers, *Sources of Christian Ethics*, trans. Sr. Mary Thomas Noble (Washington, DC: The Catholic University of America Press, 1995), 240–53, 327–53.

11 Adrienne Rich, "Compulsory Heterosexuality and Lesbian Existence," *Signs: Journal of Women in Culture and Society* 5, no. 4 (Summer 1980): 631–60.

12 E.g., Judith Butler's most recent book, *Who's Afraid of Gender* (New York: Farrar, Straus and Giroux, 2024), 64, 248, 276.

13 Judith Butler, *Gender Trouble: Feminism and the Subversion of Identity* (New York: Routledge, 1990), 11.

14 Money is now condemned by all sides for his research and clinical practices. See, for example, John Colapinto, *As Nature Made Him: The Boy Who Was Raised as a Girl* (Harper Perennial, 2006), New York; Butler, *Who's Afraid of Gender?*, 194–5.

15 John Money, Joan Hampson, and John Hampson, "Examination of Some Basic Sexual Concepts: The Evidence of Human Hermaphroditism," *Bulletin of the Johns Hopkins Hospital* 97 (1955): 301–19; Money, Hampson, and Hampson, "Imprinting and the Establishment of Gender Role," *A.M.A. Archives of Neurology and Psychiatry* 77 (1956): 333–6. See also, M. Dru Levasseur, "Gender Identity Defines Sex: Updating the Law to Reflect Modern Medical Science Is Key to Transgender Rights," *Vermont Law Review* 39 (2015): 943–1004, at 980–1, n. 214 (noting that the number and character of the elements have varied over time).

16 Jennifer Germon, *Gender: A Genealogy of an Idea* (London: Palgrave Macmillan, 2009), 63ff.

17 Robert Stoller, "A Contribution to the Study of Gender Identity," *International Journal of Psychoanalysis* 45 (1964): 220, quoted in Germon, *Gender*, at 65. See also, Stoller, *Sex and Gender: The Development of Masculinity and Femininity* (London: Karnac Books, 1968), at 40.

18 Sharon M. McGowan, "Working with Clients to Develop Compatible Visions of What It Means to 'Win' a Case: Reflections on *Schroer v. Billington*," *Harvard Civil Rights-Civil Liberties Law Review* 45 (2010): 205–45, at 234–5, citing tr. of Bench Trial at 402–3, *Schroer v. Billington*, 525 F. Supp. 2d 58 (D.D.C. 2005) (No. 05-1090). The "various elements" here echo Money's division of identity and the sexed body into parts, increasing the number from seven to nine.

19 Stoller, *Sex and Gender*, at vii, 5, 14.

20 The work of scientists, such as Money and Stoller, should serve as a cautionary example for conservative attempts to use the category "biology" to defend the integrity of sexual dimorphism, since modern biology stands partly behind the fragmenting and pathologizing tendencies we see in their work. Rather, we need a new "biology," understood in terms of *human nature* (see *The Phenomenon of Life* in note 3).

21 E.g., Ann Oakley, *Sex, Gender, and Society (Toward a New Society)* (London: Temple Smith, 1972), ch. 6.

22 Gayle Rubin, "The Traffic in Women: Notes on the 'Political Economy' of Sex," in *Toward an Anthropology of Women*, ed. Rayna R. Reiter (Monthly Review Press, 1975), 157–210, at 204, New York.

23 *G.G. ex rel. Grimm v. Gloucester Cty. Sch. Bd.*, 822 F.3d 709, 722 (4th Cir. 2016), *cert. granted in part*, 137 S. Ct. 369 (2016), and *vacated and remanded*, 137 S. Ct. 1239 (2017).

24 "Constitutive" in the sense that there simply could not be sex but for the sexes' mutually constituting relation to each other.

25 Grimm, 720–1.

26 See Section II, above.

27 Likewise, in *Who's Afraid of Gender?*, 171, Judith Butler (following a feminist trope) tries to refute the centrality of childbearing in knowing what a woman *is* by noting that some women cannot bear children. Are they not women? Do they not have a "sex"? She is able to pose these rhetorical questions only because she has lost sight of the centrality of nature and the organic wholeness of the human person. Even if most of the women in the world could not bear children, that would not detract from the centrality of childbearing to the intelligibility of "woman." This, of course, does not mean that any given woman can or must or should bear children, nor is it a normative judgment about those who cannot or choose not to have children. It means rather that a woman is intelligible as a woman because she is the kind of being who, as distinct from men and under the right conditions (both internal and external), can bear children. Central here is neither "heterosexist normativity" nor even "biology" (see Oakley, *Sex, Gender, and Society*), but rather nature and intelligibility.

28 *Harris Funeral Homes*, at 576–7.

29 Ibid., at 576, n. 4, citing and quoting Sue Landsittel, "Strange Bedfellows? Sex, Religion, and Transgender Identity Under Title VII," *Northwestern University Law Review* 104, no. 3 (2010): 1147–8, at 1172 (emphasis added).

Responses

Response to Heaton on Transgender Rights

David S. Crawford

Study Questions

1. What might Heaton mean when he says that cis people should respect trans people's identities but don't have to *believe* what trans people believe about themselves? What problems does Crawford think this leads to?
2. What problem does Crawford raise for transgenderism in light of Heaton's admission that claims to identity can be wrong?
3. How does Crawford respond to transgender claims to self-knowledge?
4. How does Crawford respond to Heaton's claim that traditional gender views are proved false by "well-rehearsed arguments"?

I have great sympathy for Jasper Heaton's argument, and in crucial ways—despite drawing on different philosophical traditions and language and arriving at very different conclusions—my own argument is fundamentally like it.

Heaton's version appeals to "epistemic communities" and "epistemic justice," the latter of which is violated when a limited or biased epistemic framework is imposed on traditionally disfavored segments of a community (minorities, women, and so forth) whose knowledge or experience is ignored, suppressed, or treated as inconsequential. Of course, like bias or prejudice more generally, control of language and the selective validation of experience and knowledge are endemic to human societies as part of the never-ending struggle for power. However, work on epistemic justice brings into focus its systemic and tacit character. Like the air around us, we are seldom aware of the epistemic communities in which we live. Viewed in this wide manner, there may be many kinds of "gaps in the predominantly held epistemic resources."[1]

In relation to "transgender rights," according to Heaton, epistemic justice requires "assent" to "trans" identity. It calls for "cis people" to agree with a "trans woman's" claim that "she is a woman and to not call her a man or tell other people that she's a man" (p. 456). A healthy epistemic community would require mutual listening and shared experience and narratives. Without this, trans experiences seem "obviously false" (p. 460).

Beyond Belief and Disbelief?

There are a few rough patches in Heaton's argument. First, it oddly concedes that "respecting trans identities" does not require people "to *believe* what trans people believe about themselves," since "there are other important epistemic relationships we have with each other, beyond belief and disbelief, that must be maintained for our epistemic communities to function well" (p. 456).

Now, belief and disbelief imply a commitment to what is true and real, and trans claims certainly purport to be about truth and reality. Heaton himself indicates, for example, that "even when . . . trans women claim to be biologically female, their claims are intelligible within trans-inclusive communities *because those communities deploy more sophisticated concepts of sex*" (p. 464, emphasis added). But to assent or agree without belief is to adopt a hypothetical or "as if" position. In effect, the claim seems to be that "cis people" must, for example, speak and act *as if* a trans woman is in fact a woman. They must, in other words, speak and act *as if* the "more sophisticated concepts of sex" were not only ideas but true ones.[2] Setting aside the problem that speaking and acting *as if* one believed appears to be closer to condescension than true respect, the deeper problem is that doing so also imposes negative implications on the moral agent. It implies, as I argued in my main essay, the internal tension ingredient in dishonesty.

But perhaps "beyond belief and disbelief" means that we should refrain from thinking in terms of truth and reality and stick to simply sharing narratives. Indeed, the argument explicitly seeks to bypass metaphysical debates over the nature of sex or gender and move directly to the ethical one. But here, again, we hit a rough patch: *reality always bites back*. Male bodies really do have advantages and really can pose risks to women in athletic competition. Children really can be seduced into "gender affirmation" medical procedures, even at very young ages. Vast cultural and traditional forms of familial, communal, and religious life really are uprooted and discredited. Their perennial value for people whose lives are rooted in them really is degraded. And so, the abstention from questions of truth and reality imposes real costs on men, women, and children of flesh and blood who must turn their lives upside down in accordance with the *as if*.

Erroneous Self-Identities

In any case, Heaton's own argument, as just noted, constantly makes claims about truth and reality. We first catch a glimpse of this in the conditions the argument lays out for when "dissent" from purported "identities" is warranted, including where "self-identity is erroneous." Two examples of this latter are given: a beginning painter and a "Lady Gaga fan" who does not *act* like a fan. If the "-er" suffix simply indicates "one who does," then even the beginner can truthfully say, "I am a painter." The purported Lady Gaga fan, on the other hand, cannot really be a fan because he does not *perform* as a fan. To be a fan is to act like a fan.

The implication of these examples and the other exceptions is that personal "experience" cannot be self-justifying; it is subject to standards exterior to experience itself. Evidently, then, claims to identity can simply be *wrong*. Yet, it is precisely the argument of those who object to the trans movement's aims that trans self-identity is, in fact, erroneous in this way, and necessarily and obviously so, however earnest and well-meaning the subject of those identities may be. My essay argues that the trans movement is wrong because it presents us with an implausibly fragmented understanding of the individual person and the natural, human communities to which he or she belongs.

Trans-Identity and Self-Knowledge

There is also a real question of what the "as if" would be an "as if" *of*. Without reference to what is real and external to the experience itself, it is impossible, as I pointed out, for a "transwoman" to be certain of having the experience of being a woman rather than having the experience of being a man who thinks he is having the experience of being a woman. In this sense, the "as if" is imported into the claimed identity itself. This point can be extended to other, less obvious examples, such as a "non-binary identity." Am I really "non-binary," or am I simply *feeling* non-binary? I do not mean to launch these last points as weapons. Rather, they are part of a more universal question: how well can any of us possess the sort of categorical knowledge of ourselves—our "identities"—implied by the trans movement?

Of course, the sort of self-experience of which we are speaking here is very different from Heaton's example of someone "wanting to leave." No one can tell someone else what he or she *wants* because wanting (simply as such) is relative only to itself, to the subjective state of the individual. This is true even when the want is directed outward, for example, in wanting a beer, since my wanting or not wanting a beer refers only to my desires and makes no special claim about the beer itself. Trans "self-experience," on the other hand, is about more than wanting. It makes a claim that matters to the wider society about the external reality of the sexes.

Well-Rehearsed Arguments?

Heaton tries to waive off appeal to the true and real by claiming without real argument that traditional views of sex are simply false, as proven by "well-rehearsed" arguments, as though the question was long ago resolved beyond reasonable dispute. But this is merely an appeal to authority, inviting its own charge of epistemic exclusion by elite authorities.

Here is where my argument begins to resemble Heaton's. The fact of the matter is that the arguments for the trans viewpoint are only "well-rehearsed" because elite institutions of knowledge (science, medicine, media, academic philosophy, and so forth) are ideologically captured. Dissenting voices, on the other hand, have been constantly stifled. In fact, the ideological capture is foreshadowed in the very metaphysical assumptions of modern, Western thought more generally, for example, in its endemic reductionism and nominalism.[3] As my main essay argues, these presuppositions need to be challenged as philosophically and humanly unsound.[4]

In any case, the talk of experience is a little pointless. Rather, the tendency is to think of gender in terms of transgressive action. In fact, Heaton repeatedly suggests that to have an identity one must take responsibility for that identity, which primarily means acting in accordance with it. Likewise, it would seem, to be a woman or a man means *acting* like a woman or a man. Hence, Heaton's list of social patterns enforcing the binary view (styles of dress, make-up, medical practices, etc.) all relate to *presenting oneself* as a man or woman.

Of course, this raises the question of whether a "natal male" *can* act like a woman in the pertinent sense. If you accept that gender is *exhaustively* constituted as performativity, in the manner of Butler and her followers, then perhaps he can so act in a *limited* way (e.g., he cannot bear children). But if you think that "gender" (insofar as we even want to accept the tendentiously redeployed term) is not *exhaustively* constituted as performativity, however much it may be shaped by culture, then he cannot act as a woman even in a limited way. Again, Heaton treats the answer as resolved long ago. But the well-rehearsed resolution is only real inside the ideological bubble that is academic gender theory.[5]

Heaton's point must be granted, of course, that transgender individuals have not possessed political or social power, at least until recently. My point is a deeper one: the bent of modern, Western rationality, in its nominalist and reductive tendencies, as exercised by social elites (examples were Money and Stoller), has skewed our view of reality, such that it is hard for us to conceptualize either sexuality or personality except in an essentially trans way. "Transgender rights," then, are both the bitter fruit and prolongation of this essentially failed form of rationality.

Notes

1. Gaile Pohlhaus, "Relational Knowing and Epistemic Injustice: Towards a Theory of Willful Hermeneutical Ignorance," *Hypatia* 27, no. 4 (2012): 719.
2. In support of "more sophisticated concepts of sex," Heaton holds up the bodies of those who do not fully conform to maleness or femaleness. Presumably, the reference

is to intersex individuals. The argument is repeatedly trotted out as a clincher in this sort of debate. Yet, anomalous occurrences cannot disprove the nature and intelligibility of something. It is only the pervasively *nominalist* assumptions of these arguments (see n. 3, below) that give them a veneer of credibility.

3 "Reductionism," in the ontological sense intended here, refers to the doctrine which understands wholes in terms of their parts. As regards human sexuality, reductionism regards the human person as a set of parts, for example, an interior subjective "identity" and an external sexual body, which is itself subdivided into parts, such as "internal morphological sex," "external morphological sex," "endocrinal sex," "chromosomal sex," and so on (see the discussion of Money and Stoller in my main essay). When Heaton speaks of "more sophisticated concepts of sex that do a better job of tracking the *different combinations of sex characteristics* and *the way those characteristics can be changed*" (p. 464), we have a perfect example of reductionism at work. Under this view, the person is understood on the model of a machine, in which parts can be swapped out or reconfigured into different patterns. The result is the illusion that a woman, for example, who identifies as a woman, does so, not because she is an organic and embodied whole personal being, but because she happens (arbitrarily) to have one identity, and its particular combination of characteristics, rather than another. "Nominalism" is the philosophical doctrine, associated with William of Ockham (*c.* 1287–1347) but perduring in much modern philosophy, which holds that only particular objects exist, rather than universals or natures. Under this view, talk of "human nature" or a "nature of human sexuality" appears either naïve or tendentious. Yet, without the concept of nature, we cannot distinguish between natural or healthy and anomalous instantiations of things. As a result, human sexuality has become more or less unintelligible to us. In Heaton's suggestion that "trans women" may be considered "biologically female"—as though talk of a "male vagina," "female penis," or "pregnant fathers" could mean anything at all—we have an excellent example of this sort of unintelligibility.

4 In the notes for my main essay, I point to some resources for thinking about and challenging those assumptions.

5 In fact, the examples Heaton provides, however much we might think of them as in some sense "identities," are nothing like being a man or woman. They are all superficial, the sort of "identity" that could come and go, that is adopted or chosen. They fail to reach to the core of personal being.

Response to Crawford on Transgender Rights

Jasper Heaton

Study Questions

1. What two preliminary points does Heaton make in response to Crawford?
2. According to Heaton, why is labeling the enforcement of rights "coercive" a Red Herring? Why does he think that it's actually the cis ideology that's being enforced?

> 3. What ignorance do cis critics of transgenderism have, according to Heaton? What three examples of this ignorance are present in Crawford's essay?
> 4. How does Heaton respond to Crawford's critique of social constructionism about sex?

I want to thank David Crawford for his essay, and also for the opportunity his essay gives me to expand a little on the original argument I made in my essay, and also to address a few points that I could not cover there. There are two preliminary points that I would like to briefly discuss before getting into my main response.

Preliminaries

First, Crawford notes that proponents of trans rights see them as a continuation of civil rights protections, and he makes a distinction between what he calls "genuine civil rights" and "transgender rights." The former, Crawford says, are based on some "naturally given attribute," whereas trans rights are based on the category of identity. But even granting this distinction, civil rights are not just in the business of protecting our naturally given attributes. For example, one of the most important and hard-won rights we have is the right to Freedom of Religion, but one's religious beliefs are not a naturally given attribute.

Perhaps Crawford wants to say that the drive toward religious belief is a fundamental, natural part of the human experience, given how widespread and enduring is the tendency for humans to hold religious beliefs. I am happy to grant that this is the case. But then, so is being transgender. The point is not that *everyone* has a "little bit of transness" in them, just like not everyone holds religious beliefs. The point is that religious belief and trans identities are two widespread and enduring parts of the "tapestry of humanity," and the need for civil rights protections around some parts of that tapestry is explained by the fact that those parts are or have been threatened.

Second, Crawford states that his critique is "of a pervasive idea, not of persons," and that his opponent is "never persons or groups but a culturally animating concept" (p. 467). This is a sentiment that opponents of civil rights often tout, and I have no patience for it. Crawford is arguing for social policies that will, as a matter of empirically demonstrable fact, harm trans people. For instance, preventing trans people from using the social spaces, like bathrooms, that align with our gender identities increases our risk of sexual assault.[1] Crawford says pro-trans policies harm cis people. I would have appreciated his providing any evidence, or even detailing any specific harms, that these policies cause. Granted, this might be difficult, as there is no evidence that pro-trans policies harm cis people and there is evidence that pro-trans policies do *not* harm cis people. For instance, pro-trans bathroom policies do not cause any increase in cis women's risk of sexual assault.[2]

So, Crawford is not just taking up an intellectual position against an idea. This, in itself, is not my complaint. My complaint is that Crawford tries to disavow the consequences of his views. I believe that Crawford should own his views, including their consequences. I will note that I, nor any other advocate for trans people's rights, have to shy away from any of the consequences of our positions, though this might be because our positions do not harm other people.

The Main Response

With these preliminary points addressed, let me now turn to my main response, which has three parts. First, Crawford points out that while there is a tendency among some people to think that civil rights function only to "protect" and "empower" specific individuals and groups of people, in fact, rights also "imply a specific social and legal order and its *coercive* application of law" (p. 468, my emphasis). Rights certainly do compel specific kinds of behavior, but I think labeling this as "coercive" is a Red Herring. If I have a right to political asylum, then the nation where I claim asylum is compelled, through its own courts or through international courts, to process my claim, to give me shelter, a lawyer, a hearing in court, and so on. If Crawford means to imply there is something especially coercive about trans rights, he needs to do more than point to the fact that rights compel action.

Granted, Crawford does say more. He says that the struggle over trans rights is, ultimately, a struggle over "what society at large will be permitted to believe is real" (Ibid). Crawford says that laws protecting trans people's civil rights will "channel the words and actions" of people in positions of institutional authority—implying, I take it, that a law that permits trans women access to women's bathrooms will also require people not just to say "trans women are women" but also to *believe* that trans women are women—and this kind of channeling, he says, constitutes nothing less than a "sustained enforcement of thought" (Ibid). This, he says, will erase cis people's understanding of their genders, and he laments that "it is increasingly difficult to think of ourselves as men or women simply because of *being* men or women in the organic wholeness of our sexually dimorphic selves" (p. 469).

It is hard to know how seriously to take this worry about cisgender erasure when one looks at the actual world around us. As I am writing, the Supreme Court of the United Kingdom just ruled that "woman" is legally defined as "female." Since his inauguration, Donald Trump has repeatedly asserted that "there are only two genders." I will step over Crawford's claim that proponents of trans rights are "so focused" on children, but I will point to the popularity of clothing for babies and toddlers with cisheteronormative messages like "ladies man" and "heartbreaker." There is an ideology being enforced, but not the one Crawford is worried about. Moreover, UK courts have ruled that anti-trans or "Gender Critical" beliefs are protected under the Equality Act.[3] Similarly, although Jordan Peterson famously argued that Bill C-16 would lead to Canadians being imprisoned for misgendering trans people, the law simply does not provide for this.

There is no reason to think that anti-trans beliefs will be Thought Policed should trans rights be secured. Of course, people may not be permitted to act on those beliefs—that is what it means for trans people to have civil rights. But Crawford is right that the debate over trans rights also involves a contest over the conceptual resources we use to understand each other.[4] These kinds of "meaning contests" are commonplace; they are how language evolves. Crawford objects, though, that these new concepts have already been "tacitly decided" for everyone, without any consultation. This brings me to the second part of my response. This objection demonstrates exactly the kind of ignorance that I discussed in my essay. Trans people have been creating new concepts and knowledge about our lives and have been trying to engage mainstream society in a conversation about this knowledge, and we have largely been ignored; and I argued that this gives trans people warrant to ignore other people's critiques of our identities. I want to highlight three examples of this ignorance in Crawford's essay.

The first is small but speaks volumes. Crawford uses the term "transwoman," rather than the standard term, "trans woman." Trans women are not a different kind of woman. "Trans" is an adjective, like "tall," and we say "tall women," not "tallwomen," because tall women are not a distinct kind of woman either. The refusal to take up standard terminology signals disrespect and a broader refusal to engage with the knowledge trans people have generated about ourselves.

In the second example, Crawford says that we "seldom ask," in "a serious way," whether the social changes that proponents of trans rights advocate for are good for people (Ibid). I'm not sure what Crawford means by a "serious" way of asking the question. But his claim demonstrates the kind of ignorance I discussed because, as I noted above, we do have evidence that pro-trans social changes are beneficial to trans people and are not harmful to cis people. Researchers have been inquiring about the benefits of pro-trans policies in a serious, scientific way, and they have been finding empirically evidenced answers that support pro-trans policies.

In the third example, Crawford argues that the concept of "non-binary gender" is incoherent because it both implies that the concept of the gender binary is unintelligible while also presupposing that concept for its own intelligibility. But transfeminist theorists do not claim that the gender binary is unintelligible, and the fact that non-binary gender presupposes the gender binary has been a central topic of discussion within Trans Studies since at least 1987. It forms the basis of Sandy Stone's highly influential transfeminist political vision, and theorists have extensively explored how politically resistant gender categories are created as explicit responses to socially dominant categories.[5] Crawford does not engage with these ideas. Overall, his essay fails to meet the conditions of epistemic participation that I argue are necessary for making ethically significant claims about people's identities.

This brings me to the third part of my response: What about the biological categories of *male* and *female*? Crawford says that social constructionists about sex take the possibility of category anomalies (e.g., infertile men) as evidence that there is no intrinsic structure to the sexes and that sexed parts can be recombined in any way whatsoever. Against this, he argues that the whole is metaphysically prior to its parts, and that sexed wholeness constitutes a natural and biologically determined integrity in two sexually dimorphic categories that ground the identities of men and women. But the wholes that Crawford appeals to are delineated by concepts that are completely culturally saturated, and do not simply track naturally given differences—the question of whether something counts as a "normal" or "abnormal" instance of a sex category is inseparable from the cultural construction of those categories and the social norms governing the context in which the question is asked.[6] Crawford does not engage with these arguments, but any plausible attempts to establish the biological reality of binary sex need to address their critiques.

Notes

1. Julia Serano, "Transgender People, Bathrooms, and Sexual Predators: What the Data Says," *Medium* (June 7, 2021) (https://juliaserano.medium.com/transgender-people-bathrooms-and-sexual-predators-what-the-data-say-2f31ae2a7c06).
2. Serano, "Transgender People." As Serano explains, opponents of trans rights sometimes cite studies purporting to show the contrary, but these studies invariably fail to distinguish between cis men and trans women and do not establish the connections they purport to.
3. "Employment Tribunal Rulings on Gender-Critical Beliefs in the Workplace," House of Commons Library (https://commonslibrary.parliament.uk/employment-tribunal-rulings-on-gender-critical-beliefs-in-the-workplace/, accessed May 25, 2025).
4. Talia Bettcher, "Trans Women and the Meaning of 'Woman'," in *The Philosophy of Sex: Contemporary Readings*, ed. Nicholas Power, Raja Halwani, and Alan Soble (Lanham: Rowman & Littlefield Publishers, 2014), 233.
5. Sandy Stone, "The Empire Strikes Back: A Posttranssexual Manifesto," in *The Transgender Studies Reader* (New York: Routledge, 2013), 221. See also Bettcher, "Trans Women." Emi Koyama, "The Transfeminist Manifesto," in *Catching a Wave: Reclaiming Feminism for the Twenty-First Century*, ed. Rory Dicker and Alison Piepmeier (Boston: Northeastern University Press, 2003), 244–261.
6. Judith Butler, *Gender Trouble* (New York: Routledge, 1990); Laurie Shrage, "Sex and Miscibility," in *You've Changed: Sex Reassignment and Personal Identity*, ed. Laurie Shrage (Oxford University Press, 2009), 175.

Questions for Reflection

1. What are the metaphysical issues at the heart of the transgenderism debate? Who makes the stronger case on these issues, Heaton or Crawford? Why?

2. Is Heaton correct that trans rights laws do not harm cis people? Why? Are trans people harmed by anti-trans policies? Why?

3. How can society resolve practical problems, such as trans people in women's sports and the use of bathrooms, in a way that is fair to people on both sides of the transgender debate?

For Further Reading

Anderson, Ryan T. *When Harry Became Sally: Responding to the Transgender Moment.* Encounter Books, 2019.

Butler, Judith. *Who's Afraid of Gender?* Farrar, Straus, and Giroux, 2024.

Jeffreys, Sheila. *Gender Hurts: A Feminist Analysis of the Politics of Transgenderism.* Routledge, 2014.

Shrage, Laurie J. *You've Changed: Sex Reassignment and Personal Identity.* Oxford University Press, 2009.

Stryker, Susan, and Dylan McCarthy Blackston. *The Transgender Studies Reader Remix.* Routledge, 2022.

Trueman, Carl R. *The Rise and Triumph of the Modern Self: Cultural Amnesia, Expressive Individualism, and the Road to Sexual Revolution.* Crossway, 2020.

15

Drug Legalization

For Drug Legalization

Chris Meyers

Study Questions

1. Who does Meyers say has the burden of proof on the question of drug legalization? Why?
2. Why does Meyers think that recreational drug use should be legal even if it is immoral?
3. What is "paternalism"? How does Meyers respond to the argument against drug legalization based on paternalism?
4. How does Meyers respond to the claim that illicit drug use harms others besides themselves?
5. What is the argument against legalizing the sale of illicit drugs? How does Meyers respond to this argument?
6. Why should we prefer regulation over prohibition according to Meyers?
7. What are the alleged bad consequences of drug legalization? How does Meyers address these?

Scholars have long questioned the wisdom and justice of drug prohibition. For example, an anthology of articles on drug policy published twenty years ago, entitled *How to Legalize Drugs*, contains original articles by thirty-two contributors—respected academics from law, anthropology, sociology, political science, philosophy, economics, criminal justice, psychology, and medicine—all of whom conclude, for various reasons, that the prohibition of drugs should be ended.[1] Among those outside of the ivory tower, however, the idea has not gained much traction. In this essay, I will offer what are, in my assessment, the best arguments for drug legalization.

Burden of Proof

For any inquiry, it is important that we ask the right question before taking a stab at the answer. With drug legalization, the question is whether the use of illicit drugs (such as heroin, cocaine, and meth) should be legally prohibited. This might seem like a simple question on the surface, but looks can be deceiving. For one, the question can be divided into two distinct questions: (1) Should it be against the law to possess and use these substances? And (2) should it be against the law to buy and sell these substances? I will argue that the answer to both questions is *No*.

We also need to be explicit about what we mean by "legally prohibited" or "against the law." Parking your car in front of a fire hydrant is legally prohibited, and so is using heroin. But there is an enormous difference between the two. Drivers who park their cars in front of fire hydrants are not treated as criminals. Drug prohibition, by contrast, involves punishing drug users and drug dealers in the same way we punish burglars, murderers, and rapists.

For this reason, the proper question is whether drugs should be prohibited, not whether drugs should be legalized. That might seem like the same question stated two different ways, but there is a crucial difference. When we ask whether drugs should be legalized, we assume the prohibition of drugs as the default. Supporters of legalization are then expected to give convincing reasons for why we should change the status quo. This incorrectly puts the burden of proof on the side of those who advocate for legalization. When there is a disagreement about whether to punish people for engaging in some activity, those who advocate in favor of throwing people in prison are the ones who need to prove their case.[2]

Thus, my argument for legalization does not posit a right to use drugs. Nor does it appeal to a more general right to autonomy. Instead, it is based on a right not to be punished without a very good reason. Those who advocate for prohibition need to do more than simply show that drug use is a serious social problem that the government should try to mitigate against. They must show that putting people in prison is an appropriate solution to the problem.

With serious crimes, this burden of proof is easily met. Why should we punish those who commit acts of armed robbery, rape, and murder? Because such conduct causes severe harm to innocent others and violates the rights of victims. People who do so intentionally deserve to be punished as a result. Consuming illicit drugs, however, does not cause severe harm to innocent others or violate the rights of any supposed victim.

We also must distinguish the legal question—should it be illegal to use drugs?—from the moral question—is it morally wrong to use drugs? That an action is morally wrong is not sufficient reason to make it a crime. For example, I think it is morally wrong to cheat on one's spouse. I assume most people agree. Nevertheless, it would be unjust to make adultery a crime and have unfaithful spouses arrested and thrown in prison. That an act is morally wrong is not sufficient reason to punish someone for doing it, but it might be a necessary condition.

Thus, some argue for legalization on the grounds that it is not morally wrong to use drugs. They claim that drug use only harms the user, and you cannot have a duty to yourself. Although I have doubts about both claims, my argument does not assume that drug abuse is blameless. Suppose, for the sake of argument, that it is morally wrong for drug users to ruin their lives by abusing intoxicating substances. It would still be wrong to punish people for harming themselves. If someone willfully harms another person, then it may be fair to punish him. But if someone willfully harms himself, we cannot punish the person responsible without also punishing the victim, since they are one and the same person. And we should never punish the victims of wrongdoing. So even if it is morally wrong to harm yourself, it would be unjust to make it a crime to harm yourself.

Furthermore, although it is true that users sometimes ruin their lives with drugs, and it might be wrong for them to do so, we should still hesitate to blame them. People who become addicts typically lead miserable lives independently of their drug use. They often suffer from emotional pain, social isolation, poverty, or mental illness. It is estimated that between 32 percent and 54 percent of people addicted to illicit drugs or alcohol suffer from major depression compared to only about 7 percent of the general population.[3] A disproportionate number of addicts suffered trauma, abuse, or neglect as children. Renowned addiction expert Gabor Maté, who spent a career treating hardcore addicts in Vancouver's notorious Eastside, sums it up this way: "The majority of my skid row patients suffered severe neglect and maltreatment early in life. Almost all the addicted women inhabiting the Downtown Eastside were sexually assaulted in childhood, as were many of the men."[4] These are the people most likely to engage in problematic drug use, and they deserve our pity more than our censure.

Paternalism

Retribution, however, is just one justification of punishment. We punish wrongdoers in part because they deserve it. But there are other reasons to punish lawbreakers. One such reason is *deterrence*. The threat of punishment discourages would-be lawbreakers from violating the law, thus lowering the crime rate. Punishment is justified not because the lawbreaker deserves to suffer but because the beneficial social consequences of punishment outweigh the harms inflicted on the person punished. For armed robbery, murder, and other serious crimes, these good consequences are protecting innocent people who would otherwise be victimized by wrongdoers. In the case of drug laws, the good consequences are preventing at least some people from ruining their lives with drug abuse. Drug laws are thus paternalistic.

Paternalistic laws restrict liberty in order to prevent people from harming themselves. Examples include laws prohibiting riding a motorcycle without a helmet or swimming at a public beach without a lifeguard present. Many, if not most, proponents of drug laws support them on paternalistic grounds. Philosopher George Sher, for example, argues that drug prohibition laws are justified because "many persons whom they deter are thereby prevented from wasting their lives."[5]

Recreational drug use, however, is not invariably or even usually harmful. Although some drug users ruin their lives through substance abuse, most do not. Only about 25 percent of heroin users develop a dependency problem, and heroin is one of the most addictive drugs, second only to nicotine. For cocaine, the addiction rate is only 15 percent, roughly the same as alcohol.[6] Other drugs are associated with even lower rates of addiction, and some illicit drugs, such as psychedelics, are not addictive at all.

Addiction, however, is just one risk of using drugs. A better gauge of the safety of various drugs might be measured in terms of fatalities. The mortality rate for heroin users is about 1.6 percent.[7] That is quite high, but nothing compared to the approximately two-thirds of smokers who eventually die from tobacco-related illnesses.[8] The mortality rates of other illicit drugs are much lower. And there has never been a single case of fatal overdose from marijuana or psychedelics. On the other hand, alcohol-related deaths in the United States outnumber deaths from all illicit drugs combined by a considerable margin (178,000 versus 106,000 in 2021).[9]

So, it is mistaken to say that illicit drug use is harmful. At most, we can say that the use of *some* illicit drugs involves a *risk* of harm. But the law allows people to take all sorts of risks with their health or even their lives. We do not outlaw horse riding, eating junk food, hang gliding, or sunbathing, even though these activities can be at least as dangerous as taking most illicit drugs. And unlike these other activities, laws prohibiting the sale of drugs only increase the risk of illicit drug use. It is unwise and unjust to threaten all drug users with prison just to prevent a very small percentage of worst-case-scenario addicts from ruining their lives with drugs. Also, putting drug addicts in prison does not prevent them from wasting their lives but only makes their miserable lives even worse.

Some might object that I am considering only the most severe harms that might result from drug use. It might be true that most people who use illicit drugs do not develop an addiction, and even fewer suffer a fatal overdose. But there are other, less dramatic harms that are commonly experienced by drug users. For example, drug legalization opponent Peter de Marneffe claims that drug use "is bad for the users themselves when it results, as it often does, in a loss of self-respect and self-esteem, and a failure to develop emotionally, intellectually, morally, and spiritually."[10]

Let us assume, for the sake of argument, that he is correct and that a substantial portion of drug users fail to reach their full potential due to their use of illicit substances. That might be a good reason for the state to discourage drug use—through education, nudging, or excise taxes. But would it be a good enough reason to make it against the law to use drugs? It seems obvious to me that it would not. It is not against the law to have low self-esteem, or to lack self-respect, or to fail to develop emotionally, intellectually, morally, or spiritually. Nor should it be. So, if it would be unjust to punish people for falling short of their full potential (in these ways or others), then it would also be unjust to make it a crime to engage in some activity that might cause people to fall short of their potential.

Another weakness of the paternalistic defense of drug prohibition is that such laws are justifiable only when they use the least restrictive means necessary to protect people from self-harm. Consider motorcycle riding, for example. There are two ways we could protect riders from harm. One is to ban the activity altogether by outlawing motorcycle riding. Another is to require wearing a helmet, as well as requiring a driver's license specifically for motorcycles. A paternalistic approach to drug use should also use the least restrictive means of protecting users from harm. Instead of banning the use of drugs altogether, we could restrict drug consumption to on-premise use or require a license to purchase drugs. (I will return to the idea of licensed use later.)

Finally, the biggest weakness of the paternalistic defense of drug prohibition is that it does not justify the harshness of our laws against use and possession. We do not put people in prison for riding a motorcycle without a helmet or for swimming at public beaches without a lifeguard present. And the reason is obvious. These laws are meant to protect people from harm. Putting someone in prison is much more likely to cause harm than using even the most risky illicit substances.

Harm to Others

So far, we have considered only the harm that drug use might cause to the users themselves. But what about harm to others? It may be unjust to punish people for harming themselves, but it is not unjust to punish people for causing harm to others or for acting in ways that risk harm to others.

Many who defend drug prohibition deny the claim that drug users only harm themselves. They claim that drugs can cause users to neglect duties to their family members or employers. "If heroin is legal," Marneffe argues, "parents can buy and use it legally. Some of them will abuse it. Parental abuse of heroin will lead to the neglect of children, resulting of feelings of low self-esteem and lack of direction."[11] The term "neglect," however, is ambiguous. Suppose Mr. Smith misses his son's piano recital because he was too high or too busy trying to score some smack. We might say that Mr. Smith is neglecting his child. But it would be outrageous to claim that Mr. Smith ought to be sent to prison for missing his son's piano recital, even if this sort of behavior is habitual and his son is worse off because of it. If it would be unjust to punish Mr. Smith for missing his son's piano recital, then it would also be unjust to punish him for doing something that might make him more likely to miss his son's piano recital.

There is, however, a different sense of the word "neglect." Child neglect in this narrower, legal sense occurs when parents fail to provide their children with basic needs, such as adequate food, clothing, shelter, or supervision. This abusive kind of neglect should be criminalized. But that does not mean that we should criminalize any activity that might lead to such abusive neglect. There have been several news stories of parents neglecting their children while they play video games—including at least two cases in which the children starved to death[12]—and over two hundred news stories between 2000 and 2014 reporting cases of children abandoned in casino parking lots while their parents gambled inside.[13] But that does not mean that we should outlaw gambling or video games. Consider these three cases:

- Mr. White abusively neglects his children because he is obsessed with video games.
- Mr. Grey abusively neglects his children because he uses heroin.
- Mr. Black uses heroin but, in spite of that, is a caring and responsible parent.

I assume most people would agree that it would be acceptable to punish both White and Grey, at least under certain circumstances. But I see no reason why we should punish one of them more than the other. And I see no reason why Black should be punished at all, just because others who use drugs do things that warrant punishment. That would be a kind of group punishment. Besides, children are much more likely to suffer neglect when one of their parents is incarcerated.

Full Legalization

The arguments I have presented so far pertain mostly to the laws against drug use or possession. Drug users do not deserve to be punished for using or possessing drugs, and threatening drug users with prison is not an effective way to protect them from harm. What about buying and selling illicit drugs?

The most reasonable argument against legalizing the sale of illicit drugs is indirect paternalism. With direct (or "pure") paternalism, we curtail a person's freedom to prevent that person from harming herself. With indirect ("impure") paternalism, we restrict the liberty of one person to prevent another person from self-harm. One example of indirect paternalism is usury laws, which prohibit offering loans at excessive interest rates. Although the law restricts the liberty of loan sharks, the aim is to prevent desperate borrowers from entering into loan agreements that will cripple them financially. Indirect paternalism also includes laws against drug trafficking. These laws limit the freedom of dealers to sell drugs in order to protect the dealers' customers from harming themselves with the use of intoxicating substances.

Although it is true that we do not, and should not, attach harsh penalties to directly paternalistic laws, such as seatbelt laws, it is a different matter when it comes to indirect paternalism. It would clearly be unjust to threaten borrowers with prison time for taking loans with exorbitant interest rates. But lenders can face up to five years in prison for offering such loans. That is acceptable because we can punish those who enable self-harm without at the same time punishing the victim of self-harm.

So, it might not be unjust to punish people who make and sell drugs. On the other hand, unlike people who murder, rape, burglarize, or commit other acts that violate the rights of others, justice does not *require* that we punish people who make or sell drugs. There might be other good reasons not to criminalize the making and selling of drugs. Justice is not the sole aim of public policy and criminal law. The government also has the responsibility to promote the public good. If prohibiting the sales and manufacturing of illicit drugs would have overall social consequences that are substantially worse than alternative policies, then we should not do so—not because it would be unjust but because it would be unwise, imprudent, or counterproductive.

There are many ways that laws against drug trafficking are imprudent and counterproductive.[14] Let us start with the enormous cost of enforcing drug laws, in terms of both money and law enforcement resources. The United States currently spends about $50 billion annually fighting the war on drugs, about as much as all other nations combined. And yet all that effort does little to reduce drug use. It is not just money that is wasted but also law enforcement resources. There are at least 100,000 rape kits in police departments throughout the country that have never been sent to a lab for analysis.[15] Meanwhile, cops arrest over 200,000 people each year for mere marijuana possession.[16] Outlawing the sales of illicit drugs also deprives the government of tax revenues. According to the best estimates, the market in illicit drugs in the United States was over $150 billion annually in 2017, about as much spent on electronic goods.[17] Virtually all of those revenues are untaxed.

Another undesirable consequence of outlawing drug trafficking is that it fuels violent crime. A comprehensive review by the International Center for Science in Drug Policy found that "Contrary to the conventional wisdom . . . the existing scientific evidence strongly suggests that drug prohibition likely contributes to drug market violence and higher homicide rates."[18] The review looked at longitudinal studies that compared rates of violent crime before and after increased law enforcement efforts. Fourteen of the fifteen studies reviewed found that increased enforcement of drug laws corresponded to increased rates of violent crime.

Drug prohibition also contributes to police corruption, with about half of all police corruption cases in the United States involving drug-related offenses.[19] And the enforcement of drug laws has contributed to the erosion of civil rights. Former superior court judge James P. Gray goes so far as to say, "Nothing in the history of the United States of America has eroded the protections of our Bill of Rights nearly as much as our government's war on drugs."[20]

More than thirty-five million Americans consumed an illegal substance in the past month. Even arresting a small portion of drug users and dealers exacerbates our mass incarceration problem. The United States has the highest incarceration rate of any country on earth. Despite having only about 4 percent of the world's population, a whopping 25 percent of the world's prison population are Americans.[21]

Prohibition or Regulation

This list of undesirable consequences of drug prohibition might be enough to demonstrate that drug prohibition is ill-advised. But there is one more reason that I think is decisive—the cost to public health. The choice we face is not between prohibition and legalization but between prohibition and *regulation*. Once we make it a crime to sell heroin, cocaine, meth, and other psychoactive substances, we put those products into the black market, where they are beyond the reach of any attempts to regulate them. We can control what chemicals go into these products and ensure consumer safety only through regulation, and we can regulate these substances only if they are legal.

Drug prohibition makes drug use substantially more dangerous, resulting in increased harm to users. Because illegal drugs are not regulated, users cannot be sure of the strength, quality, or purity of the drugs they are taking, resulting in overdoses. The average purity of heroin purchased on the street is only about 32 percent.[22] If a user who is accustomed to consuming heroin that is only 30 percent pure buys a batch that is 75 percent pure, he might end up consuming two and a half times his normal amount, severely increasing the risk of suffering an overdose. The lack of regulation means that when you purchase drugs from a dealer, you have no way of knowing if you are getting what you bargained for. Unscrupulous dealers (and most dealers are unscrupulous) have been known to substitute one drug with another, much less safe drug such as fentanyl.

The ongoing fentanyl crisis is, by itself, a sufficient reason to legalize drugs. There were about 106,000 overdose deaths in the United States in 2021. Of those deaths, 70,600—or about two-thirds—were due to fentanyl, which is cheaper to make than heroin and about fifty times stronger. Drug overdose deaths in the United States have increased fivefold between 2015 and 2021 and are continuing to climb. Almost all of that increase is due to the increased use of fentanyl. Most people who consume fentanyl do so unwittingly. Drug suppliers sell fentanyl as heroin or other drugs or boost the strength of weak drugs by adding fentanyl. Virtually no one would intentionally use fentanyl if fentanyl-free heroin were an option.

If heroin and other drugs could be manufactured by legitimate businesses, sold in licensed dispensaries, and regulated by the government, we could dramatically reduce the number of unnecessary deaths due to drug overdose. Arresting dealers and suppliers does little to reduce the quantity of drugs sold and consumed in the United States and makes it impossible to ensure the quality of these drugs or to require distributors to inform consumers about their strength or purity. Legalizing and regulating these substances could potentially save thousands of lives annually.

Preventing unnecessary overdose deaths is not the only benefit of regulating illicit drugs. We could also reduce underage use by imposing strict age limits. According to a meta-study with a sample size of over 1.4 million, medical marijuana legalization has no effect on teen use, while recreational marijuana legalization is associated with a *drop* in teen use by 8–9 percent.[23] That could be because marijuana use is no longer seen as "cool" once it is legal. A more likely explanation, however, is that dispensaries, which check IDs, have displaced street dealers who do not.

Bad Consequences of Legalization

I have addressed the undesirable consequences of drug prohibition. But what about the undesirable consequences of legalization? Critics claim that legalization will result in increased drug abuse and all the associated social ills—crime, overdose, child neglect, loss of productivity, homelessness, and so on.

All of these alleged bad consequences of legalization assume that legalizing drugs would result in increased use. But there is good reason to think that legalization would not increase use significantly. Users who quit are rarely motivated by fear of punishment or legally mandated treatment. And most people who abstain from illicit drugs do so for reasons other than the fact that they are illegal. Surveys consistently find that most people would not be inclined to try illicit drugs if they were to be legalized. In a nationwide poll published by the National Institute of Drug Abuse, only 2 percent of the 1,400 participants said they would be "very likely" or "somewhat likely" to try cocaine if it were to be legalized. A whopping 93 percent said they would be "not at all likely" to try it.[24]

Of course, it is possible that the people surveyed are not being truthful, either with the researchers or themselves. Fortunately, we can test this claim by looking at whether marijuana consumption increased after it was legalized for recreational use in the state of Washington. According to a study by the National Institutes of Health, there was an increase, but it was only about 5 percent.[25] The increase would probably be much smaller for drugs such as cocaine, heroin, or meth, which are socially stigmatized and perceived by the general public to be much more dangerous than smoking weed.

It is possible, however, that the prohibition of drugs discourages use, not as a deterrent but due to what we might call a "hassle factor." The fact that drugs are illegal makes it difficult for many people to get access to them. To procure illicit substances, one must have connections in the drug trade or be savvy enough to find a trustworthy dealer. If we make drugs too easy to procure, we might encourage impulse buyers to try them on a whim. And some of these people might develop a serious problem.

I agree that the hassle factor probably discourages some people from using drugs. But we can maintain the hassle factor without threatening to throw people in prison. One way would be to require a license to use.[26] As with a driver's license, obtaining a license to use a particular drug would require passing an exam on proper dosing, the importance of using clean needles, how to administer overdose antidotes, and the legal consequences of driving while impaired or distributing drugs to minors. Getting a license would have to be inconvenient enough to prevent impulsive experimentation without being so much of a hassle that users stick with the black-market dealers.

Conclusion

Many people think that the idea of legalizing heroin, cocaine, meth, and other dangerous addictive drugs is crazy. I used to be one of those people. Before I started doing in-depth research on drugs and drug policy, I was in favor of moderate reforms: legalizing marijuana for recreational use, increasing harm reduction programs such as needle exchanges, and eliminating the Schedule-I category from the Controlled Substances Act. I did not take the idea of legalization seriously. But critical thinking requires avoiding the trap of assuming that the intuitively obvious answer is the correct answer. The reason drug legalization seems crazy might be nothing more than status quo bias.

Notes

1 Jefferson Fish, ed., *How to Legalize Drugs* (Northvale: Aronson, 1998).
2 Douglas Husak makes a similar point in *Legalize This! The Case for Decriminalizing Drugs* (London: Verso, 2002).
3 Kathleen T. Brady and Rajita Sinha, "Co-Occurring Mental and Substance Use Disorders: The Neurobiological Effects of Chronic Stress," *The American Journal of Psychiatry* 162 (2005): 1483–93.
4 Gabor Maté, *In the Realm of Hungry Ghosts* (Berkeley: North Atlantic Books, 2008), 36.
5 George Sher, "On the Decriminalization of Drugs," *Criminal Justice Ethics* (2003): 30–3, at 31.
6 James C. Anthony, Lynn A. Warner, and Ronald C. Kessler, "Comparative Epidemiology of Dependence on Tobacco, Alcohol, Controlled Substances, and Inhalants: Basic Findings from the National Comorbidity Survey," *Experimental and Clinical Psychopharmacology* 2 (1994): 244–68.
7 Matthew Hickman, Zenobia Carnwath, Peter Madden, Michael Farrell, Cleone Rooney, Richard Ashcroft, Ali Judd, and Gerry Stimson, "Drug-Related Mortality and Fatal Overdose Risk: Pilot Cohort Study of Heroin Users Recruited from Specialist Drug Treatment Sites in London," *Journal of Urban Health* (2003): 80(2), 274–87.
8 Danielle Paquette, "The Terrifying Rate at which Smokers Die from Smoking," *Washington Post* (February 26, 2015).
9 "Overdose Deaths," National Institute on Drug Abuse (https://www.drugabuse.gov/drug-topics/trends-statistics/overdose-death-rates); and Marissa B. Esser, Adam Sherk, Yong Liu, and Timothy S. Naimi, "Deaths from Excessive Alcohol Use—United States, 2016–2021," *CDC Morbidity and Mortality Weekly Report* (February 29, 2024).

10. Peter de Marneffe, "Do We Have a Right to Use Drugs?" *Public Affairs Quarterly* 10 (1996): 229–47, at 238.
11. Peter de Marneffe, in Douglas Husak and Peter de Marneffe, *The Legalization of Drugs—For and Against* (Cambridge: Cambridge University Press, 2005).
12. Sean Elder, "A Korean Couple Let a Baby Die While They Played a Video Game," *Newsweek* (July 27, 2014); Joe Kemp, "Oklahoma Parents So Engulfed in Second Life They Allegedly Starved Their Real 3-Year-Old Daughter: Cops," *New York Daily News* (October 12, 2013).
13. Annys Shin, "Casinos Want Customers to Stop Leaving Kids in Cars While They Gamble," *Washington Post* (August 7, 2014).
14. For a more exhaustive account, see Chris Meyers, "Social Consequences of Drug Prohibition," in *Drug Legalization—A Philosophical Analysis* (Cham, Switzerland: Palgrave Macmillan, 2021), Ch. 11. A similar list can be found in Husak, *Legalize This!*, Ch. 3.
15. "Rape Kits and Sitting on Shelves, Untested," *Scientific American* (July 1, 2020).
16. Iris Dorbian, "Weed Arrests Were Nearly a Quarter Million Last Year," *Forbes* (October 19, 2023).
17. RAND Corporation, "Americans' Spending on Illicit Drugs Nears $150 Billion Annually; Appears to Rival What Is Spent on Alcohol" (August 20, 2019) (https://www.rand.org/news/press/2019/08/20.html).
18. Dan Werb, Greg Rowell, Gordon Guyatt, Thomas Kerr, Julio Montaner, and Evan Wood, "Effect of Drug Law Enforcement on Drug Related Violence: Evidence from a Scientific Review," *International Journal of Drug Policy* 22 (2011): 87–94.
19. Michael D. Lyman, *Drugs in Society: Causes, Concepts, and Control*, 8th ed. (New York: Routledge, 2017), 225–6.
20. James P. Gray, *Why Our Drug Laws Have Failed and What We Can Do About It* (Philadelphia: Temple, 2012), 103.
21. "World Prison Brief," Institute for Crime and Justice Policy Research (https://prisonstudies.org/highest-to-lowest/prison_population_rate?field_region_taxonomy_tid=All).
22. This data is from a 2018 declassified DEA Intelligence Report: "2016 National Drug Price and Purity Data" (https://ndews.umd.edu/sites/ndews.umd.edu/files/dea-2016-national-drug-price-purity-data.pdf).
23. D. Mark Anderson, Benjamin Hansen, and Daniel Rees, "Association of Marijuana Laws with Teen Marijuana Use: New Estimates from the Youth Risk Behavior Surveys," *JAMA Pediatrics* (July 2019): 879–81.
24. Lloyd D. Johnston, Patrick O'Malley, and Jerald Bachman, *Drug Use Among American High School Seniors, College Students and Young Adults, 1975–1990* (National Institute on Drug Abuse, 1991).
25. William C. Kerr, Yu Ye, Meenakshi Sabina Subbaraman, Edwina Williams, ānd Thomas K. Greenfield, "Changes in Marijuana Use Across the 2012 Washington State Recreational Legalization: Is Retrospective Assessment of Use Before Legalization More Accurate?" *Journal of Studies on Alcohol and Drugs* 79 (2018): 495–502.
26. Jim Leitzel, "Toward Drug Control: Exclusion and Buyer Licensing," *Criminal Law and Philosophy* 7 (2013): 99–119.

Eat, Drink, and Be Sober: The Case for Drug Prohibition

Timothy Hsiao

> ## Study Questions
>
> 1. How does Hsiao understand the nature of freedom? What conditions must be met to exercise freedom?
> 2. According to Hsiao, what are the immediate effects of recreational drug use on freedom?
> 3. What is corollary to the government's duty to protect freedom? How does Hsiao illustrate the truth of this point? How does this apply to recreational drug use?
> 4. What three objections to his argument does Hsiao consider? How does he respond to them?
> 5. What is Hsiao's framework for regulating drugs?
> 6. Why does Hsiao think that the failure of alcohol prohibition is not a good reason to legalize recreational drugs?
> 7. Why does Hsiao say that the "over-incarceration" of nonviolent drug users is a myth?

If you value freedom, then you should support restrictions on intoxicating drugs.[1] The reasoning is simple: the use of intoxicating drugs impairs, degrades, and, in many cases, destroys the very organ that enables us to act freely and rationally, thereby making it counterproductive to free action. Since safeguarding freedom is an essential responsibility of the government, it is justified in enacting legal restrictions on intoxicating drugs.

This point applies to all drugs, including alcohol. However, because each drug is different in physical effects, the scope of legal regulations will vary. There is no "one size fits all" approach to drug regulation. As such, I'll outline several frameworks for regulating drugs, ranging from mild to moderate restrictions all the way to full-blown prohibition.

Some argue that freedom entails the individual right to get high. But this is mistaken. Recreational drug use impairs the very faculties that enable free action to begin with, so conceiving of drug use as an extension of freedom makes as much sense as promoting seawater as a remedy for thirst. It is *self-defeating* to invoke the concepts of freedom, liberty, and autonomy to justify the legalization of substances that are used to undermine these very things.

Before I continue, a clarification is necessary. One common argument for drug restrictions is the *general harm argument*: we should ban or heavily restrict drugs because they are harmful to a variety of physical, social, and societal measures of well-being.[2] While I believe there is significant merit to this argument, this is *not* the approach that I'll be taking. Instead, my focus is on a *specific kind* of harm, namely impairment of the fundamental capacity to act. The widespread social harms of drug use may furnish an *additional* reason to restrict them, but it is not an essential part of my argument.

The Nature of Freedom

To understand why drug use is incompatible with freedom, we must first clarify what freedom actually means. True freedom is not simply the absence of external constraints; it requires the capacity for rational, self-directed action. Without this, freedom is reduced to mere impulse or compulsion rather than genuine autonomy. We can thus think of freedom as *rational agency*.

Now, in order for someone to exercise freedom in this sense, two conditions must be present.[3] First, they must be *thinking rationally*. A free person must understand what it is they are choosing, why they are choosing it, and be able to deliberate between various options. Reason confers on one's actions a certain order and intelligibility that makes them explicable and coherent. It is what makes our actions *ours*, such that we are *responsible* for them. Second, a free person must be in *control of his faculties*. Free persons must be able to exercise their physical and mental faculties without interference or impairment. For this condition to be met, those faculties must also be in proper working order.[4]

These two conditions are closely related. The ability to think rationally is dependent on properly functioning cognitive and perceptual faculties. If one's brain is damaged or if one is subject to overwhelming coercive forces, then his ability to think rationally is also negatively affected. Conversely, if one is not thinking rationally, then he likely also has diminished self-control over his actions.

In making this point, it is also important to note that the expression of freedom comes in *degrees*.[5] We can be more or less free, depending on our abilities. Nobody is free in a completely unlimited sense: we all have physical and mental limitations that constrain what we are able to do. On the other hand, even someone who is conscious but completely paralyzed retains the ability to make mental choices, even if those choices cannot be expressed physically. Since freedom is expressed in degrees, impairment likewise comes in degrees. This point is important to keep in mind because the impairing properties of drugs will differ from substance to substance, which in turn should shape our policy response.

The Effects of Drugs on Freedom

Given that freedom requires (1) reason and (2) self-control, how do commonly used recreational drugs affect these abilities? Answer: they are profoundly destructive. Any honest defender of drug legalization should admit that many recreational drugs—even if they should ultimately be legal—have seriously negative effects on reasoning and self-control (not to mention various other negative physical and societal effects).[6]

We can divide the effects of recreational drugs into two categories: immediate and long-term. My primary concern is on immediate effects, as these directly impair the physical mechanisms responsible for reasoning and self-control—the very faculties that make free choice possible. This is not to downplay long-term effects (especially *addiction*), which can severely degrade cognitive function, motivation, and emotional stability. However, while chronic drug use weakens autonomy over time in a way that may be distant or diffuse, acute intoxication overrides it in the moment, directly severing the connection between reason, self-control, and reality. Even though this disruption is temporary, it represents a direct and immediate breakdown of agency, whereas long-term effects unfold more gradually.

In the context of rational agency, *impairment* should be understood as any disruption of the proper functioning of our cognitive faculties, whether through suppression or artificial stimulation. The purpose of our rational and cognitive faculties is to enable us to perceive reality accurately, deliberate soundly, and act in accordance with truth. When we speak of drugs impairing rational agency, we are not only referring to substances that depress cognitive function but also to those that overstimulate it. Proper cognitive function depends on *homeostasis*, a balanced state that allows the mind to perceive reality clearly and process information accurately.

This is why the claim that some recreational drug use "enhances" mental function is misleading.[7] While stimulants or psychedelics may create the *feeling* of heightened awareness or sharper focus, subjective intensity is not the same as genuine cognitive enhancement.[8] In reality, these substances override the brain's natural regulatory mechanisms and lead to erratic, fragmented, or distorted cognition rather than improved reasoning. Just as a fever is not "enhanced" functioning but a symptom of dysregulation, excessive cognitive stimulation is not an enhancement but a disruption. The mind's ability to reason properly depends not just on raw mental activity but on balance and stability, ensuring it can process information truthfully rather than distorting it.

Anecdotally, we are all familiar with examples of individuals acting in ways that are erratic, irrational, dangerous, or otherwise ill-advised while under the influence of a drug. One only needs to perform a simple internet search to find thousands of police body camera recordings of individuals utterly embarrassing themselves while high or under the influence. Nevertheless, empirical research is helpful. Here is what we know about the effects of several drugs.[9]

- **Cannabis (Marijuana)**: Cannabis use is associated with impairments in verbal learning, memory, attention, psychomotor function, and executive function. These cognitive impairments are particularly pronounced during intoxication and may persist in heavy users.[10] A review of data conducted by the National Academies of Sciences, Engineering, and Medicine found that there is a substantial body of research showing that long-term cannabis use is associated with schizophrenia or other psychoses.[11] Indeed, some researchers have asserted that the evidence is so decisive as to warrant a statement that cannabis use can *cause* these conditions to develop.[12]

- **Heroin**: As measured by fMRI, heroin use damages brain function and stresses the brain, resulting in impulsive and unhealthy decision-making. In individuals with heroin use disorder, brain circuits associated with executive control show distorted connections.[13]

- **Methamphetamine**: Methamphetamine use is associated with impairments in episodic memory, executive functions, information processing speed, motor skills, language, and visuoconstructional abilities. These impairments are exacerbated by long-term use, which also damages how brain cells communicate. It also affects important brain areas that control emotions, decision-making, and self-control.[14]

Some might point out that some recreational drugs have medicinal applications. While this is true, it does not change the fact that these same substances, when used recreationally, profoundly disrupt cognitive function. The question is not whether some drugs have therapeutic uses, but whether their typical use in nonmedical settings impairs rational agency. I will return to this point later.

The Responsibility to Protect Freedom

We are now in a position to see why legal restrictions on drug use are justified. In making this point, I'll take it for granted that *freedom is a good thing*. Human beings are by nature rational agents oriented toward the perfection of their being, and the exercise of rational agency in this pursuit of perfection is an integral part of human flourishing. Virtually all moral theories recognize the value of being free, so if this explanation doesn't work for you, then take your pick. Suffice it to say that if you do *not* think that freedom is a good thing, then you shouldn't be too bothered if the government takes away freedom vis-à-vis drug use.

Accordingly, the next step in the argument is the premise that governments ought to protect freedom. I take this to be so obvious that little needs to be said in defense of it.[15] Indeed, if there is going to be *any* legitimate responsibility that we can ascribe to governments, then a good candidate would be the responsibility to safeguard the ability to make free choices. Although we might reasonably quibble over the scope of freedom and the extent to which it should be protected, there is wide agreement across the political spectrum that freedom in a broad sense should be protected. This is not to say that governments are always successful in doing this. The point is that governments are *supposed* to respect freedom as a basic responsibility. Suffice it to say that if you *don't* agree with this premise, then there is little reason to oppose drug prohibition as an act of sheer will by the government.

A corollary of all this is that, if the government has a responsibility to protect freedom, then it must also have a corresponding responsibility to protect its essential ingredients. This is because some interests presuppose other interests. For example, the right to assemble must presuppose the right to freedom of movement, for one cannot assemble if he is not free to move about. Or consider an analogy with free markets: if a government wants to recognize and protect free markets, then it must have an interest in safeguarding the conditions that make a market economy possible, including freedom of exchange, contracts, and private property. Without these elements in place, it would be practically impossible for a free market to flourish.

None of this requires endorsing any specific moral theory. Even those who disagree on moral theories can recognize the necessity of ensuring that citizens retain the cognitive capacities required to engage as full and equal members of society.

So, what are the essential ingredients of freedom? Again, freedom requires two things: rationality and self-control. Without these, a person does not truly act freely but is instead ruled by impulse, compulsion, or external influence. Thus, anything that is corrosive toward rational agency is something the government has an interest in regulating, restricting, or even prohibiting. This is not a radical or unprecedented idea—most people already accept that the law appropriately intervenes to protect our ability to make rational decisions. Consider a few examples:

- **Suicide Prevention**: The law allows for crisis intervention (including involuntary psychiatric holds) when a person is deemed a *danger to themselves*. This is based on the recognition that extreme distress can impair judgment, leading individuals to make irreversible decisions that do not truly reflect their autonomous will. Far from being seen as an unjust restriction on freedom, such measures are widely accepted as safeguards for individuals who are not thinking properly.

- **Gambling**: Many governments restrict or regulate gambling because it can exploit impaired decision-making and lead to addiction, making individuals act against their long-term rational interests. Casinos, for example, are required to display warning signs about gambling addiction, and some jurisdictions impose self-exclusion programs where individuals can voluntarily restrict their own access to gambling establishments.

- **"Cooling Off" Periods**: Many legal systems enforce waiting periods before finalizing large purchases or canceling essential contracts—not to restrict freedom, but to ensure that individuals make decisions with full rational deliberation rather than acting on impulse or external pressure.

- **Medical Decision-making**: Medical decisions can have profound consequences, so the law requires that individuals be in a competent, unimpaired state when giving consent. If a person is intoxicated, under severe distress, or otherwise cognitively compromised, their decision is not considered fully autonomous, and any consent they give is likely going to be deemed invalid.

All of this shows that the idea of government activity in protecting the capacity for rational agency is something most people already intuitively accept.

Now consider recreational drug use. The primary function of psychoactive drugs—at least in their recreational context—is to induce a mental state that is incompatible with the unencumbered exercise of rational agency.[16] From the outset, this direct impairment of cognition is unlike any other substance and as such would appear to justify strict regulation. Indeed, psychoactive drugs appear to be sui generis—a unique category in themselves, in that their use generates coercive forces that infringe upon our freedom, not through external oppression, but through interfering with the very faculties that make free action possible. It is no exaggeration to say that many recreational drug users become slaves (whether temporarily or permanently) to the drug that they are using. We may conclude, then, that the state has a strong interest in intervening to prevent the recreational use of intoxicating drugs.

Three Objections

Before sketching a framework for drug regulation, let me first address three common objections.

Objection 1: The Harm Principle and Paternalism

Although the examples that I have just offered would be accepted by many, I realize that there are some—mainly committed political libertarians—who might still disagree. Although these libertarians would wholeheartedly agree that the government's main responsibility is to safeguard freedom, they would argue that this responsibility should be discharged by *preventing harm to others*, not the individual. On this view, rational agency is only a governmental concern when it is used to undermine the agency of non-consenting parties.

Several responses are in order.[17] First, most of the examples just offered involve seemingly justifiable interventions into areas involving an individual's own decisions regarding his own life plans. Take suicide prevention. Do we really want to say that the government cannot intervene to impose an involuntary psychiatric hold in cases where someone wants to end their life because of (say) a bad breakup?[18] Such interventions are obviously justified because the government is interested in protecting that individual's rational agency, and not just his bare ability to do things.

Second, freedom (and thereby rational agency) is a fundamental good that is essential to every individual's actual flourishing. Without it, it is literally impossible to flourish. Thus, the government's interest in protecting freedom shouldn't extend only to cases where others are harmed, but also to an individual's self-regarding actions. Taking freedom seriously must start with protecting the individual's ability for rational agency. Indeed, John Stuart Mill (from whom the "Harm Principle" originated) himself said that "The principle of freedom cannot require that [one] should be free not to be free. It is not freedom, to be allowed to alienate his freedom."[19]

Third, *all* harm is bad, whether it is self-inflicted or imposed on others.[20] A harm is a setback to well-being, and well-being—particularly as it pertains to rational agency—is an objective measure, not a matter of subjective preference. It is entirely possible to harm oneself and to violate one's own rights. The mere fact that the harm is voluntarily chosen does not make it any less real or morally significant. If flourishing depends on the preservation of rational agency, then self-inflicted harm that degrades this capacity is just as much an object of moral concern as harm imposed by others. Thus, the libertarian distinction between self-regarding and other-regarding actions collapses when we recognize that all harm, regardless of its source, compromises the very conditions that make freedom and well-being possible.[21]

The libertarian may respond by arguing that restricting self-harm constitutes an unjustified form of paternalism. However, this objection misunderstands the nature of the argument. The state's role is not to prevent self-harm *as such*, but to safeguard the preconditions of rational autonomy itself. Unlike ordinary risk-taking (e.g., skydiving or eating an unhealthy diet), which leaves one's decision-making capacity intact, the consumption of psychoactive substances directly alters and degrades the very cognitive faculties necessary to make rational choices. The justification for regulation, then, is not based on protecting individuals from *every* form of self-harm, but rather on ensuring that individuals retain the basic capacity for meaningful self-governance.

Objection 2: Overcriminalization

Another objection pertains to *overcriminalization*. One might argue that, although it is plausible that the government has an interest in protecting rational agency, applying this principle too broadly could justify excessive restrictions on nearly every aspect of life. After all, many things—lack of sleep, high-stress environments, poor diet, even social media—can, in some way, impair rational decision-making. If we take this argument too far, would we not risk an overbearing state that micromanages personal choices under the pretense of protecting freedom?

This concern, while understandable, rests on a misapplication of the protection principle. Not every impairment of rational agency warrants criminal penalties, nor does every potential influence on cognitive function require government intervention. The key distinction lies in the nature of the impairment and the reason for its occurrence. There is a major difference between minor, incidental influences on decision-making and substances that are directly, substantially, and intentionally used to facilitate impairment, particularly in ways that lead to compulsive use and long-term impairment. The primary purpose of psychoactive drugs is precisely to induce an altered cognitive state—to seek pleasure through impaired cognition. This is not the case for substances like unhealthy foods, household chemicals, or even some medications, where any cognitive impairment is an incidental or unintended side effect rather than the primary reason for use. In light of all this, we should adopt the following regulatory principle:

The degree of regulation for an impairing substance should be proportional to the extent that it is used to undermine rational agency.

Take, for instance, markers and glue—they can be abused as inhalants to achieve a high, but that is not their intended or primary use. This contrasts sharply with marijuana, where impairment of rational faculties is the primary goal of its recreational use (i.e., getting "high"). For substances whose primary function is unrelated to cognitive impairment, regulation should be minimal. But for substances like marijuana and other drugs, where cognitive impairment is not merely a side effect but the very reason for their use, harsher regulations (up to prohibition) are justified.

This aligns nicely with our existing commonsense intuitions about regulation: we impose greater restrictions on substances and behaviors that pose a direct, intended, and widespread threat to public interests than those that carry only incidental or indirect risks. Factors such as intent, likelihood, and severity of impairment, rather than mere possibility of harm to rational agency, should guide regulatory decisions. The goal is not to create a legal system that indiscriminately punishes all impairments to rational agency, but one that proportionately responds to the circumstances surrounding drug use.

Another version of the overcriminalization objection contends that my reasoning would justify state censorship in order to protect rational agency. If the government has an interest in preserving a culture of clear and rational thinking, doesn't it follow that it should suppress false or irrational ideas?

This objection fails to distinguish between *protecting cognitive function* and *controlling belief content*. The state has an interest in preserving the biological and cognitive faculties that make rational thought possible to begin with, not in dictating what individuals should believe. Censorship suppresses ideas *after* they have been formed, whereas drug regulation ensures that individuals remain capable of *forming beliefs freely in the first place*. My argument is not about shaping ideological content (and is thus neutral with respect to political ideology), but about protecting the cognitive preconditions of genuine self-governance, regardless of one's political or philosophical commitments.

Objection 3: Medicinal Uses for Drugs

Some defenders of drug legalization claim that because certain substances have recognized medicinal uses, their prohibition is unjustified. This is a Red Herring. The presence of a medical application does not negate a drug's impairing effects when used recreationally. Many substances (opioids, benzodiazepines, and certain stimulants) are prescribed for legitimate medical purposes yet remain tightly controlled due to their high potential for misuse. The argument for medicinal allowances does not translate into a justification for broad legalization any more than the existence of prescription opioids justifies their widespread recreational abuse.

If anything, the fact that certain substances require strict oversight in medical settings reinforces the case for their prohibition outside of those settings. The same logic that justifies regulating painkillers or anesthetics also justifies restrictions on drugs whose primary intended use is to impair rational self-governance.

Moreover, this objection is often used as a dishonest rhetorical smokescreen to smuggle in full legalization. Legalization proponents frequently use medicinal allowances as a foot in the door to dismantle prohibitions on recreational use. This pattern is evident in the case of marijuana, where initial arguments for limited medical access rapidly transitioned into sweeping efforts for full-scale legalization.

A Framework for Restricting Drugs

So how should we regulate drugs? Earlier, I noted that the degree of regulation for an impairing substance should be proportional to the extent that it is used to undermine rational agency. Applying this principle requires an examination of (1) the actual effects of a drug on rational agency and (2) the primary purposes for which it is used.

Consider a legal drug like alcohol, which is widely consumed for a variety of reasons. Some people drink a glass of wine to unwind after a long day, others have a beer to enhance social bonding, and still others consume alcohol explicitly to experience intoxication. The key point is that alcohol is not exclusively or even primarily consumed for the sake of intoxication. Many individuals drink in moderation, experiencing no cognitive impairment, and are able to retain rational control over their actions.

At the same time, however, alcohol carries a significant risk of abuse, particularly in the form of binge drinking. An estimated 17 percent of adults in the United States engage in binge drinking (defined as five or more drinks per occasion for men, four for women), which almost certainly results in intoxication and thus obvious impairments to rational agency.[22] The effects of excessive alcohol consumption—impaired judgment, aggression, diminished impulse control, and cognitive dysfunction—are so well documented and widely recognized that they hardly require extensive elaboration.

Thus, although alcohol can be consumed apart from intoxication, it still warrants regulation due to its high propensity for abuse and its capacity to induce severe impairment. The appropriate legal response should strike a balance by permitting moderate, non-impairing use while imposing legal safeguards against excessive consumption.[23] All of this is rather uncontroversial.

Now consider a drug like marijuana. Unlike alcohol, which is frequently consumed in moderation without intoxication, the primary function of recreational marijuana use is to induce a psychoactive "high"—a state that directly impairs rational agency. Unlike social drinking, where individuals may have a single drink without experiencing significant cognitive impairment, typical marijuana use often involves consuming amounts sufficient to produce noticeable psychoactive effects, if not outright intoxication. This distinguishes it from substances like alcohol, where impairment is often an incidental consequence rather than the primary goal of consumption. Legal policy should reflect this difference.

Indeed, researchers have noted that "normal marijuana use in the United States likely resembles binge drinking more closely than it does mere drinking."[24] This comparison is instructive: whereas moderate alcohol consumption allows individuals to retain full control of their rational faculties, typical marijuana use involves *deliberate cognitive impairment* as the primary means of enjoyment. Given that the defining feature of binge drinking is the pursuit of intoxication beyond a threshold that severely degrades cognitive function, this parallel suggests that marijuana consumption should be understood not as a casual indulgence, but as an activity fundamentally structured around a loss of rational self-governance.[25]

This distinction is crucial. The defining feature of recreational marijuana consumption is the deliberate induction of a psychoactive state that degrades rational agency. This is not an incidental or avoidable consequence of its use but rather the primary motivation for its consumption. As such, it cannot be compared to alcohol. When a substance is consistently and deliberately used to undermine rational agency (both in the moment and over time), it warrants more than mere regulation; it demands *prohibition*.

This reasoning extends with even greater force to substances such as methamphetamine, heroin, MDMA, and other "hard" drugs. Unlike marijuana, which has some variance in consumption patterns, harder drugs are overwhelmingly consumed with the explicit intent of inducing a powerful and often overwhelming psychoactive effect. Their impairing properties are not just incidental but essential to their appeal. Furthermore, the cognitive disruption caused by these substances is far more severe, with methamphetamine and heroin users experiencing profound impairments in executive function, impulse control, and even basic reality perception. The immediate and lasting consequences of such impairments—ranging from reckless and destructive behavior to full-blown physical and psychological dependency—justify prohibition.[26]

But Didn't We Try This Once Already?

Critics of drug prohibition often invoke the failure of alcohol prohibition in the 1920s as evidence that prohibition of other substances is similarly doomed to fail.[27] However, such a claim rests on a "historically flimsy basis."[28]

Under Prohibition, per capita alcohol consumption declined by an estimated 30–50 percent. Key public health indicators—such as cirrhosis death rates (a reliable measure of heavy drinking), hospital admissions for alcohol-related psychosis, and arrests for drunk and disorderly conduct all dropped dramatically.[29] From an economic point of view, it should not be surprising that prohibition reduced consumption. Prohibition made alcohol more expensive and less available, which in turn discouraged and disincentivized its use.[30]

What about crime? Economist Emily Owens found that "murder rates did not increase when alcohol markets were criminalized," and that "observed crime trends during the early 20th century are primarily explained by demographic changes."[31] Other factors, such as societal changes occasioned by the First World War, immigration, and increased urbanization during the Roaring Twenties, largely accounted for the change in crime. In fact, Owens found that the "passage of legislation banning the commercial sale of alcohol had a net negative effect on the homicide rate," meaning that alcohol prohibition may have *reduced* the homicide rate. This finding "casts doubt on the assertion that legalizing the sale of illicit substances would necessarily lead to a reduction in crime."[32]

Prohibition didn't fail. It was abandoned.[33] The reason was political, not practical. The law was weakly enforced from the start, with widespread noncompliance from "wet" states. The lesson of Prohibition is not that bans don't work, but that enforcement must be serious and consistent.

Criminal Penalties for Drug Use and the "Mass Incarceration" Myth

If the government has an interest in prohibiting substances that directly impair rational agency, then it also has an interest in ensuring that prohibition is enforceable. A purely regulatory approach (e.g., taxation, licensing, or civil fines) may be effective for substances that have some non-impairing uses, but it is insufficient for drugs that are primarily used to erode the very faculties necessary for rational agency.

Activities that undermine rational agency warrant a legal response that acknowledges their status as violations of the foundational conditions of civic life. Just as the law treats fraud not as a mere regulatory infraction but as a criminal act because it strikes at the heart of voluntary agreements, so too must the law treat recreational drug use as more than a mere violation of social norms. It is a criminal transgression against the very conditions that make responsible citizenship possible.

That said, mere drug users are often both offenders and victims. We must acknowledge this reality and ensure appropriate distinctions between traffickers, distributors, and users. For traffickers and distributors, harsh prison sentences are warranted as they knowingly profit from substances that destroy lives.[34] Widespread drug use undermines the broader social environment that depends on rational, self-governing individuals. For users, punishment should still reflect their culpability, but it must also recognize their victimization, incorporating treatment alongside other penalties. In many cases, non-incarcerative forms of punishment such as fines, community service, or monitored probation may serve as appropriate legal responses.

However, incarceration may be justified for drug users whose behavior results in reckless endangerment, repeated criminal activity, or a persistent refusal to seek rehabilitation. Incarceration may also provide a "shock" deterrent effect and aid in treatment by keeping first-time users away from drugs. At the end of the day, specific penalties will have to be determined on a case-by-case basis, considering factors such as the specific drug, amount used, prior history, and other crimes that may stem from drug use. There is no bright-line rule.

Going against all of this is the widely repeated objection, which looms large in contemporary discussions about drug policy and criminal justice reform, that the "racist" "war on drugs" is responsible for mass over-incarceration and over-policing—particularly when it comes to Black Americans.[35] This is simply a myth.[36] As criminologist Barry Latzer has noted, the vast majority of inmates (including Black inmates) serving time in prison are there for *violent crimes*. Out of all the inmates within the state prison population (which houses 88 percent of the US prison population), only 14 percent are there for drug offenses. Of that number, a meager 3.7 percent are there for mere possession. The rest are incarcerated for trafficking.[37] For Black Americans, 94 out of every 100 inmates (state and federal) are serving time for *non-drug* offenses. Even if the war on drugs were to immediately end and all drug inmates released, the proportion of Black Americans in state prisons would be essentially unchanged.[38]

Conclusion

Freedom is meaningful only when anchored in reason and self-control. Recreational drug use does not expand freedom: it corrodes the very faculties that make it possible. If the state has a duty to protect liberty, then it also has a duty to restrict substances that degrade rational agency and self-governance. True freedom is not found in a chemically induced escape but in the clarity of a mind capable of making sound, responsible choices. A free society is a sober society.[39]

Notes

1 This paper contains amplified versions of arguments originally found in Timothy Hsiao, "The Case for Marijuana Prohibition," *Ethics & Medicine* 35, no. 1 (2019): 17–25; Timothy Hsiao, "Why Recreational Drug Use is Immoral," *National Catholic Bioethics Quarterly* 17, no. 4 (2017): 605–14; and various op-eds that I have written for *The Federalist* and *Arc Digital*.

2   For example, see Peter de Marneffe, "Against the Legalization of Drugs," in *Contemporary Debates in Applied Ethics*, 2nd ed., ed. Andrew I. Cohen and Christopher Heath Wellman (Oxford: Blackwell, 2013), 346–57.

3   To use some fancy philosophical jargon, some might argue that my overall argument is doomed to miss the mark from the outset because I seem to be confusing *political freedom* and *metaphysical freedom*. Not so. My argument is not about metaphysical freedom per se, but about our practical ability to make rational, responsible choices. Even if one denies free will in a deep metaphysical sense, it remains true that certain social conditions enhance or inhibit our ability to deliberate and act responsibly. The state's duty is to foster a society where rational agency can function effectively—just as it does when it regulates fraud, coercion, or threats to public order.

4   **Objection**: "What about physically and mentally disabled people? Are you saying they're not free?" **Response**: No. Lacking the ability to freely perform *certain actions* isn't the same as lacking the ability to be free *in general*. Freedom comes in degrees. Someone who is missing a leg might not be free to walk, but he is still able to make other free choices within his ability. He is still a free person, even though his freedom is limited.

5   For reasons of conceptual clarity, it's also important to further distinguish between the *ability* to act freely and the *expression* of that ability. An ability is a kind of potentiality or capacity that is real and present, even if it's not being actively used (expressed). Someone who is asleep remains a free person, even if he is not *expressing* his freedom at that specific moment. Likewise, I retain the ability to act freely even if I am temporarily prevented from doing so (e.g., I am under general anesthesia). The ability is still real and present; it is just not being manifested. That ability is only destroyed when the structure that it is rooted in (my mind) is also destroyed.

6   A useful single-volume reference that surveys the effects of commonly used recreational drugs is Cynthia Kuhn, Scott Swartzwelder, and Wilkie Wilson, *Buzzed: The Straight Facts About the Most Used and Abused Drugs from Alcohol to Ecstasy*, 5th ed. (New York: W. W. Norton and Company, 2019). Also see the NIDA chart on "Commonly Abused Drugs" at (https://nida.nih.gov/sites/default/files/cadchart.pdf).

7   This point can be challenged as well. Consider the claim that some drugs improve creativity. These are often based on *self-reported* perceptions of improved creativity, which are dubious indicators of whether creativity actually improved—especially since drug use alters our perceptions! This has been confirmed by research showing that positive self-reports are heavily influenced by a user's prior expectations of a drug's effects, not by the drug itself. See Joshua A. Hicks, et al., "Expecting Innovation: Psychoactive Drug Primes and the Generation of Creative Solutions," *Experimental and Clinical Psychopharmacology* 19, no. 4 (August 2011): 314–20; and Danielle E. Humphrey, et al., "Self-Reported Drug Use and Creativity: (Re)Establishing Layperson Myths," *Imagination, Cognition, and Personality* 34, no. 2 (October 2014): 179–201. In one study (which looked at marijuana) participants who consumed marijuana-infused biscuits were less creative than members of the control group. However, those in the control group were less creative than individuals in another group who consumed a placebo that they *thought* contained marijuana. See Maurice Bourassa and Pierre Vaugeois, "Effects of Marijuana Use on Divergent Thinking," *Creativity Research Journal* 13, no. 3–4 (2001): 415.

8   Genuine enhancement must be sustainable and aligned with the proper function of rational faculties. If a drug improves one aspect of cognition at the cost of long-term function, it is not truly enhancing but rather distorting.

9   Many of the following references are to meta-analyses. These combine data from multiple studies, increasing statistical power and reliability.

10 S. J. Broyd, H. H. van Hell, C. Beale, M. Yücel, and N. Solowij, "Acute and Chronic Effects of Cannabinoids on Human Cognition—A Systematic Review," *Biological Psychiatry* 79, no. 7 (2016): 557–67.

11 National Academies of Sciences, Engineering, and Medicine, *The Health Effects of Cannabis and Cannabinoids: The Current State of Evidence and Recommendations for Research* (Washington, DC: The National Academies Press, 2017).

12 "The preponderance of evidence . . . substantiates not only a significant, causal role for marijuana in chronic psychotic syndromes but also a strong association with mood disorders and suicidal ideation. Thus, there can no longer be any doubt that the range of negative mental health impacts of this drug, too frequently dismissed as fear-mongering rhetoric, must be positioned at the front and center of international drug policy dialogue" (See Christine Miller, "The Impact of Marijuana on Mental Health," in K. Winters and K. Sabet, *Contemporary Health Issues in Marijuana* [Oxford: Oxford University Press, 2017]). Also see M. Colizzi and R. Murray, "Cannabis and Psychosis: What Do We Know and What Should We Do?" *The British Journal of Psychiatry* 212, no. 4 (2018): 195–6, who state: "It is now incontrovertible that heavy use of cannabis increases the risk of psychosis."

13 Ayman Fareed, et al., "Effect of Heroin Use on Changes of Brain Functions as Measured by Functional Magnetic Resonance Imaging: A Systematic Review," *Journal of Addictive Diseases* 36, no. 2 (2017): 105–16.

14 J. C. Scott, S. P. Woods, G. E. Matt, R. A. Meyer, R. K. Heaton, and J. H. Atkinson, "Neurocognitive Effects of Methamphetamine: A Critical Review and Meta-Analysis," *Neuropsychology Review* 17, no. 3 (2007): 275–97 (https://doi.org/10.1007/s11065-007-9031-0).

15 Nevertheless, here's a slightly longer rationale: government exists to organize society and maintain social order. But the formation and continued maintenance of social order require cooperation, and freedom of choice is essential to cooperation. Hence, one of the government's basic obligations is to protect freedom.

16 **Objection**: Most users aren't constantly in an impaired state, and temporary impairments don't undermine rational agency. **Response**: The key issue is not whether the impairment is permanent or temporary, but whether it *actively undermines rational self-rule while it lasts*. A person who is under the influence of drugs is no longer fully acting according to rational direction—his thoughts, impulses, and actions are being shaped by an external chemical influence. Whether this effect lasts for minutes, hours, or days does not change the fact that, during that period, he is not fully in control of himself. The loss of control, even if brief, is still a genuine impairment of self-governance. The same principle applies to rational agency. That is enough to warrant concern.

17 Also see Timothy Hsiao, "You Are Not Your Own: A Critique of Liberal Social Ethics," *EPS Project on the Philosophy of Theological Anthropology* (2018) (https://www.jpgociety.org/articles/you-are-not-your-own-a-critique-of-liberal-social-ethics/).

18 **Objection**: the individual contemplating suicide will affect the emotional well-being of other people if he were to kill himself. That justifies intervention. **Response**: *Really?* The only reason that we're justified in preventing suicide is because of the fallout to *other people*? Are we not going to care about the *individual*'s own interests? Does that mean that if the individual were a loner, there would be no reason to intervene? This strains credulity to the extreme.

19 John Stuart Mill, *On Liberty*, ch. 5 (https://www.econlib.org/library/Mill/mlLbty.html?chapter_num=5#book-reader). Mill is referring to letting oneself be sold into slavery. For the purposes of this paper, we might extend this reasoning by noting that allowing intoxicating substances is the equivalent of doing just that. Someone who is under the influence of a drug is, well, literally *under the influence* of a chemical substance that disrupts their normal proper functioning. If we reject *political slavery* because it violates autonomy, then we should likewise reject *chemical slavery* because it produces the very same result: a person who is ruled by something other than his own rational will. A society that tolerates and normalizes widespread chemical enslavement is not a society that is maximizing freedom. It is a society that is manufacturing dependence and self-imposed servitude.

20 This is not to say that harm cannot sometimes be justified—only that harm, if it is to be justified, requires a good reason. In the absence of a justification, harm is a bad thing.

21 Another reason to reject this argument is that psychoactive drug use constitutes a unique exception to the libertarian framework. For the libertarian, the government's role is to protect against coercion. Self-regarding actions that we freely choose to perform are by definition not coerced, and so are outside of the domain of the state. But drug use is different: psychoactive drugs put individuals into states of consciousness in which they are subject to coercive forces that often cause them to do things they would otherwise not want to do. Hence, libertarians ought to oppose recreational drug legalization because it runs directly counter to libertarian principles. See Timothy Hsiao, "Why Libertarians Should Oppose Marijuana Legalization," *Arc Digital* (November 4, 2018) (https://medium.com/arc-digital/why-libertarians-should-support-marijuana-prohibition-32bc05d8c389).

22 CDC, "Data on Excessive Alcohol Use" (August 6, 2024) (https://www.cdc.gov/alcohol/excessive-drinking-data/index.html).

23 Some have plausibly argued that more stringent alcohol controls are needed. See Philip J. Cook, *Paying the Tab: The Costs and Benefits of Alcohol Control* (Princeton: Princeton University Press, 2007). Additionally, there is a growing body of recent research indicating that alcohol consumption in any form is not safe. See Robyn Burton and Nick Sheron, "No Level of Alcohol Consumption Improves Health," *The Lancet* 392, no. 10152 (2018): 987–8. This should inform our policy approach on alcohol. If it demands prohibition, so be it.

24 Jonathan P. Caulkins, Beau Kilmer, and Mark A. R. Kleiman, *Marijuana Legalization: What Everyone Needs to Know*, 2nd ed. (Oxford: Oxford University Press, 2016), 31.

25 It may be argued that certain forms of "moderate" marijuana use, such as microdosing or consumption of low-THC products, do not produce the same level of psychoactive impairment as standard recreational use. While it is true that microdosing aims to avoid overt intoxication, this objection does not undermine the broader argument for prohibition. First, research has shown that THC, even at low

doses, can have adverse psychiatric effects. See Guy Hindley, et al., "Psychiatric Symptoms Caused by Cannabis Constituents: A Systematic Review and Meta-analysis," *The Lancet Psychiatry* 7, no. 4 (2020): 344–54; and Carsten Hjorthøj and Christine Merrild Posselt, "Δ9-tetrahydrocannabinol: Harmful Even in Low Doses?" *The Lancet Psychiatry* 7, no. 4 (2020): 296–7. Second, such use cases remain marginal compared to the predominant recreational consumption patterns, which involve sufficient THC intake to achieve a psychoactive effect. Policy must be based on general use patterns, not niche exceptions. Consider blood alcohol limit, which, for most states, is 0.08. There are some who may still be able to drive safely at or above that level, but the law nevertheless criminalizes doing so based on a general pattern of behavior. The reality is that most recreational drug consumption is not about responsible, rational enjoyment, but seeking intoxication. If we take rational agency seriously, then we must also take seriously the policies needed to protect it from normalization and erosion.

26 Moreover, unlike marijuana, these harder substances present an undeniable and well-documented risk of compulsive use and addiction, further eroding an individual's capacity for rational decision-making over time. The distinction between voluntary and involuntary use quickly collapses as these drugs chemically rewire the brain's reward system, reducing users' ability to act as autonomous agents in the long term. Heroin and methamphetamine, in particular, create addiction pathways that not only impair decision-making but also fundamentally reshape a person's ability to exercise free will.

27 For a more detailed response to this objection, see Timothy Hsiao, "Almost Everything You Know About Alcohol Prohibition Is Wrong," *The Federalist* (April 23, 2019) (https://thefederalist.com/2019/04/23/almost-everything-know-alcohol-prohibition-wrong/).

28 Jack S. Blocker, "Did Prohibition Really Work? Alcohol Prohibition as a Public Health Innovation," *American Journal of Public Health* 96, no. 2 (February 2006): 233–43.

29 See Clark Warburton, *The Economic Results of Prohibition* (New York: Columbia University Press, 1932); Mark H. Moore, "Actually, Prohibition Was a Success," *New York Times* (October 16, 1989); and Jeffrey A. Miron and Jeffrey Zwiebel, "Alcohol Consumption during Prohibition," *American Economic Review* 81, no. 2 (May 1991): 242–7.

30 As Philip Cook explains: "The Volstead Act was successful in raising retail prices of alcoholic beverages by a factor of two or more. . . . And the Prohibition period was associated with a substantial reduction in per capita alcohol consumption. . . . Mortality rates from alcohol-related diseases were also lower, indicating that the prevalence of chronic heavy drinking was way down during the 1920s" (See Cook, *Paying the Tab*, 27).

31 Emily Green Owens, "Are Underground Markets Really More Violent? Evidence from Early 20th Century America," *American Law and Economics Review* 13, no. 1 (Spring 2011): 1–44.

32 Ibid., 3.

33 Blocker, "Did Prohibition Really Work?" 238.

34 This is based on the following principle: if it should be illegal to act in a certain way, then it should also be illegal to help, assist, or facilitate someone in acting in said way, *especially* when it involves assisting large numbers of people in ways that also exploit or victimize them.

35 The definitive statement of this argument can be found in Michelle Alexander, *The New Jim Crow: Mass Incarceration in the Age of Colorblindness* (New York: The New Press, 2010).

36 It is commonly argued that the "war on drugs" originated from explicitly racist motivations during the Nixon administration. This is not true. As Michael Huemer (himself an ardent defender of drug legalization) notes, the Comprehensive Drug Abuse Prevention and Control Act of 1970 was passed with overwhelming bipartisan support, including the support of several Black legislators. The following year, the Congressional Black Caucus met with Nixon and encouraged him to intensify the drug war. (See Michael Huemer, "Racist Drug Laws," in Huemer, *Progressive Myths* [Independently published, 2024], 94–5.)

37 Barry Latzer, *The Myth of Overpunishment* (New York: Republic, 2022), 108. Also see 95–101 for a response to the claim that Black Americans are over-policed and over-arrested. Latzer concludes that "violent crime, not the drug war, was the main reason so many African Americans were behind bars—and that is still true today" and that the "bottom line is that high rates of violent crime among African Americans are not a function of police bias. They are, uncomfortable as it may make us, a social reality."

38 Latzer, *The Myth of Overpunishment*, 90–1. Similarly, as John Pfaff points out: "The racial disparities in prison populations would barely budge if all the people serving time for drug crimes were immediately released, and it seems likely that scaling back the drug war would not on its own necessarily alter offending or enforcement patterns enough to bring about real change" (John Pfaff, *Locked In: The True Causes of Mass Incarceration and How to Achieve Real Reform* [New York: Basic Books, 2017], 50).

39 I would like to thank Thomas Alberto, Steven Cowan, and Bruce Blackshaw for comments on previous drafts of this paper.

Responses

Response to Meyers on Drug Legalization

Timothy Hsiao

> **Study Questions**
>
> 1. Why does Hsiao reject Meyers's view on who has the burden of proof?
> 2. What flaw does Hsiao see in Meyers's view of the justification of punishment? What alternative view does Hsiao defend?
> 3. How does Hsiao respond to Meyers's claims about the costs of prohibition?
> 4. Why does Hsiao think that flawed drug policies call for strengthening enforcement rather than abandoning it?

Chris Meyers claims that legalization should be the default position, but his argument rests on undefended assumptions about law and punishment. This response challenges those assumptions and defends prohibition as essential to ordered liberty. It also examines key empirical claims that Meyers makes about the effects of prohibition and legalization.

Is Legalization Really the Default Position?

Meyers begins by attempting to shift the burden of proof onto prohibitionists. He assumes that the default legal stance should be permissiveness, thus placing the burden of justification on those advocating prohibition.

But the question of who bears the burden of proof depends on the context. In this case, we cannot determine who must justify their position without first establishing what law is meant to achieve. Meyers assumes that the law should begin from a presumption of individual liberty, requiring a strong justification for any restrictions. On this view, punitive legal restrictions require clear evidence of necessity, while permissiveness requires no special defense. The burden of proof lies with those who advocate for criminalizing conduct. However, he does not *argue* for this conception of law; he simply *assumes* it. This is a serious flaw because, if his assumption is mistaken, then his entire framing of the burden of proof collapses.

If, instead, a key purpose of law is to promote ordered liberty—the conditions under which people can exercise meaningful, rational freedom—then the burden of proof shifts.[1] Under this framework, existing drug laws support the essential conditions for ordered liberty by restricting substances that degrade rational agency. Thus, it would follow that Meyers, as the advocate of legal change, must demonstrate that legalization would better serve the purpose of law. In other words, the burden of proof falls on the legalizer, not the prohibitionist.

Moreover, even if we grant Meyers's assumption that legalization should be the default, his argument still faces a major challenge: he must successfully refute every plausible justification for prohibition before legalization can be considered justified.[2] Although Meyers does attempt to refute many of the major justifications for drug prohibition, he does not engage with the argument I presented in my main essay. My case for prohibition is not grounded in traditional appeals to social harm or paternalism but instead in the idea that drug use actively undermines rational self-governance. Because Meyers does not address this argument at all, there is a gap in his analysis.

Meyers essentially begs the question against the prohibitionist. Each side must defend not only their policy position but also their underlying conception of law itself.

The Justification of Punishment

Meyers applies the same underlying assumption to punishment that he does to law in general: it is an extraordinary intrusion that must be specially justified. He suggests that punishing drug users is fundamentally different from punishing those who commit crimes such as murder or robbery because drug use does not directly harm others. Thus, punitive measures for drug-related offenses require an especially strong justification, one that is not met by prohibitionists.

However, this argument suffers from the same flaw as his burden of proof claim: it assumes without justification that punishment is an exceptional measure rather than an ordinary and necessary function of law. If law exists to maintain ordered liberty, then punishment is not an anomaly requiring extraordinary justification. Rather, it is a standard enforcement mechanism that ensures compliance with laws designed to uphold rational self-governance.[3]

Under a framework of ordered liberty, criminal punishment is distinct from administrative or regulatory penalties in that it applies to actions that directly undermine the foundational conditions of a self-governing society. Regulatory penalties, such as fines for traffic violations or environmental infractions, address matters of efficiency and risk management. They aim to shape behavior without necessarily implying moral culpability. Criminal penalties, by contrast, are reserved for actions that willingly threaten or directly attack fundamental social values. Fraud is criminalized not merely because it causes harm, but because it corrodes the civic trust necessary for free association. Likewise, drug prohibition is justified not simply because drug use has negative consequences, but because it erodes the individual's capacity for rational agency—the very capacity that makes ordered liberty possible.[4] Since recreational drug users willingly seek to undermine a cornerstone of ordered liberty, their actions are subject to criminalization.

Moreover, a purely regulatory approach (e.g., taxation, licensing, or civil fines) assumes that individuals will be able to *rationally comply* with restrictions, make informed decisions, and self-regulate their consumption. But drugs that severely and directly impair rational agency compromise the very ability to process deterrence-based incentives. A person addicted to heroin or methamphetamine is not making rational cost-benefit analyses about potential legal penalties. The more a substance weakens rational decision-making, the less effective civil penalties become as a deterrent.

The Costs of Prohibition and Legalization

Meyers makes several empirical claims about the costs of prohibition. Due to space constraints, I cannot address them all. However, I will respond to what I believe are the most important ones.

Costs of Drug Enforcement

It is true that drug enforcement is costly. In 2024, the federal drug enforcement budget totaled $43 billion.[5] However, Meyers overlooks the fact that enforcement helps contain the far greater costs of drug abuse, estimated at $193 billion annually as of 2007 (a number that has almost certainly risen).[6] Without enforcement, this figure would be far higher.[7] Research consistently shows that drug enforcement reduces use by driving up prices and limiting availability.[8] A systematic review of thirty-six studies found that a 10 percent price increase reduces consumption by roughly 9 percent.[9]

Why would drug enforcement increase prices? Enforcement makes the production and distribution of illegal drugs more difficult, risky, and expensive. When law enforcement disrupts supply chains through arrests, seizures, or lab shutdowns, the available supply shrinks and prices rise. Dealers also raise prices to compensate for the risk of being caught and punished. As prices increase, many users cut back or stop altogether. Like any other product, when the cost goes up, demand tends to go down. Even limited enforcement can reduce drug use by making access more costly and less convenient.

Real-world enforcement supports this. In 1995, the DEA shut down two major suppliers responsible for roughly half of the methamphetamine precursors in the United States. This single disruption immediately caused meth prices to triple and meth-related hospital admissions to fall by 50 percent.[10] Although traffickers gradually adjusted to this disruption, the intervention shows that consistent enforcement can sharply reduce availability and related harms when it effectively disrupts supply.

Prohibition limits overall drug use by keeping access restricted and use socially and legally discouraged. This is evident when comparing illegal and legal substances. About 13 percent of Americans report monthly use of illicit drugs, while roughly 50 percent use alcohol.[11] The difference is not random. Legality lowers the barriers to access and removes the deterrent of legal sanction. When drugs become legal, use increases. After marijuana was legalized in Colorado, adult use rose by 45 percent, and cannabis use disorder rates increased as well.[12]

Taxation

Meyers argues that prohibition deprives the government of tax revenue from a regulated drug market. This is true. However, we must also consider the negative fiscal effects of widespread drug use.

Consider alcohol, a legal drug. While alcohol generates tax revenue, its social costs are estimated to be around $250 billion, which is *fifteen times greater* than the total amount collected through local, state, and federal taxes.[13] If a legal drug with regulatory oversight imposes such massively disproportionate costs, there is little reason to expect a different outcome for legalized heroin, methamphetamine, or marijuana. Legalization may produce revenue, but it also drives up related harms that far exceed any fiscal gain. Indeed, one study looked at Colorado's marijuana legalization regime and found that for every $1 of tax revenue generated by marijuana taxes, Coloradans paid $4.50 to mitigate marijuana-related social costs.[14]

Mass Incarceration

Meyers insinuates that the drug war contributes to the mass incarceration problem. This is false.[15] A significant portion of US inmates are incarcerated for serious offenses. Data indicates that 55.7 percent of state prisoners were convicted of violent crimes, such as murder, rape, and assault. Property crimes, including burglary and theft, account for 17.4 percent, while drug offenses constitute 14.4 percent of the state prison population. Notably, only about 3.7 percent are incarcerated *solely* for drug possession.

Legalization Is Not the Answer

Suppose Meyers is right that current drug policies are flawed. That does not justify abandoning enforcement. It demonstrates the need to strengthen it. When a medical treatment falls short, we do not stop treating the illness. We adjust the method and continue the care. The same holds for drug policy. Enforcement is not an optional tool. It is essential for maintaining the legal and social conditions that make ordered liberty possible. Legalization disrupts these conditions by normalizing behavior that weakens rational agency. If current enforcement methods are ineffective, they must be improved. But the effort to control drug use cannot be set aside. Without enforcement, the framework of a free and self-governing society begins to erode.

Notes

1. For a defense of such a conception of law, see John Finnis, *Natural Law and Natural Rights*, 2nd ed. (Oxford: Clarendon, 2011). I distinguish ordered liberty from individual liberty in that the latter is just the raw ability to do things, whereas the former is the ability to make decisions rationally in light of what is true and good.

2. Even if a position is treated as the default, that does not exempt it from defense when it is directly challenged. A presumption may guide initial framing, but it cannot substitute for argument in the face of counterarguments.

3. If law is to be effective in sustaining ordered liberty, it must have the capacity not just to express norms, but to respond to their violation in a way that reinforces their authority. Punishment fulfills this role. It is the means by which the legal order says, "This kind of conduct cannot be tolerated if our shared project of rational self-rule is to continue."

4. Meyers argues that drug users should not be punished because they are victims. He writes: "If someone willfully harms himself, we cannot punish the person responsible without also punishing the victim, since they are one and the same person. And we should never punish the victims of wrongdoing" (p. 491). This argument relies on an overly simplistic view of responsibility. Being a victim does not necessarily entail being *innocent*. A person can be both the agent of their own harm and the one who suffers from it—for example, a drunk driver on an empty road who crashes and injures only himself, or someone who corrupts his own character by creating AI-generated child pornography. In most cases, victims and wrongdoers are distinct, but drug use presents a unique case: it is a case in which an individual can simultaneously be both victim and perpetrator.

5. Office of National Drug Control Policy, *National Drug Control Strategy—FY 2025 Budget Summary* (https://www.govinfo.gov/content/pkg/CMR-PREX26-00188487/pdf/CMR-PREX26-00188487.pdf).

6. U. S. Department of Justice: National Drug Intelligence Center, *The Economic Impact of Illicit Drug Use on American Society*, ix (https://www.justice.gov/archive/ndic/pubs44/44731/44731p.pdf).

7. Meyers seems to suggest that overzealous drug enforcement is the reason why other crimes are not solved. He writes, "It is not just money that is wasted but also law enforcement resources. There are at least 100,000 rape kits in police departments throughout the country that have never been sent to a lab for analysis" (p. 495). This is absurd. It assumes a direct trade-off between drug enforcement and solving other crimes, without providing any evidence that untested rape kits are a result of resources being diverted to drug cases. Police departments have specialized units that handle different types of crimes, and funding allocations are far more complex than Meyers suggests.

8. Jonathan Caulkins and Peter Reuter, "How Drug Enforcement Affects Drug Prices," *Crime and Justice* 39, no. 1 (2010): 213–71.
9. Jason Payne, et al., "The Price Elasticity of Demand for Illicit Drugs: A Systematic Review," *Trends & Issues in Crime and Criminal Justice* 606 (2020), Australian Institute of Criminology.
10. Carlos Dobkin and Nancy Nicosia, "The War on Drugs: Methamphetamine, Public Health, and Crime," *American Economic Review* 99, no. 1 (2009): 324–49.
11. Substance Abuse and Mental Health Services Administration (SAMHSA), *2022 National Survey on Drug Use and Health (NSDUH): Detailed Tables* (Rockville: Center for Behavioral Health Statistics and Quality, 2023).
12. Rocky Mountain HIDTA, *The Legalization of Marijuana in Colorado:* The Impact, vol. 5 (2018); Magdalena Cerda et al., "Association Between Recreational Marijuana Legalization in the United States and Changes in Marijuana Use and Cannabis Use Disorder From 2008 to 2016," *JAMA Psychiatry* 77, no. 2 (2020): 165–71.
13. See Jeffrey J. Sacks, et al., "2010 National and State Costs of Excessive Alcohol Consumption," *American Journal of Preventive Medicine* 49, no. 5 (2015): 73–9, https://doi.org/10.1016/j.amepre.2015.05.031; Tax Policy Center, "Alcohol Tax Revenue: 1977–2015" (2017) (http://www.taxpolicycenter.org/statistics/alcohol-tax-revenue); Tax Policy Center, *Tax Policy Center Briefing Book* (http://www.taxpolicycenter.org/briefing-book/what-are-major-federal-excise-taxes-and-how-much-money-do-they-raise).
14. Centennial Institute, "Economic and Social Costs of Legalized Marijuana" (2018) (https://centennial.ccu.edu/wp-content/uploads/2019/03/Economic-and-Social-Costs-of-Legalized-Marijuana-v1.3.pdf).
15. See Barry Latzer, *The Myth of Overpunishment* (New York: Republic, 2022).

Reply to Hsiao on Drug Legalization

Chris Meyers

Study Questions

1. How does Meyers respond to Hsiao's claim that the government should criminalize behavior that threatens to diminish an agent's autonomy?
2. How does Meyers respond to Hsiao's claim that drug use destroys agents' autonomy?
3. Why does Meyers think that concerns about addiction do not justify drug prohibition?

Timothy Hsiao and I start from the same premise, namely, that the law should protect individual liberty and autonomy. But he thinks that the best way to protect freedom is by putting people in prison, whereas I think that protecting freedom is better achieved by *not* putting people in prison. In assessing our respective arguments, you need to ask yourself this question: Which would be a greater infringement on your personal liberty and autonomy—recreational drug use or incarceration? The answer seems obvious to me.

At best, Hsiao's argument would show that the government should discourage drug use. But we can do that without punishing drug users or drug dealers. Cigarette smoking in the United States dropped from 42 percent of adults in 1965 down to less than 12 percent today.[1] This was accomplished thanks to public policies that did not put a single smoker or tobacco peddler in prison.

There are two major moves in Hsiao's argument, both of which I will challenge. The first is the claim that recreational drug use severely diminishes the user's autonomy. The second is the claim that the government ought to criminalize behavior that threatens to diminish the agent's own autonomy.

A Counterexample

This second claim is subject to counterexamples. Sexual arousal, for instance, has been shown to seriously impair judgment and moral decision-making. In one study, sexually aroused experimental participants (all male) reported being 2.5 times more interested in bestiality compared to unaroused counterparts, more than twice as likely to persist in sexual advances after being told "no," 25 percent more likely to skip the condom, and five times more likely to use a date rape drug.[2] If we should outlaw activities that impair rational autonomy, then we should outlaw activities that lead to sexual arousal. Obviously, that would be absurd.

To be fair, Hsiao would argue that activities that impair decision-making may be acceptable when such impairment is "an incidental or unintended side effect." But then he claims that with drugs like marijuana, the "impairment of rational faculties is the primary goal of its recreational use" (p. 507). That is a dubious claim to say the least. People use drugs for many reasons: pleasure, alleviation of pain or boredom, relaxation, mystical experience, personal insight, adventure, enhancement of creativity, peer pressure, rebellion, addiction, self-medication, and curiosity, just to name a few. Virtually no one gets high for the explicit goal of impairing their rational autonomy.

Does Drug Use Destroy Autonomy?

Now for Hsiao's first claim: that "commonly used recreational drugs" are "profoundly destructive" to the user's freedom. Presumably, this occurs in two ways. First, intoxication reduces users' autonomy by impairing their judgment and distorting their beliefs. Second, prolonged drug use can lead to addiction.

Hsiao seems to be especially concerned with the first threat to autonomy. "[A]cute intoxication," he writes, "overrides [autonomy] in the moment, directly severing the connection between reason, self-control, and reality" (p. 502). This hyperbolic characterization of the effects of drug use is reminiscent of *Refer Madness* antidrug propaganda and urban legends of LSD users jumping out of windows, believing that they can fly.

It is true that some drugs can seriously impair rational thinking, but only in very high doses. Prolonged heavy use of cocaine, for example, can lead to temporary psychosis. But the same is true of alcohol[3] and even caffeine.[4] Drugs like heroin and, to a lesser extent, marijuana, can sap the user's motivation. This may diminish autonomy in some sense. Users will be less inclined to act on their settled preferences while high. But if it is not a crime to be lazy, then it should not be a crime to do something that might make you lazy, even if laziness entails diminished self-control.

People who have used drugs will testify that they are not nearly as debilitating as nonusers typically suppose. Consider LSD, which is widely viewed as particularly mind-bending. In 1970, Pittsburgh Pirates pitcher, Dock Ellis, managed to pitch a no-hitter while tripping on LSD.[5] (Ellis mistakenly thought he would not be pitching until the next day.) Such a feat would not be possible if Hsiao's characterization of intoxication were accurate.

Coincidentally, the same thing happened to Carlos Santana at Woodstock.[6] He later reported that he could not bear to look at the neck of his guitar because it appeared to be slithering like a snake. The LSD affected his visual perception, but it did not impair his rational thinking. He knew the guitar's neck was perfectly rigid and that, as an accomplished musician, he could simply rely on his fingers without looking at the fretboard. His performance was electrifying, despite the visual hallucinations, and catapulted him to rock stardom. The only bad decision Santana made that day was consuming acid before performing, a decision he made when he was sober.

Hsiao also seems to assume that sober minds always perceive reality more accurately than drugged minds. But that is not the case. Those who suffer from PTSD, for example, see the world around them as threatening and dangerous. They are often racked with guilt or shame and are unable to access their own deeply suppressed emotions. A dose of MDMA allows them to perceive the world, and themselves, more accurately. As one recipient of MDMA-assisted described the experience, "I felt like myself for the first time in years."[7]

It is not just those with mental health issues who misperceive reality. All of us, to some extent or other, interpret the world through biases and faulty assumptions that we simply take for granted. A first step in philosophical thinking is to question these hidden presuppositions. Certain drugs can help us to question our dogmatic assumptions through an "epistemic loosening"—a temporary destabilization of deeply held beliefs and assumptions.[8] Wiliam James, for example, reported that his experimentations with nitrous oxide provided insights into the nature of conscious experience.[9]

Of all recreational drugs, the biggest threat to autonomy is probably alcohol, which can seriously impair judgment.[10] Alcohol is a much greater threat to rational autonomy than marijuana because people who are drunk tend to underestimate their impairment, while people who are high tend to *overestimate* their impairment.[11]

Moreover, drug use can, in some cases, *increase* autonomy, at least if used responsibly. Drugs can alter our moods in very predictable ways, and moods, in turn, have a powerful influence on our behavior.[12] If I am in an irritable mood, I will be more likely to be curt with my wife. If I am in an anxious mood, I might find it hard to be sociable at a party. If I am in a melancholy mood, I might not be able to muster up the motivation to work on an important project. Moods are very difficult to control. I cannot simply choose to feel calm, confident, or content. The best we can do is to try to control our moods indirectly. If I am feeling irritable, for example, I could meditate, or listen to soothing music, or pet my cat. I could also smoke a bowl of weed. Since moods have a substantial influence on behavior, it stands to reason that the ability to control our moods gives us more control over our actions and thus more autonomy.

What about addiction? Obviously, addicts have diminished self-control, at least with regard to the choice to consume drugs. But the vast majority of drug users never develop dependency. Preventing addiction is a worthy goal of public policy. But criminalizing drug use is not the best way to achieve this goal, especially given that the threat of criminal punishment has been shown to be ineffective in deterring people from using drugs.[13] Instead, we should treat drug abuse as a public health issue, not a criminal justice issue.

Notes

1 "Trends in Cigarette Smoking Rates," American Lung Association (https://www.lung.org/research/trends-in-lung-disease/tobacco-trends-brief/overall-smoking-trends).

2 Dan Ariely and George Loewenstein, "The Heat of the Moment: The Effect of Sexual Arousal on Decision Making," *Journal of Behavioral Decision Making* (2006), 19:87–98.

3 Gerhard Jordaan and Robin Emsley, "Alcohol-Induced Psychotic Disorder: A Review," *Metabolic Brain Disease* 29 (2014), 231–43.

4 Dawson W. Hedges, Fu Lye Woon, and Scott P. Hoopes, "Caffeine-Induced Psychosis," *CNS Spectrums* (November 7, 2014).

5 James Blagden, "Dock Ellis and the LSD No-No," YouTube (https://www.youtube.com/watch?v=_vUhSYLRw14).

6 Little Tommy, "The Story Behind Carlos Santana on LSD At Woodstock," *101.5 KGB* (February 26, 2020) (https://101kgb.iheart.com/content/2020-02-26-the-story-behind-carlos-santana-on-lsd-at-woodstock/).

7 Jesse Noakes, "Psychedelic Renaissance: Could MDMA Help with PTSD, Depression and Anxiety?" *The Guardian* (April 13, 2019).

8 David Blacker, "Psychedelics are Philosophical Tools for Demolishing Assumptions," *Aeon* (April 17, 2025) (https://psyche.co/ideas/psychedelics-are-philosophical-tools-for-demolishing-assumptions).

9 Dmitri Tymoczko, "The Nitrous Oxide Philosopher," *The Atlantic* (May 1996).

10 Judith Roizen, "Epidemiological Issues in Alcohol-Related Violence," in *Recent Developments in Alcoholism*, vol. 13, ed. Marc Galanter (New York: Plenum Press, 1997).

11 R. Andrew Sewell, James Poling, and Mehmet Sofuoglu, "The Effect of Cannabis Compared with Alcohol on Driving," *The American Journal on Addictions* 18 (2009), 185–93.

12 Chris Meyers, "Might Stoners Live Better Lives?—Drug Use and Human Welfare," in *Palgrave Handbook of Philosophy and Psychoactive Drug Use*, ed. Rob Lovering (Palgrave Macmillan, 2024), London, pp. 361–82.

13 Pew Research Center, "More Imprisonment Does Not Reduce State Drug Problems," *Pew* (2018) (https://www.pewtrusts.org/en/research-and-analysis/issue-briefs/2018/03/more-imprisonment-does-not-reduce-state-drug-problems).

Questions for Reflection

1. Does Meyers or Hsiao make the better case in defense of individual liberty? Why?

2. What ethical principles (e.g., autonomy, harm reduction, justice, etc.) should guide decisions about legalizing drugs, and which do you find most compelling?

3. What role does the government have in protecting its citizens from harm? How does your answer apply to the question of drug legalization?

For Further Reading

Caulkins, Jonathan P., Beau Kilmer, and Mark A. R. Kleiman. *Marijuana Legalization: What Everyone Needs to Know*, 2nd ed. Oxford University Press, 2016.

Husak, Douglas, and Peter de Marneffe. *The Legalization of Drugs—For and Against*. Cambridge University Press, 2005.

Hsiao, Timothy. "Why Recreational Drug Use is Immoral." *National Catholic Bioethics Quarterly* 17, no. 4 (2017): 605–14.

Inciardi, James A., ed. *The Drug Legalization Debate*, 2nd ed. Sage Publications, 1999.

Kuhn, Cynthia, Scott Swartzwelder, and Wilkie Wilson. *Buzzed: The Straight Facts About the Most Used and Abused Drugs from Alcohol to Ecstasy*, 5th ed. W. W. Norton and Company, 2019.

Lovering, Rob, ed. *Palgrave Handbook of Philosophy and Psychoactive Drug Use*. Palgrave Macmillan, 2024.

Meyers, Chris. *Drug Legalization—A Philosophical Analysis*. Palgrave Macmillan, 2021.

Index

Note: Page numbers in **bold** represents full chapters, while 'n' denotes note numbers

9/11   282, 343

Abigail Alliance v. von Eschenbach   173
abolitionism   378, 385, 397
abortion   1, 2, 5–6, **19–50**, 65, 70, 148, 179, 235, 238, 305, 337, 354
   pro-choice view   5, 6, 19–30, 39, 68
   pro-life view   6, 31–41, 44, 354
Abraham, William J.   348 n.34
absolutism (ethical)   216, 222, 229–30, 247, 299
affirmative action   2, 5
Agar, Nicholas   140, 148
agency/agent   4, 9, 20, 98, 142, 147, 228, 235, 237, 456, 459, 502, 505, *see also* rational agency
Airdale National Health Service Trust v. Bland   201, 209 n.13
Allan, James   206, 207
Anaximander   305, 313 n.5
Anderson, Elizabeth   159
animal experimentation/testing   9, 221, 222, 225–9, 244–6
animal rights   9–10, **221–51**
Anscombe, Elizabeth   439–40, 444 n.17
antisemitism   390–1, 403, 405, 406, 418
apartheid   406
Applebaum, Paul   71
applied ethics   1–3, 5
Aquinas, Thomas   64, 205, 235–6, 332
Ardern, Jacinda   383
Arendt, Hannah   316, 319 n.2
argument from autonomy   6, 63, 68–71
arguments   5, 17
   theological   435, 450–1
Aristotle   64, 205, 307, 310, 317, 337, 359, 372
Ashoka the Cruel   339

Athens   86–7, 94 n.10
Augustine   64, 314 n.11
authoritarianism   208, 265, 272–4, 316
autonomy   6, 9, 51, 56, 59, 60, 66, 68–9, 74–6, 78–81, 185–6, 188, 190, 212–14, 218, 219, 404, 405, 415, 417–18, 457, 459, 470, 490, 500–2, 506, 514 n.19, 522–6
   bodily   6, 26–7, 167, 170–1

Baker, Deane-Peter   299
Barbary pirates   354, 375
Bastiat, Frederic   384
Battin, Margaret   194
Bazilchuk, Nancy   356 n.5
Beech-Jones, Robert   199
Berns, Walter   92–3
bestiality   426, 523
Biden, Joseph   10, 252
bioethics   2, 70, 128, 141, 142, 147, 149, 206, 213, 217
biology   32, 138, 141, 151, 472, 478 n.20, 478 n.27
biotechnology   7, 142, 143, 149–50
body   15, 33–5, 67, 68, 97–8, 134, 146, 383, 461–2, 464, 466, 469–76, 477 n.18, 483 n.3
Boethius   235, 243 n.30
Boonin, David   29 n.4
borders   10, 164, 166, 169, 171, 174, 179, 193, 204, 252, 254, 262, 265–8, 271–4, 276 n.13, 279, 285
   open *vs.* closed   10, **252–89**
Bostock v. Clayton County   475
Bostrom, Nick   141, 143
Bowater v. Rowley Regis Corp.   200
Boxill, Bernard   366
Bozzo, Alexander   431–2, 434 n.28

Brady Bill 298
Brake, Elizabeth 336, 337, 444 n.7, 451
breach of contract 156–7, 162, 164 n.5
Breaking Bad 298, 299
Brennan, Gerard 204–5
Brennan, Jason 268–9, 277 n.27
Brettschneider, Corey 101
Bridges, Ruby 348 n.34
British Medical Association v. Commonwealth 198
Brooks, David 70
Brooks, Roy 359
Buchanan, Allen 120–3, 140, 141
Buck, Carrie 139
Buck v. Bell 139
Buddhism/Buddhist 338, 339
Burnham, James 310
Burroughs, Abigail 173
Butler, Judith 470, 477 n.7, 478 n.27, 482
Butterfield, Herbert 476 n.1

Call of the Hour 303, 308, 311, 313
Callahan, Daniel 76
Canadian Charter of Rights and Freedoms 53, 62 n.4, 392
capital punishment 2, 7, 73 n.10, **83–119**, 305, 314 n.14
Caplan, Bryan 267, 273, 276 n.16, 277 n.31, 282
Carter v. Canada 53, 56, 80
Cartesian ego 470
CATO Institute 275
cause/causation 66–8, 114 n.6, 122, 164, 202, 229, 254, 291, 292, 301 n.16, 312, 315–17, 331, 351, 383, 393, 409
censorship 264, 383, 403–12, 416–21, 507
Cetty, Chetan 296, 302 n.33
Chaoulli v. Quebec 173, 182, 183 n.1
Charles, J. Daryl 332–3, 353
Charpentier, Emmanuelle 120, 134, 138–9
Christ, *see* Jesus Christ
Christianity 64, 349, 400, 452
church 64, 100, 383, 408, 416
church-state separation 408, 422, 435, 450
Cicero 307
Ciceronian maxim 312, 318

cisgender 15, 457, 462, 465 n.4, 485
citizenship/being a citizen 11, 100, 101, 108 n.15, 166, 169, 179, 267, 273, 303–9, 311, 313, 320, 404, 406, 510
civil disobedience 310, 322–3
Civil Rights Movement (U.S.) 323, 348 n.34, 451
civil unions 444 n.12
Civil War (U.S.) 12, 377
Clinton, William J. "Bill" 106 n.2
Code of Hammurabi 85, 111
coercion/coercive authority 101, 142, 161, 162, 179, 186, 188–9, 192, 198, 253, 256, 257, 260, 261, 279, 285, 286, 395, 398–401, 422, 423, 440, 512 n.3, 514 n.21
cognitive capacities/faculties 6, 20–4, 27–9, 29 n.5, 42–3, 48, 280, 501–2, 504, 506
collateral damage 334, 343, 355, 404, 405
collectivism 371, 391–3, 396, *see also* government, collectivist forms
Collins, Francis 138
color-blind individualism 379, 384, 385
common good 9, 184, 185, 190–2, 194, 195, 211, 212, 214, 215, 292, 293, 296, 300
common sense 240, 272, 305, 343, 457, 468
conception 6, 31–4, 44, 47, 49, 148, 235, 237, 240, *see also in vitro* fertilization
consciousness 20, 21, 29 n.4, 34, 37, 470
conscription 198–9, 341, 344, 350
consent 8, 9, 25–8, 53, 54, 62 n.6, 66, 67, 69, 70, 126, 129, 138, 139, 141, 146–7, 186, 192, 200, 201, 205–6, 208, 209 n.13, 212–14, 216–19, 224, 226, 245, 253, 327, 328, 392, 395, 398–401, 436, 438, 447, 505
consequentialism 3, 17 n.8, 294, *see also* utilitarianism
contractualism, *see* social contract theory (of ethics)
Cook, Daniel Wayne 88
Cook, Philip 515 n.30
Coontz, Stephanie 437
Corey, David 332–3
Cott, Nancy F. 436

counterspeech   13, 397, 398, 410–12
COVID-19   9, 150, 190, 197–211, 215–16, 218, 296, 337
Cox, Kate   30 n.32
CRISPR   7, 120, 134, 137, 138, 141, 147
Crowley v. Christensen   212
Crummett, Dustin   297, 302 n.39
Cruzan, Nancy   73 n.9
Cullen, Charles   112
culture   21, 134, 148, 185, 252, 257–8, 268, 273, 281–2, 305, 339, 353, 379–80, 388, 405, 437, 468, 470, 482

Dahl, Robert   310
Daniele, Gianmarco   204
Davenport, Charles   139
deadly force   11, 326, 328–31, 333, 337, 349, 351
Deane, William   200, 205
death penalty, *see* capital punishment
death row   99–101, 104, 105, 108 n.10, 108 n.13, 113, 114 n.6, 118 n.3
Death with Dignity Act   52, 63
Declaration of Independence (U.S.)   327, 328, 391, 420
DeGrazia, David   232, 241, 291, 296, 297
Delon, Nicolas   232, 234
democracy   56, 116, 160, 181, 203, 261, 274, 288, 299, 310, 312, 321
Demy, Timothy J.   355
Dent, George   428, 430
dependence   66, 154, 159–60, 163, 181, 514 n.19
designer babies   7, 153
deterrence   92, 97, 101, 112, 118 n.3, 411, 412, 491, 519
dike   305, 309, 313 n.5
divine command theory   4
Dobbs v. Jackson Women's Health Organization   25
doctor-patient relationship   57, 76, 199, 215, 218
Doudna, Jennifer   120, 134
drug enforcement   495, 516 n.38, 517, 519–21
drug legalization   15–16, **489–526**
drugs   8, 15, 61 n.1, 69, 107 n.4, 112, 125–7, 151, 152, 155–6, 173–4, 178, 203, 337, 492, 496, 497, 500–3, 505, 507–9, 512 n.7, 513 n.8, 514 n.21, 515 n.26, 519, 523, 524
  addiction   491, 492, 502, 504, 515 n.26, 522, 523, 525
  medicinal use   503, 507–8
  prohibition   16, 489, 490, 492, 493, 495–7, 500–11, 518–20, 522
  recreational use   1, 16, 380, 489, 500, 505, 510, 511, 523
  regulation   16, 496–7, 500, 505, 508–9
  trafficking   494–5
Dukakis, Michael   106 n.2
Dworkin, Ronald   292

education   75, 170, 177, 179, 188, 190, 194, 267, 364, 367, 370, 378–80, 387, 404, 411, 426, 468, 492
egalitarianism   269–70, 359
Eisenhower, Dwight David   347 n.26
Ellis, Dock   524
el-Sadat, Muhammad Anwar   338
Emanuel Nine   348 n.34
embryo rescue argument/case   22, 42, 44, 231, 237, 238
endogamy   426, 432 n.2
epigenetic inheritance   120, 124, 126–9
epigenetics   120, 121, 123–6, 130, 146
epistemic interdependence   457, 464
epistemic problem of interventions   232
epistemology   2
equality/equity/equal rights   108 n.15, 142, 200, 216–17, 262, 268, 303, 305, 312, 320, 322, 340, 353, 359, 364, 367, 377, 388, 404, 405, 412, 425–8, 432, 446–7, 451, 475, 485
Establishment Clause (U.S. Constitution)   450
ethical naturalism   435, 444 n.6
eugenics   8, 64, 65, 70, 77, 78, 133, 139–41, 146–8
euthanasia   6, **51–82**
  involuntary   6, 58, 65, 69, 70, 72, 76–7, 79–80
  passive   6
evolution, biological   122, 123, 150, 152
existence   306, 307, 316, 318, 360, 361, 363, 364, 368

factory farming   9, 221, 222, 225–30, 232–3, 241, 244–6, 248, 249
Fairchild, Lydia   49 n.5
fairness   9, 105, 184, 185, 192–3, 195, 211, 214–15, 236 n.14, 340, 353, 362, 364, *see also* justice
fake news   403, 419
family   71, 137, 139–41, 147, 165, 257, 331, 364, 436, 468
Ferguson, Colin   370–1, 374
Ferrer, José Figueres   340
fertilization, *see* conception
Feser, Edward   95 n.30
Final Solution   353
First Amendment (U.S. Constitution)   13, 268, 276 n.8, 391, 392, 394, 399, 400, 420, 422, 450
First World War   339, 341, 344, 347 n.30, 353, 374, 510
first-person authority (FPA)   15, 455, 457–60
Food and Drug Administration (FDA)   120, 138, 173, 174
Foot, Philippa   441
forgiveness   314 n.14, 340, 344, 348 n.34
forms (Plato's)   1
Forrester, Katrina   366
Foster, Cleve   90
Foster, Gigi   204
Francis (Pope)   100, 108 n.14, 116, 190
free speech/expression   13, 101, 292, 294, **390–423**, 427
  absolutism   13, 390–402, 415, 417, 418, 420
  freedom (political)   8, 9, 11, 53, 56, 62 n.4, 69, 79, 97–100, 113, 142, 154–5, 157–61, 163, 176, 179, 185–7, 189–91, 198, 200, 205, 206, 212–13, 217, 219, 234, 293, 300, 302 n.33, 304, 305, 311–13, 313 n.4, 318, 320–3, 323 n.1, 326–8, 353, 378–9, 382, 385, 391–3, 395, 402 n.16, 405, 407, 412, 415–16, 418, 421, 426, 447, 457, 491, 494, 500, 504, 505, 511, 512 n.3, 514 n.19, 517–19, 521–3, 526
freedom of action   392–8, 400, 416, 420, 422
freedom of assembly   392

freedom of association   260–1, 270, 392, 395
freedom of conscience/thought   392–4, 401, 407
freedom of movement   268–9, 271, 272, 277 n.27, 504
freedom of movement argument   267, 274
freedom of religion   292, 484
freedom of speech, *see* free speech/expression
freedom of the press   392
freedom/free will (metaphysical)   16, 200, 470, 500–6, 511, 512 n.3, 512 n.5, 513 n.15, 518, 523
freedom-based argument   163
Freiman, Chris   266–7
French, Robert   198
Friberg-Fernros, Henri   237
Friday (of Robinson Crusoe)   167
Furman v. Georgia   97, 107 n.8
future-of-value machine   23, 42, 44, 48

Galileo   392, 416
Gallagher, Maggie   428
Galton, Francis   139
Gandhi, Mahatma   338, 340
Geertz, Clifford   468
Gelernter, David   92
gender dysphoria   15
gender non-conformity   470
gender/gender identity   8, 14–15, 97, 104–5, 111, 268, 427, 436, 455, 457, 460, 462–7, 469–76, 479, 480, 482, 484, 486
  poststructuralist view   470–1
gender-affirming care   14, 480
gendercide   337
Gendron, Peyton   373
gene therapy, *see* genome editing—therapy
general harm argument   500–1
genetic diagnosis   133, 135–6
genetic discrimination   136–7
genetic enhancement, *see* genome editing—enhancement
genome editing   7–8, **120–53**
  enhancement   7–8, 133, 137, 140–3
  therapy   7, 146–7
genuine human good   434, 435, 438, 440–3

George, Robert 430, 449
Gewirth, Alan 40 n.7
given, the 142, 150–2
Gladu, Nicole 55
Glover, Jonathan 140, 141
God 1, 4, 64, 85, 91, 257, 286, 327, 335 n.3, 356 n.3, 357 n.9, 401 n.4, 444 n.13
Goff, Robert 209 n.13
Goldberg, Steven 91–2
goodness/good 3, 13, 14, 37–9, 40 n.6, 41 n.8, 45, 56, 62 n.4, 81, 90, 101, 117, 190–2, 200, 235–8, 255, 307, 308, 310, 312, 314 n.11, 316, 340, 372, 384, 390, 393–4, 401, 406, 415, 417, 428, 435, 441, 450, 452, 453, 491, 506, 521 n.1
  natural 441–3, 453
  secondary 441
Gore, David Alan 83–4, 87–8
government (nature, purpose) 7, 8, 11, 13, 16, 54, 62 n.4, 96, 102–3, 154–5, 157, 161–3, 171, 176–9, 181, 182, 186, 193, 200, 204, 205, 218, 255–7, 262, 272, 279–80, 283 n.2, 287, 288, 293–6, 299, 310, 311, 313, 320, 324–9, 331, 332, 335 n.4, 349, 353, 357 n.9, 360–1, 390–4, 397, 405, 408, 415, 416, 419–22, 495, 500, 503–7, 510, 513 n.15, 514 n.21, 523, 526
government, collectivist form 319, 390, 392–3, 419–21
grace 340, 348 n.34, 353, 356 n.3
Gray, James P. 495
Greasley, Kate 29 n.8, 40 n.3
Greely, H.T. 127
Grimm v. Gloucester 474
Grinshteyn, Erin 292
Grossman, David 341
Gulag Archipelago 313
Gummow, William 198
gun control 10–11, **290–324**, 339
gun rights, *see* right to bear arms
gun violence 10–11, 17 n.10, 290, 296, 298, 316

Haines, Ian 72
Halappanavar, Savita 27

harassment 397–8, 400, 401, 403, 415, 419, 463
Hare, Caspar 302 n.39
Harlan, John Marshall 214
Harm Principle 9, 56, 62 n.4, 184, 186–90, 211–12, 214, 246, 292, 459, 505–6, *see also* No Harm Principle
Harris, John 194
Harris, Robert Wayne 88
Hastings, Battle of 342
hate speech 13, 390, 393, 397, 402–12, 415–22
  laws 13, 390–3, 395, 397, 402–4, 406, 408–12, 415, 417, 419–22
He, Jiankui 126–7, 138
health care, *see* right to health care
Hemenway, David 291
Herrera v. Collins 103
Henry v. Hazzard 199
hermeneutical virtue 455, 463–5
Herrera, Leonel Torres 103
Hill, Scott 243 n.37
Hinduism/Hindu 275 n.6, 282, 338, 452
Hippocratic Oath 64
Hobbes, Thomas 108 n.15, 328
Holmes, Oliver Wendell 139
Holocaust 129, 285, 343, 344, 356 n.6, 390–1, 394, 403, 417–18
hospice/palliative care 6, 58–60, 63, 64, 69, 72, 75, 77, 80, 81
Hoy, Wendy 201
Hsiao, Timothy 236–7, 357 n.7
Huemer, Michael 275 nn.3–4, 276 n.13, 277 n.26, 277 n.29, 283 n.3, 290, 293–9, 321, 322, 516 n.36
human flourishing 14, 143, 165, 503
Human Genome Project 135
human nature 4, 152, 466, 467, 470, 473–5, 478 n.20, 483 n.3
humanity, principle of 4
hunting 9, 221, 222, 225–30, 236, 244–6
Husserl, Edmund 315
Hutterites 344

identity-based hierarchies 404, 409–11
imagination 149, 229, 339–41, 352, 353
immigration 10, **252–89**, 396, 402 n.16, 416, 510, *see also* open borders
  illegal 10, 252, 262

immunization, *see* vaccination
imprisonment 7, 95, 97, 99–100, 107 n.4, 113, 114, 116, 390–1, 394, 495, 500, 510–11, 520, 523
in vitro fertilization 48, 135, 141, 429
incarceration, *see* imprisonment
incitement 294, 398–401, 403, 415, 419–20
indigenous peoples 338, 358, 362–4, 369 n.18, 388
individualism 379, 384, 385, 391
Industrial Revolution/industrialization 280, 361, 384–5
informed consent, *see* consent
intent/intention 66, 68, 81, 98, 124–5, 228, 292, 330, 332, 407, 409, 431–2, 507, 509
intentional genetic modification (IGM), *see* genome editing
intentionality 97, 98, 117, 432, 434 n.28
interconnectedness 193–4, 214
International Covenant on Civil and Political Rights 102, 205, 213
intersex 471–3, 477 n.7, 482–3 n.2
intertemporal law 358, 362–4, 368, 386, 387
intervention (in nature) 232, 249–50
intervention (in war) 331
intervention, crisis 504, 505, 514 n.19
intervention, genetic 121, 122, 124–30, 138, 141, 152
intervention, medical 159, 190, 206, 213, 219
intrastate/interstate travel analogy 269
intuition 4, 10, 43–4, 48, 121, 151, 152, 192, 231, 232, 236–8, 241, 243 n.37, 246, 269–70, 272, 308, 311, 507
Islam/Muslim 274, 338, 375, 407, 408, 420, 422, 452

Jackson, Henry Curtis 88
Jacobson v. Massachusetts 185, 190–1, 212, 214
Jainism/Jain 338
James, William 524
Jaworski, Peter 267–9
Jefferson, Thomas 382
Jermin, Kyla 367

Jesus Christ 91, 338, 340–1, 344, 348 n.34, 352–3, 355, 356 n.3, 357 nn.7–8
Jim Crow laws 373, 376, 447
John Paul II (Pope) 100, 108 n.14
Johnson, James Turner 350, 352 n.5
Joshi, Rishi 267, 268
Judaism/Jews 85, 102, 109 n.27, 116, 277 n.31, 282, 285, 288 n.1, 338, 343, 350, 353, 356 n.6, 374, 403, 405, 418, 452
Jünger, Ernst 314 n.16
jurisprudence 62 n.4, 197, 199, 309
just war criteria 11, 325, 330–4, 343, 350, 351, 356 n.4, 357
  discrimination/noncombatant immunity 333–4, 336 n.12, 355
  jus ad bellum 325, 330–3, 335
  jus in bello 325, 330, 333–5, 355
  jus post bellum 325, 330, 334, 335
  just cause 327, 329–33, 335, 343, 349, 354
  just intent 332–5
  last resort 332–3, 343, 355
  legitimate authority 332
  likelihood of success 332, 333
  proportionality 333
Just War Theory 11, 326, 337, 338, 343, 349, 351
justice 7, 11, 12, 39, 43, 45, 53, 83, 87, 89–98, 100, 102–5, 108 n.14, 112–14, 117, 130, 147, 155, 192, 200, 216, 218, 219, 230, 303–5, 308, 312, 313 n.5, 315–16, 318, 323, 330–5, 338, 340–1, 344, 349–51, 353, 356 n.3, 358, 360, 362, 364, 367, 399, 425, 429, 431, 432, 450, 451, 466, 489, 495, 526
  corrective/restorative 105, 113, 359, 360, 363, 388; *see also* reparations
  distributive 61, 359, 429
  epistemic 479
  as fairness 340, 353, 362, 364
  retributive 87, 89–91, 96, 99, 111, 343, 429
  social 8, 367
Justinian (Emperor) 86

Kaczynski, Ted 92
Kant, Immanuel 4, 222, 236, 244

Kantianism/Kantian ethics 4, 156, 164 n.4, 312
Kass, Leon R. 142
Kassam v. Hazzard 199
Kellermann, Arthur 302 n.27
Kendi, Ibram X. 377
keyhole solutions 264, 265, 268, 272–4, 288
killing, direct *vs.* indirect 44–5
killing, morality of 10, 12, 19, 21, 29 n.5, 37, 48, 65, 77, 78, 96, 99, 166, 224, 226–7, 231, 233, 234, 238–41, 248–50, 310, 329–30, 336, 337, 341, 353–4
   cognitive capacities view 20–3
   dual-aspect account 240–1, 247–50
   future-of-value view 22–3
   time-relative interest account 238–40
   two-tiered account 239, 240
King, Martin Luther, Jr. 109 n.27, 340, 451
Kirby, Michael 199
Kmiec, Douglas 428
Kohlberg, Lawrence 155–6
Koppelman, Andrew 425
Ku Klux Klan 376
Kurzweil, Ray 143

La Page, Michael 134
Lady Gaga 481
LaFollette, Hugh 291
Latzer, Barry 511, 516 n.37
Leeth v. Commonwealth 200
lex talionis 85–6, 93 n.9, 111, 112, 355
Liao, S. Matthew 237
libertarian open borders theory 264–78
libertarian rights theory 270
libertarianism 10, 265, 271, 285, 407, 505–6, 514 n.21
liberty, *see* freedom (political)
life, biographical *vs.* biological 67
life, sanctity/value of 44, 57, 78, 209 n.13, 311, 327, 337, 338
Lincoln, Abraham 318, 377
Lister, Andrew 426–7
Locke, John 177, 367
Loiacono, Rocco 206
Loth, Marc 364
Lott, John R., Jr. 316

love 142, 143, 165, 190, 314 n.11, 331, 340, 341, 344, 348 n.34, 437, 439, 472
Ludden, David 139–40

MacBeth 92–3
McCarthy, Thomas 363–4
McCleskey v. Kemp 104
McDonough, Richard 426–7
McGowan, Mary Kate 402, 409–10
McMahan, Jeff 233, 238–40, 244, 291, 293–4, 297
McMath, Jahi 29 n.7
Maitland, Frederic 311
marginal human beings 10, 233, 234
marketplace analogy 269–72, 277 n.28, 281, 286–7
Marneffe, Peter de 492, 493
Marquis, Don 19, 22–4, 50 n.11
marriage 13–14, 406, 424–5, 427, 428, 430–2, 434–6, 438–41, 443, 444 n.12, 446–8, 450–4
   male breadwinner conception 437–8, 451
   same-sex, *see* same-sex marriage
   traditional view 13, 14, 424–8, 430, 432, 434, 436–8, 446, 447, 451, 454
Martin, Leslie R. 150
Marxism 422
mass migration 273–6, 275 n.5, 276 n.8, 280–2
Maté, Gabor 491
Maynard, Brittany 63
Medawar, Peter 149
Medical Assistance in Dying (MAiD) 51, 53–61, 62 nn.6–8, 79
medical ethics 206, 217
Mendel, Gregor 134
mercy killing, *see* euthanasia
metaethics 1–2
metaphysics 1, 173, 235
migrant-citizen symmetry argument 264, 267, 269, 274
militarism 337–8, 343
Mill, John Stuart 56, 62 n.4, 76, 99, 100, 211–12, 276 n.8, 405, 413 n.14, 506, 514 n.19
Mill's Methods 292, 317
Mills, C. Wright 310
Moeller, Donald 90–1

Money, John   471–4, 477 n.14, 478 n.20, 482, 483 n.3
moral agency/agents   4, 9, 190, 228, 232, 234–7, 480, see also rational agency
moral community   96, 100–1, 106
moral conventionalism/relativism   326, 335 n.3
moral defiance   307, 308, 310, 318, 320
moral patients   9, 236, 237
moral responsibility   12, 38, 98, 200, 214, 217, 315, 371, 372, 386, 388, 521 n.4,
    collective   13, 184, 193–4
    racial   370–7
moral status/standing   9–10, 21–2, 35, 50 n.9, 231–7, 239–41, 243 n.30, 243 n.37, 244, 245, 247–50, 367
    cognitive capacities view   21–2, 67
    future-of-value view   22
    rights-based account   234
    substance view   235–7
    utilitarian account   233–4
Mosaic Law   85–6, 112
Moses   85
Muhammad (Prophet)   407
murder   2, 7, 20, 27, 64, 83–5, 87–92, 94 n.10, 94 n.13, 96, 98, 101, 105, 108 n.15, 110–12, 114–19, 291, 293, 300, 309–14, 314 n.14, 318, 322, 329–30, 341, 490, 491, 495, 510, 518, 520
Mustill, Michael John   201

Nanny State   200, 217–18
natural law theory   4, 204
Nawrotski, Raphael   277 n.26
Nazi/Nazism   57, 65, 77, 78, 102, 104, 116, 140, 201, 213, 224, 238, 285, 288 n.1, 343, 350, 356 n.6, 353, 354, 374, 375, 403, 459
Nietzsche, Friedrich   311, 314 n.11
Nilus, Sergei   403
No Harming Humans Principle   227–8
No Harming Principle   221–4, 226–30, 244–7, 251, see also Harm Principle
nominalism   482, 483 n.3
nomos   305, 306, 309
non-absolutism   216, 222, 229, 230
non-consequentialism   222, 229, 244
normative ethics   2–4, 17 n.4
Nowrasteh, Alex   273

Nozick, Robert   192
Nuremberg Code   201, 213–14

O'Neill, Brendan   70
Oakeshott, Michael   150
Obasogie, Osagie K.   148
Obergefell v. Hodges   14, 424, 447
Ockham, William of   483 n.3
Oderberg, David   40 n.7, 235–7
On Liberty   62 n.4, 211–12
open access   10, 265–9, 272–4, 284, 285
open borders   10, **252–89**, see also immigration
open residence   10, 265–7, 269, 272–4, 279, 284–5
Orend, Brian   334
organized cortical brain activity   20–2, 29 n.4, 42–3, 48
Orwell, George   383
overcriminalization   506–7
Owens, Emily   510

pacifism   11–12, 97, 326, 329–30, 335–48, 351–5
    completely pro-life   337
    contingent/practical   337
    nuclear   337
    religious   337, 338, 355
Palmer, Donald   90
parens patriae doctrine   200
Parmenides   305
Pascal, Blaise   314 n.10
Patch, Henry John   341
paternalism   16, 158, 184, 190, 200, 217–18, 253, 489, 491–4, 505–6, 518
Paul (Apostle)   257 n.9
pederasty   426, 432 n.2
people-seeds case   25–7
person/personhood   10, 31, 34–7, 39, 41 n.8, 43–4, 50, 65, 67, 72, 96, 98, 143 n.7, 235, 236, 239–41, 244, 304, 306, 312, 314 n.16, 316, 327, 466, 467, 471–3, 476, 478 n.27, 481, 483 n.3
    acquired attribute view   31, 35–7
    fragmented view of   466, 467, 470–3, 475, 481
    substance view   15, 231, 233, 235–41, 244
Peterson, Jordan   486
Petrie, Keith J.   150

Pfaff, John   516 n.38
phenomenology   304, 320
Phillips, Robert   336 n.12
physician-assisted suicide (PAS), see euthanasia
Plato   1, 64, 205, 306, 307
political authority/power   10, 101–3, 204, 265, 271, 285, 340, 383, 482
political philosophy   158, 167, 171, 172, 269–70, 303, 320
polygamy   426–8, 432 n.2, 436, 451, 454
pornography   77 n.1, 403, 419, 521 n.4
post-traumatic stress disorder (PTSD)   342, 356 n.5, 524
Powell, Lewis   106–7 n.2
Powell, Russell   120, 122, 123
preventive war   331–2
principle of fairness   9, 184, 185, 192–3, 195, 214–15
problem of wild animal suffering   10, 231–5, 241, 246, 249–50
procreation/reproduction   32, 47, 140, 147, 148, 427–31, 441–3, 448–9, 453
productivity argument   267, 277 n.27, 280
Prohibition (of alcohol)   509–10, 515 n.30
promises   14, 156–8, 161, 164 n.4, 311, 434, 438–40, 444 n.13
property (private)   87, 143 n.7, 156, 161, 181, 280, 321, 329, 333, 334, 395, 411, 504, 520
property (public), see public property
proportionality   93, 111, 112, 307, 308, 320–1, 323 n.4, 333
Protocols of the Elders of Zion   403
public goods   193, 214, 259, 281
public property   258–9, 283 n.3
public safety   9, 11, 16, 99, 100, 161, 187, 191, 212, 293–5, 300, 316–19, 319 n.2, 323, 496
Purves, Duncan   232, 234

Quarles, Charles   356 n.3
Quinlan, Karen Ann   73 n.9

Rabin, Yitzhak   338
racism/racial bias   104–5, 117, 273, 274, 287, 332, 361, 367, 377, 379, 384, 403, 405, 409, 411, 417, 418, 511, 516 n.36

rational agency   16, 108 n.15, 501–11, 512 n.3, 513 n.16, 514–15 n.25, 518–19, 521, see also moral agency
Rawls, John   192, 364
Re Bolton; Ex Parte Beane   204
Reagan, Ronald   207
realism/amoralism (about war)   326, 338, 343
reason/rationality   20–1, 35–8, 42, 46–8, 67, 108 n.15, 228, 234–5, 237, 243 n.37, 405, 501, 502, 504, 511, 523
rectius, see reparations
Rector, Ricky Ray   106 n.2
reductionism   482, 483 n.3
refugees   268, 271, 273, 285–6
Regan, Tom   222, 233, 234
rehabilitation   97, 98, 511
Remarque, Erich M.   314 n.16
reparations   12–13, 332, 334, 348 n.34, **358–89**
repentance   314 n.14, 348 n.34
Republic   306
ressentiment   307, 314 n.11
restitution   13, 98, 371–6
restrictionism/restrictionists   264, 268–9, 272–4, 283 n.3
retribution   97, 98, 100, 106, 110–13, 119, 343, 411, 412, 491, see also justice—retributive
Rice, Charles   205
Rich, Adrienne   470
right to bear arms   11, 290, 292–9, 301 n.18, 303–14, 318, 320–2
right to die   6, 54, 57, 61, 62 n.4, 66, 68–73, 73 n.9, 76
right to free speech, see free speech
right to health care   2, 8, **154–83**, 457
right to immigrate   265, 267, 269, 271, 273
right to life   6, 11, 19–28, 29 n.4, 29 n.7, 31, 37, 42, 44, 46, 48, 53–4, 62 n.4, 67, 102, 119, 165–9, 205, 234, 293, 295, 299, 300, 302 n.33, 305, 317, 318, 327–30, 349, 382
right to marry   14, 425–8, 446–7
right to property/property rights   156, 157, 163, 277, 334, 366, 383, 395
right to self-defense, see self-defense
right to vote   46, 288, 327, 425–6

rights   2, 3, 6, 13, 37, 46, 54, 67, 69, 76, 80, 102, 165–72, 174, 177, 179, 204, 205, 222, 229–30, 234, 236, 270, 292, 294–5, 304, 312, 315, 317–19, 327–9, 359, 379, 382, 383, 385, 395, 400, 401 n.4, 416, 420, 421, 427, 439, 467–9, 475–6, 485
   civil/political   11, 156, 283 n.6, 294, 303, 322, 327, 351 n.1, 467, 484–6, 495
   inalienable   205, 216, 218, 327, 380, 388, 391–2
   minimalist *vs.* maximalist conceptions   176–8
   natural   11, 204, 326–9, 331, 332, 334, 335 nn.3–4, 349, 351 n.1, 353
   negative   8, 164, 165, 167–71, 174, 180, 292, 293
   positive   8, 164–71, 179, 180
Robert, Eric   90
Robinson Crusoe   167, 177, 305
Roe v. Wade   5
Rome   86–7, 94 n.10, 158
Roof, Dylan   348 n.34, 373
Rose, Michael   123
Ross, W. D.   4
Roy, Guha   358
Rubin, Gayle   472
rule of law   9, 102, 202–5, 214–18
Russell, Bertrand   339, 341, 351–2 n.1, 353
Ryle, Gilbert   470

safety-ism, *see* public safety
same-sex marriage   2, 13–14, **424–54**
sanctity of life, *see* life, sanctity of
Sandel, Michael   151–2
Sandoz, Ellis   303–4
Santana, Carlos   524
Savulescu, Julian   140–3
scalability   164, 166, 168, 169
Scanlon, Tim   108 n.15, 167
Scheler, Max   303–11, 314 n.14, 320
Schindler, Oskar   374
Schutz, Alfred   304
Scott, John   200
Second Amendment (U. S. Constitution)   11, 18
Second World War   65, 336–8, 343, 348 n.34, 350, 354, 355, 375, 403, 437

self-authorship   457, 458
self-control   16, 501–4, 511, 523–5
self-defense   11, 44, 73 n.10, 168, 253, 290, 292–300, 329–30, 331, 354, 355
self-determination, *see* autonomy
self-identity   455–7, 459–60, 464, 481
self-knowledge   479, 481
Selim v. Professional Services Review Committee   198, 199
Sendler, Irina   374
separation of powers   204
Serano, Julia   487 n.2
Sermon on the Mount   341, 344, 348 n.34, 353, 356 n.3
sex/sexuality   14, 15, 33, 45, 274, 284 n.10, 406, 426, 455–6, 460–4, 468–6, 478 n.24, 478 n.27, 480–2, 483 n.3, 486–7
   binary   461, 462, 470, 472, 475, 482, 486, 487
   dimorphism   15, 468–70, 472–5, 478 n.20, 485, 487
   fragmentation of   474–5, 478 n.20
   non-binary   465 n.1, 470, 481, 486
sexual orientation   403, 406, 421, 426, 427, 447
Shafer-Landau, Russ   4
Sher, George   492
Sikhism   452
Singer, Peter   233–4, 240, 241, 244
Siracusa Principles   205, 213, 216
Six-Day War   335 n.6
slave trade   362–8, 371, 375, 386–8
slavery   340, 360–8, 370–80, 382–9, 391, 397, 514 n.19
Smith, Adam   378
social contract theory (of government)   262, 304, 328–9
social contract theory (of morality)   4, 100–1, 108 n.15, 251
social stability/order   8, 102, 154–7, 161–3, 179, 304, 305, 308–9, 318, 360, 363, 365, 387–8, 513 n.15
socialism   377, 396–7, 418, 421–2
Solzhenitsyn, Aleksandr   313
sovereignty relation   279–80
speciesism   47–8, 49 n.1
Spenkelink, John   106 n.1

stability-based argument 161–3
Stalin, Josef 172–3
Stanig, Piero 204
Stanton, Giancarlo 377
Starving Marvin 252, 254, 256, 258, 264, 270–2, 285, 286, 288
state of nature 177, 321, 328
Stemple, Timothy Shaun 88
Stephen (martyr) 348 n.34
Stephen, James Fitzjames 91
Stokley, Richard Dale 88
Stoller, Robert 471–3, 478 n.20, 482, 483 n.3
Stone, Sandy 486
Strossen, Nadine 397, 402 n.18
substance 31, 38, 235, 237, 240
suicide 17, 64–5, 68, 69, 75, 76, 100, 108 n.13, 114 n.6, 302 n.27, 315, 337, 339, 341–2, 504, 505, 514 n.18
Survival Lottery 194
Swenson, Philip 297, 302 n.39

taxation 161, 171, 178, 193, 264, 510, 519–20
Taylor, Gloria 56
teleology 429, 431
Thomson, Judith Jarvis 24–6, 49
threats 13, 159, 162, 320, 397–401, 403, 415, 419–20, 423
time-relative interests 231, 237–41, 244, 247–8, 250
transgender rights 14–15, **455–88**
transgenderism 15, 466, 475, 479, 484, 487
transsexuals 465 n.1, 471
Truchon, Nicole and Jean 55
Truchon v. Canada 55
Trump, Donald 14, 485
Tucker, Carla Faye 107 n.9
Tulsa murder spree 373
Turner, Edwin Hart 88
Turner, Mary 373
Tuskegee Institute 373
tyranny 9, 11, 205, 303, 305–6, 310–12, 320, 322–3, 353, 383

U.S. Constitution 11, 13, 68, 111, 173, 191, 313 n.4, 332, 363, 387, 391, 393, 402 n.16, 420, 438

UK Public Order Act of 1986 406
Universal Declaration of Human Rights 103, 205
universalizability, principle of 4, 113
utilitarianism 2, 3, 101, 173, 190–2, 194, 211, 214, 221–2, 230 n.1, 244, 247–8, 270, 295, 296, 299, 317

vaccine hesitancy/refusal 185, 186, 190, 213
vaccine mandates 9, **184–220**
value 1, 78, 186, 219, 315, 388, 429, 447–9, 453
 instrumental 293
 intrinsic 38, 43, 78, 293, 304, 307, 308, 314 n.11, 335 n.3
van Agt, Dries 63
van den Haag, Ernest 91, 92
van der Vossen, Bas 268–9
violinist case 19, 24–7
virtue 4, 12, 149, 307, 344, 354, 380, 455, 464
virtue ethics 4, 17 n.8, 173, 251, 341, 354
Voegelin, Eric 303, 309, 314 n.10, 315, 319 n.2, 320
voluntary active euthanasia (VAE), *see* euthanasia

Waldron, Jeremy 404, 406, 407
Wallenberg, Raoul 374
war 11–12, 73 n.10, 314 n.16, **325–57**, 377, *see also* Just War Theory; pacifism
war on drugs 495, 511, 516 n.36
Warnock, Mary 70
Washington v. Glucksburg 68
Waterfield, Fred 83–4
Waterhouse, Robert Brian 88
Watts, Mary T. 139
Wedgewood, Ralph 425
Weems v. United States 111
Weismann, August 151
Wellman, Christopher 277 n.27
Wheeler, Samuel, III 299
white nationalism 396, 416, 421
Wiley, Lindsay 147
Williams, Dudley 198
Williams, George 199

Williams, Reginald   427
Winslow, C.-E. A.   151
Wisco, Blair E.   356 n.5
Wong v. Commonwealth   198, 199
worldview   64, 140, 339, 344

Yuill, Kevin   70

Zakharov, Aleksandr   313
Zedong, Mao   385
Zimmermann, Augusto   201, 204